ashworth Awards
est 1965

Our Quality Always Finishes First!

www.ashworthawards.com

Medallions - Lapel Pins - Acrylic Awards - Key
Lanyards - Plaques - Belt Buckles - Pend

Phone: (800) 325-1917

Chains - Ribbons - Woodallions® - Bottle Openers
ants - Charms - Service Awards - and more!

Second Edition
Organizing Running Events
The Complete Guide to Staging a Successful Road Race

By Phil Stewart and Pam Balcke

Second Edition Edited by Susan Debad

Acknowledgments

The authors would like to thank the following individuals who wrote numerous articles in *Road Race Management Newsletter* over many years. These articles provided a valuable framework for preparing this *Manual:* Jim Ferstle, Jim Gerweck, Susan Green, Jim Hage, Mark Heinicke, Nancy Hobbs, Dave McGillivray, Irv Newman, Claudia Piepenburg, Sean Ryan, and Carl Sniffen.

We would also like to thank the following individuals who reviewed all or selected chapters in the publication and offered valuable insights: Jim Ferstle, Jim Gerweck, Susan Harmeling, Don Kardong, Becky Lambros, Dave McGillivray, Irv Newman, Keith Peters, Dr. Bill Roberts, Beth Rosenthal, Sean Ryan, and Carl Sniffen.

A number of individuals were extremely generous in providing feedback on topics where their knowledge greatly exceeded ours, including Adam Wade Bleakney, Dan Breidinger, Andy Carr, Terry Diller, Susan Harmeling, Ed Hartwell, Mark Heinicke, Nancy Hobbs, Don Kardong, Wayne Kursh, Dave McGillivray, Rachel Miller, Ryan Morris, Keith Peters, Christopher Quetant, Phil Quinn, Bill Roe, Sandy Sislowitz, Don Shulman, Anna Stewart, Mark Stewart, Danny Talmage, Steve Vaitones, and Jim Whitnah.

Finally I would like to credit the following groups and individuals for photos: Cover photo: Aerial view of the New Balance Falmouth Road Race, courtesy of New Balance Falmouth Road Race. Other photo credits appear with each photo.

ISBN Number 978-0-9701170-4-5   **Library of Congress Control Number:** 2017959231

Printed by Quality Graphics, Dulles, VA

Testimonials About

Organizing Running Events
The Complete Guide to Staging a Successful Road Race

*"I have a quote on my desk that reads, 'my job is secure, no one else wants it!' Although I am not sure how true this statement is, I do know that the race management business is very labor intensive, requires tremendous organizational skills and sometimes can feel like it is you against 20,000 customers. Thus, there is just one and only one defense against this and that is PREPARATION. The best way to be prepared is to learn from others who have "been there, done that." This is exactly what the book, **Organizing Running Events: The Complete Guide to Staging a Successful Road Race** offers. Trust me, if you follow what is offered in this book, a virtual "A to Z checklist" of what needs to be accomplished, you will become very successful in this business and your event will prosper for many, many years to come. My only disappointment is that it wasn't written 40 years ago when I was just getting started."*

Dave McGillivray, President, DMSE, Inc.; Race Director - BAA Boston Marathon

"Phil Stewart has used his decades of experience, both as a race director and as an advisor to other race directors, to produce what will surely become the touchstone for anyone involved in race management. If you want to organize a road race, or if you want to improve an existing road race, this is the book you need to read."

Don Kardong, Director, Lilac Bloomsday Run, Spokane, WA; 1976 Olympian

"This is an easy read and will provide a wealth of information for those who are organizing and producing a running event for the first time or, like me, for the 27th time!"

Susan Harmeling, Director, Publix Gasparilla Distance Classic, Tampa, FL

*"Road races, from the small community 5K Fun Run to the mega-sized big city marathons, seem to be ubiquitous these days, and their increase in numbers seems limitless. With this book, so is the knowledge to organize and produce one. Even if your only experience with racing is pinning on a number for your local Turkey Trot, Road Race Management's **Organizing Running Events** has everything to get you from the starting line of deciding to hold a race, to the finish line of sending out the results and doing the final budget and after-action reports.*

"Whether you've never organized a race or direct dozens a year, this is an invaluable reference, one that should be kept right next to your stopwatch and cell phone."

Jim Gerweck, Former Vice Chair, USATF Road Running Technical Council

Organizing Running Events *distills decades of race directing experience into an easily comprehensible text. I just wish the book had existed a few years ago when I tackled my first event!*

Sean Ryan, Race Director, Door County Triathlon; Senior Event Manager, DMSE

Contents

Index of Illustrations

Index of Advertisers

Introduction

Welcome to the second edition of **Organizing Running Events: The Complete Guide to Staging a Successful Road Race**. Much has happened in the road running world since the publication of the first edition in 2008. Social media has exploded, transponder timing has become ubiquitous and the Boston Marathon was bombed, for starters. But there have been countless other smaller changes and improvements in the craft of race directing that have been incorporated into this second edition as well. The authors feel this book represents the "state of the art" as we move through the first quarter of the 21st century.

Road races come in all different forms, ranging from 50-person fun runs at local recreation centers to the 50,000-runner TCS New York City Marathon. At the most basic level, a race director lines up a group of runners, says "go," tries to keep them safe and on the intended route, tallies the order they cross finish line, and lets everyone know how they did. At the most complex level, large organizations operate hundreds of events in the U.S. and abroad. The New York Road Runners organizes the TCS New York City Marathon and scores of other races (in addition to offering classes and programs for runners of all ages and abilities), employs a full-time staff of nearly 200, oversees a budget in excess of $75 million, manages a warehouse operation totaling 43,000 square feet indoors and 10,000 square feet outdoors for supplies and equipment, and uses the services of 12,000 volunteers just to conduct the marathon. The Chinese conglomerate Wanda Group gobbled up the venture capital funded Competitor Group, which expanded the Rock 'n' Roll Marathon series starting in the 1990s, and billionaire Sir Richard Branson has launched a worldwide series as well. Most of the estimated 30,000 organized running events that take place in the U.S. each year (and many more abroad) fall somewhere in between the extremes of the 50-person race and these large organizations.

The wide disparities among road races make it a challenge to prepare a single manual to address the needs of *all* race directors. The organizers of a local fun run won't be concerning themselves with the proper number of barricades needed to seal off the Sponsor-VIP hospitality area from the working media area, any more than the New York Road Runners needs advice about using spray paint versus flour to line the route of the New York City Marathon.

This *Manual* addresses all aspects of putting on a road race. However, the authors realize that some users will want a quick overview, while others will be seeking out more details about various facets of race organization. Users in the "fast lane" might start by reading Chapters 1-3, which cover basic committee or corporate organization, budget and finances, and timetables and checklists. They can follow up by looking at the opening section of each chapter, called "The Basics." This should provide an introductory overview in a relatively short period of time. Users desiring a fuller explanation about any facet of race directing (or "fast lane" readers who have additional questions) can immerse themselves in the second section of each chapter, called "The Details." The Second Edition includes a far more extensive Index as well, enabling users to locate quickly any topic of their choosing.

With each passing month, more and more race directors are "thinking Green," as they search for ways to reduce their impact on the environment. A number of brief suggestions are noted in various chapters under the header "Green Tip."

This *Manual* is used as the textbook for the Road Runners Club of America's Race Director Certification program. For details about becoming an RRCA Certified Race Director, visit http://www.rrca.org/our-programs-services/programs/race-director-certification.

The authors of this *Manual* envision updating it approximately every 6-8 years so that it will reflect the continually evolving ways in which race directors manage their events, and will provide information about new technologies entering the sport. We hope users of the *Manual* will let us know about experiences that have worked well for them that may not be outlined here, as well as any suggestions for modifications in the information we have presented. You may send your input to pstewart@rrm.com.

We wish you well in your organizing efforts.

Phil Stewart and Pam Balcke

Anne C. Beach

In 1976, traffic and crowd control at the front of the Boston Marathon was mimimal, as shown in this photo of race winner Jack Fultz (in between the two motorcycles) in the final miles.

Forward

A Brief History of Times

When the Road Runners Club of America (RRCA/www.rrca.org) was founded in 1958, there were only scattered pockets of organized running around the country, mostly on the East Coast. The 1958 Boston Marathon had 203 finishers. Small bands of diehard runners usually doubled as race directors and participants—*often in the same event*. The amateur rules were so strict that anyone paid to organize a road race would have been banned from competing in one because the Amateur Athletic Union would have deemed them as a "professional"! Nevertheless, this all-volunteer structure served the embryonic sport quite well for the next 15 years.

Things began to change in the 1970s, after Frank Shorter won the gold medal in the marathon at the 1972 Munich Olympics; Bill Rodgers, an affable ex-smoker and ex-hospital orderly, raced to four victories at the Boston and New York City Marathons; and Jim Fixx, a middle-aged convert to the sport, wrote a best-seller called *"The Complete Book of Running."* On the organizational side, the late Fred Lebow, while president of the New York Road Runners Club, had the vision to move the 1976 New York City Marathon from an isolated five-loop course inside Central Park to a high-visibility, five-borough, citywide course starting on the Verrazano Bridge and finishing at Tavern on the Green. The RRCA picked up steam by supporting the sprouting of hundreds of new running clubs across the country. Suddenly runners and

Phil Stewart

A bronzed statue of legendary NYRRC President Fred Lebow at the New York City Marathon finish line.

road races became mainstream, in what is called the "first running boom." A large number of new races came into being in the '70s and early '80s, and *Road Race Management* newsletter was launched in 1982 to bring information to the burgeoning race director community.

A second running boom followed the first in the 1990s, with the incorporation of charity-fundraising runners and walkers into the sport. Race participation, which sagged a bit in the 1980s, surged once again. The gurus of this era were Jeff Galloway, a 1972 Olympian in the 10,000-meters, and John Bingham, a back-of-the-pack columnist for *Runner's World* magazine writing under the pen name of "The Penguin," both of whom preached to the public that *"it's ok to be slow."* On the organizational side, race directors who previously could take down the finish line clock after 4 hours in a marathon were suddenly being pressured to keep the course open for *twice* that long. The estimated number of road race finishers rose from 2.9 million in 1987 to 4.2 million in 1997.

The dramatic increase in numbers, coupled with the upscale demographics of race participants, attracted the attention of commercial interests and charities, which *saw running events as business opportunities.* The proprietors of the first "finish line companies," who had built marginal existences by stringing together scores of events per year and had been viewed with some disdain by the old, all-volunteer network, began to set the tone for the new era. Certainly the lack of price resistance from runners, as entry fees escalated to $85 for half marathons and $140 for marathons, increased the opportunities to make a living in the sport and attracted greater interest from the for-profit sector. The dramatic growth of events and the increasingly intense competition for sponsor dollars demanded more time and professionalism as the era of all-volunteer race administration began to recede. Suddenly, race directors had to know a lot more than how to design a course and how many cups to place at an aid station; they had to become marketers and promoters as well. Clearly, running had transformed from a *sport* primarily for diehards into a mass participation *activity*. This meant that event directors, besides having to time the event and ensure the safety of the burgeoning number of runners, had to make investments to upgrade the "look" of their events, as they began to compete for sponsors with events ranging from music festivals to cultural events to Major League sports.

Tim Murphy, founder of San Diego-based Elite Racing, was one of the first for-profit entrepreneurs to realize the commercial potential of running events. He drew upon basic marketing principles used by industries as varied as auto companies, beer companies, and apparel manufacturers and created the sport's first recognizable "brand"—the "Rock 'n' Roll" series of marathons and then half marathons. His formula involved marrying running and entertainment by providing rock music during and after the races. Before long, Murphy could march his "brand" into a new city and soon draw 15,000 to 25,000 runners. Ownership of an entire series of successful events gave his company valuable leverage with sponsors and suppliers and made him wealthy when he sold it. Clearly this was a far cry from the running events of 1958.

CUCB

The finish line of the Cherry Blossom Ten Mile was significantly upgraded between 1975 and 2017.

Phil Stewart files

According to Running USA, a running industry trade association, running participation numbers continued to grow, reaching a high of 19 million finishers in 2013. (The male to female ratio shifted dramatically as well, changing from 75% men and 25% women in 1990 to 57% women and 43% men in 2013.) In 2014, the participation figures began to retrench, falling 2%, followed by an additional drop of 9% in 2015, before remaining flat in 2016. The slightly smaller pie meant that race directors had to be more savvy marketers and produce higher quality events.

The fact remains that for every New York City Marathon or "Rock 'n' Roll" event today, there are still hundreds, if not thousands, of small community events. [Running USA pegs the total number of organized running events in the U.S. at 30,000; there are currently 30 "Rock 'n' Roll" events.] Most of these events are still managed by all-volunteer, or largely volunteer, running clubs, charities, recreation centers or small for-profit event management companies, although more and more of these groups are bringing on paid staff. It is important for anyone entering the world of organized running to recognize that today's biggest running events are largely "products" being sold to a group of consumers who have choices about what they want to consume. Race directors need to ask themselves "why should a runner come to my event rather than spend time with his or her family, go to a movie, or head off to see a Major League baseball game?"

Of course the tragic 2013 Boston Marathon bombings reinforced in a major way the primary importance of runner safety that still lies at the core of every event.

Finally, event directors should be asking themselves, what is the obligation of running events to grow the sport of running? According to a survey done several years ago by United States Track and Field, running events raised $714 million for charities. Yet the budget for the nonprofit Road Runners Club of America, which promotes grass roots running in the U.S., is $3 million. Clearly a disproportionate amount of money is flowing out of the sport for every dollar that remains in the sport.

Looking Ahead

The future of road running in the U.S. and around the world looks positive. The strong links between running and health are undeniable. Increasing awareness of childhood obesity has stimulated a growing number of programs designed to get children physically active at a young age. Many of these children will make up the third running boom in the years ahead. Running events will face the inevitable ups and downs of the economy and its impact on sponsorship, and will continue to compete with an ever-expanding array of events for sponsor dollars and space on city streets. However, even with the increasing entry fees, running events remain a good "value" in the sports and entertainment world when compared to the expense of attending a professional sporting event.

On the industry side, there is a trend toward consolidation across industry lines in the direction of one-stop portals to service events—and runners—in all areas, ranging from online registration, timing and scoring services, access to large results databases, participant photography, race supplies such as bibs and awards, etc. With the collection of vast amounts of data from every click of a mouse online or social media visit, these companies are using the data to target audiences more narrowly and attempting to provide services for their every need. While there may be efficiencies in one-stop shopping (the "Amazonification" of the industry), the verdict is still out as to whether these all-in-ones can out-perform the more specialized vendors.

These are exciting and changing times in the sport of organized distance running and for the organizers of its events.

Dennis Steinauer

1 Taking the Plunge

Organizing a running event. How hard can it be? Just line up some runners, say "go" and let them get from point A to point B. Like many things in life, appearances can be deceiving. This book is designed to help aspiring new and veteran race directors produce quality events that provide the stage for millions of runners of all ages and abilities to live out their athletic dreams, ranging from running a "Boston qualifier," to simply remaining in motion for 3.1 miles, to raising funds for a favorite charity.

When individuals call the Road Race Management office and want to "start a community run" — often to raise funds for a favorite charity — frequently, we to try to talk them out of it. If they remain undeterred, we tell them that caution should be the word for anyone seriously embarking on organizing a new running event. It is not as easy is it looks.

Most of our callers fall into one of the following categories:

Nonprofit community groups: A typical caller from this group heard from a relative that a 20,000- person race in a large city nearby raised $25 million for the Leukemia Team in Training last year. Certainly, if he could raise 0.1% of that amount, a tidy sum of $20,000, through a community run, he would be the hero of the local school PTA, a community association, or the cause about which he feels passionately.

New running club officials: A second type of caller is an energetic new running club president who wishes to begin organizing events in order to augment the $1,000 that membership dues have put into the club treasury.

Municipal employees: A third type of caller is from a municipality, perhaps an employee of the recreation department or the Mayor's office, who wants to put on a road race to bring runners and dollars into his city or town.

Aspiring entrepreneurs: A final group we hear from are fresh-faced runners easing past their prime and looking to "remain in the sport," former race volunteers dissatisfied with their jobs and looking to start their own business, or recent graduates with newly-minted degrees in sports marketing or event planning. These individuals may be evaluating setting up a for-profit event management company.

After suggesting that they purchase this manual and asking if they are prepared to commit the large amount of time and effort necessary to put on a successful event, we direct these callers to visit the website of the Road Runners Club of America (www.rrca.org), a national organization of grassroots running clubs. The RRCA has over 2,500 member running clubs ranging in size from 25 to over 25,000 members each. RRCA member clubs provide a broad scope of activities in their communities, including staging races. RRCA "event members" are groups devoted to event management only. Many RRCA members who direct races have honed their skills by becoming RRCA Certified Race Directors, which involves completing an online course that uses this book as the textbook. Among numerous other benefits, the RRCA can immediately help prospective race directors solve the liability insurance issues that they haven't even thought of yet. According to the RRCA, its clubs organize over 10,000 events per year.

The Proper Questions to Ask

Here is a short list of questions to ask if you are considering directing a race:

- **Do you have plenty of time on your hands?** A road race can be a little like a hole in your running sock—at first you barely notice a rub, but over time it evolves into a pulsating blister that can bring down a PR (running-speak for "personal record," a runner's best time for a certain distance). Duties that seem quite manageable six months out—a phone call here and there and a few supplies to line up—become unwieldy as race day approaches, with great potential to place strain on jobs, families, and even your own running routine.

- **Do you have a circle of friends who have a fair amount of time on their hands?** Far too many race directors take the one-man-band approach. Developing a nucleus of similarly committed individuals will enable you to delegate freely. This group will become your "organizing committee."

- **Are you a detail-oriented person (if not, can one of the friends drafted above fill this role)?** Much of directing a road race involves creating and getting through a giant "to-do" list. A race director should be the type of person who likes to think through the myriad tasks associated with the event and to address well in advance how they will be accomplished.

- **Can you delegate?** All the friends you bring on board will be useless and will feel under-utilized and gradually lose interest if you do not give them meaningful tasks. Difficulty in delegating is the downfall of more race directors than probably any other single trait.

- **Are you a "people person?"** You are the individual who sells the enthusiasm for the event, both to those working on the race and to those sponsoring it. As race committees grow in numbers, race directors encounter all kinds of people with all kinds of needs. You need to be part psychologist to understand these needs and to keep people motivated. Saying "thank you" should be as automatic as breathing.

- **Are you patient?** There will be frustrations along the way—from potential sponsors who lead you on before saying "no," to school bathrooms that don't get unlocked. You need to be patient and loaded with "Plan Bs."

- **Do you have decent computer skills?** In today's world, computer skills are a must for a race director. Although you may be able to rely on other members of the organizing committee or outsiders for more advanced skills, such as race scoring or maintaining a website, a basic knowledge of word processing, spreadsheets, social media, and basic file management will pay off handsomely.

- **Do you have realistic expectations about raising funds for charity?** As cited earlier, many would-be event directors start with the expectation of raising money for charity. This is unlikely for a first-time event where a more realistic goal is to *raise awareness* of the charity. Although some events with 500-600 runners, managed frugally, can make a small contribution to charity, as a general rule of thumb, a road race with fewer than 1,000 to 1,500 runners is unlikely to have significant funds left over for charities, unless the race director is able to secure a lucrative sponsorship deal or the participants are raising money on their own. (A very rough approximation is that for races that offer ways for runners to raise money for charity on their own, about 10% of the entrants will raise money on their own, with the average raised per entrant of around $100).

- **Are you prepared for the possibility of losing money?** Most road races, if carefully planned, do not lose money.

However, many of the initial expenses will be incurred before registration income starts coming in. Since most beginning events rely mostly on registration fees as the principle source of revenue, if you are off on the registration projections, you can lose money. Some races may take a few years to turn a profit.

Getting to "Yes"

You say you've got time, you've got friends with time and you've passed the personality test. But why do this? Race directing does have its satisfactions, including creating an event that participants appreciate (and one that may be life changing for some of them), being your own boss, being able to place your own creative and organizational stamp on an activity, and, if you are lucky, possibly raising some funds for the cause you care about (although you may set your first year's goal as simply increasing awareness about the cause). It is thrilling to see a group of runners—whether it is 100, 1,000 or 10,000—head down the roadway at an event that you have created.

Establishing a Race Committee

Invite those friends with the time on their hands over to your house to set up the race committee. How you organize the race committee depends on the size of the event. Smaller events can have committee heads (sometimes called

GREEN TIP

The Green Patrol

Early on, establish a Green Team Captain on the race committee. This person's role will be to examine every facet of the race to see if there are ways to reduce the event's environmental impact and enhance its positive impacts on the community. Ideally, sustainability should be the only responsibility this person has.

"Team Captains") perform a number of functions. As the event grows in size, the responsibilities of each team captain become narrower because the scope of each individual task grows.

A small race (500 participants or under) might need as few as a race director and three committee heads covering volunteers, timing and scoring, and logistics.

A large race might be structured as shown below in **Figure 1-1.**

The key principle is to create a new committee head or more sub-heads when the duties of any single position become more than one person can handle. The chart below should provide some idea of the functions that need to be covered.

Consider Hiring a Race Director

This statement is not as facetious as it sounds. There are hundreds of running clubs and commercial event management companies throughout the U.S. that have experience in race directing. Event management companies can easily be found through an internet search, and a list of local running clubs is available at www.rrca.org. You need to decide if you wish to start from scratch or contract with one of these groups. This is not a black-and-white proposition—

nearly all of these groups offer a range of services, so you can decide to simply rent supplies like digital clocks (renting equipment as opposed to purchasing it is good idea if you are only putting on a single event), or you can delegate every aspect of publicity, registration, logistics, and timing/ scoring of the event. Most of the time, you can pick and choose the services that you need to fill in any gaps that might exist in the organizing committee. You are trading off some money for the time it takes your group to learn all these tasks. Frequently, organizing committees whose primary purpose is fundraising may shy away from incurring the costs of a club or commercial event manager. While possibly saving a few dollars, this decision can be costly in terms of the quality of the event and the welfare of the organizing committee.

If You Want to be the Race Director

Since the 1970s and '80s, the possibility of earning a living as a race director has been steadily increasing, to the point where, today, most major races employ a race director and support staff, clubs hire an Executive Director who likely oversees the club's own events and coordinates the club's directing events on a contract basis, and individuals see enough

Figure 1-1

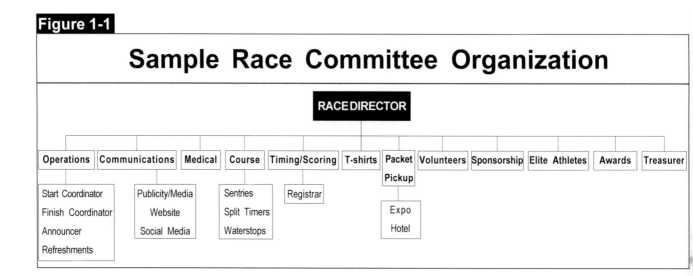

Sample Race Committee Organization

RACE DIRECTOR

| Operations | Communications | Medical | Course | Timing/Scoring | T-shirts | Packet Pickup | Volunteers | Sponsorship | Elite Athletes | Awards | Treasurer |

Operations: Start Coordinator, Finish Coordinator, Announcer, Refreshments

Communications: Publicity/Media, Website, Social Media

Course: Sentries, Split Timers, Waterstops

Timing/Scoring: Registrar

Packet Pickup: Expo, Hotel

opportunities in the sport to form for-profit event management companies and sell their services as race directors. More and more specialty running retailers are expanding their services to include event management services as well. *Road Race Management* newsletter conducts a bi-annual race director compensation survey to track employment directing running events. In 2015, the study found the following statistics among the survey respondents:

- 44% have race directing as a sole occupation

- The largest number of race directors worked for a for-profit event management company, followed closely by employees of nonprofit charity organizations. The third and fourth largest groups were independent contractors and employees of running clubs.

- For directors of a single event, 44% earned $30,000; 21% earned $70,000 and 11% earned $100,000 or more.

- For directors of multiple events, 59% earned $30,000; 33% earned $70,000; 21% earned $100,000 and 9% earned $150,000 or more.

- In general, compensation rises with race size and budget. Nearly 27% of the race directors earning over $100,000 directed races with over 20,000 entrants.

- Employment as a race director is still a relatively new career choice, with 33% of the survey respondents directing races for only five years or fewer.

Other Early Considerations

As the newly minted organizing committee gathers around your living room for its first organizational meeting, here are some items for the agenda:

- **Organizational structure:** Details about the legal requirements of incorporating, establishing a board of directors, and for-profit versus nonprofit status are addressed in *Chapter 9: Insurance and Legal* (and should

be addressed by you and the committee). Be sure to give all of these aspects of organizational structure careful consideration.

- **Goals of the race:** It would be useful to have agreement on the goals of the race—is it primarily a fundraiser; is it celebrating the opening of something such as a restaurant, shopping center, housing development, road or bridge; is it bringing more business to a client; is it celebrating a holiday or festival; or is it simply a "feel good" community event? This may seem pretty basic, but it establishes a framework against which subsequent decisions can be made.

- **Date and distance of the race:** There are two aspects to consider regarding the date—how far in advance the date should be, and the date itself. Even the date for a small community event should be set at least nine months out, and a year's lead time is preferable. As you will learn in subsequent chapters, times for everything from obtaining permits to publicizing the event require at least this much advance notice.

As for the date itself, be sure to review the running schedule in the area from which you hope to draw runners, to see if you can find a "clear" weekend. In large metropolitan areas, this probably means picking a weekend with fewer events, as it is likely that events are going on year-round. Other factors may include tying the event in with a holiday or festival, or scheduling it as a tune-up for an established area race. Not surprisingly, schedules are most crowded in the fall and spring, as race directors try to avoid the months of extreme temperatures. Be advised that you may be reduced to selecting a weekend that is "the least of the evils," meaning you will be competing for runners with some other events in the area.

Determining the race distance should be influenced by the current race schedule in the area as well, keeping in mind that runners

SIDEBAR

Race Director Code of Ethics

The RRCA has developed a "Race Director Code of Ethics," to which event directors are required to agree in order to receive insurance through that organization. The Code of Ethics provides an excellent overview of a race director's responsibilities, best practices and goals.

"The RRCA Race Director Code of Ethics outlines the expected standards of conduct of any person or a group of people that conduct an event, road race, trail race, or other similar type of event that is either for profit or nonprofit and where individuals pay a fee to participate in an organized running event. All event directors in the RRCA membership and receiving insurance through the RRCA insurance program must agree to abide by the RRCA Race Director Code of Ethics as follows:

- Race Directors shall put the safety of runners, walkers, volunteers and spectators ahead of all other aspects of the event and abide by the RRCA Guidelines for safe events as much as possible.

- Race Directors should demonstrate honest communication and not make false or misleading statements to any person or business associated with their event including but not limited to the RRCA, elite athletes, event participants, sponsors, local government, local businesses, and other related parties.

- Race Directors should avoid business transactions with any vendor or person with a proven history of a criminal conviction against them in accordance with the RRCA's Criminal Background Check policy.

- Race Directors should conduct all financial transactions in an open and transparent manner, especially when partnering with other nonprofit organizations and when accepting funds or special services from government entities.

- Race Directors should keep current and accurate records of all financial transactions.

- Race Directors who are voluntarily directing a race on behalf of a nonprofit running club, nonprofit event, or other nonprofit organization should not use their positions to profit personally, nor perform business transactions known to represent a conflict of interest with the event organizers, sponsors, vendors or staff.

- Race Directors who are hired and paid a fee to direct a race or race directors who own a race as a business venture should perform all duties to the specifications outlined in all contracts or agreements with all involved parties, including local governments, sponsors, third-party vendors, participants, nonprofit partners such as running clubs, running events and charity partners.

- Race Directors should preserve and protect the event's assets by making prudent and effective use of those assets, as well as accurately reporting on their financial condition, as applicable.

- Race Directors should not personally utilize the event's assets if the assets are owned by a nonprofit running club, other nonprofit or related partner. Assets include but are not limited to capital assets, contact information, trademarked items, etc.

- All property and business of an event owned by a nonprofit running club, nonprofit organization, or other partner should be conducted in a manner to further the event's interest, rather than the personal interest of any individual.

- Race Directors should respect the event's proprietary information. The Race Director or event staff should not disclose trade secrets, either during or after their employment,

Race Director Code of Ethics (cont.)

association or completion of consulting arrangements, except to individuals authorized by the event.

- Race Directors should make a commitment to environmental compliance as outlined in event permits. Race Directors should make reasonable efforts to conduct events in a manner that conserves natural resources within the budget of the event.

- Race Directors should make a commitment to encourage entrants to follow a "drug free" event policy and Race Directors should have athletes competing to win the event and/or earn prize money attest to being "drug free."

- Race Directors must ensure that any alcohol served in conjunction with the event is dispensed and monitored in a manner consistent with safety and adherence to all local, state, and federal requirements.

- Race Directors should be sensitive to the acceptance of gifts or gratuities attempting to influence decision-making. If there is any possibility that giving or receiving the amenity could be viewed or later construed as a bribe or improper inducement, Race Directors or staff should not give or accept the amenity.

- Race Directors are aware of local, state, and federal laws that pertain to the event and Race Directors must adhere to all such laws.

- Race Directors should keep informed and be sensitive about how their event affects the community in which their event is held. Race Directors should share that information with their staff, event committee or interested persons. They should be sensitive to community needs and work in partnership to better the health and wellness of the community and not be disruptive to citizens.

- Race Directors should demonstrate a

commitment to a nonpartisan agenda in the conduct of their event and prohibit discrimination and harassment of participants based on the basis of race, color, national origin, disability, marital status, familial status, parental status, religion, sexual orientation, genetic information, political beliefs, economic status, citizenship, veterans, military status, gender identity*, gender*, or age*. (* USATF has issued a rule of competition related to gender identity and gender transition. The RRCA follows the USATF rule on gender identity for competition. RRCA members and race directors may host women's only events. Members and race directors are encouraged to allow men to participate in these events upon request, and race directors may have a different start time for men. RRCA members and race directors may place minimum age levels on events for minors in accordance with the RRCA FUNdamentals of Youth Running.)

- Race Directors should make reasonable accommodations for adults in accordance with the ADA and USATF rules for athletes with disabilities. Race Directors should make reasonable accommodations for minors with disabilities if the minor is at or above the minimum age to participate in the race.

- Race Directors are expected to conduct themselves ethically, honestly and with integrity in all dealings. This means principles of fairness, good faith and respect consistent with all laws, permit regulations and or internal policies that govern their conduct with others both inside and outside the community.

RRCA race director members that are found in violation of one or more of the points in this code of ethics may come under review in accordance with the RRCA's Member Accountability Process found at http://www.rrca.org/about/governance/.

tend to run fewer of the longer races (over 10K), and that the longer races generally require more time to organize and to administer, simply by virtue of more streets being closed for longer periods of time (unless you are running a multiple-loop course). On the other hand, many areas get over-saturated with 5K events (due to their relative simplicity), so selecting an 8K or 10K may be a better alternative and result in a greater number of registrants.

- **Naming the race:** Naming the race is important for establishing your "brand" in the running marketplace (see next bullet point below). It is important to choose a name that generates interest and sets the race apart from other events–something that makes a runner think "I need to check this out further." For example, "Alyssa's 5K" may not mean anything except to those who know Alyssa,

but a catchy name such as the "Pike's Peek 10K," for an event that runs down a commercial stretch of Rockville Pike in suburban Washington, DC, creates a favorable impression that may entice runners to select that event out of a crowded weekend menu. Cincinnati's "Flying Pig Marathon" is a double entendre due to the history of Hormel meat packing plants in the city and as an enticement to the more gentle running crowd. Many event names reflect the location of the event, such as the Portland Marathon or the Peachtree Road Race, which runs down Peachtree St. in Atlanta. Be aware that if you give a title sponsor the naming rights to the event, the media will likely drop the sponsor's name when it refers to the event. Thus, the Credit Union Cherry Blossom Ten Mile in Washington, DC is usually — to the chagrin of the organizers — called the "Cherry Blossom" by the Washington, DC media. At

Marine Corps Marathon

Myles, the mascot of the Marine Corps Marathon, reinforces the Marine Corps brand of the event and is ubiquitous on race weekend.

the same time, however, if you make the name of the event the same as the title sponsor, such as the "Ogden Newspapers 20K," you will receive great sponsor play as long as the sponsorship continues, but suffer an identity crisis if the sponsor pulls out.

- **Establish the theme and brand of the race:** As running events have matured since the first running boom of the 1970s and the number of events has risen to an estimated 30,000 per year, individual events have become more like "brands." It is far easier to establish a brand at the outset than to try to develop or change a brand later on. So think about such things as who you want to reach, what you want to accomplish, whether you want to offer any unique features (the simple notion of bands on the course launched the worldwide "Rock 'n' Roll" series), etc. You may want to identify a single aspect or feature of the event that you want seared into the minds of the public — like the Marine Corps Marathon's identity as "The People's Marathon," or the post-race party at the Boilermaker 15K in Utica, NY, or the Maryland crabs that are linked with the Baltimore Running Festival, etc. (See *Chapter 6: Marketing and Promotions* for a more detailed discussion about marketing and branding.) For now, the point is to see if you can establish the brand early.

- **Undertake a bit of espionage:** Check out the online registration forms (or paper forms, if they exist) from other races, to get ideas on what to include and how to include it. These forms can be used for planning and as a way of proofing your event's registration form to make sure everything that's supposed to be there is actually there. This advance work will also help you to select a reputable online registration company, which can make your life significantly easier than if you attempt to manage registrations on your own.

- **Have a rough idea of where you want to stage the race:** Early on, you will want to talk to the municipal authorities, especially the police department, about your ideas for the desired course, check-in area, parking and other logistical items. It's best to know if what you have in mind is doable before investing a lot of time and energy into it.

- **Investigate resources:** As you work your way through this book, you will learn about a

host of organizations providing services for event directors. The two that you should look at right from the start are the **Road Runners Club of America (RRCA)** and **USA Track and Field (USATF).** (For an overview of additional running organizations and companies see *Chapter 23: Resources*)

- **Road Runners Club of America** (www.rrca.org): Founded in 1958, the RRCA is the nation's largest running membership organization. It provides support and programs for running clubs, individual running events and event management companies. The organization provides extensive "Guidelines" for the conduct of safe events, as well as liability and other insurance policies. The RRCA also offers a race director certification program that uses *Organizing Running Events* as the textbook.

- **USA Track and Field** (www.usatf.org): USATF is the national governing body for track and field, race walking and road running in the U.S. Its primary function is to develop and select the U.S. Olympic teams every four years. As part of this mandate, it supports programs for runners of all ages and also provides services for event directors. USATF sanctions events through 57 local associations. USATF sanctions require events to adhere to safety and other standards of conduct. The organization also oversees the accurate measurement of courses. Like the RRCA, USATF also offers liability and other insurance for events.

Moving Forward

A couple of weeks after the initial meeting, at which the preceding topics were discussed, the organizing committee can begin its real work, as outlined in the chapters that follow.

Road Race Management MEMBERSHIP

Improve Your Event

Since 1982, Road Race Management has been the industry's leading resource for the dissemination of information and exchange of ideas among those who produce the finest running events. Our portfolio of publications and meetings has helped educate thousands of race officials over the years. We are pleased to expand on this heritage by offering RRM memberships that combine our comprehensive information resources with a money-saving member benefits package.

Keep up-to-date on sponsorship, marketing, insurance and legal issues, drug testing, elite athlete recruitment, trade news, reviews of new equipment, and happenings at RRCA, USATF, RUSA, PRRO and other organizations, all while saving hundreds of dollars on RRM publications and the annual Race Directors' Meeting.

Don't be left behind! Visit www.rrm.com to join today.

Member Benefits:

▶ 11 issues each year of Road Race Management Newsletter covering event news and management in the sport of long distance running

▶ Substantial discount on registration fee at annual Road Race Management Race Directors' Meeting

▶ Discounts on Road Race Management publications

▶ Periodic E-Wire full of breaking news from the world of road running

Dennis Steinauer

2 Incorporation, Taxes, Budgets and Finances

THE BASICS

- **Establish a legal identity/corporate structure.** An important early task is deciding what kind of legal entity is putting on the race. Will it be a for-profit or nonprofit organization? Will it be a corporation, a partnership, or a sole proprietorship? There are pluses and minuses to each type of organization.

- **Set up bank accounts.** Bank accounts should be set up in the name of the race organization. A race should never be funded or financially managed out of someone's personal checkbook. In order to set up these accounts, you will need to apply for a Federal Tax ID number. Consider opening both a checking and a savings account, particularly if you anticipate having funds left over after the race that can earn interest.

- **Draw up a budget.** When drawing up a race budget, have at least one pessimist in the room and listen carefully to that person. For nearly all events—new and established—the registration fee is the major source of revenue, so considerable thought needs to be put into setting the fee and estimating the number of entrants. Generally, sponsorship fees are the other major revenue category. Even for a small race, realistically estimating the expenses in order to draft an accurate budget requires a substantial amount of legwork. Each expense item needs to be researched to determine the potential cost. Keep track of revenue and expenses electronically, either using a spreadsheet, if you have a small race without many expenses; otherwise, use money management/ budgeting software. These programs can automatically generate important reports like profit and loss, accounts receivable, and balance sheets, among others. Although the learning curve for these programs can be a bit daunting at first, down the line you will value the time spent.

- **Live within the budget.** The budget is the financial road map for the event. Make sure to consult it frequently and stay within its parameters. It is important to record expenses against the various line items on a regular basis, so you can see the "budget versus actuals." The budget can make tough decisions easier by providing a framework for spending.

- **Learn from the budget.** Once you have been through a complete cycle of the event from beginning to end, the budget will serve as an important guide for planning the following year's event. The budget should be viewed as more than merely a financial blueprint; it should also be seen as a vital operational planning document.

- **Implement some financial controls.** Make sure at least two people have access to and review the detailed financial transactions for the event. If the organization is a corporation, a nonprofit, or is operating under the auspices of an outside organization, it's your responsibility to make the finances transparent to outsiders.

THE DETAILS

Corporate Structure

At the dawn of the running boom in the 1970s, the term "nonprofit" was more often used to describe the finances of road races, as opposed to referring to a type of organization. The only people interested in staging running events were die-hard runners who put on events merely to provide a venue where members of their running clubs could compete. The largest events drew a few hundred runners (the 1971 Boston Marathon attracted 887 starters). There were few, if any, for-profit entities in the sport, because there was no profit to be had!

Today, however, there is far more interest and money in the sport of running. As a result, choosing the organizational structure for an event now requires a bit more thought.

Why Incorporate?

Many race-organizing groups are independently incorporated as a club, a company, or an event. Incorporation can help protect the personal assets

GREEN TIP

The Green Premium

In preparing the race budget, be aware that you may pay a premium for environmentally friendly items such as t-shirts and cups made from green materials, or for organic food. Research the prices for those items before finalizing the budget. You will feel good knowing that by incorporating these extra expenses you are helping the environment as well as your particular cause.

of a group's members from legal claims that could arise out of the race, eliminate disputes over who owns an event, and help with name recognition for the event. It is not required that a race be separately incorporated, but if you decide not to do so, be sure to specify in the agreements with sponsors or participating running clubs exactly who owns the race. Be aware that if you do not incorporate, you may be personally liable for any losses that the event may accrue, whether from contracts, property loss or personal injury. In addition, if you are unincorporated, both your business and personal assets will be vulnerable in the event of a lawsuit. If you do incorporate, be sure to observe all the formalities required of incorporated entities:

- Conduct periodic board meetings and membership meetings.

- Keep minutes of these meetings, especially details about the election of officers and directors.

- Sign documents and letters on behalf of the corporation.

- Use corporate letterhead and business cards.

- Use a separate corporate bank account, and don't commingle funds with the funds of any other person or corporate entity.

- Obtain required federal and state tax identification numbers in the corporate name.

- Set up online payment accounts for federal (www.EFTPS.gov) and state taxes.

- Use a separate telephone listing and email address for the corporation.

Complying with these formalities will help protect you, the officers and directors from personal liability.

For-profit or Nonprofit?

For ease of discussion, let's assume that your choice of corporate structure involves either a for-profit corporation or a nonprofit corporation. While other organizations, such as partnerships or limited liability companies, can also be used (see sidebar), corporations remain the most popular

model. And, although the terminology might differ somewhat, the critical concepts involved in the for-profit versus nonprofit decision remain the same.

Both for-profit and nonprofit running event organizers exist today, and one model is not inherently better than the other. Consider the health care industry, where for-profit and nonprofit hospitals have long existed side by side—unless you knew, you would be hard-pressed to identify whether a hospital is for-profit or nonprofit. By and large, for-profit and nonprofit events will be equally difficult to distinguish.

Most running clubs are nonprofit corporations as defined by the IRS tax code in section 501(c)(3). This designation must be specifically granted by the IRS, and offers 501(c)(3) nonprofit organizations certain exemptions from the federal income tax codes. These exemptions apply to corporations that are organized and operated exclusively for religious, charitable, scientific, literary, or educational purposes, or to foster national or international amateur sports competition. Most nonprofit running clubs and many nonprofit events in the U.S. affiliate with the nonprofit 501(c)(3) Road Runners Club of America (www.rrca.org) and are able to obtain nonprofit status under the RRCA's group exemption with the IRS. This saves a considerable amount of time and paperwork over filing for nonprofit status directly through the IRS, and there is no cost for RRCA members.

Whether you choose a for-profit or nonprofit model, you must comply with state statutes to create the entity and conduct operations.

For-Profit Business Structures

If you decide to establish a for-profit entity, there are a number of possible ways to do this. What follows is a very brief summary of each type of for-profit business structure, and some basic advantages and disadvantages of each. It is probably best to consult with a legal advisor before making a final decision.

- **Sole proprietorship:** A sole proprietorship is the most popular business structure, because it is the easiest to form. A sole proprietorship is owned by one individual and is unincorporated. The owner is taxed for the business's income on his/her personal tax return. Since there is no separate legal entity status for the business, the owner is personally responsible for all debts and legal liability, meaning that both business and personal assets are in jeopardy in the event of a lawsuit.

- **Partnership:** A partnership is a business with one or more owners that, like a sole-proprietorship, has not become incorporated and is thus easy to set up. Like a sole proprietorship, owners have personal liability for debts, obligations, and possible court judgments. Partners report their share of the business's profit or losses on their personal income tax returns. Generally, partners do not have to be equal in terms of the amount ownership.

- **LLC:** LLC stands for limited liability company. In this case, the business is a separate legal entity, offering the owner personal liability protection. LLCs allow complete flexibility with respect to distribution of profits, meaning someone can own 25% of the shares but receive, say, 75% of the annual profits, perhaps because he/she did more work than other owners in a particular year. LLCs are not, however, good vehicles to use if the end game is to try to take the company public or to raise substantial outside financing. LLCs are flexible when it comes to how you want to be taxed. Owners can choose to have an LLC taxed like a sole proprietorship, a partnership, or a corporation. Lastly, LLCs are generally easier to start up and run than S-corps.

- **S-Corp:** S-corp is short for subchapter S corporation. Like an LLC, the business is a separate legal entity, so personal liability for the owner is limited. S-corps require a board of directors and shareholders, and profits must be distributed based on shareholder percentages. Taxes pass through to the

owner(s)' personal tax returns and the S-corp does not file a corporate tax return. Although an S-corp is a good choice for a business that plans to sell stocks and look for investors, the rules that govern S-corps make them generally less flexible than LLCs.

- **C-Corp:** C-corp is short for subchapter C corporation. A C-corp, like an S-corp and an LLC, is considered a separate legal entity, so the owner is protected from liability as long as corporate formalities are followed. C-corps are taxed at the corporate level before the profits are distributed, which essentially means that owners of C-corps suffer double taxation. C-corps are the required entity in circumstances where third-party funding, such as private equity or venture capital, is used, or where the entity is setting itself up to either go public or be sold.

Filing Requirements

Whether you form a for-profit corporation or a nonprofit corporation, you will need to file articles of incorporation in the state where you plan to incorporate. Articles of incorporation contain general information about the business, such as the name, location, and type of corporate structure. Each state has separate laws that govern for-profit corporations and nonprofit corporations, and the fees for filing articles of incorporation also vary by state. Each state also requires that every corporation, whether for-profit or nonprofit, adopt bylaws, which contain information about the rules and regulations that govern the corporation. It is relatively easy to find state-specific information about articles of incorporation and bylaws on the internet - so do some research on what is required in your state. The RRCA website contains sample bylaws documents for both running clubs and event members, which can be used as a template for RRCA members who wish to obtain nonprofit status through the RRCA.

If you will do business outside of the state in which you have established the business entity, you are required to file the appropriate paperwork and pay a fee to qualify as a non-resident ("foreign") business in the chosen state. The definition of "doing business" in a state is important here. Any incidental time spent in a different state does not necessarily imply "doing business" - for example, if a race runs for a few short miles through a neighboring state, but does not start or finish in that state, paperwork is not required. However, if the race starts/finishes or is held entirely within a state other than the one in which the business is established, non-resident business paperwork is certainly required. Non-resident business paperwork is state-specific, so be sure to check the website of the particular state to determine both the fee and what exactly needs to be filed.

Governance and Membership

Corporations are governed by a board of directors—individuals who make key decisions about the goals and objectives of the corporation. Directors are considered fiduciaries and have the legal duty to act in the best interests of the organization.

For-profit corporations are owned by shareholders. Shareholders generally don't have a say in the day-to-day operations of the corporation, leaving that task to corporate officers. Many corporations are "closely held," however, meaning that there is a great deal of overlap between the directors, officers and shareholders.

Nonprofit corporations don't have shareholders, but they may have members. If a nonprofit corporation has members (many states don't require members), the members have those duties or rights that are specified in the state statutes, articles or bylaws. These rights and duties commonly include the right to vote for directors and amend the corporation's articles or bylaws.

Whether or not the nonprofit corporation has members, the articles or bylaws may reserve the election of directors to the board of directors itself. In this way, a board may be relatively self-perpetuating, although limits on the length of a board member's term are increasingly common.

Dissolution

What happens when a corporation ceases to do business, whether due to lack of activity or merger or other consolidation? For-profit corporations are generally required to distribute any remaining assets (after payment of all creditors) to corporate shareholders in proportion to their shareholdings.

If the nonprofit corporation is considered tax-exempt under regulations of the IRS (IRS code section 501(c)(3) is most common), remaining assets must be distributed to another tax-exempt organization upon dissolution.

Reporting Requirements

All corporations have reporting requirements. For-profit and nonprofit corporations are required to file annual reports in the state of incorporation and in each state in which they are doing business. Penalties for not filing these reports vary by state, but failure to file may result in eventual administrative dissolution of the corporation.

For-profit corporations file state and federal tax returns and pay income taxes on income. In the for-profit corporation known as an S-corp, the corporation files an informational tax return, and any income taxes are paid by the corporate shareholders. Nonprofit corporations that are not also tax-exempt are required to pay income taxes. Tax-exempt status is conferred upon nonprofit organizations by the IRS. The IRS has its own rules and regulations that impact tax-exempt organizations. Tax-exempt corporations are generally not required to pay income taxes. However, such organizations must file an information tax return (Form 990) with the IRS.

A nonprofit, tax-exempt corporation is also required to pay income tax whenever it generates income from activities not directly related to the organization's tax-exempt purpose. This is known as "unrelated business income," and the tax is commonly called UBIT, or unrelated business income tax. An example of unrelated business income for a nonprofit race or running-related organization would be when a third-party vendor sells goods or services at the race and you receive part of the profit. The IRS regulations in this area are complex and hazy. If you are unsure if you fall into this category, consult a tax attorney.

Control

Who controls corporate decision making? In theory, the directors of a corporation control the overall operation of the corporation, and the officers manage the day-to-day activities. In practice, it can be a little different.

Many for-profit corporations are owned and managed by a single individual or a small group of individuals. These individuals serve as officers, directors and shareholders. Agreements among the shareholders regulate how decisions are made and how deadlocks are broken. The majority shareholders in such an organization are plainly in control.

For nonprofit corporations, there are no owners. Theoretically, the corporation is owned by the public, and there is pressure for a nonprofit board of directors to make independent decisions. As a result, it may be more difficult for any individual board member or officer to exert control over the organization. It is not uncommon for an individual to take his or her dream or vision and create a nonprofit corporation to carry it out. In many cases, this individual becomes the board chair or chief executive officer. Over time, new board members have a different dream or vision and oust the founder.

Advantages of For-Profit Status

Why are running clubs, event clubs, and entrepreneurs looking at becoming for-profit corporations? There are a number of reasons, including:

- For-profit corporations usually require less paperwork in the formation stage, especially compared with nonprofit, tax-exempt corporations. Less paperwork often translates into less expense.

- Successful for-profit corporations make money for their owners, revenue that can be used to reward existing employees or attract new ones, to acquire additional assets such as other running events, or to distribute to shareholders. Value built by for-profit corporations can be used for any lawful purpose. Nonprofit corporations are more limited. While nonprofits can pay reasonable salaries to their employees and acquire assets that are related to their nonprofit or tax-exempt purpose, there can be no distribution of profits to board members or employees. Any profits are required to be used in a manner consistent with the organization's nonprofit or tax-exempt purpose.

- As noted above, it may be easier for the majority owners of a for-profit corporation to retain control over corporate decisions, because the same individuals in closely held corporations often serve as directors, officers and shareholders. Bear in mind, though, that this lack of independence between the directors, officers and shareholders can result in abuse and has led to increasing legislation in this area at the state and local levels. While much of this regulation applies to publicly traded corporations, the possibility exists that regulations regarding conflicts of interest and disclosures may filter down to smaller, privately owned corporations. Owners of for-profit corporations are well served to follow these developments and consider the adoption of corporate policies regarding conflicts of interest.

- Upon dissolution, the remaining assets are distributed to shareholders of for-profit corporations. Nonprofit corporations are required to distribute their remaining assets to other nonprofit or tax-exempt organizations.

- For-profit corporations don't have to deal with unrelated business income tax, allowing greater flexibility in the operations and income tax reporting of the for-profit corporation than its nonprofit counterpart.

Advantages of Nonprofit Status

- Nonprofit corporations, especially those that are also tax-exempt, are often exempt from a variety of taxes, including local, state and federal income taxes, and real estate property taxes.

- Nonprofit corporations may depend upon donations and contributions from individuals or grants from government entities or foundations. Many individuals give money to 501(c)(3) tax-exempt organizations because they believe in an organization's mission and goals and because they are able to deduct the amount of the gift for income tax purposes. Similarly, many government and foundation grants are available only to nonprofit or tax-exempt organizations.

- Nonprofit corporations often have a positive public image, because state law mandates that such organizations exist to provide some community benefit. For running and event clubs, this often includes education and the promotion of athletic competition. This public perception is an asset when seeking donations and grants. However, from time to time, there are public scandals involving nonprofits, generally over lavish salaries and expenses, and these scandals serve to seriously erode the positive perceptions people hold of this type of business.

Budgeting

The budget document should be easy for members of the organizing committee to review at a glance, so start with broad categories or line items. Although every budget will consist of income and expense categories, there certainly can be substantial variation among races for the particular line items. One race organization may classify its webmaster and race administrator under "Casual Labor," another may consider them "Contractual Services," while a third may consider them "Administrative Services." It is strongly suggested that you find an individual who is well-versed in some of the off-the-shelf accounting software to serve as treasurer. The accounting software programs may provide budget templates that can help you get started.

Once you have determined the major line items, you will want to create sub-groups under these broader headings. For example, you might want to have an expense category for "Supplies." In this category, include subcategories of "safety pins," "cups," "bib numbers," etc. Budgeting is a continual balance between providing essential but complete information in an easy-to-read format and providing an overwhelming amount of information, which results in a budget that is difficult to wade through. One approach might be

---

SIDEBAR

Setting Your Event's Fiscal Year

If you are setting up a corporate structure for your event, give some thought to establishing the event's fiscal year right from the start. Most businesses, more or less by default, are set up on a calendar fiscal year, running from Jan. 1 through Dec. 31. However, businesses can set their fiscal years to any 365-day period at the time the business commences operation. (Fiscal years can be changed later, but it is a cumbersome process.) It might be advantageous to set the fiscal year so that it starts and finishes during a "slow" part of the year, in terms of the event's cash flow. This means the event will take in all of its income and pay out all of its expenses during the same fiscal year. For example, a race held on the first weekend in April each year may want a fiscal year that runs from September 1 through August 31, rather than on a calendar-year basis, since August 31 is likely to be at a "slow" time of year. This means the race goes through one complete cycle of the event in the same fiscal year. If the event is part of a running club or a larger organization, you will need to operate on the same fiscal year as the parent organization.

to create three large expense categories—"Administration," "Operations," and "Marketing" and then put expense sub-categories into one of these three main categories. There are no "right" answers when it comes to making budget classifications; for example, you may wonder if you should include first aid supplies under a line item for "Medical" or under "Supplies." Either one will work; the key is to select categories and then be consistent with these categories from year to year. One of the key functions of the budget is to provide a history of the income and expenses for the event. If the medical supplies end up under "Medical" one year and under "Supplies" the next, you have lost the ability to compare these expenses from one year to the next easily and directly.

The financial information you produce will need to serve different audiences and different purposes. For example, board members tend to want to understand the big picture without a lot of operational details. Individuals involved with the day-to-day operations will need more detailed information to help stay on budget and to help plan future budgets. You may also be required to submit financial information to banks, sponsors, and local, state and federal agencies. Whatever the audience, the information should be consistent and easy to understand.

Once a budget has been developed, its adoption varies depending on how you are organized. Sole proprietorships and partnerships are relatively uncomplicated in this regard. Corporations (both non-profit and for-profit), on the other hand, must offer the budget to the Board of Directors for approval. Be prepared to defend the reasoning behind the figures being proposed.

Three sample race budgets (all fictional) appear on the following pages— **Table 2-A**: the "Twilight 5K," a low-key event with 300 participants; **Table 2-B:** the "Community Hospital 10K," a 1,000-runner 10K event offering no prize money; and **Table 2-C:** the "First City Bank Labor Day Half Marathon," a charity fundraiser with 10,000 registrants offering a $20,000 prize purse.

You can see from these budgets that account numbers have been assigned to the various line items (many budgeting programs will assign these automatically). Note that some line items, such as sponsorship on the income side and supplies on the expense side, are expanded for greater detail. A "Notes" column has been added to the budget where an explanation of the line items can be included if needed. After the first year, a column for the previous year's expenses can be added so the current year's budget projection can be compared with last year's "actuals." The budget should give the race committee a reasonably concise overview of the anticipated income and expenses for the event. A good rule of thumb is to think low on the income side and high on the expense side—despite what event promoters may be saying to the public at large.

An effective budget forces you to think through every single income and expense item in advance. For a first-time event, a great deal of time will need to be spent researching how much things will cost. (**Note:** The figures included in these example budgets are not based on actual expenses—do not rely on them as a basis for predicting your own expenses.) After the first year, you will have actuals from the previous year that will be a great aid in preparing the budget for year two. As noted earlier, a good budget is also a vital operational tool.

Our first sample race, the Twilight 5K, (**Table 2-A**) is a low-key event with a total budget of $4,500, with no sponsorship and offering no t-shirts or other amenities to participants other than a bare-bones award structure for the top runners.

Our second sample race, (**Table 2-B**) the "Community Hospital 10K," has a total budget of $40,510, with income and expenses equal at $40,510 (which means a net gain or loss of zero).

If only 800 runners showed up for the "Community Hospital 10K" in year one, then the registration fee income would need to be scaled back; if the police department announces a raise in the overtime rate for officers, an adjustment to that expense will be needed.

Undoubtedly, the budget for your event will

Table 2-A

Sample Budget #1: Twilight 5K
(a 300-runner event offering no prize money and no t-shirts)

Note: The numbers provided here are can vary widely; you should consider this budget only as a sample. The purpose is to show the types of line items you might want to include, and to give an example of how you might structure a budget for your event. You will need to research how much each of the necessary line items will cost in your locality.

		Total	Notes
4000 INCOME			**Notes**
4010 Registration Fees	$ 4,500.00		300 runners at $15 each
Total Income		**$ 4,500.00**	
6000 EXPENSES			
6020 Awards		$ 150.00	M and F top 3 Open and Masters
6050 Contractual Services		$ 1,000.00	HIJ Event Mgt. Company to score the race
6060 Copying		$ 10.00	
6090 Insurance		$ 800.00	Liability insurance through RRCA
6110 Medical			
6111 Ambulances	$ 400.00		Rental for 1 ALS ambulance
6112 First Aid Supplies	$ 100.00		
6110 Total Medical		$ 500.00	
6130 Municipal Fees			
6131 Parks Dept.	$ 200.00		Permit
6132 Police Dept.	$ 600.00		Two officers for 5 hours @$60 per hour
6130 Total Municipal Fees		$ 800.00	
6170 Postage		$ 50.00	
6180 Printing			
6181 Registration form	$ 100.00		
6186 Signs	$ 240.00		
6188 Other	$ 50.00		
6180 Total Printing		$ 390.00	
6200 Rental Equipment			
6201 Generator	$ 200.00		
6204 Porta-johns	$ 200.00		2 porta-johns @$100 each
6200 Total Rental Equipment		$ 400.00	
6210 Supplies			
6211 Bib Numbers	$ 100.00		300 bibs
6212 Cups	$ 100.00		2500 cups
6215 Pins	$ 50.00		2 boxes safety pins
6217 Toilet paper	$ 50.00		
6219 Other	$ 100.00		
6210 Total Supplies		$ 400.00	
6220 T-shirts		$ -	none
Total Expenses		**$ 4,500.00**	
Net Profit		**$ 0.00**	**Break even!**

Table 2-B

Sample Budget #2: Community Hospital 10K
(a 1,000-runner event offering no prize money)

Note: The numbers provided here are can vary widely; you should consider this budget only as a sample. The purpose is to show the types of line items you might want to include, and to give an example of how the budget for your race might be structured. You will need to research how much each of the necessary line items will cost in your locality.

4000 Income		Total	Notes
4010 Registration Fees		$ 35,000.00	1000 runners at $35 each
4020 Sponsorship			
4021 Community Hospital	$ 4,000.00		Title sponsor
4022 Jill's Running Store	$ 1,000.00		Supporting sponsor
4020 Total Sponsorship		$ 5,000.00	
4040 Virtual Goodie Bag Income		$ 500.00	5 inserts at $100 each
4060 Interest		$ 10.00	Interest on savings account
Total Income		**$ 40,510.00**	
6000 Expenses			
6010 Advertising			
6011 Your Town Sports	$ 500.00		
6012 Regional Running Pub	$ 800.00		
6013 Facebook Ad	$ 300.00		
6010 Total Advertising		$ 1,600.00	
6020 Awards		$ 800.00	Top 3 in 18 age 10-year age groups
6030 Bank Fees		$ 50.00	
6040 Casual Labor			
6041 Office Help	$ 400.00		40 hours at $10/hour
6045 Webmaster	$ 400.00		20 hours of updates @ $20.00/hour
6040 Total Casual Labor		$ 800.00	
6050 Contractual Services		$ 3,000.00	HIJ Event Mgt. Company to score the race
6060 Copying		$ 160.00	
6070 Courier & Shipping		$ 100.00	
6080 Hotel		$ 1,500.00	Rooms for 8 key staff on race weekend
6090 Insurance		$ 1,200.00	Liability insurance through RRCA
6100 Meals & Entertainment			
6101 Post-race food	$ 3,000.00		Water, muffins and bananas for 1000 runners
6103 Wrap-up Meeting	$ 400.00		Post-race committee meeting
6014 Other	$ 100.00		
6100 Total Meals & Entertainment		$ 3,500.00	
6110 Medical			
6111 Ambulances	$ 800.00		Rental for 2 ambulances (1 ALS & 1 BLS)
6112 First Aid Supplies	$ 400.00		
6110 Total Medical		$ 1,200.00	

Table 2-B

Sample Budget #2: Community Hospital 10K (cont.)
(a 1,000-runner event offering no prize money)

6130 Municipal Fees			
6131 Parks Dept.	$ 1,500.00		Permit
6132 Police Dept.	$ 1,800.00		Five officers for 6 hours @$60 per hour
6130 Total Municipal Fees		$ 3,300.00	
6140 Officials' Apparel		$ 1,000.00	Warm-ups for 10 key race personnel
6150 Online Registration Fees		$ 0.00	Service charge paid by registrants
6160 Photographer		$ 400.00	Photos for promotional purposes
6170 Postage		$ 600.00	
6180 Printing			
6181 Registration form	$ -		Donated. Value: $500.00
6183 Runner Instructions	$ 400.00		
6186 Signs	$ 2,000.00		
6188 Other	$ 300.00		
6180 Total Printing		$ 2,700.00	
6190 Professional Fees			
6191 Accountant	$ 400.00		Tax preparation
6192 Legal	$ 300.00		Review of waiver
6190 Total Professional Fees		$ 700.00	
6200 Rental Equipment			
6201 Generator	$ 500.00		
6204 Porta-johns	$ 1,200.00		12 porta-john @$100 each
6206 Tables	$ 350.00		8 tables at $50 each
6209 Tents	$ 1,500.00		
6200 Total Rental Equipment		$ 3,550.00	
6205 Storage Unit		$ 3,500.00	
6210 Supplies			
6211 Bib Numbers	$ 400.00		1200 numbers
6212 Cups	$ 300.00		8,000 cups
6215 Pins	$ 50.00		
6217 Toilet Paper	$ 100.00		
6219 Other	$ 100.00		
6210 Total Supplies		$ 950.00	
6220 T-shirts		$ 4,000.00	1000 shirts @$4.00 each
6230 Telephone/Internet			
6231 Landline	$ 200.00		
6232 DSL Connection	$ 600.00		
6230 Total Telephone/Internet		$ 800.00	
6240 Timing and Scoring		$ 2,500.00	Transponders
6250 Travel and Lodging		$ 1,100.00	Attend RRM Race Directors' Mtg.
6260 Website (incl. ISP)		$ 1,500.00	
Total Expenses		**$ 40,510.00**	
NET INCOME Net Profit		**$ 0.00**	**Break even!**

Table 2-C

Sample Budget #3:
First City Bank Labor Day Half Marathon
(a 10,000-runner event offering $20,000 in prize money)

Note: The numbers provided here are can vary widely; you should consider this budget only as a sample. The purpose is to show the types of line items you might want to include, and to give an example of how you might structure a budget for your event. You will need to research how much each of the necessary line items will cost in your locality.

Income		Total	Notes
Registration Fees		$ 600,000.00	10,000 runners @$60 each
Sponsorship			
Title Sponsor	$ 30,000.00		
Supporting Sponsor A	$ 8,000.00		
Supporting Sponsor B	$ 8,000.00		
Contributing Sponsor A	$ 4,000.00		
Contributing Sponsor B	$ 4,000.00		
Total Sponsorship		$ 54,000.00	
Expo Booth Sales		$ 10,000.00	20 booths at $500 each
Merchandise Sales		$ 9,000.00	
Interest		$ 200.00	
Total Income		**$ 673,200.00**	
Expenses			
Administration			
Race Director Salary	$ 60,000.00		
Part-time Assistant	$ 10,000.00		
Payroll Taxes	$ 5,500.00		
Webmaster	$ 10,000.00		
Race Director Travel	$ 4,000.00		
Office Rental	$ 18,000.00		$1500/month
Storage Unit	$ 12,000.00		
Telephone/Internet	$ 2,000.00		
Courier	$ 200.00		
Copies	$ 100.00		
Postage Meter Rental	$ 300.00		
Total Administration		$ 122,100.00	
Advertising		$ 6,000.00	Print media, TV, radio, online
Awards		$ 3,500.00	trophies/medals/raffle
Bags (clear plastic)		$ 4,000.00	
Bib Numbers		$ 2,000.00	
Casual labor		$ 10,000.00	Misc. extra work; volunteer coordinator
Entertainment (bands)		$ 5,000.00	Bands on course and post-race
Equipment			
Barricades	$ 1,500.00		
Gators	$ 2,000.00		
Porta-johns	$ 10,000.00		
Radios	$ 1,500.00		
Sound System	$ 8,000.00		
Stage	$ 3,000.00		

Table 2-C

Sample Budget #3:
First City Bank Labor Day Half Marathon (cont.)
(a 10,000-runner event offering $20,000 in prize money)

Tables	$ 2,000.00		40 tables @$50 each
Tents	$ 24,000.00		
Total Equipment		$ 52,000.00	
Elite Athlete Travel		$ 5,000.00	
Fees & Permits		$ 12,000.00	Municipal permit fee
Food (post-race)		$ -	In-kind donation valued at $20,000.
Graphic Design		$ 5,000.00	
Hospitality		$ 2,000.00	Pizza at committee meetings
Hotel			
Staff Rooms	$ 3,000.00		20 rooms at $150 per night
VIP Banquet	$ 15,000.00		Pre-race dinner for sponsors, VIPs, etc.
Total Hotel		$ 18,000.00	
Insurance		$ 6,000.00	General liabililty, D&O
Meals & Entertainment		$ 4,000.00	
Medals (participant)		$ 50,000.00	
Medical			
Ambulances	$ 2,000.00		
Thermal Blankets	$ 1,500.00		
Supplies	$ 1,000.00		
Total Medical		$ 4,500.00	
Merchandise		$ 10,000.00	Cost to produce merchandise sold
Miscellaneous		$ 3,000.00	
Municipal Fees		$ 25,000.00	
Postage		$ 6,500.00	Mailing out registration forms and results book
Printing			
Registration Form	$ 400.00		
Results Book	$ 5,000.00		
Other	$ 2,000.00		
Total Printing		$ 7,400.00	
Prize Money		$ 20,000.00	
Professional Services		$ 3,200.00	Legal and accounting
Security		$ 12,000.00	Police, private security
Signage		$ 14,000.00	
Supplies		$ 12,000.00	cups, bags, boxes, tape
T-shirts		$ 55,000.00	
Timing and Scoring		$ 40,000.00	Includes transponders
Transportation		$ 12,000.00	30 Shuttle buses
Travel - staff		$ 3,500.00	
Water (bottled for waterstops)		$ 10,000.00	
Vehicle Rental		$ 3,500.00	Trucks for hauling race material
Volunteer t-shirts		$ 14,000.00	Shirts for volunteers
Website (incl. ISP)		$ 1,000.00	
Total Expenses		**$ 563,200.00**	
Net Profit		**$ 110,000.00**	(to be donated to charity)

SIDEBAR

Handling In-Kind Contributions in Your Race Budget

Although a race director will want to give sponsors credit for in-kind sponsorships—such as to the supermarket that donated $20,000 towards the post-race party at the First City Bank Labor Day Half Marathon event (see ***Table 2-C: Sample Budget #3*** *on previous pages*) it is tricky to figure out how to reflect this type of sponsorship in the race's operating budget. Since most race budgets are cash budgets, the most practical solution is to set the line item ("Food" in this instance) to $0.00 and make a note of the value of the in-kind sponsorship so you will remember, if the sponsor does not return, to adjust the expense line item in the budget for the following year. The downside of this method is that the budget will not accurately reflect all the operating costs of the race, and additional income will be needed to cover the food if the sponsor drops out.

Both the event's accountant (and the IRS) and the in-kind sponsor may want a value placed on the in-kind contribution. As a general rule, all in-kind items should be assessed at fair market value as of the date of the contribution. Services contributed by a licensed professional may also constitute an in-kind contribution. For example, if a medical provider (doctor, nurse, etc.) volunteers in the medical tent, the value of his/her services should be added as an in-kind contribution. This is only the case if the individual is volunteering in his/her specific area of expertise.

In-kind contributions should be claimed on the race's tax return. For nonprofit event organizers, there are several places where you may be required to list both the type and value of donated facilities or other non-cash items. Look at the following areas on the organization's Form 990 (these lines could vary depending on the 990 form used):

1. Line 1 of Parts II and III of Schedule A;

2. Form 990, Part VIII line 1g;

3. Schedule B, Part II; and

4. Schedule M, column (c), if applicable.

If you're not familiar with the IRS Form 990, check out the available information at www.irs.gov and search the term "990," or better yet, ask your accountant. The sponsor may also wish to list the value of in-kind donations on his/her organization's tax return, especially if the event is a 501(c)(3) nonprofit organization, as the value of the donation can be taken as a tax deduction.

Credit Union Cherry Blossom

Food is a common in-kind donation to races

include line items that are not in these example budgets. For example, the "Community Hospital 10K" does not offer prize money for elite athletes, does not have an expo, and does not sell any race merchandise, so these line items do not appear. As a race grows and changes each year, the budget will grow and change as well.

Our third sample race budget, (**Table 2-C**) for a fictional "First City Bank Labor Day Half Marathon," a 10,000-runner event offering $20,000 in prize money, reflects some line items that a larger race is likely to encounter, including prize money, expo booth sales, race director salary, office rental, etc. For simplicity, the large-race budget is presented without the accounting code numbers.

During the cycle of your race, you may be tempted to revisit and revise the budget. Sometimes this is necessary, for example, if you are told that you need to pay for a Fire Marshall to inspect the expo area. Once the budget is set, however, try to keep it as static as possible. Undoubtedly you will go over budget on some items and come in under budget on others. If you are continually changing the line items to meet the actuals, the value of the budget as a planning document will be diminished. After the event is over, spend a fair amount of time analyzing which items came in high and which items came in low against the original budget.

Setting The Registration Fee and Estimating the Number of Entrants

Perhaps the most important budget decision to be made is setting the registration fee for the event and estimating the number of entrants (especially difficult in the first year). This is because, for the vast majority of races, registration fee income is the largest single income category— frequently by a large margin.

Registration fees at road races have outstripped inflation over the last decade. While a few low-key club events can be found with registration fees in the $10-$25 range, most 5Ks and 10Ks fall in the $25-$40 range; half marathons in the $80-$115 range, and large marathons are well past the $100 mark, some even surpassing $200. Quite a few events feature escalating fees, starting with discounted "early bird" fees, followed by the standard fee and ending up with higher late fees as race day approaches. Of course, many of today's races offer expanded menus of benefits, such as post-race meals, medals to all finishers, post-race parties/concerts, fancier premiums, etc., all of which drive up costs. Some race directors take a purely commercial approach and are willing to charge "what the market will bear" and, very often, these high prices do not deter runners. Other race directors, many of whom came out of the nonprofit running club culture before the running boom of the

TIP

A Reserve Fund

What would you do if you suddenly lost the title sponsor or had to cancel the event? Sponsors come and go, and over the years races have had to deal with floods, hurricanes, volcanic eruptions and terrorist attacks. Do you know how much money such a contingency might cost? To prepare for such an eventuality, all races should develop a reserve fund. How much should you put into this fund? Five percent of the budget each year seems like a good and manageable amount (consider putting in more if you have a good year). After only a few years of financial discipline, you will have a "nest egg" sufficient to provide some true relief in the event of a financial crash of some sort. Different races set different goals for their reserve funds – some will strive for one-third to one-half of their operating expenses at a minimum; others like to stash away an amount equal to what the largest sponsor pays, so that the event could go on for a year even if the main sponsor dropped out. Even if you are a 501(c)(3) organization, there is no upper limit on the allowable size of a reserve fund, as long as the amount is credible relative to the mission of the organization. Your reserve fund also becomes an investment of sorts, potentially earning some level of interest income, possibly in a CD or interest-bearing savings account.

1970s, feel it is their social responsibility to keep registration fees low. The result is a wide disparity in registration fees for events, even events of the same length. Since registration revenue is a major—if not *the* major—portion of a race's income, it is important to set the fee at a level that enables the race, at the very least, to break even. In order to set a registration fee that will allow you to break even, work backwards starting from the expenses determined in the draft budget. (In many instances, two of the most underestimated expenses are municipal and police fees. Make sure you know these costs early on. See *Chapter 13: Municipal Relations* for details about these fees). On the income side, subtract out any known sponsorship income. Based on your anticipated number of entrants, this will enable you to calculate how much income you need to raise from the registration fee. Next, try to come up with a realistic (or better yet, pessimistic) estimate of the number of registrants the event will get. Divide the costs by the number of registrants to determine the minimum registration fee needed to break even. Do some research on other local races of the same length, to ascertain that the fee is in the same ballpark. Although you need to cover expenses, be careful not to set the registration fee too high, even if you are attempting to raise money for a charity. Some charity events have done this, hoping to raise funds for the charity, and are later surprised when relatively few people register (especially if there are alternative races on the same weekend).

TIP

The Tyranny of T-shirts

Perhaps the hardest line item for a first-time event to anticipate is the premium or 'swag' expense, which is most often t-shirts. First, you must decide whether the registration fee will include a premium for every participant or whether you will allow participants to purchase the premiums separately for an additional fee. Either way, premiums are usually one of the first items that have to be ordered, at a time when it still isn't known how many runners will register or order them. If you assume 1,000 participants at $40 each ($40,000 in registration fee income) and order 1,000 t-shirts at $5 each (a $5,000 order) and only end up with 200 runners, you've overpaid for shirts by $4,000 and the registration fee income is down by $32,000 – a swing of $36,000 in income, which can put you in a perilous position! Look for a t-shirt screen printer, or a distributor of whichever premium you choose, who will allow you to place an order as close to the event as possible. Even if you pay a bit more for this ability, you may come out substantially better in the long run.

Phil Stewart

Leftover t-shirts from the Credit Union Cherry Blossom await donation.

Besides the overall philosophical bent of the event, here are some additional factors to consider when setting the registration fee.

- *What are other similar events in the area charging?* Especially during the crowded fall and spring racing seasons, runners are somewhat price sensitive when choosing from a broad array of events.

- *What is the status of the event in the area?* Some events, particularly marathons, are events that runners point to as one of their two to three major events of the year. If your event enjoys this status, you can charge a higher fee. This may require a dispassionate assessment on the part of the race director about the significance of his or her event to runners. First-time events that are not well known may benefit from lower registration fees in order to lure participants away from established events.

- *What about registration fee discounts?* The advent of codes used with online registration forms makes offering discounts on registration fees easy to do. Many events use discounts as a way to drive registrations. A few studies suggest that runners are not terribly price resistant, so if you offer discounts, track their success carefully and make sure you have planned the variable registration fees into the event's budget.

Information to assist in drawing up a budget for other line items appears in the chapters covering these areas, such as *Chapter 5: Sponsorship; Chapter 11:* *Equipment, Supplies and Key Personnel*; *Chapter 13: Municipal Relations; Chapter 15: Packet Pick-up/ Late Registration, Expo and Hotel; and Chapter 17: Timing and Scoring*.

Other Financial Suggestions

- **Establish financial protocols:** Once every

SIDEBAR

Financial Compilations, Reviews and Audits

The commonly used types of financial-statement reporting include compilations, reviews and audits.

- A compilation involves the use of an accountant to help organize financial information. A compilation does not provide any opinion as to the quality or accuracy of the financial statements. It is the least expensive alternative.

- A review is a more intensive study of the financial statements and provides additional assurance about the reasonableness of the financial condition presented in those statements. With a review, the accountant also does not offer any opinion as to the quality or accuracy of the financial statements reviewed.

- An audit is the most intensive form of review. It will come with the CPA's opinion on whether the financial statements are prepared in accordance with generally accepted accounting principles and are free from material misstatement. An audit requires a review of the organization's records and confirmations from the organization's management, governing board members, and outside professionals such as attorneys. The CPA can provide a qualified opinion, highlighting areas where there are concerns about whether certain matters may not comply with generally accepted accounting principles.

- One more type of audit to be aware of is a forensic audit, which is an investigative audit used when circumstances suggest that fraud, mismanagement or embezzlement may have taken place. A forensic audit can be used to help an organization develop internal and external controls to mitigate the possibility fraud or mismanagement, as well as to identify whether such activity has occurred and determine the responsible parties. A forensic audit is also used to help demonstrate the existence of fraud and misappropriation in court.

decade or so, a story emerges about a club or race treasurer who has embezzled funds from an event. In addition to the emotional drain of having to confront someone who appeared to be a loyal member of your organization, in many cases the money is simply gone, and no amount of legal action is going to get it back. This can be devastating. The time to implement basic financial controls—in writing—is at the front end, when everyone is enthusiastic and working well together. Financial mismanagement flourishes best in a vacuum, so make sure no vacuum exists in the financial end of your organization.

Some suggested protocols:

- More than one person should have access to all of the financial records, and the secondary person should take an active role in monitoring the financial transactions. Some races create an audit committee charged with this responsibility.
- Be sure that more than one individual has check-signing authority. This protects the event if the primary individual becomes incapacitated.
- Consider requiring multiple signatures on checks, or at least on large checks over a certain dollar amount.
- Require receipts for as many financial transactions as possible.
- Consider hiring an outside accountant to review the books periodically. This can be accomplished through a few different accounting procedures, including

compilations, reviews, and audits, as detailed in the *Sidebar* on the previous page. These procedures differ in detail/ intensity and therefore also in cost.

- Consider using an accountant to prepare the tax returns for the event.

- **Know which taxes need to be filed:** It is probably best to check with legal and financial professionals to make sure that you are filing all required taxes. The taxes that need to be filed depend on how the organization is structured—as a sole proprietorship, a corporation, a nonprofit, etc.—each structure has different requirements. Don't forget to look into state and local taxes, sales tax, personal property taxes, and real estate taxes. There may be taxes you don't even know about, so seeking advice from a CPA or attorney may be worthwhile. If you are paying any contractor $600 or more during a calendar year, you will likely have to file a 1099-MISC form and the annual 1096 form; if you have employees within your organization, you will be responsible for making monthly deposits of each employee's federal and state taxes withheld, plus Social Security and Medicare payments as appropriate. You will need to issue W-2 forms for their taxes. You will also need to file and pay federal and state unemployment taxes, generally on a quarterly basis (a separate discussion of the withholding and filing requirements for payments to elite athletes appears in *Chapter 12: Special Entrant Categories*.)

BUS LOADING, CORRAL LOADING, AND START TIMES	WAVE 1	WAVE 2	WAVE 3	WAVE 4
2015 BOSTON MARATHON	3999	10999	19999	31999
BIB NUMBERS	101–7,700	8,000–15,600	16,000–23,600	24,000–32,500
BUS LOADING	6:00 a.m. – 6:48 a.m.	7:00 a.m. – 7:48 a.m.	7:55 a.m. – 8:43 a.m.	8:45 a.m. – 9:33 a.m.
ARRIVAL IN HOPKINTON	7:07 a.m. – 7:55 a.m.	8:07 a.m. – 8:55 a.m.	9:02 a.m. – 9:50 a.m.	9:52 a.m. – 10:40 a.m.
CORRAL LOADING 1 & 2	9:05 a.m.	9:40 a.m.	10:05 a.m.	10:30 a.m.
CORRAL LOADING 3 & 4	9:10 a.m.	9:45 a.m.	10:10 a.m.	10:35 a.m.
CORRAL LOADING 5 & 6	9:15 a.m.	9:50 a.m.	10:15 a.m.	10:40 a.m.
CORRAL LOADING 7 & 8	9:20 a.m.	9:55 a.m.	10:20 a.m.	10:45 a.m.
START TIME	10:00 a.m.	10:25 a.m.	10:50 a.m.	11:15 a.m.

Please note that all times are approximate and may vary slightly.

Phil Stewart

3 Race Timetable and Checklist

THE BASICS

- **Set a long lead time.** A race director with ambitions for a successful event should start planning at least a year in advance. If you have your sights set on developing the race into a major event, even longer lead times are desirable. This doesn't mean that you will be working on the event 24/7 starting that far in advance; it means that some aspects of event planning—such as sponsorship solicitation, applying for municipal permits, and contracting for the official hotel and expo space, if they are needed—will have time to move along, even if the pace is frustratingly slow. If enough time isn't allowed for the slow-moving components to unfold, you may suddenly find yourself with no sponsor, no permit, or inadequate space when it is time to order bib numbers or to open registration. Panic will set in. Allowing enough time is like building a base in marathon training.

- **Establish a timetable.** Race directors approach setting timetables for their events in a variety of ways. Some will rely on a full-featured project management software package to create a plan;

others rely on some sort of master calendar or date book leading up to race day; others keep careful chronological files of the previous year's event and work from them; some use a standard spreadsheet to keep focus on individual items of significance; and, sadly, more than would ever admit it keep it all in their heads (not a recommended policy). A good timetable needs to have the flexibility to add and rearrange tasks to accommodate the volatile side of race organizing.

THE DETAILS

If you are a first-time race director and are feeling a bit intimidated by the length of this manual, start by using the race timetables and check list contained in this chapter. These will provide the basic framework for the event. Then, refer to specific chapters for details on each item as you work your way through the lists. As you plan and execute a race, sometimes you will want to see the forest and sometimes the trees. A long-term timetable is the forest, covering the broad tasks but without going into too much detail. This makes it easier to see the general flow of the event planning. The short-term timetable is the trees. It may cover only a few days prior to the race and should be more detailed. It covers the key tasks that everyone on the committee will be doing, in order to give you an overview of the entire operation. In other words, the long-term timetable is more of a *planning document* for the race director; the short-term timetable is more of an *operations document* to keep the race director informed about what everyone is doing during the final days.

The Long-Term Timetable

It is difficult to present a one-size-fits-all race timetable, because events come in so many different shapes and sizes. The timetable for a new major urban race weekend featuring a marathon, half marathon, 5K and Kids' Run will be significantly longer and much more complex than that for a local 5K that is an established fixture for area runners. It is not uncommon for aspiring new major events to make their initial announcements

(which presumably means at least a modest amount of planning has occurred before this time) between 12 and 18 months prior to race day (sometimes even longer); contracts with hotels and convention centers, for example, often require starting the process as much as three years in advance.

With this in mind, we have presented a timetable for a hypothetical race falling somewhere in between the two examples given above–a new event that aspires to be significant on the regional level. The timetable starts 12 months in advance of race day *(see **Table 3-A**)*.

Use this timetable only as a template. As work on your own event progresses, the timetable should increase in complexity as new tasks specific to the event are added. The timetable presented here covers only the broad tasks that are likely to be associated with a majority of events.

Remember, specific tasks are not completed in an instant, so there needs to be some fluidity in the timeline. For example, we suggest that the ordering of supplies and equipment begin four months out, even though it may lag over into the third month out. Consider the timeframe under which a task first appears as a guideline for *initiating* work on that objective.

Details about the various tasks appear in other chapters of this manual, so be sure to read those sections if you want more information. This timeline is limited to a listing of the tasks in sequential order, without going into the specifics. Also, although it is not listed here, be sure to hold regular meetings with the organizing committee, to make sure everyone is on task.

Table 3-A

Sample Large Race Year-Long Planning Timetable

10-12 MONTHS OUT

- Establish race organizing committee
  - Delegate tasks to organizing committee
  - Create mission statement for race
  - Hold initial organizing committee meeting
- Set overall timetable and budget for the event
- Set race distance, desired course, and method to be used for timing the event
- Set race date
- Initiate sponsor solicitation

8-10 MONTHS OUT

- Explore permitting process
- Set up bank accounts and financial procedures
- Identify and establish contracts or agreements with necessary contractors, especially those handling registration, timing, scoring, equipment rental, etc.
- Initiate approval process from local police and municipal agencies
- Announce creation of the race (once permits are at least tentatively approved—many jurisdictions don't issue the permit until shortly before the event)
- Identify number of volunteers needed and develop a strategy for recruitment
- Conclude sponsor search for sponsors to appear on all printed and electronic materials
- Determine site for pre-race packet pick-up
- Sign contract with race hotel and/or expo space (if necessary)

6-8 MONTHS OUT

- Formulate advertising and promotions plans
- Certify course
- Make sure website is up and running
- Establish awards structure and post on website
- Create a strong presence on social media

- Create and distribute initial press release announcing race date
- Begin development of registration form/set up online registration
- Begin development of "virtual race bag" if using
- Open registration with "early bird" pricing if desired

5 MONTHS OUT

- Begin ad placement and promotion
- Identify vendors for necessary suppliers

4 MONTHS OUT

- Develop t-shirt art
- Design staging area to anticipate supply and equipment needs
- Begin elite athlete recruitment (if any)
- Order supplies and equipment (see *Chapter 11: Equipment, Supplies and Key Personnel* for a list of supplies and equipment)

3 MONTHS OUT

- Send any snail mail-based advertising and place flyers on local sporting goods stores, etc.
- Begin "Standard" registration pricing
- Begin volunteer recruitment

2 MONTHS OUT

- Continue ordering and assembling supplies
- Distribute second press release

1 MONTH OUT

- Begin "Late" registration pricing, discuss with timers when registration should close (if applicable)
- Order race signage
- Provide final instructions to expo exhibitors
- Communicate with timing team about awards structure and other timing details

Table 3-A

Sample Large Race Year-Long Planning Timetable (cont'd)

2 WEEKS OUT

- Reconfirm all municipal services
- Reconfirm all arrangements for packet pickup
- Reconfirm all volunteers and notify about duties, time frame and where to report
- Review all permit items

1 WEEK OUT

- Close online registration, if timers deem necessary; download online database into scoring software
- Contact each committee member to check in. Troubleshoot as needed.
- Check markings for start/finish line and all mile marks on course
- Distribute final pre-race press-release
- Prepare (stuff) race packets if using

3 DAYS OUT

- Reconfirm all vendors, contractors, suppliers, etc.
- Verify that all last-minute supplies have been received or that items shipped directly to race hotel or elsewhere have arrived

2 DAYS OUT

Begin expo/packet pick-up set-up (if applicable)

1 DAY OUT

- Hold race expo (if applicable) or pre-race packet pick-up
- Hold pre-race dinner (if applicable)
- Begin pre-race set-up

RACE DAY

- Complete race set-up including race-day registration/packet pick-up
- Start race
- Hold awards ceremony
- Complete race breakdown
- Post results on website by evening, if not before
- Prepare and distribute post-race communications

1 DAY AFTER

- Start responding to post-race emails

2 DAYS AFTER

- Close protest period (if applicable)

WEEK AFTER

- Send thank you notes/messages
- Continue to respond to post-race correspondence
- Make corrections to results
- Mail out unclaimed awards (if applicable)
- Distribute prize money to elite athletes (if applicable)
- Distribute printed or electronic results to any additional sources, as needed

WEEK-MONTH AFTER

- Organize final committee/"wrap-up" meeting (ideally this should be scheduled 1-4 weeks after the event—long enough for people to recover from race day but soon enough so people don't forget the details of what happened.)

MONTH AFTER

- Send post-race report to sponsors and other applicable organizations

The Short-Term Timetable

The short-terrm timetable, which may cover only 2-3 days including race day, is more of a checklist to remind a race director exactly what is happening and when. It is less a *planning* document and more of an *operations* document. For more complex events with more staff and/or volunteers, it may be a composite covering the activities of all key personnel.

Table 3-B below provides a sample Event Weekend Timetable for a Large Race; **Table 3-C** provides a sample Event Weekend Timetable for a Small Race.

Table 3-B

Sample Large Race Event Weekend Timetable

A sample race weekend timetable for a 12,000-runner event containing a Kids' Run, a 5K and a 10K. This timetable is basically a compilation and integration of the race weekend timetables for all the race committee members combined into a single document. Besides being the "master plan" for the weekend, it is very useful for identifying any conflicts among activities or problems with the sequencing of the activities.

TIME   ACTION

1 DAY PRIOR TO RACE DAY

TIME	ACTION
6:00am	Race site logistics coordinator meets with police to coordinate day's activities
6:00am	Expo vendors begin set up
6:00am	Packet /bib/chip pick-up and t-shirt operations begin set up
7:00am	Contractor delivers porta-johns to race site
7:45am	Race committee meeting held to finalize coordination of activities
8:00am	Contractor for setup operations drops off barricades, begins to erect tents, speaker towers, etc.
8:30am	Race office opens for business
9:00am	Race expo information booth opens at expo
9:30am	Expo, packet/bib/chip pick-up and t-shirt pick-up operations open
12:00pm	Race truck is loaded at storage with supplies, such as water coolers, signage, etc. and parked until the next morning
12:30pm	Course layout team begins review of course, start to finish, looking for any last-minute trouble spots
1:00pm	Water contractor delivers bottled water to race site
2:30pm	Course layout team completes physical review of course
5:30pm	Expo closes
5:30pm	Packet/bib/chip pick-up supplies/materials and t-shirts are packed up for delivery in the morning to the race site
5:45pm	Race office closes
6:00pm	Security guards take station for overnight security at race site

RACE DAY

TIME	ACTION
4:30am	Race site logistics coordinator meets with police to coordinate day's activities
5:00am	Start/finish area closed to traffic; vehicles requiring access must have "Official Vehicle" identification
5:00am	Supply truck arrives at race site with the race equipment (coolers, signage, etc.) picked up on Saturday from storage
5:00am	Course layout team arrives at race site and begins operations; placing of cones & barriers in start/finish area begins
5:00am	Security guards go off-duty at race site

Table 3-B

Sample Large Race Event Weekend Timetable (cont'd)

5:00am	Bag check coordinator finishes setting up for baggage check operations
5:15am	Volunteer coordinator begins set up for volunteer check-in at race site; radios are distributed to key personnel/ team captains
5:20am	Course marshals and split timers (if used) check-in for specific assignments & instructions/training
5:30am	Packet /bib/chip pick-up and t-shirts are delivered to the race site
5:30am	Volunteer check-in begins
6:00am	Communications Central is established and radio checks begin
6:00am	Contractor(s) arrive to deliver necessary last-minute food/supplies (coffee, ice for medical, bagels, etc.)
6:00am	Early course marshal positions are manned
6:00am	Supply truck departs race site to deliver supplies and equipment on the course
6:00am	Transportation arrives at race site to transport course marshals and split timers to stations on the course
6:15am	Bag check opens
6:30am	Course marshals and split timers load onto buses and depart to their stations
6:45am	Race site packet/chip/bib pick-up opens operations
7:05am	Timing mats are put in place at start/finish line
7:10am	Kids' Run registration opens
7:10am	Warm-up exercises for participants from awards stage
7:10am	5K start/finish volunteers assemble
7:15am	All roads on the course are CLOSED at this time.
7:25am	Kids' Run course marshals with cones line Kids' Run course
7:30am	All course marshal positions manned by this time
7:40am	Warm-up exercises conclude
7:45am	VIP Introductions from the start/finish stage
7:50am	Kids' Run participants assemble near Kids' Run start
7:58am	All wheelchair athletes are to be in position at the 5K start line
7:59am	Wheelchair race starts
8:00am	**10K Race starts**
8:15am	Kids' Run course marshals move onto center line
8:20am	**Kids' Run starts**
8:20am	Remaining finish line structure/equipment set up
8:20am	10K finish line volunteers undergo training in finish line operations
8:30am	Food service begins
8:30 am	First male finisher
8:35 am	First female finisher
8:40am	**5K Run-Walk starts**
8:55 am	First male 5K finisher
8:57 am	First female 5K finisher
9:30am	Race site logistics coordinator begins post-race breakdown of tents, etc.
9:55am	5K course closes: no official finishers after this time

Table 3-B

Sample Large Race Event Weekend Timetable (cont'd)

10:00am	5K start/finish and course equipment removal begins
10:15am	"Soft" awards ceremony begins with random awards
10:30am	"Formal" awards ceremony begins
10:45am	Food service closes down
11:00am	Communications coordinator collects all radios not previously returned
11:00am	Supply truck returns to start/finish area after retrieving water stop supplies and various supplies from the course
11:00am	Truck is loaded up with t-shirts and packet pick-up supplies/materials
11:00am	Baggage check closes - all runner bags should be picked up by this time
11:00am	All roads on the course are reopened at this time
11:30am	Race site logistics coordinator finishes gathering equipment, etc.
12:00pm	Contractor begins breakdown and removal of equipment etc. at start/finish
12:00pm	Contractor begins removal of porta-johns
12:30pm	Supply trucks begin trips to return signage, coolers, equipment, remaining t-shirts, etc., to storage
1:00pm	Race site area is completely clear by this time
8:00pm	10K and 5K results are posted on the race website by this time

Table 3-C

Sample Small Race Event Weekend Timetable

A sample race weekend timetable for an event with one distance and 500 or fewer runners

TIME   ACTION

1 DAY PRIOR TO RACE DAY

Time	Action
6:00am	Packet/bib/chip pick-up and t-shirt operations begin setting up, along with late registration (if applicable)
7:00am	Contractor(s) deliver porta-johns and any other rented supplies, bottled water, etc. to race site
9:00am	Packet/bib/chip pick-up and t-shirt operations open for the day
12:00pm	Race truck is loaded with supplies such as water coolers, signage, etc. and parked until the next morning
12:30pm	Race director or designee reviews the entire course, start to finish, looking for any last-minute trouble spots
5:30pm	Packet/bib/chip pick-up supplies/materials and t-shirts are packed up and put in a truck for delivery to the race site in the morning

RACE DAY

Time	Action
5:00am	Race director or designee meets with police/other authorities to coordinate road closings (if applicable) or other activities
5:30am	Start/finish area is closed to traffic (if applicable)
5:30am	Supply truck arrives at race site with the race equipment (coolers, signage, packets, t-shirts etc.) picked up prior day
5:30am	Volunteer coordinator begins volunteer check-in at race site
5:30am	Course layout team arrives at race site and begins operations; placing of cones & barriers in start/finish area begins; finish line setup begins; supplies delivered to water stops
5:30am	Course marshals and other on-course volunteers check-in for specific assignments & instructions/training
6:00am	Any race-day deliveries (water, food etc.) are completed
6:00am	Water stops/aid stations are set up
6:45am	Race site packet/bib/chip operations and race day registration open
7:15am	All roads that require closing are closed at this time; all course marshals are in place at this time
8:00am	Race starts
8:30am	Food service begins
8:30 am	First male finisher
8:35 am	First female finisher
9:30am	Race director or designee begins post-race take-down of tents, etc.
10:30am	Awards ceremony begins (can be earlier depending on length of race)
10:45am	Food service closes down
11:00am	Supply truck returns to start/finish area after retrieving water stop supplies and various materials from the course
11:00am	Any closed roads on the course are reopened at this time
11:30am	Final cleanup of race site is complete
12:00pm	Contractors remove porta-johns and any other rented equipment
12:30pm	Equipment and supplies are returned to storage location
1:00pm	Race site area is completely clear by this time
8:00pm	Results are posted on race website by this time

SIDEBAR

Master Race Checklist

The following is a good checklist of the entire race operation:

REGISTRATION INFORMATION

Make sure that the online registration form contains all of the necessary information. Double check accuracy of all dates/times/pricing etc. The race director (or a volunteer of choice) should run through the entire online registration form to make sure it is working properly. Whether you are using an online registration site or a printed registration form (some events still use printed entry forms for very late sign-ups), make sure the following information is included directly on the registration platform or the form itself.

- Date of race
- Starting time
- Start and finish location(s), directions, transportation, parking information
- Race distance
- Basic course description (details of the course should be provided on the website)
- Course map (or include on website)
- Course certification number, if applicable
- Race sanction with USA Track & Field, if applicable
- Sponsoring/assisting organizations
- Municipalities involved
- Age groups and award information
- Club/corporate team categories/prizes, if applicable
- Description of premium (t-shirt, etc.)
- Packet/bib/transponder and t-shirt pick-up information/expo information
- URL for race website
- Registration fee (spell out non-refundable and include cancellation policy), registration deadline, check payable to/mailing address (if checks are accepted)
- Race limit, if applicable
- Prohibitions (no strollers, dogs, headphones, etc.)
- Clinics and other related activities (if applicable)

RUNNER INFORMATION

Most online registration forms are pre-formatted to collect the appropriate information from the registrant, so you will not need to set up this part of the form yourself. However, it never hurts to double check that the following important information is collected by the registration platform, and these fields will definitely be needed if you plan to create a paper registration form.

- Name, address (street, city, state, zip), phone number (day/evening/cell)
- Age and date of birth, gender
- Email address
- Where applicable: special categories (e.g., town, organization), team/club designation
- Emergency race-day contact name and phone number
- T-shirt size
- Any important medical conditions
- Signature (parent or guardian if under 18) acknowledging Waiver of Liability/Assumption of Risk

SIDEBAR

Master Race Checklist (cont'd)

PROMOTION

Promote the race with help of the following methods:

- Use of the race website—site should contain all relevant information about the event
- Use of social media—strong presence on all relevant platforms—Facebook, Twitter, Instagram, etc.
- Email blasts using lists from past races, club lists, or local media platforms that list and advertise races
- Distribution of postcards or other paper-based advertising materials, including paper registration forms if you will be using them, through the mail and at running stores, health clubs and races
- Distribution of posters and neighborhood flyers/signs
- Media announcements (calendar listing) to either the web or print editions of local newspapers, local and national running magazines
- Television/radio public service announcements
- Press releases
- Local running clubs, event sponsors, the local municipality and other involved organizations should assist with promotional efforts
- Advertisements (including Facebook ads and other social media advertising)
- Designation of a race photographer for participant photo sales, documentation and history, future sponsor presentations

PRE-RACE

During the months preceding the race, the following tasks should be accomplished:

- Secure municipal permits
- Secure state permits
- Obtain sanction (if necessary)
- Obtain liability insurance (through RRCA, USATF, organization's own insurance company, or other)
- Obtain certificates of insurance and additional insured documents (if applicable)
- Have course measured to USATF certification standards and submit paperwork either by learning procedure on own or by hiring a USATF course measurer
- Mark miles on course per the certified course map
- Determine how race will be timed and who will do it
- Prepare signage for course and race site
- Arrange police liaison/details
- Notify fire department
- Notify local hospital and arrange for ambulance services
- Obtain press/course vehicles
- Purchase t-shirts/other premiums
- Purchase bib numbers/safety pins
- Hire contractors for porta-johns, tents, sound system, barricades and any other necessary equipment rentals
- Create/update/maintain the race website. Make sure to add all pertinent info, including
  - medical/weather information
  - timing/starting line-up information

SIDEBAR

Master Race Checklist (cont'd)

- ◆ course map with mile markers and aid stations
- ◆ clothing/check-in/changing facilities/showers
- ◆ results posting information
- ● Create/update/maintain all social media platforms
- ● Establish online registration
- ● Deposit any mailed registration fees and file any paper registration forms received
- ● Establish volunteer committees and appoint captains for:
  - ◆ registration
  - ◆ publicity and promotion
  - ◆ sponsors and donations
  - ◆ timing and scoring
  - ◆ medical
  - ◆ aid stations
  - ◆ course security/marshals/communications
  - ◆ results posting and distribution
  - ◆ awards
  - ◆ refreshments/clean-up

RACE DAY

- ● Course/and staging area signs posted
- ● Volunteer/race official area assembled
  - ◆ tables/chairs/signage posted
  - ◆ coffee/refreshments
  - ◆ t-shirt/official identification
  - ◆ instructional briefings prepared
- ● Press area assembled
  - ◆ tables/chairs/signage
  - ◆ computer, scanner, printer and WiFi capability set up
  - ◆ race information/print-outs
- ● Race-day registration and/or packet pickup area set up
  - ◆ list/printout with runner names/numbers posted
  - ◆ number/transponder pick-up location
  - ◆ t-shirt/packet pick-up location
  - ◆ registration forms/pens/pencils or computers/tablets if online late registration will be used
  - ◆ race numbers/pins
  - ◆ race packets
  - ◆ cash box/change
  - ◆ tables, chairs, signage
- ● Help/trouble desk set up
- ● Police briefed

SIDEBAR

Master Race Checklist (cont'd)

- Course officials/marshals briefed
- Start/finish officials briefed
- Official photographer(s) briefed (provide with photo shot list)
- Press/course vehicle drivers briefed (someone very familiar with the course should serve as guide in each vehicle)
- Trail/sweep vehicle driver briefed (provide vehicle with water, cups, blankets, first-aid kit, etc.)
- Official starter equipped and briefed
- Start/finish banner(s) mounted
- Start/finish review stands assembled
- Sound system(s)/bullhorns functioning
- Restroom facilities in place
- Bag check in place
- Start/finish line equipment in place:
  - pace/seeding signs
  - finish tape
  - chute materials, if necessary
  - digital clock
  - timing equipment
  - computer system (check functionality)
  - recording sheets, clipboards, pencils for timers, select timers, bib number recorders (if applicable, for manual timing)
  - bar code spindles (if applicable, for manual timing)
  - tables/chairs
  - electric power hook-up (generator)
  - water station set up
- Medical area set-up
  - isolated, covered area near finish line
  - supervising MD and qualified nurses, EMTs
  - communications method between medical personnel and race director established
  - tables, cots, chairs
  - ice, IVs, hot and cold fluids, blankets, AED (detailed list in *Chapter 8: Medical, Safety and Security*)
  - immediate triage capability
- Aid station materials in place:
  - water/electrolyte replacement beverage
  - cups, pitchers
  - tables
  - separators for stacking multiple layers of pre-filled cups
  - barrels/trash bags
  - rakes (for clean-up)
- Course material in place
  - mile/kilometer markers

SIDEBAR

Master Race Checklist (cont'd)

- ◆ directional arrows
- ◆ water/aid station marker
- ◆ communication equipment/personnel (ham radio volunteers)
- ◆ stop watches for mile split callers (if applicable)
- ● Timing and scoring area in place and functioning:
  - ◆ secluded scoring area (tent/trailer/room inside available facility preferably near finish line) set up
  - ◆ tables/chairs
  - ◆ electric power hook-up or generator
  - ◆ computer and printer (normally provided by timing company if hiring a timing company)
  - ◆ copy machine/scanner
- ● Results kiosks/ results posting area in place and functioning:
  - ◆ tables/chairs
  - ◆ electric power hook-up or generator
  - ◆ computer and printers (normally provided by timing company)
  - ◆ Results screens (normally provided by timing company)
- ● Refreshments area in place and functioning:
  - ◆ tables, tablecloths, trays
  - ◆ ice
  - ◆ cups, knives, forks, spoons (depends on foods available), napkins
  - ◆ trash barrels/bags
- ● Awards area in place and functioning:
  - ◆ tables/chairs
  - ◆ podium/announcing stand
  - ◆ sound system
  - ◆ awards display area, with awards arranged in order of distribution
  - ◆ results posting board/area

POST RACE

- ● Clean-up accomplished (course, start and finish area, locker rooms/other rented facilities, etc.)
- ● Post results on event website
- ● Press release with results
- ● Post-race stories/photos to press/posted on website and social media
- ● Post-race email to participants with thank you, location of results, date of next year's event, etc.
- ● Thank-yous to sponsors, volunteers, contributors, municipalities, facility owners
- ● Post-race evaluation meeting with organizing committee
- ● Volunteer/officials party — then, take a vacation

Adapted, with appreciation, from USATF – New England Association

Operations Plan

After the first year's race, you should consolidate all of the checklists, timetables and other key race documents into an "Operations Plan" or "Ops Manual." This is the master race blueprint that would guide someone else to put on the race in the event the race director were unavailable. It will quickly become a key reference for future editions of the race. Because the preparation of this plan requires a fair amount of time, it may be better to prepare it during the "off season" after the first year's race, instead of during the pressure cooker period leading up to the first race. See *Chapter 21: Before Next Year* for an outline of a basic Race Operations Plan.

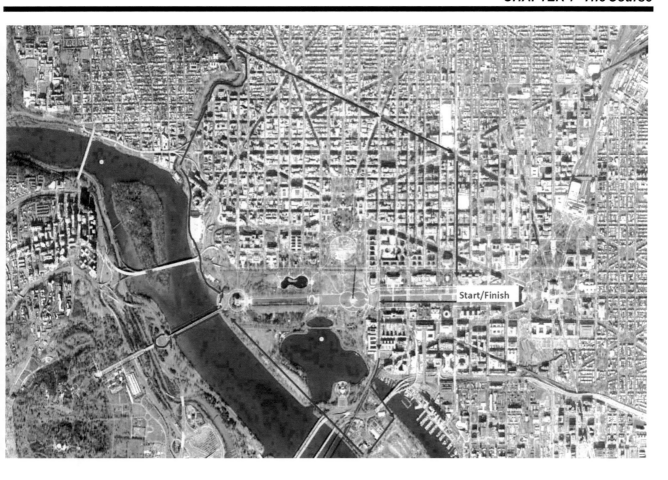

The Course

THE BASICS

- **Decide where the event will be held.** While this may seem obvious, start at the most macro level and consider such things as space for the staging area, scenery, transportation options, nearby hotels and tourist attractions, etc. You may want to look at who has the permitting jurisdiction over the prospective site and how receptive they are to running events.

- **Determine the type of course.** Once you know the general location of the course and have selected the distance for the event, you can then decide on the type of course to use. Basically there are four types of courses:

  - *Point-to-point courses,* which start and finish in *different* locations;

  - *Out-and-back courses,* which cover half of the race distance out to a turn-around and then retrace the same route back to the finish, in the *same* location as the start;

- ◆ *Loop courses,* which start and finish in the same location and make some sort of loop (or multiple loops) in between; and

- ◆ *Keyhole courses,* which are a combination of loop and out-and-back, with a common start and finish.

- **Plan the course early.** The course is the backbone of the event, so firm it up as early as possible. Once the course is set, you can obtain permits, design the staging area, place the aid stations, start publicizing the event, etc.

    Considerations in course design:

    - ◆ Safety, including the ability of the course to handle the number of runners expected

    - ◆ Character. Will the race be promoted as "flat and fast, "gently rolling" or "challenging with hills"? Will it pass by scenic and/or urban areas?

    - ◆ Effect on the community (impact on traffic, etc.)

    - ◆ Adequate location for start/finish, including proximity to parking and/or public transportation, as well as proximity to an area large enough to hold pre- and post-race activities;

    - ◆ Medical access

    - ◆ Other physical obstacles (railroad tracks, drawbridges, etc.)

- **Get the course certified.** Runners expect courses to be accurately measured. This is accomplished through a process called "certification." Certification is done under the auspices of USA Track and Field (USATF) and is coordinated by a USATF group called the "Road Running Technical Council" (RRTC). Through the RRTC, you can learn to certify a course yourself or find out where to hire a course certifier. A list of course measurers appears at http://www.usatf.org/events/courses/measurers/

- **Get all necessary approvals early.** Before the course is publicized, make sure that you have received at least tentative or informal approvals – if not the actual permits—from municipal, city, state, and/or federal authorities, depending on the event's location (be forewarned that frequently final permits are not issued shortly before race day). You don't want to find out after the fact that the course map you have been publicizing has to be completely changed because the permit was denied.

- **Publicize the course.** As soon as you have the course firmed up and permits obtained, get the word out to potential runners. They want to know where the race will run. Include a course map on the race website.

THE DETAILS

Designing the Course

Presumably, by the time you are ready to design the race course, you will have a pretty firm idea of the desired race distance (5K, 15K, marathon, etc.). The challenge is to find an area that allows you to set up an interesting course of the proper length—and one that the municipal authorities will approve. Most runners appreciate courses of one of the "standard" distances, such as 5K, 8K (or 5 miles), 10K, 15K, 10 miles, 20K, half marathon (13.1 miles), 25K, 30K, or marathon, as this allows them to compare times across races of the same distance. However, there are a number of successful races at non-standard distances, such as 4 miles and 12K. Finally, there are a few races with non-standard "odd" distances, such as the Manchester (CT) Thanksgiving Day 4.78 mile or the Falmouth Road Race, which is 7 miles – the distance between two Cape Cod bars that represents the distance of the inaugural race back in 1973. Most odd-distance races have a historical reason that overrides the usual expectation of a distance in whole miles or kilometers.

Start Planning Early

Establishing the course should be one of the first orders of business, as the course is truly the backbone of the event. Designing a course starts from a macro viewpoint, which means roughing out the route using maps or mapping software, and then progresses to the micro level, meaning a detailed map prepared by the USATF certifier, which is the final "proof" of the course's precise measurement. Don't underestimate the time it will take to go through these steps, especially if permit approval is involved, or the number of modifications you may end up making to the route. The easiest way to accomplish mapping is to use one of the numerous route-mapping software applications that exist, such as Google Maps, Map My Run, Ride With GPS or the mapping tool available through USATF (http://www.usatf.org/routes/map/). *(See **Sidebar: Mapping Software** on next page for more.)* These mapping tools may provide remarkably detailed views of city streets that will be very useful for planning purposes, and they all have a "draw" tool that allows you to trace a line that tracks the distance of the course. Users with a steady hand and patience can come very close to the final certified distance. If you are not comfortable with the software programs, you can start out with an old fashioned printed street map and your automobile odometer or a pedometer, just to approximate the route. Auto odometers should get you to within less than 5% of the advertised distance. (Look for some flexibility in the desired route —such as the ability to go an extra block or to extend the turn-around point on an out-and-back leg — in order to allow for extra distance to be added, if necessary, to bring the course up to the desired distance when it is certified. Car odometers almost always measure short.) This sort of "roughing out the course" should be, in most instances, good enough for the purpose of applying for municipal permits. Whichever method you use, spend some additional time carefully inspecting the course to look for problem areas like narrow lanes or sharp turns that may be missed or overlooked on computer maps or on a quick drive-through.

Obtain Permits for the Route

It is a tough call to decide whether to obtain permits for the course before or after getting it certified. It may be best to consult with the local authorities in advance of developing the course to see what, if any, limitations may be placed on the route by city officials. It makes little sense to go through the tedious certification process (which you will almost certainly pay for unless you train to do it yourself) until you are as certain as possible that the course will be approved by all the municipal jurisdictions through which it passes. The number of permits needed will depend largely on the different jurisdictions the course will be running through. A 5K will likely be less permit-

GREEN TIP

Have Start and Finish Do Double Duty

Out-and-back and loop courses are more environmentally friendly than point-to-point courses. In addition to eliminating transportation challenges and impacts, you are getting double duty out of more resources when a common start and finish area is employed, as opposed to duplicating many items for separate start and finish line locations.

intensive than a point-to-point marathon, which might well run through a number of different jurisdictions, each of which may require a different permit. (See **Chapter 13: Municipal Relations** for a further discussion of meeting local requirements.)

Setting the course early will also allow you to describe the course on the race website and registration form. People will want to know what the course is like when considering whether to register for the race, so the more details you can provide them, the better.

Finally, knowing the course early will allow you to take into account any special needs the course

presents as you plan for all the other aspects of the race. The layout of the course will have an impact on how many volunteers are needed, the location of the aid stations, start/finish line management, and a whole host of other logistical issues.

Types of Courses

Basically there are four types of courses—*out-and-back, loop, keyhole* (a combination of loop and out-and-back), and *point-to-point*. Each type has its own advantages and disadvantages. Out-and-back, loop, and keyhole courses share a common start

SIDEBAR

Mapping Software

One of the best places to start when designing a course is mapping software. Google Maps has made once difficult-to-obtain mapping resources available to anyone, although there are a number of alternatives. If you are slightly more ambitious, you may consult topographical maps for details about the elevation changes as well. Many runners will appreciate getting elevation information or an elevation map *(see **Figure 4-1** below)*.

Make sure that the mapping software permits easy "drawing" of the route, so you can get a rough approximation of the distance before undertaking the more precise certification process. The number of available route-mapping programs continues to grow, and many of them offer significant functionality and are free to use. Two popular free options are g-map pedometer (http://www.gmap-pedometer.com/) and MapMyRun (www.mapmyrun.com), Free maps can also be found at Mapquest (www.mapquest.com) or on Google (http://maps.google.com/maps). Topographical information can be found on Google Earth (http://www.google.com/earth/) and The National Map (http://nationalmap.gov/), as well as at http://www.topozone.com/.

There are also several mapping options available for purchase, but the free software has come so far, and is so tailored toward running, that many for-fee options no longer offer any significant advantage. Microsoft has a version called *Streets and Trips* (www.microsoft.com/streets/). Hard copies of topographical maps may also be obtained for a fee from the U.S. Geological Survey (www.topomaps.usgs.gov), although delivery may take up to 4 weeks. Last, states, counties and municipalities often have agencies that provide local maps and topographical information.

Figure 4-1

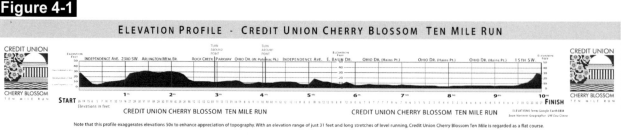

and finish line, while point-to-point courses start and finish in different locations (See **Sidebar** below for further details about course types, and **Figure 4-2** on next page for maps of common course types.)

- **Out-and-back courses:** Out-and-back courses are, as the name implies, courses that go out in one direction for half the distance, then turn around and retrace the same route back—or very close to—the finish line. Logistically, these courses are the easiest to administer, as aid and medical stations can do double duty, although they are also likely to be the most cone-intensive, as the outgoing runners must be kept separated from the returning runners. Runners give out-and-back courses mixed reviews—some like the psychological boost from seeing runners going in the other direction, while others find it repetitive to cover the same roadways twice. From a traffic-control perspective, out-and-back courses may be simpler, as they reduce

the number of different intersections that are tied up. However, they may end up blocking traffic for a longer period of time on the roads they do use, because the roads can't be reopened until after all the runners return. Another downside to this type of course is that you may have to limit the number of registrants, since the width of the roadway needs to be divided in half to handle the outgoing and incoming runners.

- **Loop courses:** Loop courses are courses that start and finish in (at least approximately) the same spot and make some sort of loop between the start and the finish. Loop courses do not have to start and finish at the *exact* same spot–the start and finish may be separated by a few hundred yards or a couple of city blocks and the course will still be called a 'loop' course. Loop courses allow for more runners to participate in the event, since they won't be going in two different directions on

SIDEBAR

Types of Courses

As described above, there are basically four types of courses—point-to-point, out-and-back, loop, and keyhole. The list below provides a clear demonstration that major U.S. events are run on every type of course (registrant numbers are approximate as of this writing):

Bay to Breakers 12K	San Francisco, CA	50,000 registrants	point-to-point
Bolder Boulder 10K	Boulder, C	50,000 registrants	point-to-point
Boston Marathon	Boston, MA	30,000 registrants	point-to-point
Crescent City Classic 10K	New Orleans, LA	17,000 registrants	point-to-point
Cherry Blossom 10 Mile	Washington, DC	15,000 registrants)	keyhole
Chicago Marathon	Chicago, IL	37,500 registrants	loop (within 50% s/f separation)
Falmouth Road Race 7 Mile	Falmouth, MA	12,000 registrants)	point-to-point
Gasparilla Distance Classic 15K	Tampa, FL	7,000 registrants)	out-and-back
Honolulu Marathon	Honolulu, HI;	24,000 registrants)	loop (within 50% s/f separation)
Lilac Bloomsday 12K	Spokane, WA	50,000 registrants	loop (within 50% s/f separation)
Marine Corps Marathon	Washington, DC	25,000 registrants	loop
New York City Marathon	New York, NY	40,000 registrants	loop (within 50% s/f separation)
Peachtree 10K	Atlanta, GA	55,000 registrants)	point-to-point
Bix 7 Mile	Davenport, IA	19,000 registrants)	out-and-back
Twin Cities Marathon	Minneapolis-St. Paul, MN	12,000 registrants	loop (within 50% s/f separation)

Figure 4-2

Common Course Types

GDCA

Out-and-back course: *Although the start and finish of Gasparilla Distance Classic 15K are a quarter mile apart, it is considered an out-and-back course.*

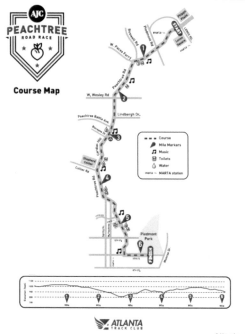

Atlanta TC

Point-to-point course: *The AJC Peachtree 10K course is point-to-point.*

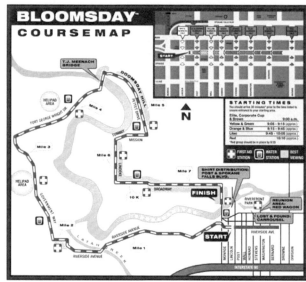

Lilac Bloomsday Association

Loop course: *The Lilac Bloomsday 12K features a loop course with a small start-finish separation.*

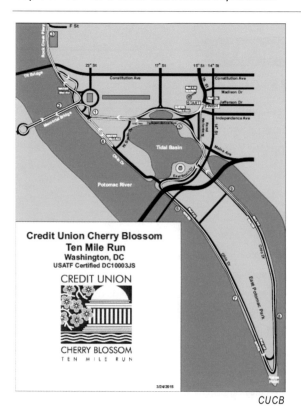

CUCB

Keyhole course: *The Credit Union Cherry Blossom features a keyhole course with the start and finish at the same location.*

the same roads, and they also offer runners a greater variety of scenery since there is no repetition. Like out-and-back courses, loops allow the same area to be used for the start and the finish. On the downside, loop courses may be somewhat more difficult to administer than out-and-back courses, due to the inability to double up on aid stations and other course services.

Multiple loop courses can help ease logistics, as you can then have aid stations/ course services doing double duty. Having a two-loop marathon course, for example, can allow you to easily offer a half-marathon option, with the runners wanting to do the full marathon going on for a second lap. Such a setup can be hard on the marathon runners psychologically, however, since they pass through the finish knowing they are headed back out again.

"Criterium-style" courses have become popular for many races limited to elite competitors, including the Olympic Trials, Olympic Games and World Championships. Modeled after bicycle criterium courses, these courses have multiple circuits (usually 3-5), in which the runners pass by the start and finish line. These courses are designed to enhance spectator viewing, as the runners can be seen multiple times during the event. In addition, the same aid stations and other on-course services can be used multiple times, as the runners pass them on each loop. However, the field of runners must be kept small and should be fairly evenly matched in ability in order to keep issues of tracking individual runners and dealing with lapped runners down to a minimum. *For an example of a Criterium-style course, see Figure 4-3.*

- *Part loop, part out-and-back courses:* An out-and-back course with side loops, often called a "keyhole course," can be a good option, as it allows placement of the aid stations and other functions such that they can do double duty on the common parts of the course, while adding in a loop at the turnaround and different side loops for variety, which runners may like. Keyhole courses work best if the loops can be kept relatively small and they aren't accessed by narrow out-and-back sections, which again would limit the number of runners that can fit onto the road.

- *Point-to-point:* Although point-to-point courses tend to be the most difficult logistically, runners generally like the concept of running from one place to another (such as from Hopkinton to Boston in the Boston Marathon or from San Francisco Bay to the Pacific Ocean in San Francisco's Bay to Breakers event). With this type of course, race facilities and infrastructure will need to be set up at both the start and the finish. Since the runners only go by each point once, you also can't double up on aid stations and other course services. In addition, there may be complex transportation issues for both the runners and their baggage, as you either have to get the runners out to the start or transport them back from the finish.

Other Key Course Considerations

1. Safety

Obviously, whichever type of course is chosen, the number one priority should be the safety of the runners. As much as possible, try to avoid busy roads and limit the number of major intersections on the course. Even though you will likely be using police at the major intersections, there will always be some crazy drivers out there. In addition, you may end up paying a lot more for police services if you are tying up numerous busy intersections. Obviously if the race is in a big city, you are less likely to be able to avoid major thoroughfares, but selecting a route that minimizes the chance of accidents and reduces the likelihood of major traffic tie-ups is the best policy.

In general, right turns are safer and simpler than left turns, since the runners remain closest to the curb at all times. This is especially true for courses where traffic is only closed in one direction and runners are running with traffic—the safest way for runners to run in a race. While you probably won't be able to eliminate all left turns, with proper planning you may be able to locate the left turns on low-traffic residential streets, where controlling the turn will be easier and safer. In the event that runners are running *against* traffic and only one lane is closed for the race, left-hand turns are preferable to right-hand turns, because, in this case, right-hand turns will force runners to cross the flow of traffic.

Make sure that the road surface is not too rough, doesn't have potholes, and is not too heavily crowned (sloped between the curbs). If the

race will take place in the summer, try to locate the course where there will be shade. Unless only bottled water will be used, also keep in mind access to water sources for the aid stations. If there is no easy access to drinkable water, bottled water or pre-filled water barrels will need to be used at the aid stations.

It may prove useful to educate yourself about other race courses that have been approved in the general area of your potential event. All USATF-certified race courses are listed on the USATF website, so that's a great place to start (http://www.usatf.org/events/courses/search/). Consider asking the local permitting authorities about past events in the area. If the police in the area have dealt with road races in the past, consider enlisting some sort of police input on course design. The police may appreciate being brought in at the beginning, and they may also have some insight into problem

Figure 4-3

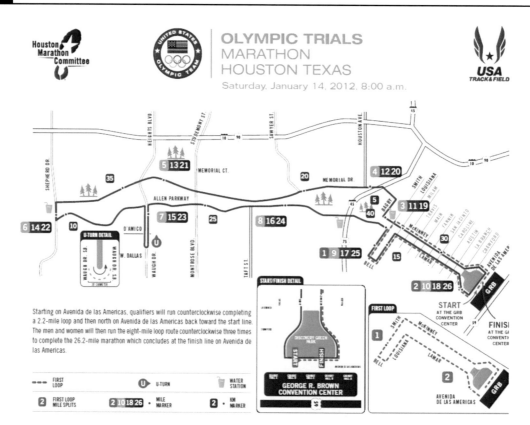

Houston Marathon

Criterium course: *The 2012 U.S. Olympic Marathon Trials were held on a three-loop criterium style course.*

areas that you may not have thought of.

2. Effect on the Community

Try to determine ahead of time if the course location and the resulting traffic will upset the residents in the area. Think of how placement of the aid stations, porta-johns, etc., will affect both residential and commercial areas.

If the race is on a Sunday (or on a holiday that may fall on a Sunday some years), consider whether the course goes by one or more churches, which may object to the race both on religious grounds and because it might conflict with church traffic. And don't forget that weddings and funerals may be going on at times you do not expect. If possible, it is easier to design the course to avoid passing directly in front of churches. Of course, this is not to say that all churches are going to object to a race; some are supportive. Some race directors have been able to bring churches on board staffing aid stations, providing entertainment,

etc. Nonetheless, keep in mind that churches are a potential trouble spot.

Area businesses might also object to the race if the runners, traffic or road closures will make it hard for shoppers to get to and from their businesses. If you can, walk around the areas through which the course will run. Talk to the businesspeople located there, and get their input. The more familiar you are with the community, the better you can work with everyone to improve the race.

3. Selecting and Designing the Start/ Finish Area

Deciding on an optimal spot for the start and finish lines is a key element of course design. Staging area design is discussed in further detail in *Chapter 16: Race Logistics and Operations from Start to Finish*, but here are some staging considerations to keep in mind as you are designing the course:

- It's a good idea to locate the start and finish

Phil Stewart

The Los Angeles Marathon uses the vast expanse of Dodger Stadium for the staging area.

away from the main street. Not only is this safer, it also allows you to set up early without interfering with traffic, and will allow more time for taking the finish equipment down.

- Be sure there is adequate parking and/or easy access to the event area. Also, ask yourself whether there is adequate space for the race to grow. Remember that growth entails not only more runners but more vehicles and equipment at the start/finish lines.

- If the event will draw a significant number of out-of-towners, make sure that there are enough hotels nearby. It is best if the runners can walk from the race hotel to the start and back from the finish. Fewer porta-johns can be ordered if many runners are staying in hotels very close to the race.

- Check to see if there are rest-room facilities already existing. This could reduce the porta-john rental bill.

- Be sure there are adequate facilities (or space for tents) in the staging area for all the necessary functions—packet pickup, medical, results processing, awards ceremony, etc. Small races can save significant money on tent rental if the start/finish of the race is held at a school or other facility with adequate indoor space that can be used in the case of inclement weather. Be aware that special permits/permission may be needed for the use of public facilities and that a fee may be charged.

- Logistics can be greatly simplified by having water hookups at the start, finish, and aid stations, and electrical power hook-ups for timing equipment and sound systems at the start and finish.

- Ideally, the first and last several hundred meters of a course should be on a flat straight-away; try to avoid turns that could cause congestion at the start or interference at the finish.

- The start should be wide enough to easily accommodate the anticipated number of runners.

4. Medical Access

Make sure you know where the nearest hospitals are relative to the course. If possible, it is better to have the hospital closer to the finish line, as this is where, statistically, the highest rate of injury/other medical issues occurs. Also, be sure that the entire course, and especially the finish area, offers easy access for emergency vehicles, and that the race doesn't cause traffic congestion that will interfere with the transport of injured runners to the hospital.

5. Other Obstacles

It is wise to try to avoid crossing railroad tracks and drawbridges. Even if you have a train schedule and it doesn't look like there will be a problem, trains can always run late. Also, avoid passing in front of fire stations and other emergency vehicle locations if at all possible. The movement of emergency police or fire vehicles can cause havoc in the middle of a race.

6. Course Appeal

- **Scenic:** There are a few races around the country where runners seem to feel that breathtaking scenery makes up for (or perhaps enhances) a very challenging course. The Mt. Washington Road Race, Pike's Peak Marathon, and Big Sur Marathon are among the country's most beautiful—and most difficult—courses. *(See Figure 4-4)*

- **Fast and flat:** Many serious runners are "PR" (personal record) seekers, usually preferring a fast, flat course to a scenic one. There are some races that manage to combine beautiful scenery with a fast course, but if you have to choose one or the other, you are probably better off going for the faster course if the goal is to attract PR-seeking runners. Of course, runners like one or two undulations in a course, since hills tend to work different muscle groups. Also, while long straight-aways are nice from both a fast-course and a race-management perspective, they can be tough for runners to take psychologically, so at least a few turns are recommended. *(See Figure 4-4).*

Figure 4-4

Course Appeal

Scenic Course: The Big Sur Marathon features one of the most scenic courses in the world. *Big Sur Marathon*

SCC Events

Fast Course: The Berlin Marathon is reknowned as a fast course. It is the site of numerous world records.

Figure 4-4

Course Appeal (cont'd)

Jan Branscome

Unique Event: *The Run Under the Lights in Gaithersburg, MD celebrates the start of the holiday season.*

- **Unique:** Many runners choose races for the uniqueness of the experience that the event provides. Although the uniqueness of a race can come from other aspects of the event besides the course itself (think of Color Runs, for example), interesting and unique courses are also a draw. The opportunity to run in places where runners are generally not allowed, such as across the Chesapeake Bay Bridge (Across the Bay 10K), through a tunnel (Tunnel to Towers 5K or Fort McHenry Tunnel Run 5K) or through a holiday lights display (Run Under the Lights 5K), are big draws to both casual and competitive runners. ***(See Figure 4-4).***

Certifying the Course

Regardless of the course distance chosen, most runners will expect that the course is accurately measured to that distance. Of all the errors a race director can make, an incorrectly measured course—either short or long—will anger race participants more than anything else. Therefore a race director should plan on having the proposed course certified by USA Track and Field (USATF). Certification is a fairly rigorous measurement process, not outside the abilities of the mathematically inclined to master, but probably more than an overburdened race director will want to take on. Fortunately there are trained individuals associated with running clubs or commercial event management firms who will certify the course for a fee. The cost of certification varies, depending on the course distance and complexity, course location (busy or quiet roads) and region of the U.S., although a very general rule of thumb is $100 per kilometer of distance Race directors should also be aware that the certifier may charge additional fees for things such as travel expenses, last-minute certification, and police escort on busy roads that are dangerous to measure. Although certification fees may seem high, amortized over the 10-year life of the certification, they generally work out to less than two average registration fees per year for a 5K or 10K, three for a half marathon and four for a marathon.

Although today's GPS devices and mapping software have a high degree of accuracy, these methods are *not* acceptable for course certification. They are extremely useful in getting *close* to the actual distance before certification takes place. Course certifiers generally use a device known as a Jones Counter, which is mounted on a bicycle and counts wheel revolutions for certification. Prior to each certification, the device needs to be calibrated on a straight line calibration course measured with a steel tape. Then it can be used to measure the course, always taking the shortest possible tangents along the way.

A good resource that can help you decide if you would like to certify a course yourself is USATF's website, http://www.usatf.org/Products-

Figure 4-5

Certification Map

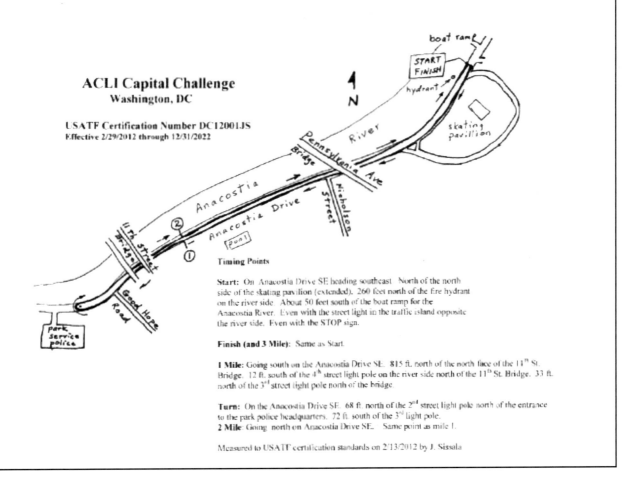

ACLI Capital Challenge
Washington, DC

USATF Certification Number DC12001JS
Effective 2/29/2012 through 12/31/2022

Timing Points

Start: On Anacostia Drive SE heading southeast. North of the north side of the skating pavilion (extended). 260 feet north of the fire hydrant on the river side. About 50 feet south of the boat ramp for the Anacostia River. Even with the street light in the traffic island opposite the river side. Even with the STOP sign.

Finish (and 3 Mile): Same as Start.

1 Mile: Going south on the Anacostia Drive SE. 815 ft. north of the north face of the 11th St. Bridge. 12 ft. south of the 4th street light pole on the river side north of the 11th St. Bridge. 33 ft. north of the 3rd street light pole north of the bridge.

Turn: On the Anacostia Drive SE. 68 ft. north of the 2nd street light pole north of the entrance to the park police headquarters. 72 ft. south of the 3rd light pole.
2 Mile: Going north on Anacostia Drive SE. Same point as mile 1.

Measured to USATF certification standards on 2/13/2012 by J. Sissala

/-Services/Course-Certifications/USATF-Certified-Courses/Certify-Your-Course.aspx. You can download a copy of a free manual on how to certify a course, or, if after reviewing the process you decide you'd like to farm out the task, you can find a list of State Certifiers in your state who will either certify a course for you or refer you to another local certifier.

Once the course is certified, you should receive a course map from the certifier (see **Figure 4-5** on previous page for a sample certification map). The amount of detail in the map may vary by certifier, but generally maps will all be marked with the start/finish and turn-around points, as well as with mile markers defined in terms of distances from fixed objects. For an example of a course map drawn up by a certfier, see **Figure 4-5** on the previous page. You will also receive a course measurement certificate from the USATF, with a unique alpha-numeric certification number. Include this number on the event website, as it serves as a sort of "Good Road Running Seal of Approval" for course accuracy. USATF course certifications are good for 10 years, after which they expire, and the course must be recertified. Keep the certification document in a safe place, and make copies, both printed and electronic. You might want to post copies on the race website and have them available on race day, so that runners can see the route and know that the course is accurate.

Be sure to have the course certificate with you when it comes time to mark the course, as it will be helpful. Most certifiers will provide very descriptive details (such as "34 feet from 1st storm sewer on Main St. after the intersection with Union St.") to help you locate the start and finish lines and intermediate mile or kilometer points, or turn around points on out-and-back segments. There's no sense in having a certified course and then incorrectly locating the splits, or worse, the start or finish. Even if you've been doing a race for years, don't rely on memory, which often just reinforces errors.

As a final note, if you inherited the course from a previous race director, you can obtain a copy of the certification map by going through USATF (http://www.usatf.org/events/courses/search/), which keeps maps of certified courses on file.

Using a course that has already been certified is also an excellent option for a new race director. Make sure the certification is still valid and does not expire until after the event. Not only has the legwork of course

TECH TALK

Record Quality Courses

There are a small number of people, many of whom serve on USATF's Road Running Technical Council (RRTC), who debate such things as the definitions of "loop course" and "point-to-point course." After all, is a 10K course with the start and finish a block apart technically a loop course or a point-to-point course? What if the start and finish are a mile apart, etc.? The impetus for precisely defining the terms "loop" and "point-to-point" grew out of the effort to create meaningful road-running records. The RRTC started with the premise that it wasn't fair to compare times from a point-to-point 10K course run straight down a mountain with a tailwind to times run on a flat 10K course with the start and finish in the same spot (where, presumably, the effect of any headwind in one direction would be neutralized by having it be a tailwind in the other direction). After much debate, USATF agreed to define a "loop course" as any course with the start and finish within 50% of the race distance (5K separation for a 10K race; 13.1 miles for a marathon) and a course that does not lose more than one-tenth of 1% in elevation between the start and finish lines (a 10-meter drop in a 10K race). In order for times to be accepted as records by USATF, the courses must meet these two "loop-course criteria;" otherwise the results are considered "aided." The bottom line is that if you have a 10K course with the start and finish separated by a mile and the elevation of the finish line is no more than 10 meters lower than the start, the course will be considered a "loop" course instead of a "point-to-point" course and will be record-eligible.

design been completed, but a new race can also save money by avoiding the fee for USATF course certification. You can search for certified courses in your area using the search link mentioned above.

Changing the Course

If you have an established race, you may have a course you're happy with; you may not want to alter the course and lose years of records, especially if the race is old enough to have developed a significant history. At the same time, don't be afraid to re-examine the course to see if

it can be tweaked to make it even better, perhaps by something as simple as modifying the start or finish location. Frequently, construction or changing traffic patterns may leave you little choice but to make alterations to the course. Just remember that *any* change in the course means it will need to be recertified. Also remember that USATF course certifications expire after ten years, so even in the unlikely event that you use exactly the same course year after year, you will need to get it recertified after ten years' time. Events that have changed the course may refer to "Event Records" instead of "Course Records."

A Jones Counter, which is mounted on a bicycle and counts wheel revolutions for course certification. Details on ordering are available at www.jonescounter.com.

Tom Riegel

5 Sponsorship

THE BASICS

- **There are several types of sponsors.** Different levels of sponsorship will require different levels of sponsor exposure from the event and different amounts of financial commitment from the sponsors. Smaller races may entice only a single sponsor, while larger events may have several sponsorship tiers, as outlined below.
    - *Title Sponsors* pay the most money, and in return get their name in front of the race name ("Credit Union Cherry Blossom 10 Mile," "TCS New York City Marathon," etc.).
    - *Presenting Sponsors* are the highest-level sponsors for events that do not wish to have a commercial name as part of the race name, or events that have a title sponsor and wish to sell a second high-level sponsorship. A presenting sponsor might be listed as follows: "The Cherry Tree 10K, Presented by Volvo," or the "Community Bank Labor Day 10K, Presented by Carefirst."

◆ *Secondary or Supporting Sponsors* generally pay less than title/presenting sponsors and receive less exposure. A supporting sponsor may serve as the title sponsor of one part of a race, such as the "ABC Company Health and Fitness Expo," or the "Company DEF Kids' Run."

◆ *In-Kind Sponsors* donate products rather than cash to the event. The products donated should save money out of the budget. The value of the products donated determines which of the above levels of sponsorship the company is eligible for. Some sponsors may be part cash, part in-kind sponsors.

● **Inventory what the event can offer a sponsor.** Before you can sell sponsorships, you need to know what you have to sell. Sponsors will want to know how many participants will be running the race and their demographics, including age, sex, hometown, income, education, purchasing habits, etc. By far, the biggest asset you can offer sponsors is access to the race participants, via email and other electronic methods. More traditional visibility includes such things as logos on t-shirts, registration forms, banners at the start and finish, links on websites, etc.

● **Draw up a list of potential sponsors and approach them with a proposal.** Consider companies in the health field, banks, investment companies and other consumer businesses in the area around the event location. Large companies that are headquartered in the area may also be good candidates. Many sponsorships are obtained through business or personal contacts. Ask committee members and friends if they know anyone who works for a company that could potentially be a sponsor of the event. Write up and either email or personally drop off a short proposal (1-2 pages) outlining why the race would be a good fit for the potential sponsor. Follow up with a phone call.

● **Prepare contracts for all sponsors.** Once a sponsor has been found, be sure to put in writing what you expect the sponsor to provide, and what you have promised to provide to the sponsor. Then, of course, it is up to you to make sure that the sponsor fulfills his commitment, and it is also vital that you do everything that you promised to do!

● **Work hard to keep sponsors.** Be sure to deliver the level of sponsorship exposure promised. Be creative in thinking of ways to keep the sponsor's name in front of spectators and participants. Give plenty of t-shirts or other race memorabilia to the sponsor(s) and make sure that the race announcements always include recognition of the sponsor's involvement in the event. After the race, send the sponsor photos of places in the staging area where their name appeared; gather analytics/tracking data from the race website and other social media outlets and prepare a report summarizing it; round-up any newspaper clippings or press coverage of the race; and send copies of any thank-you notes or emails received from enthusiastic participants, etc. These items may be assembled together into a post-race sponsor report. Finally, send the sponsor a contract for the next year soon after the current year's event concludes, while the experience is still fresh in the sponsor's mind.

THE DETAILS

For many event organizers, the topic of sponsorship is about as welcome as a stress fracture is to a runner. However, as even the fledgling race director knows, it is difficult to put on a race funded only by the runners' registration fees, unless the race is very large, in which case it is more likely to be attractive to sponsors. After registration fees, sponsorship is the second major source of revenue for most events. As a result of the necessity of sponsorship revenue, the race director must spend a lot of time courting sponsors and, once they are aboard, keeping them happy.

There has been a dramatic increase in the sophistication of sponsorship recruitment and retention over the last 20 years. While most races still rely on the race director or an assigned volunteer to procure sponsorship, some of today's largest and most successful running events are likely to have a paid person (possibly a non-runner) – or even a small staff – dedicated to navigating the complexities of the sponsorship world. These individuals talk about "building the brand," "strategic alliances", "ROI" (return on investment) and identifying ways a sponsorship could enhance the sponsor's business. Anyone going out and soliciting sponsorships should know that it is an intricate and highly competitive world – and the competition is not just with other running events, but with barbecue festivals, rock concerts, parades and charities. The information presented in this chapter should only be considered "Sponsorship 101."

Nearly all companies sponsor events in the hopes of increasing their own sales; after all, most companies need to at least break even in order to stay in business. A company can take a soft sell couched as "building good will in the community," or supporting a charity, or a harder sell, which involves getting direct exposure for the company or its products in front of a desirable audience. Physical evidence of association with a popular community event, such as the presence of the company's logo on banners, bib numbers and race shirts, or a link to the company's website on the event's site, help reinforce the company's relationship with the event. Other activities that the sponsor may undertake, such as offering discount coupons, product sampling, or hosting hospitality functions, are more directly linked to driving the company's sales.

The competition for sponsors gets tougher each year, as more and more organizations, ranging from sports to cultural events and festivals to cause-related and charitable activities, attempt to procure corporate sponsorship. Many events purposely link themselves to a charity or other noteworthy cause as a way to give the event a second hook for a prospective sponsor.

TIP

Participant Access for Sponsors

When putting together a package of items to offer potential sponsors, don't forget that participant access is probably the most important selling point. To sponsors who would like to reach an audience of runners, a list of several thousand names—with email addresses—as part of an overall sponsorship package is likely to be an extremely attractive amenity. Providing *some form* of participant access is a generally accepted practice, with the vast majority of races allowing some way for sponsors to reach participants. However, simply turning over participant information to sponsors (or selling it to outside businesses, etc.) is more controversial, with only a small percentage of races actually making registrant contact information *directly available* to the sponsors, so that the sponsors themselves can make contact with the registrants. Runners are more apt to resent having their contact information 'sold' and then receiving spam email or calls from telemarketers. Thus, it is unwise to simply provide a sponsor with the database of participant contact info. There are less intrusive ways to offer sponsors access to participants. Offer to mention the sponsor in regularly scheduled race emails, and include the sponsor's link and logo. Alternatively, offer to send a specific, sponsor-generated email to the participants at an agreed-upon time (1 week after the race, for example.) That way, you maintain control of the participant database but the sponsor can still reap the benefits of contact with the runners. If you do opt to use runner contact info commercially (highly targeted mailing or email lists can sell for significant amounts of money), be aware that this may generate some negative feelings. At a minimum, offer race participants an "opt-out" option.

Try to avoid being overly dependent on any single sponsor. You don't want to be left dangling if a key sponsor moves on. Some events try to build up a cash reserve equal to—at a minimum—the cash contribution from the event's largest sponsor. This helps ensure that the event could operate for one year without the sponsor's income.

Although procuring sponsorship for running events is a complex activity and coming up with the proper sponsorship package takes a lot of thought, some sponsorships come about because the president—or other high level executive—at the sponsoring company is a runner and wants to support the sport. For this reason, anything you can do to identify corporate executives running in the event is time well spent. Then be sure to follow up. The risk of this type of sponsor, of course, is that the running executive could move on to another company.

TIP

Review Ads and Websites Created by Others

Frequently, once a sponsor has signed on to an event, the company may want to promote its association with the event on its own – either through ads placed by the company, or on the company's website, etc. Make sure to take the time to review these sponsor-generated representations of the race. Be eternally vigilant when it comes to looking for sponsor conflicts. Consider the case of a major (non-running) retail sponsor of a national running series who put up significant dollars to take an expensive ad in a large metropolitan area newspaper promoting its involvement with the event. The problem was, the sponsor's ad featured a runner wearing shoes of a company other than the event's official shoe sponsor. Needless to say, the shoe sponsor was not very happy about the ad. If you are fortunate enough to have multiple sponsors placing ads for the event though their own advertising departments or agencies, make sure you have absolute right of review in order to avoid this type of embarrassing (and potentially costly) error.

In another lesser, but still noticeable gaffe (which, fairly or not, ultimately reflects on the credibility of the organizers), a sponsor placed an ad ludicrously showing a runner coming out of a sprinter's starting blocks for a 5K event.

Sponsorship Levels

Title sponsors: Title sponsors receive the most exposure and put up the most money. It is not uncommon for a title sponsor to be giving three to five times (or more) the amount of money to the event than the next level of sponsors. In most instances the "title" is the single most valuable item the race has to sell. Examples of races with title sponsors include the Credit Union Cherry Blossom 10 Mile and the TCS New York City Marathon. Adding a sponsor name to the race name can make for some long race names (for example, "The Indian Path Medical Center/Suntrust Bank Crazy Eights 8K"). Even if this is the case with your race, it is in your interest to always include the sponsor name in the race name whenever and however the race is publicized.. This will make the title sponsor happy, which increases the chance that the sponsor will sign on in future years. Be aware that the media will do its best to drop the sponsor's name from the race title. (If you have a media sponsor you might request that they include the title sponsor's name in at least the first mention of the event in the editorial coverage.)

Presenting sponsors: This category is usually limited to a single sponsor who has paid the second highest amount behind the title sponsor. Some events, like the Lilac Bloomsday 12K in Spokane, WA, make a conscious decision not to sell a *title* sponsorship in order to keep the name of the event unencumbered by a commercial presence. (This also eliminates the race having a new name with each new title sponsor.) In this case, presenting sponsor will be the highest sponsorship level. As the name implies, presenting sponsors are usually credited as follows: "The Cherry Tree 10K, Presented by Volvo."

Secondary sponsors: All of the non-title/presenting sponsors can either be treated equally, giving them the same amount of exposure and charging them the same amount, or several levels of sponsorship can be offered, each with a different level of exposure for a different price. Some races use designations such as "gold," "silver," and "bronze" for these sponsorship levels, while other events use terms such as "presenting," "supporting," and "contributing" to indicate different levels. The names don't matter as much as what is actually offered at each level. Be sure to allow for some flexibility in sponsorship levels, so that a sponsorship proposal can be tailored to meet the needs of a particular sponsor. The needs of a financial services sponsor are likely to be different from the needs of a supermarket chain. It is up to you, as race director, to come up with proposals that deliver equal value to sponsors at the same sponsorship level.

In-kind sponsors: Rather than providing cash, in-kind sponsors give products that can be used for putting on the event or that can be distributed to runners. Generally, from a company's perspective, in-kind sponsorships are more desirable than sponsorships that involve actually writing a check. Some sponsors will supply a combination of cash and in-kind product. Suppliers of consumables, such as bottled water, energy drinks, energy bars, or other snacks, along with printing or web-hosting companies, all make great potential in-kind sponsors. The race director should scour the race budget for items that could potentially be donated by an in-kind sponsor. Be wary of in-kind donations that don't

really help to improve the event's bottom line. Working with these sponsors and in many cases distributing their samples may be more of a hassle than the value of the in-kind item received. For example, if a local hardware store wants to provide lawnmowers, the value of this donation to the race is negligible at best (unless the event is a cross country race). Meanwhile, the sponsor gains a

Figure 5-1

Sponsor Levels

The Quad City Times Bix 7 in Davenport, IA, showcases its different sponsor levels in the event's Media Guide.

good deal of exposure in front of runners with high incomes who can afford the fanciest lawnmowers!

There is no "proper" number of sponsors for an event, although there may be a point of diminishing returns. Dealing with vast numbers of small sponsors means more work for the organizing committee, and the impact of the exposure that each one receives is reduced as sponsors

Table 5-A

Sponsor Benefits

Sponsorship Level	Number
Title Sponsor @ $100,000	1
Presenting Sponsors @ $15,000 each	3
Supporting Sponsors @ $7,000 each	3
Contributing Sponsors @ $3,000 each	6

Benefits Menu	Title	Presenting #1	Presenting #2	Presenting #3	Supporting #1	Supporting #2	Supporting #3	Contributing #1	Contributing #2	Contributing #3	Contributing #4	Contributing #5	Contributing #6
Name included in title of event	x												
Name on official race logo	x												
Name on finish line break tape	x												
Name on race participant t-shirts (20,000)	x												
Name on volunteer t-shirts (2,000)	x												
Name on official race merchandise	x												
VIP introduced to speak at start, awards, VIP dinner	x												
Logo on start/finish truss and all identifying signage	x												
Abillity to designate official race charity	x												
Interview on live stream of race and on race TV broadcast	x												
Designation as "Presenting Sponsor" of ancillary event (expo, kids run, 5K, etc.)		x											
Designation as "Presenting Sponsor" of ancillary event (expo, kids run, 5K, etc.)			x										
Designation as "Presenting Sponsor" of ancillary event (expo, kids run, 5K, etc.)				x									
Logo display on runners' bib numbers (22,000)	x				x								
Logo display on water bottles (32,000)						x							
Lead vehicle in front of race field							x						
Dedicated blast email (email done by organizing committee)	x	x	x	x									
Social media promotion	x	x	x	x	x	x	x						
Free expo booth	x	x	x	x	x	x	x						
Logo on barricade signage	x	x	x	x	x	x	x						
Free inclusion in virtual goody bag	x	x	x	x	x	x	x						
Logo on all printed materials	x	x	x	x	x	x	x						
Logo display/link on race website (500,000)	x	x	x	x	x	x	x	x	x	x	x	x	x
Right to advertise as "Official Sponsor" of the race	x	x	x	x	x	x	x	x	x	x	x	x	x
Public address recognition at all race venues including expo	x	x	x	x	x	x	x	x	x	x	x	x	x
Product sampling opportunities	x	x	x	x	x	x	x	x	x	x	x	x	x
Tickets to race VIP Banquet	20	6	6	6	6	4	4	2	2	2	2	2	2
Free entries into race	20	6	6	6	6	4	4	2	2	2	2	2	2
Goodwill	x	x	x	x	x	x	x	x	x	x	x	x	x

proliferate. Race t-shirts that are awash in logos may cause runners to zone out when looking at them or, worse, they will relegate the logo-cluttered shirts to the rag pile. Also, the cost/benefit ratio must be considered, especially for in-kind sponsors. A race director may spend so much time dealing with a high maintenance in-kind sponsor that he neglects a lower maintenance title sponsor. Always be aware of what the event's sponsors may be costing *you* in terms of time and energy.

What Does the Event Have to Sell?

It's easy for a neophyte race director to think that his "little" 5K event just doesn't have much to offer a potential sponsor. However, the hypothetical analysis of a 20,000-runner event provided in **Table 5-A** at left should open your eyes to everything that can be sold. Although the sponsor dollar figures will likely be less for most races, the categories of exposure generally apply for events of all sizes. In this sample event, estimated numbers of exposures/views have been provided in parentheses after each item, where relevant. Note from the table that not all levels of sponsors receive *exactly* the same benefits. This allows for some customized tailoring of sponsor benefits based on each sponsor's business or marketing model. For example, "Supporting Sponsor #3" is an automotive company, so it received exposure in the form of providing the lead vehicle, which was not made available to any other sponsor — even those at the same level.

Before you start looking for a sponsor, make a careful analysis of the event. If it is a new event, a number of assumptions will have to be made about who the race will attract, how it will be received in the community, and the types of sponsors the race could most benefit. If it is an existing event, make a list of the characteristics that make the race different from many of the other events in the area. What makes the race special? Think about what types of people the event attracts—does it tend to draw the real die-hard

runners, general fitness buffs, a large number of walkers, a certain ratio of men to women, etc.? Try to fit the potential sponsors with the types of runners who come to the race. Also, consider the goals of the race. Even if a company doesn't seem to be fitness-oriented, it might have an interest in or link to a specific charity that the race benefits. Finally, consider the impact of the race on the community. If the event is one of the bigger events in the community, you can offer the event to local sponsors who are interested in generating goodwill in the community. Some races will not take sponsorship from distilled spirits companies (beer and wine sponsors are generally accepted). Also, it's best to avoid selling sponsorships to competing companies (two different car dealerships or two running specialty retailers, for example).

Gathering Demographic Data

Prospective sponsors will be keenly interested in knowing *who* is participating in your event so they can see if your participants align with their prospective customers. The more participant data you can gather for potential sponsors, the better. Fortunately there are more avenues to acquire this information than ever before.

A demographic survey is a powerful tool in selling the event to potential sponsors. Such a survey provides potential sponsors important information about the event participants such as age, sex, education, household income, etc. Online survey creation platforms like SurveyMonkey (www.surveymonkey.com) or Cvent (www.cvent.com), make it easy to create and email out your own surveys. They are either free (for certain levels of service) or charge a small monthly fee. Surveys can be created and/or added to the event's social media sites. Another strategy for data collection is to add a few key demographic questions as part of the online registration process (beyond the age and sex information needed to time and score the event). However, limit these extra questions to a very small number, or you will irritate the prospective participants by slowing them down (or at least do not make these "required fields" on the online registration form). You should be able to extract some demographic information about the event's followers on its social media sites as well. Finally you may want to approach business students at a local college or university and ask them to conduct interviews at the expo or event site. Often, students are willing to conduct surveys and other types of research as school projects. If all else fails, more general demographics of runners can be obtained from a national or local running publication or national running organizations like the RRCA or Running USA. One of the strong points of running is that it attracts a "high demographic" audience, which means most participants are well educated and are at the higher end of the income scale.

Here are some questions to consider for a

Table 5-B

Sample Demographic Report

CATEGORY	PERCENTAGE	CATEGORY	PERCENTAGE	CATEGORY	PERCENTAGE
SEX		**FIELD OF EMPLOYMENT**		**SUPPLEMENT USE**	
Male	45%	Associations	10%	Use Supplements Yes	62%
Female	55%	Corporate - Defense	3%	Use Supplements No	38%
AGE		Corporate Financial	7%	**MAJOR PURCHASING PLANS**	
Age: 13-17	0%	Corporate Other	15%	Plan to purchase a home	20%
Age: 18-22	2%	Corporate - Technology	11%	Plan to purchase a car	28%
Age: 23-35	48%	Government	20%	Plan to purchase a boat	1%
Age: 36-55	43%	Military	4%	Plan to purchase a second home	5%
Age: 56-75	6%	Other	24%	Plan to purchase a computer	32%
INCOME		Retired	1%	Plan to purchase a PDA	14%
Under $25,000	2%	Student	5%	Plan to purchase a heart rate	
$25,000-49,999	13%	**JOB TITLE**		monitor	7%
$50,000-74,999	17%	Job Title - Administrative	9%	**NUMBER OF RACES RUN PER YEAR**	
$75,000-99,999	19%	Job Title - Management	34%	Run no races	1%
$100,000-149,999	22%	Job Title - President/CEO/		Run 1-2 races	21%
$150,000-250,000	17%	Partner	7%	Run 3-5 races	46%
Over $250,000	6%	Job Title - Senior Management	11%	Run 6-10 races	22%
Other	4%	Job Title - Teacher	4%	Run 11-20 races	8%
EDUCATION		Job Title - Trade	1%	Run over 20 races	2%
Some High School	0%	Job Title - Other	34%	**NUMBER OF OUT OF TOWN RACES PER YEAR**	
HS graduate	1%	**NUMBER OF TRIPS PER YEAR**		Run 1-2 out of town races	73%
Some College	6%	none	1%	Run 3-5 out of town races	21%
College Graduate	41%	Trips 1-2	20%	Run 6-10 out of town races	5%
Graduate Degree	34%	Trips 3-5	50%	Run over 10 out of town races	2%
PhD, JD, MD, etc.	18%	Trips 6-9	17%	**RUNNING SHOES PURCHASED**	
MARITIAL STATUS		Trips 10+	12%	Running shoes purchased: 1-2	56%
Single	41%	**NUMBER OF BUSINESS TRIPS**		Running shoes purchased: 3-5	40%
Married	51%	Business Trips: none	23%	Running shoes purchased: 6+	4%
Divorced	8%	Business Trips: 1-2	27%		
		Business Trips: 3-5	26%		
		Business Trips: 6-20	19%		
		Business Trips: 20+	5%		
		Business Trips: none	3%		

demographic survey. It is important to keep the survey short or the recipients will lose patience and abandon completing it. The questionnaire should take no more than 3-5 minutes to complete.

- **Basic demographics:** Age, sex, hometown, family income, occupation, education.

- **Spending habits:** how many pairs of running shoes have participants purchased in the last year; do they use a financial services company; how many computers they own; do they shop at Safeway, etc. This information helps target a sponsorship proposal to prospective sponsors.

- **Questions related to media usage:** What kinds of social media do runners use, which websites do they frequent, which radio and TV stations do they tune in to and how long do they stay tuned in, which magazines do they subscribe to, etc. This kind of data is helpful for advertising purposes and will help to target stations/websites/etc. that would be best for advertising the event.

- **Questions for out-of-town runners:** How long do they stay in the local area, how much do they spend, how many family members or friends do they bring with them, etc. This type of data helps estimate the economic impact a race has on the local economy. *(For a more detailed discussion of Economic Impact Analyses, see Chapter 21: Before Next Year.)*

- **Questions the current sponsors would like to ask:** Ask the sponsors to provide these. This gives sponsors direct feedback and is a good way to build better relations between the race and the sponsor.

Table 5-B at left shows the results of a demographic survey. These results can be very useful in determining what types of companies you should approach regarding sponsorship event.

Analyze Potential Sponsors

Once you have gathered data and considered the characteristics of the event, it is time to start trying to match the event with potential sponsors. Sponsorship proposals generally need to involve more than simply promising logos on t-shirts and race banners. You might want to sell the title to the Health and Fitness Expo to a healthcare company, or link the online registration or transponder scoring with a tech company, for example.

If you are looking for a major sponsor, the best place to start is with bigger companies. Large companies tend to have much larger marketing budgets than smaller companies. A large company with its corporate headquarters in the local area should be a prime candidate. Some large national companies now require submission of sponsorship proposals online through the company's website. At the same time, however, these larger companies are often inundated with sponsorship proposals, and you might not be as effective at getting a foot in the door as you might with smaller, local businesses. As a result, several smaller sponsorships from local companies might be easier to obtain. In general, the larger the company, the earlier it must be approached about sponsorship, since larger companies generally follow strict budgeting cycles.

Keep in mind that most races find sponsors that are locally based. As mentioned above, this means it's a good idea to look for companies that are large employers in the local area or that have their corporate headquarters located in the city or town where the event will be held. A surprising number of sponsorship decisions are made at the whim of the CEO or company president. If this person is a runner, the event could have a strong advantage. Use any contacts that have been suggested by race committee members—follow up to see if any of these contacts work at companies that could be convinced to become sponsors.

If the event already has some existing sponsors, you may have an opening with some of their suppliers. This is particularly true with a supermarket sponsor, which can lean on some of its food and beverage suppliers, who in turn hope that their support will lead to increased orders or improved shelf space in the supermarket.

Look to identify companies and products that would make a good fit with the event. Also look at other local events and see what types of companies are sponsoring them. If you notice that several sports nutrition bar companies are sponsoring events in the same area, try to get a piece of the action from those companies, or make a pitch to one of their competitors.

Be sure to do your homework. Look at advertising campaigns. If you hear of a company that is rolling out a new product that might be of interest to runners, then tailor your proposal around this new product. Years ago, Xerox was heavily involved in sponsoring marathons when it introduced its "Marathon Copier" line. Texaco once branded itself as "The Star of the American Road," which made it another likely candidate.

Most companies categorize their sponsorship dollars under "marketing," but a few place them in the corporate donations budget (especially if they are donating to a nonprofit 501(c)(3) organization). It is useful to know which category the money will be coming from in advance, in order to tailor the proposal accordingly. Proposals for marketing dollars should concentrate on how the sponsorship will enhance sales; proposals for the corporate donations budget might stress the "feel good" nature of the

sponsorship or the charity beneficiaries of the event.

Table 5-C below shows the top 10 types of cash and in-kind sponsors, compiled from a survey performed by *Road Race Management*.

Pricing Sponsorships

When the time comes, it will be necessary to negotiate with all potential sponsors regarding how much money, product, or a mixture of the two they are willing to give, and in return, how much and what type of exposure they expect. Pricing sponsorship is an inexact science. The cost will depend largely on what the market will bear in the local community. If possible, talk to other race directors and see what sort of sponsorship deals they have been able to work out, to get some sort of idea of the going rate for various levels of sponsorship. If possible, look for ways to measure the visibility the companies will receive, such as the number of people who will see their logo or name in various places, as was done in **Table 5-A**.

A sponsorship survey done by *Road Race Management* newsletter found that the 'cost' of title sponsorships varies by race size. The majority of events represented in the survey offered at least four different levels of sponsorship. In general, the higher-level sponsors provided more cash, while the lower-level sponsors were more likely to provide in-kind (or a mix of cash and in-kind) contributions. Races with large numbers of participants tend to draw larger title sponsorships, as these races are able to offer greater exposure/promotional opportunities for the sponsor. Data from this survey showing the percent of races, broken down by size, with title sponsorships within defined ranges is presented in **Table 5-D** at right.

If you're having difficulty pricing sponsorships and have some start-up dollars to spend (especially for a larger event), there is a company

Table 5-C

Top 10 Cash and In-Kind Sponsors

Primarily Cash	Primarily In-Kind
1 Bank/credit union	Media
2 Medical/healthcare	Bottled water
3 Financial services/investment	Sports drink
4 Insurance	Energy bar/gel
5 Automotive	Food manufacturer
6 Running shoe/sporting goods retailer	Beer/wine
7 Attorney	Restaurant
8 Beer/wine	Municipality
9 Fitness center	Running shoe/sporting goods retailer
10 Running shoe/apparel manufacturer	Supermarket

called IEG (www.sponsorship.com) that will, for a fee, analyze the event (the product is called the "IEG Valuation Service") and come up with a suggested "value" that can be used to set sponsorship levels. Getting someone to pay this "value" is, of course, up to you.

The Sponsorship Proposal

Allow plenty of lead-time for submitting sponsorship proposals. Many companies will let you know how far in advance of an event they like to review proposals. The largest companies will likely need 9 to 12 months or longer; smaller companies may need 3 to 6 months. Companies are going to be more deliberate when spending $100,000 than when spending $1,000.

As mentioned above, many companies now require sponsorship proposals to be submitted electronically. Generally, these online forms have templates, with specific questions supplied by the company. The forms may ask for a paragraph or two in which you "sell" the event, or they may allow for the submission of a short cover email, in which a sales pitch can be made.

If an actual sponsorship proposal is prepared for distribution to potential sponsors, it should be short, concise and interesting. Sponsors don't have time to wade through a 10-page dissertation on the merits of the race, no matter how well written it may be. Also, keep in mind that no matter how exciting the race may be to *you*, the bottom line is that sponsors really only care about how the race can help *them* reach their goals. Focus the proposal on potential benefits to the sponsor rather than offering an essay containing a glowing account of the race's features.

If you are not forced into a rigid electronic format, the elements to include in a sponsorship proposal are outlined below. Submit a short, friendly cover letter with one or two key sales points and language that will make the prospective sponsor feel special.

- **A brief race history, status in the community and value to the sponsor**: This can showcase the reputation of the event, the value of the event to the local community, and the event's effectiveness in reaching the participants. If a company's products or services are directed largely to a particular demographic, show how the event will help them reach that segment of the population.

- **A description of the market**: If you are applying to a national company, be sure to educate the sponsor on the location of the event—big city or small town (and if it is small,

Table 5-D

Percent of Races with Title Sponsorship in Given Range

Amount of title Sponsorship (cash + in-kind)	# Of Participants					
	<1,000	1000-1,999	2,000-4,999	5,000-9,999	10,000-19,999	20,000+
<$1,000	17%	0%	0%	0%	0%	0%
$1,000-4,999	33%	22%	6%	0%	0%	0%
$5,000-9,999	17%	22%	6%	0%	0%	0%
$10,000-19.999	8%	56%	31%	17%	0%	0%
$20.000-24,999	0%	0%	13%	0%	0%	0%
$25,000-49,999	0%	0%	38%	17%	20%	0%
$50,000-74,999	0%	0%	6%	17%	0%	0%
$75,000-99,999	0%	0%	0%	8%	20%	11%
$100,000+	0%	0%	0%	42%	60%	89%

what it is near). Sponsors often target a specific market location to introduce a product, to increase their "market share" in that area, or to compete with another product that may be doing better than theirs in a given area. Concentrate on showing potential sponsors how the event can increase the exposure of their product in your location.

SIDEBAR

Sponsor Likes and Dislikes

Some potential sponsors may see thousands of sponsorship proposals over the course of the year. What can be done to make sure that your proposal will at least be considered and won't immediately wind up in the trash?

- *Be persistent (although stop short of being obnoxious).* This is a fine line, but with some potential sponsors receiving 80-100 sponsor calls each day, it pays to call more than once (but not 20 times).

- *Be sure to address your letter to someone in particular.* Letters starting "Dear Sir" often get thrown away—especially at companies specializing in women's products.

- *Don't misspell the person's name.*

- *Send proposals well in advance of the event.* Many companies set their sponsorship budgets a year in advance.

- *Be flexible in your demands and dollars desired.*

- *Don't have too many sponsors.* No sponsor likes their logo being lost in a sea of logos.

- *Be incredibly vigilant about visibility for any competing sponsors.* If you have a shoe company sponsor, make sure none of your race officials or others in high visibility positions, such as your race announcer, etc., show up wearing another brand.

- *Always give a current sponsor the right of first refusal if a higher offer comes in.* Consider carefully if it is worth jettisoning a current sponsor with whom you have an on-going relationship for an unknown sponsor for just a few extra dollars.

- *Don't burn bridges with any ex-sponsors:* When the day comes that a sponsor moves on—especially if the sponsor stayed with the event for many years—don't burn your bridges with the company by disparaging them. You never know when a new CEO might be a runner or a new marketing strategy might involve running.

- *Have a passion for your event.*

- *Give different sponsors control over different areas of your event* such as an expo sponsor, a corporate cup sponsor, or a water stop sponsor, etc.

- Conduct a high-quality and safe event.

- **Demographics of participants**: If you have collected data using a demographic survey, be sure to include the basic data such as age, sex, educational status, income level, etc. In addition, highlight any data that is of particular interest to the specific sponsor being approached (i.e. the responses to the question, "Do you intend to purchase a car in the next 6 months?" would be of interest to an automobile dealer.)

- **A description of benefits for the sponsor:** As much as possible, tailor each sponsorship proposal to the specific company being approached. Let them know what sort of opportunities the race can offer, such as product sampling, promotional tie-ins, and access to participant information. This is where you show the sponsor how the event can elevate awareness of the company's products or services, boost company morale through community involvement, or give the company a chance to be a "good corporate citizen" (a claim that the company can then use in future promotional campaigns). Analyze the company's marketing strategies for possible links to runners. Think outside the usual categories of logo and banner placements for creative ways to promote the sponsor. For example, if the event has a car sponsor, be sure to use one of its cars for the lead vehicle. If the event has a bank sponsor, consider moving the race account to that bank. Sponsors with retail outlets may appreciate any opportunities that bring people into their stores. One major event approached the telecommunications company Sprint and proposed a special banner about 100 yards from the finish line encouraging runners to "Sprint to the Finish." Don't neglect social media, which can also provide a number of creative opportunities that might appeal to a sponsor.

- **Amount and type of sponsorship being requested and timetable for responding:** Although later negotiations are possible, be sure to include the dollar and in-kind amounts requested, as well as a response date.

The proposal can be supplemented with a fun, promotional video including highlights of the event, to make the race come alive for potential sponsors. It's also a good idea to include details/clips of any prior local media/social media coverage, as a way to demonstrate the media exposure the race generally receives.

One caveat in creating a sponsorship proposal: Although it is important to present the event and its potential benefits to a sponsor in a good light, be careful not to over-promise what will be delivered. A sponsor is not going to remain involved with the event if they feel that you have not been honest.

Sending the Proposal

It is important to know who should receive the proposal. The best thing to do is to call/email to see if the company has a special events coordinator, or someone whose job it is to coordinate the company's PR and advertising goals with events. If there is no special events coordinator, someone in public relations or promotions can usually direct you to the person in charge of reviewing proposals for the sponsorship of events. If you are making a proposal to a small business, direct it toward the owner or manager by name. Better yet, show up in person and ask for a few minutes of the owner's time to personally deliver the proposal.

Follow-Up

After the proposal has been submitted, wait a few days. If there is no response, follow up with an email or phone call and try to arrange a short meeting to present the proposal. If a meeting is arranged, listen closely to what the potential sponsor has say, and try to gently counter any negative responses. Even if the potential sponsor says no to the initial proposal, try to get the company to be involved in some other way, even if it is just a small in-kind donation or supplying some volunteers. If the company plays even a small role in the event for one year and has a positive experience, they might be willing to do more in the future. By listening to how the potential sponsor responds to the proposal, it may become more clear how the company and the race might benefit each other in the future.

Accept that there will be a good number of "no thanks" responses. If, despite your best efforts, you

 GREEN TIP

Create a "Sustainability" Sponsorship Category

The marketing sector is changing rapidly to meet the demands of 21st century customers. Increasingly, companies are seeking to provide great experiences and deliver feel-good emotions to win consumers' loyalty. Companies are more conscious than ever of the need for their brands to be seen in a positive light by the public. Events with an established social and ecological conscience provide lots of creative space and opportunity for sponsors to engage people, tell an interesting sustainability story of their own and create memorable experiences that can influence the future purchasing choices of both participants and spectators.

still get a negative response, consider asking for a referral that might generate some other good leads. Send an email or letter thanking the company for the opportunity to submit the proposal. One primary rule of sponsorship solicitation is never burn bridges. The management that says "no" one year may be replaced with entirely new management headed by a runner the following year!

Procuring sponsorship can be a difficult, humbling experience. No matter how good the race, a tremendous amount of work is necessary to create proposals that will interest and excite sponsors. It might help to remember that even the largest, most successful races in the country have to work very hard to land sponsors - it's never an easy job.

The Agreement

Once an agreement is reached with a sponsor, get it in writing. Clearly state who is to do what and list all of the deadlines, making sure to include the deadline for payment. If the sponsor won't provide a written agreement, send the sponsor an email confirming your understanding of the terms of the transaction. Be as specific as possible. Don't take anything for granted, even if it means stating the obvious. Do this not only for major sponsors but also for even the smallest ones, as they are all important to the event. Putting these agreements in writing will help to avoid misunderstandings between you and the sponsors, which will help to ensure productive relationships with sponsors as well as the overall success of the event. It is useful to refer back to these agreements as race day approaches, just to refresh yourself about what each sponsor has been promised and what they should be providing. You may want to create a spreadsheet with all of the items promised to each sponsor so you don't have to wade through all of the contracts as race day approaches. *See Figure 5-2 on the next page for a sample title sponsor contract, and see Figure 5-3 for a sample supporting sponsor contract.*

Billing the Sponsor

As you draw up your sponsor contract, find out what the sponsor's billing and payment policies are. These can vary widely from company to company—some may pay in 14 days; others may have much longer cycles. Many companies routinely pay bills 30 days after receipt, etc. simply to conserve cash, so factor this into the billing cycle. Include a friendly explanation of both what the bill is for and the actual due date. In large corporations, invoices may have to go through several layers of bureaucracy before they get paid. Getting an early start will probably help the payment arrive when it is supposed to. Otherwise, sending a bill very close to the due date may produce both grumbling on the part of the sponsor and a cash flow crunch for the event, since the money may not arrive for several more weeks. Many races naively think that when a signed contract contains a payment schedule buried deep within it that the payments will automatically follow on that schedule. That is rarely the case. Be proactive when it comes to billing. Be prepared to submit a W-9 tax form with the first invoice.

Make Sure To Deliver What Is Promised and Remind Sponsors to Do Their Part

Sponsors will be watching to make sure you deliver what was promised. This is frequently called the "activation" of the sponsorship. Activation works two ways—both you and sponsor have to make sure that what is in the contract actually happens. If the event has multiple sponsors, you may want to create a spreadsheet (a "**Sponsor Promises** chart") to keep track of all the promises made to each sponsor. In the lead up to race day, it is easy to forget that the pharmaceutical sponsor was promised a logo in the vicinity of the medical tent or that the retail sponsor gets a free coupon in the virtual race packet, etc. Consult the Sponsor Promises chart frequently.

Figure 5-2

Sample Title Sponsor Contract

Sponsor contracts are apt to be widely varied, but a template for a title sponsor contract appears below.

TITLE SPONSOR CONTRACT TEMPLATE

[Event name] - [Sponsor name] SPONSORSHIP AGREEMENT

Whereas, [Event Name or company or organization owning the race] has the right to establish the terms and conditions of sponsorship of the [name of race] to be conducted [race location and race date], and

Whereas, [Name of sponsor] wishes to sponsor the [Name of event] for the [term/dates of sponsorship]

Now therefore, the [name of sponsor] and [name of event or company or organization owning the race] (hereafter the "parties") agree:

Contract: This Agreement sets forth the terms and conditions by which the [name of company] will obtain sponsorship of the for [term of sponsorship] [name of event] (hereafter the "Race"), which Race event is created, owned, controlled and the property of [name of owner of the event].

Sponsorship: [Name of company's] sponsorship includes but is not strictly limited to the following rights and privileges of sponsorship of the [term of sponsorship] [name of event]:

1. Title sponsorship. The [term of sponsorship] race event will be referred to as the [name of company][name of race] or other mutually agreeable title. An additional mutually agreeable term may be included as a subhead to the race name. The parties understand and agree that the sponsorship will be a non-exclusive sponsorship *[Note: This clause allows for the race to recruit supporting sponsors and sponsors at other levels than the title sponsor]* , except that the title used in the all communications by [the event] or authorized by it shall refer to the race as the [sponsor name][event name] or such other term as the parties may agree, and no other term, title or reference shall be used by [owner of event] or others authorized by [owner of the event] unless approved by [name of sponsor]. Other entities may sponsor race-related events as "presenting sponsors" including, but not limited to, the Health and Fitness Expo, training programs, Kids Run, etc.
2. Event-Related Items. The name/logo, as approved by [name of sponsor], will appear on all event-related printed and electronic materials including entry blanks, instructions, results; race ads, etc.
3. Race Event Banners. The name/logo will be prominently displayed on the start-finish banner.
4. Race Event Competitor Numbers. The name/logo will appear on the front of the competition numbers.
5. Race Event Volunteer Shirts. The race name will appear in the artwork on the race t-shirts; name/logo screened prominently on the back of the volunteer shirts.
6. [Company name] will be provided space for one free information booth at the pre-race expo held on [expo dates].
7. Results Book. The [company name] will be provided a full-page (four-color) advertisement in the electronic results booklet (in which only sponsors may advertise).
8. Registrations Reserved. [x number] free registrations at the prevailing registration fee will be set aside for the [company name]. These registrations may be distributed to employees or customers or donated to an official charity to ensure that the recipients are able to gain entry into the race.
9. VIP-Elite Athlete Dinner. [Name of event] shall provide the [name of company] [x number] invitations to the dinner/ reception the night before the race and to the post-race brunch.
10. [Name of company] will have the right to develop promotions utilizing the tie-in with the race (subject to prior [event name] approval).
11. Official Warm-up Logo. "[Name of company][name of race] will appear on the front of the runners' t-shirts and on the back of the officials' warm-ups.
12. Term. This agreement shall cover the period [opening date of contract] through [ending date of contract].

Figure 5-2

Sample Title Sponsor Contract (cont'd)

Sponsor Commitment. [name of company] agrees:

1. Sponsorship Fee. For the right to sponsor of the [year][name of event], the [name of company] shall pay [owner of the event] a rights fee of [amount of sponsorship fee]. *[Note: If the agreement is for multiple years, the amount in each subsequent year should be spelled out.]* For each of these years, payment will be required [terms, including schedule, of payment of sponsorship fee.].
2. Right to Sponsor the Race in [year after termination of contract]. The [name of company] shall provide notice to [name of event] of its sponsorship intentions for the [year after expiration of the contract] no later than [date];
3. Good Standing. The [name of company] is a corporation in good standing at the time of the execution of this contract.

Other Agreements

1. Official Charity. [Event name] has the right to designate the official charity of the event.
2. Registration Fee. [Event name] will set the registration fee for the event.
3. Ownership of Name, Sponsorship and Relationship of Parties. It is further mutually agreed that [name of event] shall have sole responsibility and authority with respect to the organization, administration, and conduct of the run. The role of [name of company] under this Agreement shall be solely as a financial sponsor of the race. This Agreement does not create, and shall not be construed as creating a partnership, joint venture, or agency relationship between the parties, and [name of company] shall acquire no rights or obligations with respect to the run other than those set forth in this Agreement.
4. Trademarks and Copyrights. [Name of event] acknowledges [name of company] ownership of and its exclusive right, title, and interest in its registered trademarks and logos ("Trademarks"). [Name of event] recognizes that these Trademarks possess substantial goodwill and economic value to [name of company] and expressly agrees to use such Trademarks in a manner consistent with the organization's graphic standards.
5. Notice. [Name of company] will designate a single individual to serve as the contact person for [name of event] for all matters concerning the sponsorship, including implementation. [Name of event] designates [name of person] or anyone hired subsequently in the role of "Event Director" as the contact person for the event for any matters concerning [name of sponsor]. In the event that the Event Director is unwilling or unable to serve, [name of event] will select a new point of contact and notify [name of sponsor] promptly.
6. Organization/Operation of Race. [Name of event] anticipates conducting the run basically as in the past. [Name of event] agrees and understands that significant changes in the conduct of the run, unless required by applicable law or mandated by municipalities or authorities in areas in which the race is held, must be made after consultation with and agreement by [name of company], which agreement shall not be unreasonably withheld.
7. Other Sponsors. [Name of event] understands that no conflicting sponsors to [name of company] will be affiliated with the race. This include, but are not limited to [names of companies that potentially could be a conflict]

Agreed to:

_____   _____
For [Name of race or owner of race]   Date

_____   _____
For [Name of company]   Date

Figure 5-3

Sample Supporting Sponsor Contract

Agreement

This agreement between [name of sponsoring company] and [name or owner of the race] will become effective [effective date] and will remain until [expiration date]

[Name of company] will provide to [name of race]. for the [year] race :

- A [amount] rights fee payable in not more than two installments; [e.g. 50% of rights fee] on or before [date] and the remaining [balance] on or before [date];
- [Detailed outline of any in kind support, including delivery dates, etc.]

In return [event] will provide:

- Exclusive recognition for [name of company] as the "official [category of sponsorship, i.e. 'retail sponsor" or "official retail partner"] of the [name of event].
- Use of [company name] logos on print and electronic versions of registration form, race instructions, and race ads. [Company name] logo with link will appear on the race website and will be contained in the post race publication;
- One free booth at the Health and Fitness Expo
- Ten free entries into race
- Four invitations to the Sponsor-VIP Dinner;
- Two [company name] promotions in a regularly scheduled blast emails to participants. Text of email will be supplied to [event name]; emailing will be carried out by [event name];

For [name of company]
Agreed_____
Date _____

For [name of event or owner of event]
Agreed_____
Date _____

Be forewarned that you are likely to need to prod your sponsors to take advantage of the things you have promised them. Far too often, sponsors don't renew, stating that they didn't get any return from the event—when the reason is they failed to take advantage of the opportunities.

Keeping Sponsors

Once a sponsor is on board, time will need to be devoted throughout the year to maintaining that relationship. Continue to learn as much about the sponsor's business as possible, and be aware of how they market their business. Remember that they don't see their sponsorship as simply paying a fee—they are making an investment in the event. Many events refer to their sponsors as "partners" to indicate a relationship that goes deeper than merely a financial exchange. Practice this philosophy.

Before the race, make efforts to get the employees of the company involved with the event, either as participants or as volunteers. This will help build a constituency of enthusiasts within the company who will talk it up internally.

At the event, make the major sponsor(s) feel special by providing corporate hospitality for them. This doesn't have to be fancy; it can be as simple as a tent with donuts and coffee. Also, some corporate VIPs might show up at the last minute, so consider reserving a parking place or two at the start for them, if it is feasible.

Phil Stewart

Ambushed: *Citgo, an official Boston Marathon sponsor, has a large sign that is a vital landmark for runners at the 25-mile mark of the race. New Balance, not a sponsor of the Boston Marathon, has erected this sign post nearby.*

Try to document the exposure each sponsor receives on race day by assigning one or two race volunteers to go around and take pictures of signage, and anything else with a sponsor logo, that is visible at the start, finish, and out on the course. These photos can then be presented to the sponsor to reinforce the visibility they received at the event. *(For more tips on how to maximize sponsor exposure on the course, see **Chapter 16: Race Logistics and Operations**.)*

Ambush Marketing

Be vigilant for—and try to suppress—ambush marketing attempts by non-sponsors. Ambush marketing is when a non-sponsoring company attempts to steal visibility at the event for free. For example, at the Boston Marathon, many non-marathon sponsors buy up billboards along the race course *(see photo at left)*.

Post-Event Follow-up

Immediately after the race, send each sponsor a thank-you email. This should be followed up soon after with a post-race sponsor summary report (2-4 pages maximum) customized for each individual sponsor to show specifically how their sponsorship was "activated." (Use the Sponsor Promises chart discussed earlier as a guide, as well as the **Sample Sponsor Activation Report** *(see **Sidebar** at right)*. Include stats to show the reach of the event (including social media stats), photos documenting the sponsor's presence during the race, and copies of or documentation about

the media coverage. The report can contain some other basic information about the event such as size, gender ratio, dollars raised for charity and glowing testimonials from participants.

If you prepare some sort of print or online results publication, include a "Race Director's Message" for participants, with a final "thank you" to the sponsors and a reminder to participants to use the sponsors'

SIDEBAR

Sample Sponsor Activation Report

After each year's Credit Union Cherry Blossom Ten Mile, each sponsor receives a follow-up report (prepared as a PowerPoint file) outlining that sponsor's exposure. The elements of the report prepared for a healthcare sponsor include:

- Cover page with event name and sponsor's logo
- Outline of activation opportunities provided
- Samples of all blast emails with sponsor's involvement in event mentioned
- Sample of invitation to pre-race party underwritten by the healthcare company
- Photos taken at pre-race party, including photos of sponsor's signage
- Sample ad for training/educational clinic program sponsored by company
- Sample of invitation for training/educational clinic program sent to entrants
- Photos from training/educational clinic program
- List of registrants for training/educational clinic program
- Outline of event website exposure
- Timetable for all blast emails containing sponsor's logo
- Report of social media impressions
- Report of page performance of ad in electronic "goody bag"
- Photos of booth at expo
- Photos from race including photos of sponsor signage
- Copies of awards that race won in local magazines
- Photo of event receiving sustainability award
- Photo of sponsor ad in post-race .pdf results publication
- Final thank you letter for sponsor's support

products and services as well. Be sure to include links for each of the sponsors in the publication.

Sponsors, like everyone else, appreciate gifts from the race. It may be a wise investment to send the major sponsors some official race merchandise or a special gift. Lower-level sponsors should receive t-shirts or other, smaller items of race merchandise.

Include questions of interest to the sponsors on any post-event participant surveys.

Nurturing sponsors is a year-round responsibility. If you tell a sponsor you will do something for them, be sure to follow through. If for some reason you fail to deliver on a promise, don't make excuses—step up and take responsibility for the oversight and make sure it doesn't happen again. Do your best to over-deliver. This behavior will engender trust and will encourage sponsors to return in future years.

Phil Stewart

Sponsor Activation: *The water sponsor was the sponsor of the spray station at the Quad City Times Bix Seven Mile.*

CUCB

6 Marketing and Promotions

THE BASICS

S ince registration income is likely the largest single source of revenue for a running event, promoting the event to attract entrants is the most critical pre-race task. Promotional avenues have expanded massively since the days of putting printed flyers under the windshields of parked cars at other races.

- **Outline the promotional pitch**. Make sure to include the basics of the event (distance, date, registration fee, etc.) as well as what makes the event distinct from others in the same area. Customize this message for the various promotional avenues that will be chosen.

- **Utilize sources of self-generated promotion, such as:**
  - ◆ **Race website:** A good race website will greatly reduce the number of emails from participants with questions and can also be the most effective (and least expensive) means to provide

information about the event. The challenge is to keep the website current. Most online registration companies will also help an event establish a website in conjunction with using their runner-registration services.

- **Social media:** Over the last decade, a very large number of new opportunities for promotion have sprung up, most of them free, thanks to the proliferation of various forms of social media. Even in the absence of a formal event website, other forms of social media (Facebook, Twitter, Pinterest, Instagram, YouTube etc.) can be used to promote an event at no charge.
- **Press releases:** Prepare and circulate electronic press releases about the event. These can cover everything from announcing the date and registration process of the event, to a new sponsor or new course, to the elite athletes coming to the event, to the dollars raised for charity or the economic impact of the event.
- **Mass emailing of registration forms or race information:** If the event will be promoted via an email 'blast,' be sure to use up-to-date lists, targeted toward the desired demographic. After a race has been held, the list of past registrants will be the most productive source of registrants for the next event. Email platforms such as Constant Contact or MailChimp can be used for sending mass emails. These programs allow recipients to opt out of receiving your emails. Some also provide "brand-enhancing" platforms for communicating by means other than email. Many online registration providers or event management companies also provide blast email services.
- **Printed promotional materials/registration forms:** Once the backbone of race promotion, printed or "hard copy" registration forms now play a minor role, at best, in race promotion. Direct mailing is now virtually a thing of the past. Some races may still print a small number of flyers or informational postcards ("Save the date" cards) for distribution at other races, or for mailing to past participants and advertising at running shoe stores, gyms, and at other events that accept these materials, but most race directors have completely eliminated paper advertising/registration due to cost and environmental concerns.

- **Take advantage of free promotion through other sources.** These include, but are not limited to: calendars maintained by online registration providers, local/regional newspapers and their websites, local TV and radio stations, running stores, YMCAs/other fitness centers, local running clubs, other races, area hotels, and event sponsors.

- **Consider the possibility of paid promotion.**
  - **Advertising:** Paid advertising can be expensive, but effective. Advertising through social media sites provides a great opportunity for reaching prospective registrants. As an example, for a relatively small fee, a web-based ad can be placed through Facebook, targeting a very specific demographic, such as all women in the area who have 'liked' a 10K in the last 6 months. Some events still run ads in print publications, especially if there is a well-read local running publication. There is an unwritten rule that running publications (print or web-based) are more likely to cover events that have placed ads.
  - **Online marketplaces/social buying sites:** "Daily deals" services such as Groupon, Living Social and a growing number of others can provide opportunities for mass-marketing of events. Millions of people subscribe to these services, so social buying sites can certainly help with marketing/promotion and brand awareness. Although these services generally do not have up-front fees, they often require deep discounting of the registration fee and most, if not all, also collect a percentage of each sale—sometimes up to 50%. Thus, it is important to use these services judiciously.

THE DETAILS

One of the most challenging—but potentially most rewarding—aspects of putting on a road race is marketing and promoting the event. Some race organizations are extremely adept at navigating the marketing and promotions thicket, while others struggle for so much as a mention in the local paper or on its website. Working diligently to promote the event is worth the effort, as successful race promotion can pay off handsomely in terms of increased participation, stronger community interest and support, more volunteers, and increased exposure for sponsors.

The advent of social media has dramatically changed event promotions because the difficulty (and cost) of reaching prospective past participants has plummeted to next to nothing. There are more low-cost and no-cost avenues to get out the word (repeatedly) than ever before.

Keep in mind, though, that the more participants an event has, the greater the stress that will be placed on all aspects of the race organization. Make sure you can operationally manage all promotional success, meaning, ask yourself how many people the event can reasonably handle, especially the first year, and tailor the promotions to reach that number.

If you are comfortable that the event can handle an influx of new registrants, then focus on how to best increase the field as well as increase the visibility of the event in the community (both important criteria for sponsors).

Develop a Marketing Strategy

With an estimated 30,000 running events in the U.S. annually, you will need to decide what the event's selling points are in order to entice people to select your event over others and pay the registration fee. Listed below are a number of promotional avenues for events.

- *Promote the distance, date, course and special features of the event:* Distance is one of the most basic decisions, followed by date (holiday races frequently attract big crowds), but among events of similar distance, what separates yours from the crowd? Common selling points include the type of course (most runners prefer flat courses, but some like "challenging" or "rolling" courses), scenery, entertainment during or after the race, post-race party, participant medals, upgraded t-shirts, etc. However, there are also some benefits to uniformity — part of the success of the Rock 'n' Roll series or the Ragnar Relays is that the owners have created

TIP

What Makes the Event Unique?

If you live near any kind of population center, one look at a local race calendar will likely show that, no matter what weekend you choose during the racing season, your event will be up against a lot of competition. In order to attract participants to an event, the race needs to stand out from the crowd. Making an event stand out could range from scheduling it on a holiday to supporting a popular local charity, to making it a nighttime event, to including unique post-race entertainment, etc. Certainly, the popularity of MOB events (mud, obstacles and beer; also called OCRs—obstacle course events), including color runs, electric runs, costume runs and many others, illustrates the potency of such uniqueness. The challenge is incorporating the fun and uniqueness that comes with the theme into a safe and well-executed running event. If the quality of the race itself suffers because too much focus is placed on the theme, you risk disappointing the registrants and the event may ultimately suffer. The past few years have seen an increasing number of races that make this kind of mistake and, in the age of social media, bad news travels quickly.

a "brand." For Rock 'n' Roll, that means bands on the course and a post-race rock concert. For consumers, those events are much like walking into a Starbucks or McDonalds.

- **Align with a charity (or charities):** Running events have had strong ties to charities for decades. Think about which charity (or charities) will strike a chord with potential registrants.

- **Create a sense of urgency to register through registration fee discounts:** As registration fees have escalated, more and more events are offering discounts accomplished by the use of discount codes that can be used during the online registration process, or by other customizable features provided by the online registration company. The most common discount is for registering early, with fees escalating as the event draws closer. Other creative discounts include a deep discount on the day after the event for the following year's event, for a given number of days or for the first so many registrants; a one-day registration fee "sale" possibly on a holiday; discounts for runners who refer others; discounts late in the registration fee cycle for previous participants who have not registered for the current year's race; discounts for people who sign up at the retail sponsor's store; etc. Each change in the registration fee gives the event another chance to communicate with potential participants by email, social media, press releases or on the website, along the lines of "Beat the Price Increase, Enter by this Friday at Early Registration Prices," etc.

- **Offer special perks:** Provide a special giveaway (handed out at packet pick-up to avoid mailing fees) to early registrants. Create a VIP registration package with benefits such as private porta-johns and bag check, or VIP credentials for family members at a premium registration fee.

Bob Mallet

Getting charity groups involved is a good way to increase participation.

In many ways, running events have become like any other retail product from lampshades to avocados, when it comes to marketing and promotional strategies to get consumers to buy.

Certainly the ease of communicating by email and social media opens up plenty of promotional opportunities to build interest, such as announcing the t-shirt or medal design, or hyping the entertainment on the course or the post-race party. An event's social media channels are like a sponge for information — keep them well stocked. And remember, once the information is on social media it travels fast.

Make sure the marketing strategy is well fleshed out before moving into the promotions phase.

Create a Promotions Plan

The first step the race committee should take in the area of promotions is to make a promotions/media plan. First, make a list of possible promotional venues and then decide which ones are worth investing time and money into. Determine a budget for promotional activities. Once you know how much (or how little) time and money there is to spend, determine which promotional avenues to target. Some promotional avenues are free, while others can be extremely expensive. See later in this chapter under **Promotional Options** for a discussion of the promotional methods that can be used and the media outlets that can be approached.

While the country's largest races have the luxury of hiring public relations firms to do the promotional work for them, such companies are generally too costly for the average race. In most cases, it is likely that you and the race committee will have to plan to do the promotional legwork yourselves.

Keep in mind that, while the primary goal in race promotions is to attract participants, marketing efforts also can serve to attract volunteers, interest potential sponsors, and generate general interest within the community. Make sure that these secondary target audiences are all reached through the promotional plan.

Set a Promotions Timeline

Once there is a promotional plan in place, the next step is to determine what the promotional timeline should be, including key target dates and deadlines for all of the outlets you will be trying to work with. If possible, allow a certain amount of flexibility, especially if the promotional team consists of volunteers. The timeline should include a schedule for each type of promotion, including blast emails, blogs, social media, press releases, and advertising. Emails may go out every 2-4 weeks. Social media promotion takes place on an on-going basis.

Find a Promotions/Media Coordinator

If the event is large enough to attract the interest of even the local media, and to deal with the maze of promotional options outlined in this chapter, consider delegating the promotions and media coordination to someone other than the race director. The largest races, such as the TCS New York City Marathon, have several full-time staff members devoted simply to dealing with the media. If the race director goes it alone, he or she will discover in the early days that the promotional options are dizzying, and in the final days that the media are the most demanding when he or she is the busiest. (Rest assured that when a race director does not respond to the media, the race coverage suffers.)

Write a Press Release/Event Summary

With a promotional plan and timetable in hand, the next step is to prepare the message that can be used to promote the race. The best place to start may be to prepare a press release or other form of promotional event summary. (A sample press release noting the main sections of the typical release appears in **Figure 6-1**). This will force you to think about many of the details of the event that can later be expanded into other forms of advertising. Coupled with the material in **Chapter 7: Entrant Registration, Confirmation and Communications,** this should provide the basis

Figure 6-1

Sample Press Release

MAIN SECTIONS OF RELEASE INDICATED BY [BRACKETS]

[RELEASE TIME AND DATE]
For Immediate Release
2 March 20xx

[CONTACT INFORMATION]
Media Contact Information: (not for publication)

Joe Prguy, Media Coordinator, 888-881-6803 or joeprguy@10milerace.org
Website: www.10milerace.org

[MAIN HEADLINE]

2016 Credit Union Cherry Blossom Ten Mile Run Offers $10,000 Bonus for Setting American Record

[SUBHEAD]

Additional $25,000 for Americans Up for Grabs as Part of $80,000 Total Purse

[DATELINE AND BODY OF RELEASE]

   March x, 20xx Washington, DC: Looking ahead to the xxth running of the Cherry Blossom Ten Mile Run on April x, 20xx, in Washington, DC, event organizers are offering a $10,000 American record bonus for the first American man or woman to break Greg Meyer's American record of 46:13, set here in 1983, and Janet Bawcom's single-sex American record of 52:12, set here in 2014; the $10,000 bonus will be split if two new American records are set at this year's Runners Rite of Spring. As in years past, there will be an advance start for the elite women, providing them an opportunity to compete for records that will be recognized as coming from a women's-only race.

[QUOTE FROM RACE OFFICIAL]

   Event director Phil Stewart said, "With so many Americans being in top condition after the Olympic Marathon Trials last month, and ready to unwind after being so focused on the trials for the past year, we wanted to do something special for the Americans this year."

[ADDITIONAL DETAILS]

   In addition to the American Record bonus, Cherry Blossom organizers will offer a $25,000 American purse. If an American man were to win the race outright and break the American record with a sub-46:00 time, he could earn as much as $24,000. The last American man to win the race was Chris Fox in 1990. If an American woman were to win the race and break the American record with a sub-52:00 time, she could also take home $24,000. The last American woman to win the race was Joan Nesbit in 1996.

   The American record bonus and purse are part of the total open prize purse of $80,500, which includes equal payments to the top ten men and women finishers of all nationalities, totaling $40,000, with time bonuses of $1,000 and $750 available to the first two men and women to break 46 minutes and 52 minutes, respectively. The generous amount of open prize money should ensure a talented cast of international athletes as well.

   Over 27,000 runners submitted applications to participate in the 20xx Credit Union Cherry Blossom 10 Mile and 5K Run-Walk, and the list of accepted runners represents all 50 states and 14 foreign countries. The event is limited to 15,000 finishers by the National Park Service.

Figure 6-1

Sample Press Release (cont'd)

Since 2002, the Credit Union Cherry Blossom 10 Mile and 5K Run-Walk have raised over $7 million for the Children's Miracle Network Hospitals, and a significant portion of that total has been raised by Charity Race entrants.

["ABOUT THE EVENT" BOILERPLATE - APPEARS ON ALL RELEASES]

About the Credit Union Cherry Blossom Ten Mile:

The Credit Union Cherry Blossom is known as "The Runner's Rite of Spring" in the Nation's Capital. The staging area for the event is on the Washington Monument Grounds, and the course passes in sight of all of the major Washington, DC Memorials. The event serves as a fundraiser for the Children's Miracle Network Hospitals, a consortium of 170 premier children's hospitals across the United States. About one-third of the funds raised support Washington, DC's own Children's National Medical Center ("Children's Hospital"). The event also funds two $5,000 Road Runners Club of America "Roads Scholar" grants designed to support up-and-coming U.S. distance running talent.

[SPONSOR DETAILS]

Credit Union Miracle Day, Inc., a consortium of credit unions and credit union suppliers, is the title sponsor of the Credit Union Cherry Blossom Ten Mile Run and 5K Run-Walk. PSCU is the lead financial partner of Credit Union Miracle Day, Inc. Supporting sponsors include Cabot Creamery Cooperative, E-Trade, Gatorade, Gold's Gym, MarathonFoto, MedStar Sports Medicine, Navy Federal Credit Union, New Balance, Potomac River Running and Suburban Solutions Moving Company.

[SANCTIONED BY]

In addition to being sanctioned by USA Track & Field and the Road Runners Club of America, the Credit Union Cherry Blossom Run recently earned Gold certification from the Council for Responsible Sport for its many environmentally and socially responsible initiatives.

- End -

for the presentation of the event to the public. If the initial release/summary is well done, it should satisfy the requirement for many of the free listings in the sections that follow.

The press release/promotional summary should be written in a straight-forward style and be no more than two pages in length. If it is announcing the establishment of the race, or the date of the upcoming year's race, be sure to cover the well-known four "Ws"—What, When, Where and Why, along with details about how to register and the event contact information, with a website, email address, and possibly a phone number. Think carefully about the email address and contact phone number included in any promotional materials. You may want to create an email such as info@yourracename.org instead of listing someone's personal email. This "info" alias can be assigned to whomever is responsible for replying to the public. It may be prudent to obtain a

dedicated cell phone number for the event as well.

Since it is likely you will be sending the press release by email, make sure the "Subject" line of the email is written in a way that will encourage the recipient to want to read more, and be sure that the important words in the "Subject" line are visible in the recipient's email program. For the actual press release, the header for the release should contain the date of the release, the date the information in the release may be announced (most say "For Immediate Release," which means the information may be used upon receipt of the release), and a contact (name, phone and email). Sometimes the name on the release is different than the general contact for the race. It may save some wear and tear on the media contact if you note that his or her contact number is not for publication and include the "for publication" contact information in the release. The headline for an initial release might be something as simple as

"First City Bank Labor Day Half Marathon to Debut in Dubuque." Subsequent releases may deal with different topics such as "World Record Holder to Run in First City Bank Labor Day Half Marathon," but always include some boilerplate language regarding registering for the race at the end, such as "Registration is still open for the First City Bank Labor Day Half Marathon, available through the event's website, www.FCBLaborDayHalf.com." A *short* statement about sponsors may be appropriate at the end as well, along the lines of "The First City Bank Labor Day Half Marathon is sponsored by Larry's Sports and the *Dubuque Citizen* Newspaper."

With the release/promotional summary in hand, you are ready to promote! Besides your own mailing list consisting of emails of local media (especially anyone with an interest in running) and regional and national online running sites, web-based press releases can be picked up by electronic aggregators (including *Endurance Sports Wire*, *Road Race Management*, the *RRCA*, and *Running USA*). These services post releases, some requiring a fee, to a wide number of industry contacts. A listing of these outlets appears in **Chapter 23: Resources.** You can sign up to receive these releases for free, so consider doing so in order to understand what type of information is needed to get releases disseminated.

Promotional Options

The Race Website

The race website is the backbone of all race promotion efforts. Through the website, runners can get questions answered, learn important information, and register for the race, most likely through a link to an online registration provider. In addition, the internet offers a medium for selling race merchandise.

There are basically two ways to produce a race website: it can be done mostly in-house by finding a volunteer or low-cost webmaster within the race organization and contracting with an internet service provider (ISP) to get the space on the internet for the site; or it can be done by hiring an outside vendor to design and maintain the site for the organization. Both options are used successfully by races of all sizes and the option that works best for you will depend on the amount of money the event has to spend and the availability of knowledgeable people within the race organization.

Services such as Wordpress, Weebly, Squarespace, Wix and many others provide many options for website creation, some of which are free. Most of these services are very user friendly, making what once seemed an intimidating do-it-yourself task far more manageable. If you are lucky enough to have a web buff on the race committee, first make sure this person has plenty of time (well-managed websites can be labor intensive) and then sign him or her up!

The amount of work the website turns out to be is a function of how big and how complicated it is. The largest running clubs staging events and activities year round may have as many as 6-10 people working on their sites; other races make do with one part-time volunteer. One nice thing about doing the website in-house is that, as long as the webmaster has the time, changes can be made as needed throughout

---

GREEN TIP

Use Sustainability to Differentiate the Event from Others

Among the thousands and thousands of running events, relatively few market themselves as being "green." To avoid any concerns about "greenwashing," however, be sure to measure and document the event's sustainable achievements. One way to do this is to pursue certification from the Council for Responsible Sport (www.CouncilForResponsibleSport.org).

the race cycle, on almost a moment's notice. If an outside vendor is hired to do the work, you are more at their mercy regarding how many changes can be made and when. Moreover, hiring an outside vendor to produce the website will certainly be more expensive.

There are many companies that can design websites, but if you want to use a website designer that is familiar with running, there are several available that offer such services. Some online registration companies provide you with some templates for race information and photos, bundled, often for free, with their online registration services. Sometimes, this space is enough that you could choose to use just this kind of service instead of setting up an entirely separate website for the event. The drawback of this option is lack of flexibility—you will need to fit your event's information into the company's standard template. Other running-based/registration companies will create an entire website customized for the event, usually for a flat fee or an increased percentage of each registration fee. With any web design company, the cost of design will vary dramatically, depending on how complex you want the site to be.

Website Content

When determining what to include on the website and how it should be designed, keep the following tips in mind:

- **Select a unique domain name.** It is important that the URL/domain name contain the name of the event, if possible, so that it is easy to find (www.animalrights10k.com, for example). Services like GoDaddy will allow you to determine if the desired domain name is available and will provide a number of alternatives if the first choice is already taken GoDaddy and a

number of other sites will allow you to purchase/register a domain name for a small annual fee. If you decide to use an abbreviation in the domain name, consider purchasing the full name as well, so that users who don't know the abbreviation can still find you. For example, Road Race Management's web address is www.rrm.com, but it is registered at www.roadracemanagement.com as well. Any user that types in the latter address is automatically routed to the www.rrm.com homepage. This approach ensures that potential registrants are not missed because they can't find the website. While domain names ending in .com (or .org for nonprofits) remain the gold standard, there has been a proliferation of domain name suffixes in recent years, such as .biz or .info or .fit. If your desired domain name is not available as .com or .org, look for another available suffix.

SIDEBAR

Keep Control of the Site

Although what appears on the event website is of keen interest to the event's sponsors, race directors should avoid yielding control and maintenance of the event website to a sponsor. If you do this, you will be handing over your most immediate communication tool to someone outside your organization—and someone who may have hundreds of other responsibilities, or who may not work on the weekends, etc.

In addition, having the event nested within a sponsor's larger site can mean that prospective registrants have a hard time finding the event. A partial solution is to obtain the rights to the domain name (e.g., www.parkersburghalfmarathon.com), so that users entering via that address will always be directed to the most current version of the site. There are various companies who will register domain names for a small fee. Many of these can also tell you if a certain domain name is in use by someone else. Type "domain names" into a Google or Yahoo search engine and the names of these companies will surface. The bottom line is that runners aren't going to care where the race website resides; they just want to be able to get the information they need quickly. If the sponsor's "help" is going to hinder this process, then keep control of the website yourself, as much as you are able.

- *Keep the website simple and clean.* If users have difficulty navigating the event website, they won't stick around long. A clean site will be straightforward, clear, and not full of distracting clutter.

- *Don't put so many graphics on a page that it is very slow to load.* Web users generally don't want to wait around to see sixteen photos of the race on the home page, no matter how beautiful they are. A few photos and/or graphics are fine, but don't overload the page.

- *Make the site "mobile friendly."* More and more websites are viewed on mobile devices (phones, tablets, etc.), so make sure the webmaster designs the site to look good on these devices as well as on standard computer screens. There are special design features that work better in the smaller format.

- *Try to anticipate the runners' questions, and make sure the answers are readily available on the website.* Keep the content lively though; very few people want to scroll through endless pages of dull text.

- *Include links to social media.* Make sure that the website contains links to any other forms of social media being used to promote the event—the Facebook page, Twitter feed, YouTube videos, Instagram account, etc.

- *Keep things current.* Users get frustrated if they keep checking back for information, only to find that the website is out of date. Also, make sure that any new features promised, such as online registration, are operational by the date advertised on the site, or change the date. It can be pretty embarrassing if you promise to have a new training feature up at the beginning of August, only to have users logging in at the end of August and still seeing "Coming August 1." If you are going to be late, at least put a new target date up there.

- *Perform search engine optimization (SEO).* This is a process by which the amount of traffic to the website can be increased by designing it such that the site will appear early in the list of results returned by a search engine, such as Google or Yahoo. There are many techniques for effective SEO, including use of important keywords in the content and frequent updates of website content. Google provides a Search Engine Optimization Starter Guide (http://static.googleusercontent.com/media/www.google.com/en//webmasters/docs/search-engine-optimization-starter-guide.pdf) and many other helpful tips can be found by simply Googling 'search engine optimization.'

- *Analyze the performance of the site.* Use Google Analytics or another web analytics tracking software to monitor the website's traffic, how long visitors stay on each page, where visitors are from and other information that will help assess the effectiveness of the website. The basic version of Google Analytics is free and will easily provide enough data for the average race director to use to optimize his or her website.

- *Put the web address on everything.* An event might have the greatest website in the world, but it isn't going to do anyone any good if users can't find it—you have to make the web address known. The web address should appear on all official race documents and other web-based platforms used, including the registration form, the fundraising site, any printed promotional postcards/flyers, press releases, runner instructions, results book, and anything else the race office puts out.

- *Look at the websites of other races.* There are hundreds of race websites out there to examine. Decide what you like and don't like about these sites. Analyze them for aesthetics and ease of finding necessary information.

- *Think about what the event website is meant to accomplish.* What does the event have to offer the runners? If scenery is a big draw, consider including a photo gallery containing some of the more spectacular aspects of the course. Make the gallery available only to users who want to access it, however, so that those with slow internet connections or those who don't want to wait for the pictures to load don't have to.

- ***Make sure to include sponsor logos on the race website and link them to the sponsors' homepages.*** You may even want to post some information about one or more of the major sponsors on the site along with links to the sponsors' sites.

- ***Ask the major sponsor(s) if there is anything they want included on the website.*** For example, a high-tech title sponsor might want to let race applicants know about employment opportunities at the sponsor's company.

- ***Post race results quickly.*** In this internet-driven age, runners have come to expect speedy posting of results. Get the results up as soon as reasonably possible. If there is going to be a delay, post something to let runners know when they can expect the results to be up. Runners checking out results in the days after the race can comprise a large percentage of overall site traffic, so don't miss out on this chance to give the sponsors a last bit of exposure and to show the runners that the event provides excellent service. If you post results immediately, or close to it, include a notice at the top of the page to indicate that the results are unofficial, because of the possibility of errors, protests, etc. You should encourage people to email the race, or better yet, provide a feedback form on the website that goes directly to the race timers, if they feel the results are in error in some way.

- ***Follow up post-race.*** The time when people are flocking to the event website to view race results is also a good time to put up any post-race instructions that participants might have missed, such as how runners can view race photos taken by the official participant race photographer or how to pick up t-shirts if they did not get them at the expo or the race site, etc.

Remember, runners are going to the event website to accomplish specific tasks—to learn how to register, what the course is like, what the awards structure is, where their predicted time would have placed them in last year's race, etc. Once they've registered, they want quick access to race-day logistics information, such as driving directions, where to park and where packet pick-up will be. Larger races should also have lodging options, preferably with links, and, if the race tends to attract out-of-town runners, information on nearby attractions for runners who plan to bring the family and make a weekend out of it. The best way to meet these seemingly endless demands is simple—pretend that you're an interested runner who has never been to the event, and see if the site gives quick answers to the types of questions you would have. A good trick to determine the runner-friendliness of your site is to enlist the help of a handful of people who are unfamiliar with it. Give them five specific tasks to perform, such as register for the race, learn how to volunteer, contact race headquarters, find last year's winning time, etc. Sit next to them as they navigate through the site while trying to complete their assignment, but give no hints about where to look. Afterward, ask them why they made the navigational choices they did. If they mostly failed their assignment, the site likely needs to be reorganized. *For more on what to include on the event website, see under "Developing the Registration Form and Website Content" in* **Chapter 7: Entrant Registration, Confirmation and Communications.**

What Goes Up When?

Website content that is out of sync with the calendar reflects poorly on the event. (Some parts of an event's website, such as history, general information, and dates, will remain relatively constant throughout the year). The best way to avoid this problem is to work from a timeline, much as you do for race administration. In fact, the website timeline could roughly parallel the administration timeline—when the registration form is ready; when the elite athletes who are running this year will be announced; when registration closes, etc.

Link to Online Registration

The event website should link seamlessly with the online registration provider. Online registration companies have come a long way in streamlining the registration process for participants. A full discussion of online registration appears in *Chapter 7: Entrant Registration, Confirmation and Communications.*

Social Media/Marketing on the Internet

The 21st century has seen a vast expansion of free or low-cost publicity opportunities on the internet, including social networking groups such as Facebook, Twitter, Pinterest, Instagram, Snapchat, YouTube and Google+. If you are over 30 years old and you turn a blind eye to this type of marketing, do so at your own peril, as the internet is the medium of choice for individuals competing in most of the "open" (under age 40) divisions. Social media provides a nearly free, potent way to engage people with an event — a true marketer's dream.

Social networking platforms: These platforms, including Facebook, Twitter, Instagram, LinkedIn, Snapchat and Pinterest, just to name a few, enable individuals to connect and reach out to others based on a common interest such as running. Although the formats of these platforms vary, the general procedure is for people to register with the service, create a profile or bio for themselves or for an event, and then to connect with other users with similar interests by following them or inviting them to 'like'/join their group or follow their feed. Messages, photos and videos posted on the event's page or feed can be seen by all followers/members of the group, as well as shared with individuals who have not yet joined. Used properly, these social networks can effectively get the word out about an event and drive traffic to the event's website. In addition, Facebook and Google have powerful paid advertising features—see more details in the section for **Paid Advertising,** below. Once you have set up social media outlets, encourage people to join them by placing links on the event webpage and in blast emails, etc. Building followers is the name of the game for every social media outlet.

Social networking sites, as the name implies, are designed to be *social.* This means that events using them need to maintain a consistent online presence. Social media is a powerful tool for extending your brand, so make sure that the event's social media presence reinforces the overall look and feel of the event as much as possible (especially the look of the event website). Since the goal of social media sites is to create a community of followers, you should not be too heavy handed about pitches to enter the race or buy the race merchandise. Certainly, a comment about a pending price increase is appropriate, but otherwise just allow the discussions to flow (chiming in when necessary) among the followers.

TIP

A Note on Hashtags

Most people know that #hashtags are used on Twitter, but #hashtags are also being used across other platforms, such as Facebook and Instagram. It may look like words put together with a nifty "#" in front, but there's an actual method to the madness. Using a catchy, easy to remember #hashtag will help brand your message across platforms. Your followers can find all of your posts, but they can also share that #hashtag to connect their own posts to your messages. If you're thinking that #hashtags only offer a sort of slogan and way to find similar content, you'd be wrong. They also offer a boost in engagement. In fact, tweets with #hashtags offer up to twice as much engagement. But there's more to it than that—using too many #hashtags leads to a significant drop in engagement, incrementally worse the more you use. If you find a million #hashtags annoying, you're not the only one. So what's the perfect number? Research shows that you should limit your usage to one or two #hashtags.

Make sure someone is in charge of regularly monitoring and replying to user posts on behalf of the event. Sites should be monitored on at least a daily basis, if not in real time, so that those posting will be read and responded to quickly and professionally. This instant form of communication encourages participant involvement, helping them to feel engaged with the event. To further encourage participant involvement, make posts interactive—ask questions and interact with the audience. Social media gives everyone a voice, including critics. This is another reason it is important to monitor the event sites regularly, so criticisms can be responded to quickly.

Here is a short synopsis of the niches of each of the major social media sites at the time of the writing of the second edition of this book. This is a rapidly evolving area and new sites should be explored as they proliferate. A cardinal rule for social media is that it is far better to create fewer accounts and keep them active, meaning at least a couple of posts a week, more as the event gets closer. Facebook and Twitter accounts are probably the two key accounts to have and keep active. Beyond those two, just follow which social media outlets other races are using.

- **Facebook** (www.facebook.com)**:** The grand-daddy of social media sites, Facebook has over 1.79 billion active users. For an individual Facebook page, individuals request access to the page and must be approved by the creator of the page. This limits the viewership of the page to accepted "friends." However, there are two Facebook options designed for commercial use which do not require approval by the creator of the page, ensuring access to everyone who simply "likes" the page. These are Facebook Fan pages

and Facebook Event pages. Fan pages are similar to personal Facebook pages but interested users can search for the page and "like" it to receive updates and notifications without being approved as a "friend." Event pages publicize specific events, but the creator of the page must designate the page as "public" to allow anyone to visit the page without being "friended." Facebook is a good place to create a "buzz" about an event by posting news, photos, stories, etc.—anything to promote a dialog among the event's followers. You also can create surveys and hold contests on Facebook.

Many active Facebook users use Facebook messaging instead of email and expect replies just as quickly. Although more associated with Twitter posts (see below) hashtags can also be used in Facebook.

- **Twitter** (www.twitter.com)**:** Perhaps the most immediate social media outlet, Twitter

Find a Social Media Coordinator and "Race Ambassadors"

Maintaining an active presence on multiple social media platforms is time intensive, and for many race directors, especially those over the age of 40, it may be mystifying. Consider finding someone, most likely under the age of 30, who loves and is active on social media, and ask that person to be the social media coordinator. This person needs to be very keyed in about what needs to be communicated and when so that he or she can monitor and post on all the event's social media platforms and answer questions from followers. Some races coordinate with multiple individuals, sometimes called "Race Ambassadors," who blog, monitor Facebook, and otherwise promote the event on social media. It is important to keep these individuals well informed as well. Any information being posted on the website or sent to participants in an email blast should also be forwarded to the social media coordinator. As exciting as social media can be as a promotional avenue, it also carries the responsibility of more avenues to promote. Finally, most of the online registration companies have expanded their services to include social media support as part of their platforms.

members can send "tweets" or messages less than 140 characters, to all of their followers. Photos can be included on Twitter as well. Twitter works like a Facebook Fan page, in that followers do not have to be accepted. Events can create hastags (#) in their tweets, which will aggregate all the tweets containing that hashtag. For example, if the ABC 10K inserts the hashtag "#ABC10K" in all of its tweets and followers include that hashtag in their tweets, all those tweets will appear when a Twitter search is done for #ABC10K.

- **LinkedIn** (www.linkedin.com): LinkedIn is a professional network for developing business contacts. It is probably not very relevant for race promoting, but could be important for race directors looking for potential sponsor contacts or seeking to hire personnel. It is definitely beneficial for individuals seeking employment in the running industry.

- **Instagram** (www.instagram.com): Instagram is a photo sharing site in which followers do not have to be approved to view photos. It is popular among users who may want to post a large number of photos but do not wish to have their followers notified every time a new photo is posted, as on Facebook. Videos up to one-minute in length can be posted on Instgram as well. However, Facebook is likely a more effective photo outlet for events.

- **SnapChat** (www.snapchat.com): SnapChat is a photo-sharing site for individuals to share photos with people who have been accepted as friends. Photos are tightly shared and are deleted seconds after being viewed. It is not likely an applicable avenue for event promotion.

- **Pinterest** (www.pinterest.com): Pinterest is generally organized by topics – the name comes from the notion of pinning something on a bulletin board to refer to it later. Your webmaster can include a Pinterest link on the event website that will allow Pinterest users to pin the site to their "boards," which are organized by topic (i,e "running" or "10K races," etc.). Followers of the individuals who pinned your event's site will see it. Pinterest users do not have to be approved to view content on another user's page. Pinterest may have some potential use for event organizers, but time is probably better spent keeping Facebook and Twitter accounts more active.

- **Google+** (www.plus.google.com): Google's late entry into the social media arena has remained a distant

SIDEBAR

Should I Hire a PR Firm?

The amount of information provided in this chapter should give you an idea of the vast number of options available for promotion. If the event has a large enough budget and the PR task seems daunting or never-ending, consider hiring a PR firm to handle all or part of the event promotions. The plus side is that, presumably, these firms are pros at getting media attention for events; the biggest downside is that they can be expensive. Make sure the firm—or individual—has experience carrying out PR and media campaigns in the sports arena, and ideally understands the running industry. Get bids from a number of firms and ask for details about what is and what is not included in the fee.

If you hire a firm, make sure the firm has a clear understanding of exactly what you are trying to accomplish and a clear outline of the goals. Know what you are getting for your money. Are you being charged an hourly rate, a flat fee, or fees plus expenses? If you are charged an hourly rate, you will probably want to put a ceiling or cap on the amount you are willing to spend. If it's fees plus expenses, find out exactly what those expenses are and how much they are likely to cost. While it's often tempting to just hire the agency and pay the bill, you may end up paying a lot more than you need to for a project.

Finally, if you don't like the way things are being done and want to make changes, try to do them early in the process, as invariably the later you make a change, the more it ends up costing.

second to Facebook as it tries to carve out space in the crowded social media world. Nevertheless, with Google ubiquitous with its search engines, Gmail accounts and mapping programs, do not underestimate the potential synergies pulling all of these together under Google+ at some point in the future. Content posted on Google+ would be similar to what is posted on Facebook.

- **YouTube** (www.youtube.com) **and online videos:** YouTube, in conjunction with a digital video recorder, provides race directors–and anyone else–the opportunity to record and upload videos and reach a mass internet audience quickly. Go to www.youtube.com, search on the name of your race, and there is a good chance you will find videos posted by race participants already! Posted videos are then rated by viewers (with the results posted alongside the videos) and a counter keeps track of the number of people who have viewed the video. Videos created for YouTube can be uploaded either as a link to YouTube or directly onto Facebook.

- **Blogs:** These are usually narratives that can be written by anyone and then posted on a website or a blogging platform. A small but growing number of race directors will blog on their event websites about event-related subjects. Most blogs allow comments from readers, making the blog an interactive experience.

- **Online marketplaces/social buying sites:** The two most popular social buying sites, as of this writing, are Groupon and Living Social, although there are a growing number of others. These platforms help buyers find the best deals on whatever it is they are interested in purchasing. Millions of people subscribe to these services, so social buying sites can certainly help with marketing/promotion and brand awareness. The sites often work by offering "deals" that are only "on" if a certain number of people sign up for an offer before it expires. For example, a race could provide

40% off registration fees, but only if 300 people sign up for the deal. If the deal doesn't meet its 'tipping point'—meaning that less than the required number of people sign up— then the deal is off. This incentivizes potential registrants who want the deal to convince their friends to sign up for the deal as well. These sites are effectively a method of mass-marketing and they can often prove advantageous for generating excitement about events and increasing the number of registrants. However, although these services generally do not have up-front fees, the drawback is that they often require deep discounting of the registration fee and most, if not all, of these platforms also collect a percentage of each sale—sometimes up to 50%. Thus, it is important to use these services judiciously.

- **Forum:** A forum is an open-ended discussion group that takes place on a website. Internet service providers can generally provide (for a fee) special software designed to set up a forum. A number of specialized forums for race participants have been established by companies such as Cool Running (www.coolrunning.com) and LetsRun.com. Individuals can start a discussion thread and others can chime in by making posts on the site. Forum moderators can delete posts that they find objectionable or ban individuals from posting.

From a marketing point of view, the downside of the internet is that *anyone* can post a message, or a video, or write a blog–and say or show almost anything. Hypothetically, a disgruntled runner who didn't like the finisher's medal could vent to a lot of people in short order, just as easily as a race director could post a video showing the highlights of an event. It's still a bit like the Wild West in cyberspace, but the number of people tapping into these social media platforms and other networks makes this method of marketing too massive to ignore.

Email

Just as the website is the backbone of event information, blast emails are arguably the best way to keep registrants updated as race day approaches. In addition to the immediacy of communication, email is clearly the best option, budget-wise. A simple illustration says it all: the cost to send out 10,000 first class flyers via 'snail mail' at $0.49 each is $4,900. The charge to send out 10,000 emails could be $10.00 or less (the cost of one month's fee at an ISP). While this is somewhat simplified, the point is clear. Email promotion costs a small fraction of mail promotion, making it simply irresistible for businesses of all kinds to use in marketing. Email is also much more environmentally friendly than paper mailings. There is virtually no reason to use 'snail mail' to promote an event these days.

- Prepare an email promotional timeline starting with announcing the event, moving into selling the event, and ending up with a "time is running out" final pitch.

- The subject line of each email is critical, as it will determine whether or not the recipient will open or delete the message. Try to make it engaging. In the body of the email, keep the message relatively short. Consider adding photos.

- Emails can be created in .html format, giving them the visual look of a website with graphics and color. The days of text-only emails are long gone.

- Personalize and target the emails as much as possible. Many email programs can insert the name of the recipient directly into the text. If you have lists of email addresses from different sources (last year's entrants, first-time runners, local running club members, etc.), consider personalizing the message for each specific group.

- As with the race registration forms, make the emails mobile friendly and pre-test all links contained in the email.

Below are a few more tips for communicating with runners via email.

Email Etiquette

With the explosive proliferation of spam, or junk, email, the issue of what is an "acceptable" email and what is intrusive is a tough question. Attitudes vary from staunch privacy advocates who don't want any commercial email, to more laid back approaches.

Many businesses and individuals have settled on a standard that, if individuals have been identified as a member of a certain interest group, they are fair game, since they are likely to be tolerant of receiving email in the area of interest. Thus, if you are a runner, emails about running are OK. Emails from other races, running clubs, and running retailers are acceptable under this system.

A more narrow standard is to assume that if people have an opportunity to "opt-out" (decline to receive emails from outside the event for which they have registered) and do not do so, they are open to receiving outside emails about running. In theory, this gives consumers control over what type of messages they wish to receive. The most common strategy is for sites to assume that people *want* emails as the default position and allow them a chance to click a checkbox to opt out of future emails.

A more proactive method is for businesses or events to collect email addresses by offering an email training newsletter or the like, which requires people to register their email addresses in order to receive it.

The website and printed materials for an event should state the "Privacy Policy" and events should also have an "Unsubscribe Policy." The Privacy Policy outlines how email addresses collected from participants will be used. A restrictive policy would state that the email addresses will not be used in any manner other than communication about the race; a less restrictive one would be that the addresses are only used to send information about other running events, etc.; a still less restrictive one would permit use by running-related products or use by the event sponsors only. The difficulty, of course, is that once the list is passed along, you also pass along control of who uses it. As a result, it is strongly recommended that, if a sponsor or other type of partner wants to send a blast email to your event's email list, have the partner create the email, then you send it out *yourself*, rather than handing the list over to the sponsor or some other entity. This allows you to maintain control of the list.

The event's "Unsubscribe Policy" should allow customers to remove their email address from the email list, so that they receive no emails at all. Remind them that this would mean they would not receive even the most important information about the race.

Managing Email

For a fee, commercial email marketing services such as Constant Contact, MailChimp, and many others will allow individuals or businesses to upload their email address lists, send mass emails and easily manage the lists—a tedious job if done manually. These services can often streamline the emailing effort by eliminating duplicate addresses, managing bounced emails and opt-outs, and allowing recipients to customize their email preferences. Despite the ease, remember to use caution, however, and email responsibly. If these companies receive too many complaints from email recipients about spam from your organization, they may ban you from using their service.

- **Targeted emails.** Make an attempt to

SIDEBAR

Recommendations for E-mail Address Usage

1. **Maintain an up-to-date email address list.** Make sure runners who wish to opt out are actually removed, that bad addresses are removed or changed, and that duplicate emails are not sent to the same recipient. Consider using a commercial email management service for these functions.

2. **Keep the number of emails to a minimum.** If you send out too many emails, the recipients will begin to ignore them. Try to send out only one or, at most, two well-timed messages per month leading up to the race.

3. **Keep sponsors happy.** Consider including a short message from the sponsor in one of *your* race emails, rather than simply giving the sponsor the list. This seems acceptable to most runners and actually works to the sponsor's advantage, while allowing you to maintain control of the registrant contact information.

4. **Maintain control of the message.** Even if you decide to allow use of the registrant list for a separate mailing (i.e. from a sponsor), be mindful of the kind of company that will be using it. Is the message likely to be appreciated by most runners? Retain the right to approve any copy, and do the actual emailing yourself.

5. **Allow runners to opt out.** Provide a check box at the time of registration that runners can mark to avoid receiving mailings, and include an "unsubscribe" option in the emails you send out. Remind people, however, that they will miss important race information if they choose to opt out of receiving all emails.

6. **Inform runners of the privacy policy.** This information can be included on the event website. Who, if anyone, might have access to the runners' addresses or other information, and in what circumstances?

Remember—as important as generating revenue from sponsors and other businesses may be, a solid long-term relationship with the running community is absolutely crucial to a race's success.

---

personalize emails instead of using a one-pitch-fits-all strategy. Take any information you have about event participants and build a message around that information. For example, individuals who took part two years ago but not last year should receive an email inviting them back; people who have run three years in a row might receive a special offer on the fourth race. When collecting registrant information, consider asking a few questions designed to find out more about individual customers and use what you find to customize marketing emails.

- *Sources of email addresses.* The best email address list for an event is going to be the list of past registrants in that event going back 2–3 years. If you wish to expand the email list beyond your own race registrants, consider contacting another local race that is similar to yours in character, a local running club, or a timing company, to see if they will either provide you with their email list or send a message out to their list on your behalf (keeping the list under their control but still enabling you to use it). Organizations often charge a fee for access to their participants, but if their list contains your target demographic, the fee might be worthwhile.

One final note about email— it is a two-way street. Just as it is easy for you to send out a message to thousands of runners with just a couple of clicks of a mouse, it is easy for irate runners to let you know how they feel about anything that you are doing, including sending them possibly unwanted email.

Direct Mail

Even more than a decade after the widespread launch of online registration, there are still some races that use direct mail (frequently in combination with email) to get registration forms or other promotional materials such as informational postcards/flyers out to runners the "old fashioned" way. Many events now offer online registration only, as this saves money and is more environmentally friendly. Most runners have come to expect event registration to be online only.

The few runners not registering online (and even some who will) will be looking for a print version of the registration form. The easiest, cheapest, and most environmentally friendly way to do this is to include a downloadable/printable version of the registration form on the event website in .pdf format. The Adobe company created free .pdf software (called Adobe Reader) that allows people to open .pdf files. However it requires *creators* of .pdf files to purchase software (called Adobe Acrobat) to create them.

If, for some reason, you still wish to send the registration form by direct mail as well as providing it online, make sure that the mailing list used is very targeted. The same applies for any other types of promotional materials mailed from the event. Don't just purchase a random list of fitness enthusiasts; make sure the mailing is going to runners who often participate in events of your specific race distance. The list with the highest rate of return will be that containing previous race registrants, going back 2-3 years. If yours is a first-time event and you have the funds, consider purchasing or renting targeted mailing lists from local race-timing companies or a local running club. In addition to the registration form, you may want to include a personalized letter or postcard with the mailing, especially in the mailing to previous participants. Such communication can help convince a fence-sitter to run the race again. The timing of the direct mailing depends on the distance of the event—most marathoners select their marathons months in advance, so if the event is a marathon, mail the registration form/promotional materials 6-9 months before race day. For races of 10K and under, 6-8 weeks lead time should be fine.

The United States Postal Service (USPS) has strict regulations for different classes of direct mail, the requirements for each class, the proper indicia and the preparation of the mailings. To avoid the need to decipher the arcane fine print of the USPS procedures, consider using a commercial direct mail house for distribution.

Mainstream Media Coverage

The bad news for running events is that, despite years of impressive growth in numbers and a high demographic clientele, coverage of running events by the mainstream media has declined dramatically in the last few decades, especially in beleaguered print newspapers and on major cable and network TV outlets. Space on the sports pages is dominated by the NFL, NBA, NHL, MLB and NASCAR, all of which bring in ad revenue and employ high-powered public relations firms to ensure their primacy. The good news is the mainstream media has splintered over the last two decades with the proliferation of cable networks, streaming video sites and do-it-yourself options like YouTube. The bottom line is if the mainstream media turns a deaf ear to your event, there are plenty of other ways to pass them by and focus on media outlets targeted more narrowly on runners. These options are covered in the "Running Media Coverage" section below.

If you are still undaunted and decide to pursue promotion of an event through the mainstream media, here are some points to consider. Running events will fare better in online versions of print newspapers as well as online-only outlets where space is cheaper than in print publications. You will be more likely to get either print or online coverage in a small, local newspaper than a larger, more regional newspaper. Identify the small, local outlets in the area and determine which section would be appropriate for an article about the race. Do not assume that the event could only get coverage in the sports section. The article can be written in such a way as to appeal to readers of lifestyle section, for example. Keep in mind that your top runners are not the only people with stories — there may be human interest stories anywhere in the pack. Social media may be a productive place to find people with stories. Statistics are frequently inviting. Reporters like to have quotes from original sources, so round some up from the race director, elite athletes or whomever you are highlighting in the release. If a reporter contacts you, follow up quickly. A speedy reply (an email is fine) will be appreciated and may mean that the story makes the next deadline.

- Get to know the reporters who might cover the event either in print or online. Learn what their "beats" (what areas they write about) and personal interests are. Tailor your pitches accordingly. Do not pressure them for coverage; simply supply them with information that should make them *want* to cover the event. Begin to build an electronic "media list" to send out electronic press releases, etc. Encourage the media to join the event's social media sites.

- Consider developing an electronic 'media guide,' with race stats, history, possible storylines, etc. This can be posted online in .pdf format.

- Identify the relevant editors for the media outlets of interest and send them an email with the media kit attached.

- If you wish to promote via television, you will have the most luck with small, local cable channels. The steps are similar to those outlined above for online and print coverage. If you are lucky enough to land a TV spot, makes sure that the presentation will generate excitement. Think of an angle that will be of interest to local viewers—famous local figures participating, money for a popular local charity, etc.

- If you will have members of the mainstream media at the event on race day, make sure to have a specific point-of-contact for them. Ask them to describe the angle they wish to convey and help them by providing any relevant information and/or photographs. Offer suggestions about the best places to cover the race. Make sure to have a spokesperson prepared in advance for race-day comments. Assist the media in connecting with any individuals they hope to interview.

Running Media Coverage

The internet has changed much about the media coverage of events, both prior to and during the events.

Pre-race print and online coverage: The print editions of running publications tend to be more feature-focused, while race calendars and results, if covered at all, are primarily found online. However, a few regional print running publications still devote space to pre- and post-race information. There are three types of coverage possible when it comes to running media—an advance calendar listing, a feature story on the event, or coverage as part of the publication's race results section.

Calendar listings: Information for most of the online and print (if still offered) calendars is compiled electronically. This means the user must go to a website, click a link, and complete a form with the details about the event to be listed. Receiving the information in electronic format allows for easy manipulation by the publication or website.

Getting listed in a publication's calendar is easy to do, although many of the sites require you to register with the site and receive other marketing materials in exchange for the free listings. Here is an overview of the calendar policies of a number of publications (at the time of the publication of this manual):

- **Runner's World** includes races in a section called "Race Finder" in the back of the printed magazine, for a fee. The online edition contains a searchable database of basic race information and accepts listings for free at http://www.runnersworld.com/race-finder. Race directors will need to register with the magazine at www.racedirectorresource.com in order to submit a listing.

- **The Running Network**, a consortium of many of the regional running publications, publishes a national online calendar at http://calendar.runningnetwork.com/

- **MarathonGuide.com** (www.marathonguide.com) has established itself as the leading website focusing exclusively on marathons. If your event is a marathon, getting listed here is a must. Other sites can easily be located by a Google search.

- **Regional publications** may list race calendars on their websites. Be sure to send event information in to all online calendars that are likely to be visited by runners possibly interested in your race.

- **Online Registration and Transponder Timing Sites,** such

TIP

Press Packet for an Event with Elite Athletes

Whether or not you have an actual pre-race press conference, it is important to give the media all the information that they need, but don't overwhelm them with data. Many races now provide information on elite runners online, which allows for a greater amount of information to be presented, including the runner's history, detailed facts and figures, etc. However, if the event has an elite field, it is still a good idea to have a basic press packet available on race day, with info about the elite athletes. This might include:

- A numeric list (bib numbers) of the elite athletes
- Bios of top men and women
- A course map (listing miles, street names, and landmarks) with an elevation map inset
- Course records
- Last year's top 25 men and women (with prize money amounts)
- The current year's prize structure
- Event timetable
- Top age group competitors
- A "Highlights" sheet with number of starters, finishers, and men's and women's winners, along with any "human interest" registrants

This information can be provided on a thumb drive (with the race or a sponsor's name printed on it).

as Active.com and RunSignUp.com, list events in an attempt to become one-stop portals for both race directors and runners. Databar Events (www.databarevents.com) will get an event posted on over 100 calendars for a modest fee.

Editorial coverage: If you try to interest a running media outlet in doing a story on your event, try to utilize a more personal approach— the editorial staff is more likely to prefer to hear from you, at least initially, by email instead of taking time for a phone conversation. When you contact them, try to sell them on an unusual or exciting aspect of the race. How is it different from the many other races around? Do not always focus on the elite competition; publications these days are frequently hungry for stories about "average runners."

Race-day running media coverage: Certainly all of the strategies outlined in the "Mainstream Media Coverage" section above should be employed to attract running media to the event. However, race-day coverage in the running media is most likely to be done by a small number of specialized companies such as **Salmini Sportfilm** (www.sportfilm.com), **RunnerSpace** (www.runnerspace.com) or **Flotrack** (www.flotrack.org), which contract with events and produce coverage for a fee. Salmini Sportfilm contracts with various regional cable networks to carry its running magazine show, which airs videos the company has been hired to produce. These same videos can be posted on YouTube, Facebook, or on the event's website. RunnerSpace and Flotrack produce live streaming videos that can be viewed in real time on the internet as well as through other internet outlets after the race.

Post-race running media coverage: With the speed at which media moves today, results are practically old news within hours of the event. However, it is still worth making sure the running media outlets receive the electronic post-race release. If the event offers prize money, be sure to send results to *Race Results Weekly* (www.raceresultsweekly.com). The results will probably be data-mined by some of the results aggregator sites such as Athlinks.com.

Other Outlets

There are a number of other promotional avenues that can pursued—many of them at little or no cost. More than likely, you will be providing material for their websites. You can also ask if they are interested in any printed postcards or flyers. As you consider approaching each of the outlets listed below, keep in mind that you may need to tailor the strategy and message for each particular outlet:

- ***Stores, YMCAs, fitness centers.*** Compile a list of sporting goods stores, YMCAs, gyms and fitness centers in the target area. Check to see if they have websites (virtually all of them will) where they list area running events. Specialty running stores may be one of the last bastions to take printed registration forms or other kinds of printed promotional materials like postcards or flyers. For those stores,

---

TIP

Let Everyone Know When the Event Will Be Broadcast

If the race, or a story about the event, will be broadcast on TV or on the internet (either as a live stream during the event or afterwards), make sure that the spectators and participants know about it. On race day, have the announcer hype the broadcast. One race even mounted a banner on the race's lead vehicle announcing the channel and time of the broadcast—this could be done with the URL of the webcast as well. Consider sending out a blast email about the TV spot/webcast, and be sure to announce it on the event's website and all social media platforms. Simple steps like these enhance viewership. If you are posting a link to a webcast, track the volume of traffic to the link via Google Analytics or similar software.

SIDEBAR

Press Conferences

For 98% of the races in this country, scheduling of either a pre- or post-race press conference is likely to be like the sound of the tree falling in the forest with no one around. At the other extreme, the largest events have cavernous "media centers" with banks of screens tracking elite athletes, rows of media stations and scores of media representatives scurrying around to distribute lists of finishers at intermediate points in the race or to simply answer questions or provide support.

You will need to decide when the event merits an initiative to host a press conference; if no one shows, change your decision.

Here are some brief pointers for hosting a press conference

- **Facility:** Make sure the facility it easy to find, able to accommodate the number of attendees, and contains both adequate electrical and WiFi capabilities for the attendees. Have a podium for

the emcee and microphones in the room for media members to ask questions. Make sure the sound system is adequate.

- **Timing:** Pre-race conferences should be held two days prior to the event so the media will be able to prepare "advance" stories that will be out the day before race day. Post-race conferences should take place as soon after the race as possible, either at the race site if there is an adequate facility or very close by.

- **Spokesperson:** Have a knowledgeable media spokesperson convene the session. This person should be candid about any delays in the appearance of athletes or other key individuals at the conference. If he or she does not know

The Press Room at the Boston Marathon   FayFoto/Boston

Press Conferences (cont'd)

the answer to a specific question, be frank about not being able to answer, but promise to assist the media member in getting an answer.

- **Format:** The moderator may ask a few questions to get the athletes talking but then open to questions from the media. Some large events with a large number of elite athletes will assign them to tables after the formal part of the conference, for individual questioning by the media. If language is

Post-race inteviews at the TCS New York City Marathon

Phil Stewart

a barrier, try to line up an interpreter. The formal part of the conference should not run more than 15-20 minutes.

- **Content:** At the pre-race conference, have plenty of copies of the numeric list of top competitors and their bio information; post-race, get the results out as soon as possible but after taking the time to review them

The bib presentation provides a great "photo op" at pre-race press conferences.

SCC Evemts

internally for obvious errors. All results should be identified as "unofficial" at this point. See **"Tip — Press Packet for an Event with Elite Athletes"** for additional suggestions. If a pre-race media guide was prepared, consider having it available on thumb drives for the media. Event sponsors can be sprinkled into any printed materials made available to the media, so as not to waste the media's time with sponsor credits in the actual press conference. With most on tight deadlines, members of the media want the facts with little fluff.

don't just go in and drop the materials off—make the effort to get involved with the store manager and "sell" the event. Running store personnel can be great allies in helping to get the word out about a race. Many runners rely on the recommendation of their favorite store when it comes to choosing which races to run. Visitors to town may check with the local running store if they're looking for a race. Make sure that any stores or fitness centers you are working with are provided with enough promotional materials so that they will not run out. Contact them on a regular basis to see if they need more forms/postcards.

- **Running clubs.** Once again, a combination web/print strategy should be pursued. Mail a cover letter and a supply of 10-20 promotional postcards/flyers or printed registration forms to any running clubs in the target area. Or, if you are not using any printed materials, send an email to the appropriate club contact person – likely either the club president, administrator or webmaster – telling them about the event. You may even want to let the clubs know that you are available to speak about the race at a club meeting. The personal touch can be effective, especially when you are a new face in the running community. Also, if the local running club puts out a newsletter, ask if they will include race information in the newsletter or other material distributed to club members. If the club has a website, ask if they will post information about the race and be sure to include a link to the race website or registration.

- **Other races and expos.** These are another outlet for printed promotional materials/registration forms, if you have them. Try to find volunteers to distribute information about your race at other races, especially if those events are similar in nature to yours. If the event is a fall marathon, for example, distributing materials at spring marathons or fall events in the half-marathon range leading up to your marathon can help reach the appropriate

target audience. Some race expos have "flyer tables," where race promotional materials/registration forms can be placed for free, or volunteers can be sent to other races to hand out promotional materials to participants. You can even try putting postcards or registration forms on the windshields of cars parked at other races, though some people think this is poor etiquette.

Think about joining forces with another race by asking that race to include promotional materials for your event in their race packets, and then reciprocating. These can be actual printed materials, or for races that use virtual race bags, you may be able to swap or purchase an advertising spot within the virtual bag. You can go a step further and offer a discount to individuals who find the event in this way, or cooperate with the other race to offer a discounted registration to runners who enter *both* events. To reach faster local runners, link one or more other races as part of a series and offer prizes to runners who place well in all events in the series. The Lilac Bloomsday 12K in Spokane, WA sets up a relationship with other races, which serve as qualifiers. The winning athletes receive "special seeding" near the front of the massive Bloomsday field of 45,000. This helps support the smaller events and gives publicity to Bloomsday as well. Of course, the Boston Marathon is the grand-daddy of events that have qualification standards. Every marathon in America wants to promote itself as a "Boston Qualifier, or "BQ" in runner parlance.

- **General recreational sports and fitness media outlets:** These outlets are usually free to the public and will often publish both feature articles on various events and calendars listing a variety of sporting events. Visit sports-oriented retailers and health clubs to find these publications, then contact the editors to see what they can do for you, both in print and online.

- ***Community bulletin boards:*** These free boards are a great place to post race flyers or postcards. Local libraries and government centers are good places to start, but always be sure to ask about posting regulations on the various boards before you start sticking race flyers all over town. Some may require that you be a nonprofit organization.

- ***Local entertainment media outlets:*** Don't ignore these entertainment guides just because you consider a running event to be more sports-oriented. People deciding what to do on the weekends often look at these tabloids or their websites for ideas.

- ***Public service announcements:*** Commercial radio stations are required by law to make public service announcements as part of their programming. Give the basic information about the race to the programmers at as many popular local stations as possible, and find out when and how often the announcement will be made.

- ***Regional and community newspapers:*** Local print newspapers and their websites are often more interested in community news than are the larger dailies. Be sure to emphasize the community nature of the event when talking with them. Small races should send names of local finishers to these outlets, with a good-quality photograph. Although these papers may not send a reporter to the event, they will often print a photo if the local connection can be emphasized.

- ***Area hotels.*** If the event will be held in a large metropolitan area, contact hotels—either the concierge or health club—to see if they would be interested in a few postcards/flyers or registration forms, especially during the week just prior to the race.

- ***Sponsors.*** If the event has sponsors that are community-oriented (grocery stores, banks, etc.), ask them if they would be willing to help with promotion. Provide them with printed promotional materials, and ask if they will put

information about the race on their websites. Even if you don't get a whole lot of participants out of this, you will make the sponsors feel more involved with the event. You can also encourage sponsors to distribute promotional materials to their friends, families, and associates.

- ***General distribution.*** Think of the promotional postcard/flyer or registration form as a "calling card." Include one with most race correspondence and have plenty to distribute anywhere you go—other races, expos, stores, etc. Be sure to have plenty on hand for those who may contact you to request them.

- ***Clinic or autograph session.*** A pre-race training clinic or autograph session with a celebrity (who may or may not be a runner) may generate additional interest and publicity for the event and may also help attract more registrants. For more about using elite athletes or celebrities at races to generate media interest, see ***Chapter 12: Special Entrant Categories.***

Race-Specific Training Programs

If you have a few volunteers who are willing to put in plenty of time, or a local running retailer or health club that may be willing to partner with the event and benefit from the publicity, you may want to consider setting up a training program with the race as the end point. Many clubs and running retailers charge for these programs, so the programs can turn into a profit center for the race. Make sure these programs are tailored to runners of all levels of experience. Beginning runners have swollen the ranks of road races everywhere, and attracting some of these beginners to the event is definitely worthwhile. Even the more experienced runners often enjoy training programs for the structure and camaraderie they provide.

Instituting a training program is not for every race—before commencing, take a deep breath and ask yourself candidly, "Is this race significant enough in the community so that runners will focus two to three months of training geared toward the event?" If this answer is "yes," see *Chapter 20: Special Types of Races and Participatory Events* for details on starting a group training program.

Web-Based Training Programs

Although it is likely that nothing can replace an actual, physically present coach, web-based training programs are a lot less labor-intensive, from a management perspective. A basic program requires setting up a schedule and posting it on the event's website or sending out daily or weekly emails outlining the training program. Some online registration companies and other commercial companies offer–and charge for–these services, potentially adding a nice revenue stream (for a discussion of online registration companies, see *Chapter 7: Entrant Registration, Confirmation and Communications.*) At some major races, between 10-40% of participants have used web-based training programs of some sort (for details about organizing training programs see *Chapter 20: Special Types of Races and Participatory Events.*

Some races have runner bulletin boards as a part of the race website or use their Facebook pages for training participants to exchange comments about their training. A few races have coaches who monitor the boards and reply to messages. As the level of user support goes up, so does the likelihood that the event can—and will—charge for the service.

Customized training programs—of all types—build solid relationships between events and their customers.

Paid Advertising

If you can afford it, consider purchasing some paid adverting. Options include web-based advertising, print advertising (or a combination of the two), and email blasts by companies and other races. Running media companies that still publish print publications provide web and email options as well. A good place to start is to review running-related websites and print publications to see what other events are doing and to examine the nature of the ads.

Web advertising: The trend is strongly shifting towards web advertising, because web-based ads can be targeted narrowly to prospective entrants and they can be tracked. Ads can be purchased through the major social media sites and search engines, or through targeted running media company sites.

All of the *search engines* such as Google (Google Ad Words), Yahoo (Yahoo Gemini) and Bing (Bing Ads) take ads. (This is how they raise income for the sites, which are free for users.) When these ads are written to contain targeted key words, they will pop up first in the list of search results that is returned when a user searches on one of those key words. The *social media platforms*, such as Facebook, Twitter, Instagram, and Google+, have powerful advertising options as well. These ads can be targeted to a very specific demographic. For example, race ads can be tagged to appear before people of a given age range in a given area who are interested in running (or any criteria set by the advertiser). Facebook will even assign a "Relevance Score" to your ad, based on how effective they feel the ad will be. Facebook will also allow you to "boost the reach" of any post to a wider audience—for a fee. The effectiveness of these ads is tracked using analytical software, allowing the success of each advertising campaign to be assessed. With most social media sites, you can set whatever amount—say $300 or $3,000—you wish to spend on advertising, and the company will run the number of impressions that corresponds exactly to that budget.

Online running outlets also should be considered as an important part of a paid advertising program. After all, these are the websites (and the magazines) that runners seek out. It may be more beneficial to have a running ad appear on a running-related webpage at a time when a runner is focusing on entering a race, instead of having it appear in the margin of a webpage when a runner is thinking about buying a coffee pot.

In addition to running-media companies offering both print and web ads (more on print ads below), there are a host of running websites without a corresponding print edition that take race ads. (There is no shortage of opportunities to spend the advertising budget, and this section does not include all of them.) The RRCA publishes nationally circulated online *Footnotes* for all its members; MarathonGuide.com targets marathoners specifically; Road Race Management's *Online Guide to Prize Money Races and Elite Athletes* provides a chance to reach elite athletes with details about prize money at events. Analyze who you are trying to reach and select options accordingly.

Print advertising: Although print advertising is more expensive and becoming less effective as the years go by, placing a print ad in a national, regional, and/or local running publication can still be a valid option for events that can afford it. A few races still include registration forms in race ads in printed running publications, but most go for a dramatic "image ad" about the event with the event website included but no registration form.

The budget and the target audience will determine whether print advertising should be national or regional, as well as determine the size of the ad. *Runner's World* and *Competitor Magazine* are the two remaining national running magazines with a print edition. *Runner's World* is available by subscription and on newsstands; *Competitor Magazine* is distributed free at events and at specialty running stores. In an effort to keep the cost down for races, *Runner's World* takes small race-display and classified ads in two sections, called "Race Spotlight" and "Race Finder," in the back of the magazine. *Competitor Magazine* takes print race ads as well. In addition, there are several print regional running publications. There are two groups, The Running Network (http://runningnetwork.com/) and the Endurance Sports Media Group (http://endurancesportsmedia.com/),

that represent multiple regional running magazines across the country. If you are advertising in a single regional publication, you may do better to contact that specific publication directly. However, if you want to spread the word outside your region, a group buy through one of these organizations may be the way to go.

Blast emails by other groups: As mentioned in the email section above, your own email lists of past participants will be the list with the single highest rate of return. However, running media organizations, running retailers, and other events do regular blast emails to their lists and sell advertising in these blasts. These ads will generally consist of a small graphic contained in the e-newsletter, highlighting a race and linked to its website or online registration page.

Purchasing Expo Space/ Advertising Through Other Races

If you want more interaction with potential race participants than you get by placing flyers on an expo "flyer table," including the opportunity to sign them up directly, consider a buying a booth at the expo of another local event (if the budget allows) – one that seems likely to attract the type of runners who might be interested in your event, too. Expo booth prices vary widely from a few hundred to several thousand dollars, generally based on the size of the race. (**See Chapter 15: Getting Ready to Race – Packet Pick-up, Late Registration, Expo and Hotel** for details about expo booth prices.)

Generally cheaper than renting an expo booth, but also effective, is paying for promotional postcards/flyers or printed registration forms to be inserted in the other races' runner race bags. Even small races may provide runners with a race bag to hold their bib numbers and t-shirts. Race directors like to have the bag filled—it gives a good impression—so contact local races and find out what they will charge to include promotional materials. If you're looking to draw runners from outside the local area, contact race directors who have events within 100-200 miles of the event location. If the race with which you wish to advertise uses a virtual race bag, ask them if you can purchase space within that. One significant advantage of using a virtual race bag ad is that it allows you to assess the effectiveness of the ad—you can receive a report on the number of 'click-throughs' to determine how many people actually looked at the ad. Skeptics of race bag advertising feel that if there are promotional materials from too many races in the bag, they may get ignored or tossed collectively.

A Word on Post-Race Promotions

Just because the race is over doesn't mean that you should stop trying to promote the event. The natural post-race let down experienced by many race officials makes post-race promotion a frequently overlooked task. The harsh reality is that promotional work for the next year's edition of the race begins on race day, with the posting of results. You will be repeating many of the tasks outlined above, only this time with results instead of advance information. Make sure to prepare a summary sheet with the top overall finishers and the top finishers in each age group. This, along with a short narrative with quotes from the front runners that can be used in stories, should be the heart of a post-race package.

Phil Stewart

7 Entrant Registration, Confirmation and Communications

THE BASICS

- **Most registration is now done online.** Although some very small races still use "hard copy" registrations, the vast majority of events employ online registration, usually through one of the numerous commercial online registration providers. Make sure the online form is mobile friendly, since more people go online via a mobile device than via a computer. Races with online registration will generally include a printable version of the registration form on the race website.

- **Registration forms are a two-way information exchange.** Obviously, participants need to provide important information about themselves, including age, sex, contact information, and t-shirt size. But it's also a good idea to provide some basic event information on the form itself, and then provide all the race details on the event website.

- **Preparing the registration form.** For online registration, either you or a representative at the chosen online registration company will create an electronic registration form based on a discussion about the specifics of the event. Generally, registration companies will charge a fee for each registration, so there is no set-up charge for the form itself. Be sure to "road test" or proof the online registration form to ensure that it works properly (i.e., when the user hits "submit," you actually receive the data that he/she has supplied) and to see if the form contains all of the information that needs to be collected. Familiarize yourself with the administrative tools provided by the company in order to review, make changes to, and download the online registration data. The administrative tools are generally on a "private" site at a different link available to administrators only through a user ID and password. If you choose to have an actual printed form, consider having a graphic designer or someone familiar with desktop publishing software design it. Get quotes from several printing companies if you wish to print the form, so you can get the size and style (two-fold, three-fold, etc.) that work best at the least cost. The printable version of the form should be available for download from the event website as a .pdf file.

- **Confirmation.** Online registrants will receive immediate confirmation that they are registered for the race, usually by both an on-screen receipt and by email. The email should contain key information about packet pick-up, along with other important instructions and information about the event (or should refer runners to the event website for this information). Confirmation for mail-in registrants should either be emailed to them or should be available on the event website. Any type of confirmation communication should include the runner's bib number, name, address, age, sex and t-shirt size.

- **Communication.** Communication through email, social media and various apps makes staying in touch with race registrants easier than ever. It is important to strike a balance in the amount of communication with runners. Tell them what needs to be communicated, but don't overload runners' inboxes, as that could turn them off to the event.

THE DETAILS

Registration Forms

Before you even get started creating the registration form for the event, take some time to examine a few forms from other events in order to get a feel for what is included. Although most races these days prefer that the majority of registrations occur online, some race directors still feel the need to use both printed/printable and online registration forms. It may be best to think of each type of form as serving a different need—printed forms for handing out at other races or at local running stores, etc., and online forms for runners who wish to register from home without having to mail anything.

Online Registration

The registration form is one of the most important components of an event. Most events that register participants in advance use primarily online registration. This method is much simpler and environmentally-friendly than using printed registration forms. Every race that opts to use online registration should also provide a printable .pdf of the registration form on the event website, for those people who may not want or are not able to pay by credit card. Most online registration providers allow you to enter the mailed-in registrations directly into the online database, or to upload a separate database of mail-in registrants to the site.

Getting Online Registration Up and Running

The easiest way to offer online registration to participants is to hire a vendor that sells online registration services, of which there are many. A very small number of races may have a tech-savvy individual or sponsor who can set up a system specifically for the race. Based on stories from a few directors who went in-house, however, the do-it-yourself option is not for the technologically faint of heart. Make sure you have a pro in the business—who is both a computer programming expert and knows the unique nature of running events—before embarking on in-house, online registration.

There is generally no start-up fee for setting up a registration form with most online providers. These platforms usually make their money by charging a small percentage (generally 5-7%) of the registration fee per registrant, which includes the processing fee (usually 2-3%) paid for the online transaction to the credit card company or financial institution providing e-commerce services. For most online registration platforms, this amount can either be absorbed by the event (meaning that the race pays the fee, so the race nets 93-95% of the listed registration fee), or can be passed on to the runners. Nearly all race directors elect to pass the fee on to the runners as a 'service fee,' which also includes the percentage taken by credit card companies, and certainly many runners seem to think that the convenience of online registration is worth paying a few extra dollars. A few race directors do choose to absorb the cost themselves, but even those individuals generally bump up the cost of registration to make up for the amount lost to the fees.

Hiring an Online Registration Provider

Do some homework before selecting an online registration platform. Contact other race directors to find out about their experiences with various registration companies. Many of the online registration companies are moving toward becoming "all in one" companies that provide online registration services, timing services, event apps, social media services and more. The lines between registration and timing and scoring, once two distinct processes, are now blurred.

Some things to look for when considering a vendor include:

- *User experience and reliability.* What will the user experience be like? Is the site customized for different platforms (desktops, phones, iPads, tablets, etc.) How often is the site down? How 'glitchy' is the process?

- *Registrant account required*? Some companies want everyone to set up an account with the registration provider, with a unique user ID and password. While there may be good reasons to do so, such as the ability of the registrant to log back in to amend a registration, many race directors—and runners—would prefer creating an account to be optional, so that runners can register without this extra step.

- *Responsiveness/customer service.* Evaluate customer service from both the registrant side and the "back end" or administrative side. On the registrant side, do the customer service providers handle calls quickly and rapidly and implement requested updates? How are refunds and other special services provided? On the administrative side, does the company respond quickly to requests for assistance and technical support with things like generating special reports, downloading data, etc.? Are you able to speak directly with technical personnel or do you need to communicate through customer service representatives who are not the ones implementing the support?

- *Additional/optional services.* Can the company provide a fundraising platform, handle team registrations, provide special discount or free codes for use by participants? For large events, can the company handle a lottery and lottery groups? Does the company provide a merchandise sales component?

Does the company offer a social networking component? Do they offer a mini-webpage, where you can include information about the event?

- **Blast email capability.** Can the company handle blast emails to the participant database? This will eliminate the need for a separate email platform.

- **Administrative ease of use.** Is it simple to perform functions such as editing the registration form, deleting/making changes to registrations, and downloading the database? What reports are available through the administrative tools? Can the provider create customized reports based on specific criteria?

- **Method, frequency, and security of payments.** How and how frequently will you receive registration proceeds from the provider? What guarantees do you have to protect you if the company defaults or falls behind on payments?

- **Integration with the timing and scoring system.** Most commercial platforms easily integrate with timing software, but be sure to check. Many of the all-in-one companies have merged the registration and timing/scoring processes so that no downloads from the online provider to the timer are necessary.

- **Ability to customize the process.** Can you add specific questions or information about things that are unique to the specific event? Are there costs associated with customization?

- **Use and security of data.** Ask the company how they will use your data. The answer should be "not at all." Some companies may use data gathered from races for their own marketing purposes or make it available to other races. Obtain a guarantee that data will not be used in this manner. Companies may consider that they "own" data from individuals who set up accounts when registering for a race and believe that they can use this data for

their own purposes. Find out what the company's policy is in this area. Also, find out what efforts are made to ensure that all data is secure. Has the online provider ever been hacked?

Test out various online registration companies by actually registering for a few races online. Ask any prospective companies whether they can provide you with an admin comp code so that you can do this for free. This is also a good way to see what you like and don't like about the types of questions the online registration process asks. You can then see how you may want to customize this process for your own event.

Note that you do not *need* to have a race website in order to use online registration (although, as is mentioned in **Chapter 6: Marketing and Promotions**, it is probably worthwhile to have an event website). Most online registration platforms will provide an informational web page for each event, accessible through their website, at no charge. If you decide to use the online registration company as your race's main online source of information, instead of setting up the event's own website, just be aware that the pages provided by online registration companies for this purpose are often highly templated and not very customizable. Plus you may not be able to edit the pages at 2:00 a.m.!

When selecting an online registration platform, be sure to carefully read the contract that the company provides to you. The contract should tell you how often payments will be made (payments should be made at least monthly if not more frequently), how the company collects its percentage (paid by the event or by the participant), if the account is insured, liability for non-performance (i.e. what if your data is lost?), and where (what court in what state) disputes are to be resolved. It's never a bad idea to have a lawyer read over the contract. If these questions are not answered to your satisfaction, contact the company and ask again, or try a different company.

Developing the Registration Form and Website Content

Both online and print registration forms have dual purposes: to provide at least basic race information to participants and provide registrant information to race officials. The seam between the event website and the online registration form itself is becoming increasingly transparent. Whereas print registration forms or brochures traditionally contained more details about the race, this same information now appears on the event website, with the online registration form more streamlined to capture the key registrant data. In either case, here is an overview of the information runners will need to know about the race (either from the registration form or the event website) and the information race directors will need from the runners.

Information Provided *To* Runners

Below you will find a comprehensive list of things that runners need to know about an event. These days, the majority of this information is usually available on the event's website, and that's the best place for it, since that's where runners generally go first to find information. Events with their own websites will not need to include all of the information below on the registration form itself, but some of it still bears repeating on the form. If the race does *not* have a website, or if the race registration form (whether printed or online) is the primary means of providing runners with information about the event, then make sure to include *all* of the relevant items from the list on the registration form.

- *Race name*
- *Date*
- *Time*

- *Location*
- *Race website URL:* Make sure this is prominent and direct registrants here for more information about the race.
- *Sponsor logos:* The registration form is an additional opportunity to give the sponsors visibility, so be sure to include their logos. The presence of sponsor logos/links on the registration form as well as on the event website can increase the overall number of impressions the sponsor will receive. Whether online or in print, the relative size and positioning of the sponsor logos is generally proportional to the size of their contributions. Title sponsors obviously get the biggest play. See *Chapter 5: Sponsorship* for further information.

Make sure to obtain crisp, clear copies of the sponsor logos to use on the website and/or registration form. Be aware that any logo used in print must be of higher resolution [usually 600 dpi (500-600 Kb) or higher] than

TIP

Proofing the Registration Form

Careful proofing of the registration form is key, even if it is only appearing online. Errors in the registration form can result in big headaches as registrations start to come in. There are two different types of proofreading that should be employed, and each requires a different focus. The first (and the easiest) is to proof *what is already there* and make corrections to it. Check that all details are correct— particularly the pricing structure and the dates of price increases. The second (and infinitely more difficult) is to think about what *might be missing* (a sponsor logo, a section containing a key piece of information, etc.) and add it. This is where looking at registration forms from other races can be helpful. The best way to avoid both of these types of errors is to have several people, including a non-runner, run through the online form before it is 'live.' Make sure this person reads all of the event information included on the form and fills out the form as if he/she were actually registering. In doing so, the proofer may find mistakes, instructions that are hard to follow/questions that are unclear, or typographical errors.

logos used on websites (150 dpi or 100-300 Kb). Many neophyte designers make the mistake of copying a logo off a website for use in print application. The poor quality of the resulting logo reflects badly on both the sponsor and the event itself.

Note: Directors of nonprofits wishing to mail registration forms or informational post cards at nonprofit rates must be careful about the use of sponsor logos and promotions on these forms, or they may run afoul of nonprofit mailing regulations. Consult with the post office to see if a mailing will qualify for the nonprofit rate. For more on postal regulations, see *Chapter 6: Marketing and Promotions.*

- *Refund and Cancellation policies:* Nearly all races clearly state on the registration form and on the website that there are "No Refunds" for any reason, including event cancellation. This is reasonable, since many of the costs associated with the event will have already been incurred before race day. A few events that have been cancelled over the years have ended up offering a reduced rate for the following year or some other type of concession. This is generally not spelled out on the registration form, but is usually done as a goodwill gesture after the event. Some events offer cancellation insurance to runners (see *Chapter 9: Insurance and Legal for details*). A small number of races allow numbers to be transferred (*see Sidebar: Number Transfers on the next page for more on creating a number transfer program*).

- *Packet pickup location and times*

- *Pricing and procedures for standard/late/race-day registration:* Many races charge a late registration fee after a certain deadline and an additional premium for race-day registrations. These fees generally reflect the added burden for the organizers imposed by late registrations. Some races accomplish the same thing by having a lower "early bird" registration price and then a higher "standard"

registration price. Although there is quite a bit of disparity among cut-off dates for standard registration, many are set 2-4 weeks prior to race day. If there is no race-day registration, state "No race-day registration" in bold letters in a high visibility location (and plan the response to runners who show up race morning to register). For a complete discussion about setting registration fees, see *Chapter 2: Incorporation, Taxes, Budgets and Finances.*

- *Field size limit (if any)*

- *Awards:* Include all divisions and the number of places in each division that will receive awards, and types of awards given—trophies, prize money, etc. Make sure that this is unambiguous, such as "Trophies to the top 10 overall and top 5 in the following age groups, 19-and-under, 20-29, 30-39, 40-49, 50-59, 60-and-over." State the policy on "double dipping," i.e., whether or not the race allows an *individual* runner to receive *multiple* awards. For a complete discussion about "Double Dipping," see *Chapter 18: Awards, Awards Ceremonies, Entertainment and Results Posting.*

- *Time and location of awards ceremony* (if applicable)

- *Course map:* Provide both a narrative and an easily readable map of the course for maximum impact. The course is a key selling point of the event. An attractive map can be produced using many graphics or mapping programs, such as Google Earth or MapQuest. Many race directors use the map prepared by the course certifier. If you do not use the certification map, include the certification number that was assigned by USATF's Road Running Technical Council when the certification was approved. For more information on course certification, see *Chapter 4: The Course.*

- *Payment options:* Online registration nearly always requires payment by credit card or PayPal, and the online registration provider will ensure that all the information necessary to satisfy the credit card companies is required. On the printable version of the registration form, make sure that payment options are clearly stated. Some mail-in registrations will allow runners to supply credit card information as a form of payment as well. In this situation, you must be equipped to process credit card payments. Your bank will usually supply detailed instructions stating what is needed in this case. There are other e-commerce payment services such as PayPal that can be set up as well. If checks are to be accepted, make sure to include the name to whom checks should be made payable, as well as the address to which the form and check should be mailed.

- *Prohibitions and time limits:* Let runners know if strollers or headphones are prohibited or discouraged in the race or if there is a time limit for runners to complete the event.

- *Travel and lodging information*

- *Transportation, parking and bag check information:* If the race is on a point-to-point course, make sure that all information regarding shuttle buses is supplied. For races on all types of courses, it is useful to provide details about available parking. If baggage check is provided, that information should also be indicated.

SIDEBAR

Number Transfers

A small number of races throughout the U.S. that either limit their fields, cut off registration in advance of race day, or are simply hugely popular are faced with considering a number transfer policy. Headaches for the race director can ensue if a participant, realizing that he can't run the race, decides to give or sell his number to someone who either wasn't able to get into the race or could have signed up but wants to run for free. This type of undocumented transfer can cause two problems: first, there are significant liability issues, since the person now running will not have signed a waiver, and second, it can wreak havoc with age-group scoring, as the new runner might be in a different age group and/or be a different gender than the original registrant.

Race directors have generally tried to discourage such transfer of numbers by stating "No Transfers or Refunds" on the registration form and website, but the job has become harder. In the case of some very popular races like the Boston and New York City Marathons, runners have found a marketplace for their numbers on websites like eBay and Craigslist. Some race directors make an effort to ban runners who sell their numbers, but enforcement is time-consuming and unpleasant. Some events require runners to show identification when they pick up their numbers. This won't stop people from giving their number to someone else once they have it, but at least they will have to go through the effort of picking it up.

Due to increasing pressure from runners, a small but growing number of large races–especially those with registration limits–have begun instituting a transfer policy, whereby a runner who knows he can't run is able to transfer his number to a new runner. This can be done either through the online registration service, or the new runner will fill out and submit a runner-number transfer form (a sort of mini-registration form containing authorization for the transfer, information about the original registrant, and registration information and a signed waiver from the new registrant). The replacement runner may pay a transfer fee, but does *not* typically pay the original registration fee (though the original runner and the new runner may come to a private agreement about reimbursing the original runner for the fee). Most races close the transfer program a significant amount of time before the race in order to minimize last-minute changes to the race database. Races with transfer policies generally find that fewer than 10% of the registrants take advantage of them, but it does make it easier to insist that people not transfer numbers on their own. If you decide to allow transfers, make sure that the transfer policy is clearly stated—both on the race website and on the registration form—and include instructions on how to perform a transfer. If the transfer process occurs through the online registration provider, be sure to test the transfer process before it opens to make sure that it works properly.

- **Post-race amenities:** Many races feature unique post-race celebratory activities with parties, bands, fireworks shows, etc. The post-race activities are frequently a popular draw, so they should be well-publicized.

- **Registration confirmation details:** Runners should be informed as to the email address their confirmation email will be received from, and told to "white list" the sender or to watch for the email and make sure it does not end up in their spam folder, since races sending thousands of emails to accepted runners may have their messages flagged as spam.

- **Where and when results will be published/distributed.**

Additional Information Runners Might Like to Know

It is important to strike a balance between the key information that must be supplied to every registrant and information that sells the event. The additional information below should definitely be available on the event's website, and it can also be sent to the runner in the registration confirmation email. If you decide to also supply it on the registration form (online or otherwise), make sure it is done in a visually appealing manner so runners don't feel overloaded.

- Typical weather conditions on the date the event is going to be held
- Previous winners and course records
- Course elevation profile graph
- Amenities such as shower facilities
- Area hotels and contact info for out-of-town runners (this will endear you to the Chamber of Commerce)
- Local attractions that might be of interest to visiting runners

In summary, the race registration form and the race website work in conjunction to provide a key opportunity to sell the event, as well as to provide all of the relevant details of the event to prospective registrants. The website should also contain a clear and obvious link to the online registration form as well as to a printable .pdf version of the form for those who prefer to register by mail. **Note:** After spending lots of time including all the information outlined above, race directors will learn quickly that runners won't spend much time reading it. You will be asked questions again and again about information that is clearly stated on the registration form and website. Accept that as a given and move on.

Information Collected *From* Runners

Online registration forms from most registration providers are templates that require the provision of critical information, such as name, age, address, etc. If a registrant forgets to put in his or her age, he or she will be prompted to enter the missing information before continuing. Most forms are also easily modified to include any non-standard, race-specific questions that you might wish to ask during the registration process. Carefully check through the templated information requested by the chosen online registration platform to make sure that all necessary data is collected. Add custom questions as necessary to collect any other event-specific information not included in the templated portion. Be sure to collect all of the relevant information listed below on either an online or printed registration form.

- **Runner name**
- **Address:** If bib numbers, results, or awards will be mailed to runners, address information will obviously be needed. Addresses can also be useful to the race timers, particularly if there are two registrants with the same/similar names. These addresses may also come in handy the following year, if you wish to mail promotional materials to previous participants.
- **Email address:** Email is the best way to communicate with runners. Getting a runner's email address means that if there is a problem with that runner's registration, it will be easy

to contact him/her. Email is so critical as a method of communication that many online registration companies will require entrants to reconfirm their email addresses immediately after typing them in just to reduce the chance of typos. Still it is inevitable you will have emails bounce because someone types ".con" instead of ".com." Sometimes by reviewing your email "bounces" you can correct an obvious typo

You can also send "blast" emails with news and announcements about the race in the weeks leading up to the event. While nearly all registrants are willing to receive blast emails *from the race organizers,* you should supply a check box that allows them to opt out of receiving these messages. Include a "Privacy Policy" somewhere on the event website, so registrants know exactly how their email addresses may be used. *For a more extensive discussion on race use of emails, see* **Chapter 6: Marketing and Promotions.**

- **Phone number:** Cell phone number is preferable, since it can be used to contact the runner on race day by voice or text message, if necessary.

- **Age on race day (or date of birth, or both):** Consider specifying age *on race day,* rather than just age, as some people will forget they have a birthday coming up between the date they are completing the form and race day. This could put them in a different age group by the time race day arrives. Most online registration programs will instead request the registrant's birth date and will calculate age on race day from that information. Many runners will list the *current* year instead of their *birth* year in the DOB field,

which is why it might be a good idea to ask for both DOB *and* age on race day.

- **Sex:** This is also a required field on most online and print registration forms. The word "sex" is preferable to "gender," as "sex" is biological while "gender" may be elected by choice.

- **T-shirt options:** If t-shirts will be offered, make sure to request each registrant's size and make this a required field if every runner receives a t-shirt. At packet pick-up, make sure there is a way to know which size t-shirt each runner requested. Often, this will be printed on the labels on the runners' bib numbers. Otherwise, you may run out of a particular size.

- **Emergency contact name/phone number:** This contact should be the name of someone who will be available while the participant is running the race.

- **Waiver:** This portion of the registration form spells out the liabilities the registrant is accepting by running in the race. Waivers are standard legal statements that are designed to protect the race sponsors, race administrators, organizers, and municipalities from liability from accidents or injuries that

TIP

Races with Limited Fields and Charities

Many races that limit their fields become powerful charity fundraising events. These events will set aside a certain number of guaranteed registrations to the sold-out event for charities, and the charities then offer them to individuals who raise specified amounts of money. Charity entries for the Boston and New York Marathons require $2,500 to $5,000 or more to be raised in order to secure a registration. (Nearly 20% of the registrations for the Boston Marathon are set aside for "charity participants.) These events have raised hundreds of millions of dollars for selected charities in this manner. Other lottery-limited events at shorter-than-marathon distance can bring $250-$500 for charity registrations. This can be very lucrative for the charity and is excellent publicity for the race.

may occur during the race. Many races also include a sentence that asks the participant for the right to use photographs and/or video of the runner for commercial purposes. You may also wish to add a line stating that the runner understands that registration fees are non-refundable and that the race could be cancelled with no refunds. (Since very few runners actually read the waiver, you will want to indicate this again somewhere else on the form—you can even include a separate required check-box question on online registration forms stating *"I understand that my registration fee is non-refundable..."*) A print waiver will have space for the runner to sign his or her name, and a space for the date, as well as another set of lines for a parent or legal guardian to sign if the runner is under the age of 18. The last line of the waiver should have words to this effect: *"I have read the foregoing and certify my agreement by my signature below."* With online registration, applicants will sign the waiver electronically by checking a box to accept the waiver and possibly adding their initials. The default is set either to unchecked or "decline," so the applicant must take an action in order to accept the waiver. Make sure the waiver acknowledgement is a required field. Online waivers are nearly universally accepted, just like printed waivers. With mailed registration forms, some races return the paper registrations if the waiver is not signed, or will flag the form and require the runner to sign it before issuing a number at packet pick-up. For information on the importance and validity of waivers, as well as sample waiver language, see *Chapter 9: Insurance and Legal*.

- *Payment information:* This is part of the standard information requested during online registration. If you wish to allow payment by credit card for mail-in registration, make sure that you are collecting all of the information needed for proper processing by the credit card processor being used. Usually, you will need the registrant's name as it appears on the credit card, credit card billing address, credit card type (Visa, Mastercard, etc.), number, expiration date, and security code.

Other Information (Not Quite as Important—But Still Useful)

Besides the critical data listed above, you may also want to request ancillary information on the registration form, depending on the needs of the event::

- Whether the athlete will be competing in a wheelchair (if applicable to the event). It is always helpful to have wheelchair athletes identified in advance so accommodations can be made.

- Team or club that the runner belongs to or competes for.

- Number of races that the runner has completed of that distance (usually only applicable to marathons).

- Personal best time or expected finishing time for the race distance (if runners will be seeded by time). Some forms will allow runners to submit times for a different distance if they have not run a race of the distance of the event. Just be sure to ask for both distance and time.

- Whether they will attend the pre-race dinner and number of tickets needed (if applicable).

- If the race is raising money for a charitable organization, ask if the registrant is a member of a charity fundraising team. Also, it may be a good idea to ask the registrants if they want to make a donation to the race's charity during the registration process. Many race directors have been surprised at how effective this strategy can be as a fundraising tool.

- Race directors can directly help their sponsors by including questions on the registration form that relate to the sponsor's business, such as "do you use the services of an investment company?" or by gathering other demographic information that the sponsor might find useful. However, some race directors prefer to keep the registration form simple and save these types of questions for a separate demographic survey. See *Chapter 19: Post-Race* for details on post-race surveys.

- If race merchandise will be sold, make sure to include a link to the 'store' somewhere on the registration form.

When designing the non-templated parts of the online registration form and adding the event information to the registration site, limit the use of **bold** font to a small number of the most key items. (**"No race-day registration"** or **"No refunds"** are good examples of where bold might be used.) It is easy to fall into the trap of putting so much text in bold font that the enhanced importance of what appears in bold is lost.

Special Considerations for Designing Print Registration Forms/ Promotional Postcards

Although, as mentioned above, the majority of races have now turned to online registration providers, there are still a few reasons to have hard-copy registration forms available, or at the very least, a printable version of just the entry form that can be downloaded from the event website. Many events with online registration still use print forms for race-day registration. (*Note:* If a printable registration form is posted on the event website, be sure to take it down when the registration deadline is reached!) There are still a few people without easy computer access, and some people are just uneasy with supplying credit card information online, or unable to do so. These individuals will appreciate the "hard-copy" alternative. On printed/printable registration forms, use *boxes* where information can be entered one character or one number at a time, as opposed to lines for the registrant to write on. Make sure that there are sufficient boxes for people with long names and that these boxes are large enough that the information being entered can be read. Nothing is more frustrating for registration personnel than

not being able to read what's inside the boxes because they are too small.

Printed promotional materials can be as simple or as sophisticated as you would like. You can create a simple postcard with some photos, event information, and the event's web address and/or a link to online registration, or a glossy oversized sheet with photos and multiple folds. The decision will depend on how much money has been budgeted for printed promotional materials and how "green" you want the event to be.

If you do decide to mail out promotional materials, be sure that they are 'self-mailing,' meaning that an address label can be affixed directly to the postcard/form so they do not have to be mailed in a separate envelope. Find someone who is very current on postal regulations at the U.S. Postal Service—or a mailing house—and ask that person to review the design of the promotional materials, especially if you plan to mail at bulk or nonprofit rates. There are very specific requirements for various mailing rates and you have little easy recourse if the piece is rejected. If you are mailing at reduced nonprofit rates and the piece does not comply, you may be charged the higher for-profit rate.

How Many to Print?

A small, low-budget race hoping to attract 300-500 participants might print no more than 2,000 registration forms/promotional postcards (4-5 times the target number of runners), perhaps fewer, since a .pdf of the registration form should be available on the event website for runners to print themselves if they wish to mail in a form. The number of promotional materials printed should depend somewhat on how aggressively the race officials are willing to work to get them out. You might want to work backwards from a distribution plan. In coming up with the distribution plan, consider the types of outlets through which you might want to distribute the materials. *Chapter 6: Marketing and Promotions* details a number of venues for disseminating printed materials.

SIDEBAR

Registration Limits

A number of races across the country cap the number of registrants at a certain level—usually due to limitations of the course, frequently mandated by the permitting jurisdiction—and many of these reach that number well before race day. In some ways, this can be very helpful — the race director knows exactly how many t-shirts, runner bibs, porta-johns, tents, and other supplies will be needed on race day, and will avoid the potentially frantic ordeal of race-day registration. Moreover, if the event fills early, time and money can be saved on advertising. At the same time, however, limiting the field can create its own set of headaches.

Events with a limit usually start with a first-come, first-served registration system—open registration, let people register, and shut it down when the race is full. The advent of online registration has leveled the playing field so that a runner in California has an equal opportunity to get into an East Coast race as a runner who lives in the city where the event is held. If the event grows so popular that online registration fills in just hours or minutes (frequently causing the online registration system to crash), the event will usually turn to a lottery system, in which all registrations are collected over a few days or weeks and then some are selected electronically by the online provider. Once again, this is easier with an online registration system, where a random selection process can be applied to the submitted registration forms. Generally, events with lotteries will collect credit card information when people sign up for the lottery but only charge the card if the runner is accepted. With mail-in registrations, the forms (and checks) must be returned once the race is full. (See **Chapter 9: Insurance and Legal** for details about conducting lotteries.)

In either scenario, expect to spend time dealing with runners who call asking to get in. Inevitably there will be "special cases" to be reviewed.

Luring Volunteers

Having a limited field that fills early can provide a way to encourage volunteerism. The Cherry Blossom Ten Mile, for example, notifies all rejected applicants in the *current year's race* that they can receive a guaranteed registration for the *following year's race* by volunteering to work at the current year's event. The Falmouth Road Race also encourages volunteerism in its rejection letter.

Guaranteed Entry Forms

If your race limits registrations, gaining entry after it is closed will be a "hot ticket." You can take advantage of this situation and offer "guaranteed" registrations (registrations that will be accepted after the race is closed at the regular registration fee) to certain groups that are supportive, such as local running clubs, sponsors, expo exhibitors or certain charity supporters. The possibilities are as limitless as the good will. Most online registration systems easily allow for these 'special' registrants, usually by providing a code or a special link that the registrants can use to access the registration form even after it is closed to the general public. Check with the registration provider regarding how this process works in their platform.

Unofficial Entrants ("Bandits")

Races with participant limits generally attract more unofficial runners (often called "bandits") than races that allow registration on race-day. Some runners feel they are entitled to run even if they haven't registered. These unofficial runners create safety and liability issues, especially if they are injured during the event, since they have not signed waivers and often cannot be easily identified. Bandits also place added stress on race supplies, the course, and volunteers. Often these non-registered runners simply do not understand the problems they may cause for a race director. It is important that race directors do what they can to protect themselves from these situations by strongly discouraging bandits.

Processing Paper Registration Forms

If you are receiving even a small number of paper registration forms, set up an orderly processing system for opening the envelopes and separating the checks from the forms. The checks will need to be recorded and deposited into the race's bank account. It is probably best to associate each registration form with a specific check, so if there are questions about payment, you can locate details about every check on the deposit slip. If checks bounce, you will need to decide whether you will simply reject the registrants or give them an opportunity to make good on the checks. Paper registrations will need to be added to the online registrant database, or merged with it before the full database is entered into the scoring software. Information about race scoring software appears in *Chapter 17: Timing and Scoring*.

Runner Confirmation and Instructions

An advantage of online registration is that registrants receive a confirmation email minutes after completing the registration process, provided the email doesn't end up in the spam folder, which is an important reason to remind registrants to make sure their email service accepts emails from the race's email address. Through the use of .html, or by using one of the templates offered by any of the blast email companies, emails can be made visually appealing instead of appearing simply as text. For registrations that are mailed in, a similar confirmation email should be emailed to the registrant, or mailed by USPS if no email address is provided. Many races require that runners bring a copy of the confirmation document to packet pick-up as confirmation of their registration (although few events actually deny individuals without it). This confirmation email provides another opportunity to provide important race details.

Confirming Registrant Information

One important purpose of the confirmation is to verify that the information that has been entered into the race database, including the following key information.

- Name
- Address
- Contact information
- Sex
- Age (DOB)
- T-shirt size

Emails can be personalized with this information, which is an effective way to confirm the data that the race has on file.

Some races assign bib numbers at the time of registration and will include them in the follow-up correspondence, while others prefer to post an alphabetical list of registrants at packet pick-up with each runner's name and bib number. Runner information contained in the confirmation message might look like this:

> **Bib #:** 100   **Sex:** F   **T-shirt size:** Med   **Age:** 29
> Suzie Runner
> 123 Oak St.
> Anywhereville, MD 20816

If you send out elaborate confirmation and instructions, there may be a fair amount of repetition of information on the registration form and the event website, in terms of details about the course, awards, staging area, etc. The runner confirmation message should also contain more information about items of interest to confirmed registrants that may not have been included on the registration form, such as:

- How to make changes or corrections to registration information
- Number/transponder/packet pick-up information

- Details about transponder use if the event is using this technology
- Race weekend timetable
- Parking instructions
- Detailed medical instructions and warnings
- On-course amenities, including the exact location of aid and medical stations
- Travel and lodging options (including the "official hotel" if applicable)
- Packet pick-up and/or expo information
- Information on volunteering
- Details about official race merchandise, clinics, pasta dinners, etc.

On-going Communication with Confirmed Entrants

As race day draws near, information can be conveyed in blast emails to all confirmed registrants who have supplied email addresses. (See *Chapter 6: Marketing and Promotions* for a detailed discussion about using email as a method of communication. Also *Table 7-A* at right shows a sample plan for communications about the race, including both press releases and blast emails.) Avoid oversaturating confirmed registrants with emails or they will start to tune them out. Most larger races limit pre-race emails to 1-2 emails a month leading up to race day. Smaller races may only send a pre-race confirmation email with final race instructions and runner data and a post-race email with links to the results.

Make sure emails to registrants are fairly short and to-the-point, and ensure that the information in the email is consistent with what appears on the event website. The best way to ensure consistency is by using plenty of links back to the website. An abbreviated sample "final race instructions" email appears in *Figure 7-1 at the end of this chapter*. (The information in blast emails should be considered for the event's social media sites as well.)

Race Apps

More and more events are communicating with participants through an official race App that can be downloaded by participants onto their phones. There are a number of commercial companies that will build apps for events and will go through the approval process necessitated by Apple or Google. Once the app is created, you will have access to an "Administrative Tools" back end where you can upload content that will be seen by users of the App. Be aware that only about 1/3 of race participants may choose to download the App, so it should not be used as an exclusive communication tool, but rather as a supplement to your race website, social media presence, and blast email communications.

A number of on-line registration companies and timing companies are offering Apps, either as an add-on to an on-line registration or timing contract or as a stand-alone product. There are a number of companies offering Apps and we can't list them all here, but several providing Apps to a significant number of races include EventApp (from MYLAPS), Race Joy (from RunSignUp), Xacte, and Active.

These companies all offer full-blown Apps for Android and iOS. In most cases the company provides the template for the App and will teach you how to use their Content Management System (CMS) to upload your content into the App. The uploading will typically be done by a volunteer or someone on your race staff. The CMS is generally pretty straightforward and can be handled by pretty much anyone with some tech familiarity, but having a basic knowledge of html can prove helpful at times for achieving exactly the right look.

What Can an App Provide?

To some extent you have discretion over what you want to provide in the App, but there are a number of things that your App should include:

- Course map
- Race weekend schedule
- Weather information

Table 7-A

A Plan for Communications with Confirmed Entrants and the Media

It is a good idea to plan out an overall communications plan for the event. A sample communications plan for a large event appears below. The communications plan should be based on the major deadlines for the event and include media releases and blast emails to prospective and confirmed runners. The communications plan below is for a large race that conducts a participant lottery about five months before the event. (**Note:** This plan is aimed at *confirmed entrants* and others associated with the race, and is completely different from the Promotions Plan discussed in **Chapter 6: Marketing and Promotions.**)

Date	Audience	Topic
Mid October	**Media**	**New Presenting Sponsor Signed**
Late October	Prospective entrants	Fall Kick-off Coming Soon
Fall Kick Off	EVENT	FALL KICK OFF CELEBRATION
Mid-November	Prospective entrants	November Newsletter
Mid-November	Sponsor participant blast	Join the Retail Sponsor's Training Program
Mid-November	Prospective volunteers	Guaranteed Registrations for Last Year's Volunteers
Late November	Seeded runners	Seeded Runner Instructions
Late November	Prospective entrants	Entry Lottery Opens Soon
Late November	**Media**	**Entry Lottery Opens Soon**
1-Dec	EVENT	RACE LOTTERY OPENS
12-Dec	Prospective entrants	36 Hours Remaining for Lottery
13-Dec	EVENT	RACE LOTTERY CLOSES
Mid-January	**Media**	**Race Certified as Environmentally Friendly**
Mid-January	Confirmed entrants	January Newsletter
Mid-January	Lottery rejects	Charity Entries Available
Late January	Training program registrants	Training Program About to Start
Mid-February	**Media**	**Prize Purse**
Mid-February	Confirmed entrants	February Newsletter
Mid-March	Confirmed entrants	March Newsletter *(with entrant confirmation info for packet pickup)*
Mid-March	**Media**	**Elite Athletes and Clinic Speakers**
Week before	Confirmed entrants	Final Instructions
Week before	**Media**	**Final Pre-race Release**
Race Day	EVENT	RACE DAY
Race Day	**Media**	**Race Story and Top Finishers**
Week after	Confirmed entrants	Immediate Post Race News, including how to obtain results
Week after	Sponsor participant blast	Post Race Offer From Retail Sponsor
Mid-April	Finishers	April Newsletter
Mid-May	Finishers	May Newsletter
Mid-May	**Media**	**Results Are Official**
Mid-June	Finishers	June Newsletter

Press releases are in bold
Blast emails in medium
Key event dates are shaded

- Leaderboard
- Tracking of participants
- Live updates for specific participants
- Race results
- Links to Social Media
- News tab for information updates

Other things you might want to consider including that spectators and runners will find useful are:

- Local area map (wider than the course map)
- Nearby restaurants
- Nearby hotels
- Nearby sighseeing or other attactions
- Training plans geared toward your event

Race app for the Honolulu Marathon   MyLaps

Live Tracking

Live tracking of athletes can be done in one of two ways: through GPS or through timing mats placed along the course.

Some Apps, such as RaceJoy, use GPS tracking, which offers the most up-to-date and seamless tracking because you can see exactly where a runner is at any given time. The runner will appear as a moving dot on a map on the spectator's phone, much as a car does on GPS map Apps. For the tracking to work however, the runner must be carrying his or her phone while running. For the more recreational athlete, this may not be viewed as a problem, but the more serious contenders might not want the added burden of carrying a phone with them on the course.

Other Apps track by noting when an athlete's transponder crosses a timing mat on the course, at the start and at the finish. An alert is then sent out to a spectator who has requested to track that athlete during the race. For the most part, the alerts can go to Facebook, Twitter or SMS— whichever platform the spectator chose at signup. The number of alerts sent will depend on the number of timing mats on the course.

App Technology

As was noted above, the CMS is usually pretty easy to work with and user friendly. In addition, the well-known App companies are used to working with a variety of timing software and timing companies, so getting the participant data uploaded so alerts can be sent and results can be posted should be pretty seamless. Finally, once you have your App structure in final form, the App company will take care of submitting it to Google and Apple for acceptance into their App stores. You can still update content after the App has been approved.

Branding on the App

Apps are typically customizable to your event —you can use your logo, background photos, and other images to brand your App in the minds of runners and spectators. In addition, a number of

---

Figure 7-1

Sample "Final Race Instructions" Email

Dear Entrant [this can be personalized]:

We wanted to share some last minute announcements and instructions. The weather forecast looks favorable. Check the race website at [website link] for the latest information. Here are some highlights.

- **The App:** If you haven't already downloaded the official [Name of Race] App, you (and your friends) should do so. Click here: [insert link to app]
- **Race-Day Timetable and Course Maps**: [insert link]
- **Lost Your Confirmation Email?** Click here [insert link] to generate a new one and save any delay picking up your packet on Friday or Saturday.
- **New Bag Check System**: Clear here to learn about our new bag check system. [insert link]
- **Pace Groups:** Click here [insert link] to learn about pace groups.
- **Practicing Sustainability Can Pay Off:** Learn more about things you can do to make our event more sustainable. [insert link]

Reaching Us Between Now and Race Day:

We will be making a gradual transition from the race office to the packet pick-up and expo site. We strongly urge that people check the race website [insert website address], which contains information for 99% of the questions that we receive on race weekend, a time when we are very busy.

- **Saturday** [day before race day], we will cut off all responses to emails. After this time, the only way to reach us — for critical situations only — will be on the race hotline, which is [insert race weekend phone number].
- **Race day:** The only way to reach us is on the race hotline at [insert race weekend phone number]. No emails will be responded to.

And Finally... Our **Most Frequently Asked Questions** [insert link]

Want to Know More?

- **Friend us on Facebook:** Connect with your fellow runners and ask your questions as the excitement builds toward race weekend. [insert Facebook link]
- **Check out our Tweets:** Find out the latest tidbits during the run up to race day on our Twitter site at [insert Twitter link].

Good luck to everyone. See you on race day!
[Sponsor logos included somewhere on email].

---

the available Apps offer ways to promote sponsors with links and banner ads.

Social Media

Most Apps are set up to make full use of Social Media, giving users the ability to upload photos to at least Facebook and Twitter, and often to Instagram and other platforms as well. Depending on the App you choose, users can create branded photos with race specific hashtags. The event itself can also upload race photos and video to create excitement about the event.

Participant Race Progress Updates Without an App

If you are using a timing company for your event, you may want to see if the company offers an App, and if they are willing to throw in the App at a reduced rate (or better yet, free!) as part of your timing contract. If that isn't an option, and you don't have the time or money to offer an App to participants, some timing companies offer a way for people to request live tracking of athletes to Facebook, Twitter and SMS. There is no App, there is simply a signup on the race website, and then alerts are sent out as timing mats are crossed. This allows for a significant increase in spectator engagement while hopefully eliminating your expense of a full-blown App.

App as Communications Tool

Most Apps give the race director the ability to send out alerts through the App. This can be useful if you want to promote, say, a clinic or some other race-related activity, or to remind runners to bring their confirmaion with them to packet pickup. It can become extremely helpful, however, in cases of emergency, for example if you need to delay or cancel the race or make a sudden change for some reason. As mentioned above, not all participants will download the App, so it must be used in conjunction with your other methods of communication (website, Facebook, Twitter, email, etc.), but it can give you another good tool for disseminating critical information in a near immediate fashion.

Phil Stewart

8 Medical, Safety and Security

"Marathons are not exercises in sports medicine; they are exercises in disaster planning."

— Marvin Adner, Retired Medical Director, Boston Marathon

THE BASICS

- **Runner safety should be the backbone of every running event.** Incidents in which runners go off course or are timed improperly pale in significance to a serious injury or death at a road race.

- **Medical services vary greatly based on the size of the event.** A small race may need no more than a first-aid kit and a plan for transporting an injured runner to the hospital, while a large race will need a comprehensive medical operation. The percentage of runners needing medical attention varies greatly with distance and temperature. A large non-marathon race under good conditions might result in a 2% treatment rate rising to 3% for a marathon. As temperatures rise, these figures can increase to 5-8%.

- **Determine the need for a medical director.** For the smallest of races, the race director will undoubtedly double as the medical director and will need to make sure that the basics of medical care are provided. Events with over a few hundred runners should have a separate medical director and an on-site medical presence.

- **Notify the appropriate medical authorities**. For small races, at a minimum the race director should identify and notify the nearest fire station, 911 ambulance service, and closest hospital emergency room (and possibly even a back-up ER at the second-closest hospital) in advance of the event, letting these groups know when and where the event will be taking place. The race director should determine the best route to the hospital and share that information with race personnel. Local EMTs can be helpful in determining this information. Cell phones can serve as a communications network at smaller events. Emergency responders in the area should be given maps of the course and told how long the roads will be closed.

- **Assess the event's need for security.** Security at running events was virtually an afterthought until the 2013 Boston Marathon bombings shattered the age of innocence that running events are immune to terror. Smaller events may not need to do anything more than remind runners of the "see something, say something" mantra. Larger events should develop plans for monitoring backpacks, both checked and unchecked, and work with law enforcement personnel about the need for a security plan. The largest events may spend hundreds of thousands of dollars on extensive security to identify and screen runners, cordon off secure areas, and perform sweeps for explosives on and adjacent to the course.

THE DETAILS

Pre-Race Medical Planning/ Preparation

Estimates for death rates at races range from about 1 in 50,000 to 100,000 at marathons to about 1 in 300,000 at shorter-distance races. Estimates for percentages of runners needing some sort of medical treatment range from 1-3% under optimal weather conditions to as high as 10% or more during extreme conditions. A 1–3% treatment rate translates into 5–15 interventions at a 500-runner event; 50–150 at a 5,000-runner event and 500–1,500 at a 50,000-runner event.

A well-conceived medical plan is even more important today than in the past, given that baby boomers, who fueled the initial running boom, are aging, and an increasing number of less-well-trained, more social runners are joining the participant ranks.

Medical Personnel

As road races have grown over the years, participants (and their lawyers) have come to expect a certain level of medical preparedness. This has led to a steady increase in the complexity of medical management at running events. Today, medical-management issues represent some of the race director's most pressing concerns. You will find discussions of many medical issues in this chapter, but other sections of this book, especially those on communications and legal issues, also address medical concerns.

There is no doubt that well-informed and prepared medical personnel are essential to race operations. While there is no way to eliminate medical risk at a race, the medical staff can do much to minimize the possibility of a medical emergency and can facilitate the effective treatment of medical incidents through proper planning, information dissemination, and learning from the experiences gathered at previous races.

Selecting a Medical Director

The medical director, who should be an M.D., R.N., P.A. or other trained medical responder, is responsible for all medical decisions and should be involved with and knowledgeable about all aspects of race planning that could affect the safety of the event. In addition, this individual should be the race spokesperson to the media—with the race director close by (or vice-versa)—should a tragedy occur or should questions arise about race medical operations. For larger events, the medical director should create a committee to help plan and implement the medical aspects of the race.

Since many physicians may be hard-pressed to deal with the more mundane aspects of pre-race planning, such as ordering ambulances and supplies or communicating with volunteers, etc., some larger races have a medical coordinator assigned to this job. The medical coordinator need not be an M.D., but should have enough medical background to understand the necessary issues. He or she acts as the administrator while the medical-degreed medical director sets policy and makes the actual medical decisions.

Here is a short checklist of the responsibilities of a medical director:

- Recruit medical staff to help at the event.

- Order the necessary medical supplies. Sample medical supply lists for small (300-400 runner) and large (10,000-runner) races appear later in this chapter. Some smaller

races will have a first-aid kit and an automatic external defibrillator (AED) on hand, but will arrange for an on-site ambulance to provide the rest of the necessary medical supplies.

- Pay attention to the weather forecast and prepare for heat- or cold-related illnesses or problems as needed. Utilize a wet bulb globe thermometer (WBGT) to gather information about potentially hazardous conditions and advise runners accordingly.

- Develop contingency plans for emergency weather conditions. See *Chapter 21: Before Next Year* for details about developing a contingency plan.

- Calculate the amount of water needed based on anticipated weather and length of the course. A hot-weather half marathon needs far more water on the course than a mid-winter 5K. The planning and operation of water stops is covered in *Chapter 16: Race Logistics and Operations.*

- Develop a medical communications plan that covers receiving information about downed

---

TIP

Check the Good Samaritan Laws

"Good Samaritan" laws are laws that afford some legal protection to individuals who come to the aid of others in need of medical help. The laws were designed to increase the likelihood—by reducing the liability—that citizens would help others in emergency situations. The laws vary widely from state to state—some are broad and extend protection to both non-medical and medical personnel; others may exclude medical personnel such as nurses and doctors (especially if they are paid even a small amount). Race directors and race medical officials should be very familiar with the statutes in their state. It is risky to simply assume that all race personnel are covered by this type of law. Doctors may want to explore obtaining coverage for volunteer activities through their own medical malpractice insurance. Also, organizations that obtain liability insurance through the Road Runners Club of American (RRCA) have the option to purchase additional coverage for volunteer medical personnel. (See *Chapter 9: Insurance and Legal*.)

runners on the course and contacting local emergency providers for assistance. Races using multi-channel radios should designate a specific medical channel.

- Ensure adequate on-course medical presence through the use of ambulances, roving medical personnel on foot or bicycle, and golf carts or medical gators (small, specialized vehicles that can access sections of the course that are not accessible to an ambulance).

Recruiting Medical Staff

The medical director, either alone or with a committee, should also be responsible for recruiting the medical staff to work at the race. Expect attrition on race day; therefore, recruit more medical volunteers than necessarily needed. The primary responsibility is to ensure that medical help and an ambulance can reach any point on the course quickly, and that aid stations and the finish line medical tent are adequately staffed and supplied. Medical staff should be identified with special shirts or vests with "Medical" screened on

them, or by some other easily recognizable screened or embroidered garment and/or hat. It is a wise idea for race officials to verify the medical credentials of all medical volunteers. Depending on the size of the event and the number of medical volunteers, this may necessitate a separate volunteer who can focus on this.

Obviously, the size of the medical staff needed depends on the size of the race, the distance, and the anticipated weather conditions. Use experience gained from previous races or talk to other race directors to determine where the medical personnel should be concentrated. For a large race, staff the finish line medical tent with a cardiologist and/or an emergency room physician, if at all possible, as well as several general practitioners who are used to treating a wide variety of injuries and illnesses. In addition, especially for very large events, have nurses, physical therapists, IV therapists and podiatrists, as well as volunteers to help these professionals and to fetch blankets, drinks, dry clothes, medical supplies, etc.

On-course aid stations should also be properly staffed with at least a nurse or emergency medical technician (EMT). A lot of people visiting the on-course aid stations will be seeking Vaseline, band-aids, etc., so make sure that those items are readily available.

Many races also use EMTs on bicycles roaming the course looking for runners who need first aid. In addition, position teams of spotters at the finish line and in all the post-race areas to look for runners who may be experiencing problems. As in other medical areas, trained medical professionals should be used as spotters, if at all possible. Race directors might also want to consider the presence of 'medical runners' out on the course. Runners with medical training can be provided with free registration in exchange for running the race while keeping their eyes

---

TIP

What On-Course Treatment Is "Allowed"?

Back in 1984, as millions watched the Olympics on TV, overheated Swiss marathoner Gabrielle Andersen-Schiess waved off medical help that would have meant disqualification and staggered to the finish of the first Women's Olympic Marathon. Subsequently, USATF changed its rules. Now medical personnel can make a hands-on examination of a runner in medical distress without resulting in disqualification, as long as the aid does not shorten the runner's distance to the finish line. While medical officials should never hesitate to remove runners at serious medical risk, the new rule makes it possible to examine a runner in order to make such a determination, without disqualifying that athlete from the competition. Of course, runner safety should be of the highest priority for every race director. In smaller, less competitive events, the 'rules' for disqualification may not matter as much as they do in large-scale competitive events.

---

open for any participants who might be in trouble, medically speaking. These medical runners should be carrying race radios or cell phones so that they can easily be in contact with race officials if they spot an injured/ill runner on the course.

Also, consider having a medical presence at the expo (if one is held), along with a first aid kit and an automatic external defibrillator (AED).

The Medical Plan

Once selected, the medical director should create a written medical/safety/medical operations plan that outlines how the medical staff will handle various types of medical emergencies. All race-day medical personnel should be educated on the types of injuries to expect and the treatment for those injuries. It is important that the plan be both written and orally communicated, so that if a lawsuit is brought, there will be clear and easily available evidence that race organizers took reasonable and necessary steps to anticipate the event's medical needs. Both the medical director and the race director should be well versed in all aspects of the plan. The Medical Operations Plan should be present at each medical station for quick and easy reference.

In addition to having a written plan, race organizers should also hold a pre-race briefing for race workers, to reinforce the information that is contained in the medical plan and to answer questions that may arise. It is important that both volunteers and medical staff be aware of the many different kinds of medical emergencies that can come up during a race. The emphasis of this training should be to describe the symptoms that should signal a call for medical assistance, to describe exactly who should be contacted in each type of situation, and to make sure race workers know what *not* to do.

Having quick access to a runner's medical history can make

a difference in treatment. Runners' bib numbers should have space on the back for runners to list any previously existing conditions that medical providers should know about, as well as any type of medical condition that might affect treatment. There should also be space on the back of the bib number to provide the phone numbers of contacts available *during the time the race is being run,* in case of a medical emergency. Many races now require supplying the name and cell phone number of a race-day contact during the registration process and print that information directly on the runner's bib. An extra level of caution might entail asking all registrants to complete a brief medical history sheet that medical personnel can have access to for use in the medical tent, if necessary.

Finally, the race policies should state that race officials have the right to remove any participant whom they perceive to be in danger.

Preparing Medical Supplies

The medical director or medical coordinator should also be in charge of ordering all medical supplies and equipment. Obviously, supply needs will be completely dependent on race size and distance. Included in this chapter are sample medical supply lists for a 300-400 runner event (**Table 8-A**) and a 10,000-runner event (**Table 8-B**). Race directors of some smaller races (under 1,000 runners) recommend that every race have a first-aid kit on hand, as well as an AED. (AEDs and

---

TIP

Family Waiting Tent

Most races deal with the problem of family members reuniting with a race participant by creating a family reunion area somewhere near the race finish. You can take this a step further by creating a "Family Waiting Tent" adjacent to or near the finish line medical tent, where family members can wait for runners who have to be treated in the medical tent. This keeps family members out of the treatment area, but still enables the race medical team easy access to the family to get extra information about the runner being treated.

heart problems are discussed in further detail later in this chapter.) For other medical supplies, directors of small events generally contract to have an adequate number of ambulances and/or medical gators on hand and ensure that these vehicles are stocked with necessary medical supplies.

Medical Supply and Personnel Lists for a 300-400 Runner 5K and a 10,000-Runner 10 Mile

Table 8-A contains a list of the medical supplies and personnel that the average 300-400 runner 5K could be expected to need; **Table 8-B** lists the medical supplies and personnel a typical 10,000-runner race would need. These lists should be used as a guideline only, as each race may have its own unique needs.

Pre-Race Medical Communication

In the months leading up to the event, communication is vital for a successful medical operation. Make sure emergency personnel and local hospitals are informed about the event. Communicate with runners about the possible risks involved, and be sure to properly and efficiently collect medical information from all participants. These are important steps toward making sure medical operations run smoothly on race day. For larger races, a meeting between the head of the EMTs and ambulances and the medical director and coordinator is important for full understanding of every person's role and to review procedures for when a runner is injured.

Medical-Related Communication with Race Participants

Medical communication with the runners begins with letting them know, on the registration form, about the risks of taking part in the event, what medical services will be available, the fact

that they can be removed from the course if medically necessary, and the details of any weather contingencies. The risks and removal policy should be incorporated into the participant waiver on the race registration form, which is discussed in detail in **Chapter 9: Insurance and Legal** and in **Chapter 7: Entrant Registration, Confirmation and Communications**. Below is a brief overview of medical information that should be communicated to all race participants:

- **Warning signs of medical distress.** Many registration forms or pre-race materials will outline the warning signs of a variety of common medical emergencies and tell runners experiencing any of these symptoms to seek medical attention.

- **Medical services on the course.** Provide an overview of the number and location of medical aid stations on the course and at the finish line.

- **Removing runners from the course.** Registration forms should state that race officials or medical personnel have the right to remove runners from the course for any medical reason.

- **Cancellation policy.** All events, but especially those in the summer, should raise the possibility of cancellation, shortening of the course, or changing the event to a non-competitive fun run in the event of extreme weather conditions. Many races publish the American College of Sports Medicine guidelines (see under **Heat** below) on their websites or registration materials.

In addition, runners should provide the race organizers with the name of a contact who can be reached in an emergency *during the race* and of any personal medical conditions. This information can be collected during online registration. Alternatively, some races provide space to include this information on the back of the bib numbers. It is important that this information be readily available to medical personnel. As a minimum, there should be a participant list, preferably in

Table 8-A

Medical Supply List for a 300-400 Runner 5K

Item	Quantity	Item	Quantity
SUPPLIES FOR MEDICAL TENT			
2nd skin larger 'burn pads'	1 box	Purell	2 (large size)
2nd skin blister pads	1 box	Q-tip applicators	5
Albuterol	4	rescue blankets	At least 20
alcohol prep pads	1 box	safety pins	1 jar
aspirin	1 bottle	saline solution	1 bottle
athletic tape	10 rolls	scissors	2
bandaids	1 box (regular)	scoops for ice	2
bandaids	1 box (large)	sharps container	1
Ben Gay	1 tube	sunscreen	1 bottle
Benadryl	1	tampons	1 box
Betadine	1 bottle	thermometer covers	1 box
biohazard bags	2 bags	tissues	2 boxes
BP cuffs (adult)	2	tongue depressors	20 (1-1/2 inch)
butterfly/steri-strips	1 box	triple antibiotic ointment	1 tube
clipboards	10	tufskin spray	1
Coban	4 rolls	Tylenol	1 bottle
corn pad packets	10	vaseline	1 jar (large size)
crutches	2 pairs (different heights)	velcro tourniquet	1
		waterproof tape	3 rolls (large)
digital thermometers	2	wheelchair	4
disposable scalpels	1 box		
duct tape	1 roll	**SUPPLIES FOR ON COURSE MEDICAL STATIONS**	
emesis basins	12	antibiotic ointment	1 tube (4x4)
epi pen	3	aspirin	small bottle
E-Z wrap plastic film to hold ice		athletic tape	2 rolls
bags in place	1 roll	bandaids	20 small, 20 large
flashlights	1	Betadine	1
garbage bags	5	biohazard bag	1
gauze (kling) Rolls	10 rolls (4")	blister care	4 kits
gauze (kling) Rolls	5 rolls (3")	clipboard	1
gauze pads	4 boxes (4"x4")	gauze pads	15
gauze pads	2 boxes (3"x3")	hydrocortison cream	1
glucometer	1	ibuprofen	small bottle
hydrocortisone cream	1 tube	kling roll	1
ibuprofen	1 bottle	latex-free gloves	20 pairs
latex-free gloves	2 boxes (large)	medical forms	10
medical forms	100	pens	5
medical vest	Enough for med. Vols	Purell	1
Moleskin	5 packs	saline solution	1 small bottle
name tags	25	scissors	1
non-adhesive dress	10 packs (3" x 8")	sunscreen	1 bottle
paper towels	2 rolls	tampons	1 box
pens	20	tissues	1 box
plastic bags for ice	75	Tylenol	small bottle
powder	1 (large size)	vaseline	1 jar
prewrap	5 rolls		

Table 8-B

Medical Supply List for a 10,000-Runner 10 Mile

This list should be used as a guideline only. There may be particular variables associated with different events that might require different quantities than those listed below or additional items not listed here. *Note:* This race does not have on-site IV supplies (they would transport if IV were needed), so races with onsite IV provided would need to have IV supplies added to this list for the finish line station.

Item	Size	Quantity	Item	Size	Quantity
SUPPLIES FOR MEDICAL TENT:					
2nd skin larger 'burn pads'		2 boxes	gauze (kling) Rolls	3-inch	5 rolls
2nd skin blister pads		2 boxes	gauze pads	4x4	4+ boxes
ace wraps	4-inch	2 big boxes	gauze pads	3x3	2 boxes
ace wraps	6-inch	3 rolls	glucometer		2
Albuterol		4	hydrocortisone cream		2 tubes
alcohol		2 bottles	hydrogen peroxide		1 bottle
alcohol prep pads		4 boxes	ibuprofen		1 bottle
angio cath		weather	medical vests		100
		dependent	Moleskin		10
aspirin		1 bottle	name tags		100
athletic tape	(1 1/2 inch)	20 rolls	non-adhesive dress	3x8 inch	10 packs
bandaids	regular size	2 boxes	non-latex gloves	large	6 boxes
bandaids	large size	2 boxes	paper towels		3 rolls
bandaids	4-wing	2 boxes	pens		50
Ben Gay		2 tubes	plastic bags for ice		400
Benadryl		1 box	powder	don't need to	2
Betadine		1 bottle		designate big	
biohazard bags		4 bags	prewrap		1 box
BP cuffs (adult)		3	Purell	big	4 bottles
butterfly/steri-strips		4 boxes	Q-tip applicators		10
callus relief		2 packs	Q-tips		1 box
clipboards		15	rescue blankets		at least 20
Coban		10 rolls	safety pins		1 jar
combine dressing 8-inch		5	saline solution		1 bottle
corn pad packets		15	scissors		4
cotton balls		1 box	scoops for ice		3
coveroll bandage 6-in		1	scotch tape		1
crutches		2 pairs,	sharps container		1
		different	tampons		1 box
		heights	thermometer covers		3 boxes
dental kit		1	tissues		2 boxes
digital thermometers		2	tongue depressors		plenty
disposable scalpels		3 boxes	transparent tape		1 box
duct tape		2 rolls	triple antibiotic ointment		2 tubes
emesis basins		12	tufskin spray		2
epi pen		6	Tylenol		1 bottle
E-Z wrap plastic film to hold ice			vaseline	big	1 jar
bags in place		2 rolls	vaseline	little	2 jars
flashlights	medium	1	velcro tourniquet		1
flashlights	little	3	waterproof tape	large	3 rolls
garbage bags		plenty	waterproof tape	small	3 rolls
gauze (kling) Rolls	4-inch	10 rolls	wheelchairs		8

Table 8-B

Medical Supply List for a 10,000-Runner 10 Mile (cont'd)

Item	Size	Quantity	Item	Size	Quantity
SUPPLIES FOR ON COURSE MEDICAL STATIONS					
antibiotic ointment	(4x4)	1 tube	ibuprofen		small bottle
aspirin		small bottle	kling roll		1
athletic tape		2 rolls	pens		5
bandaids		plenty	Purell		1
Betadine		1	saline solution		1 small bottle
biohazard bag		1	scissors		1
blister care		4 kits	tampons		2 boxes
clipboard		1	tissues		2 boxes
gauze		15	Tylenol		small bottle
gloves		20 pairs	vaseline		1 jar
hydrocortisone cream		1			

electronic format for easy sorting, in the medical tent, to help with identifying runners. Some events print QR codes directly on the bib numbers to streamline this process even further. There is a movement toward establishing a medical database where runners can enter any personal medical conditions that should be known by the medical teams at races. Although there are privacy concerns, a number of medical directors have said that such a database would help ensure that runners receive the proper care in the medical tent.

Communication with Emergency Rooms

Well before race day, the medical director or medical coordinator should inform local hospitals to which runners might be transported as to the nature of the event and the types of emergencies that are likely to arise. Establish the first hospital to which a runner will be transported and a back-up in case the primary hospital's Emergency Department is full and not accepting transfers. It is a good idea to have a list of all of the hospitals in the area. While emergency rooms deal with

crises every day, race crises may differ enough from everyday trauma that it is helpful to brief the hospitals on what to expect. If a runner is transported to the hospital, a member of the race medical staff needs to track the individual's status. Sometimes a member of the medical team might be allowed to accompany the individual or can drive to the hospital shortly thereafter, in order to act as a "patient advocate" or to assist the runner's family and answer any questions they might have. Be aware that HIPAA laws may limit the information that hospital personnel will release to race officials (see sidebar). If possible, medical staff should ask the patient to sign a HIPAA form that allows the medical team to inquire about the runner's care at the hospital. If you are unable to obtain the runner's signature, the medical director or coordinator should contact the runners' family members to follow up.

In addition to notifying local hospitals about the event, someone from the race should provide the nearest fire station with pertinent race information, including when the race will take place, where the course will go, and how long the roads will be closed.

Race-Day Medical Operations

Communication among all the key medical players, including medical personnel and local emergency rooms, is vital for a successful medical operation. For details on how to set up a communications network for both medical and non-medical use, see *Chapter 16: Race Logistics and Operations from Start to Finish.*

Location of Medical Tents

Most events will position their primary or main medical tent between 100 and 200 yards beyond the finish line. Statistically, most runners who collapse do so right at the finish line or within steps after finishing. Placing the tent in front of the line or right at the line may result in medical personnel having to go against the flow of finishers in order to bring collapsed runners to the tent. Ideally, the tent will be readily accessible both to ambulances, in case runners need to be transported to the hospital, and to the post-race area, in case runners need medical aid some time after finishing. Statistics from marathons, for example, indicate that there tends to be a mini-peak of injury and illness between 15-20 miles, a decrease between miles 20-25, and then the highest level of injury at the finish. As much as possible, put the most experienced medical personnel in the high-risk locations.

There should be some medical presence on the course at larger events. Ideally, medical personnel should be present at each on-course aid station, and a small (10' x 10') tent with medical signage may be provided for this purpose. It is vital that on-course medical personnel have access to the event communications system (either radios or by cell phone). On-course medical tents are designed to treat only the most basic, non-life threatening injuries, such as blisters and abrasions. Runners needing more medical support should be transported to the main medical tent or directly to a nearby hospital.

Design of the Main Medical Tent

The medical tent itself should offer a degree of privacy for runners who are being treated, as well as room for several cots and supplies, and room for medical personnel to maneuver. The size of the medical tent will increase with the size of the race, ranging from perhaps a 10'x10' or 10'x20' tent for a small event to a block-long tent like that at the finish line of the Boston Marathon, which can treat up to 300 runners at a time. If the tent has siding (which it should for privacy purposes), add power for lighting inside. In addition, if the event is held during cold weather, a heater is essential.

The medical tent at large events should have designated areas to treat acute, serious injuries/complaints such as chest pain. Designate appropriate medical volunteers, such as those who work in an emergency room, to staff that area of the tent. Also, designating two

Design of the indoor medical "tent" at the Chevron Houston Marathon.   Phil Stewart

people to triage all runners at the entrance of the main medical tent will help manage the flow of the injured. These two people should have experience determining who needs minor care and who has more acute needs. Those with acute needs should be escorted to the section of the medical tent set aside for these runners.

On-course Medical Presence

If the event is large enough to consider on-course medical aid to supplement the finish line operation, most events put the on-course medical personnel—and ambulances—at or adjacent to the on-course aid stations. The locations of the aid stations are generally well known to the runners, which makes them a logical position for medical aid as well. In addition, the officials at aid

Phil Stewart

A pop-up medical tent suitable for a small race or on-course at a larger event.

stations are usually on the race's radio network. Most on-course medical stations are not as full-featured as the main medical tent at the finish line, but are designed for general first aid and minor injuries and as communication points with the main medical tent. If the medical professionals on the scene feel that a runner needs to be transported either to the finish line tent or directly to the hospital, arrangements can be made quickly. Many people visiting the on-course aid stations will be seeking Vaseline, band-aids, ice packs, and aspirin or ibuprofen (although some mostly longer distance races—half marathons and longer—have stopped providing ibuprofen due to the effects on the kidneys), so make sure that those items are readily available. Problems on the course should be handled on the spot, or the individual in trouble should be transported to the main medical tent at the finish line or, if the injury is severe, directly to a nearby medical facility. Transport of injured runners can be accomplished with medical gators – small, specialized motor vehicles used to transport injured or sick participants from areas inaccessible to standard ambulances. Companies that supply

ambulances may also be able to supply gators. A patient can be transported on a gator to an aid station or the main medical tent, where he or she can receive further treatment or be transferred to an ambulance and taken to the hospital if necessary. The gator should be stocked with first aid supplies, medications and life-support equipment, and staffed with a paramedic or an EMT.

Finding Downed Runners

One of the biggest challenges for medical personnel is locating the runner in need of medical attention. Oftentimes, medical personnel and volunteers may not be familiar enough with the race course to relay precise instructions about where to dispatch medical aid. One solution is to prepare a "Grid Map" of the course that divides the course into small sectors. A volunteer can more precisely position himself by saying something like, "I have a downed runner in Sector E-4." Grid maps should be distributed to all medical and course volunteers. A sample grid map appears in **Figure 8-1** on the next page. (Note that the emergency call-in procedures have been included.).

It is also difficult to locate downed runners in crowded finish areas. Some events actually have their medical personnel carry ID flags that they can wave to show the location of a downed runner. Many events place medical volunteers in elevated "life guard" or tennis umpire chairs to provide a broader view of the finish line area.

Tracking the Runners

It is desirable to have a system for tracking runners who are receiving medical attention at various points in the race—both on the course and

Figure 8-1

Sample Grid Map

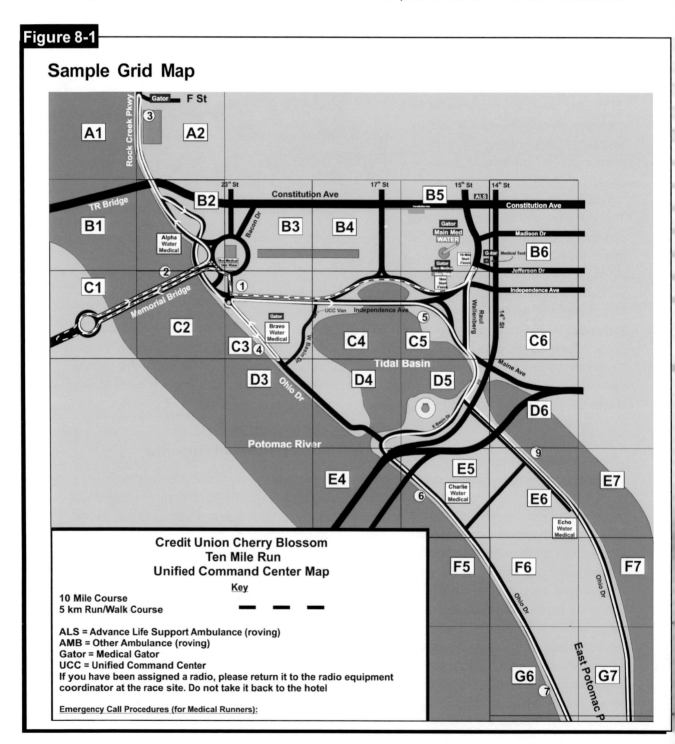

at the finish—so that family members and friends can be notified of the status of any runner who is reported "missing." Volunteers on the course should note the race numbers of runners who drop out or are being treated, as well as their location on the course, and this information should be relayed back via radio or cell phone to the central communications unit and/or the finish line medical area. Wherever the information goes, that area should have an electronic or printed listing of race registrants by number, or access to the registrant database, so that identifications can be made. Some races print barcodes or QR codes on the bib numbers, which can be scanned by medical personnel to quickly establish the identity of the runner/patient. Also, create an "exit system" to indicate when a runner has been released from the event's medical system, so that relatives or friends searching for that runner can be informed if he/she has left the medical area. It is helpful to have a non-medical volunteer at the entry/exit point of the main medical tent to keep track of the names of the runners and the time of day that they entered and exited.

Record Keeping

Make sure that records are kept of all incidents of injury or need for medical treatment. Volunteers in the medical tent should be instructed to fill out an online form or printed data card on each injured or sick runner who comes in to the tent. This record-keeping can be extremely helpful in planning for the next year's event, because it gives a fairly accurate account of what medical problems were encountered and how to adjust the system to be better prepared for them. In conjunction with this effort, it is particularly useful to keep accurate weather data on race day. Heat is the best gauge of the number of runners who might need medical attention. Use this medical data to project staffing and supplies that might be needed depending on the race-day weather. Make sure to keep all injury records for as long as the waiver forms are kept, in case of a later lawsuit.

Post-Race Evaluation

After the race, hold a meeting to go over what went right and what went wrong in the race medical operation, or make sure to discuss this topic in the general post-race meeting. This discussion will help enable the medical team to assess what they need to do to improve operations at next year's race.

Serious and Life-Threatening Medical Conditions

Medical treatment of runners at races should be left in the hands of highly qualified medical personnel who are part of the medical team. These individuals are trained in dealing with the type of medical emergencies that are most likely to arise

Phil Stewart

An elevated chair gives medical officials an excellent overview of the post-race staging area.

at races. However, here is a brief overview of some of the life-threatening, serious, and common medical conditions most likely to be encountered at a road race.

Heart Attacks

"Heart attack" is a catch-all term for three main heart-related ailments that can cause death. The etiologies of each are different, but all three require immediate intervention to restore the heartbeat. *Arteriosclerosis,* or clogged arteries, generally strikes older, frequently overweight individuals with previously existing high cholesterol and/or blood pressure. The clogged coronary arteries deny blood flow to the heart, which then cannot function. *Sudden cardiac arrest* is a disruption in the heart's electrical signals. This causes the heart to stop pumping blood. *Congenital heart defects* cover a wide assortment of often-undetected heart abnormalities and are the most frequent cause of cardiac death in runners under age 30. A congenital heart defect was the cause of the tragic death of U.S. marathon champion Ryan Shay at the 2008 Men's Olympic Trials Marathon.

Treatment for these heart conditions must happen quickly, before blood flow to the brain and other vital organs is cut off for more than a few minutes. CPR can be administered immediately by individuals certified to do so, but should only be thought of as a stopgap measure until the victim can be shocked with an AED (Automatic External Defibrillator) and transported to an emergency room. Any race large enough to have a dedicated medical presence should have an AED on hand, as well as someone trained in how to use it. The device applies an electrical shock directly to the heart in an attempt to restore a normal heartbeat. The four-pound device is simple to operate, and trained personnel can easily carry one in a backpack. AEDs can be purchased for between $1,500 and $2,000, as of this writing. Many larger races use medical teams with AEDs on bicycles to rove the course and/or include an AED at every on-course medical station (or on ambulances deployed out on the course).

Heat Exhaustion and Heat Stroke

Heat exhaustion and heat stroke occur when runners become dehydrated in warm weather conditions, frequently at summertime events. With heat exhaustion, the body's cooling mechanisms are still working, although they are not keeping up with the body's need to eliminate heat. With heat stroke, a far more serious condition, the body's mechanisms for dealing with heat have stopped working. Failure to address heat stroke can lead to death.

A runner experiencing heat exhaustion will initially feel faint, dizzy and fatigued. As the condition progresses, the runner's skin becomes cold and clammy. The individual will generally be sweating profusely, will have a rapid but weak pulse, and the body temperature will be about normal or slightly below normal. Other symptoms may include thirst, giddiness, weakness and lack of coordination. Runners should be warned in advance of the race that if they experience any of these symptoms they should stop running and seek medical aid. A rectal thermometer can help determine the degree of hyperthermia.

To treat a runner with heat exhaustion, volunteers or medical personnel should lay the individual down in a cool shady location, loosen his clothing and offer him water, telling him to sip it instead of chugging it. If the individual begins to vomit, immediate medical attention is required. Remember, untreated heat exhaustion can lead to heat stroke if the body continues to heat up. Heat stroke can be fatal.

A runner with heat stroke usually stops perspiring (the body's normal defense against heat has shut down) and the skin is hot, dry and red. The individual's pulse will be rapid and strong, and his temperature will rise above 103°F. He may collapse or stagger and will exhibit confusion or delirium. Death can occur when the temperature reaches 107°F.

A runner with heat stroke needs immediate medical attention in order to dissipate the accumulated heat as quickly as possible. He should be moved to a cool place and have his clothing removed. He should have a cold sheet placed over him or be immersed in a cold ice bath. Medical stations at warm-weather events should be stocked with a tub suitable for this purpose. Transport to a hospital may be required.

Allergic Reactions

Insect stings can easily happen at races, especially in warmer weather when insects tend to hover around food and garbage cans. Bee, wasp, hornet and yellow jacket stings can result in dangerous allergic reactions in some individuals, sometimes culminating in a life-threatening condition known as anaphylactic shock. Signs of an insect sting allergy include swelling of the face and throat, difficulty breathing or swallowing, and rapid, shallow pulse. In the most severe cases, unconsciousness, shock and cardiac arrest can occur in under ten minutes in the absence of medical intervention.

Emergency treatment of an anaphylactic response includes an injection of epinephrine. Often, people who know they have severe allergies will wear a medical alert bracelet and may carry an Epi-Pen auto-injector with them at all times and can often treat themselves. Instruct the medical team to look for the alert bracelet, or, if the runner is still conscious, ask if he/she has experienced a prior insect sting allergy. If at all possible, the medical tent should contain a supply of Epi-Pen auto-injectors, which come in both adult and child dosages. Epinephrine should only be administered by a trained medical professional, as it can have serious side effects. Even if the administration of epinephrine appears to be effective, the runner should still be transported to an emergency room for further evaluation.

Hyponatremia

Hyponatremia, or "water intoxication," has become more prevalent as more and more slower runners and walkers participate in longer events. Hyponatremia occurs when an individual ingests so much water that the sodium concentration in his blood drops to a dangerously low level that can be life threatening. The issue can get complicated for medical professionals, because some of the symptoms of hyponatremia can be similar to those of dehydration, but treating for dehydration, with a quick fluid replacement, can be life-threatening for an individual with hyponatremia. An increasing number of medical tents at major marathons are now using iSTAT instruments that measure instantaneous sodium levels before treatment is started, in order to determine if the runner is hyponatremic.

Hyponatremia virtually never appears in runners who are completing events in under four hours. This makes it primarily a consideration for slow marathoners (and walkers who may take more than 4 hours in shorter events) or ultra-marathoners. If the event does not involve this amount of time, it is extremely unlikely that hyponatremia will be an issue. Still, the condition has caused many medical directors to rewrite the rules of hydration from "drink, drink, drink" to advising runners to "know your own hydration needs and drink to replace the fluids that you have lost during exercise." If the medical team suspects a runner is hyponatremic, the patient should be

SIDEBAR

HIPAA Laws

The Health Insurance Portability and Accountability Act of 1996, commonly known as the HIPAA laws, were designed to protect the privacy of medical records. These laws can result in a complicated situation for race directors, because they limit the amount of information a race director can receive once a runner has been transported to a hospital. This may put the race director in the awkward position of being unable to keep distraught family members abreast of the status of a transported runner. Although difficult, the best option may be to direct the family members to the hospital treating the runner, telling them that HIPAA limits the information that can be relayed to you.

transported to the hospital. For races that will encounter runners or walkers that take longer than 4 hours to finish, consider stocking the main medical tent with an iSTAT device to help determine if someone has hyponatremia.

Hypoglycemia/Insulin Shock

Diabetic runners, especially those who require regular administration of insulin, may be at risk for post-exercise hypoglycemia, or low blood sugar. This happens when larger-than-normal amounts of glucose are used by the cells of the body during exercise, creating an imbalance in the amounts of insulin and glucose in the blood stream and resulting in abnormally low blood glucose levels. Most diabetics are well aware of the early symptoms of hypoglycemia and can treat themselves with glucose tablets or other quick-acting carbohydrate and quickly stabilize their blood sugar. However, in a small percentage of cases, a more severe reaction called insulin shock can occur, and this is a diabetic emergency. Symptoms of insulin shock include dizziness, shaking, sweating, confusion and poor coordination. If not treated quickly, symptoms can progress to unconsciousness, seizures and coma.

Often, diabetic individuals wear a medical bracelet that can alert medical staff that they may be experiencing a diabetic emergency and that immediate transport to a hospital is warranted. Treatment of insulin shock involves getting sugar into the blood stream immediately, most often via an injection of glucagon, which should be administered by trained medical personnel.

TIP

Free Registration for Doctors

Assuming that the Good Samaritan laws in your state cover doctors who volunteer at events (most state laws allow this), you might consider providing free race registration for a small number of physicians—with the understanding that they will help address any medical emergencies they see on the course. The medical director may be able to help you in recruiting, or try a local hospital.

Complications from Falls

Although the medical team will commonly encounter numerous non-serious fall-related injuries such as cuts and bruises, serious complications can also sometimes result from falls and the medical team should be trained to recognize and treat these, as well. Serious fall-related injuries experienced by runners include broken bones and head trauma. Although not often life-threatening, situations involving either of these fall-related complications may necessitate transport to a local emergency room.

Non-Life Threatening Conditions

Other typical non-life threatening conditions that commonly occur at road races include sprains, cuts, bruises and blisters. First-aid supplies to deal with these types of injuries should be on hand. In addition, under cold and wet conditions, you may want to have hot fluids and blankets to treat runners with hypothermia. If runners are wet, they can begin to experience the symptoms of hypothermia at temperatures as high as 50°F. In cases of hypothermia, have blankets on hand, as well as warm chicken broth for runners to sip.

Other Functions of the Medical Staff

If possible, get the medical director's input when designing the course. People with medical backgrounds can often think of issues that even an experienced race director might not think of. Research has shown, for example, that events with a downhill finish generate more problems because the runners are expending a great deal of effort to finish fast, then they come to a sudden stop.

The medical director's opinion will also be important if weather issues, such as heat or lightning, spark debate over cancellation or delay. Determine in advance who has the final authority on these decisions, the race director or the medical director.

Drug Testing

Drug testing at road races for elite athletes is supervised by the United States Anti-Doping Agency (USADA). For a full discussion of this topic, see *Chapter 12: Special Entrant Categories.*

Weather- and Safety-Related Issues

Lightning

Nationwide, anywhere from 150 to 300 people are killed by lightning each year. About twice as many are struck and recover, according to the Maryland Institute for Emergency Medical Services Systems. Since many running events are held outdoors on summer evenings when the risk of thunderstorms is greatest, race organizers should be aware of the risks that lightning poses, and of the steps that should be taken to cope with the threat.

Lightning Safety Points to Consider

Clearly, race directors cannot lightning-proof their events; a summertime race has inherent risks. Options are more clear cut if a storm is approaching prior to the start of the race when runners are still in the staging area. Once runners are out on the course, options are more limited. The best on-course strategy may be to have volunteers make announcements that the race has been cancelled and runners (and volunteers) should seek shelter. Here are some things you can plan in advance:

- *Make the start and finish areas as safe as possible.* Locate these areas near indoor facilities where runners, spectators and volunteers can safely stay during a storm. Keep in mind that only fully enclosed buildings or cars are safe; shelters, canopies, trees, etc., should be avoided.

- *Develop an evacuation plan.* Identify and obtain approval for the use of nearby shelters (buildings, underground subway stops, parking lots, etc.) and prepare evacuation protocols and announcements prior to race day. Check with municipal officials in advance regarding how long the event can be delayed in the face of a storm before it needs to be cancelled.

- *Closely monitor any approaching storms.* Use a reputable weather app that can accurately track an incoming thunderstorm and advise you of the storm's progress. Some apps have specific lightning alert features that will warn of potential danger from lightning in the area.

- *Determine how communications will be maintained during a storm.* Keep in touch with people out on the course.

- *Make sure that some members of the race staff are trained in CPR.* It's also advantageous if some are educated about how to handle lightning-strike victims.

- *Use the race announcer to keep runners, officials and spectators informed.* Let everyone know what to do in case of an oncoming storm. Do **not** leave the announcer atop a metal platform. Here are some general pointers that can be conveyed to runners trapped in a thunderstorm:

  - *Don't carry metal objects.* They are good conductors of electricity.
  - If you feel your skin tingle or hair stand on end, *drop to the ground and curl up immediately.*
  - *Spread out from others and crouch down on the ground (don't lie down). Avoid being the highest object in an area.* If you are out in an open area, walk with a shuffling gait, or crouch down on the ground with your hands on your knees and lean forward. Don't stand with your legs spread apart. Do not seek shelter under a tree or near tall buildings.
  - *Get away from water.*

Lightning First Aid

- If someone at the race is struck by lightning,

the person is no longer carrying any electrical current, so you can apply first aid immediately. The person will be burned and will have received a severe electrical shock.

- People who may appear dead after a lightning strike *may* be able to be revived if quick action is taken. If you must make a choice between injured individuals, treat those who are not breathing first—those who are unconscious but still breathing are more likely to come out of it on their own.

- For victims not breathing within a few minutes after being struck, an AED should be used, or CPR should be administered by trained personnel, if possible, according to recommendations of the American Heart Association or American Red Cross.

When to Cancel or Delay for Lightning

Thunderstorms can develop quickly on hot, humid days. This means race officials must always be prepared to make a decision based on rapidly changing conditions. For the most part, though, storms will necessitate only a delay in the event, not an outright cancellation. This is why communication with weather officials in the vicinity of the event can be key. The old adage "If you can hear it, clear it," is frequently put forth as the standard for delaying the start of the race. Consider implementing the "30-30" rule, which says if the lightning and thunder are within 30 seconds of each other, delay the event until 30 minutes after the last clap of thunder. Cancellation must be considered when the storms continue over a longer period of time.

Heat

Other than potentially deadly lightning, heat and humidity are a runner's greatest enemy. Activity at medical tents rises dramatically when temperatures move much above 60°F, especially if accompanied by high humidity.

Aid stations will become more important in warm weather. The operation of aid stations is covered in *Chapter 16: Race Logistics and*

Operations.

The American College of Sports Medicine has produced guidelines regarding how a race should consider reacting to various weather conditions. The ACSM has purposely avoided creating a strict cancellation standard, stating that it does not want to handcuff race directors; rather it offers recommendations about the course of action that should be taken in various weather conditions. The temperatures in the ACSM guidelines are all wet bulb globe temperatures (WBGTs). The WBGT is an index that takes into account heat (dry bulb), humidity (wet bulb), and the ambient temperature (black bulb, which factors in additional variables such as reflected heat and wind). A WBGT thermometer can be purchased from a medical supply house. The ACSM guidelines are as follows:

WBGT >82°F (>28°C) Black Flag: Cancel or recommend voluntary withdrawal. (Races that are always held in these conditions should acknowledge the extreme heat risk to the poorly acclimated and non-resident competitors in the pre-race literature and the pre-race announcements.)

WBGT 73°F - 82°F (23°C - 28°C) Red Flag: Recommend participants at increased risk for heat collapse withdraw from race and others slow pace to match conditions.

WBGT 65°F - 72°F (18°C - 22°C) Yellow Flag: Recommend participants at increased risk for heat collapse to slow their pace. Warn participants of increased risk of heat collapse.

WBGT <65°F (<18°C) Green Flag: Collapse can still occur. Decreased risk of hyperthermic and hypothermic collapse.

WBGT <50°F (<10°C) White Flag: Increased risk of hypothermic collapse.

When to Cancel or Delay for High Heat or Humidity

Fortunately for the safety of race participants, it has become much more acceptable in recent years for events to cancel due to excessive heat and humidity. Many races use the ACSM guideline for black flag conditions as the standard to cancel or shorten their events, or at least turn them into non-competitive fun runs. For more on cancellation, see *A Cancellation or Alteration Plan,* below.

Obtaining Heat Information

If you are planning a race and would like to know about the likelihood of high temperature and humidity on the proposed event date, visit a very helpful website maintained by the Zunis Foundation at www.zunis.org. The site provides historical heat index values for over 100 U.S. cities hourly for an entire year. In addition, the site provides a wealth of information on the effects of heat on various sporting activities, including running.

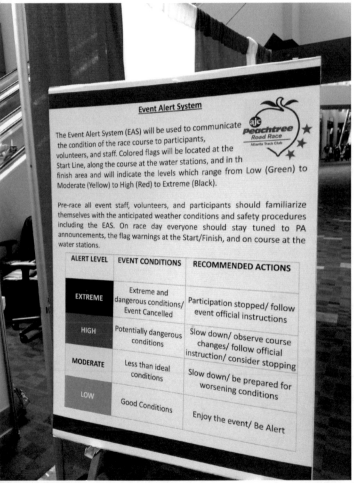

Phil Stewart

The "Event Alert System" is used widely by many large events as a guide to weather conditions. This sign was used at the Peachtree Road Race, held in hot and humid Atlanta, GA every July 4; hence there was no need to include White Flag conditions.

High Winds

The biggest danger from high winds is injury from blowing debris or falling trees. When the wind exceeds 20-30 mph, race officials should go into a heightened risk-management mode. The entire race site should be evaluated for objects that could turn into projectiles. Overhead scaffolds are a primary risk—if they are draped with nylon banners, the banners can act as giant sails, with a chance that the entire structure can blow over; if the scaffolds have fixed cardboard or metal signs, these signs can be ripped off and fly into the crowds below. Other potential hazards to consider include hanging signs, signs mounted on barricades at street level, feather banners on poles, balloon arches, and digital clocks. As wind speeds increase, even items such as staked tents and porta-johns also become hazards.

When to Cancel or Delay for High Winds

Frequently, winds will accompany other forms of severe weather. Cancellation should be considered when flying debris poses a significant threat to runners, spectators or volunteers.

Cold, Ice and Snow

The effect of extremely cold temperatures is certainly less dramatic than the effect of excessive heat. However, runners can begin to experience hypothermia starting at temperatures as high as 50°F. This is most likely to happen in situations where they have dropped out of the race and are being exposed to wind and cold in their still-damp running clothing. If the race will be run in the dead of winter, try to finish at a location that has an indoor space for the runners to warm up and enjoy their post-race refreshments. A large tent, possibly with space heaters, can also serve this purpose. Be sure to provide hot drinks and warming blankets. A few very large races provide warming buses along the course. Ice and snow can create additional risks due to slippery footing. Consideration should be given to canceling or altering the course of a race if there are significant ice patches that could result in slips and falls to participants, as well as present hazardous conditions for official vehicles or participants traveling to or from the event.

When to Cancel or Delay for Cold or Snow

The decision to cancel or delay may depend on the typical weather in the area in which the event is held – basically what the runners are used to. The director of a race in southern Florida may see fit to cancel his event for low temperatures that would be perfectly acceptable in New England, for example. The Twin Cities Marathon in Minneapolis-St. Paul sets a cancellation policy of 0°F for the October event. As a race director, use your best judgment when it comes to winter weather-related cancellation. Race directors should be aware that municipal governments may cancel events on their own volition if ice and snow force them to concentrate their resources elsewhere. The small print on most permit applications gives them this right.

A Cancellation or Alteration Plan

In 2012, the New York City Marathon was cancelled in the aftermath of "Super Storm Sandy." A couple of years earlier, the Boston Marathon came very close to being scrubbed in the face of a nor'easter. These incidents prove that cancellation is possible for any event—even very large ones that require massive planning. So, advance preparation for such a contingency is necessary. Large events and/or those run on city streets may have their fates dictated by the permitting jurisdiction, taking the decision out of the hands of the race director. It is worth establishing a rapport well before race day with the municipal officials who may decide the event's fate, so that they may involve you in the actual decision-making process.

Thus, it is certainly best to come up with a plan for cancellation, postponement or alteration of the race course. For smaller events, the final choice to make a change may be more or less a "gut" decision. Still, race directors should have some agreed-upon parameters to begin the evaluation process. Be aware that, whatever option you choose, someone is going to complain about it.

Most race directors reserve the right to cancel by stating directly on the registration form and/or as part of the waiver that organizers have the right to cancel, postpone or alter the event. While postponement may be an option for small, local races, it is generally not viable for larger events with significant numbers of out-of-towners, who cannot reschedule their travel on short notice. This means that, for larger races, the choice typically comes down to cancellation or alteration (either shortening the course, turning the event into an untimed fun run, or both).

A note about the waiver: Even if it is stated on the registration form that the "event will be held rain or shine," you will still want to include a disclaimer in the waiver about cancellation. While the event may go forward in a heavy downpour, hurricane conditions may warrant cancellation.

Whatever you end up deciding to do on race day, the issues listed below should be addressed in advance. Make as few policy decisions as possible in the heat of the moment, when circumstances will not be conducive to calm reflection.

- *Refunds?* Nearly all races state that there are no refunds in the event of cancellation. Some have softened this stance, offering discounted registrations to the following year's event or some similar type of concession. It is extremely rare for an event to offer a full refund because many expenses are incurred prior to race day. In general, runners seem to be understanding of this fact. Some events offer cancellation insurance for participants. (For details about these policies, see *Chapter 9: Insurance and Legal*.)

- *Prize money.* If the event offers prize money, what will be done with it? Some races give it away as random awards; most put it into the race reserves or use it to offset other expenses resulting from the cancellation.

- **Timing and scoring:** If the format of the event is changed to non-competitive, most directors remove clocks from the mile marks and finish line and do not record any times or places. Aid stations, medical facilities, communications networks, and other amenities remain in place.

- **Timetable for making and announcing the change:** Certainly, if the possibility of cancellation or alteration exists, the runners should be informed as soon as possible. This

is often a difficult call because, especially with weather, conditions can change quickly. For a large event, the decision may have to be made as much as 24-48 hours in advance, when tents and other equipment need to be placed, or hours before, when shuttle buses start rolling to the staging area; for smaller events, the call can be made as close as 15 minutes before the start. The public relations problem is, of course, that weather forecasting is an inexact science and conditions may not end up as extreme as the advance forecasts

Frank Nielsen

Although few races are cancelled due to just rain unless there is lightning, the 2017 Copenhagen Marathon was stopped at the two-hour mark when these conditions prevailed at the finish line of the concurrent Copenhagen Half Marathon.

predicted. Once a decision is made, don't look back or second guess the decision. Others will; the race director should not.

Social media is an excellent way to keep runners aware of the possibility of cancellation or alteration of the event, especially more 'immediate' forms of social media, like Twitter, that users often set up with push notifications that pop up on their mobile devices. As soon as there is even a question as to whether the event will proceed as planned, social media can be used to tell runners to stay tuned for further updates about the status of the event. Consider posting the same information prominently on the event website, as well. If the event provides text messaging services or has an app, those provide excellent avenues for quickly reaching the runners who have signed up for those services. Get the word out via every possible avenue and encourage runners to spread the word to other race

registrants that they know. And of course, make frequent updates to the status, letting runners know as soon as possible if the event actually does need to be cancelled or changed.

If the weather changes for the worse quickly, or for some other reason possibility of cancellation arises when the runners are already at the race site, be sure to have the race announcer alert runners to the situation as soon as he or she begins announcing.

- **Late registration?** Registration can remain open until the decision is made, as long as registrars let everyone know that the race may be altered.

Security

The world of organized running events changed forever on Monday, April 15, 2013 when two brothers detonated two pressure-cooker bombs

Police presence in the post-race interview area at the TCS New York City Marathon.

Phil Stewart

12 seconds apart on Boylston Street, near the finish line of the Boston Marathon, killing three spectators and injuring over 250 others. Ramped-up security had certainly been on the minds of many event directors — especially for the New York City Marathon — in the aftermath of the September 11, 2001 terrorist attacks, but conventional thinking was that even the largest running events paled as potential terrorist targets in comparison with huge, compact venues like the Super Bowl. However, increasing numbers of "lone wolf" terrorists—like the brothers in Boston, who were not formally trained or part of an organized attack by a formal terrorist group—have pushed security concerns more into the forefront of race planning.

Security planning extends beyond terrorist attacks, since running events have also been sites of protests and other forms of civil disobedience. This is the potential dark side to the success and visibility of large-scale, urban running events.

Size Does Matter

The need for a security plan is very closely correlated with the size and visibility of the event. (Size itself is not the only factor— what events like the Olympic Trials Marathon and the Olympic Marathon lack in size, they more than make up for in visibility.) Still, even smaller events can take the most basic step of educating volunteers and participants in the "see something, say something" mantra, telling them to notify the race organizers or law enforcement personnel if "something doesn't seem right." Larger races have definitely instituted or tightened security procedures in the

wake of Boston, while for smaller events, it's been pretty much business as usual.

The Challenges of Running Events

From the perspective of security personnel, running events are a nightmare. Unlike the security at stadiums or arenas where entry is controlled at a limited number of locations, running events may be spread over vast sections of cities, making the scanning of both participants and spectators a huge challenge, if not, in many instances, impossible. This makes races "soft targets," in security parlance. In the years since the Boston Marathon bombings, race officials and security personnel have agonized over how to provide for the safety of the participants and spectators while still allowing everyone to enjoy the experience of the event, mirroring the public sentiment about not letting the terrorists "win" by causing massive disruptions in people's lifestyles.

General Security Measures

Security measures undertaken by running events can range from very simple steps that are easy to implement and free/very low cost, all the

Security fencing at the Bank of America Chicago Marathon.   Phil Stewart

way to advanced, personnel- and cost-intensive measures. As previously stated, the degree of security appropriate for a given race is dependent on how much of a 'target' the event poses. Unfortunately, this can never be known with certainty, so these days all race directors would be wise to adopt at least the most basic of security measures. The general security measures outlined below are divided into two categories — preparations focused on runners and preparations focused on event organizers. They are listed from simple and widely applicable to increasingly complex measures that are more appropriate for high-profile, higher risk events. The simplest measures cost little to nothing to implement, while the more advanced measures can be quite expensive, particularly if you need to contract with a security company. Very high-profile events may have certain security measures 'enforced' by local authorities or even by the DHS or other federal enforcement agencies. In all cases, if security measures will be implemented that directly impact the participants or spectators, for example 'no backpacks' or 'spectators must go through security,' make sure to communicate these procedures to the participants and spectators well in advance, through emails, the event website and social media. Pre-race communication about measures that may be viewed as 'inconvenient' will prepare the participants and spectators to cooperate, which will both help the security procedures to move along more smoothly as well as reduce potential race-day frustration for all parties involved.

Activities Focused on Runners

- **Provide "see some-thing, say something" warnings.** This is the simplest possible security procedure. It doesn't cost anything, take much time, or require a large number of volunteers. Through email, social media, and postings on the event website, encourage everyone at the event—participants, spectators, volunteers, sponsors—to immediately report any and all suspicious activity to a race official or to law enforcement. Some obvious examples include unattended backpacks or packages, individuals acting furtively, and vehicles in inappropriate locations. Make sure that the volunteers and race officials know exactly what actions to take in the event that suspicious activity is reported to them. Establish a chain of command so that everyone immediately knows who to call with the information.

- **Require IDs for bib pick-up.** While certainly not foolproof, this straightforward, no-cost security measure at least assures that the individual picking up the bib is the same person who is registered for the race. If you decide to implement this procedure, have a clear plan for how to deal with runners who come in without ID, or those

Phil Stewart

Security signs for participants at the TCS New York City Marathon.

who want to pick up multiple bibs for their family/friends.

- **Use clear plastic bag-check bags.** This is a fairly easy measure that has been successfully implemented by many races with bag checks. In the past, runners would check everything from back packs to duffle bags to coolers to luggage, but the clear plastic bags make it easy for volunteers to do a quick check to see whether there may be something suspicious inside. For an increased level of security, bags can be scanned using an airport-type scanner, or bomb-sniffing dogs can be employed to examine the checked bags. The clear plastic bags can either be distributed at bag check itself or earlier, at packet pickup.

- **Ban hydration packs for runners.** In the months immediately following the Boston Marathon bombing, some races went so far as to ban runners from wearing hydration packs, out of concern that these packs could conceal an explosive device. Although most races have softened their stance on this over the intervening years, some still insist that runners use a bladder-type bag only, not the type with a backpack attached.

- **Scan bags as participants/spectators enter controlled areas.** Bag scan can be performed either manually, using trained security personnel to look inside bags, or via an airport-type bag scanner. Bag scan can be performed wherever there is restricted

access—at the expo or at the entrance to cordoned-off areas around the start/finish.

- **Perform security scans on participants/ spectators themselves.** If the highest possible degree of security is necessary at the event, you will want to scan individuals as well as any bags they may be carrying. Security companies will be able to provide walk-through, airport-type scanners, so that you can establish security check-points at any locations that have restricted access, including the expo and the start/finish areas. All individuals involved with the race should be scanned, including sponsors, vendors and charities—just make sure to notify these individuals in advance so that they can arrive early enough to get through security before beginning any set-up they need to do, either at the expo or at the race site.

Phil Stewart

An elevated police viewing station at the Publix Gasparilla Distance Classic.

- **Ban bags or backpacks (for spectators and/or runners) in race area.** Race directors who want to amp up security at their events but do not wish to employ higher-tech security measures   such as manual bag-check procedures or airport-type scanners can choose to completely ban backpacks (or all bags larger than a small purse) at the event, particularly in the start/finish areas. Be aware that this can be extremely difficult to enforce, unless there is strictly controlled access to these areas. No matter how well this rule is publicized in advance, there will undoubtedly be individuals who attempt to bring such bags into the start/finish areas. Be aware that some individuals may heatedly object to the 'no bags' rule, so if you are using volunteers instead of security personnel for enforcement, make sure they are thick-skinned and well-trained in the chosen manner of handling potentially difficult individuals.

Activities Focused on Event Organizers

- **Monitor social media activity.** This is another free measure that can easily be implemented for any race with a social media presence. The race director or a designated volunteer should keep an eye on all social media postings, looking for anything hateful, unusual, or otherwise suspicious. If such messages are observed, local law enforcement should be notified. Depending on the visibility of the event, law enforcement personnel may themselves monitor the social media activity for the race, but race directors or their designees can certainly be on alert or suspicious postings as well.

- **Develop a rigorous credentials program:** For most races, the credential programs are not extremely vigorous; badges are generally used to easily identify key personnel with "All Areas" or "Staff" credentials. If security is tight, you will need to develop a much more detailed credentialing program with more levels and specific areas of access (and more stringent

monitoring of credentials). Some high profile races will include photos on credentials for the most key individuals. (See *Chapter 16: Race Logistics and Operations* for details about a credentials program.)

- **Establish a clear chain of command within the race organization** and develop job descriptions for all personnel who might be involved in an emergency response.

- **Prepare, rehearse and disseminate evacuation procedures.**

- **Encourage dialog and relationship building among members of emergency response teams, local law enforcement and organizing committee members.**

- **Develop scripts and protocols for various groups for different security threats:** These groups might consist of runners near the site of the security breach, others on the course, spectators and the public not present at the event.

- **Use roving security personnel.** Work with local law enforcement to discuss their recommendations for the event. If you are holding a fairly small, low-profile event, the visible presence of a few uniformed police officers can serve to deter possible incidents as well as to put participants and spectators at ease about event security. Directors of large, high-profile events may want to hire a security service or work directly with DHS. Long-distances races like marathons might even choose to monitor course security from the air using a helicopter. Of course, the more manpower and equipment that is used, the higher the security costs will be.

- **Sweep the course for suspicious packages.** Course sweeps should be performed by individuals in the security field who are trained for such work. Depending on the particular security concerns and budget for the event, multiple sweeps can be performed—the week before, the day before, and the morning of the event, for example.

- **Check/seal mailboxes and garbage cans along the course.** In order to avoid the possibility of explosive devices being planted in hidden locations such as garbage cans or mailboxes, directors of some races choose to work with local municipalities to either seal or remove trash cans/mailboxes from the course. Never tamper with public trash cans or mailboxes yourself—always work through the channels appropriate for the particular jurisdiction. Removing all garbage cans from the course clearly creates a whole new set of problems, since runners will have nowhere to properly dispose of cups, empty water bottles, wrappers, or anything else they may need to throw away. Obviously, additional volunteers will need to be employed for trash collection/cleanup if garbage cans are removed. Have the volunteers collect the trash in clear plastic garbage bags, so the contents can be easily seen.

- **Employ bomb-sniffing dogs.** Trained personnel with these dogs can be used for multiple purposes—for sweeping the course, searching checked bags, or just walking through/scanning crowds at the expo or in the start/finish areas.

- **Institute controlled access to start and finish areas.** The difficulty of restricting access to the start/finish areas will clearly vary by venue. For some courses, it will be relatively easy to restrict access using snow fencing or French barricades, while for other courses this may prove logistically impossible or cost-prohibitive. Analyze the start finish area(s) carefully to determine whether restricted access is even an option. If you are designing a race course from scratch, consider selecting start/finish areas based on the possibility of restricting access, if it becomes necessary. Access to the start area should be limited to two points—one for runners and the other for spectators. Depending on the security needs of the event, spectators can pass through the necessary security (bag check/

scan, metal detector, etc.) and then receive a pass/wristband indicating that they are "allowed" in the restricted area. Only runners wearing bibs should be allowed through the runners' entrance, a method that also helps to prevent bandits from running in the event.

Working with Law Enforcement and Security Firms — "Tabletop Exercises"

Virtually every race should work to establish a good relationship with local law enforcement, regardless of the security measures needed for the event. However, if security is warranted, solid relationships with these authorities are particularly important, since local law enforcement can certainly assist in implementing the event's security procedures. Early on in event planning, contact and set up a meeting with the appropriate individual(s) from the local police department to discuss the security concerns and plans for the event. Ask that the individuals who will be directly involved in the event's security procedures attend the meeting. Sometimes called "Tabletop exercises," these discussions involve coordinating anti-terrorism plans and other action plans for emergency scenarios among all relevant agencies and will help to assure a professional, effective response to any threat that is faced by the event.

While the involvement of local law enforcement will definitely increase security at the event, some of the more involved security measures, such as performing security scans on bags and/or individuals, may be beyond the purview of local authorities, especially if the event is held in a small jurisdiction. In such a case, the race director may wish to employ the services of a private security firm. Be sure to carefully check the reputation of any security firm you consider hiring, and get a detailed, written quote for the services they will provide, to make sure that the event's budget can accommodate the additional cost.

Whether you choose to employ only local law enforcement or a private security firm, work hard to maintain a good relationship with them and listen to their advice. Not only do they have far superior expertise in these areas, but law enforcement and security personnel will also do much behind the scenes to keep the event safe—possibly things that the participants, spectators, and even the race director might never know about.

Unified Command Centers

In the event of a race-day emergency, such as an accident or fire on the course, a terrorist incident or unsafe weather conditions, the decision to close the course or cancel the race needs to be made and communicated quickly. To facilitate this rapid response, many larger events set up a unified command center. an office or trailer where representatives of the race and all the federal, state and local agencies needed to make the decision are all in a single location. If the race passes through multiple police jurisdictions, all of them are represented. This ensures that everyone who needs to have input into the decision is in a single location at the same time. The largest UCCs will have live feeds from security cameras out on the course

shown on monitors to monitor security. Even smaller races should plan to have a race official alongside law enforcement personnel in an established location to facilitate a rapid response to any emergency.

Contingency Plans

Certainly, the 2013 Boston Marathon bombings reinforced the necessity of contingency plans to cover such items as suspension of the race, mass evacuation procedures, on-course shelters, as well as scripted messages provided to runners and spectators regarding any emergency situation. See *Chapter 21: Before Next Year* for details about creating a contingency plan.

Terrorism/Other Additional Insurance

Unfortunately, the standard RRCA and USATF insurance policies for road races do not cover acts of terrorism. Although policies can be purchased that do include some combination of terrorist threat, terrorist act and bomb threat riders, these policies may prove prohibitively expensive for most races.

Another insurance option to consider, if it's

Phil Stewart

Inside the Boston Marathon's Unified Command Center near the finish line.

within the event's budget, is sporting event spectator insurance, which offers general liability coverage protection for all spectators at a given sporting event. If you are interested in this type of coverage, make sure that it covers events of your particular distance and size, and check out the limits to ensure that they are adequate. Also, be aware that many sporting event spectator insurance policies also have terrorism exclusions, so again you may have to pay extra to obtain that type of coverage.

To prepare for the contingency of race cancellation due to an act of terrorism *prior* to the start of the race (and other contingencies such as adverse weather and natural catastrophes), some races decide to purchase event cancellation coverage. This coverage serves to refund registration fees to all of the registrants at no cost to the race, which can really make the participants happy in the event of a cancellation. While, like all non-standard policies, this insurance may often be prohibitively expensive, some reasonably priced options are becoming available. For example, certain online registration companies (or at least one that we are aware of at the time of this writing) may provide cancellation insurance for only a slight percentage increase in the existing service fee (which is often paid by the registrant). This type of insurance may be an extremely viable option for cancellation coverage, however, be aware that, at least in the case of the currently existing example, this coverage only applies to terrorist acts that have *already occurred*, not to the *threat* of terrorist activities. So, if you are forced to cancel an event because security officials have obtained information about a *potential* terrorist attack directed at that event, the cancellation insurance will not apply. This insurance also does not cover an event that is cancelled after it has officially started.

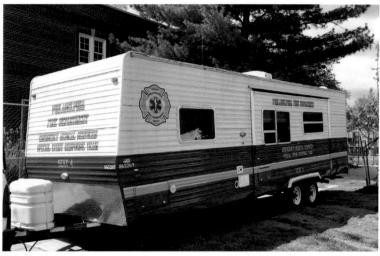

Phil Stewart

A mobile UCC van used at Philadelphia's Blue Cross Broad Street Run

Budgeting for Security

Although all race directors want their events to be as safe as possible, these security needs must be balanced with the reality of the race budget. As mentioned above, some simple security measures, such as "see something, say something" are basically free to implement, but many others come with significant additional costs. Fees for additional police and/or security personnel, as well as the rental of security equipment such as airport-type scanners, can add up very quickly. The cost of additional fencing to enclose a large start/finish area or to keep spectators off of a roadway can also be staggering. Additional security costs may include other expensive items such as the insurance options described above, down to relatively less costly items such as additional security-related signage. The bottom line is this: no matter how much money is spent, there is no guarantee that a violent act will not occur at the event. But if the appropriate steps are taken, you will be doing the best you can to keep the event participants and spectators safe. First, work with the race committee/security team to honestly assess the security needs of the race and make a list of the

Law enforcement officials have responded to terror attacks involving vehicles being driven into crowds by blocking roadways with heavy vehicles like dump trucks, snow plows or trash trucks.

security measures the team would like to implement. Then, do the requisite legwork to find out how much these measures will set the event back, monetarily. Last, hold further discussions with the security team to determine the best way to balance the security needs of the event with the additional costs involved, possibly focusing on ways to obtain the additional revenue necessary to implement the appropriate security measures.

In the Event of an Emergency...

Despite the tightest of security measures, the unthinkable can still happen. In the event that a terrorist attack or other violent incident *does* occur at the event, the best you can do is to be prepared for it. Well in advance of the event, talk with the race team and possibly with security experts (even DHS if the race is high-profile) about various potential scenarios that the event could face. Try to have solid, written plans in place for dealing with every possible contingency and make sure the entire team is well aware of these plans.

Communications

In the event of a terrorist attack of the magnitude of the Boston Marathon bombings, be aware that cell phone service may be turned off by security officials or the cell networks may simply be overloaded. Both HAM radios and walkie-talkie type radios are more likely to be functioning. If the event is a plausible venue for a terrorist attack, make sure to have a robust, back-up communications network.

Closing the Course

In the event that a violent incident occurs while the race is in progress, it is very important to have a plan for shutting down the race and getting everyone off the course quickly and safely. Since it is impossible to predict where on the course an incident might occur, the shut-down plan may need to include several different scenarios. Depending on the distance of the race, runner transportation back to the finish (or to an alternative, pre-determined location, if the finish is the site of the incident) may need to be arranged from various points on the course. The shut-down plan should be established well before race day, and the entire race team, including volunteers, should be aware of the procedures that will ensue in the event of an incident. If it's possible, hold a meeting with the race committee to specifically discuss these procedures, or even better, perform "drills," so that everyone can be as prepared as possible for the various potential scenarios that could occur.

If runners do need to be evacuated from the course and cannot return to the finish area, they will still need to be reunited with their bags at some point. If a terrorist incident occurs in the vicinity of the checked bags, it is possible that the runners will not receive their bags for quite a while, since the area will be treated as a crime scene during the investigation. Be prepared to deal with runners who may have left important items like cell phones, wallets, and car keys in their checked bags, since some runners will invariably check these items even if they are clearly told not to check valuables. In advance of the event, determine a plan for getting the bags back to the runners, if need be. Even if they have to wait a few days, most runners will be understanding and cooperative if they get clear information and feel that there is an established plan in place.

Dealing With Injuries

The race's medical team will likely serve as the first responders to any casualties incurred in the event of a violent incident at the event. Qualified medical personnel, especially EMTs or those who work in emergency rooms, will already be trained in the methods necessary to turn the medical tent from a site to treat simple things like dehydration and ankle sprains to an emergency response center. Work with the medical team to come up with a written plan, including a triage system to sort patients with critical injuries from those with minor injuries. The emergency medical plan should also specifically detail which hospital emergency rooms will be contacted, as well as specify the individual who will be responsible for hospital contact. If there are a large number of injuries or only a small number of local hospitals, the triage plan becomes especially important to ensure that the most critically injured individuals are transported to the hospital first.

After an Emergency

Communication With Participants

If an act of terrorism or other violent event does occur at or before the race, follow-up communication with participants in the days following the incident will be crucial. This communication can take many forms, including local emergency alert systems, information on the event website, emails, texts and social media postings. The event participants will look to you both for the details of what happened as well as for information about what's next, both for them personally (e.g., how they will recover their checked bags) and for the event (e.g., whether a race cancelled before the start will be rescheduled) Expect lots of questions, and prioritize them so that the most important questions, such as those that affect the greatest number of participants, get answered first. As the event director, you will feel that you should answer all questions immediately, but it's very likely that you will not be able to do so. Accept that it is OK not to have all the answers, but stay in close communication with the public and ensure them that all questions will be answered in time.

Participants Who Do Not Finish

If an act of terrorism or other violence results in cancellation of the race while some participants are still on the course, you will want to consider how to deal with these individuals, in terms of whether to consider them finishers. In the weeks following the 2013 Boston Marathon bombing, the BAA declared the 5,000+ runners who were past the half way point on the course when it was closed to be finishers. Not only were these participants sent medals along with their projected finish times, but they were invited back to the 2014 race without having to re-qualify. A similar policy is advised for any event in this situation, as it will definitely engender goodwill in the wake of an otherwise traumatic experience.

Tribute/Memorial Runs

The events in Boston clearly demonstrated the cohesiveness of the running community—the response to the bombing was nearly instantaneous and very heartfelt. Within days after the bombing, a number of tribute/memorial runs were organized in the region and across the nation. It is likely that the same response would happen in the wake of another violent incident at a running event.

What happens if........

Electrocuted Participant died after race Race committee member hit a bystander in **trying to** Property stolen after **Runners collided** Pulled muscle cart-vehicle **move a** lock cut on race truck **at a group run** while running **Bit by dog** **tent** Runners collided at an event Course support person fell off bike **during a race** Participant struck by car on race Fell on wet Volunteer dropped table on Participant struck in the face course pavement leg while moving expo items by feather banner Rental van hit car **Struck by** Tripped - broken teeth **Slander charges** **a baby stroller** Tripped on Event spectator collapsed and **during a race** broken road was airlifted to the hospital Fall in finisher chute - broken surface Fell out of truck while dropping Fell, Finish line fencing finger **Runner** off aid station supplies injured wrist fell and knocked **fainted at 5k** **Wild animal attack on course** over participants Phone ruined during rainstorm Fractured ankle on trail run Race officials damaged city fountain with rental truck Runner hit during group run Heart attack during group run Fell on ice, fractured leg **Tripped -** in busy intersection after not **Wind blew tent** Participant **fractured / hurt leg** following traffic signals **into participants** hit their head at an expo vendor's booth

The Road Runners Club of America has you covered!

The RRCA offers a variety of programs and services designed to support local running clubs, events, run specialty businesses, and more.

- General liability coverage for athletic events including participant accident coverage
- Volunteer medical personnel malpractice liability coverage
- Business and operations insurance coverage
- Group music license program with discounted rates for BMI and ASCAP
- And much more!

RRCA.ORG

Phil Stewart

9 Insurance and Legal

THE BASICS

- **Insurance.** If you are putting on a road race, you must have insurance. There are simply too many risks for which you, or the organizing club or committee, could be held responsible. Liability insurance is the most essential coverage to obtain, but there are a number of other types of policies to consider, including equipment, cancellation and directors/officers coverage (if you are incorporated). Fortunately, insurance is easy to obtain from the Road Runners Club of America (RRCA, www.rrca.org) or USA Track & Field (USATF, www.usatf.org), or an independent provider can be used.

- **Contracts.** Everything contracted for should be put in writing. You may think that a verbal agreement is sufficient for small deals, but the best way to avoid miscommunication and ensure that you have recourse in the case of non-delivery is to get everything in writing.

- **Waivers.** Make sure the registration form includes a waiver and that *all participants* sign it. While not absolute protection against a liability judgment, it certainly strengthens your case to enter a courtroom with a signed waiver in hand. Make sure the waiver *specifically enumerates* the risks specific to running a road race, such as potholes in the road, excessive heat and/or humidity, excessive cold, etc. Do not let anyone run without signing a waiver. Races should have their volunteers sign waivers as well.

- **Music Licensing.** Legally, no one can publicly perform copyrighted works without the permission of the copyright owner, and the owner has the right to be paid for the use of his or her property. Music licenses are required from the licensing agencies whenever copyrighted songs are performed live or otherwise played at public events. This means that virtually all races are legally required to obtain music licenses.

THE DETAILS

Putting on a road race can be a lot of fun and is rewarding, but few race directors would put coping with insurance and legal issues at the top of their list of job highlights. Nonetheless, there are some issues in these areas that need to be considered, regardless of the size of the event.

When the race committee is assembled, you might find it worthwhile to consider including someone with a background in risk management and insurance. This individual can help you anticipate the risks associated with the event and evaluate the insurance coverage, seeking to fill any holes. This expertise could prove invaluable if the race is later hit with a lawsuit.

It All Starts with Risk Management

One of the most important aspects of race management is to reduce, as much as possible, all risk of accidents or mishaps to all associated with the event. This should be the main goal of the entire race organization. Obviously, not all problems can be foreseen and prevented, however, so obtaining sufficient insurance will also be critical for the continued success of the event.

As you plan the event, consider everything that can go wrong, examining how course route and traffic control can best be arranged to minimize hazards and provide adequate security, medical coverage, etc. These are all part of the standard planning that any well-run event should engage in.

What can you do to minimize the potential for an accident? How can you best manage access to the course while maximizing security? What is the best way to handle crowd control? Is the scaffolding designed to withstand high winds or is there a wind-speed guideline for taking it down? Does the race have a "disaster" or contingency plan? Whatever can be done to reduce exposure and make the race safe *should* be done. A risk management plan also identifies in advance the available options and alternatives to be put in place in the event that an identified risk occurs.

Obtaining Insurance Coverage

Most U.S. running events obtain coverage through policies offered by the Road Runners Club of America (RRCA) or USA Track & Field (USATF). If a race is being organized by a parent organization (for example, when the race is a fundraising event for an established nonprofit corporation) the parent organization may have insurance that will cover the event. A small number of events obtain insurance on their own, but these policies are likely to be more expensive because the event is not coming in as part of a larger group. (In rare instances, insurance coverage can be provided as an in-kind contribution from a sponsoring insurance company.) While these basic insurance packages, whether from the RRCA, USATF, or a third-party provider, cannot insulate the event from every type of lawsuit, they do offer excellent coverage for many of the run of the mill occurrences that can happen in the course of putting on a running event.

The RRCA's information is at www.rrca.org (click on "Services" on the horizontal links near the top of the page and then click on "Insurance") or through the RRCA National Office: Phone: 703-525-3890; Email: membership@rrca.org. RRCA insurance is sold to RRCA club members and event members on an annual basis and covers all events conducted by the club or event member.

USATF's information is at www.usatf.org (click on "Resources For..." in the upper right corner of the horizontal links across the top of the website and then click on "Event Directors"), or through the office: Phone: 317-261-0500; Email: sanctions@usatf.org. USATF insurance is sold on an event-by-event basis and is tied to purchasing a USATF event sanction (a sanction is basically the organization's imprimatur that the event is safe and conducted in accordance with USATF rules and regulations), so on the "Event Directors" link, click the option for "Event Sanctioning," which will eventually lead to details about purchasing insurance.

Disclaimer: When arranging for insurance, it is extremely important that you understand the terms of the policy. General details about each organization's policies are included below, although any policy should be reviewed by an experienced insurance professional. In addition, changes can occur in these policies from year to year, so you should go to each organization's website for the latest information. The information below represents details about all of the policies *at the time of publication of this book.*

General Liability and Participant Accident Insurance

Very few race directors today would be foolish enough to put on even a small event without General Liability and Participant Accident Insurance. A general liability insurance policy is the most critical. No event should take place

without this type of policy in place. Proof of liability insurance coverage is mandatory for any event that is sanctioned by USATF or any club or event member of the RRCA. Both organizations will accept proof of insurance from the other organization (e.g. an RRCA member event can use USATF's insurance and a USATF-sanctioned event can use the RRCA's insurance—or the event must hold an equivalent insurance policy from another source).

General liability insurance covers litigation and any settlement costs caused by negligence on the part of the race organization. Settlements have been awarded for such things as collapsing structures, electrocutions from exposed wires, porta-johns blown over by high winds, and injuries from extreme weather conditions, etc.—anything that a court determines occurred because the organizers behaved in a manner that put the participants (or volunteers, etc.) at an unacceptable level of risk. People will file suit even if their claims have no merit, and defending a claim, even if it is frivolous, can run into the tens of thousands of dollars, often even more; settlements can reach millions of dollars. Since few clubs or events have the financial resources to deal with these claims on their own, general liability insurance is a must. With the proper insurance, the cost of legal expenses and settlements can be passed on to an insurance carrier rather than having to come from the coffers of the club or event. By contrast, a Participant Medical Policy (discussed below) provides coverage of costs associated with treating an injured individual regardless of any liability on the part of the event organizers.

General Liability Insurance

The basic USATF policy provides up to $1,000,000 for each occurrence, with a general aggregate ceiling of $3,000,000 per event. The RRCA offers a tiered program with the choice of either $1,000,000 or $2,000,000 for each occurrence, each with no general aggregate ceiling (meaning there is no cap on the total amount that it will pay for all claims combined).

USATF does offer an additional excess policy that carries up to $10,000,000 in coverage after the first $3,000,000 is paid by the liability policy. The single-occurrence limit on the RRCA policy can be increased in increments of $1 million as well. Additional premiums must be paid in all of these instances.

The RRCA's insurance policy requires that clubs, events, or event management companies be dues-paying members of the RRCA to obtain RRCA insurance coverage. For organized running clubs, the RRCA insurance covers all events owned and organized by the club, which includes expos, race set-up, and tear down. Coverage also includes a club's ancillary activities, including training runs, social events, banquets, meetings, seminars, and picnics. For events and event management companies, coverage includes expo, race set-up, the event, and tear down. Event and event management companies conducting training programs will need to purchase an additional policy to cover these activities. It is important to note that clubs and event management companies hired by a third party to conduct a race on behalf of the third party **are not covered** under the club's or the event management company's insurance. Transference of RRCA insurance coverage to a third party is fraud. The third party must obtain insurance on its own through the RRCA, USATF or privately. The RRCA policy excludes coverage for fireworks, terrorism, fungi or bacteria and pollution or asbestos. The standard coverage also does not include high-risk events such as overnight relay races run on open roads, mud-runs, "warrior dashes," and urban-athons that include man-made obstacles.

USATF's insurance policy requires that events purchase a USATF sanction. A USATF sanction commits the organizer to certain basic standards of conduct and to using USATF rules. Unlike the RRCA policy, which allows an organizer to insure *all events* conducted by the organization with a single application, USATF sanctions are sold on a *per event* basis—event directors obtain a specific sanction and insurance policy for *each* separate

event (multiple events on a single day may be insured together). The USATF policy covers ancillary events including expos, awards ceremonies, etc. Post-race concerts and entertainment are excluded if a separate paid ticket is required. Running clubs can purchase liability coverage from USATF for their "*bona fide* club practices" (this means that they must be regularly scheduled and a certified coach must be present). If running clubs need insurance for additional activities, USATF will review their needs on a case-by-case basis.

If an event has RRCA insurance but is applying for a USATF sanction, USATF requires that the event submit a liability insurance waiver form. If an RRCA member event elects not to use the RRCA insurance but instead decides to get a sanction and insurance from USATF, no additional action is required on the part of the event to so notify the RRCA.

A word about exclusions: If a certain class of entrants, such as entrants with strollers, or those wearing headphones, or those running with dogs, is *excluded* from a liability policy, this means the insurance *will not cover* participants in these categories. While these are categories that race directors frequently discourage—or even ban—from participating for safety reasons, they will find relief if they are **not** excluded from the liability policy. So check the exclusions. The RRCA policy provides coverage for all the categories mentioned above because there is no exclusion for these groups. Be aware that drones are excluded from the RRCA policy.

Participant Accident/Medical Insurance: It is important to be aware that a general liability policy may or may not contain *participant accident coverage,* also referred to as *accidental medical coverage.* One should closely review insurance policy information to determine if participant accident coverage is included or if an additional policy is required. Participant accident coverage is not linked to liability on the part of the event, but provides coverage for medical costs if a runner, for example, falls or trips on the course and breaks his arm or teeth. The purpose of this type of policy is to provide coverage for unreimbursed medical costs to make an injured participant financially whole. This may reduce the possibility of a future liability lawsuit.

The RRCA participant accident/medical coverage comes as part of the general liability policy for events and includes coverage up to $10,000 per occurrence, over and above any other health insurance the injured party holds, with a $500 deductible. *Participants and volunteers for the event are not required to be individual members of the RRCA.*

The USATF participant accident/medical coverage is sold separately from the liability coverage and *is sold to individuals only, not to events.* The policy offers up to $10,000 of coverage over and above any other health insurance the injured party holds, with a 20% deductible on the first $5,000 of expenses. *Individuals must be USATF members and the event must be USATF sanctioned to be eligible for coverage.*

Below are some additional considerations regarding insurance for running events.

Additional Considerations

- **Costs for liability and participant medical coverage.** The USATF policy is offered as part of the USATF sanction. The sanction fee is the sum of a fixed national fee based on race size, plus an association fee that is also based on size but is variable from association to association (e.g., a 1,000-person race in the New England Association pays an association fee of $260; the same sized event in the Southern California Association pays $400). There are 57 USATF Associations in the U.S., each with their own Association sanction fee schedule. Exact pricing can be found on the USATF website (www.usatf.org). The cost of the RRCA policy is determined by a formula that, for running clubs, takes into account the number of club members, or for events or event management companies, takes into account the number of event participants. Exact pricing can be found on the RRCA website (www.rrca.org).

- **The application process.** The RRCA has a yearly application and fee for three main types of organizations: running clubs, events, and race management companies. Event membership is designed for stand-alone independent events that are not owned by a race-directing company or a running club and that occur only once a year. Event management companies are defined as companies that own multiple events that are hosted annually. RRCA insurance covers the activities of these organizations during the entire year for which they have paid for RRCA membership. USATF requires that each event apply for a sanction, which includes the general liability insurance on its own.

- **Certificates of additional insured:** Occasionally, a third party, such as a municipality or property owner, requests to be listed as an additionally insured party under an event's general liability insurance policy and will request an "additional insured certificate." Accepting this responsibility should not be taken lightly, as it means that *the event's* insurance company is taking on an additional exposure. If organizations— most likely sponsors and municipalities— require additional insured certificates, the certificates can be obtained through either the RRCA or USATF policy. Both the RRCA and USATF provide the certificates at no additional cost (although both require a rush fee when the request is submitted on short notice). There are a number of exclusions regarding who may be named as an additional insured, including timing companies, police departments, and other independent contractors who are paid for their work, as these organizations should have their own general liability policies and should be required to show proof of coverage. Be sure to check with the relevant organization to make sure that the third party you are attempting to add is not excluded for some reason. Think about turning the tables and asking for *your organization* to be named as an additional insured on the policies of the vendors, hotel, etc.

- **A note for events *not* using the standard RRCA or USATF policies:** If an event obtains insurance from a carrier on its own, make sure the policy at least matches the level of coverage provided by either the USATF or RRCA policy, especially when it comes to participant liability coverage. In addition, find out if the policy will cover race-related activities in the days before and after the event, such as packet pick-up, pre-race banquet/party, pre-race setup and post-race tear down. You may need to obtain a special endorsement from the insurance provider to cover these extended time periods. Look very closely at the policy exclusions. Are support bicycles excluded? Are headphone-wearers excluded? Is damage to property included in the policy? If these items are excluded, you are not receiving coverage comparable to RRCA or USATF policies. As noted above, the USATF policy will cover these activities for a specified timeframe, and the RRCA policy covers all customary ancillary activities pre- and post-race, so no additional endorsement is needed.

Other Types of Insurance

Unfortunately, once you have the general liability insurance and participant medical policies in hand—either from one of the two organizations discussed above or from a private insurer—you still aren't quite done. There remain some additional types of insurance that you will want to consider. It is important not to lose sight of the fact that a general liability insurance policy is not designed to be an "all-inclusive" policy. Both the RRCA and USATF provide an a la carte menu of additional types of policies (at additional fees).

Directors & Officers (D&O) insurance

Liability insurance protects against the acts of an event or its agents that result in injury or damage to another. Directors and officers insurance, by contrast, protects those individuals in the case of errors in judgment. For example, if the race director or board makes a decision that results in discrimination against a particular group, or if an event is sued over a decision to cancel a race, directors and officers insurance would offer protection. The RRCA requires that all nonprofit member organizations also purchase D&O insurance or provide proof of coverage elsewhere. USATF offers all nonprofit member organizations the option to purchase D&O insurance.

One thing to keep in mind in considering D&O coverage is whether the coverage is stand-alone or a "pool" arrangement. In a pool arrangement, a national organization, for example, covers its directors and officers with its policy at a set limit or ceiling, and "extends" or sells this coverage as a D&O policy to member clubs. This may be fine if there are no or few claims generated by the national office or the member clubs, but the worst case scenario is that multiple claims are filed, and your claim is the one filed after the limits to the policy have been reached. Technically, you were covered, but you're still left paying the bill. The D&O insurance available through both the RRCA and USATF does not pool with other clubs. Each club buys its own coverage and has its own limits.

Equipment

Neither RRCA nor USATF cover equipment in their basic liability policies. (USATF does cover track & field equipment such as hurdles, javelins, starting blocks, etc. for up to $5,000 per event or practice, with a deductible.) However, both organizations offer equipment insurance for an additional premium. If purchased, the equipment policy covers items such as clocks, computers, radios, etc. The cost of the equipment policy varies slightly between RRCA and USATF. The

USATF policy can be purchased through USATF's insurance broker as part of USATF's "Event Directors Program."

Coverage for Volunteer Medical Personnel

USATF's policy includes medical volunteers under the general liability policy, but charges an additional fee for each medical volunteer (the rates were $56 for each physician and $20 for other medical professionals at the time of publication of this book); the RRCA requires the purchase of a separate policy for a flat rate of $250-$300. You should have an insurance professional compare coverage terms and limits as well as the types of medical professionals covered (i.e. PAs, EMTs, PTs, nurses, DPMs, chiropractors, etc.) for each of these policies. Generally, these policies provide liability coverage over and beyond any personal coverage held by the medical professionals. The USATF policy covers a *paid* Medical Director (the single person in charge of the overall medical operation) but not the other medical team members; the RRCA policy does not cover any paid medical staff. Both policies require all medical personnel to have current medical licenses, so events should verify the licenses for every member of the medical team. Although the USATF policy states "volunteers who receive a small stipend and/or expense reimbursement are eligible for coverage," events should be cautious about giving medical personnel anything that could be construed as payment, such as gift cards, etc.

As was noted in ***Chapter 8: Medical, Safety and Security,*** in a few states, such personnel might find some protection under Good Samaritan laws. Good Samaritan laws are laws that afford some legal protection to individuals who come to the aid of others in need of medical help. The laws were designed to increase the likelihood—by reducing the liability—that citizens would help others in emergency situations. The laws vary widely from state to state—some are broad and extend protection to both non-medical and medical personnel; others may exclude medical personnel

such as nurses and doctors (especially if they are paid even a small amount). Race directors and race medical officials should be very familiar with the Good Samaritan statutes in their state. It is risky simply to assume that all race personnel are covered by this type of law.

Even if Good Samaritan laws don't protect medical personnel in your state, most doctors are probably still covered by their own personal malpractice insurance. It is a good idea to let them know if you will be relying on their medical malpractice policy. Ask them to check with their carriers to make sure their coverage extends to services they perform outside of their offices. The "outside the office" exclusion is also sometimes a problem for nurses, physical therapists, etc. Be sure to have all of the health care professionals involved in the event ascertain any restrictions in their malpractice coverage.

The easiest way to be sure that all medical personnel are covered for liability is to obtain a separate insurance policy for medical personnel. Both USATF and RRCA offer separate insurance packages for members with general liability coverage. These policies cover emergency medical treatment provided by properly licensed personnel working as volunteers. Coverage limits are similar to those stipulated in the general liability policies of the organizations.

Vehicle Insurance on Rental Vehicles

If the race committee members rent vehicles, they should take the rental company's collision damage insurance. The RRCA general liability policy does include liability coverage for hired and non-owned (rental) vehicles up to a certain size, but does not pay for damages to these vehicles. In addition, individual automobile policies, which normally cover rental vehicles, may not cover vehicles that have been rented for commercial purposes. The individual should either check out his or her own policy in advance or simply take the rental company's policy, just in case.

Insurance Coverage if Alcohol Is Served: "Host Liquor Liability"

If the event *gives away (for free)* beer (or any alcoholic beverage) at a post-race party, the service of this alcohol should be covered under a general liability insurance policy *as an inclusion for host liquor liability coverage.* The RRCA general liability policy includes host liquor liability coverage, so long as the host club or event *is not* "in the business of selling, serving, manufacturing, distributing, or distilling alcoholic beverages." *If alcohol is served, there should be **no charge,** and the event registration should not make any reference to alcohol being included as part of the registration fee.* Check local ordinances and regulations for more information about alcoholic beverage service. If a vendor sells alcohol at an event, incidents arising from the sale of alcohol are not covered by the RRCA's general liability insurance policy. An increasing number of permitting entities ask that clubs and events secure a temporary liquor license, sometimes called an ABC license, even if they are not selling or serving the alcohol. In that case, you may be required to secure a liquor liability endorsement or policy, which could cost anywhere from $400 - $700 or more. The RRCA's insurance broker works with all members needing additional liquor liability coverage.

Cancellation Insurance for Events

Races always have to face the possibility of cancellation, as clearly demonstrated by the cancellation of the 2012 New York City Marathon. Severe weather is always a concern—snowstorms, flooding, lightning, etc., can all wreak havoc with the best-laid race plans. Many regular insurance policies have exclusions for "acts of war," "acts of God/nature," etc., so the event's current insurance policy may not be of any use in such a situation. If the race is held during months when weather makes cancellation a possibility, you might want to look into finding some sort of cancellation insurance that would help the event cope with the huge financial hit it would suffer if it were cancelled completely for a year. This is especially true if the race is large enough, and the race city busy enough, that rescheduling would be difficult or impossible.

Weather is not the only occurrence that can produce cancellation. The September 11th attacks and the Boston Marathon bombing produced a wave of interest in "terrorism insurance"—a policy that would cover cancellation resulting from a terrorist attack during the event itself or any other serious security risk occurring prior to the event. This type of insurance is not offered by either RRCA or USATF, so it would need to be obtained independently of those organizations. Be aware that the premiums for this type of insurance can be steep, particularly if the event is located in a high-profile city such as New York City or Washington, DC.

Carefully read and understand policy exclusions if you obtain a cancellation or terrorism policy. The insurance industry's definition for a covered act of terrorism is very specific and aligns with the U.S. Federal Government's definition of a certified act of terrorism. For example, the Boston Marathon bombing, from an insurance standpoint, was actually considered a domestic act of violence, which would be covered under a general liability insurance policy.

TIP

Protect Yourself with Good Record-Keeping

In many instances, when a participant sues an event, the decision will turn on whether the participant or the race (if either) was negligent. Race directors can go a long way toward protecting themselves from suits based on negligence claims by keeping detailed and accurate records of the steps they have taken to obtain medical care for the race and to train volunteers. If an injury occurs, be sure to make a detailed account of exactly what happened.

Cancellation Insurance for Individual Participants

Escalating registration fees have created a market for participant-based cancellation insurance. These policies are purchased *by the participant* (as opposed to the event), generally at the time of registration. The most basic policies provide reimbursement of the registration fee if the covered individual is injured or unable to participate in the event (documentation of some sort is required). If an event were cancelled by the organizer, the insurance would pay all the individuals who had purchased the coverage, but not those who did not. Coverage can be expanded to include travel costs, race items purchased, etc. The principal role of event organizers is to contract with a provider and to offer the coverage to participants. Adjudication of claims takes place directly between the insured individual and the insurance provider.

Record Insurance

Nothing generates the excitement of runners and the press like the prospect of a big payout for a record-breaking performance, whether it is a world record, course record, or beating some other time. Of course, this means if a certain time is achieved, the race organization has to come up with a substantial prize. One way to be able to offer such bonuses and still protect yourself in the event that they are triggered is to purchase "record insurance," which will pay if the record or time incentive is broken. The underwriters of these policies may require that the record be certified by USATF or make other stipulations for payment. Review these restrictions carefully. Although premiums can vary widely depending in part upon the insurance company's calculation of the likelihood of a payout, a rule of thumb is to expect to pay about one-third of the amount you wish to offer as a premium (i.e., to insure a $30,000 record bonus, you could expect to pay a premium somewhere in the neighborhood of $10,000).

Record Insurance companies offering this insurance will want to see a list of your elite athletes before quoting a premium. Coverage is limited only to those athletes; late entrants not on the list would not be covered.

Bonding

Bonding is also a form of insurance. Typically, businesses that handle large amounts of cash will bond their employees. If monies turn up missing, the company that issued the bond will pay the amounts that are missing. Thereafter, the bonding company may pursue the person suspected of misappropriating the funds. Although rare in a running context, you may wish to consider bonding race volunteers or paid staff who handle large amounts of money in conjunction with the event, such as the treasurer, for example. With online registration companies handling large amounts of registration fee income, you may want to be sure that the company you select is bonded, so that you can recover the funds if the company happens to go out of business before you are paid.

The RRCA offers an "Operations Package" for members that can help to cover losses when a volunteer or employee embezzles funds through the club or event. Please see the RRCA website (www.rrca.org) for more details.

Contracts

Although contract law can be extremely confusing and, yes, downright dull, there are a few things that every race director should know about contractual agreements. Every race director, regardless of the size of the race, should draw up contracts with sponsors, suppliers, vendors and race service providers, so a little knowledge can be helpful.

Contract Enforceability

A contract exists when two or more parties make an agreement to do or refrain from doing something. One party makes an offer (for example, you offer a t-shirt vendor $300 to print the t-shirts), and the other accepts the offer (the t-shirt vendor agrees to do the job). In order for the contract to be enforceable, the terms and conditions of the contract must be certain and understandable by a reasonable person. The contract must also include what is called "consideration," i.e. something of value must be given in exchange for something else. In the t-shirt example, the consideration is the t-shirts for the $300.

Race organizers should try to put all contracts in writing. PDF copies of signed contracts saved electronically are satisfactory, as long as they are backed up externally. Written contracts make it far more likely that all parties know and understand what has been agreed to, and they also provide an excellent chance of redress in court if the other party fails to perform his part of the bargain. A written contract should specify who the parties to the contract are, what they are expected to perform (and what constitutes adequate performance), the relevant dates for performance, payment terms, delivery terms, and what remedies are available if one of the parties fails to perform. *See Figure 9-1 for a sample contract/letter of agreement.*

Specifying remedies can be very important if it will be difficult to determine what the damages should be. For example, if a speaker agrees to speak at the expo and then fails to show, it can be hard to determine what damages have been suffered. For this reason, include in the contract what the damages will be if the speaker fails to perform. This is called a "liquidated damages" clause, and it states that the parties have agreed that damages would be difficult to prove with certainty, and therefore the parties agree that if the speaker fails to come to make the speech, the speaker will pay the race a certain monetary amount as liquidated damages. You and the speaker (or the speaker's agent) will need to agree to the amount when the contract is created.

If you don't have a written contract, oral contracts can be enforceable, with the exception of contracts involving the sale of goods priced at $500 or more, which are generally required to be in writing. Although it is good to have everything in writing, many races often fail to do so, relying on oral communications or notes to make the deal. This is generally not a good practice, as you could find yourself spending a lot of time in court trying to prove that an oral contract actually existed and what the terms of that contract were.

Even if you don't get an actual written contract, be sure to make notes of what you understand the terms of the agreement to be and send the vendor or other party an email or letter that states those terms. That way, you may be able to avoid a misunderstanding if the other party has a different understanding of the agreement, and you will also have something to take to court if the vendor fails to keep his part of the bargain. After you talk to the t-shirt supplier, for example, you might send him an email stating, "This message confirms our discussion of Nov. 1, 2017, in which you agreed to supply 125 t-shirts by March 9, 2018, for the Heaven and Hell Hill Run, for a cost of $450." Put in any relevant specifics, for example the sizes, color and other details of the shirts.

If you have no written contract or written email or letter, you may still be able to prove the existence of an oral contract if you have had a prior course of dealing with the other party, if you have a receipt or invoice from the other party, or if you or the other party took any actions indicating you were relying on an apparent agreement.

Broken Contracts

If you think that another party has broken a contract, you can sue the party in court, but it is worth suing only if the following conditions have been met:

1. **You can prove you had an enforceable contract and what the terms of the contract were.** Can you show that you had an agreement, that there was consideration (i.e., some right or benefit was exchanged as part of the contract), and that the terms of the agreement were clear and understandable?

2. **You did all that you were required to do under the contract.** If you failed to perform

Figure 9-1

Sample Contract for Services Template

There is no great mystery to preparing a basic contract—the two parties identify themselves, set the respective duties and responsibilities for each party, and set up a term and payment schedule. If lawyers are involved, there will be a host of legal boilerplate about dispute resolution, protections of intellectual property such as logos and trademarks, etc. (this language is only hinted at here). A simple, sample contract for a club or event management company to perform event services for an organization desiring to host an event appears below.

[Organization/Contractor Supplying Services] and [Organization Desiring Services] Contract for [Year] and [Name of Event]

[Name of Organization Desiring Services] wishes to engage the services of [Name of Contractor] for the purposes of consulting on, planning, and conducting the annual [Event Name] on [Date, Time and Location of Event].

[Contractor] will provide the following services:

- Securing all permits necessary for the conduct of the event, including scheduling and attending all necessary permitting meetings
- Pre-event logistical services, including the following:
  - Establishing and obtaining certification of the race course
  - Overseeing and consulting with the design of day-of race activities to be held during the event
  - Developing a site plan and determining the number of tents, porta-johns, information booths, pre- and post-race food and water, location of post-race activities, etc.
  - Ordering specific items and billing them to the appropriate organization as outlined in the attached budget
  - Preparing maps of the staging area site and course as needed, as the site plan evolves
  - Developing and keeping current a timetable for conducting the event
  - Meeting in person or by conference call with [Event Owner] and key volunteers on a regular basis for updates and integrated planning
- *Other pre-event day services, including the following:*
  - Recruitment of key volunteers responsible for overseeing operational areas of the race, including water stops, permitting, parking, signage, post-race food service, course marshals, bag check, and site management zones.
  - Oversight or development and management of the online registration
  - Securing a [x dollar] liability insurance policy covering the event and naming additional insureds as directed
  - Developing a signage plan for the event and overseeing the production and delivery of this signage
  - General consulting on all aspects of the event
- *Administration of the event, including the following:*
  - Conducting a safe and well-organized event in accordance with accepted standards of race management
  - Managing all on-site contractors and labor
  - Recruiting or hiring event medical personnel
  - Consulting on [or operating] pre-race packet pick-up
  - Consulting on [or conducting] timing and scoring of the event, including preparation of results for race-day awards ceremony, making corrections to results as needed after the event, and posting results to the event website within 24 hours of the start of the race
  - Setting up visible timing clocks at the start, on the course and at the finish line

Figure 9-1

Sample Contract for Services Template (cont'd)

- ◆ Setting up and staffing of pre- and post-race water and refreshments at the start and finish area and one water stop on the course
- ◆ Setting up medical stations in the start-finish area and one on-course location
- ◆ Supplying a medical coordinator and medical personnel for all of the event medical stations
- ◆ Developing a parking plan for the event
- ◆ Operating race-day activities in the staging area
- ◆ Coordinating on t-shirt order and support of t-shirt delivery with chosen vendor to off-site packet pick-up locations and race-day location
- ◆ Design and ordering of race bibs
- ◆ Coordinating production, delivery and posting of signs on race day, including the following:
    - Start-finish line banners
    - Signs mounted on barricades
    - Other identifying signage for tents, activity areas, etc.
- ● *Event Summary and Review*
    - ◆ Providing a detailed analysis and review of event
    - ◆ Providing recommendations for future events that will focus on increasing sponsorships and participants, reducing expenses, and augmenting the event experience for all stakeholders

[Name of Organization] will provide the following:

- ● Developing the theme and look of the event
- ● Publicizing and recruiting participants and volunteers
- ● Developing and maintaining the webpage for the event
- ● Conducting all of the fundraising aspects of the event, including the collection of all funds raised.
- ● [Name of Organization] retains final authority on graphic elements and will oversee the graphics for the race t-shirt design and the design and ordering of staff apparel

Other Agreements

- ● The event will be referred to as the [Name of Event]
- ● [Name of Organization] understands that its role under the agreement is the hiring of [Contractor] as a contractor to perform the services outlined in this contract for the agreed-upon fee.
- ● [Contractor] acknowledges [Name of Organization's] ownership of and its exclusive right, title, and interest in its registered trademarks and logos. [Contractor] recognizes that these trademarks possess substantial goodwill and economic value to [Event Owner] and expressly agrees to use [Name of Organization] trademarks in a manner consistent with the organization's graphic standards

Term of Contract and Fee for Services

[Name of Organization] agrees to provide the services outlined as being covered by [Contractor] for a total of [Agreed-Upon Fee].

[Name of Organization] agrees that, should it desire to expand the scope of services provided by [Contractor] significantly beyond those outlined in this agreement, the contract may be amended to reflect the additional cost of those services.

Figure 9-1

Sample Contract for Services Template (cont'd)

Payment Schedule:

[Name of Organization] will remit payment of [Fee] to [Contractor] on the following schedule

- [X] by [Date]
- [X] by [Date]
- [X] by [Date, most likely after the event is over]

Intentions regarding the [following year's] event:

Both [Name of Organization] and [Contractor] shall provide the other party notice of its intentions regarding the [Following Year's Race] race no later than [Date].

[Possible legal boilerplate about dispute resolution]

Term:

This agreement shall cover the period between [Opening Date] and [Ending Date]

Agreed to:

_____   _____

For [Name of Organization]   Date

_____   _____

For [Contractor]   Date

your end of the bargain, you may not have a claim.

3. **The other party failed to perform what he had promised to perform, and that failure materially affected the agreement.**

4. **You suffered damages as a result of the other party's failure to perform.** If you end up having to contract with another vendor at a higher cost because of the first vendor's failure to perform, then damages are measured by the difference between what the cost would have been using the first vendor and what the costs actually were using the second vendor. If, however, the second vendor agrees to perform the same tasks as the first vendor at the same cost, a court will find that you have not suffered any damages. The frustration, energy, and time spent running around getting a second vendor is generally not considered when determining damages.

Contract Contents

Whenever you reach an agreement with a supplier, vendor, or sponsor, before you sign it, be sure to review it carefully and ask many "What if" questions. What if the supplier fails to supply the product? What if a vendor produces a product that is competitive with one produced by a sponsor? If you adopt this strategy, you will be more likely to draft a thorough contract and to have a backup plan if something falls through at the last minute.

At the very least, the following documents should be "on paper" (hard copy or electronic):

- Sponsor agreements
- Supplier contracts
- Insurance policies
- Race promotional materials
- Pre-race instructions for runners and volunteers
- Race waivers

Waivers

Participant Waivers

As every runner who has entered a race knows, registration forms almost universally contain language releasing a host of entities from liability for any injury sustained during the event. Enforcement of waivers varies from state to state, but a race director can never be wrong to have in his possession a signed waiver from each participant. Even if a waiver is not given legal effect, a specific waiver listing potential risks and hazards may be useful in proving that a participant was aware of the risk. A participant's knowledge of a potential risk could serve to reduce any damages awarded.

These waivers should be kept in storage until the statute of limitations has expired in the state where the race is held. The statute of limitations in most states is two years, but in some states it might be as long as six years. In addition, in the case of minors, the statute of limitations does not begin to run until a minor reaches the age of majority (typically 18 years of age). This means that in a state where the statute is six years, the minor could bring a claim until he or she reaches the age of 24. Therefore you may want to store the waivers of minors for 10-20 years, depending on the age of those participants.

Waivers are greatly strengthened by enumerating the *specific risks* that a runner may encounter during an event, as opposed to simply having the runner "waive any and all risks" without further elaboration. Thus, you will find that typical language, as taken from the Credit Union Cherry Blossom Ten Mile Run waiver, specifically mentions "falls," "the condition of the road," "contact with other participants," both hot and cold weather, etc. The full text of the Cherry Blossom waiver is as follows:

Sample Participant Waiver:

"I know that running a road race is a potentially hazardous activity and that I should not enter and run unless I am medically able and properly trained. I agree to abide by any decisions of race officials relative to my ability to safely complete the run. I understand I must follow the directions of police or course marshals, including leaving the road if I fall behind the 14-minute per mile pace required of 10-mile runners. I assume all risks associated with running in this event including, but not limited to, injuries from: falls, contact with other participants, the effects of the weather, including high heat and/or humidity, high winds, lightning, and extreme cold, snow and ice, traffic and the conditions of the road, all such risks being known and appreciated by me. I further acknowledge that the organizers reserve the right to refuse or revoke my registration into the event for any reason. Having read this waiver and knowing these facts and in consideration of your accepting my registration, I, for myself and anyone entitled to act on my behalf, waive and release [name of event], event volunteers, the [name of municipality], [names of other sanctioning groups, etc.], and all sponsors, their representatives and successors from all claims or liabilities of any kind arising out of my participation in this event or carelessness on the part of the organizations and persons named in this waiver. I am aware that the foregoing organizations assume no liability in the event of cancellation of this event for any reason and that the registration fees are not refundable. Further, I grant permission to all the foregoing to use my name and images of myself in any photographs, motion pictures, results, publications or any other print, video graphic or electronic record of this event for legitimate purposes. I agree that I will use only the procedures authorized by the race organizing committee for the transfer of my bib number and I agree that I will not charge a premium over the event's registration fee."

Just because you have a signed waiver, though, doesn't necessarily mean that the event is completely safe from liability. U.S. courts have not had many occasions to scrutinize waiver language in road races, but in the few times they have looked at them in the context of participatory sporting events, the results have been far from clear. In one case in Georgia, a man sued the Peachtree Road Race after he suffered heat stroke. The court found that the registration form and waiver had clearly stated the possible risks and that therefore the signed waiver was valid and protected the race from liability. Other states have viewed waivers less favorably, however. In Virginia, a triathlete was injured during an event and sued, and the court refused to uphold the waiver. The Virginia court indicated that, in the future, it would likely continue to find such waivers void as against public policy. The bottom line is that the attitude of the courts toward waivers varies from state to state.

Obviously, the case law regarding waivers is somewhat murky, so it is hard to predict how a court will react to a waiver. As a result, it is a good idea to make sure that the event is adequately

insured and to follow a few simple rules in dealing with waivers to increase the chances of their being viewed favorably by a court. Make sure that:

- The waiver on the registration form is specific to road races (or even your particular race)
- The waiver is clearly visible and not printed in extremely small type (as is frequently the case)
- The waiver is signed and dated by each participant
- The waivers are kept until the statute of limitations has run on them (note that waivers for minors have to be kept longer than adult waivers)
- Most important, in all cases, take responsible precautions to prevent causes of injury and provide specific warnings to race participants of any unusual hazards on a course that require participants to take special care
- Have a race policy prohibiting anyone from registering for another person. This guarantees that each runner will personally sign a waiver

Volunteer Waivers

Race participants are not the only people out on race day who can get injured; volunteers can trip and fall or be struck by collapsing scaffolds or windblown signage. It is a good idea to get all volunteers to sign waivers as well. Once again, it is important to enumerate the risks. In addition, volunteer waivers should require the individual volunteer to acknowledge that he/she is volunteering his or her time with no expectation of compensation, in order to provide insulation from laws governing unfair labor practices. General language for a volunteer waiver, which should be adapted to cover the conditions at a particular event, is included below:

Sample Volunteer Waiver:

"I, for myself as well as for my heirs, executors, administrators, trustees, and assigns, hereby waive and release any and all rights and claims for any fatality, injuries and/or damages, including, but not limited to, demands or actions for negligence, premises liability, emotional injury, intentional conduct, tort claims, and any other actions or demands of whatsoever nature I have or may have in connection with my participation as a volunteer in the [name of event] against all sponsors of the [name of event] and otherwise agree to hold these entities harmless. I acknowledge that I am aware of the inherent risks (physical and otherwise) involved in volunteering for the event including, but not limited to, injuries from falls; contact with race participants; the effects of the weather, including high heat and/or humidity, high winds, lightning, and extreme cold, snow and ice; and traffic and the conditions of the road, and I voluntarily assume these risks. I further attest and certify that I am physically capable of performing the tasks required for the volunteer job(s) I have selected.

I further acknowledge that I am volunteering my time and energy to support the [name of event] without any promise by the [name of event] or expectation by me of receiving compensation or any other thing of value for my services."

Kids' Run Waivers

Kids' Run waivers are obviously being signed by the child's parent or guardian. The language must reflect this fact. Here is a template for a Kids' Run waiver:

Sample Kids' Run Waiver:

As the parent of legal guardian of the minor registrant entered on this form, I know and have explained to the minor registrant that running a road race is a potentially hazardous activity and that the minor registrant should not enter and run unless he or she is medically able and properly trained. I agree to abide by any decisions of race officials relative to the minor registrant's ability to complete the run safely. I understand and will inform the minor registrant that he/she must follow the directions of police or course marshals, including leaving the course. On behalf of the minor registrant, I assume all risks associated with his/her running in this event, including, but not limited to, injuries from: falls, contact with other participants, the effects of the weather, including high heat and/or humidity, high winds, lightning, and extreme cold, snow and ice; traffic and the conditions of the road, all such risks being known and appreciated by me and explained to the minor registrant. I further acknowledge that the organizers reserve the right to refuse or revoke the minor registrant's entry into the event for any reason. Having read this waiver and knowing these facts and in consideration of your accepting this entry for the named minor registrant, I, for myself and anyone entitled to act on my behalf, waive and release [name of event], event volunteers, the [name of municipality], [names of other sanctioning groups, etc.] and all sponsors, their representatives and successors from all claims or liabilities of any kind arising out of the minor registrant's participation in this event or carelessness on the part of the persons named in this waiver. I am aware that the foregoing organizations assume no liability in the event of cancellation of this event for any reason and that the entry fees are not refundable. Further, I grant permission to all the foregoing to use the minor registrant's name and images of himself/herself in any photographs, motion pictures, results, publications or any other print, video graphic or electronic record of this event for legitimate purposes.

Club and Training Group Waivers

The sample waiver below covers just about everything else—participation or volunteering for club activities, participation in training programs, etc.

I agree that I am a member of _____ (name of club), and I know that running in, participating in and volunteering for organized group runs, social events, and races with this club are potentially hazardous activities, which could cause injury or death. I will not participate in any club organized events, group training runs or social events, unless I am medically able and properly trained, and by my signature, I certify that I am medically able to perform all activities associated with the club and am in good health, and I am properly trained. I agree to abide by all rules established by the club, including the right of any official to deny or suspend my participation for any reason whatsoever. I attest that I have read the rules of the club and agree to abide by them. I assume all risks associated with being a member of this club and participating in club activities which may include: falls, contact with other participants, the effects of the weather, including high heat and/or humidity, traffic and the conditions of the road [insert any specific risks related to your event here], all such risks being known and appreciated by me. I understand that bicycles, skateboards, baby joggers, roller skates or roller blades, animals, and personal music players are not allowed to be used in club organized activities and I agree to abide by this rule. Having read this waiver and knowing these facts and in consideration of your accepting my membership, I, for myself and anyone entitled to act on my behalf, waive and release the _____ [name of club], the city of _____, and the [RRCA, USATF or other national organization with a relationship to the club], all club sponsors, their representatives and successors from all claims or liabilities of any kind arising out of my participation with the club, even though that liability may arise out of negligence or carelessness on the part of the persons or club named in this waiver. I grant permission to all of the foregoing to use my photographs, motion pictures, recordings or any other record for any legitimate promotional purposes for the club.

Signature: _____

Date: _____

Parent's Signature if under 18 years: _____

Date: _____

Customized Waivers

An examination of the sample waivers provided above reveals a lot of common language in all of them. If you have activities that seem to fall outside any of these waivers, you should be able to draft a waiver to cover that activity (with the advice of a lawyer). The key point with waivers is to be as specific as possible in enumerating the risks.

Validity of Online Waivers

Unlike the waiver on a printed registration form, which must be signed by the participant, online

TIP

Low-Key Run Waivers

Many running clubs hold runs that are so informal that no one even registers for them, much less fills out a registration form that contains a waiver. One way to "cover yourself" for informal club events is to have a waiver that members sign when they join the club. This waiver should contain all of the same language that an individual race waiver has, but can be broadened to cover all club runs instead of just a single event. While it is preferable to have a waiver for each event, this method can serve as additional protection. Of course, having members sign a universal waiver when they join doesn't help a race get a signed waiver from non-members. Some clubs have one long sign-in sheet at each low key run that every participant can sign, with a waiver at the top.

waivers typically appear at the end of the online registration form, and registrants must simply check a box that says "Accept," then click "Submit" to send in their registration data. The online default setting is to reject the waiver, so that the individual must take an action (click the "Accept" option) to accept the waiver. If you want to be extra certain, you may require runners to type their initials into a box to indicate their acceptance. Regardless of the system in use, acceptance of the waiver must be a requirement for participation in the race. Thanks to the Federal Electronic Signatures in Global and National Commerce Act (also known as the E-SIGN bill or the Millennium Digital Commerce Act), both hard-copy and online waivers are considered to be on the same legal footing, so race directors do not need to be concerned that online waivers will not be treated in the same

fashion as their counterparts signed on paper.

Note that the Act has no bearing on whether or not waivers *per se* are acceptable in a given state or judicial circuit. For example, in the Virginia case described above, the courts have up to now found waivers to be void as against public policy, a position that the E-SIGN Act will not alter. The Act merely places electronic signatures on the same footing as written ones.

Music Licensing

Most runners and race directors would agree that music plays an important role in determining the atmosphere of just about any running event. Among other things, music can be used to pump runners up before the start, entertain them along the race course, and keep them around for a while after the event. For much of the history of the sport, race organizers thought nothing about the legality of playing music at their events, but over the past few years this issue has come sharply to the forefront, especially for larger races.

A song legally belongs to the songwriter who creates it, the artist who performs it, and the music publisher who markets it. No one can publicly perform copyrighted works without the permission of the copyright owner, and the owner has the right to be paid for the use of his or her property. In the U.S., two main music licensing agencies (BMI and ASCAP) represent the artists who write, produce and sing nearly all recorded music. (A third, SESAC, licenses a small number of songs.) Music licenses are required from these agencies whenever copyrighted songs are performed live or otherwise played

Phil Stewart

Music performed by bands must be licensed by the event organizers.

at public events. This means that virtually all races are legally required to obtain music licenses, with very few exemptions, even for nonprofits/charitable organizations. Failure to obtain a license to perform copyrighted music publicly is copyright infringement under the copyright law.

Although musicians typically align themselves with only one of the agencies, it is often very time consuming and difficult to determine which songs are licensed by which agencies. To further complicate the matter, the agencies actually co-license many songs, so in effect, events that want to incorporate music are coerced into purchasing licenses from both BMI and ASCAP. The cost of obtaining music licenses varies by the agency and is determined by the expected attendance at the event. ASCAP issues licenses per event,

while BMI issues licenses for a year at a time. The sidebar provides links to online applications for the three licensing agencies. Once the initial license is issued, renewal notification will be sent directly to the address shown on the license.

If a band or DJ will be hired for the event, please be aware that the responsibility for obtaining music licenses falls on the event director, not on the performer or DJ, except in some extremely narrow instances. The bottom line is the event bears the ultimate liability, meaning that if the DJ does not actually possess the appropriate license, the event itself will be liable. Licenses are also needed if radio stations will broadcast at the event, and also if karaoke will be performed, Be aware that, if there is a separate post-race concert, a concert performance license must be obtained as well.

SIDEBAR

Music Licensing Resources

For more information about music licensing rules, visit:

- **Better Business Bureau Guide to Music Licensing**
  http://www.bbb.org/council/for-businesses/toolkits/bbb-brochure-music-in-themarket-place/
- **ASCAP General FAQ**
  http://www.ascap.com/licensing/licensingfaq.aspx#general
- **ASCAP Guide to Using Copyrighted Music**
  http://www.ascap.com/~/media/655449c494b748ba89edc4864655e1b6.pdf
- **BMI Website**
  http://www.bmi.com/news/entry/C_in_a_Circle_Exceptions_To_The_Rule_When_Unlicensed_Uses_of_a_Copyright_Are_Not_Infringements
- **SESAC FAQ**
  http://www.sesac.com/Licensing/FAQsGeneral.aspx
- **US Copyright Law**
  http://www.copyright.gov/title17/

PRO REPERTORY SEARCHES
Use the links below to find out which artists are represented by each agency—but be aware that co-licensing is common!

- **ASCAP** — https://www.ascap.com/Home/ace-title-search/index.aspx
- **BMI** — http://repertoire.bmi.com/StartPage.aspx
- **SESAC** — https://www.sesac.com/repertory/terms.aspx

Blanket ASCAP and BMI music licensing coverage for events and clubs is available for members of either the RRCA (www.rrca.org) or Running USA (www.runningusa.org), with slight variations in the terms (at the time of the publication of this manual). The RRCA's ASCAP license is on an event-by-event basis; the BMI license can be purchased for all of a club's or event member's events on an annual basis. Running USA's coverage for both ASCAP and BMI is sold on an event-by-event basis. The RRCA's policy can be purchased at the same time as the organization's annual insurance policies.

Outside of the RRCA and Running USA programs, if you want to play music legally at an event (the penalties for playing music illegally are steep, and BMI in particular has aggressively threatened many larger events), there are very few ways to avoid purchasing a music license. One solution would be to hire a band that plays only original music. An intermediate solution might be to license only a few songs and continually rotate through them. If the race has a lawyer or other legal advisor, consult with this person. The crackdown on unauthorized use of music is still evolving, so it is in every race director's best interest to stay as up-to-date as possible on current events, litigation and other activities related to the use of all forms of musical entertainment connected to their events.

Tax Matters

- **Federal Taxes:** Details about Federal and State taxes are beyond the scope of this manual because they are dependent on the structure of the race directing entity—nonprofit, for-profit, S-corporation, etc. (For further details about corporate structure, see *Chapter 2: Getting Ready: Incorporation, Taxes, Budgets and Finances.*) Needless to say, the event organizing group must check to see what Federal and State tax forms need to be filed and when.

- **Sales Taxes:** Sales tax laws vary widely from state to state, so little more can be said other than to check into sales taxes at state, local, county and city levels to see if you are responsible for registering and collecting them. Be aware that being a nonprofit organization does not automatically exempt the organization from sales tax.

- **UBIT:** UBIT stands for "Unrelated Business Income Tax," which are taxes that are levied on items sold by tax-exempt nonprofit entities and fall outside the nonprofit's core mission. Merchandise sales are the most frequent area in which UBIT comes into play—items sold over race weekend may be viewed differently from items sold year round on the event website. It is best to seek advice from a tax professional about UBIT.

Employees and Contractors

- **Employees:** If your organization hires employees, you will need to set up a payroll operation and open Federal and State accounts to make payroll tax deposits (Federal and state withholding and employee and employer shares of Social Security and Medicare), pay unemployment taxes, and issue employer tax forms annually (W-2 and W-4 forms).

- **Contractors:** Many events pay small stipends to key personnel who work on critical functions, such as being the volunteer coordinator or expo coordinator, in addition to being race weekend volunteers. If these individuals earn $600 or more, the race organization will need to issue a 1099 form to each contractor each year, and submit an annual 1096 form to the IRS along with copies of the 1099s. Contractors are not subject to employee taxes.

- **Employee or contractor?:** This can be a grey area. The IRS (www.irs.gov) provides guidelines about when an individual is an employee versus a contractor. The starting criteria are the employer's control over the individual's time; whether the business aspects of the worker's job are controlled by the payer; and whether the payer offers any benefits. If the IRS determines that contractors should have been classified as employees, it can assess all of the back payroll taxes. Seek professional advice here as well.

Other Legal Concerns Worth Investigating

- **Intellectual Property:** These include copyrights, trademarks, and right of publicity versus privacy rights.
  - **Copyrights:** Copyrights should be obtained to protect any unauthorized use of streaming webcasts, photos or videos of an event. If you hire photographers, make sure to determine whether the event or the photographer holds the copyright on the photos. It is best if the event owns the rights to all of the photos.
  - **Trademarks:** Get state or federal trademark or service mark protection for the race name and any distinctive race logos. Federal protection is preferable, as state laws typically only protect a name or logo within the state. Trademarks are generally narrowly defined—it is unlikely a race could trademark "Cherry Blossom Ten Mile," but it could trademark "Credit Union Cherry Blossom Ten Mile." If you acquire a trademark, you must vigorously police any unauthorized use of it. This is generally done through a "cease and desist" letter to the offending party.
  - **Right of Publicity:** There are some state laws (but no federal laws) that provide privacy protections for individuals so their likeness cannot be used for commercial ("exploitive") purposes without the individual's consent. Include language in the waiver granting the event the right to use photos in any manner. The laws do not cover "fleeting use of identity" in crowd shots, etc.

- **Civil Rights Issues**
  - **Inclusion of Physically-Challenged Participants:** The Americans with Disabilities Act (ADA) requires that events provide reasonable accommodations for athletes with disabilities. These accommodations can range from the design of the race course to competitive accommodations for physically-challenged participants (push-rim or hand-cycle wheelchairs), and logistical accommodations such as ramps and handicapped porta-johns. It is generally best for events to do whatever is possible to handle physically challenged athletes, because of the ADA and the "court of public opinion," which generally sides with the physically-challenged participants.
  - **Transgender Participants:** Laws are still changing—and inconsistent among various organizations—in this area. An IAAF rule that defined gender by testosterone levels was thrown out by the Court of Arbitration for Sport. USATF rules require male-to-female participants to have received two years of hormone therapy after reassignment surgery. State laws in the U.S. have been controversial, with some states allowing "declaration of gender" to be the determining factor, while others state that the gender at birth is the person's gender for life. Recent guidance from USATF is to allow individuals to declare their own gender at the time of registration. If a protest is filed, the USATF rules will be tested.
  - **Gender-Neutral Participants:** At the time of publication of the second edition of this book, both the IOC and USATF require participants to declare themselves either as male or female. You may want to use the word "sex" instead of "gender" as "sex" is more closely associated with a person's body or biology while "gender" is more closely associated with an individual's sense of self.

- **Lotteries:** Lotteries consist of three criteria—*"consideration"* i.e. a fee to enter the lottery; *"chance,"* i.e. not everyone gets in; and a *"prize,"* what those who are selected receive. Private lotteries that meet these criteria are illegal in all 50 states. A race that charges $10 *to enter* its lottery meets these criteria; a race that conducts a lottery with no lottery fee does not, given that there was no "consideration" to enter the lottery. The bottom line is, if you conduct a lottery, do not charge to enter the lottery (obviously those selected will still pay the registration fee for the event). Even if the lottery does not meet the three criteria outlined above, it is generally good advice to research the lottery laws in your state.

- **Data Breaches:** Protections of personally identifiable information (including credit card information) are covered by varying state laws. Some of these laws outline what type of notification must be given to individuals whose personal information is breached and what other action needs to be taken. Check these laws in your state.

Miscellaneous Beneficial Legal Practices

- **Make sure race materials contain accurate information and adequate warnings.** On the race website and registration form, be sure not to promise more than you can deliver. If you promise a course that is closed to traffic, be certain that all streets and access points are controlled. In addition, be sure to place all aid stations and medical support stations where they have been promised. Also, include all necessary safety warnings against dogs, baby strollers, and headphones. You may want to use language like "the event strongly discourages" when referring to these hazards, instead of "prohibits," because if "prohibited" items are seen on race day, liability may increase. If something goes wrong, courts are going to look very closely at what the event promised and what it actually delivered, and what warnings were given to race participants.

- **Obtain necessary permits and licenses.** Permits must often be obtained from several different jurisdictions, based on where the race course goes, so be sure you know exactly whom you need to contact and when to get the appropriate permits. Remember that bureaucratic red tape may slow the permitting process down, so allow plenty of lead time. There are numerous cases of events that have been forced to cancel fairly close to race day, due to failure to obtain a necessary permit. *See **Chapter 13: Municipal Relations** for more detailed coverage of permits.*

  In addition to permits to hold the race, certain related activities may also require licenses. If you will sell anything, such as at an expo, state and local revenue authorities may require a sales tax license. If food will be served, you may need food permits. The necessity for food permits and the food handling procedures these permits require vary by municipality. Check with the local permitting office to determine the specific requirements where the event is held. Be aware that inspectors may show up on race day to make sure all required procedures are being followed. If proper procedures are not implemented penalties may be incurred, including shut-down of food service.

  As was mentioned above in the section on insurance, if beer or other alcoholic beverages will be sold at the event, you will be required to have a liquor license. Providing alcoholic beverages at a race can be tricky, so if a sponsor is providing the alcohol, it is always best to have the sponsor serve it themselves; if the alcohol is being sold, it is definitely best to have the sponsor serve it.

Some races have an enclosure for alcohol consumption to make sure that minors are not given alcohol; others use a hand-stamp procedure after an ID check. The race should do everything it can to avoid being considered the host that served beer to an individual who was later injured in an accident as a result of intoxication.

- **Designate certain individuals to talk to the media.** Make sure everyone knows who is authorized to talk to the media in the case of an accident or other problem. Having a chain of command will allow a proper investigation of the accident and improve the likelihood that the information that is released is based on fact, not speculation. Discourage volunteers from speaking to the media.

- **Publish the fact that the race director's decisions are final.** State on the race website, registration form, and in any other pre-race instructions that all decisions of the race director are binding. Such a provision designates the race director as the final arbiter of race-related judgments and disputes. Certain championship events may be required to have a jury of appeals. In that case, the race director should select the members of the jury, and all race publications should state that the decisions of the jury of appeals are final. Disputes involving USATF rules are covered in *Chapter 14: Rules of Competition*.

- **Always reconfirm everything with the police and city each year.** Don't assume that policies and requirements will remain static from year to year. Employees may be replaced without your knowledge, and the new people may have completely different ideas of what you need to provide to them to get the permits and their cooperation. One event realized at the last minute that the city had hired a new city manager who was much more risk conscious than his predecessor and required more stringent and increased

insurance coverage. Check with the local municipality every year!

- **Try to get a lawyer on the race committee.** Having a lawyer on the race committee can help the event tremendously. This individual can help with contracts, insurance, obtaining permits and licenses, identifying liability risks, and with monitoring compliance with laws, regulations, and corporate bylaws. If you give an interested lawyer a position on the race committee, he or she may be willing to provide advice on these matters for free or at a substantially reduced fee.

Dealing with Problem Runners

At some time or other, just about every race director has had to deal with runners who are annoying, obnoxious or even worse. These problem runners can create massive headaches, requiring you to take immediate action at a time when you may already be stressed out over a hundred other things. If the problem does not need to be dealt with on the spot, buy yourself some time to resolve the matter, if possible. The important thing to do is to remain calm, think things through, and arrive at a common-sense solution. Below, we outline some of the more common scenarios that problem runners can create and offer some suggestions. (Remember, while there are a small number of individuals who may try to "beat the system," many of the scenarios below are more likely honest mistakes.)

- **A runner comes on race day to pick up his packet and claims that he registered weeks ago, but there is no record of registration.** Let him run (after he signs the waiver), with various stipulations. Remember, this is a customer service-oriented business, and in most instances the runner is not intentionally trying to deceive. It is possible that the runner experienced a problem with online registration and did not realize he/she was not actually registered. Ask for a confirmation number or other proof of registration. If the runner cannot provide that data, but insists that he/she registered, you can avoid potentially forfeiting the registration income by requiring that the runner pay again, but providing him/her with contact info for a race official who can reimburse runners if they can prove that they actually paid twice. Make a note of the runner involved to see if the problem recurs in subsequent years.

- **A runner pays his registration fee by check and it bounces, or a runner's credit card is declined.** Very few runners pay by check these days, but in the case that a check bounces before packet pick-up, ask the runner to pay the fee, plus any bank charges, to the race account when he picks up his packet (you might want to insist on cash or credit card, however). If you don't learn of the bad check until after the event, send a letter requesting payment. Make a note of the runner involved and be on the lookout for a recurrence. If a runner wishes to pay by credit card and the card is declined, give the runner a chance to use a different card or to pay by another method.

- **Someone runs with someone else's number.** Most often, this will be an honest mistake. Maybe one person picked up the race packets for several friends or family members and numbers/transponders got confused. In those cases, the situation can usually be resolved without a serious problem. In some cases, you may need to quietly disqualify the offender(s). Make sure to talk to the race timers about how to deal with this situation, if it arises. It's also a good idea to post something on the race website, and make announcements in advance of the race, about the importance of not switching bibs/transponders with another runner. Again, if this situation occurs, make a note of those

involved for future reference.

- **Runners start making off with loads of post-race refreshments, leaving little or nothing for late finishers.** You can either add more volunteers to police the food area and have them instruct the runners to only take a certain amount of food, have the volunteers hand each runner the proper amount of food, or restrict access to refreshment areas.

- **Cyclists, rollerbladers, runners with headphones or runners with dogs or pushing strollers insist on staying on the course.** Don't try to forcibly remove someone from the race course yourself, as the risk of an accident occurring is too high. Instead ask firmly that those people leave the course. Talk with local police officers before the event to create a strategy for safely removing such individuals from the course, if necessary. If you choose to do so, you can inform the race timers that these offenders should be disqualified. Be aware that running with headphones is so ubiquitous in today's events that attempting to enforce a ban is virtually impossible. Nearly all events 'discourage,' but do not prohibit, headphone use.

- **A man threatens to sue because he can't enter an all-women's race.** This has happened at several women's races over the years, and different events have used different tactics to handle it. Some events allow the men to enter and run if they want to, although they don't publicize that this is an option. Directors of events using this approach point out that even when a man does complain, often he won't show up to run if he is told he can. Other races offer men a list of other events being held in the area on the same day.

- **Someone gains access to the race registration or results area of the event website and tampers with computer data.** Although this doesn't happen very often, it has happened, so don't think it is impossible.

It might not be feasible to completely prevent this kind of hacking from occurring, but it is important to closely monitor any sensitive data that is available to hackers. Wherever possible, increase website security for this type of data. Also, make sure that all data posted online is backed up. Online registration providers should already have adequate security in place to protect registrant data. When choosing an online registration provider, ask for some details about the security of registrant data. For example, are credit card numbers stored on the site for any length of time? These companies should also have procedures in place stating how they will respond if a breach does occur. If a security breach occurs involving data from the event website, and if you can identify the individual(s) involved, you can invoke the criminal and civil justice systems, although it might be more trouble and expense than it is worth.

- **You publish the photo of a participant from last year's race in the race brochure. The participant then wants compensation for use of the photo.** In general, you do not need to compensate someone if they appear in a photo of a public scene. To be on the safe side, however, you might want to mention in the waiver that participants consent to the use of their photographs for promotional purposes.

- **You suspect a runner may have cheated.** The best way to prevent cheating is through course monitoring. Small races tend to use the honor system and take no advance precautions, but will try to reconstruct and

review evidence if a complaint is received. Higher profile events may utilize video cameras, a crew of spotters, or a combination of these, stationed at random spots along the course. The locations of these spotters should not be revealed to the runners prior to the race. The spotters should make note of runner bib numbers or record the race using a video camera. The cameras and course monitors need to have a clear view of all the runners. If you are using a transponder timing system, have one transponder mat at an undisclosed location (preferably not at a mile mark or split time location) and check the data produced at that point to see if the runner in question crossed the mat. Many timing companies place mats at multiple locations on the course and can provide a list of intermediate splits. If a runner's splits vary widely—such as running 10-minute miles for the first 5K and 3-minute miles for the final 5K—you have some evidence to explore the possibility that the runner cut the course.

High-profile events should also have a referee and an adjudication committee to handle disputes or review the evidence if cheating is suspected. This group should get together before the awards ceremony to sort out any potential problems, and when there is doubt, the awards should be delayed. Most races declare that their results are unofficial until they have been reviewed and verified. For more on enforcement of the rules covering road races, see **Chapter 14: Rules of Competition**.

CUCB

10 Volunteers

THE BASICS

- **Find a volunteer coordinator:** This person should be high-energy, hard-working and enthusiastic. Praise and reward the volunteer coordinator with abandon. Unless the race is very small and needs few volunteers, the volunteer coordinator should be someone other than the race director.

- **Recruit volunteers from everywhere:** Look for volunteers from local running clubs, event sponsors, event charities, area service clubs, friends, neighbors, and any group that you and/or your friends belong to. In addition, solicit volunteers on the race website through social media outlets, especially Facebook, and the registration form. Tell everyone you meet!

- **Keep track of volunteers and no-shows:** A spreadsheet or database is an excellent way to maintain a list of volunteers with some basic contact information such as address, phone, email, and job assignment. Many online registration companies offer volunteer management modules, and specific online volunteer management platforms also exist. If the race requires a lot of volunteers, assign a team captain for each major aspect of the race. Each team captain should tell the volunteer coordinator approximately how many volunteers he or she needs. Be aware that as many as 20—30% of the volunteers who sign up will not show up on race day, so this no-show factor needs to be incorporated into the total number of volunteers needed for each job. Keep track of the volunteers who show up to work on race day, so that you can thank them later.

- **Have someone respond to volunteers quickly:** The volunteer coordinator or the applicable team captain should be in touch with volunteers soon after they sign up. If the volunteer coordinator or team captain can send out at least one personalized email to each volunteer who signs up, that effort will be very much appreciated and will increase the likelihood that the volunteer will show up on race day. Generic emails to all volunteers are a bit less effective—the personal touch really goes a long way toward establishing volunteer commitment.

- **Make sure that volunteers receive adequate training and instructions so they will know what they are supposed to be doing:** Volunteer training can take place race morning, or through scheduled pre-race meetings, depending on the needs of the event. Likewise, instruction sheets can be distributed on race morning or provided in an earlier email to the volunteers. If volunteers will be provided with instructions via email, make sure those emails aren't sent out too early—volunteers will either lose or forget about them. A few days to a week prior to the event is a good timeframe.

- **Make sure all volunteers are utilized:** Volunteers will quickly become unhappy with their choice to help with the event if they show up (often very early!) and end up standing around. If there are too many volunteers, be creative and make up something for them to do, or shift them to another area of the race that might be understaffed. It is very important to make sure that volunteers feel useful!

- **Thank volunteers over and over:** Be sure to reward volunteers in any way you can afford—with a party, race apparel, or even a drawing for a weekend away or another large prize!

THE DETAILS

Volunteers are the Lifeblood of the Event

Without volunteers, a race would be chaotic at best and potentially dangerous to participants. Volunteers are the worker bees, the people who get the job done. No matter how hard-working you are as a race director, there is no way that you can put on a quality event without the enthusiastic support of numerous volunteers. Ask any race director who has gone into his or her event with a shortage of volunteers, and that person will tell you that nothing is worse. Recruiting, training, retaining, and rewarding volunteers should be one of the

highest priorities of both the race director and the race committee. It will be essential to keep the volunteers happy and well-organized if you want to make the race a success.

The Volunteer Coordinator

One of the most important positions you will fill on the race committee is the volunteer coordinator. Unless the event is very small, the race director should not attempt to perform this function. As a race's staff and budget grows, the volunteer coordinator should be one of the first few positions to be paid. It takes a special type of person to be a volunteer coordinator—positive, upbeat, unflappable, personable, attentive to detail, possessing of good verbal and written skills, and proficient with spreadsheet/database programs and/or online volunteer management platforms. It is also vital that this person has a lot of energy and can get by on a little less sleep over the final few weeks before race day.

How Many Volunteers Are Needed and Where Do They Work?

If the event is being held for the first time, it is difficult to predict how many volunteers will be needed. You will have to rely on statistics from other similarly sized races to calculate volunteer needs. There are many variables that go into this calculation, including the number of runners, race distance, nature of the course (out-and-back, loops, point-to-point), expected weather conditions, pre- or race-day registration, number of splits on the course, type of scoring (pull tags or transponders), etc. You should be able to fine-tune the estimates in year two.

The best way to determine how many volunteers will be needed is to break the race down into tasks and estimate how many volunteers will be required to complete each task. Remember, some volunteers may be willing to do multiple tasks (one person may want to help with registration, packet stuffing, and at the awards ceremony, for example). If you break things down and assign people to tasks, you will be able to determine whether you will have enough help for each assignment.

Large races utilizing team captains will rely on the team captains to place an "order" for

Table 10-A

Sample Volunteer Needs for a 600-Runner Race

(Distance: 10 Miles and 5K; Course Type: Out-and-back;
Likely Weather Conditions: Variable—event held in October)

Prior to race day (9 total):

Packet stuffing	3
Pre-race packet pick-up	6

Race day (approx. 60 total):

Race day registration and packet pick-up:	8
Set out mile markers:	1
Set up and removal of aid stations:	4 (2 trucks)
Coning the course:	3 (1 truck)
Parking:	3-5 (depending on venue)
Course marshals and split timers:	10-12 (depends heavily on the specific course)
Serve post-race refreshments:	3-5
Medical:	2
Staff for two start lines and one finish location:	8
Aid stations:	4 at each of 3 stations; total of 12
Timing and scoring:	2
Assemble awards:	1
Emcee awards ceremony:	1

volunteers. Be sure to determine whether the individuals have factored the usual 20-30% no-show rate into their requests (if the race is early in the morning or race day dawns nasty, the no-show rate is likely to be in this range), or if they have given you "hard" numbers to which you will need to add the no-show percentage.

To help you come up with a ballpark number of volunteers, we have supplied the volunteer breakdown for a 600-runner race (*see* **Table 10-A**) and for a 4,000-runner race (*see* **Table 10-B**). In addition, we have listed some basic race functions and suggestions about the number of volunteers

needed to carry them out. These are "hard" figures, not including any adjustments for no shows.

Estimates by Task

- *Packet pick-up:* This job is completely dependent on the number of runners in the race. Assume at least 4—5 volunteers per every 1,000 runners.

- *Course marshals:* This is a difficult area to calculate, since it depends on the nature of the course, particularly on the number of turns/intersections and the amount of traffic. If you are using volunteers (as opposed to

Table 10-B

Sample Volunteer Needs for a 4,000-Runner Race

(Distance: 10K; Course Type: Point-to-point;
Likely Weather Conditions: Warm—event held in August)

Prior to race day (126 total):

Course set-up:	6	Parking - registration site:	12
Escort VIPs (2 days before race):	12	Sign distribution:	6
Finish set-up:	6	Start set-up:	6
Packet pick-up:	60	Aid station set-up (day before race):	6
Packet stuffing:	12		

Race day (approximately 400 supplied by event; 100 supplied by Fire/Rescue):

Announcer help:	4	Packet pick-up:	15
Awards:	10	Parking - starting line:	25
Baggage bus or bag check:	24	Parking - finish line:	20
Banner set-up:	6	Post-race party:	20
Chute (if using disposable transponder timing):	10	Rescue/Fire (provided by vendor):	100
Communications:	2	Runner escorts:	5
Course marshals:	50	Start breakdown:	6
Finish breakdown:	15	Timing and scoring (if using pull-tag system):	20
Finish food:	10	Volunteer Party:	6
Finish trash:	12	Aid station at start:	6
Human chain at starting line to keep		Aid station #1:	10
runners behind start:	10	Aid station #2:	16
Info Kiosk:	4	Aid station #3:	16
Kids Event:	20	Aid station #4:	30
Lead cyclists:	12	Aid station #5:	20
Massage:	25	Aid station at finish:	10
Medical:	30		

cones) as course marshals, consider planning for a course marshal every 100-200 yards.

- *Split timers:* For small races where the majority of runners cross the start line at the same time, split timers may be useful. Two volunteers per split time is ideal, so they can trade off shouting out the elapsed times. Alternatively, a digital clock could be placed at each mile mark so that runners can view their times themselves, in which case split timers are not essential, although volunteers will be needed to set up and start the clocks. For larger races with wave starts, split timers become less important because the times are based on the first wave only.

- *Aid stations:* Assume 3-4 volunteers *per table*, maybe more at earlier stations where the runners come through tightly bunched.

- *Finish line personnel:* The number of volunteers depends on the number of runners and the type of scoring system employed. The range is 6-8 for the smallest races, which may be handing out index cards or other placeholders to runners as they finish, to 15 and up for a pull-tag system (depending on the number of chutes). The personnel requirement for collection of reusable transponders approximates that of a pull-tag finish line system, although the job descriptions are quite different. Events using disposable transponders, like those that adhere to the back of runners' bibs, need far fewer volunteers for the finish line, but could still use 5-7 volunteers to keep runners moving through the immediate post-finish line area, as well as to offer congratulations, direct runners to refreshments, etc. See **Chapter 17: Timing and Scoring** for a complete description of timing systems.

    Note: For information on the specific duties of volunteers, see the chapter relating to the topic that would need that volunteer type. For example, medical volunteers are dealt with in **Chapter 8: Medical, Safety and Security**, course marshals

and aid station volunteers in **Chapter 16: Race Logistics and Operations**; and finish line volunteers in **Chapter 17: Timing and Scoring**.

Finding Volunteers

Volunteers are everywhere. We're a nation of volunteers; in fact pollsters have found that over half the adult population of the country has volunteered at one time or another in their lives. Volunteers can be recruited as individuals, although it is more efficient to try to focus on groups. *Volunteer opportunities* are also everywhere, and some traditional volunteer sources may be getting tapped out. Today, many large events make some sort of donation to one or more organizations to attract some of their volunteers. These donations are usually in the $100-500 range for a *group* of volunteers. When looking for volunteers for the event, consider these sources:

- **Local running clubs.** Traditionally one of the very best sources of volunteers, running clubs may be increasingly hesitant to tax their own volunteer base for races that are not "club events," or for an event that does not accrue income for the club. Attracting a volunteer base is one of the compelling reasons to hire a local running club for at least some aspect of event management. As a bonus, you can be assured that nearly all volunteers from running clubs are going to know something about the sport.

- **Event sponsors.** Most large sponsors will provide volunteers, and you can stipulate this in the sponsor contract.

- **Charity beneficiaries.** If the race will be held wholly or in part to raise money for one or more charities, those charities are usually more than willing to supply volunteers to make the event happen.

- **Service, church and school groups.** You will have better luck with these groups if you make a small donation, as outlined above. A $200 donation to a high school cross country team may possibly double their budget. Some schools require "community service hours" for students. If the event is a nonprofit, you can register it as an eligible event so that volunteering counts towards a student's community service hours quota. In general, volunteers should be at least 16 years of age, or they may require more supervision than the value of the volunteer labor you get from them.

- **Friends, neighbors and co-workers.** It's amazing how friends will volunteer for a project if it's something that doesn't require a lot of training and that they can do in a group with other friends.

Creating a Volunteer Form

Begin the volunteer recruitment effort by establishing some sort of registration form for volunteers. Like runner registration, volunteer registration certainly should be done online. Enough options are available that you should not have to create a volunteer registration/management system yourself. If the race uses an online registration provider, ask them if they have a volunteer management system as part of their platform. Most companies do, since the process of signing up volunteers is similar in many ways to signing up runners. The more sophisticated of these programs can help you manage the communications with each group of volunteers as well as track the number of volunteers that have signed up for each volunteer job (and can often automatically close down jobs once the desired number of volunteers for that position has been reached). If you do not have the

option (or do not wish) to manage volunteers using the registration provider, a number of other excellent sets of volunteer tools exist. Do a web search for "volunteer management" and you will find many platforms to choose from. If the race is small and only a few volunteers are needed, they can be managed manually using a spreadsheet or database program. Whichever system you decide to use, be sure to test it out before committing to use it, so that you will be less likely to run into problems as you move forward.

In addition to basic contact information, including a cell phone number and an email address, you should ask for the following:

- Any special skills, such as CPR or other medical training, knowledge of foreign languages, sign language, etc.

- Time frame for which they are available

- Any physical conditions that might impact their placement

- T-shirt size, if you are giving t-shirts to volunteers

Some events will list the various types of volunteer positions available, the hours of work, and a brief description of duties, such as aid station, course marshal, packet pick-up, finish line, etc., and let the prospective volunteers express a preference. You may want to include a check box they can use to indicate their willingness take any other assignment if their preferred choice is not available, as well as an option of "anywhere you need me." Also state that preferences cannot be guaranteed.

Recruiting Volunteers

When you are ready to begin the hunt for volunteers, use these tools as a starting point:

- **All communications designed to attract participants.** Include information about how to volunteer in any blast emails sent to potential race registrants, on the race

GREEN TIP

Going Green Can Take More Volunteers

If the event is undertaking labor-intensive green initiatives, such as separating compostable and recyclable materials from trash going into the landfill, additional volunteers will be needed both to help educate participants and perform these functions.

registration form (either online or in print), and in the confirmation email that runners receive after they register. This information is targeted at the family and friends of the runner.

- **Social media.** Advertise for volunteers on every form of social media that is employed by the race—post on the event's Facebook page, Tweet about volunteer opportunities, etc. If the race has a blog, consider some "Volunteer Spotlight" blog posts, highlighting the fun experiences past volunteers have had as well as any perks that volunteers receive.

- **Race website.** Put a notice on the race website requesting volunteers, and include information about what is involved in being a volunteer. Include a link to volunteer signup, if it is automated, and the email address of the volunteer coordinator. You may also want to provide contact information for the team captains in charge of certain areas, so volunteers can reach them directly with special requests, questions, etc.

- **Contact friends and family members of race participants.** Some races send emails to runners who are already registered, requesting that they ask their friends or family members (who might be accompanying them to the race anyway) to volunteer. If you use this approach, try to place these folks out on the course—either at an aid station or as course marshals—so they can cheer on the runners they know while they are volunteering.

- **Newsletters.** Spread the word through any print or online newsletters to which you have access—those of your employer (or the employers of other race officials), local running clubs, churches, volunteer service clubs, sponsors, etc.

SIDEBAR

Medical Volunteers

Licensed professional medical volunteers bring a unique set of challenges. Most states have Good Samaritan laws that shield volunteers who provide medical assistance. However these laws vary widely from state to state and should be researched in advance. Some states actually *exclude* individuals with medical training (MDs, EMTs, RNs, PTs, MTs, etc.) from protection under their Good Samaritan laws. You might consider purchasing additional insurance coverage for medical volunteers. See **Chapter 8: *Medical, Safety and Security,*** and ***Chapter 9: Insurance and Legal*** for details. It is a good idea to ask for proof of credentials from medical volunteers, including doctors, PTs, MTs, RNs, etc.

Medical volunteers should be distinctly identifiable.

Bob Mallet

- **Newspapers.** Especially if the event is a nonprofit, local print or electronic newspapers may publicize (at no or reduced charge) the event's need for volunteers.

- **Radio and TV public service announcements.** Local radio and TV stations always want to look like they are involved in the communities they reach. Use this mindset to your advantage—particularly if the race is benefiting a charity—and send them details about volunteering that they can use as a public service announcement.

- **Previous years' volunteers.** After the first year of an event, the volunteers from the previous year(s) are arguably the most important pool of prospects, especially if they felt useful when they helped out in the past. Send an email to all previous volunteers telling them it's time to sign up to help out again, and encourage them to ask their friends to join them!

- **Tell everyone you meet.** Many people will volunteer for a project if you get them excited about it.

A note on young volunteers: Most races set 16 as the minimum age for volunteers. Volunteers younger than 18 should have their parents sign a waiver authorizing participation. Anticipate that, in most cases, younger volunteers will want to be placed alongside their parents. When possible, keep younger volunteers out of situations where they are telling adults what to do, and never place underage volunteers out on the course alone.

Follow-up Communication

Initial confirmation: Since volunteer recruitment frequently begins months before race day, make sure that all volunteers receive a confirmation of their volunteer registration as quickly as possible after they sign up. Volunteers who sign up online can receive a confirmation email immediately. Volunteers who sign up via email or other means should also receive a confirmation soon after they apply.

Regardless of how the volunteer signs up, the initial communication should be a simple confirmation that the registration was successful, should let them know when they can expect to receive more details, and should be the first of several "thank you for volunteering" messages.

Communication as race day approaches: A final pre-race communication should be sent out to volunteers about 7—10 days before the race. If the event utilizes team captains, it is best for this communication to come from the team captain to whom the volunteer will be reporting. The communication should contain all the necessary race-specific information, including the following:

- A clear description of duties

- Start and finish times

- Parking instructions or details about getting to the volunteer location

- Check-in time and location

- Any special apparel, supplies or equipment that might be needed

- Instructions about any training that will take place prior to the race

If there will be a volunteer meeting in the days prior to the race, you can hand out instructions at that time, but many race organizers find that volunteers end up taking them home and then losing or forgetting them. It may be better to wait and hand them out at the race site itself. If you do provide instructions in advance, be sure to at least have backup printed copies at the race site on race day.

In addition, each team captain should email every volunteer 2-3 days prior to the race, just to reconfirm that they will be attending. This last bit of personal communication will drive the no-show rate down and may also help to alert you in advance of race day if you are facing a sizeable no-show rate. This is especially important if weather on race day is expected to be bad.

Finally, although telephoning volunteers may seem old fashioned, don't underestimate the value of an actual human connection versus another email in a crowded in-box, especially if you are only responsible for a small number of volunteers.

Volunteer Waivers

Every event should have all volunteers sign waivers. A sample volunteer waiver appears in *Chapter 9: Insurance and Legal*. The waiver can be signed as part of online volunteer registration or handed out for signing at volunteer check-in on race day.

SIDEBAR

Volunteer Psychology

It's important to suit the volunteer job to the person. If you want to play amateur psychologist and can get a chance to talk to volunteers, you can try to match some of the personality types with specific jobs. Here are three distinct personality orientations and a description of the types of job each is likely to prefer:

- **Achievement-oriented**—These are the people who seek out challenging work and enjoy solving specific problems. They like to work independently and to create systems. Achievers like results that can be measured. Volunteers motivated by a sense of achievement do well in such tasks as recordkeeping, database management, even fund-raising. They will be bored stuffing envelopes!

- **Affiliation-oriented**—These are the team players. They like being around other people, the more the better. They'll fit right into a job like packet pick-up, working an aid station, or staffing the finish line, because they like conversation and camaraderie while they're working. Make sure to thank them often, and don't give them a job sitting alone in a corner typing labels.

- **Power- and responsibility-oriented**—These are people that every race needs, because they are going to be the leaders. They may soon "graduate" to become one of the "team captains" or organizing committee members. They are the teachers, the people who can influence others. These people like a job with status, a job where they are in a position to motivate others. They are the people to whom you can assign a task and then step back and let them do it. Make sure to give them the authority to accomplish their mission, and keep in mind that once they get the project designed and started, they may get bored. Give them something else to do, and let your "affiliation-oriented" team players take over the actual implementation of the project.

Dennis Steinauer

There are a myriad of tasks for volunteers. Try to match the volunteer's skills with the work needed.

Volunteers on Race Day

On race day, volunteers can either check in at a central location or report directly to their team captains. Consider telling the volunteers to show up 15 minutes to half an hour earlier than you actually need them, to account for the fact that some will be late. Having a central check-in means that t-shirts do not have to be distributed to each team captain to give to his/her volunteers, but checking in directly with team captains saves volunteers an extra step in the process. If there is one centralized volunteer check-in point, determine how the more remotely located volunteers will get to their stations—can they walk, will they drive themselves, or will the race transport them somehow? You could also institute a hybrid system of volunteer check-in, in which volunteers serving at remote locations on the course (aid stations, course marshals, etc.) report directly to their team captains on-location, while volunteers close to the start/finish area check in at a central location. Whichever method you decide to use, someone should be taking attendance so no-shows can be tracked and the no-show rate can be calculated. The no-shows should be eliminated from any of the volunteer perks. If you are technologically savvy, consider implementing various 'advanced' methods, like sending QR codes in volunteer confirmation emails, that can be scanned by mobile devices at check-in to speed up the process.

Some things to keep in mind to ensure that volunteers can do their jobs effectively:

- Don't set one time for all volunteers to show up, as volunteer jobs will start at different times. Volunteers setting up registration tables will need to be there earlier than those who will be working the finish line, for example.

- If volunteers are wearing official race t-shirts or apparel, runners will assume they are experts on everything regarding the event. Some events will distribute FAQ sheets to all volunteers that address questions they may be frequently asked by runners. Include such information

as the location of the porta-johns, medical tent, aid stations, etc., along with a timetable for the event. It is advisable that on-course volunteers have a grid map that enables them to identify their precise locations quickly and easily, if necessary (i.e. "There is a runner down in quadrant F6!") (See *Figure 8-1 in Chapter 8: Medical, Safety and Security* for a sample Grid Map.)

- Since most volunteers will have cell phones, provide detailed instructions about when and how volunteers can use their cell phones in performing their duties.

- Make sure that volunteers can partake of any

Phil Stewart

"Ask Me" volunteers rove the race site to answer questions.

post-race food given out to the runners. Also, volunteers arriving very early always appreciate coffee and donuts.

- Inform volunteers about where to seek medical aid in the event they are injured while on the job.

- A Golden Rule of volunteer management is to make sure all volunteers have enough to do. Underutilized volunteers will leave the event with a vague feeling of resentment if they feel that they got up at 4 a.m. on a weekend morning and then stood around and did nothing. They will be unlikely to return the following year.

- Don't expect volunteers who have been working in another capacity on race day to help with post-race clean-up. Have a cadre of people assigned specifically to clean-up detail and nothing else.

Appreciation and Recognition

In order to keep volunteers committed to the event, you should constantly show appreciation. For starters, it's amazing how much the words "thank you" mean to volunteers. After saying "thank you," here is a list of some other tried-and-true methods to show appreciation:

- **T-shirts**: Volunteer t-shirts actually serve two functions—first to identify volunteers and second to serve as a reward for volunteers. For this reason, volunteer shirts are usually distinct from the basic runner t-shirts in either color or design. Many shirts include the word "Volunteer" somewhere on them. If you decide to give volunteers the same t-shirt as the runners, be sure to have another way for the runners to recognize volunteers, either with name tags or a different item of clothing such as hats, vests, jackets, etc.

- **Food:** Feed the volunteers well! On race morning, be sure to have coffee/muffins/bagels or the like for all of the help. Have it available

as soon as they arrive, no matter how early this is! If people are working before the race with setup (even in the days before) or at the registration/expo, have a plan for all of them to get food. For those who are working on the course or otherwise off-site, consider a per-diem policy for purchasing their own food. It's also a good idea to feed people at all pre- and post-race meetings. When volunteers are fed, they are more likely to work harder and to come back in future years.

- **Volunteer party:** People love a party, particularly if it's being held in their honor. There are differing schools of thought as to when to hold volunteer recognition parties: some race directors like to hold them in the afternoon or early evening after the event; others prefer to wait for another weekend so people won't be so tired and can appreciate the festivities to the fullest. Some races have better success with a party *before* the race to "rally the troops," as interest can often wane quickly post-race.

- **Gifts/premiums**: You can give something as traditional and simple as a plaque, or something more useful, like a mug or mouse pad with the race logo. These gifts should be used to thank specific volunteers, perhaps team captains, or you can give a special "volunteer of the year" award.

- **Media recognition:** If a local newspaper is an event sponsor, you may be able to get the paper to include a list of volunteers in either the print or online version. An alternative is to include the list in the results publication, if you have one, or to post it on the race website. This is another reason why taking attendance on race day is so important.

- **Photographs:** Have the race photographer shoot pictures of volunteers. Someone can even take pictures in the days leading up to the event. The photos can be used as a volunteer recruitment tool or given to the volunteers who are pictured. If a famous athlete or local celebrity is coming in for the race, perhaps you can arrange for him or her to sign photos that will be framed and given to team captains.

- **Random awards:** Some races offer random prize drawings at the award ceremony. Volunteers can be included in the drawings. Just give volunteers the same raffle tickets that are given to the runners.

- **Sponsor giveaways:** Sponsors can be excellent sources of products (or discount coupons for their products) and incentives for volunteers.

ORBITER ★ CHIP TIMING

TIME YOUR OWN RACE STARTING AT

$295

15LBS • 3 MINUTE SET UP • AC OR BATTERY POWERED • USED BY US MILITARY

SYSTEM RENTAL

ORBITER.COM // 888.816.4366

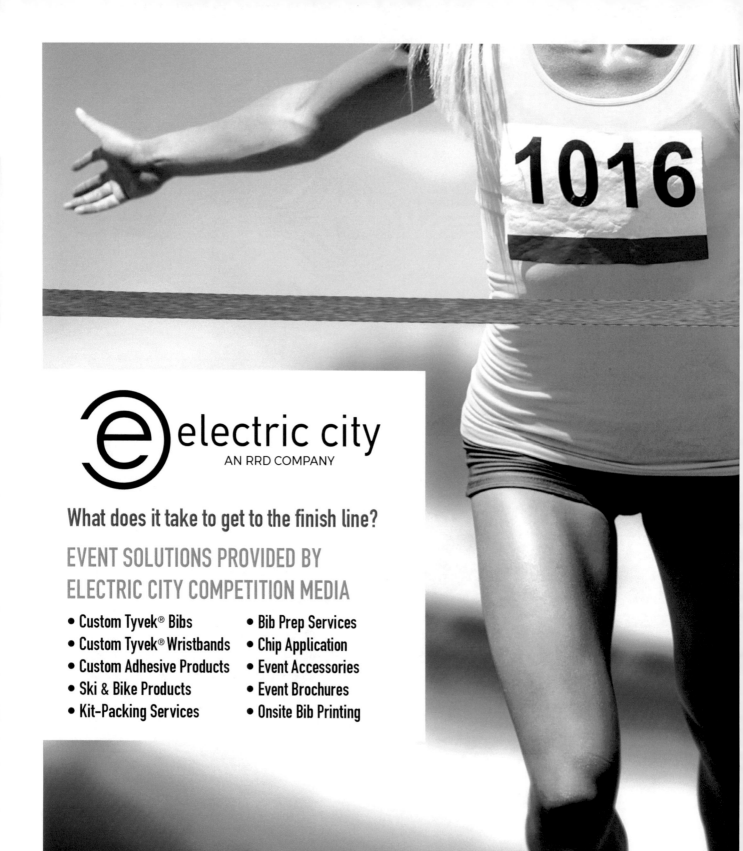

Bob Burgess

11 Equipment, Supplies, and Specialized Personnel

THE BASICS

Equipment

- **Porta-johns**. Count on at least 1 porta-john for every 75-100 runners. Order closer to the 1 per 75 figure if the event is longer than 10K or is an all-women's event. If the race is longer than 5K, consider adding 1-2 additional units at the aid stations. Also take into account the needs of the elite athletes, wheelchair and physically challenged participants, and volunteers. Plan to have a number of restricted-use staff, VIP, and handicapped porta-johns to serve their needs. These frequently need to be fenced off or accessible only through the inside of a tent or located in a building.

- **Sound system.** A bullhorn, or a loud-voiced race director, may be sufficient for a small race. Sound systems for larger events can be rented.

- **Generators:** If the event is in an area without access to electrical outlets and it lasts long enough to outlast the fully charged batteries of any electrical equipment, or if the event has a big demand for electricity for a variety of functions (sound equipment, computers, printers, timing and scoring devices, etc.), you will need to rent a generator. Check with municipal authorities about any special permitting requirements for using generators.

- **Communications equipment.** The operation of a communications system is dealt with in detail in *Chapter 16: Race Logistics and Operations*. While an increasing number of races, especially smaller ones, may rely on cell phones for communications, consider renting walkie-talkie-type radios, which often come with a repeater that boosts reception to cover a wider area; and consider using local ham radio operators as the event grows more complex.

- **Scoring equipment.** The type of scoring equipment needed depends entirely on the size of the race and the scoring method being used. It can range anywhere from bulletin boards for posting index cards, to extensive chute building materials if a pull-tag system is used, to transponder timing/ scoring apparatus if this system is employed. See *Chapter 17: Timing and Scoring* for details.

- **Stage.** If possible, find a start or finish area with a conveniently located stage already in place, either outside in a park or inside a building such as a school or recreation center. Otherwise, you will be in the market for a rental stage.

- **Barricades and scaffolding.** Metal barricades are useful for crowd control, to line up corrals, to indicate course direction and for hanging sponsor banners. Scaffolding with an overhead truss can be used to provide a structure for hanging start/finish or sponsor banners. Both barricades and scaffolding can be rented from event supply companies.

- **Tents.** Small 10' x 10' pop-up tents are relatively inexpensive and quick to assemble. Avoid tents that are so light-weight and inexpensive that they will be carried aloft by a gentle breeze. Tents can provide a focus and shelter for various tasks like race-day registration or t-shirt distribution. Many clubs and events keep an inventory of pop-up tents on hand. Larger tents (10' x 20' and larger) are usually rented from commercial event suppliers and can run into the thousands of dollars for rental and setup. The largest tents will need to be anchored with stakes, water barrels, or concrete blocks.

- **Tables and chairs.** If volunteers will be doing a stationary job for long periods of time, give them a place to sit down while they work, and a place to put papers, boxes, etc. Small races can make do with card tables; larger events should look into renting 6' or 8' tables.

- **Digital clocks.** If you don't want to bother with people calling splits and the race budget is large enough, you can rent clocks for each mile, or at least for key points along the course. If you can afford little else, it is pretty essential to have a digital clock at the finish. Clocks can frequently be rented from local running clubs or event management companies, or they can be purchased for $1,000+, depending on the size of the digits and whether the digits are on one side or both sides of the clock.

- **Lead vehicle** (this can be someone on a bike). While you can just send the runners off and hope they stay on course, it is helpful to at least have a car or a bike leading the way. Just make sure that the driver or bike rider knows the course! For a more detailed discussion of lead vehicles, see *Chapter 16: Race Logistics and Operations*.

Supplies

- **Runner premium. T-shirts** are still the most common premium offered by races of all distances. These days, many events offer performance shirts made of wicking fabric. These are more expensive than cotton t-shirts, but runners generally like them better. Instead of shirts, some races have taken to giving out other types of unique premiums, such as towels, hats or duffel bags. Runners tend to like unique premiums, so the premium provided can be something that sets the race apart from the competition.

- **Runner bibs/numbers.** As discussed in *Chapter 17: Timing and Scoring*, a small number of low-key races are still scored by handing runners numbered index cards for their order of finish and may not use bib numbers. Virtually all other races—even transponder-timed events—provide bib numbers, simply to give organizers a way to identify everyone quickly and to provide some high-visibility real estate on which to place a sponsor's name. Nearly all commercial bib numbers are made of Tyvec, which resists inclement weather well. If using transponder timing, in most cases, the timing transponders may be part of the bib and will need to be applied to the bib by the race timers or volunteers.

- **Course-marking materials.** Chalk or non-permanent spray paint to mark the course is essential, along with a supply of cones.

- **Signs.** Try to use signs to mark key sections of the staging area (starting line, porta-johns, registration, etc.). Place signs above head height so people can see them, even in a crowd. Many sign-making companies create signage quickly and relatively inexpensively.

- **A finish line tape.** Make sure the winners have something to break when they (the top male and top female) win the race. This may be the highest photo op of the event.

- **Awards.** These can be anything you want them to be, from inexpensive plastic trophies, to custom-designed works of art, to gift cards (consider approaching a sponsor to donate these, possibly instead of cash). Decide what the event can afford, and how you want to allocate awards among open (the top overall finishers, usually under-age 40) and age-group runners. For details on structuring an awards ceremony, see *Chapter 18: Awards, Awards Ceremonies, Entertainment and Results Posting.*

- **Vests/credentials.** Volunteers and race officials should be easily identifiable. Volunteers who are out on the course should have safety vests and/or other clothing that will both keep them safe and distinguish them from the runners and spectators. If you have a large race with restricted areas and/or security, you will want to provide credentials to race officials so that they can easily access all parts of the course and start/finish areas. (See *Chapter 16: Race Logistics and Operations* for details about a credentials program.)

- **Plastic fencing.** This can be useful for creating a finishing chute or keeping spectators out of the fray in situations where metal barricades are not necessary.

- **Miscellaneous.** Finally, be sure to have plenty of pencils or pens, clipboards, something to start the race (bullhorn or whistle), sharpie markers, boxes or bins to stack late registrations, safety pins (for the bib numbers), cable ties for hanging banners and signs on tents, and plastic sheeting in case of inclement weather.

Specialized Personnel

- **Heavy lifters.** Volunteers can be counted on to perform many race functions, but some activities may involve physical labor that goes beyond what can be expected of most volunteers. In advance of the race, consider finding individuals who are prepared to do the "heavy lifting," as needed.

- **Information specialist.** Even after receiving instructions and with plenty of signs on the race site, runners still will have plenty of questions. Try to have a knowledgeable person to cover the "Information Table" or booth.

- **Media consultant.** It's helpful to have someone skilled in managing and coordinating the platforms primarily used to get information out to runners. This person should be familiar with website management, social media platforms, fundraising platforms and the like.

- **Timers.** The personnel needed for timing and scoring are outlined in more detail in *Chapter 17: Timing and Scoring*. In brief, have an experienced head timer at the event who keeps the official time, and enough helpers to adequately perform whichever type of timing is employed.

- **Announcer.** Someone needs to tell everyone what is going on and when they need to be where. This person should be well-versed in the vernacular of runners and provided with all of the instructions given to the runners in advance of the start. The announcer's script should have ample mentions of the title sponsor and slightly less frequent mentions of the other sponsors.

- **Photographers.** To get photos of the race for the website, the media, sponsors, etc., consider hiring a professional photographer. If that isn't in the budget, try to find a skilled volunteer. Whoever is used, make sure that, in addition to the standard start and finish photos and runner photos, the photographer gets photos to document the visibility the sponsors have been given, as well as the layout of the staging area. Larger events may consider hiring a participant photographer or participant photography company. A participant photographer takes photos of every runner in the race and then offers them for sale to the participants. Runners generally appreciate this service, especially at longer races such as marathons.

Various other types of specialized personnel—a social media coordinator, a sustainability coordinator, a volunteer coordinator—are covered in detail in the chapters addressing these functions.

THE DETAILS

The Master List

There are two key questions in assessing *equipment, supplies,* and *specialized personnel* needs—*what* you need and *where* you need it. **Table 11-A** aims to show *what* you need in these three categories, for small and large races. Some items may be optional for either a small or large race and are labeled as "Possibly." **Table 11-B**, based on a 5,000-runner event, is designed to show *where* various items are placed. Keep in mind that a small event may have special needs that require

items from the large event list, or a large event may not need all the items on the large event list—or may need them in different locations than those outlined in the second chart. The tables are designed to offer guidance; you will need to tailor the list to the unique requirements of your own event. Just because there is a "No" in the Small Race column does not mean you are not permitted to offer it.

(*Note:* These lists do not include a comprehensive list of medical supplies. These supplies are covered separately in *Chapter 8: Medical, Safety and Security*.)

Table 11-A

Equipment and Supplies List

EQUIPMENT	Small Race (600 runners)	Large Race (5,000 runners)	Comments
AED	Yes	Yes	Strongly recommended for races of all sizes
Ambulances	Possibly	Yes	Small races may rely on 911 for emergencies
Barricades	Possibly	Yes	Metal barricades or plastic fencing for crowd control
Batteries	Yes	Yes	Extras for any battery-operated items including sound systems and lanterns
Buses	No	Yes	
Cell phones	Yes	Yes	
Chairs	Yes	Yes	
Clocks (digital)	Yes	Yes	At least at finish for small race
Computer and printer	Yes	Yes	For on-site access to database, late registrations, printing results
Cones	Yes	Yes	Sizes and quantities dependent on course
Credit card processing system	Yes	Yes	For handling race day registrations
Easels	Possibly	Possibly	Use for signage
Generator	Possibly	Yes	Need to assess power needs in staging area; may need drip pans underneath
Ladder	Possibly	Possibly	Step ladder or 8' ladder may be useful for hanging signage
Lead vehicle (car or bicycle)	Yes	Yes	
Medical "Gator"	No	Yes	
Megaphones	Yes	Yes	
Mile marker signage	Yes	Yes	
Porta-johns	Yes	Yes	
Radios	No	Yes	At low key events cell phones can be used for communications
Scaffolding	No	Yes	
Scoring trailer/tent	No	Yes	
Signage	Possibly	Yes	Type and quantity depends on needs at site
Sound system	Yes	Yes	
Stage	Possibly	Yes	
Tables	Yes	Yes	
Tents	Possibly	Yes	10' x 10' pop-ups for small races if available
Trucks/vehicles	Possibly	Yes	To get materials to site and out on course
Timing and scoring equipment	Yes	Yes	Type depends on scoring system used
Water tables	Yes	Yes	Count and then order 10% more
SUPPLIES			
Apparel - officials	No	Yes	Identification and a perk for key race officials
Awards	Yes	Yes	
Bag check bags	No	Yes	

Table 11-A

Equipment and Supplies List (cont'd)

SUPPLIES (cont.)	Small Race (600 runners)	Large Race (5,000 runners)	Comments
Banners	Possibly	Yes	Good exposure for sponsors even at small events
Bulletin board	Possibly	Possibly	Need someplace to post results on site
Cable or zip ties	Yes	Yes	For hanging banners and signs and locking porta-johns if they arrive day before race day. Lots of them.
Cash box/change	Yes	Yes	
Clip boards	Yes	Yes	
Coolers	No	Yes	
Course marking materials	Yes	Yes	Duct tape or non-permanent spray paint are best
Credentials	No	Yes	Staff, All-Areas, Medical, VIP, etc.
Cups	Yes	Yes	Range of 2-3 per runner per aid station in cold weather to 6-8 per runner per aid station in hot weather
Duct tape	Yes	Yes	Can be used to mark start and finish lines as well as mile marks
Extension cords (heavy duty) and outlet boxes	Yes	Yes	
Finish line tape	Possibly	Yes	
First aid kit	Yes	Possibly	For larger races items included on medical supply list; may still want kit for on-course aid stations
Flashlights, lanterns	Yes	Yes	
Hats – VIP	No	Yes	
Hats/vests – medical	No	Yes	
Hoses (clean) for dispensing public water	Yes	Yes	
Ice	Yes	Yes	
Maps	Possibly	Yes	At least one map posted for small races
Medical supplies	Yes	Yes	See *Chapter 8: Medical and Safety Issues* for a detailed list
Merchandise	No	Yes	
Numbers	Yes	Yes	
Office supplies	Yes	Yes	Scissors, pens, clips, clip boards, rubber bands, push pins, safety pins, scotch tape, string, markers, tape, post-it notes, etc.
Parking permits	No	Yes	To all access for race vehicles; parking for VIPs
Participant mementos	No	Yes	

Table 11-A

Equipment and Supplies List (cont'd)

SUPPLIES (cont.)	Small Race (600 runners)	Large Race (5,000 runners)	Comments
Permit	Yes	Yes	Always have copy of municipal permit on site
Podium signs	No	Yes	Self-adhering sign with race name and/or sponsor logo for podium
Post-race food	Yes	Yes	Even a single item to supplement water at low key races1
Press kit covers	No	Yes	
Rakes and brooms	Yes	Yes	For clean up
Registration forms (blank)	Yes	Yes	For late registrants
Rope	Yes	Yes	
Safety pins	Yes	Yes	Copious amount (over 4 per runner number to allow for runners who forget them on race day or who drop them)
Signs	Yes	Yes	Many sign stores can make signs quickly.
Toilet paper	Yes	Yes	Over and beyond what porta-john vendor may bring
Toolbox and tools	Yes	Yes	Pliers, hammer, sledge hammer, electric drill, screw drivers, carpet cutters, nails, screws, etc.
Trash bags	Yes	Yes	For use at water stations and for clean-up
Trash cans (plastic) and liners	Yes	Yes	For use at water stations
T-shirts - participant	Possibly	Yes	Low-key club races that only charge a few dollars to enter do not need to offer t-shirts
Volunteer apparel	Possibly	Yes	Volunteer t-shirts or tyvec vests to indicate volunteers at low key races
Watches	Yes	Yes	Even if using transponder timing, hand time the winners
Water or access to water supply	Yes	Yes	Check water potability in advance; 5-gallon jugs if from bottled water company
Waterstop supplies	Yes	Yes	Includes coolers if mixing electrolyte drink; latex gloves for volunteers, separators for stacking cups, pitchers, etc.
Wire cutters	Yes	Yes	For cutting zip ties
Writing implements (pens, sharpies, etc.)	Yes	Yes	
SPECIALIZED PERSONNEL			
Announcer	Possibly	Yes	Usually can find a volunteer to do this at low key races
Heavy lifters	No	Yes	"Labor" for jobs too big for volunteers like moving barricades or water tables

Table 11-A

Equipment and Supplies List (cont'd)

SPECIALIZED PERSONNEL (cont.)	Small Race (600 runners)	Large Race (5,000 runners)	Comments
Lead vehicle operator	Possibly	Yes	In car or on bicycle
Participant photographer	No	Yes	Commercial service that photographs each runner
Photographer	Possibly	Yes	Photographer to be assigned duties by race director
Police officers	Yes	Yes	For traffic control and safety
Security guard	No	Yes	
PRINTED MATTER (and/or on website as .pdf files)			
Registration form	Yes	Yes	Even if the registration form is online, you may want some paper forms for race day registration.
Post-race results publication	No	Optional	
Pre-race program	No	Optional	
Printed runner instructions	No	Possibly	Most are available electronically
OTHER			
Insurance - Equipment	Possibly	Yes	
Insurance – Liability	Yes	Yes	Available through RRCA and USATF. See *Chapter 9: Insurance and Legal* for a detailed discussion of insurance options
USATF Sanction	No	Possibly	USATF sanction required if 1st place earns $500 or more in prize money

Table 11-B

Equipment and Supplies by Location
(for a 5,000-runner event)

Qty.	Item	Qty.	Item
REGISTRATION/PACKET PICK-UP AREA		**COURSE**	
1	Registration box (pens, paper, scissors, tape, rulers, etc.)	40	Tables (4 tables each side x 5 aid stations)
		10	Porta-johns (2 at each of 5 aid stations)
1	Cash box (change)	24	Water barrels
Variable	Registration signage	10	Trash barrels with trash liners
1	TV monitor and computer to show last year's race coverage (optional)	24	Water pitchers
		125,000	Cups (5 per runner x 5 aid stations)
Variable	Banners	Variable	Signs
1	Each alpha and numeric registrant listing	6	Course clocks (1 at each mile and half way)
100	Confirmation brochures		
5000	Race packets	Variable	Water hoses
5000	T-shirts	5	Balloon arches each mile
5000	Envelopes with bib number, chip, chip flyer	15	Rakes and brooms (3 per aid station)
1	Chip reader set-up		
20,000	Safety pins (4/runner x 5,000 - but be sure to have extra on hand)	**FINISH**	
		1	Food tent (20' x 30')
Variable	Refreshments for volunteers (coffee, bagels, etc.)	2	Awards tents (20' x 20')
		1	Timing tent (20' x 30')
		1	Medical tent with sides (30' x 60')
STARTING LINE AREA		1	Press/elite tent (20' x 40')
1	Starter's and announcer's platform (5' x 7'x 4') with canopy	1	VIP tent (20' x 40')
		1	Merchandise tent (20' x 20')
25	Tables for water, elite tent and bag check	1	Massage tent (20' x 20')
15,000	Cups for pre-race water	1	Operations tent (20' x 20')
625 gal.	Water (assume 16oz/runner)	1	Awards platform (8' x 20' x 32') with wheelchair ramp
20	Folding chairs		
50	Barricades	Variable	Electricity for tents, PA, computers (1 generator at finish line)
1	Tent at start for elite athletes and wheelchairs (20' x 30')		
		20	Trash barrels
5	Trash barrels and liners for water supply	60	Folding chairs
1	PA system with wireless microphone	2	PA system (need one main system for finish area; need one microphone at announcer's location at finish line)
1	Generator for electricity		
3	Bullhorns		
45	Porta-johns	50	Tables (6')
1	Airhorn	3000 ft	Fencing
1	Lectern	174	Stakes
2	Flags (U.S. and State flag)	Variable	Fencing with sponsor logo imprinted on it
1	Set of scaffolding towers	20	Medical cots; medical supplies
20	Stakes to hold down scaffolding towers	1	Finish line clock (2-sided)
1	Balloon arch	4	Bullhorns
20	Road cones	1	Finish truss system
1000	Safety pins for runners who forget	1	Balloon arch
Variable	Bags and markers for runner baggage	Variable	Signage and banners

Table 11-B

Equipment and Supplies by Location (cont'd)
(for a 5,000-runner event)

Qty.	Item	Qty.	Item
FINISH (cont.)		**PARKING AREA**	
15	Porta-johns	200	Road cones
Variable	Water hoses	2	Golf carts
1	Results board	80	Fluorescent vests
2	Lecterns (announcer and press tent)		
1	Interview platform (9' x 15' x 16')	**MISCELLANEOUS**	
1	Finish announcer's platform (5' x 7' x 32')	50	(2-way) radios
1	Bleachers	14	Cellular phones
Variable	Ice	Variable	Rope
2	Golf carts/Gators for finish	Variable	Vehicles
25	Cones	2	Start, finish banners
1	PVC for sponsor banners	2	Breaktape (and back-up)
1	Awards banner	Variable	Zip ties, tool box
10	Clipboards	Variable	Credentials
50	Pens	Variable	Duct tape
10	Flowers (awards)	Variable	Stencils and spray paint
2	Laurel wreaths (awards, top male and female)	25	Sandwich boards
Variable	Refreshments for runners	**PRE-AND POST-RACE FUNCTIONS**	
		1	Tent for clam-bake (60' x 80')
KIDS' EVENT		1	Generator for clam-bake
1	Tent (20' x 20')	1	Tent for drinks at clam-bake
50	Cones		(20' x 40')
1	PA system	30	Round tables
1	Generator	3	Tables (8')
Variable	Fencing and stakes	300	Folding chairs
1	Set of scaffolding towers	1	PA system
1	Banner	1	Lectern (for start platform)
1	Balloon arch (can be relocated from start)		
6	Trash barrels		
3	Bullhorns		
10	Tables (6')		

Table 11-B shows the equipment/supply needs *by location* for the 5,000-runner Beach to Beacon 10K in Cape Elizabeth, ME. As noted above, the table is to be used as a guideline; not every item in this table will be needed for every race, and some races may require items that are not on the list.

Quantities

There are four key numbers to consider in planning supplies and equipment ordering and logistical planning for an event (see also *Chapter 16: Race Logistics and Operations)*. These numbers will vary depending on race distance and weather conditions, so consider these figures as a starting point. You should keep careful track of these numbers at each year's event to provide guidance for the following year.

- **How many register?** This is the largest number and determines things like how many bibs to order (every registrant needs a bib assigned). Some of these participants won't show up, but if you allow race-day registration you will be adding possibly 10-20% to this figure at the very last minute.

- **How many show up?** This figure should be the basis for ordering items like t-shirts that will be given out on race day. As a rule of thumb, this figure may be 10% less than the number of registrants, although races that require early registration may experience no-show rates as high as 20-25%.

- **How many start?** This figure determines how much space to allow in the staging area. This figure is likely to be around 90% of the show-up rate for events that do not have race-day bib/transponder pick-up and slightly higher for events that do allow race day pick-up and late registration.

- **How many finish?** This

determines the amount of post-race space and quantities of post-race amenities that are needed. At most races, the finisher rate is 95% to 98% of the starter rate.

Be cognizant of these numbers throughout *Chapter 11: Equipment, Supplies and Key Personnel;* and *Chapter 16: Race Logistics and Operations*.

Equipment

Outlined below are descriptions of some of the major categories of equipment needed for a race, and details to help determine the appropriate quantities, as well as other tips for selecting these items. In some instances, we have referenced other chapters where further details about the use of these items can be found.

Porta-johns

While hardly a glamorous task, providing porta-johns at an event is an absolute necessity, unless there is a sufficient quantity of fixed restroom facilities available at the race site. Unless the event is a small race, few venues outside large sports stadiums are likely to have adequate numbers of fixed restrooms on-site. This means you will be renting porta-johns.

SIDEBAR

Porta-john Entertainment

Some races try to interject a bit of humor into their porta-john operation. The following sign appeared *inside* a porta-john at a Midwestern half marathon.

WELCOME!
Thanks for taking part in the
SUPERBOWL of MIDWEST ROAD RACING,
The Annual Hospital Hill Run
Whether you're a World Class Runner a Jogger or a Walker—
This one's for you! You're A Winner! Now Hurry Up!
There are people waiting!

The first order of business is to determine how many porta-johns are needed. Be forewarned that, in the view of the runners, there will never be enough. For many years, the standard formula for porta-john numbers was 1 porta-john per 100 runners, but recently some race directors—especially for events over 10K—have dropped that proportion to the vicinity of 1 porta-john per 60 to 75 runners. Large races, especially those with wheelchair athletes, should be sure to have one or more special porta-johns for disabled participants. Remember, if you skimp on porta-johns, runners will find other places to go, which may not make the neighborhood around the staging area very happy.

Most events have porta-johns delivered the day before race day. This allows time to contact the vendor if they do not arrive by the appointed hour. Plan to inspect them to make sure they are clean and in good working order. One disadvantage of early delivery is that other individuals may use the porta-johns during the time between delivery and when the race participants begin to arrive on the site. To deal with this situation, many rental companies will provide some sort of "lock" for the porta-johns, which can then be unlocked just prior to the runners' arrival. Alternatively, some companies will come and clean them just prior to the race. Some race directors take a do-it-yourself approach and simply string cable ties through the latches and clip them off just prior to the race. In any case, make sure that you get an emergency cell phone number for someone at the rental company to better your chances of getting a quick resolution to any difficulties.

Before the porta-johns are delivered, give careful thought to where they should be placed. Most race directors recommend putting them within easy access to the start/finish area, if possible within view of the registration area, so that race volunteers won't have to repeat over and over where they are located. Many large events place all the porta-johns in a single location, sometimes with two rows back-to-back so the lines can spread out. Some municipalities require breaks every 5-6 units in long lines of porta-johns, in order to allow quick evacuation of the area in the event of an emergency. Other events will have smaller numbers of porta-johns grouped together in different locations throughout the staging area. Obviously, in deciding where you want to locate the porta-johns, you will need to consider the unique circumstances of the event, including whose

Phil Stewart

Porta-johns locked with cable ties to prevent early use before race day.

property is being used and relations with neighbors who might complain. Use volunteers to direct runners to create shorter lines *in front of each* porta-john instead of one really long line for all of them. When runners see a really long line, they are likely to get impatient and find another (possibly inappropriate) place to go. Also, if the race start is not at the same location as the finish, some porta-johns will be needed at each location, though you should plan on 4-5 times as many at the start than at the finish. Allow about 4'x4' of space for each porta-john—keep this in mind during staging area design.

Some races, mostly longer ones, have porta-johns available on the course, frequently 2-3 at each aid station for larger events. This is obviously up to the discretion of the race director. You also may want to consider some staff and elite athlete porta-johns, to give race personnel and invited athletes some relief from standing in long lines with the race participants. These can be cordoned off with snow fencing and monitored with volunteers or can open inward into the staff or elite athlete tents so that they are not accessible to anyone outside the tents. Have signage indicating these are "Staff Porta-johns" and be prepared to assign volunteers to "defend" them.

Some final tips: Be sure to have plenty of extra toilet paper on hand. Also, distributing some race t-shirts to the company supplying the porta-johns can go a long way toward achieving good service year after year. Finally, consider renting a stand for washing hands. While not essential, it is a nice touch.

Sound Systems

Unless a race is extremely small (under 100 people), some sort of sound system will likely be necessary. Sound systems—using the term broadly to include both substantial electronic systems at the start and finish lines of large races, and small

portable systems or bullhorns that work well for small races (and at large races for splits and some finish line announcements)—are invaluable for many different functions on race day.

Use at the Start and Finish Lines

The primary sound system will be located at the start and finish lines and should fulfill the following objectives:

- ***Disseminate important instructions to runners on race day.*** It is a sad but true fact of life that most runners don't bother to read instructions provided before the race. Therefore, if you want the runners to know what they are supposed to be doing, you will need to announce all of that information prior to the race and then repeat it. The fact that you have announced in advance possible hazards or other circumstances that might affect the safety of the runners may prove very helpful if someone is injured and sues the event.

- ***Create ambience.*** Many races like to pump out music at the start and finish areas to create an upbeat atmosphere. Most sound systems with speakers, an amplifier and a microphone will allow you to plug in an ipod or phone to play music from a pre-established playlist. For details about music licensing, see ***Chapter 9: Insurance and Legal.***

- ***Provide spectator announcements.*** At

TIP

Life Guard Chairs

Quite a few races rely on small sound systems to keep runners moving, either toward the start or through the finish area. These "sound systems" frequently consist of a volunteer with a bullhorn, so the instructions are heard only in the immediate area where they are relevant. Race directors might consider putting some of these announcers in elevated chairs like those used by lifeguards or by umpires in tennis matches (Google "*Tennis Umpire Chairs*" to locate a supplier). This gives the volunteer a place to sit down and elevates the sound over the heads of the runners for better sound quality.

many races, the announcer at the finish line informs the spectators of how the race is progressing while the runners are on the course, and announces the names of runners as they cross the line. This helps create excitement at the finish line area.

- ***Keep runners moving at the end of the race.*** No matter what type of scoring a race uses, it is important to keep runners moving through and out of the finish area after they finish the race. Small races using pull-tag finish line systems *(for an explanation of this system, see **Chapter 17: Timing and Scoring**)* use the sound system to keep runners moving through the chutes in the proper order and to remind runners to remove their pull tags. In transponder-timed races, runners should be told to keep moving when

they cross the finish line to avoid a traffic jam there. In addition, you will want to let the runners know the locations of the refreshment tables, baggage check area, family reunion area, etc. Events with large finish areas may have a main sound system at the finish line and distribute bullhorns to volunteers in the finish area to keep the runners moving and let them know the location of various race amenities as they proceed through the post-race area.

- ***Announcing awards ceremonies.*** It is hard to hold runners' attention at the awards ceremony, and it is nearly impossible if they have to strain to hear you. A good sound system is essential for a smooth and efficient awards ceremony. Smaller events with awards ceremonies in the finish area can use the main sound system. However, if the event is large enough to merit a stage for the awards ceremony, it is likely you will want a separate sound system for the ceremony, particularly if slower runners and walkers are still finishing by the time the ceremony starts. (***Note:*** For a detailed outline of duties for the race announcer, see the section titled "***Specialized Personnel***" below.)

Use on the Course

- ***Announcing split times or upcoming water or medical stations.*** In general, the most effective equipment for performing these tasks is the bullhorn, as it can be pointed directly at the oncoming runners.

- ***Providing sound for bands and other on-course entertainment.*** With more and more large events featuring bands and other entertainment on the course, you may end up planning for multiple sound systems along the course. Be sure to check with the entertainers to

Bob Burgess

A small portable sound system suitable for small events.

find out what their power and sound needs are. Make sure there is adequate fuel available for any generators that are needed. Most bands bring along their own sound equipment, but it never hurts to check.

What Kind of Sound System?

Several factors will affect the choice of type and complexity of sound system. The first of these is the area the sound needs to cover. For very small events (200-300 participants), or for the on-course uses at larger events outlined above, you might be able to get away with just a bullhorn, as long as the runners are fairly quiet and you can point the bullhorn directly at them. (If some of the runners are behind you or to the sides, they will probably not be able to hear you very well.)

If you are trying to announce to over 300 people, and the start area is fairly large, you will probably need to move up to an electronic sound system complete with amplifier, speakers, and microphone. There are some portable models that work well for races with 300—1,000 runners and range in price from $500 to $2,500+, depending on their features. For even larger races, you will be looking to rent a more substantial system with an amplifier, microphone and larger speakers strategically placed throughout the staging area. Be aware that you can only add a certain number of speakers, though, before the sound will start to become garbled due to the dynamics of sound waves. Most event rental companies will help assess the type of system needed, given the size of the event and the characteristics of the staging area. (Placing speakers next to a concrete freeway creates quite a different sound than placing them by a pine forest.) Once you add on generators, microphones, multiple speakers, mixers, etc., the cost of a major sound system can run $10,000 or more. At this level, you should get the sound vendor to provide on-site personnel in order to maximize use of the system and to troubleshoot any issues.

Another consideration is whether to use corded versus wireless microphones. Corded microphones have better sound quality but are not mobile; wireless microphones allow the announcer to move around (they have a range of no more than 100 feet), but at the expense of sound quality. If you choose to go with the wireless variety, make sure to have enough extra batteries on hand.

Obviously there are many factors to be considered in determining what an event's sound needs will be. The best thing to do is to consult with the sound technicians and contractors to determine what type of system is best for the event, and to solicit bids from a number of companies.

You—or the company renting the sound equipment to you—should have a plan in place to cover the sound equipment in the case of a downpour. Water and electricity can be a dangerous mix, so if the sound system is outdoors, be sure that the amplifier and power cords are protected from rain. One thing you can do is cover the system with extra large plastic trash bags with holes punched on one side so the sound can get through. Have a bullhorn as a backup in case of a power failure.

Finally, if there is no power supply at the race site, you will need to rent one or more generators. Make sure that the generator will supply sufficient wattage to power all the amplifiers, lighting, etc. that will be hooked up to it. Check with the contractor from whom you are renting the sound system to make sure that you will have sufficient power. Also, carefully consider where the generator is placed. The noise often overpowers the PA system, which makes it hard for runners to hear instructions or awards ceremonies. (See section below on "*Generators*" for more details.)

Digital Clocks

Most digital clocks used at races have either LED displays or day-glow digits. They come in one-sided and two-sided versions and are usually placed on a tripod that comes with the clock. The clocks may contain mounts so they can be attached to an overhead finish line structure as well. One-sided clocks are satisfactory for splits

out on the course, while two-sided clocks are best for the start and finish line areas, where photographers may be stationed behind the clock that the runners are approaching. A double-sided clock allows the time to be viewed by both groups.

While most races of any size have a digital clock at the finish, many races are using digital clocks at mile markers throughout the race. If you don't own enough clocks to do this and don't want to purchase them, you can rent them. Many running clubs have clocks available for rental, as do most finish line companies—even if you don't contract for their services for timing and scoring. The purchase price for most clocks runs between $1,000 and $2,500. Note that on-course clocks may be less necessary in large races with wave starts, because the times on the clocks will only be meaningful for the first wave.

You may be able to recoup some of the money spent on clock purchases or rentals by offering to hang sponsor signs from the clocks in exchange for a modest fee. Take a picture or two of the runners passing by the sponsor's sign and send it to the sponsor to show the company the exposure that it has received.

Generators

Portable electrical generators are powered by small fossil-fuel engines similar to lawnmower or motorcycle motors. Technically, the "generator" is just the magnet, windings, and transformer part of the machine, but in practice, generators are usually identified by the manufacturer of the motor that drives the generator—Briggs & Stratton, Honda, Yamaha, etc. If you are not provided with the name of the *motor manufacturer*, then ask. For example, one established generator brand is "Winco," which is powered by a Honda motor—probably a good thing.

For the amount of power required at a typical race, a small gasoline generator is adequate. Diesel generators are more efficient and durable, but generally much heavier and harder to start, and therefore suited primarily for permanent installations.

Phil Stewart

A generator with the type of enclosure required by many municipalities.

Assess Wattage Needs

The most basic requirement for a generator is to supply enough power for everything being operated at the site. This is most easily understood in terms of *wattage*, since most of our electrical devices have a rating in terms of watts. This is *not quite* as simple as totaling the wattage for all the devices to be used—speaker system, computers, printers, lights, etc., but that's a good start.

It gets more complicated if you have any device with an induction motor—such as a refrigerator or air conditioner. Their compressors call for a *lot* of power at startup. For example, a modest 800 BTU A/C unit in a trailer might be rated at 800 watts under continuous usage, but still require more like 2000 watts every time the compressor kicks in. As a result, a rental generator should probably be sized to handle the *peak demand*—continuous wattage plus the oomph to power up the A/C compressor—just in case that occurs when the finish line data are being fed into the results program.

Generators are typically rated for peak wattage—i.e., a "5,000-watt" generator can handle 5,000 watts for brief periods, but only 4,000-4,500 watts of continuous demand.

In cold weather, you might want to factor in a space heater—a notorious energy hog (check the label). Similarly, in summer, A/C may be required just to keep the computers at a safe operating temperature, not to mention the personnel.

It's also advisable to add a fudge factor for the inevitable extra device that will get plugged in when nobody's looking—"I have to have my own coffee!"

Try to get as many receptacles (outlets) as possible. Preferably you'll have at least one to three 120-amp (120 volt) outlets, and/or one to two 15-amp (120-volt) outlets, and maybe one 240-volt outlet for heavy-duty uses (e.g., big A/C unit). Check with any subcontractors, particularly the finish line/results people, to confirm their power needs.

Transportability, Ease of Use, and Reliability

Generators are heavy—250+ lbs. for a 4,000-watt gasoline unit—and bulky, making them hard to fit into the trunk of a car. (Weights can be twice as much for diesel units.) If you can't get a wheel-mounted unit (you may need large wheels to trundle it over grass), get a cart or large dolly to move it around—that or a couple of NFL offensive linemen.

Starting the motor could be the biggest headache. Make sure the person who is going to start the generator on race day knows how the choke and/or primer works, and preferably has tested it beforehand. A recoil (pull rope) is the simplest and most reliable starting method, as long as the starter has a strong elbow and an unbreakable starter cord. Electric starters are great, as long as the battery is charged up. The best option is an electric (battery-powered) start with a recoil backup. If you're renting the generator, have the rental personnel demonstrate a start at the shop before you drive off with it.

Engine oil is critical. Make sure oil is topped up (but not overfilled!) prior to every use. Most generators today have an automatic low-oil shutoff, which is good, but if it malfunctions, the engine may refuse to run even if oil levels are sufficient.

Computer-friendly "Clean" Power

Unstable voltage, or "unclean" power, was a problem with older generators. This arises when *inverters*—which take the direct current from the generator coils and transform it into the alternating current coming out of the receptacles—fail to produce the smooth "sine wave" form which computers like. If you see a claim for "clean" or "superclean" power for a generator, that's what it's talking about—*not* a claim for low pollution. Most generators available these days are compatible with computers and other electronic devices. Any doubts, ask your vendor or rental business.

Phil Stewart

Power cord covers should be placed in all areas with foot traffic.

Green Power: Consumption and Emissions (Noise Included)

As is the case with other fossil-fuel engines, the issue with generators is not "more green" but "less brown." Efficiency of fuel use is not a huge issue with an engine that can run for hours on a few gallons of gasoline. But why not reduce carbon footprint and air pollution when you can? For example, some generators automatically adjust engine speed, and therefore fuel consumption and air pollution, to the usage load.

Noise pollution strongly affects the quality of an event. The steady racket of a generator detracts from the mind/body harmony we like to associate with our sport. But it's hard to compare "apples with apples" in the generator market, since the distance from the machine is a key factor, and vendor claims of "quiet" and "superquiet" are made over a range of distances. The good news is, generator noise can be reduced simply by moving the machine farther from the runners. Every time the distance from the generator is doubled, the noise level is reduced by 6 decibels, and a 6-decibel reduction is defined as "clearly noticeable." You might also consider a sound barrier—something as simple as a plywood screen could make a significant difference.

Determine Availability—and Make It Stick

Make sure the generator will be on the scene and running on the appointed day. If you own the generator, problem solved. If you are renting (more likely), make sure to *reserve the unit well ahead of time and reconfirm the reservation days before the event.* Since the rental fee for a week is typically equal to the 3-day rate, it often makes sense to fetch the generator on the Monday before a weekend event and return it the Monday after. That gives five days in which no one can rent it out from under you and provides the opportunity to check it out before race day.

The reason for these precautions? Demand for generators can quickly explode due to power blackouts or brownouts from a variety of causes, typically a local storm. Also, be aware that rental businesses often tell you a piece of equipment will be available based on an expectation of its being returned by another customer as of a certain due date—only to find that the earlier customer wants to keep it for a while longer. (Building contractors are notorious for extending generator rentals when a job gets delayed from unforeseen circumstances.) For all these reasons, it's good to let the rental business know the time-critical nature of your use.

Municipal Regulations

Make sure to check whether the municipality in which you are holding the event has any specific municipal regulations concerning generators. These might include a requirement for the use of drip pans under the generator, barricades surrounding the generator, or any specific refueling policies that may apply.

Communications Equipment

While cell phones are increasingly used for person-to-person communications at races, they have one significant drawback—generally, the communication can take place only between two individuals at the same time. Using portable radios provides the ability to communicate instantly with many people at the same time. Although there are some inexpensive "walkie-talkie" systems on the market today, it is likely that these systems are not robust enough to serve as the primary radio communications network for a running event. If you think you might be able to get by with a few of the inexpensive radios, be sure to test them at the race site in advance—do not rely on the manufacturer's claims about the range.

Most larger races still rent heavy-duty radios, similar to the type used by law enforcement officials. (Rentals are definitely the way to go—the units are very expensive to buy.) Most of these radios have multiple channels (usually 5-8), which means that different channels can be designated for different communications networks. There is a dial or knob on the radio which can be turned to different channels. A channel can also be selected for private "off line" conversations that don't need to be heard by everyone on the network. Generally, races will have a primary network that covers just about everyone (channel 1) and may have a separate medical network (channel 2).

Talk to the radio vendor about the terrain of the race site and the distances between people who will be on the radio network. If people are very spread out, the vendor may recommend use of a repeater, which is a distant antenna, usually on high ground somewhere in the vicinity of the race, where the radio signals can be relayed and boosted in strength for better reception. Even with the use of repeaters, there are some areas where the geography limits the effectiveness of hand-held radios—especially mountainous or craggy coastline areas. Testing the radio network in advance to locate any "dead" areas is critical.

The radios are battery operated, so they need to be charged before race day (if you use them over two days—at an expo on Saturday and the race on Sunday—charge them overnight). The vendor will supply chargers for each radio. Ask for some extra charged batteries as well. This means if someone's battery goes dead, another battery can be snapped into the unit quickly.

The radios work by depressing a button on the side of the radio when you talk. Radio users should be instructed on how to use the system. For example, they must press the "talk" button and wait 1-2 seconds before speaking or their first few words will be clipped. Also, if someone keeps the "talk" button depressed, the system does not allow anyone else to use it.

Finally, you might want to investigate insurance for the radios. Tired and harried race personnel have been known to put them down, get distracted, and fail to pick them

back up, leaving them vulnerable to being stolen. Make sure to have a communications or radio coordinator whose responsibilities include the distribution and collection of the radios. A more detailed description about the operation of a radio network appears in *Chapter 16: Race Logistics and Operations.*

Ham radio operators can be a useful addition to a race communications network, but should be used in conjunction with a hand-held radio network. This is because ham radio operators must be licensed, and they can only communicate with other licensed ham radio operators. However, ham radios may operate in remote areas where the hand-held radios do not.

Tents, Stages, Barricades, Tables and Chairs

These items will likely be rented from an event supplier. Some tips and comments regarding

Jane Monti
Barricades are crucial to keeping people where you want them—in this case off the roadway as Shalane Flanagan finishes the Boston Marathon.

each of these items appear below; a more complete discussion of the set-up and use of each appears in *Chapter 16: Race Logistics and Operations.*

- **Tents** come in almost any size, with the rental fees for larger, more elaborate tents running into the thousands of dollars. 10 'x 10' or "pop-up" tents may be purchased for under $2,000. The larger tents are almost always rented. Consider whether or not some type of "flooring" is needed inside a rental tent—this can make life a lot more pleasant on rainy, muddy race days. You will also want to know the wind tolerance of the tents. Tent heaters should be available to rent as well, if needed. Some municipalities may require engineering drawings of larger-sized tents. The rental companies should be able to provide these easily. *(See Figure 11-1 for some tent options).*

- **Stages** should be placed on as level ground as possible, although the vendor should be able to level the stage to a certain extent. Consider the orientation of the stage when you design the staging area. If possible, have the stage face into the sun. This means the faces of the individuals on the stage will be lit for better photos.

- **"French" barricades** are the most frequently used barricades at running events. These barricades come in 8'-12' sections and can be interlocked to form an entry-resistant barrier. Banners or coroplast signs with sponsor logos can be easily affixed to these barricades using plastic ties. When setting up barricades, leave a few of them "unlocked" (i.e. one unlocked for every five that are locked) to allow rapid access to the roadway in case of an emergency.

Look for barricades with flat "legs" that won't be a tripping hazard for runners as they pass by.

- **Tables and Chairs** should always be over-ordered. Order 10% more than you think you will need. People will come asking for them on race day.

Gators or Golf Carts

These vehicles, generally rented, are extremely useful if the staging area is spread out. Gators generally operate with a single common key. While a basic gator will be like a traditional golf cart, there are also medical gators, modified to carry stretchers, and gators that are like mini-trucks. Ask for gators with headlights if your setup takes place in darkness. Gators tend to bring out the playful side in adults (and should never be entrusted to young teens), so remind users to drive them slowly and cautiously. Plan on being able to refuel them on site.

Other Rental Vehicles

It is possible that some members of the race committee will need to rent vehicles—including vans, box trucks, and for larger races, fork lifts (a license is needed to operate a fork lift)—for their specific duties over race weekend. Try to line up someone with experience operating each type of

A medical gator.

Bob Burgess

Figure 11-1

Tents

Tents come in all sizes and can be upgraded with windows and features for sponsor hospitality, etc. *Phil Stewart*

Tents being anchored by concrete blocks. *Phil Stewart*

Tents being anchored by stakes. *Phil Stewart*

vehicle. Tell anyone renting a vehicle to go ahead and take the Collision Damage Waiver offered by the rental car company (which most people decline because they believe their own auto insurance policies cover rental cars). Many personal auto policies do not cover *non-passenger vehicles* such as trucks. Rather than reviewing the auto policy of each person who might be renting a vehicle, the safest action is to tell *everyone* to take the CDW offered by the rental company and have the race reimburse them for the few dollars more per day. See *Chapter 9: Insurance and Legal* for details about insurance.

Buses

If buses may be needed to take volunteers out on the course, to shuttle runners between the start and finish of point-to-point courses, or to take elite athletes from the hotel to the race site, etc., the buses will be rented with drivers. Ask to have the race named as an additional insured on the rental company's policy. (*See* ***Chapter 16: Race Logistics and Operations*** *for details about running a busing operation.*)

Supplies

Listed below are descriptions of some of the major categories of supplies and details to help determine the appropriate quantities and other tips for selecting these items. The use of some of these items is discussed in greater detail in other chapters; references to the appropriate chapters are included in the text.

T-Shirts

There is probably no single item with a more powerful association with running events than the race t-shirt. A race t-shirt can be a potent advertising tool, both for the event and for the sponsors. The goal is to create a shirt that the runners will want to wear to other races or just around town. It doesn't do you or the event sponsors any good to create a cheap, ugly shirt that the runners will just stuff into a drawer and forget about, or use for painting their homes. Long-sleeved shirts are popular for cool-weather races, as are tank tops for hot-weather races.

Runners are savvy when it comes to t-shirts,

A t-shirt pick-up area

Phil Stewart

THESE AREN'T SOUVENIRS, THEY'RE TROPHIES.

The effort it takes to earn bibs is the inspiration behind every piece in the Champion® Athleticwear performance collection. It's the difference between claiming performance and truly performing. To see the complete line-up of performance apparel for runners, volunteers and staff, go to Championlocator.com, call 800-685-7557, or email us at hbi_service@hanes.com

Champion

so don't get cheap shirts that are likely to shrink, fade quickly, or feel "thin" to the touch, just to save the race a little money. If you're going with traditional cotton t-shirts, remember that 100% cotton or 50/50 (percentage of cotton to synthetic fiber) shirts are better quality. Many races now opt for performance/moisture-wicking fabric shirts, which runners tend to greatly prefer over cotton t-shirts. If it's in the budget, performance shirts are a great option and may actually provide the race with more of an advertising boost, since runners will wear them running! You could also consider offering a cotton t-shirt as the 'standard' premium while also offering a performance shirt as an upgrade, for an additional amount that will cover the cost. Performance shirts can cost twice as much as cotton or 50/50 shirts.

Manufacturing and screening of t-shirts is a big, highly-competitive business, and race directors are likely to be approached by many companies, all promising the best art, the lowest prices, and outstanding service. Talk with other race directors before choosing a t-shirt supplier. A satisfied race director can tell you a lot more than an ad or a catalog. Moreover, race directors are far more likely to understand the unique requirements of race t-shirts—and tell you if a prospective vendor was able to meet them. In general, place a greater value on service (i.e. will the vendor deliver t-shirts to the race hotel, ship shirts to various committee members, react quickly if you run out of shirts, etc.) than on saving a few pennies per shirt. Also, be sure to ask for samples of the actual shirts you will be purchasing to check the quality and the sizing.

T-shirt Art

There is no single route to successful t-shirt artwork. Event directors use pre-selected designers, design contests, in-house artists, t-shirt screening companies, sponsor-designed shirts and other methods to come up with a "keeper." Below, we discuss some of the benefits and drawbacks inherent in each of these t-shirt design methods.

Pre-selected Artist

Probably the most frequent method used to come up with a t-shirt design is to assign the design to an artist (or a small group of artists) designated in advance. This arrangement permits the event to secure the services of an artist with a known track record. The downside is that it limits the designs and styles to those of a single artist, and a certain "sameness" may appear in the designs after a few years. However, pre-selected artists are apt to be the most flexible in terms of reworking or altering designs, since they have a guaranteed payday at the end of the process. This method ensures the race director the most control over the design process, with the least investment of time.

If you hire an artist or designer to provide samples for review, make sure to ask the designer if he/she is providing the artwork "on spec" (payment only if the design is selected) or if a "kill fee" is expected if you do not use the design. If nothing is agreed upon in advance, it is possible the artist may expect to be compensated for his time even if his design is not selected. Many artists will not work on an "on spec" basis, so don't be surprised if a "kill fee" is expected. Just be sure to set, in advance, what that fee will be.

T-shirt Company Designers

Some of the screenprinters who sell shirts to events will include design services in their proposals, or make them available for an additional cost. The downside to this approach is there are likely limits to the amount of time the company wishes to expend on any one design (especially for smaller shirt orders) and the designs may be formulaic.

In-house Artists

Some larger event management companies are able to keep a staff artist busy enough working on shirts for multiple events (or they find a multi-talented graphic artist who can design shirts as well as event printed matter and, perhaps, do the website as well). Smaller races might be able to identify a volunteer with the artistic and technical skills necessary to come up with a t-shirt design and other graphics that might be needed by the race.

Sponsor Artists

As a variant of the in-house artists above, some events have their sponsors design the t-shirts (and other graphic items). The downside of this method is that it may be a delicate (or impossible) matter to tell a high-priced title or major sponsor that the runners on the shirts look more like sprinters than distance runners, etc., and, besides, you just don't like the design. Event directors going this route should be aware of the authority they are giving away.

Repeating the Same Design

A small number of events, like the Falmouth Road Race and the Boston Marathon, keep things simple by repeating the same shirt design on different colored shirts each year.

T-shirt Design Contests

This method is best suited for larger races that are well-known in their communities. While labor intensive (event organizers have to keep the process moving along), design contests bring additional publicity for the event at times of the year other than race weekend, while at the same time expanding the event's reach into the non-running community. If you plan to take this route, make sure you have an "escape clause," publicized in advance, to cover the possibility that you don't like any of the submitted designs. Some events offer the winning artist a small stipend, ranging from a few hundred dollars to as much as $1,000. In many communities, and for larger races, the artist will hope that having his or her design selected will provide a boost in visibility. This may mean the amount of remuneration can be kept small or non-existent.

Who Decides?

Some race directors are autocratic about selecting the t-shirt design and consider it one of the prerogatives of the job. Other directors will present multiple options to the entire race committee, which, more than likely, will be deeply divided. The best route may be somewhere in the middle, with a small group of four to five people reviewing the designs. These people can serve in an advisory capacity to the race director, or the final design can be determined by a vote of the committee. Be prepared for a range of opinions about the race shirts from the runners as well. If most like it, you've done well. If you see runners running in the shirts for years after the race, give yourself (and whatever system you used to select the shirt) a gold star. Next year, things could turn out completely differently. If you plan to use the t-shirt art on other race merchandise such as mugs, posters, fanny packs, etc., you might want to consider how well the art will work on those items—or have the artist prepare a variant of the art for those items.

Cost Factors

- **Printing.** Printers will charge separately for each side they print—printing the back and front is more expensive than just printing on the front. Printing a small logo on the sleeve may be more expensive than a large area of printing on the back, because sleeve printing requires special positioning of the shirt, which slows down the process. Most printers quote prices for six colors, although there may be a price break if fewer colors are used. Printing may be done using traditional screen inks or by a process called "sublimation." Sublimation printing, which is more expensive, uses heat sensitive inks that combine with the fabric itself to create a smoother feel to the design, instead of the thicker feel of traditional screening, in which inks are layered on top of one-another.

- **Color of the shirt.** In general, white or light grey (often called "ash") shirts tend to be the cheapest; light colors cost a little more; and dark colors (including black) cost the most. Try to stick with stock colors for the best prices. Whatever color shirt is selected, be sure that it will go with the color(s) you choose to have printed on the shirt. Some colors may require a special dye lot that will add to the cost. Printing white or light inks on dark shirts is difficult and may require a second printing, which will add to the cost and may produce a heavy ink feel to the design, unless sublimation printing is used.

You should be able to get different colored shirts for the race volunteers at no additional charge beyond the charge for the shirt color selected, as long as you don't change the design or print color. For example, if the race shirts are blue with yellow print, you should be able to get red shirts with yellow print for the race workers. If you are really cost-conscious, you may be able to save money if you allow the printer to provide his own selection of shirt colors. This allows the printer to liquidate his extras at a savings to you and will give a rainbow effect to the race.

If the race is tied in with a holiday that is associated with a specific color (Halloween, St. Patrick's Day, etc.), order the shirts very early, as it is more difficult to get special color shirts, such as orange, black, or green, in sufficient numbers if you wait until close to the event.

- **Number of ink colors.** Most screeners can handle almost any design with five or six screen colors—this is the number that is used on most estimates. However, when getting an estimate, it is worth confirming how many colors are included and, if you have the artwork available when getting the estimate, how many colors the design requires. Sometimes if you are using a dark-colored shirt, the screener will suggest adding a solid block of white

ink, called "flash printing," as a base and printing the design on top of it. When flashing is required, there most probably will be an additional color charge for that extra step.

- **Sizes.** Although most races experience similar size ratios of t-shirts at any point in time, the long-term size trends are a bit like hemlines, they migrate up and down. During the 1990s, big was in. The combination of a greater number of slower runners, who tended to be larger, and women of all sizes migrating to larger, looser sizes meant the rush was on toward increasing numbers of large and extra-large shirts. Starting with the turn of the millennium, however, sizes have drifted downward. Today, women, who now make up over 50% of the field in many road races, want smaller, tighter fitting t-shirts, so the number of small and medium shirts is on the rise (and extra-smalls are making an appearance). Women runners also greatly prefer shirts that are specifically cut for them, as unisex shirts tend to be cut for men and thus are generally larger and more boxy. If you go with a generic unisex shirt, many women runners will be unhappy with the fit. It is definitely worth the extra effort to provide both men's and women's shirts, especially for "performance" wicking shirts.

Also, it is worthwhile to get sample shirts of each size from the shirt vendor. Not all "smalls" are created equal, and this is

 GREEN TIP

Consider Offering a More Sustainable T-Shirt

If you choose to provide a more responsibly produced t-shirt, expect to pay a premium for t-shirts made from organic cotton or recycled PET plastic. Event participants may be willing to pay more for such a t-shirt, or the race may be able to absorb the additional cost. One thing is certain: providing a more responsibly produced t-shirt is a great way to make a very visible statement about an event's commitment to sustainability.

especially true for children's shirts. If the actual sizes of the shirts you order run significantly different from what runners expect, you will end up with a lot of unhappy runners who want to switch sizes.

There is enough variation among races that directors are advised to keep year-to-year statistics on the number of t-shirts in every size that was ordered. To serve as a starting point, **Table 11-C** shows the overall t-shirt size breakdown for the Credit Union Cherry Blossom Ten Mile Run, an event that has about a 60:40 female-to-male ratio. The chart also includes information about the women's sizes only, in case you are directing an all-women's event. It also shows the breakdown of volunteer t-shirts (which indicates that the sizes run larger for volunteer shirts than for participant shirts) and Kids' Run shirts.

T-Shirts as Rewards

Once you have calculated the t-shirt needs for the participants, be sure to add some extra shirts for key sponsors and suppliers, as well as for volunteers. The additional shirts cost very little, but they can go a long way toward ensuring the continuation of a valued relationship. Keep a special stash of shirts readily accessible on race day as an immediate reward for a job well done. (Shirts back in the office are of little value.) As a way to enlist volunteer services, some races offer volunteers a long-sleeved version of the participant shirt, emphasizing that this shirt is only available to volunteers.

Ordering

For a first-time event, deciding how many shirts to order is a tricky business. Since most races take registrations right up to race day, and shirts need to be ordered *in advance* of race day, you are going to have to make some projections about the number of people you think will enter the race *after* the t-shirt order is placed. On the other hand, most races experience a certain no-show rate (generally about 10% but variable for races that don't close registration in advance, and as high as 25% for races that close registration well in advance of race day) among runners who have pre-registered, which serves to depress the count. To minimize this uncertainty, *consider a t-shirt vendor who will let you place the final order as close to race day as possible.* On one hand, you don't want to over-order and pay for more shirts than are needed (and be left with the boxes of leftovers); on the other hand, you don't want to under-order and be forced to re-order (you may not get the same price break as you did on the large initial order) and be faced with shipping and handling charges for all the runners who didn't get shirts. In year one, try to order as many shirts as you have registrants and count on

Table 11-C

Sample T-Shirt Size Distribution

% of Unisex Participant Shirts in a Race with 60% Women

T-shirt sizes	XS	S	M	L	XL	2XL
All Runners	n/a	34%	37%	21%	7%	1%

% of Gender Specific Participant Shirts

	XS	S	M	L	XL	2XL
Males	1%	10%	35%	36%	15%	3%
Females	7%	30%	37%	19%	6%	1%

% of Unisex Long-Sleeved Volunteer Shirts

	XS	S	M	L	XL	2XL
All Volunteers	5%	21%	27%	29%	12%	6%

% Unisex Kids' Run Shirts

	Youth-S (6-8)	Youth-M (10-12)	Youth-L (14-16)	Adult S	Adult M	Adult L
All Kids	45%	38%	10%	6%	1%	0%

using the leftovers (representing the no-shows) as rewards. If you have volunteers and you are planning to give them shirts, add the number of volunteer shirts to the number of runner shirts as well. Fortunately, once you get past year one, you will have your own history to fall back on, so keep careful records the first year, including how many people registered after shirts were ordered, how many pre-registered people did not show up, and how many shirts were distributed to volunteers, sponsors, etc. Keep the same data in subsequent years.

T-shirts are one of the largest expenses for any race, so using a t-shirt vendor who offers flexibility on adding to or reducing the shirt order can be crucial to the overall profitability of the event.

Don't despair if you over-order shirts the first year—if you have an expo, you may be able to sell the leftovers the next year. Some races have Christmas sales or find other creative ways to unload extras. As a last resort, they can be donated.

In any case, make sure to work with a screenprinter who can accommodate an additional order to supplement the original order (at a reasonable price). If they can't, find another printer. In addition, be sure to tell the printer to save the screen(s) after the original order is printed. This will save the screen/set-up charge on a supplementary order.

Set a Policy for T-shirt Exchanges

If runners pre-registered, the pre-ordered t-shirt size should be printed on the runner's bib or included in the confirmation document. However, it is not uncommon for runners to receive their t-shirts at packet pickup, assess the size and ask if they can exchange their shirt for a different size. Since shirts are ordered in advance, if on-the-spot shirt exchanges are allowed, it is quite possible that you will run out of shirts of a given size, denying a later arriving runner the shirt size he/she pre-ordered. To prevent this from happening, you may want to have a 'no exchanges' policy, letting people know that they need to stick to the size shirt that they pre-ordered.

If you want a bit softer policy on exchanges, you can always tell runners that they are not allowed to exchange their shirts until after the race. By then, all registered runners should have already picked up their shirts, so letting runners exchange for the leftover shirts on a first-come, first-served basis should not cause a problem. Some races set up a pre-race informal *t-shirt exchange area* separate from the location where the shirts are picked up and allow runners to exchange among themselves, with no guarantees provided of any size availability. If you want to allow t-shirt exchanges, be aware that most people will want smaller sizes than they ordered, so adjust the t-shirt order accordingly, bumping up the order numbers for the smaller sizes.

Bib Numbers

Only the most low-key races don't use bib numbers for participants. For everyone else, bib numbers are used to identify race participants for administrative and medical purposes, for scoring,

---

TIP

Forgotten Bib Numbers

Because many events have runners pick up their numbers prior to race day, there's more of a chance for these runners to forget to bring them along to the start. One way to handle this is to have an extra supply of "blank" or unassigned numbers on race morning. This can be especially important if one or more of the elite athletes arrives at the race site with no number. Well in advance of the race, talk to the race timers about how to handle incidences of forgotten numbers. Chances are they already have a system in place for dealing with that problem.

and to provide sponsor visibility. The increasingly widespread use of transponder-based timing systems has reduced the necessity of bib numbers for scoring purposes (although most transponders are adhered to the bib), but the other reasons remain compelling enough to ensure that bib numbers are here to stay.

Most bib numbers today are made of Tyvec, a durable material that is lightweight, doesn't tear easily, and holds up well in inclement weather.

The basic runner number is about 8"- 9" square, large enough to be seen easily, but small enough so it is not cumbersome on the chests of participants. Race numbers are available from a number of suppliers across the country. Check out the suppliers' websites. Make sure to order numbers specifically designed for running events, not cycling or ski events. This will ensure that you receive numbers in the proper size range.

Typically, you can order basic numbers in lots as small as 100, while more customized numbers may have a minimum order of 500 or more.

You may want some special features incorporated onto the bib number. If you are scoring the event using a pull-tag system (see *Chapter 17: Timing and Scoring* for an in-depth discussion of scoring options), order bibs with a perforated tag and a spindle hole below the number itself. This tag (on which a mailing label is placed

with the runner's name, address, age, and sex) is removed by finish line volunteers (or by the runners themselves) after the finish line and placed on a spindle. These tags are then used to determine the order of finish. If the event is being scored with a pull-tag system using bar code readers, the printers of the bib numbers can print the barcodes directly on the pull-off tags as well.

If the event will be timed by transponders affixed to the bibs, it might be possible for the printer to affix the transponders to the bibs for an additional fee. Talk to the race timing company to see if they typically attach the transponders to the bibs or if they would prefer that the printer (or race volunteers) do this job.

As you can see, it is very important to know how the event will be scored before ordering the bib numbers. If you are ordering the numbers yourself but are hiring the services of someone to time and score the event, be sure to inquire about how they will be scoring the race so you get the correct bibs.

In addition to the pull-off tag for scoring, some numbers may have additional perforated pull-off sections—either above or below the numerals—for such things as a bag claim check or a ticket for a random drawing.

Many race directors also print, directly on the back side of the main bib number (avoiding the backs of any pull-off tags or allowing space for disposable transponders), a "form" for runners to include any special medical needs they may have and/or the phone numbers of emergency contacts who are available while the race is being run. Be aware, however, that most runners won't fill these sections out, so make sure you have this information as part of the main race database that is on-site on race day.

Advances in printing technology mean that bib numbers today can be customized in a number of ways and each number can be unique.

Bib numbers can be individually customized with athlete names. Jane Monti

- While the most inexpensive numbers will be black numerals on white Tyvec, color printing is now more affordable than ever before. This means sponsor logos can be reproduced in color, or the numbers themselves can be color coded to indicate things like different corrals where runners should line up. The individualized printing capability also means each runner's name can be printed on his/her number (the printer will need to be provided with a spreadsheet with the names). If you want colored backgrounds (often called "floods"), make sure that there is adequate contrast between the color of the digits and the color of the background, so that identification remains easy. Some events that color code their numbers will run stripes of color above and below the numerals, while the numerals remain black on white to enhance readability.

- Numbers can be printed in blocks. This means you do not necessarily need to order numbers in consecutive order, say 1-1,000. If you want to use the bib number itself as a way to designate different groups of runners within the entire race, you can order the same 1,000 numbers, but in blocks of 1-200, 401-600, 801-1,000, 1,201-1,400, and 1,601-1,800.

Just about anything is possible—for an additional cost. However, the costs may be more reasonable than you think. Just discuss the ideal number distribution with the bib number printer and you may be surprised that it is possible to create it inexpensively.

Start/Finish Line Banners

The start-finish banner is an often-photographed item, so give a good deal of thought to how it will

TIP

Check Those Numbers

Checking bib numbers for accuracy should be done as soon as they arrive from the printer. Check through them to ensure that no numbers have been omitted or printed twice. The latter poses the biggest problem if undetected, as it means that two runners could be in the race with the same number. The computer at the finish could have a hard time digesting more than one runner with the same number.

Errors are most likely to occur if late sign-ups are allowed and numbers are distributed, most likely in a hurry, just prior to the race start. In these hectic moments, registrars are more likely to be unaware of exactly what number they are giving out. Furthermore, if late registrants come in sporadically or if different sequences are used for age or sex categories, the registrar could lose track of the last number distributed.

Omitted numbers pose less of a scoring problem, but may create anxiety for a director about whether or not a runner is missing.

The bib number companies do their best to ensure that the sets are complete, but a quick and early check is certainly worthwhile.

look and what will appear on it. (For purposes of the discussion below, we will assume that the event starts and finishes in the same location; if the event starts and finishes in different places, plan to have a banner at each location.)

Start-finish banners generally contain the name of the race, along with some sponsor names and/or logos. Reserve space on the banner for, at most, only a small number of high-level sponsor logos; cluttering the banner with a horde of logos creates a "junky" look and reduces the impact of any single logo. The banner may not necessarily need to have the words "Start" or "Finish" on it. Generally, it is apparent—or it can be imprinted on the road under the banner—and the space can be put to better use with the event name or sponsor logos.

For low-budget, smaller events, stores that specialize in quickly preparing banners may be the best bet. Most of the banners obtained from these types of outlets are likely to be heavy-duty plastic. If you need something more customized, consider some specialized event signage companies. Consider getting a banner with some sort of holes or vents, so that it doesn't act like a giant sail in windy conditions. Nylon banners have the advantage of being lighter. For information about companies that provide various types of banners, check the internet.

When purchasing a banner, consider how it will be hung. If the banner will simply be tied to two fixed points on either side of the road, such as light posts or trees, you will need a banner that has rope stitched into a seam along the top and bottom of the banner. If the banner will be hung on some type of overhead metal structure, on the side of a building, on a wall, or on a French barricade, you will need grommets (metal eyelets) in the corners of the banner—and spaced along the top side, if the banner is long—to help set it up. Cable/zip ties are an effective way to affix banners to barricades, scaffolding, or other structures.

Some events use "hard" or "fixed" banners, which may be made of plasticore or some other type of more rigid material. These banners offer a "cleaner" look, as they do not ripple in the wind. The downside is that they are not usually prepared with holes or vents, so under extremely windy conditions you may not be able to use them due to safety concerns. Avoid using plastic or metal for banners, as banners made of these materials can be a safety risk in high winds if they are blown off their mounts and end up striking nearby runners.

Figure 11-2

Designating the Finish

Dave McGillivray

A finish line banner with "Finish" on the road way. This may allow more space for sponsors, etc.

Dave McGillivray

A finish line banner with "Finish" on the banner. This is visible from further away but may not allow as much space for sponsors, etc.

Finish Line Tape

The finish line tape is the crème-de-la-crème location for visibility of the race name and sponsors. This is because the most frequently used photograph from a race is the winner breaking the tape. Therefore, make sure you have a finish line tape if you expect there to be any media attention given to the event! There is a story in running lore about a race that forgot its finish line tape and replaced it with some yellow construction tape with the word "Caution" on it. This is not the

Figure 11-3

Finish Line Tapes

A finish line banner that splits in the middle at the end of the Boston Marathon.

BAA

A finish line banner that is a single piece held by finish line officials

RunCzech

effect you want to create at your finish line.

Finish line tapes are usually made of out nylon and are about 9"-12" high and 6'-10' long. Most races reserve this location for their highest level sponsor. If the race has a title sponsor, the banner most likely will contain the official name of the race, as in "Credit Union Cherry Blossom Ten Mile." There is about an even split among race organizers regarding the type of finish line tape preferred. About half like to use finish line tapes that consist of two halves held together in the middle with Velcro, which pull apart when the finisher crosses the line. Others prefer tapes that are a single piece and are simply pulled out of the hands of the race officials as the winner finishes. Advocates of the Velcro banners think

it creates a cleaner break, rather than having the banner wrap around the winner after the finish line. Advocates of single-piece finish tapes point to the tendency of the Velcro tapes to sag in the middle. If you decide on a Velcro tape, make sure that the Velcro is not too loose, so that it breaks before the runner hits it, and not too strong, so that the runner is unable to break it.

Most events have the finish line tape lettered on one side only. Since it is likely made of a lightweight fabric, if it is printed on both sides the letters may show through. This results in the letters on the banner looking like gibberish. Make sure you have the single side with the letters on it facing the finish line photographers, who are generally in *back* of the finish line. If you decide to print on both sides (just to make sure an over-eager volunteer doesn't put the "blank" side facing the cameras), be sure the fabric of the banner is heavyweight enough to avoid the lettering show through.

Signage

Signs are obviously a great way to let runners know the location of various areas such as registration, porta-johns, bag drop-off, start, etc. Races have great variability in their sign budgets and can choose to be either minimalist or extravagant with their signage. The better the signage, the less time the volunteers will have to spend answering repetitive questions from runners, and the more likely the runners will feel that they know what is going on and where it is taking place.

The same type of store that you may have contacted about banners is a good candidate to produce signage as well. Professionally made signs, rather than hand-scrawled ones, greatly improve the "look" of an event and are likely to be taken more seriously by those reading them. Some races add the name of the race or race logo to their signs in a small font, in order to link them to the event.

As a general rule of thumb, signs printed and then mounted on foam core board are appropriate for indoor use (in the race hotel, for example), while signs with adhesive lettering affixed to Coroplast boards are more substantial and may be better outdoors. The Coroplast signs are quite durable and can be used for a number of years. If the race is on an extremely tight budget, you should at least try to print the signs with a laser printer. These can be laminated quite inexpensively at a printing or office supply store.

If signs will be made professionally, be sure to ask for grommets to be included either in the corners of the sign, if it is going to be hung on a fence, or centered on the top and bottom edges of the sign, if it is going to be hung on a pole. Some

signs to consider include a course map, staging area map and a timetable of events. Finally, have some generic left-pointing and right-pointing arrows made, which can be affixed to existing signs or placed above or below them to indicate which direction people should be heading.

Strive to create a uniform look and design for all of your signs. Often signs ordered by different people at different times create a haphazard look, with different designs, graphics, type fonts, etc.

Plan Ahead

It is a good idea to appoint a "sign czar" from the race committee. This individual will pester everyone on the committee to think through their sign needs and will order the signage well before race day. Many of the sign-making stores have "rush" service, but you will pay dearly for it. Sign orders should be turned in at least 2-3 weeks before race day. It is practically inevitable that someone is going to have a sign emergency and you will be ordering something at the last minute. It is a lot cheaper to minimize this method of doing business.

Think Big

Keep in mind that the primary objective of signage is to convey information, at a glance, to a group of people. This means the signs must be large enough to be read at a considerable distance. No sign should be smaller than 24" x 36," and some may be considerably larger. At mega-races with thousands of people, the signs may end up being banner-sized for a few key functions and may be hung from scaffolding.

Hang Them High

Logic dictates that signs need to be hung from eye-level on up, depending on the number of people who need to see them at the same time. As mentioned above, nearly all signs need to have grommets. The exceptions are signs that can be placed on easels. These are most likely to be signs used indoors at the race headquarters hotel or expo site. For outdoor signs, place cable ties

Figure 11-4

Show Me a Sign

Barricade signage.

Expo map sign. Phil Stewart

L-pole signs create a festive effect. Bob Burgess

Feather banners. MPA Event Graphics

Three sided race day directional sign. Phil Stewart

Figure 11-4

Show Me a Sign (cont'd)

MPA Event Graphics

Use of a giant inflatable start-finish structure is an alternative to a truss structure.

Mile marker. Phil Stewart

Family Reunion area signage. Phil Stewart

Novel directional "Spinhead" sign Phil Stewart

through the grommets for signs that are being affixed to tent poles, French barricades, etc. Signs that will be secured to poles should have the grommet holes centered on the pole, although you may end up simply securing the sign to the pole using duct tape. You may want to tape the sign pole to a smaller piece of wood that can be pounded into the ground with a sledgehammer. This is a far easier solution than trying to hit the top of a 8' stake with a sledgehammer.

Dog-eared or worn out signs do not reflect well on the look of the event. Many events consider their signs as disposable items.

Saving the Signs

Most of the materials that signs are made of are not very durable and are very lightweight. This helps keep the cost down, but it also means that signs will inevitably become dog-eared or marred relatively easily. Some large races (with large budgets) consider all of their signage to be disposable and simply make a new set of signs each year. If the signs are treated with care, however, you may be able to get several years of use out of them. They can be wiped with a damp cloth after the race to remove dirt and stored for the next year.

Water

Very small races may be able to meet their needs for water with a garden hose hooked up to a spigot in a nearby building. (Be sure to check with the authorities to make sure the water is potable.) As races increase in size, though, the demand for water will outstrip this supply method quickly. While some events may tap into municipal water through fire hydrants (although again it is important to check with the municipality about the potability of city water), more and more events purchase water from a bottled water company. In a perfect world, every race would have an in-kind spring water sponsor that would agree to provide (and maybe even deliver) enough water for the entire event. These sponsors are difficult to come by, however, so it is likely that water will have to

be purchased. It's possible that a water vendor may be amenable to negotiating a favorable cost. Shop around. See if the bottled water company is willing to work out a deal for a "standby" water supply. This is water that will be delivered to the race site but will remain on the company's trucks and only be used if the event runs out of the off-loaded water. Since the water is not unloaded from the company trucks, it can be returned.

Bottled water can be packaged in different volumes. For races, 5-gallon bottles or case packages of six 1-gallon jugs are best for situations where the water is being poured into cups or mixed with electrolyte replacement powder. Anything smaller than one gallon can be a nightmare to use out on the course. Don't underestimate the challenge of picking up the water and transporting it to the staging area and the aid station locations along the course. If the race budget will allow it, consider paying the company or directly paying employees of the company to handle the pickup and delivery. This is much easier than recruiting race volunteers to load and unload 5-gallon jugs into and out of box trucks. Although runners certainly don't want to pick up the standard 16.9 ounce bottles at aid stations on the course, it is possible that pre- and post-race water needs can be met by passing out individual-use bottles instead of pouring water into cups from larger containers. Of course, the smaller bottles generate more trash to clean up.

Finally, take some time to consider what will be done with leftover water. Empty jugs will need to be returned to the vendor as well. *See **Chapter 16—Race Logistics and Operations*** for a complete discussion of the operation of aid stations.

Refreshments

As a group, runners love to eat, and a good post-race spread will keep them coming back year after year. Although some races go all out with a post-race breakfast or lunch, you don't have to get fancy to be successful —just have lots of food! The type of refreshments provided at an event can serve to set it apart from the competition. If an event provides something other than the typical fare of bagels and bananas, that may make the race more memorable to runners. You can choose to offer a seasonally appropriate food—for example, if the event takes place in the winter, consider some sort of hot food offering, like soup or chili or at least hot chocolate/cider. Often, you can get food items donated. If you do, remember that these in-kind sponsors can be just as valuable to the event as cash sponsors, so be sure to give them the recognition they deserve. Let local permitting officials know if you will be serving food—there may be additional permits required, especially for serving hot food.

Other things to consider in choosing food (aside from digestibility) include:

- Popularity
- Ease of handling and storage, including refrigeration and/or heating
- Health issues, including concerns about spoilage in warm conditions
- Ease of distribution to participants/requires the least number of volunteers to serve
- Amount of trash (wrappers, containers, etc.) produced—try to minimize

Also, in the refreshment plan, assign volunteers to monitor food consumption, so there will be food left for slower runners. Have the volunteers encourage runners to take only one of each item. Volunteers should also be watchful that rogue participants don't try to make off with whole boxes of food or drink! If you have leftovers,

check with the local homeless shelter or food bank about making a donation. Finally, if companies want to use the race to offer samples of a new product, ask them to provide staff and trash cans.

Other Miscellaneous Supplies

Here is a brief checklist of additional supplies that may be needed. Consult **Table 11-A: Equipment and Supplies List** for a more complete list.

- ***Cones:*** Cones come in a variety of heights, from about 12" through 36". Larger, heavy-duty cones should be used to separate runners and automobiles; smaller cones can be used to indicate the route of the course if it is on streets that are entirely closed to traffic, or off road on grass/trails, or for other less critical functions. If the event is not held in broad daylight, you may want to get some cones with reflective tape on them.

- ***A well-stocked tool box:*** You will never go wrong having hammers, screw drivers, pliers, heavy duty scissors, cable-tie clippers, etc. on hand.

- ***Something to start the race with:*** A bullhorn, a marine horn, or a whistle can serve this purpose.

- ***Something to measure the weather conditions:*** While not vital, it is possible to pick up an inexpensive anemometer at a marine supply store. An anemometer measures wind speed, temperature, humidity and dew point to provide the announcer with the "instant" weather conditions. Weather apps on cell phones can serve this purpose as well. A slightly more sophisticated product is a Wet Bulb Globe Thermometer which measures the WBGT temperature that the American College of Sports Medicine flag conditions are based on. (See ***Chapter 8: Medical, Safety and Security*** for a full discussion of the ACSM Guidelines.)

- ***Miscellaneous office supplies:*** Have a

container full of potentially useful items like clip boards, scissors, Sharpies, tape (including duct tape or other strong tape), extra batteries, etc.

Specialized Personnel

In addition to plenty of volunteers (volunteer needs are discussed in **Chapter 10: Volunteers**), the members of the organizing committee, (discussed in detail in **Chapter 1: Taking the Plunge**), and the medical personnel (covered in **Chapter 8: Medical, Safety and Security**), there are some other "specialized personnel" you should consider enlisting to assist with the event. The necessity for the types of personnel outlined below grows proportionately with the event size.

Heavy Lifters

There is often a good deal of heavy lifting involved in putting on a running event. Do not leave it to chance that you will have some current or ex-Marines or ex-football players show up as

volunteers on race day. Make sure to recruit some volunteers who are willing/able to do this work. Many races pay a small fee ($100 or so) for a morning of moving barricades or hauling pop-up tents, etc. Consider approaching a local moving company to hire some seasoned movers.

Race Announcer

The race announcer is a critical link between the runners and the race organization, the sponsors and the event, and the event and the public. Race announcing is a key function that needs to be performed well. There is no shortage of people, many with smooth-as-silk deep baritone voices, who will step forward (or propel themselves forward) in quest of this high-visibility position. Here are some characteristics to look for in a race announcer:

- ***Knowledge of and sensitivity to running and race organizations:*** Find a race announcer who truly understands what he/she is talking about. Don't allow anyone who

Bob Burgess

Race announcers can use a good support team to feed them information.

doesn't know the difference between a marathon and a 10K to speak into the microphone for very long! Nothing can make a race look worse than having an announcer who cheerfully tells the crowd that "it's a great day for a race" when it's 80 degrees with 70% humidity!

- **The ability to "read" a situation:** The announcer must have a sense of what needs to be said and when. If there are 3 minutes to go and runners are not behind the starting line, the race announcer needs to know that this is what needs to be announced with some urgency.

- **The flexibility to adapt to a rapidly changing situation:** If the race is not going to start on time, the announcer must be prepared to convey this information to the runners in a manner that keeps them relaxed during the delay. The probable length of the delay should be communicated as well.

- **Not thin-skinned and argumentative in high-pressure situations:** The race announcer serves the race director. When the race director asks for a certain announcement to be made, there should be no second-guessing on the part of the race announcer. If the race announcer has just made an announcement and the race director asks him to make it again, the announcer should do just that, rather than wasting valuable seconds saying,

"I just made that announcement." Bottom line: The race director is the boss.

- **Invisible except when the race director needs him:** On race day, the announcer should not pepper the race director with questions, etc. unless it is an emergency. Any questions should have been asked in advance.

- **A good voice (and a long-lasting one):** The announcer's voice should help the runners sort through the relative importance of the announcements—sponsor announcements can carry an upbeat tone, while a reminder to drink plenty of fluids before the race start should carry a hint of gravity, etc.

A note regarding deejays: Sponsoring radio stations frequently want to have their deejays/radio personalities do the race announcing. While good voices may be their strong suits, they will more than likely have shortcomings in the other areas listed above. If the sponsor is insistent, see if the deejay can be limited to greeting the runners, or be assigned to the awards ceremony or some other less critical function.

Items for the Announcer

The most critical duty of the race announcer is to relay accurate information to the runners. This means that the announcer must be provided with the most up-to-date information about the event. The website should be the announcer's first place to look for race information. Other information sources might include:

- The race registration form
- The runner instructions (if separate from the registration form), including medical information and warnings
- A current list of race sponsors
- Pre-race program
- Details about use of transponders, if the event is using this method of timing

---

TIP

A Strategy for Lost Person Announcements

Nearly every race announcer gets beset with requests for lost person announcements. Races have differing policies about what can become a long litany of names and meeting places. One solution is for volunteers to write the names on small dry-erase boards and hand them to the announcer. This is a vast improvement over trying to yell the names to the announcer or handing the announcer scrawled names on tiny slips of paper.

- Copies of press releases

- A list of the top athletes

- Event records

- Historical material

- A copy of the course certification map

Provide the announcer with a detailed timetable covering everything from the opening of race-day packet pick-up through the closing of the awards ceremony. If possible, check the announcer's information if he collected it himself from the race website or registration form. Frequently, the information on registration forms and websites is out-of-date, which may cause the announcer to omit a sponsor who signed up on the late side.

Finally, the race director should work closely with the announcer, in advance of the race, on scripted announcements, including introductions that may need to be made just before the start of the race or at the awards ceremony.

Other Considerations

Some other things to consider to help the announcer include:

- *Wireless versus corded microphones:* Wireless mikes provide the convenience of mobility, but their range is limited and they generally have a longer delay between the moment when words are spoken into the microphone and when they are heard over the speakers. This delay can be disorienting to speakers, including the announcer. If the announcer doesn't need the mobility of a wireless mike, a corded microphone may be more reliable. Always try to get a mike with an on-off switch so off-line conversations and comments aren't broadcast to everyone.

- *An AC outlet:* This allows the announcer to plug in various items, ranging from a computer for announcing names of finishers to the announcer's cell phone.

- *Introduce the sound system crew to the announcer:* Have the head of the sound team and the announcer get to know each other. Most of the time the sound engineers control

the volume level of the sound system. When the announcer is making announcements, the sound team will need to turn down or turn off the music.

- *Review the physical layout:* Provide a good physical layout for the announcer, including a platform about 5' - 10' off the ground, a good line of sight to the start-finish line, a podium, a table for a laptop and an AC outlet if he/she will be announcing names entered into a computer, and a couple of chairs.

- *Provide the announcer with at least one race-day assistant and a radio tied into the main race operations network.* The assistant will have a variety of jobs, ranging from listening in on the radio for instructions that might need to be relayed while the announcer is announcing, to helping to pick out key runners as they finish, to getting the announcer something to drink when he/she starts to get hoarse. In addition, the volunteer assistant can relay any important messages to the announcer if it's information that the runners truly need to know.

- If you plan to have on-course reports phoned in from the lead vehicles, have one assistant dedicated to getting reports from the men's race and another assistant getting the women's updates. If you hire an out-of-town announcer, select an assistant who knows the local runners, so he or she can provide the announcer with the names of key individuals to announce.

- *Have the announcer wear official race clothing.* The announcer is one of the most visible race officials and should dress accordingly.

- *Think about adjustments for Mother Nature:* How will you help the announcer if it is raining or if there are high winds? If the announcer will be reporting the race from a TV monitor or will be announcing names from a laptop, can the announcer's platform be positioned so that the sun is not shining directly onto the screen?

Information Specialist

Even with more ways than ever to disseminate information about an event, runners will not read most of the race information and will show up on race day with lots of questions. Runners expect any person wearing a volunteer t-shirt to be able to answer any question they may have. The reality is that a volunteer serving pre-race water most likely will not know what time late registration ends. Therefore, consider assigning someone to be the "Information Specialist," who is briefed on everything and can answer runners' questions on race day. Many larger races have a small army of information specialists wearing shirts or holding signs that say "Ask Me," etc.

Media Consultant

These days, event information is distributed to runners using a wide variety of platforms, including traditional methods like postcards, blast emails, etc. and web-based methods, including the website and any social media platforms employed by the event, such as Facebook, Twitter, or Instagram. It is a good idea to have an individual on the race committee who is knowledgeable and skilled in using each of these platforms, but it is even *more* important that the message conveyed via all of the various platforms is consistent. That's much easier to accomplish if *one* individual oversees all of the communication methods employed by the event.

Photographers

Good race photos can help to promote the drama, spectacle and beauty of the race, give sponsors recognition, and capture the elements that make the event unique. As a result, you may want to designate someone with the job of taking photos on race day. Depending on the size of the race and the race's budget, this official race photographer may be a volunteer or a paid professional. If you do hire a photographer, try to be sure that he has some experience in photographing running events, as that will make it more likely that he will get the types of shots you want. You also will want to draw up a contract covering the rights you have to use the photos. If you are paying a photographer a "day rate" (a single sum to shoot the event) you should ask for "unlimited use" of the photos. Unlimited use gives you the right to use the photos for promotion (next year's promotional materials, brochure, website, etc.) and even give photos to magazines/other publications without any additional payment to the photographer. If you have unpaid photographers submit shots, you should expect the rights to be far more limited, unless you secure broader rights in advance.

Prior to race day, plan out with the official race photographer what shots you need, and give him a list—don't forget to include shots showing each sponsor's exposure. Once you have a list, see if it is humanly possible for him to get all the shots you want. If not, set priorities or get additional photographers.

If you have a press truck, make sure that it will allow photographers a good view as the race progresses. Let the photographers know what their vantage point will be, and alert them to particularly good opportunities for getting dramatic or unique shots.

If you plan to have a photographer taking photos at the awards ceremony, dress up the stage, which will be the backdrop for the photos. Often, the stages used for the ceremony are in disrepair and unsightly, but a little window dressing on your part can do wonders. One suggestion is to put a skirt, like the type used at exhibit hall display tables, around the front

---

TIP

A Race Committee Photograph

Consider taking a photograph of the entire race committee at some convenient time. It can make a nice memento for all the committee members and serve as an adult version of the class pictures we received as kids.

of the stage. In general, just look at the stage in advance and visualize how it is going to look in the photographs. Dress it up accordingly.

Ask the race photographer (or assign someone) to take photos to record the logistics and course set up. This will help immensely when planning for the next year's race.

Once you have some good shots, email them (or share them via file-sharing site) to various running publications, along with the race results. Post them on social media. Even if the local newspaper came out and took pictures (and hopefully published some of them the day after the race), they probably won't allow you to have them for use in other publications, so if you want a photo to appear somewhere else, you will probably have to provide it.

Participant Photography

The combination of digital photography and the internet have revolutionized participant photography from the days when companies mailed proofs to participants several weeks after the event. Now photos are emailed or accessible by links within hours to minutes after participants finish. Increasingly sophisticated processing capabilities allow the company to automate the identities by bib number (or even by facial recognition with photos in their databases) and post photos quickly. Pre-ordered photos can be posted directly to Facebook or Instagram accounts.

This streamlining has opened alternatives to the traditional model where participants purchase and download selected photos of themselves. Some companies now offer the photos for free, with the cost being covered by a sponsor whose name may appear on the edge of the photo.

Frequently, these participant photography companies will take some general shots of the race to give to the race director as a goodwill gesture. You might ask the participant photographer to take some shots of the staging area, including runner assembly area, start-finish lines and post-race assembly area.

Prague Half Marathon

12 Special Entrant Categories

THE BASICS

- **Elite athletes.** Most smaller races do not have much of a planned elite component. As a race grows and its budget increases, you may find that you want to attract elites, as an elite field can generate greater media interest in an event and more excitement among the back-of-the-packers who feel inspired by the elites. Enticing elites to an event usually takes prize money or appearance money, or a combination of the two. Generally, you will also need to offer expense reimbursement and lodging to elite athletes, unless you are offering a very large amount of prize money. If you don't pay expenses and have only a moderately-sized purse, you will probably only draw local or regional elites. Paying out prize money, especially to foreign athletes, brings a host of payment rules to satisfy the IRS.

- **Wheelchair and physically challenged athletes.** Most small races don't attract wheelchair competitors unless there is a wheelchair athlete in the immediate vicinity of the event or unless the charity associated with the event somehow involves disabled athletes. Wheelchair divisions in higher profile events reinforce the inclusiveness of the running community and may enhance media coverage, runner support and spectator interest. Most race directors will strive to accommodate wheelchair participants if they contact the race organizers in advance. Wheelchair competitions bring an additional set of organizational challenges, and race directors will need to consider whether the course is safe for wheelchairs, the length of time the course must be open (the fastest chairs are faster than the fastest runners, and the slowest chairs may be slower than the slowest runners), and other special accommodations that may be necessary. In addition, there have been issues over the use of push-rim versus hand-cycle wheelchairs. Physically-challenged participants may require guides in addition to the special accommodations outlined above, and if they are very slow may come into conflict with any time limits set by municipal authorities on how long the course can remain open.

- **Slower runners, walkers and children.** The runners of the first running boom in the 1970's tended to be faster and to train harder than many of today's back-of-the-packers. As a result, races today have to be prepared for a number of slower runners and walkers at their events. Keep this in mind as you plan, as you may need to keep the course open longer than you had originally thought, to accommodate all who wish to participate. Time limits may be imposed by the municipality that force you to develop a strategy for closing the course at a certain time. Because the walkers will get so spread out, have a race official accompany the final one, so that the volunteers will know when they can leave the course. Also, be sure you keep enough food, water, finisher medals, etc. on hand for these later finishers. Young children generally should be discouraged from starting on or near the front row.

- **Charity fundraisers:** If the event is a charity fundraiser with "charity runners," the charities may want to work with you to create special amenities for the fundraisers who have raised thousands of dollars for their causes in order to gain entry into the race. These amenities may include charity tents (often grouped together in a "charity village"), extra food, dedicated porta-johns and the like.

THE DETAILS

Elite Athletes

There is no question that having elite athletes at a race heightens the prestige of the event and increases the chances of a course record that may generate media coverage. Members of the media and the community generally take more notice if you can lure some big names to run the race. At the same time, however, including an elite field adds another layer of logistics to an already hectic schedule. Travel arrangements, hotel reservations, course tours, pre-race instructional meetings, and press conferences are just a few of the issues that will need to be tackled if elite athletes participate in the event. In addition, elites generally don't work for free, so you will have to add a prize structure or pay appearance fees, which will also require planning and decision-making. After the race, there will be tax issues to contend with when the elites are paid. Clearly, before you leap to pursue an elite field, it is wise to consider the costs and benefits.

Elites? Yes or No?

To have, or not have, an elite field at a race is a decision that will usually be made in the very early stages of event planning, and the event sponsors might play a key role in making this determination. If the race has a majority of "in-kind" sponsors and only a few (or no) cash sponsors, the decision on elites will be an easy one—you probably won't have them! As noted above, elite athletes cost money: airfare, hotel rooms, meals, prize money and appearance fees add up quickly. Many major races, marathons in particular, budget from $100,000 to over $1 million or more for elite runner expenses including prize money. As a result, if an event is going to be small, low-key, and monitoring expenses down to the last paper cup, you will probably have to forego an elite field.

Even if an event has a big cash sponsor, or several small ones, you may find that elite runners are not something that event sponsors are interested in. Particularly if the race is a fund-raiser for charity, sponsors may not want to support an elite field. From a public-relations standpoint, sponsors may feel that it would not be appropriate to pay money to elite runners if the public perceives the funds are being ill-spent. Even if the event isn't supporting a charity, sponsors may still have no interest in an elite field. As race fields have swelled with more casual runners and walkers, there is more of a disconnect

between the elites and the rest of the field, which, on a practical level, means that for many races, elites are not as big of a draw as they used to be— for sponsors OR participants.

It may be, however, that event sponsors have just never considered the idea of elites. If so, it will be up to you to bring up the issue. If the money is there and the sponsors do not seem to have an opinion on elites one way or another, you may need to educate them by laying out the pros and cons on elite runners. It may depend on variables such as the size of the city or town, what area of the country you are in, and the attitude of both the local media toward running in general, and the interest from the local running community.

Pros—The Reasons to Have Elite Runners

The major reason to bring in elite runners is that they usually create excitement, particularly in the media. If you have enough cash to afford to bring in several elite runners, the race will gain immediate prestige, especially if the event will take place in an area with no other races that pay

Chris Lotsbom

American elite athletes are well-received at many U.S. events. Olympian Amy Hastings shows the colors after winning the AJC Peachtree Road Race 10K

prize money. Local runners (and the media) will view the event as being "the" race to run. Some back-of-the-pack runners find the elite runners inspirational. One of the truisms frequently uttered about running is that it is the only sport where back-of-the-packers can take part in the same event as Olympians. Savvy newspaper sports writers can tease their readers in the weeks leading up to the race with the list of invited athletes and their stories. All of this added publicity makes the sponsors happy. Large races have grown up over the years in smaller cities and towns such as Utica, NY and Davenport, IA, in part because the areas have embraced the elite athletes from around the world. Interestingly, both of these events have the local newspaper as a sponsor, which provides opportunities for extensive coverage of the international field.

Sometimes an elite runner (provided he/she is charming, well-spoken and interesting) can act as a spokesperson for the event, or you can have him or her do a clinic prior to the race that is open to the public. These options usually will require an appearance fee, which can range from several hundred dollars to $15,000 - $20,000 for the most marquee distance runners,

Some events employ a patriotic theme and target their prize money toward U.S. runners only, as support for up-and-coming U.S. Olympic prospects.

Cons—The Reasons Not to Have Elite Runners

If your primary motivation is to grow the event quickly, carefully examine whether dollars spent on elite athletes (prize money, etc.) might be better spent on direct promotions to attract more runners.

The reality is that most big name runners are relatively unknown to the general public outside running circles. This may result in the local media being relatively uninterested or simply clueless. Moreover, if local sportswriters don't have an understanding of the sport and an appreciation of the times being run by the elites, they may be unable to convince their readers that the race has merit (at least based on the elite field). Finally, the use of performance enhancing drugs by a small number of elite athletes has dampened enthusiasm.

Don't discount the fact that you might be better off relying on local elite athletes to "talk up" the event, rather than runners from somewhere else in the country or world, who may or may not have any appeal in the community, and whose broken English may make interaction with the media, the public and race organizers problematic. A positive word from the town's former high school track star who came back home after college and wins all the local races may mean more than a national-class athlete who races in a different city every weekend.

Prize Money Issues

If you decide that you want an elite field, there are a lot of decisions to be made. First, do you want to try to lure one big name to the race and pay him or her an appearance fee of say $5,000 to $10,000 (much higher for a marathon), or do you want to put that amount up as the prize purse and hope it will attract high caliber regional runners? This decision will depend largely on what you hope to accomplish with the money. The single running star may lead a clinic, which will generate media coverage, then win the race by a minute the next day and leave, taking the money with him. This may be exactly what event sponsors are after, so it might work well for the race. In contrast, a purse of $5,000 is likely to generate interest among a number of top regional and local runners—and perhaps even a national-class athlete if it happens to fit in with his or her training schedule—which could make for a highly competitive race, again generating greater media interest. Advocates of prize money feel that it provides the "purest" competition—the prize money is announced and *anyone* can run for it. Everyone is equal on the starting line and the fastest runner earns the most money. Nearly all mixed-gender races in the U.S. offer equal prize money for men and women. Still other race directors opt for a hybrid of the above, offering some appearance money and some prize money. This option will leave you with a much smaller prize purse once the appearance money is paid. The appearance-fee recipient is likely to win a share of the prize money as well.

To attract more than local interest, a non-marathon race should offer a minimum of between $1,000 and $3,000 in prize money. By the time this is divided equally between men and women, you will see that even $2,000 doesn't go very far. A three-deep prize structure of $500-250-100 for men and for women gets you to $1,700 in total prize money. Most races tend to offer a fairly significant break between the first and second place prizes (the $500 first place drops to $250 in the example above) to provide an incentive for an athlete to win the race. Most races don't go below $100 for a minimum amount of open division prize money. A few events offer age-group prize money as low as $15-25.

Other Prize Money Considerations

- **Marathon prize money:** Because most elite runners run a maximum of two marathons a year, they will want to maximize the payday for the marathons they run. This means prize purses at marathons must be significantly higher than the purses at shorter-distance races to attract an equal caliber athlete. For example, the major *non-marathon* events in the U.S. have prize purses between $30,000 and $75,000, while the major marathon events, such as Boston, New York City and Chicago, *start* at 3 to 4 times those amounts and go up from there. In addition, most elite athletes will be looking for appearance money in addition to prize money for the major marathons. The bottom line is that marathons are expensive.

- **Masters and age-group prize money:** A fair number of races offer prize money to masters athletes (40-and-over) as well. This is a good way to bolster competition in this division, but it stretches the prize-money budget thinner. Including masters money also means that, in addition to open-division

runners, there will be an additional population of masters runners looking for travel and lodging expenses. A far smaller number of races offer prize money in 5- or 10-year age groups. Again, the tab can run up quickly. Offering even $100 in seven male and female 10-year age groups costs $1,400. Another option for age groups is to offer age-graded prize money (see ***Sidebar*** *next page*).

- **Bonuses:** Many race directors have discovered over the years that paying out bonuses leads to both faster times and more publicity. A bonus is a payment in addition to the prize money for bettering a certain time standard. Often the world record, American record or the course record is set as the time standard, because bettering one of these records is likely to attract better media coverage. Other races will simply set other times as the standard, such as a $1,000 bonus for a sub-2:15:00 marathon for men and a sub 2:45:00 for women, or something similar. Like prize money, bonuses are equal opportunity, meaning if a bonus is offered for the men, one should be offered for the women as well (taking into account the difference in the men's and women's times).

As discussed in ***Chapter 9: Insurance and Legal,*** nearly all large time-incentive bonuses (such as a $100,000 bonus for a new marathon world record) are funded by insurance premiums. The race pays an insurance company a fraction of the bonus for coverage—usually about a third of the amount insured—and the insurance company pays the bonus out if someone wins it (if not, they keep the premium). The insurance companies will likely want to know in advance who is in the elite field. The premium may vary based on the credentials of the top athletes. Make sure that the event's timing procedures conform to USATF timing standards if you are offering such an insured bonus, and that the course is properly certified as described in ***Chapter 4: The Course***.

- **U.S.-only money:** After the U.S. failed to qualify a full team for the Olympic Marathon in 2000, many races started to offer U.S.-only prize money, which would be awarded only to U.S. citizens, as a way to support Americans in the sport of running. Nearly all USATF National Championships offer U.S.-only money. Some races provide both "open" (or "international") prize money—available to athletes of all nationalities—and separate U.S.-only money. In this type of event, if the first American finisher finishes third overall, he or she will earn the third place open prize money and the first place U.S. prize money.

- *Preems:* Another way to use money to generate excitement about an event is to offer "primes" or "preems," a concept borrowed from bicycle racing. A preem is a payment to the first athlete to reach an intermediate point on the course, such as the one-mile mark, the half-way point, etc. Over the years, many races have used preems, some successfully, others not so successfully. One of the major problems with preems is the tendency for athletes who know they don't have much chance of actually winning to blast through the first few miles, pick up the preem money, but then not finish the race. After getting burned a few times, many race directors wised-up and started tying the receiving of preems to completing the race. Some races went even further, establishing rules that stated an athlete had to finish high enough to earn prize money to collect any preems he/she may have won on the course.

Prize Money Sanctions

The battles and contortions over payment of prize money necessitated by the need to preserve an athlete's "amateur status" are, thankfully, long since passed. The only remaining vestige is a USATF requirement that, regardless of the total purse, any event that offers any *single prize* of $500 or more must obtain a USATF "National" or "Regulation 14" sanction. (This means if you offer a single prize of $500 or more you must obtain the sanction; if you offer 100 prizes of $499 or less, you do not.) Enforcement of the rule is lax, but higher profile events, especially those dealing with international athletes, should apply for the sanction. (A USATF sanction is required if an American record is set, so if this is a possibility, plan on getting a sanction regardless of the amount of prize money being paid out.) Details and an application can be obtained from USATF at www.usatf.org or through your local USATF Association. An associated "national sanction fee," which should run less than a few hundred dollars, and a follow-up report to USATF are also required. Plan to apply for the sanction a good three months prior to the event. The *national sanction fee* is separate from the *local sanction fee* charged by each USATF association. Those local fees are frequently bundled with insurance coverage, and you should only pay for them if you purchase USATF's liability policy. (See **Chapter 9: Insurance and Legal**.)

SIDEBAR

Age-Graded Prize Money

If you want to offer prize money in age groups but don't want to spend money in all of the five- or ten-year age groups, consider offering age-graded prize money. Age grading is a method of comparing times run by different ages over the same distance, such as a 38:00 10K by a 48-year-old male to a 47:00 10K by a 57-year-old female, using a set of tables (an age-graded calculator is available at http://www.runnersworld.com/tools/age-grade-calculator; many timing companies can provide age-graded quotients for all finishers as part of the results). Using this system, you could offer prize money to the top five age-graded performances, which would be the five best performances by runners taking into consideration their sex and age. In our example above, the 57-year-old female with an age-graded quotient of 79.54 would place ahead of the 48-year-old male, whose age-graded quotient is 77.76.

Appearance Money Issues

Appearance money gives race directors greater control over the elite field, and some high level athletes will only come to an event if offered an appearance fee. Unlike prize money, which is open to all comers, appearance money can be used to bring in select athletes only. Appearance money may also reduce the number of no-shows in the elite field, which can be a problem for prize-money-only races. On the other hand, appearance money may reduce the incentive for a chosen athlete to perform on race day, since the compensation is based on his or her showing up, not upon how he or she finishes the race. *As a result, most races that offer appearance money do it in conjunction with prize money.* This ensures that there is still a financial incentive for an athlete to perform. As mentioned above, in the U.S, the combination of appearance and prize money is much more prevalent in marathons than in shorter distance events. Some athlete agents take a hard-line attitude that if the race does not offer appearance money, then the athlete owes the race nothing more than to show up, run, and take the winnings home. In the minds of these agents, anything beyond simply running the event, such as showing up at VIP functions, doing a clinic, talking to the media, or even showing up at all, merits appearance money. In the eyes of many, this is viewed as a disservice to the sport of running, which needs all the media attention it can get as it competes for the public's attention with the various major league sports. Not all agents operate in this manner (and for some, it depends on the athlete involved). If you decide to offer appearance money, use it on athletes who will work for the race (make appearances, be cordial to sponsors and the public, etc.) to earn the fee, not those who will merely show up and run fast.

Even races that publicize themselves as "prize money only" events may offer athletes a stipend for doing a clinic. Clinic fees can range from several hundred dollars up to $5,000 or more, depending on the quality of athlete.

If you decide to pay appearance money, negotiate with the athlete's agent or directly with the athlete about exactly what is expected for the appearance fee. Get the terms in writing. Ideally, these talks should take place 6-12 months before the event. It is hard to place a dollar figure on appearance fees, as they are mostly dependent on the name recognition of the athlete, how the event fits into the athlete's training schedule, and your personal relationship with the athlete or the agent. Appearance fees for non-marathon events might run in the $1,000 to $15,000 range; for marathons the range can be from $5,000 to well over $100,000.

Appearance money for pacesetters or rabbits: Since nearly all pacesetters are not supposed to finish the race and earn any prize money, if you are planning to use pacesetters in an event you will likely make an appearance money arrangement. Pacesetters are designed to set up a fast pace for the true contenders. This relieves the contenders of the burden of "worrying"

SIDEBAR

Prize Money and College Athletes

There have been some cracks in the NCAA's rules about collegiate runners earning prize money and maintaining their NCAA eligibility. ***Currently, the loosening of the rules only applies to athletes in track and field in NCAA Division I schools.*** Division I athletes may now earn prize money at races, as long as they provide justification that the prize money is used to support their training expenses. If you have college athletes earning prize money, you must determine if they compete for Division I schools before making any payments. Division II and III athletes may not receive prize money. A group called the Collegiate Running Association (https://www.collegiaterunning.org/about) offers extensive information on this topic and actually conducts a limited schedule of prize-money championship events for NCAA-eligible (Division I) runners.

about the pace. There are some athletes who have established reputations as a pacesetters, thereby earning a reasonable amount of appearance money. Generally, only a small number of highly competitive events, nearly always marathons, use pacesetters. However, there has been a bit of a backlash in recent years against the use of pacesetters because, in the eyes of the public, it confuses the issue about who the actual competitors are in the lead pack. Major events are going back to emphasizing "the competition" rather than fast times. The Boston Marathon has never used pacesetters; the New York City and Chicago Marathons have dropped the use of pacesetters. The London, Tokyo and Berlin Marathons, among the World Marathon Majors events, employ pacesetters. It is always controversial—though done in a few marathons—to use male athletes to pace females.

Do You Need an Elite Athlete Coordinator?

Elite athletes are exciting—and labor intensive. Tasks associated with an elite field include negotiating with athletes' agents or athletes themselves, making travel and lodging arrangements in advance, coordinating airport pick-ups and returns on race weekend, hosting an elite athlete hospitality suite, getting all of the elites to and from the race site on race day, and possibly dealing with language and cultural issues, just for starters. In nearly all instances, race directors should not consider doubling as elite athlete coordinators.

An elite athlete coordinator, also referred to as a "professional athlete coordinator," needs to be passionate about the competitive side of the sport and interested in interacting with the elites on a more personal level. Sometimes, recently competitive local runners (or retired local runners) like to take on the role as a way to stay connected to the sport. There are a few individuals who serve as elite athlete coordinators for multiple races around the country (expect to pay these individuals some type of stipend or travel allowance). Since

many of the same athletes compete in races around the country, these elite athlete coordinators truly get to know the runners.

Make sure any prospective candidates have:

- A good understanding of the travel and hospitality industry (they will be booking hotel rooms and researching airline fares)

- Good organizational skills for keeping track of runners' flight schedules and making sure athletes get the right hotel rooms

- An even temperament

- Patience

- An outgoing, upbeat personality

- Tolerance for midnight phone calls and mad dashes to the airport to pick up runners who missed their flights or who were delayed for some reason

- A good relationship with the media to promote the possibility of coverage

Even if you are not going to have national- or world-class athletes at the event, but you are planning to invite fast local and regional runners capable of winning or finishing in the top five overall, you should still designate someone on the race committee to work with those runners. You will want to make sure that there is one individual responsible for getting registration fees waived for those faster runners (if this perk is offered), and then making sure that they get to line up at the front on race day.

The Care and Feeding of Elite Athletes

If you decide to have elites at the event, keep in mind that communication is the key word when it comes to dealing with them. That communication takes place in three segments: pre-race, race-day and post-race.

Pre-Race Communication

The athlete or his/her agent should be contacted well in advance. Most runners who compete regularly set up their racing schedules months in advance. Don't expect to call four weeks before the race to see if they're available. Success will be limited.

Once an initial contact has been made with either the athlete or agent, keep the lines of communication open. Send him/her an invitation letter or email; in fact, many races will send out the invitation as the first contact with the runner or agent. With the letter, include a link to the event website and registration form, course description, prize structure and instructions regarding any activities that the runner will be expected to attend, such as clinics or seminars. If you are offering appearance fees, and/or a per diem, those amounts should be clearly spelled out. This is the time to explain arrangements for any ground transportation from the airport, as well.

Once an athlete has committed to participate in the event, send a confirmation letter or email reiterating the terms of his or her visit.

Race Weekend Communication

If you have promised to pick up an athlete at the airport rather than having him or her take ground transportation, make sure that someone is there to meet the athlete. The driver should be at the airport well ahead of the arrival time, and should have a sign and apparel clearly indicating that he or she is with the race. You should also have given this person's cell phone number to the athlete and/or the athlete's agent, in case there are travel delays or problems connecting at the airport.

Most elite athletes expect that there will be a hospitality suite at the host hotel. Make sure to ask for a room that can serve this function when you are negotiating the contract with the host hotel. Athletes will use the suite to pick up their race packets, get information about course tours (if they're being provided) and relax. Often the elite athlete coordinator will use the suite or an adjoining room for sleeping the night before the race.

The hospitality suite is a good place to have information about transportation to and from the start/finish areas, drug testing procedures (if any), aid stations (especially important if runners will be supplying their own bottles for fluid replacement), and any responsibilities runners are expected to fulfill with the media following the race. Many larger races, marathons in particular, will also dispense this information along with a review of the rules of competition (see **Chapter 14: Rules of Competition**) to athletes at a "technical meeting" the day before the event.

Make sure that someone is available in the hospitality suite on race morning for any crises that might arise. Runners have been known to lose their numbers, oversleep and miss the bus to the start, or become ill and need medical attention. These instances are all rare, but anything can happen! At the race site, if at all possible, try to provide an area away from the rest of the field where the elites can warm up, stretch and access porta-johns that are just for their use. A building adjacent to the start is an excellent location.

Make sure that there is a good system for the athletes to drop off and retrieve their warm-ups. This is particularly important if the race is in late fall or winter when the weather may be inclement. A post-race massage is another service you can offer to the elites.

Post-Race Communication

Try to hold the awards ceremony as soon as

SIDEBAR

Elite Athlete Circuits and Championships

Being part of a series or circuit or being designated as a championship race can generate additional excitement for an event. Below are listed some well known circuits and championships. Some of these are very exclusive and require significant prize money commitments, while some of the smaller championships require very little in the way of a prize purse.

- **Abbott World Marathon Majors:** This circuit consists of six (as of this writing) major marathons around the world—Berlin, Boston, Chicago, London, New York and Tokyo. Elite athletes earn points by placing in the top three at these races over a two-year period that rotates. Highest point earners split a $500,000 circuit purse. Criteria for joining are to be one of the top marathons in the world, investing upwards of $1 million or more in elite athletes and willing to contribute a share of the circuit purse. Even that might not be enough. ""We know that for any race to become an Abbott World Marathon Major, there has to be a strong alliance and desire to succeed from government, emergency services and event organizers," according to Tim Hadzima, general manager of AbbottWMM. "The benchmark for any race to join the Series is high. . . ." (Details at www.worldmarathonmajors.com)

- **PRRO Circuit:** This is a U.S.-based circuit of races (five at the time of this writing) at less than the marathon distance that offer approximately $20,000 or more in prize money and are committed to funding drug testing out of their own race budgets. Events can offer an international or U.S.-only purse. Winners of each circuit race qualify for the circuit championship, which rotates among the member races that pay international prize money. Additional prize money is offered at championship to winners from other circuit events. Approximate financial commitment outside of prize money but including drug testing and share of championship purse is approximately $15,000 annually. (Details at www.prro.org.)

- **USATF Championships**: National championships for men and women in open and masters divisions at all standard distances are awarded at annual USATF Convention in December. Nearly all open events offer U.S. prize money, and a few offer an international purse as well. Championships also awarded in ultra and trail categories. Criteria include a significant U.S. purse—most non-marathon championships fall in to the $20,000 - $30,000 per gender, while the marathon championship can be double those amounts ($500,000 if the marathon championship is the U.S. Olympic Trials, which has a separate bid process). Masters championships have more modest prize money dedicated to masters runners. Selected events must sign a contract with USATF. USATF's local associations also host association championships, which are far more lowkey, and some may not require any prize money. All championship events must be USATF sanctioned. National championships: http://www.usatf.org/groups/EventDirectors/bids/process.asp; Association championships: contact local association.

- **RRCA Championships:** The RRCA offers annual championships for men and women, generally at 1 mile, 5K, 10K, 10 mile, half marathon, marathon, ultra-marathon and cross country at the National, Regional and State levels. Championships must include an open division and five-year age groups. Selection is by championship committee. There are no criteria for prize money, although most *national* championships will offer at least a modest prize purse. Prize money can be international or U.S. only. Prize money at state and local championships is flexible; races designated as state or local championships sometimes offer no prize money, a small purse, or somewhat more. Championships may receive product free or at reduced rates from select RRCA sponsors. Events must be hosted by RRCA Member Clubs. (http://www.rrca.org/our-programs-services/programs/rrca-championship-series/hosting-an-rrca-championship-event)

- **Bring Back the Mile Grand Prix Tour:** A U.S. based tour of road miles offering tour prize money of $2,500-$1,000-$750-$500 in addition to prize money at the individual tour events. Visit www.bringbackthemile.com/tour or contact media@bringbackthemile.com.

possible after the race, and don't drag it out. Often, elite athletes are on a tight time schedule and need to catch a flight soon after the race. Of course there are sometimes problems with results that cannot be helped. Keep in close contact with the timing/scoring personnel, so that if there is a problem, athletes won't be waiting around for a ceremony that might not take place. (For more on awards ceremonies, see *Chapter 18: Awards, Awards Ceremonies, Entertainment and Results Posting.*)

Make sure that the athletes get to the airport on time. Many races will post the schedule of shuttles to the airport in the hospitality suite. Encourage the runners to return to the hospitality suite after the awards ceremony to make sure that they are clear on the arrangements. There should be a race representative in the suite at all times, ready to answer questions.

Paying Athletes

Like any contractor or vendor, elite athletes have the expectation and the right to be paid in a timely fashion. There are, however, a number of reasons why athletes *should not be paid on race day*, including the resolution of any protests about the competition, drug testing, and the provision of time for the race director to sort out IRS obligations. In the event that there are no protests (protest procedures are dealt with in *Chapter 14: Rules of Competition*), and no drug testing (a positive test has the potential to hold up payment for two to six months while the test result is adjudicated), race directors should be able to disburse checks within a week after the event, and certainly no later than the 30-day standard that applies to most businesses.

The reporting and withholding aspects involved with paying athletes used to be a double-headed demon with a significant amount of red tape required by both USATF and the IRS. With the demise of the rules covering amateurism, obligations to USATF are limited to filing a post-race report as part of the "national sanction" if the event offers a single prize of $500 or more *(see under **Prize Money Sanctions** earlier in this chapter).*

That leaves only the IRS. In practice, many small-prize-money races simply write out checks for the published amounts of prize money and hand them out on race day along with the trophies. While Road Race Management, Inc. does not condone this sort of *laissez-faire* approach, we certainly are aware that it is surprisingly prevalent, even among some large races. We are not aware of the IRS auditing and penalizing a race for simply paying out prize money, but the fact remains that if you pay prize or appearance money, you have the same obligations as any business paying its self-employed contractors. If you have foreign athletes in the field, the headaches become more substantial. Below appears a short overview of the basic rules for U.S. and foreign athletes; for additional details, contact your accounting professional.

- *U.S. citizen athletes earning less than $600 in a year: These athletes can be paid directly and no paperwork is required to be filed after the event with the IRS. However, if you award*

SIDEBAR

"Seeded" Runners

If you bring an elite field that is likely to claim the bulk of the prize money, you may want to provide some special accommodations for the top local runners who may not be quite on a par with the elite athletes but nonetheless are well-known in the community. Many races go out of their way to make sure the top locals feel welcome into the race and frequently "seed" them so they can start either with the elites or immediately behind them. You may want to assign someone on the committee as the "Seeded Runner Coordinator," whose job is to offer (possibly free) registrations and extend hospitality to this group. Some races offer separate prize money to the top local runners (be sure to define "local," both in terms of residence and length of time in the area). The bottom line is, in the rush to serve the elite athletes, don't forget the local stars.

any prize of $600 or more, or if an athlete may win $600 or more in multiple races conducted by your organization in a calendar year, it is advisable to have all U.S. citizens complete an IRS Form W-9 in advance.

- **U.S. citizen athletes earning $600 or more:** You must obtain an address and social security number for U.S. athletes (and green card holders) using a Form W-9. This form can be downloaded from the IRS website. You can pay the athletes the full amount of their winnings directly, but you must file a 1099-MISC form and a 1096 summary form with the IRS by February 28 of the calendar year following the race. A copy of the 1099 must be sent to the athlete, one to the IRS, and one retained for your files. *Note: Foreign athletes presenting a social security card are* **not eligible** *to be paid in this manner (despite what their agents may claim) unless they have a green card.*

- **Foreign athletes earning any amount of money:** Foreign athletes are subject to tax procedures upon receipt of *any* amount of prize money. Well before race day, obtain copies of IRS Publications 515 and 519. Prior to race day, each foreign athlete should complete an IRS Form W-8BEN. This form establishes an athlete's country of citizenship. Once the prize money disbursements are set, refer to IRS Publication 515 to see the withholding requirements for each athlete based on his country of citizenship. The withholding requirement calls for withholding 30% of the payment regardless of the amount of prize and/or appearance money, *unless there is a tax treaty that stipulates a different withholding amount.* (The tax treaties vary from country to country which means the withholding can vary from nothing to a certain percentage depending on the country's treaty. As a result, the tax treaty for each country has to be reviewed.) In most cases—including for Kenyan and Ethiopian runners since there are no tax treaties with these countries—you will need to withhold 30% of the athlete's check,

give the athlete the balance, and deposit the 30% with a Form 8109 tax coupon at a bank shortly after the athlete is paid. Early in the year following the event, prepare a Form 1042-S, which lists the amount withheld. By mid-March, a copy of this form needs to be filed with the IRS, sent to the athlete, and retained for your files. There are two additional exceptions to the withholding in addition to the athlete being from a country with a tax treaty exemption. These exceptions are for an athlete claiming his income is connected to the conduct of trade or business in the U.S. (Form W8-ECI), or an athlete who has a central withholding agreement with you and the IRS (obtain IRS form 13930 for details).

This is a greatly simplified version of what is a complicated process. Please carefully review IRS Publications 515, 519, and Form 1042-S; consult the IRS website (www.irs.gov); and consult your tax or accounting professional.

Foreign Athletes and Visas

Red tape has always plagued athletes and agents seeking visas, and the situation has only grown more complicated with the increased security implemented in recent years. An athlete's agent should be responsible for getting his or her athletes into the country with the proper type of visa. Once an athlete is in the country, he or she can generally move about freely. Here is a list of the types of visa granted to foreigners entering the U.S. Only athletes with Q-1 or P-1 visas are eligible to earn money at road races.

- **Q-1** For individual athletes of extraordinary ability. Usually limited to athletes with established credentials (i.e. world or Olympic medalists).

- **P-1** For individuals or teams of athletes of extraordinary ability. Groups can come in under this visa, and the criteria for establishing extraordinary ability isn't as strict as for the Q-1 visa. This is the type of visa used by most athletes coming into the U.S. to compete in road races.

- **F-1 Student visa.** Holders of student visas are technically not supposed to "work," i.e. earn prize money, while in the country under this visa, but can compete in charity events or do promotional work.

- **B-1 or B-2. Visitor's visa.** Designed for "vacationers," holders of this type of visa are not supposed to work or earn money during their stay.

Race directors need to decide for themselves how much checking they will do to ensure that an athlete has the proper type of visa to earn money at their events. Theoretically, there could be penalties assessed by the U.S. Government for allowing a foreign athlete with an incorrect visa to compete.

A small but growing number of race directors report receiving emails from individual athletes abroad who are seeking invitations to U.S. events to include in their applications for visas. It is probably best to rely on athletes coming through one of the established agents rather than taking on the responsibility of vouching for an unknown athlete.

Drug Testing

The drug-testing landscape has changed significantly in recent years, with the testing program now *administered* by the United States Anti-Doping Agency (USADA) or another licensed commercial drug testing company. The results of drug tests are *analyzed and adjudicated* by USADA. There are three types of testing—"in-competition" testing, which is testing that takes place at an event, "pre-competition" testing, which is unannounced testing that takes place at the race site in the one to two days before the race, and

"out-of-competition" testing, which is unannounced testing that takes place when athletes are at home, at a training center, or anywhere else outside of a competition. USADA is charged with conducting both in-competition and out-of-competition tests for all of the Olympic sports, but given its limited budget, the reality is that very few road races outside the major marathons, such as Boston, New York and Chicago, along with selected USATF Long Distance Running

Bob Burgess

Drug testing chaperones prepare to greet elites elected for drug testing. The chaperones stay with the selected athletes until the athletes are turned over to the drug testing personnel.

Championships, get selected for testing. However, a small but growing number of events, such as

SIDEBAR

Race Policies Regarding Past Drug Offenders

The IAAF hands down three different lengths of suspensions for athletes who fail drug tests, based on what the organization believes to be the severity of the offense, the athlete's intent, and how the athlete behaved in the aftermath of the positive test. The mildest suspension is a "Public Warning," which means the athlete only forfeits earnings at the event at which the positive test was taken, but is eligible to compete immediately after the event. The next level is a "minor suspension," which generally lasts six months but can be anything less than two years. Minor suspensions may be imposed if the IAAF believes the use was "inadvertent" or the substance was one frequently found in medications or supplements such as ephedrine. A "major" suspension is two years to life for willful use of steroids, EPO and a variety of other substances, use of masking agents for these substances, and "biological passport" violations. [An athlete's biological passport establishes a base level blood chemistry profile. If a subsequent test shows a changed level in the athlete's blood chemistry consistent with the use of performance-enhancing drugs (PEDs), the athlete can be suspended.] Both the IAAF and USATF maintain lists on their websites of athletes *currently* serving drug suspensions. However, once an athlete has served a drug suspension, in the eyes of the IAAF and USATF he or she is eligible to compete and is removed from the list. An increasing number of race directors, including all of the events on the PRRO Circuit, are taking the stance that they do not want to *invite* athletes who have served major suspensions but who have regained eligibility in the eyes of the IAAF and USATF. These events would be on shaky ground if they did not let the athletes enter their events, but they certainly can elect not to pay any expenses or to extend any elite athlete amenities to these athletes.

Neither the IAAF nor USATF maintain a list of *formerly suspended* athletes, making it difficult to track past offenders who have returned to competing. In 2014, *Road Race Management* launched its "Doping Sanctions Site" (www.dopingsanctions.com), which lists all *current and past offenders*. Race directors can check the drug testing history of any athlete by visiting this site. This is particularly helpful because a number of athletes with active suspensions continue to compete in small prize money events that are "under the radar" with no testing program. An event's entire elite field can be checked at this site.

those on the PRRO Circuit, have decided to be proactive and contract with USADA to test, at the races' own expense, as a way to combat the perception of drug use in distance running.

If you would like to have drug testing at an event (nearly all athletes publicly endorse the concept, so you will be enhancing the reputation of the event, not scaring athletes off), contact USADA at www.usantidoping.org for details. The usual arrangement is to test the top three male and female finishers, plus two randomly selected additional finishers from among the prize money winners, for a total of 10 athletes. The complete budget (including the expenses of the testers who come to the event) should run between $8,000 and $12,000. USADA will provide a manual outlining what is expected from the event. Plan to designate a committee member as the liaison with USADA, establishing a tent or building near the finish line with private bathroom stalls or handicapped porta-johns (these units are large enough to allow for testing), and recruiting about a dozen volunteers. (Don't worry, none of the race volunteers will be involved with "sample collection.") The USADA representative will arrive a day in advance and may conduct a pre-competition testing at USADA's own expense. USADA will work with you to train the volunteers. Most of the volunteers will be "chaperones," who will stay with the athletes until the drug testing process is completed.

USADA will work with you to try to make the drug testing process as unobtrusive as possible on post-race activities such as the awards ceremony or press conferences.

However, there are specified guidelines USADA must follow to ensure the uniformity and integrity of the testing. If you are considering contracting for drug testing, consider visiting another event that is already conducting testing to watch the entire operation.

If you have drug testing at an event, hold off paying prize money until the drug test results are confirmed. The time it takes to receive the results usually ranges from 6—12 weeks. If there is a positive test result, you will need to hold up the money even longer while the issue is resolved.

USADA will inform you if you have a positive test and ask you to keep the information confidential. The athlete's identity cannot be released publicly until the B-sample confirms the positive A-sample and the athlete has completed or abandoned the appeals process. Ask USADA if you can "pay around" the athlete who tested positive, which means that you can go ahead and pay all the other athletes except for the affected athlete. If the athlete ends up being suspended, you will redistribute the prize money to the athletes finishing after the suspended athlete. One of the nettlesome aspects of this period of confidentiality is that some athletes will continue to compete while going through the appeals process and before their identities are known publicly. Once convicted, the suspension takes effect on the date of the positive test, which means any prize money earned in subsequent events after the positive test, but before his or her identity was revealed, are null. Race directors who paid out prize money during this time period may be tasked with trying to get the money back in order to pay it out to the rightful winners, not to mention stripping the convicted athletes from their race results, etc. Rita Jeptoo, a Kenyan athlete who won the 2014 Boston Marathon in a course record time, was stripped of her title and record after her suspension dates were amended to include the date of the marathon. The BAA was faced with the daunting task of recovering and redistributing over $150,000 in prize money.

Wheelchair Competition

Wheelchair competition can provide a truly appreciated mainstream opportunity for disabled individuals to compete, as well as add an element of uplifting drama to an event. (With drafting being a much more significant strategy in wheelchair competition than in running, many wheelchair races are decided by inches like bicycle races.)

Wheelchair competition may also involve a significant outlay of time and organizational resources for race directors—all for only a few competitors, some of whom may go faster than the fastest runners, and others who may go slower than the slowest runners. You should consult with local and state authorities, as well as the federal Americans With Disabilities Act, to see what your obligations might be with regard to physically-challenged entrants. The key standard is the event should make "reasonable accommodations" to include physically-challenged individuals. [Note that this standard may be different for a road race than for a trail run, etc.] It is almost certain you will receive negative media publicity if wheelchair participants are banned. Therefore, it is best to work with members of the disabled community to integrate them into the event. Most members of the wheelchair community will be more than happy to work toward this end.

Practical Matters

As with able-bodied participants, the foremost consideration for wheelchairs should be safety. Look at the size of the event; the road surface—is there gravel, sand, grass, water, bridge grates, etc., that would be difficult for a wheelchair to traverse; the course typography—are there steep grades that would make it difficult to control a wheelchair; and the course layout—is there a crossover point or some other problem in the course that could become dangerous in the presence of swiftly moving wheelchairs? Be sure also that spectator safety will not be threatened if wheelchair athletes participate, and that the course is wide enough so that able-bodied runners and wheelchair racers can be side by side at all times. Finally, let the police know that there will be wheelchairs in the race.

If you determine that wheelchairs can be safely accommodated, check with police and the event's major sponsor(s) to ensure that they agree to having wheelchair participants.

Be sure to indicate on the website and registration form that wheelchair athletes are welcome, and provide a check-off box on the registration form so registrants can indicate that they are wheelchair racers. It is very helpful to have wheelchair athletes identified in advance, and to know how fast they intend to complete the race. If the number of wheelchairs will be limited, be sure to include that limit on the website and registration form as well. Strongly encourage wheelchair racers to sign up in advance. Planning for wheelchair racers can be complex and have implications for the implementation of the race. If a wheelchair racer shows up on race day unbeknownst to the race organizers (especially if the entrant is the sole wheelchair entrant), it can add a significant degree of complication for the operations team.

Don't start wheelchairs out front at exactly the same time as the able-bodied runners, as the wheelchairs take longer to get started, and this slower start might be hazardous to the runners. Most events start the wheelchair division between one and 15 minutes early, depending on the unique course considerations and the speed of the chairs.

Hand-crank Wheelchairs

To add to a race director's confusion, controversy has arisen over whether hand-crank (also known as hand-cycle) wheelchairs should also be allowed to participate in road running events. Hand-crank cycles are powered by hand by turning a handle connected to bicycle-style gears. Such chairs have the potential to go much faster than the more traditional push-rim chairs (up to 40 miles per hour), thereby raising even more safety concerns. The hand-crank operators have asked a number of races that already have wheelchair categories to add a hand-crank category as well, and allow them to compete for similar prizes.

Many push-rim proponents have argued against inclusion of hand-crank chairs, insisting that such chairs are more akin to bicycles, and that the hand-crank participants should use push-rim chairs to compete on a level playing field. The hand-crank operators contend that the Americans with Disabilities Act (ADA) requires their inclusion in running events where push-rim wheelchairs are allowed, and that not all wheelchair-bound athletes can utilize a push-rim chair in a race without extreme difficulty or pain related to their disability. Under no circumstances should hand-crank and push-rim wheelchairs compete against each other. Separate divisions are a must.

Race directors have found themselves in the middle of this debate, and there are no clear-cut answers. The issue of whether the ADA applies has not yet been fully litigated in court, so race directors who refuse entry to hand-crank chairs may risk being sued. Adaptive Sports USA (www.adaptivesportsusa.org), the governing body for wheelchair track, field, and road racing in the U.S., maintains that wheelchair racing and hand-cycling are two different sports and that they should not compete for the same prizes. Both Adaptive Sports USA and the International Paralympics Committee (www.paralympic.org) provide rules governing the participation of wheelchair athletes in road races.

For Further Information

If you want more information on including a wheelchair division in an event, you may want to get a copy of *How to Conduct a Wheelchair Race: Guidelines for the Administration of a Wheelchair Road Race Division*, by Brad Hedrick, Martin I. Morse, and Ann C. Walters (published in October 1994). This 28-page book covers nearly every facet of race management, including the start, course monitors, aid stations, lead vehicle position, awards, etc., from the wheelchair competitor's point of view. A supplement in the back provides guidance on key wheelchair rules.

An updated version of this book can be downloaded from the Road Race Management website (www.rrm.com) under "Resources" at the bottom of the homepage.

Other Physically-Challenged Participants

Race directors should make a major effort, in advance of the race, to identify other physically-challenged racers who may need some type of special accommodation on race day. Blind runners or runners with cerebral palsy may need guides, for example. The toughest situations are going to be those that bring pressure to keep the course open longer than planned. Reach out to every physically challenged participant registered for the race and request information about how they will participate, their special needs, and what their expected pace or finish time will be. Race/start line procedures can then be adjusted as necessary, if possible. The immense appeal of many of these physically challenged participants' stories makes it hard not to find some way to accommodate them. This is why it is so important to identify them early and allow plenty of time to see what, if anything, can be done to enable their participation. You might want to contact the Achilles Track Club at https://www.achillesinternational.org/ for advice.

Figure 12-1

FayFoto/Boston

Push-rim wheelchairs are propelled by hands pushing the wheels and contain no gears.

FayFoto/Boston

Handcycle (also called hand-crank) wheelchairs are propelled by hands cranking a chain with gears like a bicycle. They can attain speeds of over 40 mph.

Celebrities of the Slower Sort

Some races look for celebrities who are not known as fast runners but still capture the public's interest. Years ago, the Crescent City Classic 10K in New Orleans received more "ink" from bringing in the "Playboy Racing Team" than from being the USATF National 10K Championship. Similarly, Oprah Winfrey's run at the Marine Corps Marathon in 1994 and Drew Carey's in 2011 were both huge media generators. The NYRRC has recruited personalities ranging from sex expert Dr. Ruth to former heavyweight champion Ingemar Johansson, to rapper P. Diddy. Before his drug ban, cyclist Lance Armstrong received almost as much coverage for his participation in the New York City Marathon as did the elite runners. If you import a celebrity, make sure to brief him or her on the message you want the media to hear. The real "professionals" among the celebrities will know exactly what you mean and will make sure to say exactly what you want them to say.

Pace Groups

Although the use of pacers is controversial and may be illegal in elite competition (for details about pacing rules see ***Chapter 14: Rules of Competition***), the use of pace groups further back in the pack is an appreciated feature in larger and longer events (half marathons and marathons in particular). Pace groups are led by runners recruited to run at a certain pace—6:00 - 6:30 - 7:00 - 7:30 - 8:00 minute pace (generally in :30 increments), etc.—or pre-set times—sub-3:00, sub-3:10, sub-3:20, sub-3:30, (generally in ten-minute increments) etc. for a marathon. Pace group leaders who can comfortably run the pre-set paces must be recruited (consult local specialty running stores or local running clubs to locate these individuals) and should be given at least a free race entry in exchange for their service. The pace group leaders generally line up with and run holding a light-weight sign with the projected pace or time. Some events offer extra back bibs with the pace printed on the bib that individuals can obtain at packet pick-up to wear on their backs on race day. This gives a larger amount of visibility for each pace group.

Slower Runners and Walkers

The growth area in running since the 1990s has been among slower runners and walkers. The median finish times for marathoners have slowed nearly an hour during that time, and many charity events draw thousands of participants in what is truly a blend between a run and a cause-related walk. Analytical race directors must look at the costs (both in terms of dollars paid for

Dan Reichmann   *John Elliott*

Large pace group signs used at the start of a race; a pace group team leader on the course.

police services and wear and tear on volunteers) of keeping a marathon course open longer than 7 hours so only a handful of the slowest participants can finish. There has been a bit of a cultural clash between slower runners, who may feel that their dollars are driving the economics of the sport, and faster runners, who don't like the slower runners lining up near the front and then walking ten abreast, effectively blocking the route. Beleaguered race directors are caught in the middle. Some forthright communication in advance and special accommodations on race day can go a long way toward easing tensions.

The following are some recommendations for dealing with these slower-moving participants.

- ***Decide how long the course can be kept open, publicize it, and stick to it.*** Making this decision will involve input from local officials and an analysis of the costs. As a rule of thumb, allow time for up to a 15- minute-per-mile pace for runners, and up to 20-minutes-per-mile if "strolling" walkers are expected. Once the time limit has been established, make sure it is mentioned prominently on the website and regis-tration form, as well as in the runner instructions. Let participants know that any athletes not maintaining the cut-off pace will be required to move to the side of the road or to an adjacent sidewalk (or will be removed from the course—in some

sort of "sag wagon" if possible—if that is the policy). If you do advertise that the course will be open for say, six hours, be sure that it actually *does* stay open that long—and that includes aid stations and other supporting facilities.

- ***Explain any changes in services slower runners can expect after course time limits are reached. Have these details included in the waiver.*** For example, if aid stations will be dismantled at six hours in a marathon, include language in the waiver stating that there will be no aid on the course after this time. Elaborate the risks and have participants sign the waiver acknowledging the risks.

- ***Create a separate, shorter event.*** If the race is 10K or longer, you might want to add a

Phil Stewart

Slow runners bring the challenge of how long the course must remain open.

companion fun run/walk (perhaps between 1 mile and 5K) to the event. Instruct runners who expect not to be able to complete the longer race within the time limit to sign up for the shorter event instead.

- *Identify the last participant.* Although many races use a police car or ambulance to follow the last runner, both can be called away for an emergency. It is therefore preferable to use a volunteer in a safety vest or other distinguishable clothing to follow that last participant on foot or on a bicycle. That way, the volunteers on the course and at the finish line can be sure of the last finisher and begin course breakdown after this person passes.

- *Maintain at least a skeleton finish line for as long as the course is advertised as being open.* If necessary, the finish line can be broken down, but keep at least part of it open for any stragglers. If logistics allow, move the finish line, and even the last few miles of the course, to an adjacent sidewalk or bike path.

- *Aid station considerations on course and at the finish.* If aid stations on the course need to be closed down because of time limits and cannot be moved to the sidewalk or the side of the road, leave cups of water on the curb for the last finishers. Make sure there is enough water and post-race refreshments for everyone at the finish line and ensure that the post-race clean-up crew goes back to dispose of the discarded cups on the course.

- *Be sure slower runners get their finisher medals, etc.* For many slow runners, finishing is the main goal—they often don't care about their times. All they want is the medal showing that they made it. Often, they want that recognition as much as, if not more than, the other runners in the race.

  Keep in mind that, for these slower runners, the race is a social event, not a competition. As a result, competition rules and times mean little to these participants, but amenities and recognition for participating are huge.

Charity Participants

The majority of charity participants are likely to be among the slower runners and walkers discussed above, and the policies in the previous section apply to this group as well. However, charity running is big business for both the charities, which reap millions of dollars annually from charity participants, and the events, which gain immense positive publicity (and justification for closing down the city streets) for being the vehicles for raising all of this money. (The Boston Marathon raises over $30 million dollars annually for charity through runners who raise $2,500 or more to gain entry in a special "charity wave," which comprises nearly 20% of the field; the Chicago Marathon amasses between $15 and $20 million dollars annually for charity.) However, charity runners who have collectively raised these massive amounts of money expect VIP treatment from the events. Generally, this takes the form of a "charity village" in the staging area, where the charities can provide a place for their runners to gather before the race (and after, if the race is on a loop course). Event organizers generally foot the bill for these charity villages, which may contain dedicated porta-johns, bag check areas and other amenities just for this group.

TIP

Make the Race Accessible to Under-Represented Groups

Ask yourself whether the event you are directing truly represents the community in which it is held. Are there underrepresented groups, such as disadvantaged youth, minorities or senior citizens, who might like to be included as participants and/or volunteers? Reach out to these groups and the nonprofit organizations that serve them to see what can be done to encourage their participation and to generally create a more inclusive environment.

Charities of all varieties have realized the huge fundraising potential of running events, so race directors are likely to be approached by charity groups seeking status as an official event charity. Some races limit themselves to one official charity; others will have multiple official charities that may remain the same or change each year. Likewise, many of the largest running events, especially marathons, recognize that they provide an important fundraising for charities to raise millions, so they charge a fee to the charities to be charity partners (to cover some of the event's extra expenses).

It is hard to gauge what percentage of the field will raise funds on their own for the event's designated charity. Certainly, after the Boston Marathon bombings, a high percentage of runners opened their wallets. Absent an exceptional emotional appeal for a certain charity, though, event directors might expect 5-10% of the field to raise funds for charity, with the average amount raised of $100 to $150 per person. These figures can trend higher if the event is clearly linked to the charity, as in a "5K

Run to Cure Autism," or "Race for Every Child to Raise Funds for Children's Hospital," etc.

Children

Although the medical science about young runners participating in road races may not be definitive, most marathons set a minimum age of 16 or 18 to participate. Half marathons are more likely to set the age limit at 16. Age restrictions at shorter distances are rare as long as the young runners can finish the course in the time allotted for the course to remain open. Most "Kids' Runs" top out at 12 years old, implying that by age 13 kids might consider the "adult" event. A more subtle way to discourage participation by very young runners is to make the age-group award categories start at 14-and-under or even 16-and-under rather than having a 10-and-under age group. (See *Chapter 14: Rules of Competition* for details about records for young runners.) Whatever minimum age you may have (if any)—

MPA Event Graphics

A charity village features tents for each participating charity.

and there certainly are many children under the age of 12 who enjoy running road races on their own or as a family activity—you will want to *discourage* young children from starting at or near the front of the race for safety reasons. This should be made very clear to parents (some of whom might actually encourage their children to line up in the front, not realizing that they may be run over by the crowd). You should also be vigilant for parents who go overboard excessively pushing or even verbally abusing their children during the event. *(See Chapter 20: Special Types of Races and Participatory Events* for more details about Kids Runs.)

Phil Stewart

13 Municipal Relations

THE BASICS

Without the support of local government, law enforcement, business and tourism organizations, churches and local running clubs, all but perhaps the smallest races have little chance of succeeding. No matter how big or small a race, the initial planning must involve every group and organization in the community that will be affected. Those groups include:

- **Local government.** If an event requires road closures, a municipal permit will be needed. For smaller events, or those in less-urban areas, permits are usually approved by someone in the police or recreation or parks departments. Once an event swells past several thousand participants, it is likely you will work through the mayor's office, which will bring in other departments as needed. Try to get preliminary approval of the staging area and route very early in the planning process. You don't want to spend hours working out details for a course that will not be approved by the authorities.

- **Police.** Law enforcement support is critical to producing a safe race; whether a race takes place on the streets of a big city or on country roads, local (and sometimes state or county) police and emergency personnel must be included in the planning from the beginning.

- **Chamber of Commerce**. Even the smallest towns and villages usually have a chamber of commerce. Chambers are a valuable resource for making inroads into the local business community.

- **Convention/conference and visitors bureau.** In larger jurisdictions, these organizations have the same goals that you do: to attract visitors/participants to the city/race. They may be able to help you promote the event.

- **Churches.** If a race will be held on a Sunday and the course goes by any churches, you may have to make modifications to the start time of the event or work with church officials to somehow engage them in the day's activities.

- **Neighborhoods and neighborhood associations.** You want to be welcomed by the residents on the streets the race uses. Explain the event to neighborhood associations and consider placing flyers announcing any street closures at the homes along the route.

- **Running clubs.** Running clubs are a valuable resource: their members are an excellent source of volunteers, they may have contacts in the local government and/or business community, and many larger clubs have equipment for rent.

THE DETAILS

Getting Permits

One of the earliest tasks for a race director is to learn the procedures for obtaining municipal permits for the event. If you are unsure where to start, call City Hall or go to the city's website and look for information about conducting an event on local streets and obtaining a permit. It is important to have a least a rough course map established before starting the permitting process since, in many cases, a course map is required for permitting. The permitting process will move slowly and may involve multiple meetings with various city agencies that may be affected, *so allow plenty of time—at least six months—for the application* and approval process. Many jurisidictions accept permit applications 365 days in advance of the event—on a first-come, first-served basis. Keep in mind that, while the event may be important to *you*, your special event application may be one of hundreds received by city workers. If the proposed course runs through multiple jurisdictions, you may be conducting this process separately for each jurisdiction! The municipalities' websites may have a listing of departments and agencies, with descriptions of which departments are involved in granting various special use permits.

Permits, or possibly just contracts, with the school or recreation department will likely be required if you wish to use school or recreation center buildings at the start and finish line areas. Having access to a building is a valuable asset, especially in cold or inclement weather. Plus, you may be able to use the restroom facilities in a building, reducing the porta-john rental bill. It would behoove the cautious race director to confirm,

GREEN TIP

Have a Waste Diversion Plan

More and more municipalities are looking for waste management and recycling plans as part of the permitting process. Address these issues prior to applying for a permit, that way you won't be taken by surprise if such a request is made. Showing sensitivity to these issues may be an asset to the application.

the day before the event, that arrangements are truly in place to have the school open and ready at the correct time.

Over the years, cities have seen special event promoters make money by staging events on city streets, such as food festivals, craft fairs and road races. Today, financially-strapped municipalities generally want part of the action. Many jurisdictions charge simply for applying for a permit, then come the additional fees for police securing the streets and for city workers collecting trash, restoring the parkland, and conducting general cleanup. Some cities even charge events for lost parking meter revenue if the event closes streets with parking meters that would otherwise have been used. Any city employees who work the event usually get paid overtime rates for weekend and evening work and often require a minimum of a 5-hour shift, even if the event takes less time. Some larger cities will require you to post a bond against these anticipated charges. You can argue about the economic impact of the event to the city until you are blue in the face, but don't expect much relief from these fees.

With the proliferation of all types of events, some municipalities have reached a state of "event overload." As a result, you may discover that there are limits on the number of permits issued. Particularly with running events, there has been pushback from local residents about the number of days the streets are closed. You may also find that cities will limit the size of the field or limit the time that the roads may be closed. As mentioned, most municipalities review permits on a first-come, first-served basis, so it is important to find out how far in advance of the event date you can apply for the permit—for many jurisdictions it is one-year prior to event day.

You will likely unearth a bevy of municipal rules and regulations that will have to be complied with. These may range from the size of traffic cones, to maintaining fire lanes, to the limits of commercial exposure on city streets. Brace yourself.

If you are serving food at the event, you may have to obtain approval from the local health inspector before a permit will be issued. The 'rules' of serving food vary considerably by location and also by the type of food being handled. There may be requirements for tents to cover the areas that serve food, requirements for hot food to be kept at a certain temperature, or requirements to add hand washing stations, complete with water of a specific temperature, to the porta-john order. Make sure to look closely into the local health department regulations in order to avoid any unexpected hassles on race day, should the health department show up to inspect the event.

Most municipalities don't issue the final permit to conduct the race until several weeks to several days before the event. This leaves race directors in the uncomfortable situation of not having final approval to conduct the event until long after registration fees have been collected, t-shirts, supplies and equipment have been ordered, etc. This is why building relationships with the permitting authorities is so critical—if something is likely to cause a permit to be denied, you want to see it coming so it can be addressed and resolved well in advance of race day. (The late issuing of permits has provided cover for an extremely small number of unscrupulous race directors to cancel events and pocket the registration fees. Frequently these individuals never applied for them at all—or waited until too late.) Doing your due diligence with permitting officials should ensure that you are not denied a permit. However, you should be aware that municipal officials always have the right to cancel any event held on their roadways for any purpose at any time. Last-minute revoking of permits is most likely to be due to weather or security concerns.

Even if an event has existed for many years, do not assume that the local municipality will do things the same way year after year. Cities frequently pass new rules governing events, or new personnel may interpret existing rules differently. Always check early every year to make sure there are no changes in the city's requirements.

Finally, look for ways to create goodwill with permitting officials. You can improve your chances to have favorable interpretations of regulations if you have built good relationships with the permitting authorities. While laws prohibit large gifts or payments (which can be construed as bribes), most permitting officials can receive race t-shirts or plaques thanking them for their support. Consider putting on an event for which the city is a beneficiary or find some way to support city recreation programs. Invite a city official to be a part of the organizing committee. Conversely, be extremely cautious about going over the heads of permitting officials to higher city, state or federal authorities. Even if you "win," it will create ill-will in the minds of the officials whose decisions were reversed.

Working with Police/Law Enforcement

Depending on the size of the event and where it takes place (urban or rural area), you will need law enforcement personnel monitoring the course. This personnel may take the form of the local town police force, or the county or even state police or highway patrol. The route of the course determines who will be responsible for traffic control. A 5K run in a town of 30,000 people will probably require only a few officers from a single jurisdiction to control traffic at intersections, while a marathon in a major metropolitan area may require the expertise of scores of personnel from several law enforcement jurisdictions to protect runners from traffic and keep motorists relatively happy. Since the 2013 Boston Marathon bombings, the scrutiny of road races by law enforcement personnel has increased, with the race directors generally footing the bill for enhanced security-related coverage. If deemed necessary, you may hear from federal security agencies such as the FBI, the Department of Homeland Security or the Secret Service. (A complete discussion of security appears in *Chapter 8: Medical, Safety and Security*.)

Coming up with a course is one of the first responsibilities of the race director. The earliest drafts of the course should be shown to local municipal representatives, local running groups and law enforcement. Never underestimate the value of bringing the police into the discussion early on (after you have an initial idea of the route but before you spend time and/or money to have the course certified). Since local, county and state law enforcement personnel deal with traffic issues daily, they may have some important ideas about where the course can run. They will also tell you if a road you want to use simply cannot be closed due to traffic concerns. It is better to know this earlier rather than later.

Make contacts with law enforcement early in the process of developing the course, and keep them in the loop at every opportunity. As race day approaches, you may want to schedule at least one meeting with law enforcement personnel that will include driving the course and stopping at key intersections as necessary, particularly if the course requires traffic control assistance from more than one jurisdiction. Where multiple jurisdictions will be involved, the value of a general meeting of the race organizers and police officials representing each of the various jurisdictions cannot be overstated—just to make sure nothing falls between the cracks. Talk to law enforcement or local officials about the possibility of posting temporary "No Parking" signs along the course on race day. Race setup and teardown will be infinitely easier if non-race-related parking is restricted. You will want to set up the policy with the municipal authorities for having vehicles that ignore the no parking signs towed from the course. Many cities simply tow them "around the corner" to the nearest street which is not posted as a no parking zone instead of to an impoundment lot. (Some races absorb the cost of towing so they don't end up dealing with angry drivers whose vehicles are towed.) Make sure that official race vehicles, marked with "Official Vehicle" signs, will be able to park in the "No Parking" areas and move about freely on the course after the roads are closed.

Some large cities will charge for lost parking meter revenue if they need to post "no parking" in metered areas.

It is important to develop and maintain good relationships with law enforcement personnel; to a large extent they can make or break the race. Supplying coffee and pastries on the mornings of the course tour and race day is a simple, inexpensive gesture that will win support. A supply of race t-shirts or merchandise (sized slightly larger than the typical participant sizes) is also a good investment. You might also want to give a special award every year to a particular policeman or policewoman deemed to be important to the race's success. If the event features team competition, include a division for law enforcement and emergency responder teams. If the race has a board of directors, consider having someone from law enforcement represented on the board.

Ideally on race day you will have a way to communicate directly with the police. It is unlikely that a member of the committee, unless he or she is a police officer, will have access to a police radio tied into the police network, so make sure that one of the officials on the *race radio network* stays right at the side of a police officer tied into the *police network,* in order to facilitate "cross-over" conversation. (A complete discussion of radio communications appears in *Chapter 16: Race Logistics and Operations.*)

If possible, you may want to see if some sort of "Unified Command Center" can be set up, with representatives from the all the police departments involved in race coverage, the fire department, emergency responders and the race team assembled side by side in a single location. The group will to be able to quickly and decisively address any emergencies that may arise. This

Phil Stewart

Police motorcycle officers are a fixture at the front of all but the smallest races. These officers lead the wheelchair race at the Boston Marathon.

UCC can be in a trailer, a tent or a nearby building.

Even after all the advance planning with the police department, it happens frequently that officers arriving on race day are only minimally briefed about the event. (You may wish to have extra copies of the course map within easy reach to hand out to the officers as they arrive.) However, their word is law on the streets. Inform the volunteers never to get into a heated discussion with a police officer—they will lose 99% of the time. Have the volunteer contact the race director, who can then work with his police contact in an effort to resolve the situation. One cardinal rule of police-volunteer interaction—no race volunteer *ever* moves a barricade put in place by a police officer. If something is not correct, approach an officer and explain the situation; if that fails, radio the race director. If the local police department will allow it, see if you can have a race official who knows the course ride in the lead police vehicle. Police very often won't know your course as well as they should, so having a race official riding along can help keep everyone on the correct route.

Much of the burden of controlling crowds on race day will fall on the local police force. Law enforcement officials are authorized to deal with any problems that may be encountered in keeping the course secure. Count on the police if you need to physically remove someone from the course. If you or a volunteer attempt to do so, you could be opening the door to possible legal action if the individual being removed is somehow injured. Police should also get involved with missing person incidents, especially those involving lost children, and all race volunteers should be notified of where police will take lost children to be reunited with their parents.

After the race is over, send a note of thanks to the police chief for the services provided.

Working with Churches

Many races, marathons in particular, are held on Sundays. If the race you are directing is on Sunday, pay attention to how it will affect the churches on or close to the course. Depending on the length of the race, the best way to avoid conflicts with churchgoers is obvious: don't design a course that will affect any churches. If this isn't possible due to the length of the race, the size of the community, and/or the number of churches in the area, there are steps you can take to avoid or ameliorate potential conflicts.

- Meet personally—well before race day—with church officials; nothing succeeds as well as

Phil Stewart

Sunday morning races frequently have to work with churches to minimize the impact of the event on their congregations.

the personal touch. Showing respect by having a face-to-face meeting with disgruntled groups or organizations makes a good impression, and allows the parties to openly discuss the situation and develop workable solutions that will make everyone happy.

- Get church members involved in the event in some way; invite the church choir to sing the national anthem at the start, or station them outside the church to sing as the runners go by.

- Suggest that if church officials are willing to move the times of their services on race day, and congregation members will man an aid station, the race will make a small donation to the church, or perhaps to a local charity that the church supports.

It is still likely that a few church leaders will be unwilling to compromise, taking the position that the services that they provide on Sunday mornings are of a higher calling than a local road race. In these instances, it is likely you will be the one making adjustments.

Working with Neighborhoods and Neighborhood Associations

Engage in building solid relationships with neighborhood ("Citizen's") associations and local residents. Plan on attending neighborhood association meetings to explain the event you will be holding (be sure to talk about the charities) and solicit their support well in advance of race day. Some municipalities require the relevant neighborhood associations to sign off on permit applications. At the root neighborhood level, many events distribute leaflets about pending road closures or otherwise attempt to get the word out via neighborhood association newsletters/emails or other forms of mass communication.

Working with Convention and Visitors Bureaus and Chambers of Commerce

A Convention and Visitors Bureau (CVB) or Chamber of Commerce can be found in most cities and towns in America. In smaller communities (under 50,000 people), the CVB may be referred to as the "meeting and visitors bureau" or sometimes just the "visitors bureau." Their input, assistance and approval can help make an event successful. As race director, it is your responsibility to learn all you can about how these organizations operate in the local community and what their goals are; chances are you'll discover that the goals are very similar to yours. The upscale demographics of runners make them an attractive group to bring into town. Websites are the best way to find out about each organization's priorities. You can also learn a lot by looking at the official website for the local community and the community's calendar of public events.

Generally speaking, CVBs and chambers of commerce have mission statements and goals that include showcasing the city, maintaining strong business and community relations, and providing positive economic and financial benefits. You must demonstrate to them how your race is compatible with their goals. For instance:

- If the CVB needs to fill hotel rooms during slow tourism times of year, provide them with statistics showing how many out-of-town runners you expect.

- If the chamber, or perhaps the department of economic development (in a larger metropolitan area), is trying to improve the area's image, explain to them how the race will provide positive media exposure.

- If there's a civic event in town, like a festival, highlight the positive economic impact of the two events being held the same day or weekend.

Take the time to get to know the executive directors and other key players in these organizations. Attend events and other functions, like luncheons and round-table meetings. Arrange to speak at a meeting so you can answer questions that their board members may have. Ideally, have a representative from the CVB and local chamber on the event's board of directors. CVBs and chambers of commerce can assist you in many ways:

- Helping with the permit process
- Working with local law enforcement
- Securing specific services such as porta-johns, trash pick-up and signage
- Recruiting volunteers
- Marketing support, such as direct-mail or email campaigns, calendar listings and website links
- Coordinating and booking hotel rooms (the CVB may be set up to send out the hotel proposal to *all* of the hotels in the area, which saves you having to contact each of them individually)
- Advising on sponsorship possibilities

Keep in mind that these groups are made up of the movers and shakers in the community; they are important—potentially the most important—individuals you will work with to ensure that the race is a success. The ultimate goal is to develop a strong, mutually beneficial relationship. Remember that you're not putting on the race only for the runners, you're putting it on for the community. As any successful race director can tell you, a successful event usually reflects the character of the community where it takes place.

Economic Impact Report

For larger events that attract a fair number of out-of-town participants, an economic impact report is one of the best ways to tout the financial benefits of the event, which can help win the cooperation of municipal and civic groups and organizations. The report should include:

- The amount of money that participants and family members spend on hotels, restaurants and rental cars during race weekend
- Direct spending by race organizers for services like policing intersections and rental fees for portable toilets
- The amount of tax revenue generated by the event

(For information on how to prepare and distribute an economic impact report, see *Chapter 21: Before Next Year*).

Working with Running Clubs

Chances are there is a running group or club in the area whose members should be included in the planning and production of the event you are directing. Many clubs provide general race consulting services, frequently for a small and usually reasonable fee. If you are a neophyte race director, don't underestimate the potential value of such an arrangement. If you are unfamiliar with the Road Runners Club of America, check out its website (www.rrca.org) to find out how to get in touch with a local club. Put a member of a local club on the board of directors for the event, and if you're in an area where there are several running clubs, find a way to include all of them in the event. Running clubs can be invaluable in several ways:

- Members can help design and certify the course and consult with you on other issues.
- Members make excellent team captains and volunteers.
- Members may work for potential sponsors or have other contacts in the community.
- If the club is a large one, it may own a finish line clock and/or timing equipment that you can rent. Some clubs will even do the finish line set-up and timing, often at a lesser fee than a professional company.

SCC Events/Jiro Mochizuki

14 Rules of Competition

THE BASICS

- **If a race is sanctioned by USATF, the distance running rules in USATF's *Rules of Competition* must be followed.** For non-sanctioned events, USATF rules provide a solid framework. The only races required to obtain a USATF sanction are those that purchase liability insurance through USATF, or those that award at least one individual prize greater than $500, or invite foreign athletes. However, many races that are not sanctioned by USATF fall back on USATF's rule book for the rules covering their event. *USATF's Rules of Competition* can be downloaded as a .pdf file for free at www.usatf.org/About/Competition-Rules.aspx. USATF-certified officials can advise on the application of USATF rules. Visit https://www.usatf.org/about/directory/info.asp?parent= Administrative+Division&group=Officials+Committee for a directory of USATF-certified officials by USATF Association..

- **The Road Runners Club of America (RRCA) offers "guidelines" covering the conduct of**

road races. These guidelines provide standards for directing races; RRCA advises member clubs and events to use the USATF rules of competition. (The RRCA guidelines can be viewed at www.rrca.org/resources/event-directors/guidelines-for-safe-events.)

- **In some cases, it's "your race, your rules."** Outside of USATF rules and RRCA guidelines, there are not a lot of standards or rules for many aspects of the race. Set reasonable rules for the event and publicize them.

THE DETAILS

By fiat or default, USATF rules are those most likely to be used at running events. However, there are still plenty of events that are not sanctioned by either USATF or RRCA and thus go off "rule-less." It is best that unsanctioned events fall back on USATF rules, so there is some uniformity among road running events.

A copy of the current edition of USATF's *Rules of Competition* can be downloaded for free from USATF's website at www.usatf.org/About/Competition-Rules.aspx. Users will quickly find that the rules governing road races are not neatly contained in one place within the book, but tend to be scattered among rules covering everything from the javelin throw to "bantam" youth competition. Even rules governing road races are divvied up between rules that apply only to USATF Championships (local or national), and rules for all other (non-USATF championship) events. One way to cut through the morass is to consult a USATF-RRCA-certified long-distance running official, or at least someone who is experienced (but maybe not certified) in USATF rules. You can find certified officials through your local USATF association (contact information for local associations is on the USATF website), or through experienced officials found in many local running clubs. You should also be aware that the USATF rulebook is not static. Every other year at the USATF convention, hundreds of rules (most of which have to do with track and field events, not road races) are revisited (amended) and new rules are introduced. Some examples in road running include new rules allowing for the use of transponder times as official times. Other rules have gone back and forth over the years, including

the rules regarding male pacers in women's events and the rules about the use of headphones in events.

Opening Words About Rules

USATF's mandate is governing the competition that selects U.S. Olympians, and its rules are designed to resolve disputes that may mean Athlete A goes to the Olympics and Athlete B stays home. Every other year at the USATF convention, a horde of officials, coaches, administrators and athletes debate rules such as whether the hammer can have an all-metal or steel head, or the maximum allowance for the inclination of a track. Meanwhile, the vast majority of road race participants are non-competitive and are running for social, fitness and recreational reasons. The problem is where to draw the line for the rules governing the competitive and recreational road racing fields. Elite athletes have rules about who can pace them during an event, while back-of-the-pack family members may run along with mom or dad for a mile or so during a local 10K. During the Boston Marathon, elite runners can only pick up aid from official aid stations, where the bottles cannot be handed to them, while back-of-the-packers may stop at a lawn party to refuel. USATF has struggled with defining the "professional" or "elite" section of a race, where its rules apply, and the recreational section, where only some of the rules apply. Race directors are left to figure out which rules to use and which to ignore with their split fields. This frequent dichotomy is discussed below in the review of relevant road running rules.

Common Distance-Running Rules

Below are brief overviews of a number of situations that most commonly arise in road races and an outline of the USATF rules that could apply. Remember that, technically, these rules **only apply to events that are USATF sanctioned or have chosen to use USATF rules to govern the event,** but the rules generally provide a good framework for most races.

General Protests

If a runner has a complaint about something that happened at an event, the USATF rules outline a mechanism for resolution. In brief, in advance of the race, the race organizers should appoint a *referee* (the race director can serve in this capacity) and a *"Jury of Appeals,"* ideally consisting of 3-5 people. In addition, it is useful to have 2-3 *finish line judges* to assist in the event of a photo finish (see below). The names of these individuals and contact information for the referee should be publicized in advance of the event, generally through posting the information on the race website.

There are two broad categories of protests, each with different procedures.

- **Protests concerning the eligibility of a participant or a team to enter the race.** This type of protest is very unlikely to occur at a road race. Examples would be a participant from a banned country or a competitor banned due to a current drug suspension. These protests must be made to the referee *prior to the start or during* the competition.

- **Protests concerning the conduct of a participant or the results of an event.** This is the most common type of protest. Things that occur *during the race* that may result in a protest range from a photo finish, to a participant cutting the course, to a runner impeding the progress of another runner. Things that occur *after the race* that result in a protest generally involve the results, and

examples include bib switching or an erroneous age. The person filing the protest, who may be another runner, a coach, or a race official, has a certain time period in which to file a protest with the referee.

If the event is offering prize money and the protest involves one of the elite or professional runners earning prize money, the protest must be made within *30 minutes* of the posting of the results. Smaller events that do not have a designated "elite" or "professional" division may consider that this time standard applies to anyone earning an open award. If the event does not have a "professional" section—or for any protests outside the professional section—the time to file a protest is *24 hours* from the posting of results. This time period applies to all competitors in most events and *includes all age-group protests in all events*—even age-group protests in events with a professional section.

Event directors should be deliberate about the posting of results, because results posting is what starts the protest clock ticking. If the event is tabulating results on-site, post a printout of the results in a conspicuous place (i.e. near the stage where the awards ceremony will be held, if you have one) and state that this represents the "official posting of results." If the event is not scored on site, the referee should state when the results will be posted (and where) and that this posting represents the "official posting" that starts the protest clock ticking. In events where results are NOT posted on the race/event day, the race itself may determine and announce/post results at a later date, a period not to exceed 7 days in which protests can be made is allowable.

Within the designated protest period, the individual making the protest may make the protest verbally or in writing. The referee will hear the facts and make a ruling. The aggrieved party can appeal the ruling of the referee in writing to the Jury of Appeals, if a Jury of Appeals has been established by the event. This appeal must be made within 30 minutes (for the professional section) or 24 hours (for the non-professional section) of the receipt of the decision by the referee. USATF strongly suggests that the Jury of Appeals consult with USATF officials about the application of the rules before making a decision. The decision of the Jury of Appeals is final.

To summarize these technical protest procedures—all events not paying prize money should appoint a referee, have and announce a formal "posting of results" policy; have the referee ready to receive protests for 24 hours after the posting of results; and let the referee make a final ruling on the protest. If the event offers prize money, the process is the same, but the time period for filing a protest is only 30 minutes after the posting of results for those athletes competing for the prize money.

Eligibility Requirements

Several decades ago, some of the most bitter legal battles both inside and outside USATF were fought over athletes losing their eligibility when they accepted prize and appearance money in defiance of the amateur rules in effect at the time. Fortunately, thanks to the legalization of prize money at road races by the sport's governing

bodies, those days are over. Now just about the only infraction that will result in an athlete being banned from participation is if the athlete has been convicted and is currently serving a suspension for a doping violation. The ban for a first-time serious infraction starts at two years, minor infractions can last six months. In addition there are "public warnings," which result in the voiding of results from the event where the test was performed but include no subsequent ban. Multiple doping convictions may result in lifetime bans. The most comprehensive list of athletes serving current or past suspensions for doping can be found on the Road Race Management website, (www.rrm.com), or at www.dopingsanctions.com. The IAAF and USATF also maintain lists of currently suspended athletes. *(See **Chapter 12: Special Entrant Categories** for further details.)*

Some events may choose to limit prize money payments to U.S. athletes only or have separate U.S.-only purses. An event can make such an eligibility policy, although it is not a USATF rule (except in the case of U.S. championships and qualifying races for U.S. national teams). In this case, a "U.S. athlete" is defined as an athlete who is eligible to be on a U.S. Olympic team. This would exclude green card holders but would allow naturalized U.S. citizens to qualify. Another eligibility rule that could affect prize money payout calls for restricting payment in USATF Association Championships to athletes who are members of USATF. U.S. athletes competing in an event that serves as a qualifying event for a U.S. International Team (such as the IAAF World Half Marathon championship) *must be current USATF members to qualify for the team.*

Course Certification

USATF requires courses to be certified in order for times to be accepted as World or American

SIDEBAR

Eligibility to Qualify for the Olympic Marathon Trials

There are stringent eligibility requirements for American runners to qualify for the U.S. Olympic Marathon Trials. Both men and women can qualify for the U.S. Olympic Marathon Trials by bettering specific time standards during specific time periods leading up to the trials. These standards are set by USATF approximately three years before the Olympic Marathon Trials, which are generally held in the early months of the Olympic year. There are time standards for both the *marathon* and *half marathon* distances. In order for a half marathon or marathon to serve as an Olympic Trials qualifier, the course must be USATF certified *and the event must be sanctioned by USATF.* Simply having the course USATF certified is not sufficient to have the event serve as a qualifier. Participants in the qualifier events do not have to be USATF members, but if they better the Olympic Trials qualifying times, they will need to join USATF in order to compete in the Olympic Trials.

records (including age-group records) or as qualifiers for any other event. The Boston Marathon requires that marathon courses be USATF certified in order to serve as Boston qualifiers. Certification means that the course has been rigorously measured according to procedures set out by USATF's Road Running Technical Council (see **Chapter 4: The Course**). Even if an event is not USATF sanctioned, it is a good idea to get the course certified anyway. An accurately measured course is one of the most basic expectations of runners and should never be compromised. Courses measured by an automobile odometer are not accurate and are thus a disservice to everyone. Meticulous individuals who are comfortable with numbers can learn how to certify courses, or the certification task can be contracted out to an experienced measurer for a fee. You can find a list of USATF Course Certifiers for each state on the USATF website (www.usatf.org) or the USATF Road Running Technical Council website (www.rrtc.net).

False Starts

Unlike track events, there are no false starts in road races. It simply is not feasible to call back 100, 1000, or 10,000 runners. Your timers must be schooled to start their watches or timing devices when the runners on the front row move—regardless of whether the "go" command has been issued.

Cutting the Course

The rules in this area are pretty self-evident for the runners—they must run the course as certified or they are subject to disqualification. Some European races appear to be looser about elite runners cutting the course by leaving the roadway and going on the sidewalk to shave off a corner here and there. A few foreign runners accustomed to this policy have been disqualified from U.S. races over the years for course cutting that would have been acceptable in Europe.

Going Off Course Unintentionally

Things get more ambiguous if improperly

trained course marshals or poor course markings result in runners going off course. In this instance, officials may take into consideration whether the inadvertent course cutting "materially" affected the outcome of the race, meaning if a runner was leading a race by two minutes and was unintentionally misdirected off the course by 100 feet, the runner could still be declared the winner (although the time would not be considered accurate for the distance if the course was shortened). This is determined on a case-by-case basis. Some races have taken matters into their own hands and offered duplicate prize money or made other gestures to offset an error that was made by the organizers or, inadvertently, by volunteers.

Short Course

If the course is short due to a measurement or course-marking issue, the results can still be considered official, but any records set on the course will be rejected. The Boston Athletic Association may consider adjusting qualifying times for marathoners who missed qualifying times for the Boston Marathon due to marathon courses that wound up being short—or long—due to race director error or an emergency that necessitated re-routing on race day.

Pacing and "Unfair Assistance"

Pacing and "unfair assistance" have been two of the thorniest protest issues, particularly in women's racing. The pacing rule states that pacing is permissible "by a person entered in the event for that purpose." However, pacers cannot *talk* to the runners whom they are pacing or they are in violation of the "unfair assistance" rule, which defines assistance as "the conveying of advice, information or direct help to an athlete by any means, including a technical device." In addition, a pacer must be entered in the race and must start at the start of the race. If a friend or coach jumps into the race and runs alongside an athlete once the race is underway, this would be deemed unfair assistance. Finally, a coach or friend who runs into the roadway to offer aid or advice—or shouts from a lead vehicle that the leader has a 200-yard lead—could result in the athlete receiving this information being in violation of the unfair assistance rule as well. There is perhaps no rule with a greater discrepancy in enforcement between the front of the pack, where unfair assistance is taken seriously, and the back of the pack, where an "anything goes" spirit prevails, with organizers establishing and promoting "pace groups" at various pre-determined paces, runners conversing while pacing one another during the race, and friends jumping in for a couple of miles along the way. If you are conducting an event with significant prize money or with the possibility of World or American records being set, you would be well advised to pay attention to these rules for the front runners, in order to avoid having a protest lodged by another runner or coach.

Unfair assistance rules also cover how aid can be dispensed out on the course. These rules are rarely enforced outside major U.S. championships and international competitions, but are in the rule book and could be cause for a protest to be filed. The rules permit runners in the professional section to take aid only at official aid stations. The aid can only be handed to them by approved race officials. Runners in the professional division are prohibited from taking aid from spectators along the course who are not working at an official aid station. They are allowed to share water bottles and pass cups with other runners alongside of them.

The Finish Line

While a finish line seems pretty self-explanatory, it's not quite that simple, and USATF has a rule defining the finish line: a vertical plane extending perpendicularly up from the *front edge*

SCC Events/Camera4

Pacers (the runners with numeric bibs in this photo) have been employed successfully by many events seeking world records. Critics feel they dilute the competitiveness of the event.

of the finish line that should be clearly visible on the roadway. The finish line may be painted, a piece of tape, or the leading edge of a transponder timing mat. The recommended width is 15 cm. (Many races far exceed this figure with elaborate finish lines with the name of the race or sponsor logos, etc.) The winner is the first runner whose chest breaks that plane. This rule also makes it clear that the *finish line tape is not the finish line*. Although the finish line tape is assumed to be directly over the finish line, this may not always be the case due to wind or to the banner holders being slightly out of place. The judges must look for the breaking of the imaginary plane based on the leading edge of the line on the roadway, not the finish line tape.

Intentional Ties

USATF rules don't prohibit ties, and this is presumably the case whether the finish judges are unable to determine a clear winner or whether the athletes themselves voluntarily decide to tie (usually by clasping hands as they cross the line). If the two runners truly intended to tie and judges affirmed their intentions, then it is unlikely the athletes would protest. The situation could get more delicate if a recalcitrant judge elected to over-rule this intent and declare a winner. In the event of a tie, the first and second place prize money should be added together and split in half.

Records

The rules and procedures governing the setting of World or American records at events are complex, and there are slight differences between World and American records in the open division and in the masters or age-group divisions.

World records are kept by the IAAF (https://www.iaaf.org) at only a select number of distances, which include 10K, 15K, 20K, half marathon, 25K, 30K, marathon, and 100K.

Courtesy of Hong Kong Marathon

Judges had to determine whose chest broke the vertical plane at the front edge of the timing mat which marks the actual finish line.

USATF (http://www.usatf.org) keeps records at all of the IAAF distances plus 1 mile (road), 5K, 8K, 12K, 10 miles, 50K, 50 miles, 100 miles, 24 hours, 48 hours, 144 hours, and 1,000 miles.

In addition, the Association of Road Racing Statisticians (http://www.arrs.net/) keeps world records as well as records for each country. The ARRS U.S. records include single age records for runners as young as four years old.

Open division records. The criteria for setting

an open division record are that the event must be USATF sanctioned, the course must be certified and "record quality" *(for a complete discussion of "record quality courses" see **Chapter 4: The Course**),* the course must be "verified" (re-measured) to confirm that it is at least the certified distance (this can be done either before or after the event), and the record setter must be drug tested immediately after the event. There are timing requirements as well—the record must be a gun time and, even with transponder timing, there must be three stopped watches on *the first place time.* (In the case of an American record being set in an event with international athletes, the person setting the American record will not necessarily be the winner of the race; in that case, *the three stopped-watch times would need to be on the overall non-U.S. race winner and not on the American setting the American record.* The American's record time will be taken from his or her transponder time once it is calibrated with the stopped-watch winning times.) If an IAAF world record is set at a U.S. event, the event would submit the time as a U.S. record to USATF and USATF would submit it for consideration as an IAAF record.

Masters and age-group records. The criteria for masters and age-group records are the same as the open division, with the exception of drug testing not being required and verification being at the discretion of USATF's Masters Records Committee. Net times are also acceptable, as long as the record setter wins the division based on order of finish.

19-and-under records: USATF publishes records in the "junior" division, which is ages 16-19, and maintains single age records for all ages based on data submitted by race directors. The Association of Road Racing Statisticians keeps records for ages as young as four.

If a race organizer thinks a record has been broken, after fulfilling these requirements he or she will need to submit a "record application" form (available on USATF's website, www.usatf.org) to USATF's Records Committee, which will officially ratify (or reject) the record at USATF's annual convention held in early December each year. Until approved, records should be listed as "pending."

Use of Headphones

USATF opened up a hornet's nest of controversy when it passed a rule banning headphones in races for safety reasons in 2006. Armed with stories about ear-budded runners being struck by cars or getting entangled with their cohorts and suffering injuries, USATF was well intentioned but

Dennis Steinauer

Headphones became so ubiquitous in road races that a rule to ban them was shortlived. Today their use is "discouraged" for safety reasons.

ran into the face of the worldwide popularity of digital music players (and a marriage of commercial titans like Nike and Apple promoting these devices for runners). A few years later, USATF changed the rule to discourage but not to ban headphones. Likewise, the RRCA guideline discourages but does not recommend banning the use of headphones. (The RRCA will not insure events that *actively encourage* the use of headphones.) Currently, most race directors simply discourage the use of headphones by pointing out the safety issues. A few races still state a "no headphones" policy in their race materials, but do not generally enforce it.

Hands-on Medical Examinations

At the 1984 Olympics in Los Angeles, Swiss marathoner Gabriela Andersen-Schiess staggered toward the finish line in serious heat distress while medical officials agonized about whether to intervene to examine her—which would have disqualified her under the rules in place at the time—or whether to let her finish—which could subject her to serious injury. After this incident, viewed by millions on TV worldwide, USATF passed a rule that allows for a hands-on, on-course medical exam by officials, *as long as it doesn't shorten the distance the runner has to travel to get to the finish line.*

Timing and Scoring

The introduction of transponder-based timing in the mid-1990s produced many difficult issues for rule makers. Suddenly runners had both traditional "gun" times based on the elapsed time from the starting gun, and "net" times, which are based on each runner's elapsed time between crossing the timing mats at the starting line and crossing those at the finish line. The problem was that the use of net times as official times could potentially be at odds with the order in which runners

cross the finish line. Not surprisingly, net times became a big hit with runners further back in the pack, because they were no longer "penalized" for the time spent waiting to cross the starting line at big events, especially those with wave starts. As with a number of other rules, the needs of the runners at the front of the pack (where order of finish is key) is at variance with the needs of the runners at the back of the pack, where not being penalized for having to wait to start the race is key. USATF responded by creating a bifurcated set of rules—one set for the "professional division" (i.e. prize-money winners), which requires the use of gun times as the official times, and another for the masses, in which net times can be considered as official times. Age-group competitors are caught in the middle—the rules allow for the use of net times for age-group winners, as long as the runner with the fastest net time places first in the age group based on gun time. (For a complete discussion of transponder timing, see *Chapter 17: Timing and Scoring*.) At many smaller races, these USATF rules are not necessarily followed. The use of gun versus net times for prize winners can be at the race director's discretion and should be discussed with the timers well in advance of the event. It's perfectly acceptable for directors of small races to do this, as long as the

SIDEBAR

IAAF "Label" Events

The IAAF offers a program of "Gold-", "Silver-" and "Bronze-" label events based principally on the competitiveness of the professional fields and standards of event conduct. While prominent among European and Asian races, the labeling system is not widespread in the U.S., outside of a few major marathons and other events with top-flight international fields. Events seeking one of these labels are subject to more stringent IAAF rules on the conduct of these events, including rules governing the size of logos on athlete uniforms and a requirement to perform in-competition drug testing. The IAAF label events are promoted internationally by the IAAF. Details about this program are at https://www.iaaf.org/competitions/iaaf-label-road-races.

methods are publicized so that all runners are aware of the scoring rules.

Team Competition

Although there is a labyrinth of rules covering team competition in the USATF rulebook, many race directors set their own rules, especially for corporate divisions, fund-raising teams, etc., that would never hold up under USATF rules. Whatever team rules you set up, make sure they cover who can be on a team, the number of runners on a team, the genders of those runners (mixed-gender teams are frequently incorporated into team competitions), the number of runners who score, and the method of scoring. Then, make sure the rules are clearly spelled out and enforced. For the record, the USATF rules generally allow for up to five members on a team, with the top three serving as scoring members. Team scores can be tallied either by adding up the *finishing places* of each team member or the *finishing times* of each team member. The team with the lowest number of points or lowest combined time is the winner. If places are used, they can be tallied either by including or eliminating the finishers who are not part of any team. Consider the mixed gender competition below, with the top three finishers on each team to score:

1. Mark Heinicke, Team Q, 15:05
2. Dave Kayser, Team Y, 15:12
3. Pam Balcke Team Q, 17:20
4. Phil Stewart (no team affiliation), 17:21
5. Claudia Piepenburg, Team Q, 17:22
6. Rick Platt (no team affiliation), 17:23
7. Susan Debad, Team Y, 17:24
8. Bruce Robinson, Team Y, 17:25

Including non-team runners means Team Q scores 1+3+5 points for a total of 9 points and Team Y scores 2+7+8 points for a total of 17 points. If non-team runners are eliminated, then the 4th and 6th place runners are eliminated and Team Q scores 1+3+4 = 8 points and Team Y scores 2+5+6 = 13 points.

Scoring by time, the competition is much closer, with Team X's time 15:05 + 17:20 + 17:22 = 49:47 and Team Y's time: 15:12 + 17:24 + 17:25 = 50:01.

Other Miscellaneous Rules

USATF offers a host of other rules— sometimes worded as "guidelines"—that reflect sound race management principles, including such things as clearly marking the course, having adequate medical aid, and allowing official vehicles on the course. Other rules cover the verification of competitor ages (birth certificates and passports are acceptable proof), and the payment of prize money in the event of a disqualification (the money shifts down to runners finishing after the disqualified runner). If an event serves as a USATF National or Association Championship, there are additional rules governing these competitions. In National Championships, elite athletes have limitations on the sizes of logos that appear on their uniforms. The logos should be measured prior to the competition. Consult the USATF rulebook for details.

Cheating

Cheating in a road race should be a cause for immediate disqualification. However, the event should spell out its cheating policies (as well as the ramifications of being "convicted" of each offense) prominently in advance of the event, in order to avoid having the suspected cheater use the "I didn't know" defense.

Bib Switching

Bib switching sometimes happens because participants do not realize the implications of giving (or selling) their bibs to other runners; at other times, bib switching is more calculated, such as when marathon runners switch bibs with faster participants in order to obtain Boston qualifying times. Bib switching is particularly prevalent in events that sell out, and escalating registration fees have made the selling of bibs more enticing, as well. In many cases, bib switching is undetectable and will not cause an overt problem. The most common negative ramification of bib switching is likely to be seen in the age-group awards. For example, a 52-year-old mother gives her bib to her 25-year-old son and the results show that "mom" broke the age-group record for 50-54 year old women by 10 minutes, because her son ran 10 miles in 53:21 wearing her bib. A good way to detect bib switching would be to have someone familiar with local age-group runners scan the results for unfamiliar names among the age-group winners. You could then follow-up by contacting these suspicious runners. If the race uses a commercial participant photography company, you could search the digital photos by bib number to see if the finisher matches the gender and age of the suspect. Some events mount a video camera at the finish line to record all the finishers. This can be valuable in detecting bib switchers as well.

Obtaining a Bib Fraudulently

This practice can vary from runners who sell bibs on sites such as Craigslist, despite a race policy banning the practice (some races do have authorized bib transfer procedures), to running with a counterfeit bib, or having a faster runner run with a slower runner's bib in order to qualify for a race (usually the Boston Marathon). These cases are labor intensive to pursue and difficult to adjudicate (i.e. if a runner buys a bib on Craigslist, should the runner who bought the bib be penalized in addition to the seller?)

Course Cutting

The most famous case of course cutting took place in the 1980 Boston Marathon, when Rosie Ruiz hopped on the course at the 25-mile mark and denied Canada's Jacqueline Gareau her rightful spot on the victory platform. It did not take long for Ruiz's story to unravel. Course cutters may hop into the competition

Table 14-A

Using Transponder Splits to Locate Cheaters

The use of intermediate splits generated by transponders can help detect cheaters. Shaded splits are suspect in this diagram.

Age Grade	0.9442	0.9432	0.4670	0.4223	0.2913	1.0771	0.9249
Total Pace	4:40/M	4:40/M	10:07/M	11:41/M	17:20/M	—	—
Chip Diff	0:01.0	0:01.0	15:01.0	18:41.0		31:21.0	9:28.0
Gun Time	46:36.0	46:39.0	1:56:07.0	2:15:33.0	2:53:16.0	—	—
Chip Time	46:36.0	46:39.0	1:41:06.0	1:56:52.0	2:53:16.0	—	—
10 Mile Pace	4:31	4:34	9:46	11:50	14:52	—	—
Incremental 10 Mile Time	4:32.0	4:35.0	9:47.0	11:51.0	14:53.0	—	—
10 Mile Rnk	1	2	10522	15421	17422	DQ	DQ
9 Mile Pace	4:35	4:35	9:52	13:28	17:18	10:43	
Incremental 9 Mile Time	12:52.0	12:51.0	27:38.0	37:44.0	48:27.0	30:01.0	
9 Mile Rnk	3	1	9394	16682	17661	12233	
10k Pace	4:40	4:40	10:04	11:49	17:07	9:48	
Incremental 10k Time	5:37.0	5:37.0	12:06.0	14:12.0	20:33.0	11:46.0	
10k Rnk	1	2	9221	14299	17481	8223	
5 Mile Pace	4:43	4:43	10:19	10:37	17:52	0:38	10:00
5 Mile Time	23:37.0	23:37.0	51:38.0	53:07.0	1:29:23.0	3:10.0	49:59.0
5 Mile Rnk	7	12	11166	12398	17688	1	9723
Age	27	28	45	26	38	55	45
Bib No	51	55	16460	16477	21710	10239	7431
Place	1	2	10195	15022	17728	DQ1	DQ2

in the later stages of the race, or start the race with everyone else but cut portions of the course along the way. Courses with out-and-back sections are particularly vulnerable to course cutting. In the pre-transponder timing days, concerned event directors would put security volunteers out on the course to monitor the sections of the course most prone to cutting. Today, both transponder timing and internet search engines serve as potent tools to detect cheaters. Many races will place transponder mats out on the course to record intermediate splits for all competitors. This data can be analyzed to see if a suspected cheater crossed all the mats out on the course, or if the intermediate splits between the mats are unrealistic (i.e. a runner passes the 5K mat at a 12:00 per mile pace but records a 3:30 per mile pace between the 5K mat and the 10K mat). **Table 14-A** on the previous page illustrates how split times can be used to detect cheaters. Events wishing to use this system will need to pay for the extra mat set ups on the course. Search engines (and various race results-aggregating sites such as Athlinks) allow race directors to research runners to see if their performances at other races are in line with their performance in the questioned race.

Adjudication

Races should publicize their policies, and the penalties for infractions, on their website in advance. Runners suspected of cheating should be given due process by race organizers. A race director may want to involve the referee or another individual as the adjudicator. In a fair number of cases, runners will admit cheating when confronted with the evidence. In the case of bib switching, there may be complete ignorance of the scoring ramifications. Other runners maintain their innocence in spite of overwhelming evidence that they did cheat. In these cases, the race organizers may want to consult their legal counsel to make sure the process is well documented in case of a lawsuit. Convicted cheaters are frequently banned

from participating in future editions of the event. (Bib switchers may receive shorter-term bans of 1-3 years.) However, banning runners imposes the burden of scanning the registration database in subsequent years for the names of the cheaters. There has been some discussion among race directors about starting a "convicted cheaters" database, which would enable them to share data on known cheaters. However, concerns about legal action have stymied these efforts to date. Some information is informally shared among race directors.

A Final Word

Outside of the USATF competition rules and RRCA guidelines, unfortunately there are not a lot of "standards" in the race directing business that all race directors can go by. Frankly, most race directors just determine what is best for their customers and their individual race. Race directors need to anticipate, well in advance, all the issues and unique concerns specific to their particular race. In doing so, they will often need to determine their own rules or policies specific to all these concerns, some which are unique to just that particular race.

Some of these policies include dealing with runners lining up in the wrong corral or wave, a person pushing another in a wheelchair, dogs, baby joggers, headphones, whether young kids have to register when participating with their parents, etc. Reasonableness and common sense are usually the ideal guide. Set rules in advance and publicize them on the race website or registration form. Include the most important rules in the confirmation email sent to all runners. Also consider what the penalties will be for those who break the rules, and whether the rules and penalties are actually enforceable. If it's really not enforceable, maybe it should not be a rule. In general, the fewer rules the better. Keep the atmosphere upbeat and positive, don't come across as a heavy-handed regime.

Phil Stewart

15 Packet Pick-up, Expo and Hotel

THE BASICS

Packet Pick-up Considerations

- Prior to showing up at the starting line, runners need to pick up a few key items including bib numbers, timing transponders (if used and not directly incorporated into the bib) and in most instances t-shirts. The type of venue in which all of this is taking place—as well as the timing of these activities—is dependent on the size of the event.

- The key elements of packet pick-up, wherever it occurs, are to have an *alphabetical* printout of all the pre-registered runners (this may be supplemented with an electronic version of this information in the form of an email or on the race app) posted near the packet pick-up tables with the runners' bib numbers indicated after their names (you may want to add their ages and hometowns to help confirm the identities), enough volunteers behind the tables to keep the lines down to a manageable level, and the packets or bib numbers/transponders organized in numeric order and ready for easy distribution.

- Separate tables for late registrants, goody bags, and for t-shirt distribution (with the various shirt sizes clearly separated and plenty of signage about which sizes are located where) should be established. If late registration will be held, you may want to separate this activity a short distance away from both the packet pick-up and t-shirt tables. Have plans for dealing with both cash and credit card transactions at late registration.

Expo-Related Considerations

- Once a race grows to at least 2,000 participants, consider augmenting packet pick-up and late registration activity with an expo. You might receive an inkling that the event is big enough for an expo when businesses and other races start asking if they can promote or display items at packet pick-up. Expos also serve as a nice benefit for sponsors. Most event sponsor contracts provide free booth space for sponsors of a certain level.

- The largest events host multi-day "Health and Fitness" expos, with hundreds of exhibitors, race merchandise sales, clinics and more. These expos are truly pre-race celebrations of the sport and can be hugely profitable for the race organizers and popular with participants.

- Holding an expo can be as intensive a task as putting on the race, so find an individual dedicated solely to managing the expo. Expo management has four distinct components—finding a suitable site and time frame, soliciting and working with the vendors, creating a floor plan, and managing the expo itself. Never lose sight of the fact that the most important aspect of the expo should be the ease of packet pick-up and late registration for the participants. Runners will be unforgiving if this is not the case.

Hotel-Related Considerations

- The hotel business is all about occupancy rates. The equation looks like this—you bring more people into a hotel and the hotel gives you "concessions" in return. These concessions can range from reduced room rates to free/reduced price meeting space for committee meetings or the expo, to reduced rates for meals in the hotel. The standard unit of measurement for occupancy rates is the "room night." One person staying in one room for one night equals one room night. If the same person stays for two nights, that equals two room nights, etc.

- Running events have some pluses and minuses in the minds of hotel operators. The plus is that they represent repeat business year after year, unlike many meetings or conventions that may be one-time only events or rotate from city to city. The downside is that most runners only stay in the hotel the night before the race; convention attendees tend to stay multiple nights.

- Food functions greatly increase the value of the contract with a hotel, so things like a VIP dinner for the race committee or a pasta dinner for participants are a big plus. When working with a hotel, you will quickly learn that the room block, meeting space requirements, and food functions are inextricably linked and will be negotiated as a package.

THE DETAILS

If the event you are directing is small and does not attract a significant number of out-of-towners, you may be able skip the second half of this chapter, which is all about expos and hotels—the expo and hotel business is all about numbers. However, all but the smallest races—those with race-day registration only—will have packet pick-up, so the first part of this chapter is important for both large and small races. Bear in mind, though, that "small" in a small town is different than "small" in a large city, so it may be worth at least checking with some local hotels to see if participant numbers are large enough to justify a room block and/or expo space, and check with local vendors to see if they are interested in purchasing an expo booth. Even in a small town, you probably should have at least 500 to 1,000 runners to interest hotels in setting aside room blocks, and as high as 2,500 runners to interest companies in shelling out fees to participate in an expo. Small races might want to consider a "Health Fair" instead of an expo, with local hospitals taking blood pressure and BMI readings, as well as podiatrists, massage specialists, etc. participating at no or a very low cost.

Packet/T-shirt Pick-up and Late Registration

Whether the event you are directing is small, with packet pick-up taking place only at the race site, or large, with these activities taking place in the context of a full-blown expo at a hotel or convention center, the basic packet pick-up functions remain pretty much the same as those outlined below. Activities that are more likely associated with expos at larger events, such as sales of race merchandise and clinics, are covered in the Expos section later in this chapter.

Packet Pick-Up: Pre-Race and Race-Day

Organization of Packet-Pick-Up

Nearly all but the largest races offer *race-day* packet pick-up, and for the smallest races this may be the *only* time to pick up bib numbers and transponders. However, if a race is larger than about 500 runners but still does not have an official expo, consider having a pre-race day packet pick-up/late registration location for the convenience of the runners (especially for events with early morning starts).

Pre-race packet pickup can take place at a local school or recreation center, or perhaps at the a sponsor location or local running store, either of which may be eager to provide space due to the increased foot-traffic generated. A successful pre-race day packet pick-up can help to prevent runner frustration over long lines on race morning. But remember, if you are providing pre-race packet pickup at an off-race site location *and* on race day at the race site, you will need to arrange to transport all of the materials as well as the t-shirts from the pre-race site to the race-day site.

If packet pickup will be held outdoors, prepare for inclement weather by arranging for the option to move it indoors or under a tent (a 10' x 10' pop-up, at a minimum). In addition to serving as shelter, a designated packet pickup tent at the race site provides runners with a visual cue directing them to the most important pre-race stop before they head to the starting line. Make sure that there are plenty of tables, chairs, and volunteers in the packet pick-up tent. In addition, you will need a flat posting surface on which to post the alphabetical printout of the confirmed registrants and their bib numbers (unless computer kiosks are being used—see *"Bib Number Information"* below.)

For either pre-race or race-day packet pickup, the easiest way to distribute bib numbers to runners is to keep the bibs organized in numeric order (this is the way they will arrive from the bib number vendor). Packet pick-up tables should be set up with the numbers divided equally at several stations and there should be lots of clearly visible signage, ideally placed at eye level and *not* on the tables, where it will be obscured by the lines of runners. The signs should indicate where the runners should line up, based on bib number (1-200, 201-400, etc.) The number of stations will vary according to the size of the event, with the goal being to keep the lines as short as possible. Once runners determine their bib numbers (see *"Bib Number Information"* below), they will then proceed to the correct table to pick up their packets. Make sure that the location chosen for packet pick-up has adequate space to accommodate the crowd of runners that will occur during the 'rush' periods. The busiest times for most pre-race packet pick-ups are immediately after they open and an hour or so before closing. If you are holding packet pickup under a tent, the easiest strategy is to set up tables around the perimeter of the tent so that the runners remain outside. Volunteers and supplies can be located behind the tables under the tent.

Finally, set up a separate area or table for runners with registration problems (some races call this the "Solutions Table," the "Help Desk" or the "Trouble Desk"). The most common problem packet pick-up staff will encounter will be runners who say they have registered but are not in the scoring database. The volunteer at the trouble desk will need access to the participant database generated by the scoring team in order to search for the missing registrant. It is also advantageous to have internet access at the packet pick-up location, so that the help desk volunteer can

Phil Stewart

The bib pick-up process generally starts with runners checking an alphabetical list to determine their bib numbers.

access the online registration site directly to determine whether the runner appears there. In case the runner's name was accidentally misspelled during the registration process, it may prove useful to search the participant database for the runner's mailing or email address. If the runner cannot be found in either the scoring database or the online registration site, it is possible that he/she encountered a problem during registration and was unaware that the registration did not go through. In that case, the runner will have to register as a late registrant. Often, on-site registration is more expensive than early registration, so make a decision in advance as to whether you are willing to waive that extra charge to maintain goodwill in these situations.

Other problems the help desk staff may encounter will be simpler, like changes in t-shirt size or other runner information. Whether these last-minute changes should be entered into the online registration platform itself or into the scoring software will depend on the method being used for late registration (see "*Late and Race-Day Registration*" below). Make sure the person working at the trouble desk is in communication with the race timers about how to handle changes that need to be made to runner information at this point. The bottom line, of course, is that the timers will need the most current version of the runner database before the start of the race. It will simplify scoring if the late corrections and adjustments to the database can be completed before the race is over.

Bib Number Information

There are several ways to get bib number information to the runners, incorporating varying levels of technology. The least technology-based method is to print out an alphabetical listing of all registrants by last name, with their corresponding bib numbers, and post it at the packet pick-up venue (*see* **photo** *previous page*). If you are using a timing team, they will generally be responsible for assigning the bib numbers and providing this name/number list. Post the list at the entrance to the packet pick-up area (if you have a very large race, you might want to post this printout in more than one location to distribute the crowds). As an alternative to the paper method, some races have computer/tablet kiosks, at which runners can look up their numbers or even register on-site (see "*Late and Race-Day Registration*" below). Other races have volunteers with tablets who can look up runners' numbers for them. While having runners look up their numbers at packet pick-up is a common practice, packet pick-up will run even more smoothly if you can inform runners of their bib numbers *before* they even arrive at the packet pick-up site. Once bib numbers have been assigned by the race timers, many races will post

Phil Stewart

Once participants know their number, they can report to the bib pick-up stations.

a list of runner names/bib numbers on the race website. Additionally, some online registration systems/scoring software will allow you or the scoring team to generate an email or text message to each registrant, with their general information, bib number and t-shirt size. If the event has an App, this information can be made available on the App. Even if bib number information is made available electronically in advance, you need to have some way for runners to look up their numbers at the packet pick-up location, as not all of them will have read the email, checked the App or necessarily remembered their number.

Note: A very small number of races arrange the bibs in alphabetical order; this method can be useful for events that attract a good percentage of participants who are not usually runners (like kids' runs or charity races that pull mostly from supporters of the charity, not the general running populace) and don't 'know the drill' as far as how packet pickups generally work. However, this method is far more labor intensive for race volunteers, who will have to alphabetize the numbers in advance. Most races view this as too much additional work just to save the participants the extra step of determining their bib number by one of the methods outlined above.

Late and Race-Day Registration

If runners will be allowed to register at pre-race packet pick-up or on race day, the most important objective is to determine, with the timing/scoring team, the procedure for entering the late registrants into the database in a timely fashion, so that they will be scored in the race. Have a clear plan as to how to assign bib numbers/transponders and how to get data from paper registration forms, if they are used, into the database. Whether occurring at pre-race packet pickup or on race day, the late registration process should take place in a location separate from packet/bib/transponder pickup for pre-registered runners. This is because late registration takes more time than simply picking up race materials, and it is also nice to reward those who signed up early with a more efficient process. Some races only allow late registration at pre-race packet pickup and not on race day. This method has the significant advantage of streamlining the pre-race process on race day and gives the timing team more time to enter the late registrant data and otherwise prepare the scoring database for race day.

Bob Mallet

Expos at large events require a substantial amount of floor space. The expo at the Credit Union Cherry Blossom is held in the historic National Building Museum in downtown Washington, DC.

Using a low-tech late-registration system, registrants will complete a printed version of the registration form, ideally available on a table away from the registration area, and they will then get in line to turn the completed form in to the registrar and pay. Make sure that plenty of blank registration forms are available, and have a printer/copier nearby for printing additional forms. Each registrar will have a pile of unassigned bib numbers (with transponders taped to the bibs if reusable transponders are employed) and will write the assigned bib number on the paper registration form before giving the bib to the runner and sending the registration form off to a data entry volunteer/team (closeted away from the actual registration table to avoid distractions) that will enter the new registrants into the scoring database.

A more high-tech late-registration system will allow participants to register on computers, tablets or even on their phones, using the online registration

TIP

Expo Signage

Large and well-placed signage is an important component of a successful race expo. All signs should be at eye level or higher, and the signs should be designed and properly placed with the goal of keeping people moving through the expo. Signs directing runners to packet pick-up and late registration are especially important, so that runners know exactly where to go. In a crowded expo without proper signage, runners can easily get frustrated. The expo venue should be able to provide easels for displaying these signs. Some expos will hang signs or banners for the race sponsors high around the walls of a hotel or from the rafters of a convention center. The venue may charge for hanging these banners. The banners add a festive atmosphere and give additional visibility to the sponsors.

Phil Stewart

Large expos require lots of signage including the large row numbers along the back wall to help vendors find their booths. Pipe and drape must be ordered to set up the individual booth stalls.

platform—the same way that they would have registered weeks in advance of the race. This method, sometimes referred to as "registration on the fly," eliminates the need for volunteers or the timing team to manually enter the information from late registrants into the scoring database. However, using the online registration platform for late registration generally only works if the registration platform in use has the ability to assign bib numbers and notify the new registrants of those numbers, since these runners will need to receive their bib numbers immediately in order to pick them up. Check with the online registration provider to see if the platform has a bib number-assignment feature. Timing teams are also generally familiar with a variety of registration platforms, so the race timers may be able to tell you if the chosen registration platform works in this way. The timers will also most likely be able to help set up the platform properly for automatic number assignment. If online registration is kept open in this way, then the timers will download the full list of registrants, with bib numbers, and upload that data into the scoring software once late registration closes. Make sure to work out all of these details with the timing team well in advance of the race.

Whichever method is used for late registration, remember that the process takes time and that the more 'high-tech' the process, the greater the possibility for electronic glitches and registrant confusion, especially for the non-tech savvy. Make sure to have plenty of volunteers to assist and answer questions, and encourage prospective race-day registrants to arrive early. Do not delay the start of the race for more than a few minutes on their behalf. Most races widely publicize the fact that late registration closes 30-60 minutes prior to the start of the race, to allow for adequate time to complete the process before the start.

For both pre-race and race-day late registration, provisions will need to be made for handling cash and credit cards on-site. Decide in advance if you are going to accept checks, with the awareness that bouncing, and thus lost revenue, is a possibility.

Cash will need to be counted and stored in a safe location and then deposited at a bank. Runners will expect to be able to pay by credit card. Many easy and inexpensive methods, including credit card swipe readers that jack into mobile devices, now exist for credit card processing. Most online credit card transactions have a per-charge fee paid by the registrant. Make sure to inform the registrants very clearly about any additional fees they will have to pay for late registration by credit card and how the charge will be listed on their credit card statements.

Obviously, you will need to have access to electricity in the late registration/packet pick-up area, either by running an electrical cord from a nearby outlet or by purchasing or renting a small generator. It is likely that the timing team will need power as well, so you may be able tap into this power source. Make sure there is adequate internet connectivity at the late registration site.

Expos

The decision of whether to hold an expo in association with the event will be based partly on the size of the race. While expos can offer a means to bring in some extra money and increase sponsor visibility, an event should have at least 2,500 runners before an expo is even considered. Without a critical mass of attendees, you will be unlikely to attract vendors to exhibit, so the expo will not be very successful. If the race is smaller but you'd still like to hold some sort of pre-race event, consider a small health and fitness fair that will be held in conjunction with packet pickup and will most likely be free for vendors. It will become obvious that it may be time to consider holding an expo when sponsors and outside groups/vendors begin making inquiries about promoting products or services to the race participants. Done properly, an expo is not just a money maker for the race, but can also provide a desirable venue for runners to learn about the latest training tools and to buy shoes and clothing, usually at discount prices.

Logistics

Start planning the expo as early as possible. The decision of whether to have an expo should be made at the initial race meeting. Unless the event is very large and hires an outside firm to manage all aspects of the expo, the first task will be to find an expo coordinator. An expo is a big enough undertaking that it should be one of the first tasks the race director delegates. Ideally, the person in charge of the expo should have experience with hotels, caterers, convention or meeting planning, and sales (to market the booths). If no one on the race committee has that type of background, choose someone who is well organized, slow to panic and able to think on his or her feet. You also will want to draw on the expertise of the hotel's event staff and, if the budget allows, consider hiring a commercial decorator who is familiar with the chosen hotel.

- **When to hold the expo:** Most commonly, expos are held the day before the event, with expo set-up occurring two days before the event. A small number of events have race-day expos, and an even smaller number keep the expo open after the race is over. Pre-race anticipation is what drives enthusiasm for the race expo, and this enthusiasm dissipates quickly when the event is over. Nearly all events stage the expo in conjunction with packet pick-up and late registration (if registration is still open). These activities will drive the runners to the expo.

- **Where:** Give careful thought to the location of the expo. If the race is large enough to warrant it, stage the expo in a hotel or convention center, instead of a school or a large tent. This will enable you to rely on the hotel and meeting/convention staff to assist you and the race staff with expo management. Hotels will frequently provide the expo space for free

Phil Stewart

Tata Consultancy Services (TCS), the title sponsor of the New York City Marathon, produces an elaborate booth at the event.

Many large expos provide interactive opportunities for runners to leave messages on a "wall."

Phil Stewart

in exchange for a room block and banquet functions; most convention centers will charge for the space. If the race is small and you will have a low-key, pre-race event, a tent or some rented space in a school or other public facility may suffice. Also, check with the event sponsors to see if any of them have enough space to accommodate the pre-race fair/packet pick-up. (A specialty running retail store is a prime candidate.) Not only will this save money on room/tent rental, but it can provide significant extra exposure for the sponsor. Make sure that whatever space is chosen is well lit and well ventilated, and that there is adequate parking or easy access to public transportation.

- **How much space?** This is a tricky question— you want to have enough space to accommodate all of the booths plus the packet pick-up and t-shirt operations, but not so much space that the hall dwarfs the expo and makes it look small. The goal should be to have the expo look bustling and vibrant, but not gridlocked and overwhelming. Diagram a floor plan in order to best understand how to use the available space (allow plenty of space for aisles). In subsequent years, you will be able to consider how the space worked the previous year. There is no single way to design an expo; take into account the size and shape of the room, the location of the entry and exit doors, etc. It is likely you will make some tweaks to the expo design if the same space is used the following year.

- **Duration:** A reasonable goal is to have the expo last just long enough to accommodate packet pick-up activities, providing the vendors with a steady flow of traffic during the hours the expo is open. Vendors do not want such a crush of attendees that merely being in the expo hall is unpleasant, nor they do not want to stand idly by their booths. Remember that staffing an expo is a significant expense for vendors, especially if they are coming from out of town and have transportation and hotel expenses on top of the booth rental fee. Expos for events with up to 10,000-12,000 runners should be able to take place in a single day. Only the largest races—those with 15,000 or more runners—have two- or three-day expos.

- **Set-up time**: While many booths can be set

up in 10-15 minutes, others, especially those of large retailers, may need several hours to construct clothing racks, set out merchandise, etc. Be sure to factor adequate set-up time into the expo plan. Information about the amount of set-up time needed can be directly requested in the vendor contracts. Remember that the event will also need sufficient time to get the packet/t-shirt pick-up and late registration operations up and running. If the race has the funds, hiring a professional decorator, especially one familiar with the venue, will save hours of time and give you an ally who 'speaks the language' of the trade show business. A decorator is of particular use if the expo is taking place in a large, open space like a convention center. The decorator will let you know how much time he/she needs to prepare the room, so you can factor this in to the overall plan.

- **Hours of operation:** A one-day expo with

Some creative branding at the TCM New York City Marathon expo hall.

Phil Stewart

set-up the night before usually opens between 8:30 and 10:00 a.m. If the expo will be held for two days, consider opening later in the morning or in the early afternoon of the first day, to give the exhibitors a chance to set up that morning (and save an extra night in a hotel). Some Sunday events will open their expos on Friday evening to allow for after-work pick-up. Remember, however, if you require the exhibitors to set up prior to early pick-up, you may end up frustrating them with light attendance. If they set up for a Saturday expo and packet pick-up opens on Friday evening, the exhibitors may fret about losing the Friday attendees. Most expos close between 6 and 9 PM. If the same room will be used for the race banquet, etc. the expo will have to close on the early side to allow the room to be reset by the hotel or convention center staff.

- **Designing the expo:** Before selling a single booth, a floor plan for the expo will need to be designed. The size of the space—minus the aisle space needed for the flow of runners—will determine the space available for selling booths. Allow a minimum of 10' for the aisles between the rows of booths, more if possible. Some hotels and convention centers require 20' in front of fire exits and do not allow exhibitors to block fire exits with booths. If there is a foyer outside the expo room, ask the hotel if you can use this space as well. Standard booth sizes are either 8' x 10' or 10' x 10' (a "standard booth unit"). You will soon learn that some exhibitors, especially discount running retailers, actually take multiples of the standard booth unit. Once the floor plan is set, it is likely the hotel will need to obtain approval of the design from a fire marshal. (A fire marshal may also show up during the expo and can shut it down for violations of fire safety regulations.)

- **Flow pattern:** To keep the exhibitors happy, set up a flow pattern that will ensure, as much as possible, that attendees will circulate through the entire expo hall. There are two basic designs that accomplish this objective. *Option 1* is to place late registration and/or bib pick-up at one end of the expo room, and t-shirt pick-up at the opposite end. This ensures that runners will need to traverse the entire length of the expo hall in order to complete their pre-race processing. *Option 2* is to place both the bib and t-shirt pick-up together along the far wall opposite the set of doors participants use to enter the expo room. In general, runners like to complete the bib and t-shirt pick-up before starting to browse the expo booths. There may be variations on these options (*see **Figure 15-1** at right*), but the principle is to maximize traffic flow past the booths, while not making packet pick-up so burdensome that participants want to leave as soon as they can. Be cognizant of the runners' mindsets, which generally are to complete the packet pick-up process *before* starting to browse the expo. If runners are slowed too much—or find it difficult to locate the packet pick-up area—because of the expo design, they will be in sour moods not conducive to spending money at the exhibitor booths.

- **Number of booths:** Determine how many standard booth units are needed for official race functions ("house booths"), including packet pick-up and t-shirt distribution, a separate information table and/or a "Help Desk," and official race merchandise table(s), if you have race merchandise. Finally, decide if you are going to give the sponsors "free" booths as part of their sponsorship packages. If so, these should be added into the total of "house" booths. Now subtract all the house booths from the total number of available booth units and arrive at the number of standard booth units available to sell. If this sounds overwhelming, consult with the hotel meeting planner to get his/her opinion regarding the approximate number of standard booth units that will fit in the space.

- **Pricing booth space:** The pricing of expo booth space is an inexact science. It is loosely correlated with the size of the race. Marathons generally command a premium over non-marathons of the same size. **Table 15-A** on the next page provides some of the vital statistics for a *standard booth unit* at a number of expos. Very roughly, booth prices

range between $.04 and $.08 per attendee. The expos are sorted based on the number of finishers in the event. [***Note:*** most expos, justifiably, cite a higher number of expo attendees than race finishers because the expos are open to the general public, and often families and friends of race participants attend as well.] If an event is holding an expo

Figure 15-1

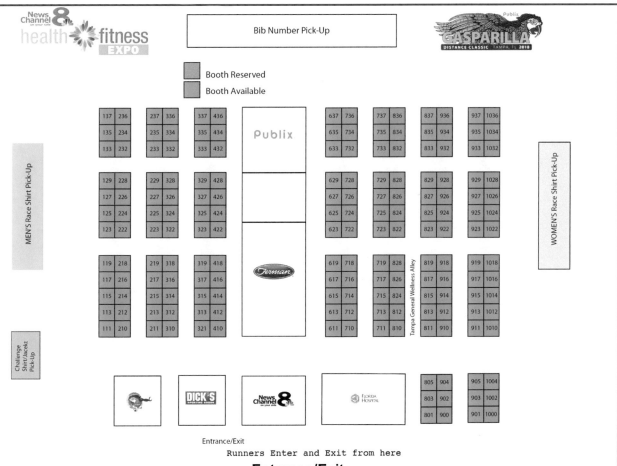

This expo floor plan from the Gasparilla Distance Classic is designed so that the runners enter through the opening marked "Entrance" on the bottom of the diagram and need to pass by all of the booths to get to the bib number pick-up tables, located along the top of the diagram, followed by the t-shirt tables along the sides. The only way out is to return across the expo floor for a second pass through the exhibitors, back through the same doors that were used to enter the hall. Note the large booth spaces set aside for sponsors. Some of the single booth units are sold as multiples, but are not indicated as such on the diagram.

for the first time, it is advisable to keep the booth price on the low side until the event has a track record.

Not all expo spaces are created equal. Most expos will charge a premium for corner booths or other booths that are in the most highly trafficked areas. If you are not sure of the most desirable booth locations in the layout, charge a uniform rate the first year and then, in year two, raise the prices for booths that sold out the quickest the first year. In addition, many vendors (especially large retailers) want multiple booths. If a vendor asks for a double booth, you might want to charge twice the single booth rate; if a vendor

asks for 10 booths, you may give him a "volume" discount. Once you agree with an exhibitor about a booth location, do not change it, at least not without letting the exhibitor know (and being prepared to offer a rebate of some sort if the new space is less desirable in the eyes of the exhibitor). The exhibitors have put much thought into selecting their spots and generally don't like to be moved. Avoid placing competing booths right next to each other, if at all possible. If you want to provide an incentive for exhibitors to pay early, set a policy of not making any booth assignments until payment has been made in full. In addition to the booth space, vendors

Table 15-A

Vital Statistics for Standard Booth Units

Name of Race	Distance(s) of All Events	Race Size	Facility	Length	Set up Day	Basic Booth Unit Price	# of Booths	Attendance	Cost per Attendee
Lake Tahoe Marathon	5K, 10K, 13.1M, 16.6M, 26.2M	2,000	Hotel	1 day	Day expo opens	$300	12-18	4,000	$0.08
Boilermaker Road Race	15K, 5K	18,500	College Athletic Ctr	2 days	Day before expo opens	$350	70	30,000	$0.01
IMT Des Moines Marathon	5K, 5M, 13.1, 26.2	9,000	Convention Center	2 days	Day before expo opens	$600	70	15,000	$0.04
Quad-City Times Bix 7	7M, 2M, Kids Run	20,000	Convention Center	2 days	Day before expo opens	$650	50	15,000	$0.04
Illinois Marathon	26.2M, 13.1M, 10K, 5K, Kids Run	20,000	Rec Center, other public building	2 days	Day expo opens	$650	68	20,000	$0.03
Vermont City Marathon	26.2M + relay	8,000	Hotel	2 days	Day expo opens	$725	40	15,000	$0.05
Lilac Bloomsday Run	12K	42,500	Convention Center	2 days	Day before expo opens	$800	250	38,000	$0.02
GO! St Louis	26.2M; 13.1M; 5K	25,000	Sports/Concert Arena	2 days	Day before expo opens	$850	60	15,000	$0.06
America's Finest City Half Marathon	13.1M, 5K	9,000	Hotel	2 days	Day before expo opens	$900	50	12,000	$0.08
Flying Pig Marathon	26.2M, 13.1M, 10K, 5K, Kids Run	40,000	Convention Center	2 days	Day before expo opens	$950	135	60,000	$0.02
California International Marathon	26.2M, Kids Run	15,000	Convention Center	2 days	Day before expo opens	$1,050	75	25,000	$0.04
The Cowtown	50K, 26.2M, 13.1M, 10K, 5K	28,000	Convention Center	1 day	Day before expo opens	$1,100	180	60,000	$0.02
Credit Union Cherry Blossom	10M, 5K	19,000	Museum	2 days	Day expo opens	$1,100	70	25,000	$0.04
TCS New York City Marathon	26.2M	50,000	Convention Center	3 days	Day before expo opens	$6,000	100+	150,000	$0.04

expect the basic price to include a 6' or 8' draped table, 1-2 chairs, and a trash basket. Let the exhibitors know if the booth will have 'pipe and drape,' or curtained dividers between exhibition spaces. These items may be provided by the hotel or convention center (some free and some for a fee), but if not, they will have to be procured from an outside provider.

- **Fact sheet and exhibitor contract:** Once you determine the number of booths available to sell, the prices, and the design of the floor space, draw up a fact sheet and a contract to provide to potential exhibitors. The fact sheet will contain all the basic information about the dates, set-up times, operational hours, tear-down times, and prices for standard booth units, multiple booths and premium positions, along with the floor plan. The contract will ask for contact information from the exhibitor and the amount of booth space the exhibitor is purchasing. Ask about the nature of the activities that will take place in the booth, so you can identify any exhibitors you might want to reject as inappropriate. Try to get a good mix of exhibitors as opposed to just a number of competitors in the same field. It is best to require payment in full with the contract, since collecting money after the race can be difficult. Most exhibitors will want to pay with a credit card, so make sure you are prepared to handle this method of payment.

- **Electrical and other special services:** In nearly all cases, expo exhibitors (including yourself for "house booths") must order any "special services," such as electricity or WiFi, directly from the venue where the expo is held. Provide information in the vendor contract about ordering these services from the venue.

- **Union labor:** Many hotels and nearly all convention centers use union labor for set-up and tear-down of expos. Be sure to check in advance to see if this is the case with your venue. If union labor is being used, there may be very strict rules about what exhibitors can and cannot carry into the expo area. Exhibitors should be reminded that the cost of union labor is not included in the basic booth price and in nearly all cases this cost will have to be negotiated directly between the exhibitor and the venue (the venue should supply the union contract forms for review).

- **Shipping of exhibitor materials:** Most venues charge for receiving and shipping out exhibitor packages and maintain strict rules about how soon before the expo they will accept delivery. Make sure the exhibitors are informed about the venue's policies, including language directly from the venue about how the boxes should be addressed. Most venues will accept boxes 4 to 5 days in advance of the expo date; many charge a storage fee for holding the boxes.

- **Security:** Although you may want to supply security guards to watch the expo area during off hours, be sure to inform the exhibitors that the event organizing committee is not responsible for theft. Exhibitors should be told to secure their booths when leaving the expo site.

- **The exhibitor mindset:** Smaller expos will attract mostly local exhibitors, including running retailers, other races in the area, and local doctors, podiatrists, and specialists who serve the running public. Larger events will also draw national companies, many of whom are on the "expo circuit" and attend an expo nearly every weekend of the year. These larger, national companies include a number of online or mail-order retailers that sell many items on closeout. These companies are attractive because they frequently purchase multiple booths and set up what amounts to a retail store at the expo. A few events discourage participation by these companies because they do not like the "flea market" appearance of the booths, as well the fact that these companies provide lower-cost alternatives to the official race merchandise. Generally, however, the large number of booths ordered by these companies silences the critics. Other national exhibitors include those that sell sunglasses, sports drinks, physical therapy devices, etc. Instead of taking a booth themselves, the larger running shoe companies will generally contract with local retailers attending the expo, who will then feature their brand of shoes. While most exhibitors are cordial and easy to deal with, some can be a bit competitive and aggressive—monitor the exhibitors to make sure they do not extend their booths outside the space that has been allotted to them, and be prepared for some grousing if the booth space they received is not what they imagined. Nearly all exhibitors would prefer not to be placed directly next to their competition, so when exhibitors are placed into the overall expo plan, be sensitive to this mindset.

- **Expo announcer:** Having an expo announcer is generally a good idea, especially in larger venues. The announcer should make periodic (not non-stop) announcements about the expo schedule, race schedule, clinics (if any) and perhaps include some sponsor recognition.

Phil Stewart

Events that sell official merchandise plan the expo so participants pass through the official merchandise store after picking up their bibs and t-shirts and before they reach any other vendors.

Vendors may want the announcer to plug activities at their booths, including elite athlete appearances. This may be acceptable in moderation.

- **Extras:** Provide a clearly designated information table, and make sure the volunteers who work at this table are well informed about the race and events taking place race weekend. The information table should have an ample supply of paper registration forms (if online registration is no longer available), runner instructions, and course maps, to help answer any questions. Provide the information table volunteers with the answers to the most frequently asked questions and also with information about area restaurants and attractions.

  - **Race flyer/postcard table.** Many expos provide a table for race flyers/ informational materials from other races. While you don't want to compete with races that are paying for booth space, a flyer table will fill up so quickly with promotional materials that it will hardly be competition for a booth dedicated to a single race. If there is no race flyer table, the materials will likely appear mysteriously at other locations at the expo.

  - **Customer service.** Remember that the exhibitors are your customers and treat them with respect. Be honest with them about expo attendance.

Official Race Merchandise

A relatively small number of events, usually only the largest and most high-profile, (and especially marathons) make considerable money selling official race merchandise. Other prominent events just a stride or two behind this elite group can invest a lot of time developing a race merchandising program and end up with only a modest profit. Race merchandising may still be worth it for these events, since the race merchandise provides the event with year-round visibility. The race expo is the place where the lion's share of official race merchandise will be sold. Web sales before and after the event represent only a modest portion of the sales for most events.

If you decide to offer official race merchandise, make sure to find a merchandise coordinator with retail sales experience, since you are basically making the decision to open your own store. This person should be as thrilled about ordering the correct mix of merchandise as a runner is excited about running along the rim of Lake Tahoe. Certainly, the fashion aspects of running-related merchandise are way beyond the scope of this book. If you wish to sell official race merchandise, here are some pointers:

- **Set modest expectations.** Set modest expectations (added for emphasis).

- **Start the design process early.** Especially if you plan to sell items on the event website, have the following year's design set no later than a couple of months after the current year's race. The lead time for designing, approving, selecting and imprinting the product line is long.

- **Think hard about whether the extra effort needed for web sales is worth it.** The answer may become painfully apparent after the first year.

- **Order fewer products and colors rather than more.** This is known as keeping a smaller number of SKUs.

- **Get volunteers with retail sales experience for every phase of this operation.**

At the expo, place the official race merchandise booth in one of the highest visibility locations possible. Most races design the expo floor plan so that all runners have to pass through the official race store immediately after picking up their t-shirts—usually the last stop in the packet pick-up process. This ensures that the store gets first crack at the runners after they complete their required activities and shift into browse-and-buy mode. Invest in some racks and merchandise display equipment to showcase the items in the store. Prospective buyers like to be able to touch the items. Full-length mirrors around the booth are a plus. Changing rooms can be a nice addition. Plan to have the volunteers wear the merchandise, and select volunteers who can operate the check-out quickly and efficiently, with good customer-service skills. The official race store should have only a single exit, to minimize shoplifting.

If the event has a shoe and apparel sponsor, that company may want to work jointly with you on the merchandise operation and may require you to offer their branded merchandise. Try to determine if this is the case before signing the sponsor agreement with that company.

Goody Bags

Providing runners with goody bags—either an actual physical goody bag stuffed with race flyers,

TIP

Licensing Race Merchandise

A few races license their race merchandise with a merchandising company. Under a licensing arrangement, the merchandising company takes all of the risks—they select the products; decide the quantities, the colors, and the sizes; produce the products; develop both a physical "store" for the expo and a virtual store for the website (including preparing the site and setting up the mechanism to take electronic payments online); sell the products at the expo and on the event website; fill the orders; handle complaints and returns; and pay the event a small percentage of gross sales, usually in the range of 5 to 15%. These vendors are most likely going to want to work only with more established events.

brochures, and product samples, distributed at packet pick-up or at the expo, or a "virtual goody bag " sent by email to race participants shortly before race day—is a good way to add value for the sponsors by giving them an avenue to reach the participants directly, or to raise additional income by selling inserts into the bags. Events should have at least 1,000 runners before goody bags are likely to attract much commercial interest.

Virtual goody bags are an online method of providing runners with sponsor messages and special offers. Races pay a fee for the service, which has several advantages over traditional bags. The online platform makes it simple and easy both for sponsors to provide their content and for race directors to compile and manage sponsor material. Also, virtual goody bags are clearly better for the environment, as they drastically decrease the amount of paper and plastic used by an event. Despite their growing popularity among race directors, however, many runners often still prefer to receive a traditional goody bag containing actual items such as water bottles, energy bars and other 'gifts,' so be sure to consider the pros and cons of each method before making a choice between real and virtual goody bags.

The main drawback of physical goody bags is that they can be both labor intensive and logistically intensive. Approach one of the race sponsors to see if they are interested in donating bags (covered with their logos, no doubt) as another form of visibility. Otherwise, you will need to order the bags. Many vendors who sell promotional items stock these bags. As mentioned above, the bags can do double duty as gear check bags. (For a complete discussion of Gear Check, see *Chapter 16: Race Logistics and Operations.*) If you plan to sell inserts into the bags, include this option in the pitch to potential sponsors and expo exhibitors. The fees charged for including an insert depend on the number of runners in the event, with most ranging between $100 and $800.

If you go the physical goody bag route, make sure to set enough lead time to receive the materials for the bags and allow time for stuffing—at least 2-3 weeks before race day. To avoid the tedious job of getting volunteers to attend a bag-stuffing party, you may want to check your area for local organizations, such as those for the physically/intellectually challenged, to see if they will perform this task, generally for a fee. Alternatively, there are commercial outfits that prepare goody bags for events in exchange for the rights to market the bags to large commercial companies. Arrange to transport the bags from the stuffing location to the expo and—if race-day, on-site registration will be offered—from the expo to the race site. In sum, be sure to consider the cost:benefit ratio of goody bags before proceeding. An alternate distribution system for inserts is to have the handouts distributed by race volunteers as they hand out race numbers.

Races with increased security, or races that choose to provide a virtual goody bag, may still distribute goody bags with no "goodies" inserted to serve as the "clear, plastic bags" needed for bag check.

 GREEN TIP

Consider Environmentally Friendly Race Merchandise

When deciding which apparel items to order as official race merchandise (or even for the standard participant t-shirt and race committee/volunteer apparel) don't forget to consider organic cotton, recycled PET plastic and other environmentally friendly fibers. They will cost a bit more, but runners—and the environment—will appreciate the gesture.

Clinics

Some larger races will incorporate a clinic, or a series of clinics, into their expos. Clinic topics can range from elite athlete or other celebrity appearances to local doctors, PTs, or nutritionists offering training advice, to experienced race participants talking about running the course, etc. In general, most expo clinics attract only modest crowds, so do not set expectations too high. The clinics should be heavily promoted in any last-minute emails to registrants or in other late race communications. It is important that the space in which the clinic will be held is situated as close to the packet pick-up and expo areas as possible (if not within it), and to have the expo announcer hype the clinic frequently. Even a large race should be able to make do with a room with 125 chairs set up theater-style for a clinic. A microphone and a podium will also be needed, and most speakers expect a laptop computer, a screen, and a projector that handles PowerPoint-type presentations as well. Many local sports medicine practitioners are willing to speak for free or for a small fee because they gain good visibility among potential clients.

If the event features elite athletes, you may be able to ask some of them to do a clinic. (For foreign athletes, make sure their English is understandable.) It is common for elite athletes receiving appearance fees to do a clinic as part of their fee. Events offering prize money only will sometimes offer a modest clinic fee ($500-$1500) as a way to provide an extra inducement for an athlete to run the race. Many leading running celebrities and coaches can command fees in the $5,000-$15,000 range, plus travel and lodging expenses, to speak at a clinic.

With more and more first-timers entering races, consider adding on a special "first-timers" clinic. Topics might include the absolute basics, such as pinning the race number on the front side of the body, lining

up based on expected finish time, how to warm-up, how a race is scored, and a review of the course.

Make sure to have an emcee for the clinic who will introduce the speakers, keep the clinic on schedule and handle questions coming from the audience. If the clinic includes an autograph session, pre-print copies of a photo of the speaker for him or her to sign. Don't forget the Sharpies. For hugely popular speakers signing autographs, you may need to put a volunteer as the last person in the autograph line in order to cut off the process without causing disappointment among those who are waiting in line when time runs out. Many autograph seekers will also want a photo with the celebrity, which slows down the lines. Provide a volunteer who takes the phone/camera and snaps the photo in order to keep the line moving.

Finally, make sure the sound system is adequate and, if the clinic is held in the expo area, confirm that the sound does not overwhelm any announcements being made on the expo floor.

Phil Stewart

Clinics and autograph sessions should be positioned in the heart of the expo if at all possible. Otherwise attendance may suffer.

Hotels

An official race hotel is only necessary if the race is large enough, and attracts a large enough number of out-of-town participants, to justify a room block. When a race reaches a minimum of 500-1000 participants, it may be time to consider a race hotel. The hotel can serve exclusively as a place of lodging for out-of-town runners, or in addition it can be the location of a number of pre-race activities, such as the race expo, packet pick-up, clinics, meals and committee meetings.

Identifying Hotel Needs

Start with a list of needs for the race hotel. Generally, this will include a certain number of rooms for a certain number of nights for the anticipated participants and the race committee members, meal functions, and meeting space for the expo, packet pick-up and clinics. If you are directing a first-time event (or are a first-time user of a hotel), it will be difficult to come up with figures for these items. Make conservative estimates for the first year and keep detailed records that will guide you in the second year. (Continue to keep detailed records in subsequent years, as they can prove invaluable in making future projections.)

Start hotel negotiations early, and if you are confident of the race date and participation level in subsequent years, go for a multi-year contract. The longer commitment will both lock in the space and possibly secure a lower rate.

Assuming that a hotel has the rooms and the meeting space to meet the needs of the event, the hotel will generally be happy to accommodate you—for a price. That price will vary based on the number of rooms you block, the location, and the time of year. For example, you will get a substantially lower room rate for booking rooms in Florida in August than you will in February or March. The heart of the negotiations will revolve around how much the hotel will discount its normal fees in exchange for a commitment from the event to produce a certain level of income (through rooms booked and food functions). Be conservative in estimates of room nights and attendance at food functions, as you will be giving the hotel an attendance "guarantee." If you fall below that "guarantee," you will be charged the difference between the commitment and the actual number of people who showed up. This can very quickly add up to a significant amount of money.

Calculating the number of rooms needed is more straightforward than calculating the necessary meeting space. The amount of meeting space depends on how the space will be used. For example, a 1,000 square foot room should be able to handle about 90 people for a stand-up reception, but only about 25 people around a "hollow square" for a meeting, or about five 8' x 10' expo booths. The best bet is to know the number of people who will be using each room and the type of activity in which they will be engaged. From this point on, a knowledgeable hotel sales person should be able to help with the necessary square footage. Again, once you have your own history, you will be better prepared to fine-tune your needs.

TIP

Hotel Booking Services

If the prospect of sending out proposals to multiple hotels and directly comparing their responses seems daunting, you may be able to get some help. There are a number of commercial services that will work with clients in search of hotels. They earn the commission from the hotels, so there is no charge to the client for their services. The companies will send out and screen proposals based on the client's needs. Oftentimes these companies are already familiar with many of the hotels you are considering, which can help streamline the search process.

In some major cities, the local Convention and Tourism Bureau may be willing to circulate your proposal to hotels that meet the criteria for room nights and meeting space. The hotels that have availability on the chosen dates will follow up with you directly. There is no charge for this service.

Hotel Visits

Armed with an outline of the event's needs, plan to visit several potential hotels. You will quickly discover that some hotels are better configured to handle the flow of runners or have meeting rooms that are more conveniently situated. Inquire as to whether the hotel has upgraded suites and a health club, and find out what other groups will be using the hotel on the weekend of the event and how close their functions will be to your functions.

Ask about the possibility of a "show office" as part of the package. This might be a small room, near the rooms where your activities will be held, where you can set up a "command post" and possibly use as a storage room. If you anticipate many items to store, inquire about an additional storage room.

Be sure to look into wireless internet service in the hotel—for guest rooms, the expo area and any ancillary rooms you may be using. If the hotel does not offer free internet to guests, you may be able to negotiate free internet in the contract.

Negotiating the Contract

The Language of the Contract

Here is a brief overview of some of the terms that may be encountered when negotiating the hotel contract.

- *Room night*: This is the basic unit of hotel room bookings. It refers to one room booked for one night. If two people stay in a room for one night, the hotel counts that as one room night. If one person stays in a room for three nights, the hotel counts that as three room nights. One of the major drawbacks of most running events is that most of the people only stay in the hotel the night before the race. This means the hotel may be near capacity for one night (the "peak" night) but well under capacity for the night before and the night after the peak night. From a hotel's perspective, this is less desirable than a smaller convention whose attendees stay for 3-4 nights.

- *Guarantee*: As outlined above, this is the commitment that you make to the hotel for the number of room nights, and the number of individuals that will attend the banquet events. If you fail to meet these guarantees (or usually a certain percentage of these guarantees, such as 80% of the room nights), you will be penalized by the hotel and will have to pay them a certain amount of "damages" for the lost income on their side of the ledger. The amount of these fees should be outlined in the contract. Pay close attention to them.

- *Service fee*: This is an amount, generally ranging from 20-24%, simply tacked on by the hotel for "service" at banquet functions. It covers tips to the wait staff. It is unlikely that you will be able to negotiate these fees down. Most of the time they *are not* added into the figures quoted for the banquet functions (the contract will read "plus 22% service fee"). Read the contract carefully to see how these fees are handled. The fees may be added into other hotel services such as the audio-visual charges.

- *Single/double room rates*: Pay close attention to how the contract handles a second person in a room. While most hotels charge the same rate for single or double occupancy, a few hotels charge an additional fee for a second person in the same room. The contract should read "$169 single/double" if the rate applies to the second person; otherwise it will read "$169 single/$189 double." It is likely that the hotel will break down the number of room nights into "kings" and "doubles," so be aware of how many of each type of room you may need (if it matters). Most races with elite athlete fields will double up the athletes, and some events will ask their committee members to share rooms in order to save on hotel costs.

- *Concessions*: This is a part of the contract where the hotel will outline any concessions it has made to you in negotiating the contract. A list of possible concessions is provided in the section entitled "*Negotiable Items*" below.

- *Banquet event order (BEO):* The BEO is a detailed document supplied by the hotel to the client, usually within a week of the event, which outlines in great detail all of the services that are scheduled to be provided by the hotel. The hotel will require you to sign the BEO, which serves as the confirmation and acceptance of receiving the services as outlined. It supersedes (but should agree with) what is in the contract. It will be broken out by day and function location. Review this document very carefully. Once you sign it, you are locked in.

Negotiable Items

Many items in the contract with the hotel may be negotiable. The room rate is usually the primary negotiable item. Do your homework and check the room rates at different hotels for the same time of year, so you will know the average before starting to bargain. The standard complimentary room ratio is one comp room for every 40-50 room nights, meaning that for every 40-50 room nights you book, you will receive one free room for one night. This is pretty standard and not often negotiable. Some hotels will offer a "room rebate." This is a credit on the bill for every room booked. If the hotel won't budge on the room rate, it may be willing to give you a lower price on something else, such as banquet prices. If this saves money, it really doesn't matter whether the savings comes through a lower room rate or lower banquet prices. So take a look at all of the charges that are outlined in the contract and see which can be moved from the "charges" field over into the "concessions" category. Here are some likely items that you may want to negotiate (outside the basic room rate and meeting room rental rate, which may be free already, in exchange for the room block).

- Free space for banquets, hospitality suites, office or storage space
- Reduced rates for rental of tables, easels, bulletin boards, etc. for the expo
- Free hotel parking (some hotels do not own the lots at the hotel, so in these cases, parking fees may not be on the table)
- Reduced or waived banner-hanging fees
- Extra hors d'oeuvres at a reception or meal function
- Complimentary weekend for two, for use as a race or committee award
- Reduced or waived storage fees for packages shipped to the hotel prior to race weekend
- Extra complimentary use of a suite or suite upgrades at the standard room rate
- "Staff rooms" at a lower rate than the room block rate (races with an elite field frequently use these rooms for elite athletes)
- Reduced audio-visual fees (AV fees are usually overpriced, so obtain the AV price list in advance and try to hack the high prices down. Some hotels use outside contractors for AV services so this may be difficult—but not impossible—to do.)
- Late check out for committee members
- Free WiFi
- Double hotel points (this can be a nice perk for the hotel coordinator, as the points can be applied to anyone's account)

Other Contract Considerations

Here are some additional notes on the hotel contract:

- ***Set as late a cut-off date as possible for room reservations in the block.*** Most hotels will want to set the cut-off date for the room block at least 2-3 weeks before the event. Try to get the hotel to set the date as close to the event as possible, so you can still put people into the rooms. The hotel is not obligated to hold the rooms in the block after the cut-off date. This means if you have not met the room block, you could lose the chance to do so over the last few weeks. Runners are notoriously late reservation-makers (and elite athletes may not commit until just days before the event), so you want all the time you can get.

• ***Make sure the hotel knows in advance if you are exempt from sales tax.*** The hotel will most certainly want a copy of your tax exemption certificate. The exemption applies only to the expenses incurred by the tax-exempt organization and will not apply to the general public reserving rooms. Tax-exempt organizations may still be subject to local tourist taxes.

• ***Review the contract carefully.*** Make sure that all the meeting space requested is reflected in the contract. The hotel will likely rent out the meeting rooms that you are not using to other groups, so if a room is missing on the contract, it may be unavailable by the time you notice that it was not included. It is a good idea to set up a spreadsheet or some sort of timetable showing all the meeting rooms you have on an hour-by-hour basis over the course of race weekend. This will serve as a good check that nothing has been omitted.

Race Hotel Operations

Once the contract is signed, your primary point of contact will most likely change from someone in the sales office to someone in the event services office (or a similarly named office). This individual will be your contact from this time forward. Try to establish a good rapport with this individual, since you will be working closely together (and there may be discretionary favors that he or she can do for you). Depending on the size of the hotel, you may end up working with banquet staff, reservations staff, meeting room staff, and shipping-and-receiving staff as well. You may want to offer some race t-shirts to the key hotel staff (or provide some to the event manager and let him arrange to have the shirts distributed). The bottom line is that good relations with the entire hotel staff will make race weekend run more smoothly.

If the contract is signed well before the event

Phil Stewart

Some creative branding at the headquarters hotel at the Chevron Houston Marathon

date (or if you are returning for a second year on a multi-year contract), meet with the event manager well before the event to review the contract.

Promote and Check the Room Block

Since you are now responsible for bringing a certain number of people into the race headquarters hotel, do whatever you can to promote the hotel and its association with the event. Before doing any promotion, obtain the hotel's web address, so that people can book their rooms online, and the appropriate reservations phone number. Find out the name of the room block that individuals will need to use to receive the negotiated rate (such as "The Big Labor Day 10K rate"). Using the block name is important both for the individuals to receive the discounted rate and for you to ensure that the reservation is credited to your room block.

Once you have the room block name, you may want to call the hotel yourself and try to make a reservation for the event, just to make sure the system works (you can cancel the reservation later). If it does not work, let the event manager at the hotel know at once.

Do not be shy about encouraging runners to stay in the headquarters hotel. With the growing number of internet booking options, some individuals may be able to find lower rates at other nearby hotels. (If a guest finds a lower rate *at the race hotel*, you should complain. This has happened.) Let runners know that the event receives benefits from the hotel based on the size of the room block, and if they book down the street to save $5 it may mean an increased registration fee the following year because the event failed to meet its room block guarantee.

Check on the status of the room block with increasing frequency as the event approaches. If you are lagging behind projections, think about additional ways to promote the block. Most hotels will set up an administrative section on the hotel website where you can check in with a user ID and password to see the status of the bookings and other details.

Rooms for elite athletes can be problematic, because many athletes and their agents don't firm up their attendance until after the room block closing date. Ask the hotel if you can use "dummy" names to hold the rooms, such as "Elite Athlete #1" and "Elite Athlete #2." They may be willing to accommodate this request, as long as you let them know that you will be responsible for the room if it goes unused. If not, you may have to put fictitious names into those rooms to hold them.

Communicating with the Hotel

Although several members of the race's organizing committee, including the expo coordinator, elite athlete coordinator, clinic coordinator, registrar, etc., may need to discuss race operations with the headquarters hotel, it is best to have a single point of contact (or two at the most) with the hotel event manager. This will cut down on the potential for miscommunications.

Banquet Functions

You will need to guarantee the number of attendees at any banquet functions approximately 72 hours before the banquet. This gives the hotel a chance to order and prepare the food. The banquet staff will be prepared to handle a figure either 5% over or under the number that you guarantee. The guarantee should not be lower than the number in the contract or you may be charged for failing to deliver on the contract guarantee. Keep careful records so that you will have a history of what you guaranteed for the meal and how many individuals actually attended.

Check the Bill Carefully

When the hotel bill arrives after the event, review it carefully and make note of any charges that do not seem correct. Quite a number of different people, including the reservations manager, banquet manager, expo manager, parking attendants, restaurant staff, etc., will be placing charges on your master account. It is worth making sure the charges are what you expected and that no charges from other groups ended up on the bill. If you had a staff room block that was charged to the master account, be particularly sure that none of the rooms reserved by *participants*, not for race staff, end up on the bill. The hotel should be willing to trace the charges and make any corrections that you can justify.

Phil Stewart

16 Race Logistics and Operations

THE BASICS

Getting to the Race

· ● Participants and volunteers begin to evaluate their experience at a race the moment they leave home or from their hotel. Research and publicize the public transportation and parking options that are available (and those that are open, if the event has an early starting time on a weekend). If streets will be closed for the course, consider how that will affect runners' ability to reach the race site and publicize the time the closures will take place. If you will be offering any VIP or "Official" parking, develop a VIP parking plan and send out passes in advance.

Staging Area and Starting Line

- When designing the staging area, keep the flow of the runners uppermost in your mind. Where will the runners come from; where will they congregate; how will they use all the services available in the staging area before the start; how will they line up for the start? How much space will be needed?

- Consider how any buildings that are in the staging area might be utilized (make sure to get permission and check that the buildings are unlocked on race day) and whether you will need to supplement the buildings with tents. Shelters will become extremely important in rainy or cold weather.

- The key locations in the staging area should include late registration or packet pick-up, pre-race water, medical, porta-johns, a place for timing and scoring, and a place for runners to leave their belongings (at their own risk). If race-day registrations are accepted, have a secure location to keep the money (and someone to watch over it).

- There will invariably be questions from runners, so make sure an information tent or table is one of the first things people see as they enter the staging area—have good signage. Be sure that the volunteers manning the information area are extremely knowledgeable.

- Place sponsor signage, banners, etc. such that they provide maximum sponsor exposure. Be sure that participants, spectators, and photographers have a good view of this signage. The sponsors' logos should appear in those finish area shots!

- Have runners approach the starting line from the rear, if possible.

- Encourage runners to line themselves up according to predicted times. Warn children who line up at the front that they might get trampled. Hopefully their parents will hear this and move them further back; if not, you might need to insist the children move on their own.

- Don't make runners stand around for endless announcements once they are lined up and ready to go. Try to make remarks as brief as possible. Warn runners of any hazards on the course.

- Check the staging area to make sure it is usable in all kinds of weather (for example, that it doesn't turn into a lake if it rains).

On the Course

- Make sure the course is well marked. Use a variety of directional markings such as temporary spray paint (if allowed), duct tape directly on the roadway, signs, cones, course marshals, etc., especially at critical turns. (Flour or lime, once standard marking mediums, are less reliable because they tend to spread when runners run over them—although they may be usable for very small events in conjunction with course marshals at key turns and intersections.) Remember that markings put out the night before could be obliterated by wind or a sudden rainstorm.

- Make a plan for delivering and picking up all on-course resources like water or aid station supplies, mile markers and medical supplies.

- Nearly all races place signage at the mile marks; if clocks or split timers are used at the mile markers, you will need to coordinate the setting of the clocks based on the actual start time, or let the split timers know when the race has started so they can start their watches.

- If a police officer is driving the lead vehicle, have a race official who knows the course extremely well go with him, if allowed. You don't want the lead vehicle to lead everyone the wrong way!

- Have someone go over the course in the weeks and days leading up to race day to look for such hazards as potholes, branches, paving, new construction projects, etc.

- Recruit course marshals who are loud and assertive and make sure they are absolutely clear about which way they are to direct runners. Remind them to stay alert and vigilant. Try to place race veterans at especially critical intersections. Alert the course marshals to the possibility that the front runners may be spread out, which will make those following the leaders more dependent than ever on the marshals to keep them on course. The same logic applies to runners at the very end of the pack, who may be out of sight of the runners just in front of them.

- Think about what you will do if runners do run off course—how will you get them back on course and how will you handle the distribution of prizes if the error affects the finish order? (See USATF Rules about short courses in *Chapter 14: Rules of Competition*.)

- If a number of slower runners and walkers are expected and the course can't be kept open long enough to accommodate them, consider having a shorter event or an earlier start for those participants. If these options are not possible, plan to have a trail vehicle ("sag wagon") to pick up runners outside the time limit.

At the Finish Line

- If the finish line is separate from the starting line, develop an entirely distinct finish area site plan. Be aware that the runners' needs will be somewhat different at the finish—the finish area will require more fluids and medical support, as well as a location for post-race food, if it is supplied.

- If the finish area is the same as the starting area, some efficiency is gained through double use of facilities; however, think about what adaptations will need to be made during the race so that the area is ready when the runners finish. Good staging area planning will keep these changes to a minimum. Keep in mind that there will be more time to accomplish these adaptations during a half-marathon than during a 5K event—the length of the race dictates how much time there is to get these changes made.

- Plan carefully for the flow of runners at the finish line, including removal of tags if using a pull-tag scoring system or reusable transponders, and providing post-race amenities, which should include water and medical services, and may include food, medals, and foil "blankets." Finally, devise a plan for getting the runners easily to the awards ceremony and then to their cars.

- Figure out where the finishers and spectators can reunite. Make efforts to ensure they don't reunite right at the finish line. Barricades may be needed to separate the runner and spectator areas. Remember, once the groups co-mingle, the flow will slow down considerably.

Spectators and Local Citizens

- Put flyers in neighborhood mailboxes along the course. Not only is this good public relations (people will often get very upset if they have no idea a race is going on and they suddenly find they can't get out of their driveways), but it might also get a few spectators outside to see what is happening. In addition to mentioning street closures, use the flyer as a promotional and recruiting tool. Include an upbeat message about the excitement of the event and provide details about volunteering. Prepare and circulate a map of local road closings and a timetable.

- Work closely with local police. Develop plans to minimize traffic delays. Police will frequently let cross-traffic through when there are gaps in the flow of runners.

- Contact the local radio station and ask them to run a public service announcement about the best places to watch the race.

- Post a spectators' guide on the event website and on the mobile app (if you have one), including a course map, and note the best locations from which to watch. Include approximate times for when the lead men and women should go by each point.

- Ask the local newspaper to publish, in print or online, a spectator's guide. This may have to wait until the race is more of a force in the community, but it doesn't hurt to ask.

- Provide space for spectators in the staging area plan. Once efforts have been made to attract spectators, make sure the staging area can accommodate them if they show up.

Communications

- Be sure to have a communications network that is up to the demands of the staging area and course. Cell phones may work for very small events, but "walkie-talkie"-type radios, which enable more than two people to talk at once and have multiple channels, are still the staple for most larger races.

- Plan to have one individual who will serve as the "command central" and is tied in to police and EMS radio networks. This person serves as the "cross-over" between the race network and the external networks. Larger races may arrange for a unified command center, a tent or trailer where representatives from the race and all municipal agencies are side-by-side to coordinate responses.

THE DETAILS

The starting area, the course, and the finish area are truly the stage upon which the drama of the race unfolds—whether it is elite athletes in quest of thousands of dollars in prize money or back-of-the-packers chasing after personal fulfillment. In this chapter, we first discuss how to successfully get runners to the race site, then we look at the staging area, the line-up and start, the course, and the finish line, followed by an examination of the communications network, which is the glue that holds everything together. Be sure to also review the material in **Chapter 11: Equipment, Supplies and Key Personnel**, since the material in that chapter is closely intertwined with the logistics and operations topics covered here.

Getting to the Race Site

The key to getting runners to the start of the race on time (and in a good mood) is communication—both pre-race (using the website and runner confirmation email) and on race day (using clear signage and knowledgeable volunteers).

As early as possible, provide accurate information on the race website about how to get to the race. These days, this can be as simple as providing the address of the staging area/start line, so that runners can plug it into the map function on their phones. Maps or directions from Google Maps or similar mapping software can also be directly embedded into the website, so that runners can see the location and get directions right from the site itself. If the race will have a specifically designated parking location, be sure to provide the address to *that location*, if it is different than the staging area. The address should be included in the confirmation email that runners receive upon registration, as well as in any last-minute email blasts or social media postings.

If the event is being held for the first time or if it will attract a lot of out-of-town runners, signage on the main roadways leading to event parking will provide runners with a level of confidence that they are going in the right direction. Consider placing these signs on the most commonly traveled routes leading from the main highway(s) to the race site.

Parking

Participant parking is an important aspect of race planning. Even for areas well-serviced by public transportation, many runners will still choose to drive to the event. Don't make the mistake of thinking that all it takes is the provision of a suitable parking lot, and runners will then smoothly and appropriately park their cars. A successful parking operation requires a significant amount of planning.

Determine Parking Needs

First, estimate the size of the parking area that will be needed for participants, volunteers and race officials. Of course, parking needs will vary based on the location of the event and how strongly runners are encouraged to carpool or use public transportation, if it is available. If most participants will drive to the event, assume that most will come alone, unless there is incentive to carpool. To be safe, estimate no more than a 10% no-show rate, since it's always better to have empty parking spots as opposed to too few spots. So, for a 500-person race, have space to park at least 450 cars. An exception to this would be a kids' run or other type of family-oriented race. In that case, a figure of .75 runners/car can safely be

used to calculate the number of spots needed, meaning 375 parking spots for a 500-person event.

If a paved parking lot with spaces clearly painted on the pavement is available for the event, it will be relatively easy to determine the number of cars that can be parked in the lot. However, if a field or other unpaved parking area is used, this determination becomes more tricky. Measuring the number of cars that can be safely parked while allowing enough space for traffic to continue to pass through is important. Check the field for ditches, holes, muddy spots, etc., so that those areas can be coned or roped off, and take those areas into account in the parking spot calculation. Remember that SUVs and vans take more space, so don't measure for compact cars only. Also be aware that, without close monitoring by volunteers, drivers will not naturally park in a way that promotes the most efficient use of the space. Either factor this into the calculation of how many cars the lot can accommodate, or be sure to have plenty of parking volunteers to guide drivers into the pre-established parking pattern. If an unpaved lot will be used for parking, it's very important to make sure the lot is still safe and useable after a few days of heavy rain (or a snow storm, if the event is held in the winter).

Of course, the appropriate permissions need to be obtained before a lot can be used for event parking. If the lot belongs to a school, church, or other public-use facility, in addition to getting permission, ascertain that there will be no other events taking place at the same time that will limit the number of available slots. The owners of some parking lots may request a certificate listing them as an additionally insured party on the event's policy (See **Chapter 9: Insurance and Legal**).

In some cases, there may be fees involved for using a particular parking lot. For example, it is fairly common for state and regional parks to charge a per-car fee (usually only a few dollars per car) for parking. It is entirely up to the race director whether that fee is absorbed by the event or passed on to the individual registrants. Some events, particularly mass-participation events like obstacle course runs, regularly charge participants for parking during the registration process. Although this is not typically done for standard running events, some races with remote off-site parking also charge parking fees to offset the high cost of transporting the runners back and forth to the race site. Finally, charging a small parking fee per car can sometimes be used to encourage carpooling. If parking fees will be collected on-site, be sure to factor in the amount of time this will add to the entire parking process, and clearly instruct runners as to the appropriate time to arrive at the event site so that they will have time to pay, park, and make it to the start on time.

Parking Logistics

Many parking lots are easy to set up for race parking, particularly if a clearly defined entrance and exit can be established. For more challenging lots, and particularly for completely unmarked parking areas like fields or other pieces of open land, the parking area should be clearly delineated with cones or stakes and caution tape. Arrange the lot so there is only one entrance. Do some legwork in advance to determine not only the best location for the entrance, based on the direction most drivers will be coming from, but also the most efficient and safest traffic flow pattern within the lot. Use as many cones and markers as possible to make the traffic flow pattern obvious to drivers, and block off any unsafe areas such as ditches or large potholes that could be safety hazards to cars or pedestrians. Place highly visible parking signs at the main entrance, readable from all directions of approach to the lot. If the race will be held after dark (or if it starts early enough in the morning that people will be parking before it is completely light out) make sure that there is enough lighting for the safety of participants walking from the parking area to the staging area.

Parking cars quickly and safely is critical. A back up in the parking process can have implications for the rest of the race, particularly if enough participants are affected that the start must be delayed. The importance of pre-planning and good volunteers cannot be stressed enough. Also, if the parking lot is accessed from a main road, or if participants have to cross a busy road to get from the parking lot to the staging area, consider hiring a police officer, or possibly a crossing guard, to help with traffic control on the streets around the lot and to ensure pedestrian safety.

Parking Volunteers

Volunteers are essential for a safe and efficient parking operation. If drivers are allowed to park however they choose, spots will

Phil Stewart

Bank of America Chicago Marathon vehicle pass - large enough to be seen from a distance.

inevitably be lost to those who park too far apart, and cars will be parked in different directions, which will impede a safe and hassle-free exit from the lot after the event. Free-for-all parking can also be a safety hazard, particularly closer to start time, when fewer spots are left and anxious runners, in cars and on foot, are rushing to get to the event site. Volunteers who are experienced in parking cars are a big plus, particularly if they are a group of people who know each other and work well together. Older Boy Scouts with their Scout Masters can be a very good choice, as they are accustomed to working together and they follow instructions well. In general, however, children should not be used as parking volunteers, for safety reasons. Parking volunteers should be friendly but assertive, calm under pressure, flexible, and able to think on their feet. The majority of runners will show up within a very short time period, and unfortunately they are not always cooperative, making the parking job somewhat stressful on occasion. Volunteers should be clearly attired in bright orange safety vests, with orange flags or bright traffic wands to direct drivers. Last, parking volunteers need to be at their posts *early,* often even before the majority of the other volunteers arrive, in order to get them parked properly, too.

Although fewer parking volunteers are needed after the race to empty the lot, it's a good idea to have at least some volunteer support at this time, especially in the case of a night race, since those volunteers can help to move the cars out of the lot in a safe and organized fashion. Again, depending on the venue, a police officer may be useful to get cars out of the lot, particularly if the lot empties onto a busy road. Parking lot gridlock is not the final impression runners should have of an event!

VIP Parking and Official Vehicles

Determine if you will need any special, limited-access parking for VIPs or official vehicles close to the race start. Individuals to be considered are companies or parties involved with the set-up and tear down of the race site, race-day deliveries to the race site, race officials, physically challenged participants, media, and sponsors or other VIPs to whom you want to give a special perk. Designate a VIP parking area, large enough to accommodate these special groups, into the overall staging area start plan. Create some VIP parking passes and instructions to provide to the appropriate individuals and, most likely, send them out prior to race morning. On race day, have strong-willed volunteers (with the flexibility to let in a TV truck without a credential arriving at the last minute to cover the race) to monitor the VIP parking area.

Some parking accommodations may involve vehicles that need to be positioned out on the course for set-up and teardown of aid stations or mile markers, or as lead vehicles, etc. These vehicles can be identified with "Official Vehicle" tags. Law enforcement personnel should be provided with a sample of these passes and informed that these vehicles should be allowed access to the course even when the streets are closed.

The Staging Area

A well-thought out staging area for the event will put the runners in a good mood by the time they line up for the start and save wear and tear on the volunteers and race officials. Plus, "the look" of the event can impress the runners and, perhaps more importantly, the sponsors. The vast majority of races have a common start and finish area, so we will deal with setting up a staging area in a single section and provide special notes about changes when the areas are not the same. A few items related solely to finish lines appear at the end of the chapter.

Find a Logistics Coordinator

If the event is small, the race director will likely serve as the logistics coordinator. However, as the race grows, this should be one of the first jobs he/she passes along to someone else on the race committee. The job requires a passion for detail— the ability to design and map the staging area down to the nearest foot, and to compile a list of all the items needed; persistence in getting other committee members to identify what their supply and equipment needs are in a timely manner; and a balance of firmness and diplomacy in dealing with the vendors who need to show up on time and get their work done well and quickly, usually on a very specific timetable. For events that are

extremely spread out, the logistics coordinator may want to subdivide the staging area or the course into sectors, with a sector captain overseeing each particular part.

Setting the Footprint

It is best to start considering the needs of the staging area when the course is selected. For a

---

SIDEBAR

Credentials

For small and mid-sized races, a volunteer t-shirt or vest is all that is needed to identify key race personnel as they go about their duties. As races grow in size, preparing some sort of credentials, usually worn on a lanyard, may become necessary in order to indicate specialized roles for key individuals, such as distinguishing the "Media" from the "Medical Staff," etc. Credentials may be used to indicate areas of access for different individuals as well. Sample credentials for a large race might include "All Areas" for race staff with total access, "Medical" for medical personnel (allowed in the medical tent), and "Media" or "Photographer" for access to the finish line for photos, "Course" for on-course personnel with less than "All Areas" access, and "VIP" or "Sponsor" to allow access to hospitality tents (and to make them feel important). Individuals with the highest level of access may have customized credentials containing their photographs. The other half of the credentials equation is how much of an enforcement plan you will create. For most races, little more is done than self policing. At high-visibility events identified as security risks, enforcement becomes much more strict and a sizeable number of security personnel will need to be present. (See ***Chapter 8: Medical, Safety and Security*** for details about the use of credentials at high security events.) Most printing companies can print laminated cards suitable for credentials. Have a hole punched in each credential that matches the type of clip on the lanyard. Decide the best method for distributing the credentials—some may need to be shipped out in advance, while others can be picked up on race weekend. Race

Phil Stewart
Media credential from the Boston Marathon. Punched out circles indicate various access levels for security personnel to see quickly.

directors should always have a supply close at hand for individuals who need credentials of some sort and were left off the master list.

complete discussion of designing a course, see *Chapter 4: The Course.* Once the course is set, the staging area is limited to the ground within walking distance of the starting line.

- Don't scrimp on space for the staging area. A ballpark figure is to allow no less than **10 square feet of *usable space* (i.e. not in a grove of trees) for each participant.** This works out to 120,000 square feet for a 12,000-runner race; 20,000 square feet for a 2,000-runner race, and so on. This figure allows for placement of tents, tables, a stage, etc., within this space. If you have access to more space, take it! Here are some other considerations:

- *Adequate drainage.* Check out the proposed site after a heavy downpour and see how it drains. You do not want to be setting up in a swamp on race day. Assume the worst when it comes to weather—that means it will rain on race weekend.

- *Level terrain.* Especially if tents and stages will be set up, make sure that the ground is level. Most tent companies can handle a small amount of slope and still construct the tents and other structures, but flatter is better.

- *Adequate parking for staff vehicles and participant vehicles (see section above).*

- *Grass is better than concrete.* Keep in mind that runners will be waiting around before the start of the race. It is more comfortable and friendly for them to be standing on a soft surface such as grass instead of on hard concrete. The downside of grass is that it can turn into mud in wet conditions. An ideal set-up might offer both options.

- *Accessible underground water supply.* If you will be tapping into the municipal water supply, either for drinking water or to fill up weights to anchor tents or to spray down runners on hot days, make sure there is access to a fire hydrant in the staging area. Obtain permission from the municipal authorities before tapping the hydrant;

frequently there will be special wrenches, connectors, and hoses needed to complete this task successfully. If the water will be used for drinking, double-check that it is potable, have water barrels (usually large, clean plastic trash cans filled with plastic trash bags as liners) for filling with water, and have a way to move them from the hydrant to the locations where water is needed.

- *Easy vehicle access to the starting area.* Keep in mind that there will be vehicles unloading equipment and supplies in the staging area. Ideally, there will be a driveway or some sort of break in the curbing so vehicles can drive to where they need to be. Some curbs are deliberately made to damage tires. If this is the case, a driveway is crucial (or a temporary ramp should be constructed—most likely with two-by-four or four-by-four pieces of lumber).

- *Good sightline to the starting line.* It is preferable if runners can see the starting line—or the banners or start line truss—from the staging area. This allows them to orient themselves. A corollary to this guideline is to minimize the distance the runners need to walk from the staging area to the starting line.

Designing the Staging Area

Once you have determined the site for the staging area, you will begin the "design" process. A list of *possible* facilities needed in the staging area appears below. Smaller races may need only the basics—registration, water, scoring, and porta-johns—while larger races may need all of the facilities on the list. If you have access to a building, many of these facilities can be located indoors; if not, consider renting some tents in case of inclement weather.

- **Registration and/or packet pick-up tent**

- **Scoring tent:** Select a somewhat out-of-the-way area for scoring, in order to ensure quiet and privacy —a room in a nearby building, a tent in a less heavily trafficked area, or an RV.

If the scoring facility is in the thick of the staging area, expect the scorers to be peppered and distracted with questions by impatient runners waiting for their results.

- **Pre-race water**

- **Post-race food distribution area:** Post-race food may be distributed from a tent or tables.

- **Porta-johns**

- **Barricades or fencing:** Necessary in situations where you want more control of the flow of runners as well as separation between the runners and the spectators, or need to designate certain areas as off limits to everyone.

- **Medical tent:** Medical tents are covered in more detail in **Chapter 8: Medical, Safety and Security**. In brief, the medical tent should be located just past the finish line, as this is where the highest incidence of injuries/illness occurs. The tent should be easily accessible from the finish line and well marked.

- **Volunteer check-in tent**

- **Information tent**

- **Elite athlete tent**

- **Sponsor hospitality tent(s)**

- **Media tent**

- **Bag check tent:** These tents are typically very space-intensive, since bags need to be laid out in a rapid and organized fashion for pickup.

- **Raised platform for start/finish line announcer and dignitaries**

- **Equipment tent:** For equipment and supplies that may need to be distributed and collected from race officials and volunteers on race day.

- **Lost and found**: This may be able to be consolidated with one of the other tents, such as the information tent.

- **Awards stage**

Once you determine which items on the above list are needed, figure out how to arrange them in the staging area. An easy flow of runners into and through the staging area is critical. If the event is small, it will be easy to set up the various staging area components almost anywhere and be ready to go.

If the event is large, a bit more planning will be needed. Start by thinking about the direction from which the majority of runners will be approaching the staging area. If the event starts and finishes in the same location, consider post-race flow as well. Then think about *the order* in which the runners will do things once they arrive. If the event has race-day registration or race-day packet pick-up, the runners will most likely go there first, followed by a trip to the porta-johns and the pre-race water tables. Finally, if gear check is provided, that is likely to be the runners' last stop before heading to the starting line. After the race, the runners may have pull-tags or reusable timing transponders that need to be removed (if the event is using one of these types of timing) then they will seek water, food (if it is being offered), medals, and their gear. If the event is very large, a designated family reunion area may be needed as well. Finally, it is usually the case that only a relatively small number of folks will stay around for the awards ceremony unless there is one heck of a post-race party. (For further information on post-race awards ceremonies, see **Chapter 18: Awards, Awards Ceremonies, Entertainment and Results Posting**.)

Make sure to allow enough space between the various tents/tables for people to stand and be out of the way of the activities taking place as they wait for the time to line up at the start. (Don't forget to calculate the amount of space the lines for the porta-johns will occupy.) Make sure that runners and spectators can move about freely.

Most large races use some type of barricades to keep runners out of restricted areas such as the medical tent, to keep spectators separated from runners, and to improve the flow throughout the staging area. The metal barricades that link together (frequently called French barricades), are common; plastic staked fencing is an alternative, but it provides less resistance to individuals who may try to breach it. The type of barricade selected depends on the likelihood that the crowd will need to be controlled. With any type of barricade, it is important to figure out where openings may be needed to allow rapid access or egress for emergency vehicles or personnel. The metal barricades can be linked with plastic ties instead of locking them. These ties can be snipped easily with scissors by race officials in the event of an emergency that requires quick access. Try to avoid excessive use of barricades that will limit runners' access to areas where they must be, or limit spectators' view of the action at the finish line.

If the event will have a number of spectators (more on spectators below), try to leave the curbside along the course unencumbered with race equipment to enhance the spectators' viewing experience.

Tables, Chairs and More

Once you have decided on all of the facilities needed in the staging area (tents, porta-johns, post-race food service, water, medical, etc.), focus on the supplemental items that will be required at each of those facilities. The most essential items to consider are tables, chairs, and electricity. Other items may include flooring for the tents, heaters if cold weather is a possibility, and food and beverages for the volunteers. If the event starts before daylight, consider providing lighting for some of the tents. Consult with the race committee or each team captain about his or her specific needs for the staging area. Collect all of this information on a master spreadsheet with the exact number of items needed for each facility, total the categories (adding in a few extra tables and chairs), and place the order with the appropriate vendor.

Map and Timetable

Once all the items needed in the staging area have been determined, develop a map, preferably to-scale, clearly showing where all the items will be set up. Depending on the location of the race,

you may be able to use Google Maps or another commercially available mapping software as the jumping-off point for the development of this map. Depending on the size of the event and the sophistication of the "map maker," the staging area maps may range from simple (and not to scale) to highly technical to-scale CAD drawings, **Samples appear in the following pages in Figure 16-1.**

Create a delivery timetable for the equipment needed in the staging area. In some instances, the deliveries need to happen in a certain sequence, such as tents before any items that will be stored inside the tents. In other instances, limited access to the staging area may dictate that large items such as the stage and the porta-johns do not arrive simultaneously. (See **Chapter 3: Developing a Race Timetable and Check List** for further details about timetables.)

Operations in the Staging Area

Packet Pick-up and Late Registration

Except for the smallest and most informal races, most events should consider providing—and encouraging—packet pick-up *before* race day. This allows the process to take place in a more relaxed atmosphere, in a location more likely to be indoors, and with more time to fix errors and add late registrants. (Information about pre-race day packet pick-up appears in **Chapter 15: Packet Pick-up, Late Registration, Expo and Hotel.**)

If circumstances mandate race-day packet pick-up, it's very important to have some sort of covered facility in case of inclement weather—a building is preferable to a tent, but a tent is better than nothing—with plenty of tables for the packets or numbers, chairs for volunteers, and electricity for the computers. Try to be overstaffed with volunteers, to allow for the possibility of a large race-day influx. If race-day registration is offered, many runners will wait until the last minute (checking the weather forecast, no doubt, even knowing they will be incurring late fees) before

Figure 16-1

Staging Areas

Cellcom Marathon 3D View

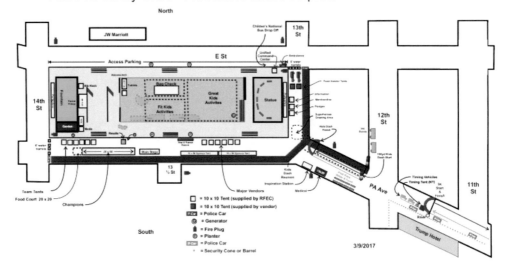

Race for Every Child Staging Area

Figure 16-1

Staging Areas (cont'd.)

START MAP

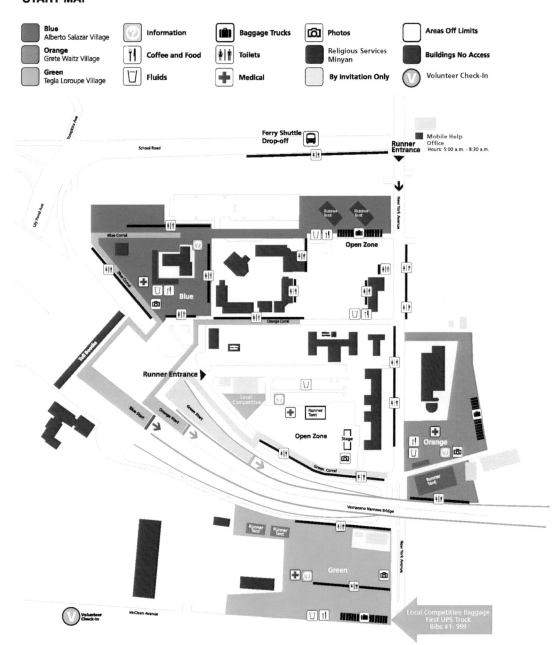

Baggage drop-off will be located in each start village (blue, orange, and green). **Baggage drop-off will close promptly at 9:30 a.m.** NYRR strongly advises marathoners to drop off their bags **no later than one hour prior to their wave start time.**

*Locations of amenities are subject to change. Visit www.ingnycmarathon.org for updates.

Layout subject to change

New York City Marathon Staging Area

deciding to participate. It is simply not fair to the pre-registered runners to face a late start due to a race-day registration surge coupled with a lack of volunteers. The best way to ensure this doesn't happen (and to ensure that the extra income for those late-fee paying customers comes into the race coffers) is to overstaff for race morning.

Bag (Gear) Check

Having a bag or gear check (many races prefer the term "bag" check if they require items to be placed in plastic bags and want to discourage participants from using the service to check larger items such as backpacks and suitcases, etc.) for runners is a labor- and space-intensive process, but it is appreciated by participants, particularly at larger events. (Some smaller events may designate an area, preferably cordoned off with barricades or plastic fencing, for a non-monitored gear check, but warn runners that it is not secure and that items are left at the runners' own risk. If no gear check is provided, runners are apt to find their own nooks and crannies to deposit their extra clothing or bags, or will simply leave their personal items in their automobiles.)

If gear will be checked near the start/finish line, plan to have a large tent—or multiple smaller tents, each with a designated bib number or alphabetical ranges—to keep checked items and volunteers out of the rain in case of inclement weather. The bag check tent for a 16,000-runner event may measure as much as 210' x 60', which could be subdivided into five 50' x 60' tents. However configured, a copious amount of space is required because the bags must be placed side-by-side with the bib numbers or alphabetical ranges easily visible, for ease of retrieval. The bags can't just be thrown into a massive pile.

Most races, especially since the Boston Marathon bombings, require that runners use specifically provided clear plastic bags to check their gear, and they do not allow runners to check anything that cannot fit into the bag. Backpacks and luggage, for example, are generally not accepted. The clear plastic makes the contents more visible, which is preferable from a security perspective. It is always best to use drawstring bags so that the contents remain inside. Forcing the runners to use the bags that the race provides also places a limit on how much gear can be checked. (You don't want to become a luggage check!) Runners are issued some sort of baggage tag, usually a pull-off tag as part of their bib number, which can be affixed to the checked bag. Many races require the runners to write their bib numbers on the bags with a Sharpie pen so the bags can be located even if the tags fall off.

The bag check area should be enclosed in such a way that runners cannot hop in and attempt to retrieve their own bags. For example, it could be

Bag check tents arranged by bib number.

Phil Stewart

surrounded by tables, each marked with a sign indicating the number ranges for checked bags available at that table (1-250, 251-500, etc.). The number ranges should not be too broad, because each bag will be put in a pile with other bags in the same number range. If the total number of bags is too large, it will take longer for volunteers to locate the proper bag after the race. Each table should be staffed with at least two volunteers, one who greets the runner and inspects the bag, and the other who takes the bag and places it in the area inside the tent marked for bags in that number or letter range.

Volunteers should be warned that runners will wait

Kath Mallet

The interior of a bag check tent. To facilitate locating the bags quickly requires a lot of space.

until the last possible minute to check their bags (meaning activity will be heaviest just before the runners line up to start the race). If an efficient process is not in place, the lines for bag check can get very long. Have volunteers walking the lines, instructing runners to fill their bags (and handing out bags if they were not distributed at packet pickup or forgotten by the runners) as they are waiting, instead of doing this only once they reach the bag check table. Post-race bag retrieval is a bit more laid back, because the runners are finishing over a longer time span, but the act of locating the bag and returning it to the runner takes a bit longer as well.

Very small, local races may opt to establish a 'self-serve' bag check that is less labor intensive. At the entrance to the secured tent/bag check location, runners show their checked bags to a monitor, who makes sure that the proper bag is being used, that it is marked with the runner's number and that the contents are appropriate. The runners then enter the tent and place their own bags near signs corresponding to their bib

numbers. After the race, they come back into the tent, retrieve their bags and, on the way out, show their bib number and the bag number to the bag check monitor. This method is quicker than a 'full-service' gear check and uses fewer volunteers. However, an appropriate space is needed, with one-way traffic flow, and it will only work well for races with a few thousand participants or fewer. Also note that this method is a bit riskier in terms of security than a 'full-service' gear check operation.

It is critical to clearly state in the written runner instructions that the race is not responsible for any lost bags or articles and that the runners should not check anything of value. Most races have a stated policy that leftover bags are returned to the race headquarters, held for 30 days, and then discarded or given to charity. If valuables such as cell phones are in the leftover bags, the race may try to locate the owners.

Bag Check for Point-to-Point Courses

If the event starts and finishes in different locations, checked gear will need to be transported from the starting line to the finish line. This is often done using rented trucks or buses, which are convenient because the gear can remain on the vehicles at the finish line. Instead of a large tent, lots of curb space will be required in the start and finish line areas for these vehicles to park. The number ranges (or alphabet ranges for the few races that collect the bags in alphabetical order by last name) can be posted on the windows or sides of the vehicles. If buses are used, runners can drop off and retrieve their bags directly through the bus windows. The Boston Marathon allows a series of 50 numbers for each bus window, with about 500 bags stored on each bus. Another method is to accept the bags at the back of a rented box truck in the starting area, and to transport them to the finish line where they are laid out in a systematic manner for retrieval after runners finish the race.

Busing Runners

Some point-to-point courses—such as the Boston Marathon—or courses with extremely tight staging areas or parking areas that are far away from the start of the race, may need to bus runners to the start (and/or from the finish back to the start). These buses also serve as a convenient repository for the runners' baggage and as warming vehicles in extremely cold weather. Here are some pointers:

- **Have a race committee member assigned to this function.** This person should be in radio contact with the race site to keep everyone informed on the progress of the busing operation. If possible, have radio contact with the individual buses as well, so adjustments can be made if needed. This individual should also let the race director know if there are any delays that may result in some runners not making it to the starting line in time. (Then decide if the start should be delayed.)

- **Minimize the number of busing locations.** Although a few races have an extensive system of satellite busing locations, fewer is better.

- **Find a local vendor who rents school**

Boilermaker Road Race

If you provide shuttle bus service make sure to have lots of buses so runners won't be anxious about making it to the start.

buses. These are the cheapest and are more than adequate. Costs may range from $200-600 per bus.

- **Have plenty of buses and allow plenty of time.** If runners think there are not enough buses, panic may set in (buses may be recycled if time permits); try to have at least one bus loading participants at all times to give them a high comfort level that there will be seats for them. Most events have buses start rolling between 1.5-2 hours in advance of the start.

- **Aggressively publicize the departure time of the last bus.** Then run a final bus 5-10 minutes after the cut-off time.

- **Plan for the highest concentration of runners to arrive at the last minute.** This means having a large number of buses available for this period of peak demand. Do not assume an even flow of participants throughout the designated busing period.

- **If buses are leaving the race site after the race for multiple locations (different hotels, parking lots, etc.), make sure clear signage is visible on each bus as to its destination.** Use volunteers to reinforce this message.

- **Bus companies should carry their own insurance.** Be aware that shuttle buses are not covered under the RRCA insurance policy and that some small companies that might agree to transport runners might not have insurance policies that cover them when they operate at a race, since it is outside of their normal area of business. Make sure that any service used to transport runners definitely has its own liability policy. Get the race organization listed as an additional insured on their policy and obtain a copy of the additional insured certificate.

The Aesthetics

Once the essentials are laid out, turn your attention to the aesthetics (or "the look") of the staging area. There are numerous design touches that can be used to give the event a professional look in the eyes of the runners and the sponsors.

- **Within the staging area**: Have all of the signs professionally prepared by a quick sign company or a graphic artist. Runners greatly appreciate having large maps of the staging area, the course, and a timetable of events readily available in the staging area. Consider placing these signs near the packet pick-up tables and announcer's platform, as many runners gravitate toward these areas in search of information. Each tent should have a sign indicating its function. There are many varieties of signage available for events, and as long as the signs perform the basic functions, the race director may get an opportunity to indulge his or her creative side in developing the look of the event.

- **At the finish line:** The photo on the next page taken at the finish line of the Chicago Marathon provides an excellent example of how to create a sponsor-pleasing finish line. Note the following in the photo on the following page:

  - **Crisp-looking banners on fencing**: The organizers prepared all the sponsor banners themselves, thereby standardizing the sizes and styles (instead of taking a mish-mash of banner sizes and styles supplied by each sponsor) and had the banners imprinted on a rigid material such as Coroplast instead of on nylon or canvas. The rigid signage does not blow in the wind (nylon or canvas signs can, which can make them harder to read), and does not become wrinkled.

  - **Overhead banner:** Although the overhead banner is only partially visible in the photo, you can see that it has the race logo directly in the center. The banner is not too far off the ground, so it gets captured in the finisher photos. (7'-8' should be the maximum—just make sure the press truck can get underneath it if the truck is not leaving the course before reaching the finish line.)

+ **Hanging signage:** Note the Clif Bar signage over the runner's head. This concept, borrowed from cycling races, works well and provides a classy look while getting the sponsor's name out.

+ **Logo on roadway:** This is printed up-side-down to the runners, but right-side-up for the photographers. Make sure the logo is not slick—especially when wet. Years ago, the winner of the Chicago Marathon suffered head injuries when he slipped on the finish line logo in the roadway.

+ **Finish line tape:** Sponsor names are printed in large type.

+ **Clock signage:** The "Citizen" name is located *under* the clock. This ensures that, to have the time on the clock appear in the photo, the "Citizen" name will appear as well.

+ **Finish line directly over the front edge of the first transponder mat:** This eliminates the unsightly mats from the photo and makes for an unambiguous finish line that is compliant with USATF rules.

+ **No stray officials in the finish line area:** The organizers go to great lengths to make sure that no race officials, photographers, or on-lookers mar the background. Many races look like a rock concert with officials, timers, race personnel, photographers and gawkers crowding the finish line area.

+ **Finish line lighting:** The only drawback of this finish line is that the face and body of the runner are in the shade (after breaks of sunlight). This makes the lighting more problematic for photographers, especially when shooting dark-skinned runners.

Other Nice Touches

A few additional suggestions for dressing up the finish line:

● **Balloon arches, flags, etc:** Balloon arches over the start and finish lines certainly add a festive touch. These can be ordered from party-supply businesses or professional decorators. Be sure to hand-pop each of the balloons when the event is over in order to minimize the environmental impact of letting them drift away. Flags mounted on the barricades near the finish line can give the event an international flavor.

● **Scissor lift for media:** If you want to give the media a chance to photograph a smartly-attired staging area, consider renting a scissor or bucket lift to allow for some shots of the area from above.

Attracting Spectators

The largest group of spectators that attend most running events are the friends and families of

Bob Ramsak

A sponsor and spectator pleasing finish line at the Chicago Marathon

the participants. While many running events start too early in the day to become mass spectator events, others, such as the New York City Marathon and the Quad City Times Bix 7 Mile in Davenport, IA, have successfully drawn out their own citizenry to cheer on the runners.

Getting the Word Out

Obviously, you can post announcements aimed at spectators on the event's website, social media and in other materials sent to the runners, but the major challenge is to get the word out to the public beyond those individuals with a direct tie to someone in the event.

If the event is in a smaller town, you may be able to get the local media to encourage the public to come out and watch—especially if you are able to sign the newspaper on as a sponsor (as is the case at Bix and at the Boilermaker Road Race in Utica, NY). Consider publishing a Spectator's Guide, complete with basic race information and a course map, for distribution to the public. If the race has a media sponsor, they may agree to help with this. Similarly, if the race has a radio or TV sponsor, they can target announcements toward spectators. Some races promote spectator parties—running's version of tailgating—along the route.

In addition to newspaper articles, radio shows and websites, potential spectators can also be reached by distributing flyers to some or all of the residences and businesses along the race route. Again, include all the relevant information on the race, as well as information on when the runners will reach each particular neighborhood.

Spectator-Friendly Course Design

Some race directors have specifically designed their courses or events to enhance their appeal to spectators. Some events feature citizens' races, followed by elite races that are run on multi-loop, "criterium-style" courses. Spectators can stand in the same spot or walk only a few hundred feet to see the elite competitors pass by several times. These multi-loop courses work well only for

Phil Stewart

A balloon arch adds a festive touch.

invitational races with small fields, however, as much of the field would be lapped in mass fields with hundreds or thousands of ordinary runners. This criterium-style course design is generally used with great success at the U.S. Olympic Marathon Trials. These events have no mass-participation event as part of the day's activities, but rely solely on the star power of the fields and drama of making an Olympic team to draw out the crowds. Spectators at these events are usually able to watch the progress of the races on Jumbo-tron TV screens located at the finish lines. These courses keep TV production costs down as well, since fixed camera locations can be used multiple times. (For more information on course design, see **Chapter 4: The Course**.)

Spectator-Generated Aid Stations— Be Careful

Do all that you can to encourage spectators to volunteer through the race organization, rather than having them set up aid stations on their own. If the race will be run under hot conditions, no doubt the runners would appreciate having spectators turn on their hoses and hand out supplemental aid in addition to the official aid stations, but such practices could turn into a liability nightmare for the event. Clearly, a race director cannot police the actions of every spectator, but race organizers could find themselves in trouble if they encourage spectators to create their own aid stations and someone is injured. IAAF and USATF rules prohibit elite athletes from accepting aid from unofficial stations.

The Start

For most races, the start is the only place in the event where all the participants are assembled the exact same place at the exact same time.

The Mallet Team

Very large races may use corrals to stagger the volume of participants on the roads.

Thus, the way in which the start is planned and executed is critical. During the planning stages of the event, it's important to determine how much space will likely be needed in the starting area. *Conventional wisdom is that 3 square feet per runner works well.* Of course, this can be a little more or less—it depends on how much elbow-room you'd like the participants to have, as well as on the amount of space that is actually available. This number helps to determine both whether there is enough space at the start and will also give you an idea of how far back the lineup will extend. So, if a race has 3,000 participants, approximately 9,000 square feet of space should be available in the start area. If the road is 30 feet wide, at least 300 feet of road will be needed to adequately handle the field.

For smaller events, the line-up and start of the race are pretty basic—call the runners from the staging area onto the roadway, make sure that all the timers and scorers are ready, check that the course is clear and send everyone off. When participation in an event reaches 500 or more runners, the line-up gets a bit more involved, primarily because it is advantageous (at least to the organizers) for the runners to "self-seed," whereby faster runners line up in the front and slower runners in the back. This configuration helps ensure a safe and orderly start. As events swell into the thousands of runners, the seeding imperative increases. Often, organizers create seeding signs with anticipated paces (i.e., 6:00 miles, 7:00 miles, etc.) that volunteers hold aloft to help runners line up in the proper position. Placing the pace signs is a bit of a guessing game and varies based on the nature of the event. More competitive events mean more runners hoping to run faster times; charity fundraising events tend to attract more slower runners and walkers, so the bulk of the runners will be slower. **Table 16-A** at right breaks down the finishers by pace in a more competitive event that cuts off finishers at 14-minutes per mile, and a charity event with no time limit. The charts show that while the largest number of runners in both events finishes between 9:00 and 11:00 minutes per mile, the competitive event finishes over twice as many runners in the 8:00-8:59 range, and the charity walk has only finished 62% of its finishers when the competitive event has finished 100% of its field. So the only way you can truly know exactly where to place each pace sign is to know the breakdown in the ability level of the entire field. In year one, race directors won't

know this, so it will need to be estimated. In year two the year-one results will be a guide. Overall, the faster the pace (there will always be fewer runners running sub six-minute miles than 10-minute miles), the less space is needed between the signs. The signs should not just be placed equidistant from each other.

Some of the largest events, notably the Boston Marathon, assign runners to specific starting corrals based on seeding or qualifying times submitted in advance. Volunteers rigorously monitor entry into the corrals, and each corral is a self-contained pen cordoned off with rope or

Table 16-A

Distribution of Finishers by Pace: Competitive Race versus Charity Race

Competitive Race		15000 Total number of entrants			Charity Race		15000 Total number of entrants		
Pace	%	Cum. %	Finish Place	# of finishers at this pace	Pace	%	Cum. %	Finish Place	# of finishers at this pace
<6:00 pace	1%	1%	135	135	<6:00 pace	0%	0%	48	48
<7:00 pace	5%	6%	842	707	<7:00 pace	2%	2%	366	318
<8:00 pace	13%	18%	2764	1922	<8:00 pace	4%	6%	895	530
<9:00 pace	21%	40%	5966	3202	<9:00 pace	9%	15%	2282	1386
<10:00 pace	26%	65%	9803	3837	<10:00 pace	11%	26%	3938	1656
<11:00 pace	19%	84%	12612	2809	<11:00 pace	11%	37%	5526	1589
<12:00 pace	10%	94%	14079	1466	<12:00 pace	9%	46%	6874	1348
<13:00 pace	4%	98%	14682	603	<13:00 pace	7%	52%	7851	977
<14:00 pace	2%	100%	14936	254	<14:00 pace	5%	58%	8631	780
<15:00 pace	0%	100%	14989	53	<15:00 pace	5%	62%	9310	679
>15:00 pace	0%	100%	15000	12	<16:00 pace	4%	66%	9931	621
Total finishers				**15000**	<17:00 pace	5%	71%	10639	708
					<18:00 pace	5%	76%	11409	770
					<19:00 pace	6%	82%	12323	915
					<20:00 pace	5%	87%	13094	770
					<21:00 pace	4%	91%	13719	626
					>21:00 pace	9%	100%	15000	1280
					Total finishers				**15000**

Possible corral breaks	# in corral
Sub 8:00 pace	2764
Sub 9:00 pace	3202
Sub 10:00 pace	3837
Sub 11:00 pace	2809
Over 11:00 pace	2388
	15000

Possible corral breaks	# in corral
Sub 9:00 pace	2282
Sub 11:00 pace	3244
Sub 14:00 pace	3105
Sub 18:00 pace	2778
Over 18:00 pace	3591
	15000

barricades. If using corrals, the data in **Table 16-A** will be key in calculating the space, as well.

These charts give the breakdown of finishers by pace for a "competitive" event and a less competitive, charity fundraiser event with walkers. These charts are useful in calculating the amount of space between pace signs at the start as well as the finisher density at the end.

For all but the smallest events, it is important to have the runners approach the start from *behind* the starting line, whenever possible. This avoids the situation where the runners must walk *past* the starting line and then make a U-turn to face in the proper direction. Most runners will try to make this U-turn as soon as they cross the starting line, which will make it nearly impossible to get everyone behind the starting line and will create chaos in any attempt to self-seed them. If they are approaching the starting line from the back, they are more likely to ease themselves behind the

proper seeding sign or into the proper corral. If the staging area must be in front of the starting line, try to restrict access to the roadway with some type of barricades or fencing and march the runners *past* the starting line on the grass or sidewalk and have them turn around so they can enter from behind the start.

Many races provide a special corral for the elite athletes, even if corrals are not being used for the masses. Entry to this corral is limited to runners with bib numbers in the elite range. This corral may initially extend in *front* of the starting line in order to provide the elite athletes with a larger area for warm-up prior to the start. More importantly, it should *extend about 5-10 yards in back of the starting line* to keep the masses from edging toward the starting line. The barrier between the elite corral and the masses can be rope, plastic fencing or metal barricades. This is sometimes called a "false starting line" for the

FayFoto/Boston

The Boston Marathon uses a "human chain" to keep starters in back of the starting line.

masses. The barrier keeps the masses from surging *forward* over the starting line, making it impossible for the elites to get in *back* of the starting line for the start. With about 1-2 minutes to go, race personnel ease the elite athletes back behind the starting line, and the barricade is removed (quickly, by volunteers) from in front of the masses. This enables the masses to move slightly *forward* to immediately behind the elites, who are now in *back* of the starting line. Once everyone is in position, the race is started generally within 1-2 minutes.

Remember this caveat: *you can never get runners at a starting line to move back, they will only move forward!* If you allow the field to start lining up on the actual starting line at the outset, eventually they will crowd the people at the front and soon you'll have hundreds of runners standing well in front of the actual start. Once that happens, it is *very* difficult to get them to move back.

Starting the Race

Before the race can start, the timers must be ready to activate the timing system. It is best to have more than one timing system in place, so that there is a backup in case of some sort of failure. For example, if a race is timed by transponders, timers could also use stopwatches and 'time machines' as backup systems. The starter should identify, in advance, a single member of the timing team who will give him the "all set" signal, which means the timers are ready for the start at any time. The starter may also want get clearance from someone tied into the police team that all the roads are secure before starting the race. Once the starter has these assurances, the race should begin within 60 seconds. Never, ever allow anyone except a race official to determine when to start the race. Although it is always ideal to start the race precisely at the advertised time, it is more important not to start until everything is ready and safe. Going over and over the details of the start with all key race officials and with the official race starter is critical. Precision is extremely important. How the race starts can be the difference between a good race-day experience and a complete disaster.

The race may be started in one of two ways. Races have used either method successfully; just choose the one that you think will work best for your particular event.

● **By a starter standing on the roadway adjacent to the front of the pack.** With this method, the announcer in the front row will go off the microphone with a minute or less to go. A race official will stand in front of the athletes, get the all-clear from the timing team, and start the race, frequently in a low voice that

SIDEBAR

Starting Devices

The majority of races use one of two methods—either a starter's pistol or a marine air horn—to start the race. Some races use the simple and least risky route of simply announcing into the PA system at the start, "runners set, go!" Each method has its pros and cons. As for the starter's pistol, not everyone has easy access to one, and in many cases, local public safety officials simply won't allow them to be used, given local gun laws and the sheer perception of the presence of a gun. As for the air horn method, if it is cold out, many times the sound just won't come out or will be muffled. This can become not only dangerous in terms of creating a false start, but very embarrassing to the official starter, given his/her honorary task of starting the race. As for simply yelling "go" into a PA system, not much can go wrong, but it is not very imaginative, nor does it create a crescendo of excitement to the proceedings. Creative race directors might want to come up with a starting device that not only gets the job done, with minimal risk of failure, but is unique to the event and will become a memorable moment for all the participants and spectators. No matter the method chosen, it's important to have a backup plan in case of a starting mechanism malfunction.

can only be heard by runners in the first few rows. The advantage to this method is that the masses in back of the front athletes won't hear the starting command and will not start moving (which means no pushing) until they see the people in front of them move.

- **By having the race announcer serve as the starter from a raised platform adjacent to the starting line.** The announcer, from the elevated announcer's platform, explains the instructions for the start. (It is advisable to avoid the word "go" when giving the instructions.) The announcer should explain to the runners that they will be given two or three commands and then they will hear the starting sound (starter's pistol or cannon or air horn or whatever is being used to signal the start—*see **Sidebar** for details*). Once the instructions have been given, there should be no more than twenty seconds until the start, and during that time the announcer should keep silent. If you have a VIP whom you wish to let "start" the race, have the announcer simply drop his arm to signal the start, at which time the VIP can blow the whistle, fire the gun or sound the horn to start the race. Never allow a VIP to start a race without a direct signal from a race official. It is important for race management to keep complete control over this critical event.

It is best to avoid a countdown all the way down to the exact second of the start (as in 10, 9, 8, 7, to "go", because the runners may try to anticipate the start and break across the line before "zero" or "go" is said. If this happens, experienced timers are trained to start their watches with the *movement of the runners* across the starting line—even if that takes place before the official start. With race participants numbering into the tens of thousands, there can be no false starts or re-dos. Make sure the timers are knowledgeable about this policy.

Special Types of Starts

- **Wave starts.** As races have increased in size, the sheer volume of runners can result in too many runners on the roadway, causing congestion. To minimize the crowding, event directors may implement a wave start, in which smaller groups of runners are sent off in separate waves at several-minute intervals. This timed-release serves to reduce the density of runners on the roadway, but scoring is complicated if a pull-tag timing system is being used. Today, with transponder-based timing systems producing net times for *each* individual runner (each runner's time is recorded from the moment he crosses the mat at the start until he crosses the mat at the finish), accurate times can be recorded for *all* runners, regardless of which wave a particular runner starts in. The mini-races scored on a wave-by-wave basis can be merged into a single set of results based on net times. (For a complete discussion of timing systems, see **Chapter 17: Timing and Scoring.**)

Most races using a wave start create separate waves of between 1,000 and 2,500 runners per wave. The exact number depends on the capacity of roadways near the start. Runners are assigned to a wave based on their previous race times. The waves are generally started at anywhere from 1- to 4-minute intervals. Since runner density is a function of the width of the roadway, you may have to experiment with different intervals between the waves to find the one that works best for the event. In general, more time should be allotted between the slower waves, because the runners do not spread out as quickly. **Table 16-A** provides data that is useful in determining the time ranges for the waves.

- **Advance starts for elite women.** This is really just a variation of the wave start, in which the elite women start well in advance of the men, in order to create "an all-women's event" (at least for the elites). This practice was instituted primarily to address the issue of elite women being paced by men in races, which officials decided represented unfair assistance. Race directors soon realized that it also served to give more coverage to the women's race, because the women were no longer immersed in the men's race and difficult to locate. With this format, press trucks and TV cameras can track the women's competition far more extensively.

USATF has rules that are applicable to events with women's advance starts. For details on relevant rules, please see *Chapter 14: Rules of Competition.*

- **Early starts for the physically challenged, walkers, and wheelchair participants.** The influx of slower runners, walkers, and physically challenged participants into road races nationwide has caused some races to institute early start procedures for these special groups. An early start allows for extra time for those who need it. For more on early starts, see *Chapter 12: Special Entrant Categories.*

- **Dual and multiple starts.** The New York Road Runners pioneered the first dual start in a high-profile event when the field for the New York City Marathon grew so large that all the participants could no longer start on the same side of the Verrazano Bridge. (Today the race uses both sides of the road on the upper level and one side of the road on the lower level for a triple start.) The runners run different routes for the first 8 miles and then merge together for the final 16 miles. Using dual starts and separate courses for a number of miles allows the field to stretch out before being assimilated onto a common route to the finish. Assuming that both starts can be serviced by the same staging area, the major requirements are to make sure that the distances from each start to the merge point are certified independently (only one certification needs to be done from the merge point to the finish), that everyone knows a single starting sound applies for both starts, and that the different starts are kept separated until the merge point in order to

minimize cheating. In most cases, the starting lines are in slightly different locations rather than side-by-side, because of the separate measurements. Obviously if the starts are too far apart, entirely separate staging areas are needed for each start, and a system for getting runners to their designated starting area needs to be developed.

On The Course

Runners going off course, whether it is the leaders or stragglers, is one of a race director's biggest sins. Just telling runners where the course goes, or putting a map in the runner instructions, is not enough. It is very common for runners to go off course, even in professionally managed, long-time events. Here are a number of redundant measures designed to reduce the chance of runners going off course. Pay close attention.

Marking the Course

The two most important things a race director owes the participants are keeping them on the correct (certified) course and providing them with an accurate finish time. (See *Chapter 17: Timing and Scoring* for details about scoring.) Failing in either of these areas is often viewed as an impeachable offense. Course marking can either be done by the race staff itself, or a company can be hired to place cones/barricades/other course markings shortly before the race. If an outside company is employed, it is essential that they are very clear about the route and where the markings are to be placed. If possible, have a knowledgeable member of the race staff accompany them as they lay out the cones/course markings.

It is best to obtain a copy of the *certification map* of the course (See *Chapter 4: The Course* for details about course certification), and then go out and identify the crucial turns and mile marks on the course *several weeks before race day.* The certification map provides information about how the course was measured, where cones may be required (if any) to ensure that the runners run the course as certified, and exactly where each mile mark is located. The maps contain detached verbal descriptions of key points on the course, such as "Mile 4—345' past light post #1410" or "Mile 8—123' past the first storm drain after Main St., etc." You may want to put down a small dot or a 2"-3" line at the curb with the initials of the race (i.e. "CB1" for mile one of the Cherry Blossom 10 Mile)—or freshen up the previous year's marks

within a few weeks of race day if the course has been used before—in day-glow paint, so that the point will be easy to find on race day, when everyone will be operating under more pressure. Some course certifiers hammer masonry nails directly into the asphalt to serve as unobtrusive markers.

On race day, marking the course should be an exercise in overkill. Your best bet is to mark turns with both course marshals and directional markings

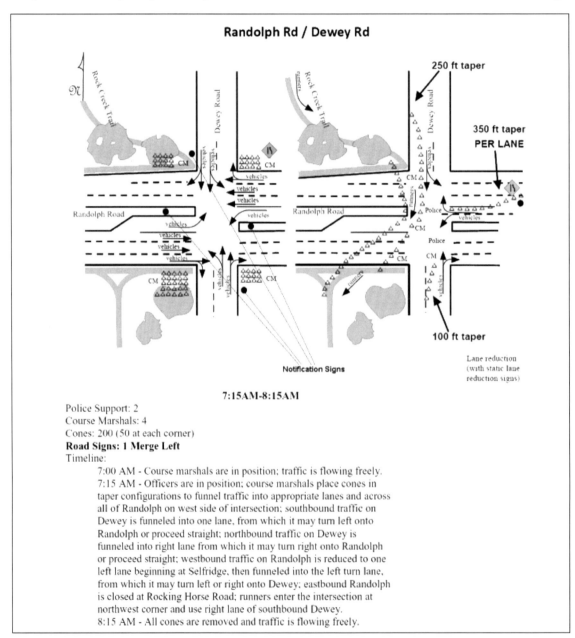

Randolph Rd / Dewey Rd

250 ft taper

350 ft taper
PER LANE

100 ft taper

Lane reduction
(with static lane
reduction signs)

Notification Signs

7:15AM-8:15AM

Police Support: 2
Course Marshals: 4
Cones: 200 (50 at each corner)
Road Signs: 1 Merge Left
Timeline:

    7:00 AM - Course marshals are in position; traffic is flowing freely.
    7:15 AM - Officers are in position; course marshals place cones in taper configurations to funnel traffic into appropriate lanes and across all of Randolph on west side of intersection; southbound traffic on Dewey is funneled into one lane, from which it may turn left onto Randolph or proceed straight; northbound traffic on Dewey is funneled into right lane from which it may turn right onto Randolph or proceed straight; westbound traffic on Randolph is reduced to one left lane beginning at Selfridge, then funneled into the left turn lane, from which it may turn left or right onto Dewey; eastbound Randolph is closed at Rocking Horse Road; runners enter the intersection at northwest corner and use right lane of southbound Dewey.
    8:15 AM - All cones are removed and traffic is flowing freely.

A detailed coning plan is vital to ensure correct set-up.

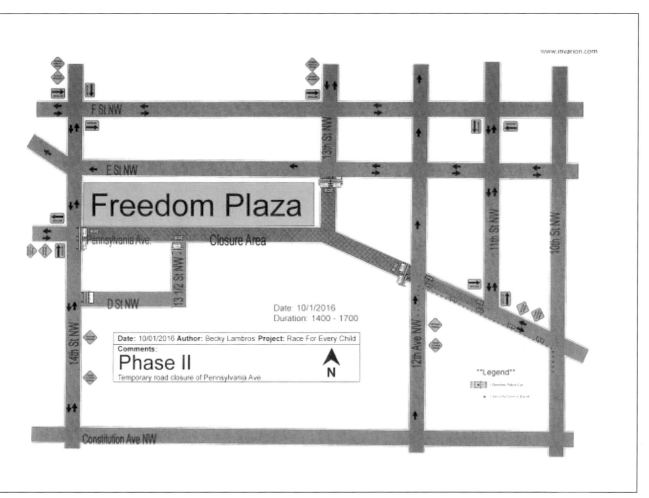

A detailed traffic plan is essential.

like spray-painted arrows on the roadway, cones, and signs (with arrows also). Don't worry about overdoing it with course markings—runners concentrating on a race will probably miss most of them. Err on the side of too many markers, rather than too few.

- **Arrows:** Most small races use *temporary* spray paint to mark the course (flour or lime are less permanent and tend to lose definition as runners run over them) or even duct tape, which can be pulled up after the race. While these markings are the least durable, they are the most likely to be acceptable to the municipality in which the race is run. The city will not be enamored with course markings that last longer than the stripes applied by the highway department for traffic control.

While it is best to have course marshals at each turn, they are an absolute necessity if flour or lime are used to mark the course, as flour arrows can be obliterated quickly by weather or by the first few hundred runners trampling over them.

Start the directional arrows about 25-30 yards before the actual turn. Be sure to paint them thick and long enough that they can be seen easily, and paint them through the turn. Also be sure that the arrows are far enough away from the curb so runners who are further out toward the middle of the road can also see them (This can often be accomplished with several sets of parallel arrows).

- **Cones:** Cones, which are usually day-glow orange, are a good supplement to arrows. Set the cones on the outside perimeter of the turn, allowing plenty of extra room so that even where the pack is the most crowded, runners can easily make the turn without anyone having to run outside the cones. Place cones no more than 10 yards apart from one another, and, as with the arrows, put them at least 25-30 yards before the turn (some large races start the cones even further out—up to 100 yards—and use them to gradually funnel the runners down as everyone approaches the turn). Instruct course marshals to return the cones to their original positions should any get knocked over by a runner or blown over by the wind. Larger-sized cones (18"-36") are preferable to smaller cones, which are less obvious and more likely to be kicked around.

- **Directional signs:** Use directional signs only in conjunction with arrows and cones; they don't work well alone, since most runners are usually looking slightly down and in front of themselves when racing. Signs should be big and attached to poles or stakes so that they can be positioned aloft, above the runners. Directional signs are also a great place for sponsor logos, as long as they don't interfere with the directional information.

- **Mile/kilometer markers:** Runners are more accustomed to looking up for mile markers, since there may be a digital clock at each mile as well, but many races still indicate the mile markers directly on the roadway, too. Mile marker signs provide an excellent opportunity for some sponsor logos printed discreetly underneath the number indicating the mile or kilometer. Make sure that the digit indicating the mile is the largest graphic image on the sign. Some races, especially marathons, provide distance markings at other distances such as 5K, 10K and the half marathon distances. A few place markers with 1200m to go, 800m to go and 400m to go, so finishers can gauge their kicks (or know how much more suffering they have to endure).

- **Other signs:** Some races add amusing signs or signs offering encouragement along the route.

Other Considerations

- **More than one distance.** If there will be more than one race going on at the same time (e.g., a 5K and a 10K that share the course for a time), be sure that the spot where the shorter race splits off from the longer is extremely well-marked, and that there are course marshals (preferably with megaphones) announcing, repeatedly, which way to go for which race.

- **"Reassurance" arrows.** If the course has long straight-aways, consider putting arrows pointing straight ahead along the way, just to reassure runners that they are still on the correct course. Runners are apt to be uneasy if they feel like they've been running for a long time in one direction with no reinforcement that they are doing the right thing.

- **Transponder "splits."** With the advent of transponder-based

---

TIP

Find a Course Checker

Assign someone on the race committee to ride or run the course once a month throughout the year and as often as once a week during the month prior to the race. It's a good way to spot construction, potholes, etc. far enough in advance of race day to provide the time to react and perhaps get the authorities to fix the problem (or provide the time needed to develop an alternate course, if necessary). Far too often, race directors discover a problem on the course very late and face limited options in solving the situation.

Also, have someone inspect the course the day before the race, and again on the morning of the race, especially if there has been recent bad weather. In high winds, a tree or large branch can fall on the course, or heavy rainfall can cause a low-lying area to become suddenly flooded.

---

timing and text message-based reporting of splits to those who sign up to receive such information, some events place a set of transponder mats at several mile/kilometer marks on the course. The transponders record individualized splits at these points, which the runners (and the people following their progress) appreciate. These transponder-monitored splits can also be used to detect cheaters.

Course Marshals

Assign the loudest and most demonstrative volunteers to course marshal duty, but be sure that they can temper this with a dash of diplomacy, as these volunteers will often need to deal with irate drivers. Course marshalling is not the job for shy, retiring types. Besides being physical and vocal human directional arrows, course marshals serve as eyes, ears and cheerleaders out on the course. Marshals should have their duties outlined clearly in advance of being deployed and most likely will require some sort of transportation to the far-flung outposts on the course. (For details about recruiting volunteers to be course marshals, see *Chapter 10: Volunteers.*)

Most events have course marshals check in at a central location, receive their official race garments and instructions about their duties, and then transport the marshals to their on-course locations. Course marshals often need to be among the earliest-arriving volunteers to allow time for all of these pre-race activities. The race committee official overseeing the course marshal operation will need to find out when

the marshals can be transported out on the course. Check with the police to see if this needs to be done *before* the streets are closed to traffic (in which case the course marshals will need to wait *off* the roadway until the course is closed) or if it needs to be done *after* the roads are closed, in which case the vehicle transporting the marshals must be allowed access to the closed roads (it will need an "Official Vehicle" sign of some sort). Alternatively, course marshals can drive directly to their assigned areas and park nearby. In these cases, it is helpful to have an area captain who can distribute the instructions and volunteer t-shirts or reflective vests.

Course marshals should be given some sort of unique race apparel that will clearly identify them as volunteers or marshals. Some races use a different-colored version of the race t-shirt (or a long-sleeved version) to indicate the course marshals. In cold or rainy weather, however, the marshals may put outerwear over the event-supplied volunteer shirts. For this reason, consider providing reflective volunteer vests or special

A course marshal serves as a back-up to the cones.

Phil Stewart

Tyvec bibs with the word "Volunteer" or "Course Marshal" imprinted on them. The volunteers can then pin these bibs to their outerwear. (If you go this route, still plan to give the marshals some type of t-shirt in appreciation of their work.)

The course marshal coordinator should prepare a one- to two-page handout for distribution when the marshals check in. These instructions can also be sent by email a few days before the race, but expect that at least some course marshals will not read them before race day, so have some hard copies on hand. The directions should include the following instructions:

- Exact location of the course marshal post, where the marshals should situate themselves in relation to the post, and what instructions they will be providing to the runners

- Instructions about getting to the post

- Timeframe to remain on duty and instructions about leaving the post

- Procedures for dealing with an on-course emergency. These instructions should include what to do if a runner goes down. As outlined in the "*Communications*" section that follows, course marshals with cell phones should be instructed to call the special cell phone number for Command Central, call "911," or otherwise communicate with any nearby medical officials. (Course marshal duty is a good place to assign volunteers who are CPR certified.)

- A map of the course: This could be a "Grid Map" (*see Figure 8-1 in Chapter 8: Medical, Safety and Security*)

- Locations of the nearest medical and aid stations: This information can be included on the course map

- A reminder to encourage and cheer for the runners

Course marshal duty may be a good opportunity for volunteers from a single group to be assigned together (although they may be told that they have to stand a certain number of yards apart and not stand together and chat).

Course marshal duty is probably not the spot for parents volunteering with their children, as parents are unlikely to feel comfortable standing apart from their children, which they would likely have to do. Marshals should be strong, assertive, and loud.

Other types of specialized on-course volunteers, including water-stop volunteers and split-timers, are covered in the sections on each of these functions provided below.

Aid Stations

The design and function of aid stations is essential to keeping the runners hydrated and preventing serious illness or injury out on the course. Even if the event is held during the cold winter months, an aid station should be provided at events that are 5K or longer. Depending on the time of year and the length of the race, be aware that the aid stations can be the most labor-intensive program in the entire race. Don't underestimate the challenge in what may initially seem like a very simple aspect of the event.

Here are some things to consider as the aid station operation is planned:

- **How many aid stations are needed?** This will depend largely on the distance of the race, the number of participants, and the expected weather conditions. Most races today will plan for aid stations about every 2-3 miles, give or take a bit. This means a single station during a 5K, two for a 10K, and four to five for a half marathon. There are exceptions to every rule, however; Atlanta's July 4th Peachtree Road Race 10K, which draws 50,000 participants (a sizeable number of whom come off the couch just for this event), has aid stations at every mile through mile 5. While the likelihood of hot weather is the primary driving force, the more frequent aid stations also reduce the pressure on runners to get water at every station, since the next aid station is only a mile away. Interestingly, many marathons have *scaled back* the number of aid stations from one every mile to one every 2 miles, because of a serious medical condition called hyponatremia, or "water intoxication." Hyponatremia is most likely to affect slower runners and walkers out on the course for longer than four hours. (For details on hyponatremia, see *Chapter 8: Medical, Safety and Security.*)

- *Where should they be placed?* Most races try to place the aid stations on long straight-aways at relatively even intervals throughout the course. For many events, if municipal fire hydrants or buildings with water connections are needed for the water supply, the location of aid stations will be determined by the location of water sources. (Be sure to check the potability of those sources.) It is certainly far easier to tap into an existing water source than to transport water to the aid station in

barrels (although most races will use bottled water these days and completely avoid this necessity). If this means an aid station ends up at the 2.75-mile mark instead of the 2.5-mile mark, this is acceptable. (Just make sure the exact locations are listed on the runner instructions.) Other factors that may influence the exact location of aid stations include the features of the course and the terrain surrounding the station where the tables and supplies will be set up. It is not a good idea to locate an aid station right at a turn or a turn-around point, at the bottom of a long downhill, at the crest of an uphill, along a narrow stretch of roadway, or on a bridge with metal grating that gets slippery when wet. Most races avoid placing aid stations directly at the mile markers, as runners may be pre-occupied with checking their splits.

Dennis Steinauer

A waterstop features layers of cups separated by a "separator" to allow for quick water distribution during peak periods.

Aid stations may be placed shortly after the mile marks.

- ***What other race functions can be placed at the aid stations?*** Aid stations frequently serve as the organizer's eyes and ears out on the course, doing double duty as on-course first-aid or medical stations (and locations for ambulances or medical gators) and as communications hubs back to the staging area. This means the runners can be told that on-course medical aid or rides back to the finish line for drop outs, etc., are available at the aid stations. Information regarding a security or weather issue once the race is underway can be communicated to runners on the course at the aid stations (you may want to have a bull horn at each aid station for this purpose).

The Design and Operation of Aid Stations

Aid stations are generally lines of tables along one side of the roadway, designed to facilitate rapid handing out of water/ electrolyte replacement drinks to the participants. Very large races may have lines of tables on both sides of the roadway. The key is to assure the runners that there will be ample opportunity for them to pick-up their aid, and that *this does not need to happen at the very first table!* A second consideration is to have the serving of the aid have as little impact on the progress of the race as possible. If

possible, the tables should be placed just above the curb instead of on the roadway, in order to minimize the impact on the course. (If the tables must go on the roadway, place them as near the curb as possible.) Since runners will generally be running the roadway's tangents, it is best to place the stations on the tangents so that runners will not have to deviate far from their planned route to get water. Better yet, place them on straight-aways, if feasible.

If both water and an electrolyte replacement drink will be served, allow for separate tables for each type of fluid and be consistent about which is being served first at every station throughout the course—runners do not want to pour cups of sticky electrolyte replacement drinks over their heads thinking they contain water. Most races tend to serve water first and alternative beverages second. If both water and an alternative will be served, have signs indicating which beverage is being served at which tables, and ask the volunteers to shout out which type of beverage they are

CUCB

Waterstop volunteers extend their arms to allow access to the water cups by participants.

serving. Some events will serve water on one side of the road and the electrolyte replacement drink on the other side, although this requires meandering across the roadway for runners who may desire a little of each type of beverage.

Aid Station Supplies

Equip aid stations with the following:

- Trash cans with plastic liners that water can be poured into and scooped out from, to fill the cups (if bottled water is not being used)

- Pitchers to scoop the water from the cans into the cups

- Water dispenser crocks or other dispensing mechanism, if using 5-gallon jugs of bottled water

- Slabs or flat dividers to separate levels of pre-poured cups of water stacked in advance of the runners' arrival. This procedure provides a buffer for the period when water is being handed out faster than new cups can be filled and placed on the tables.

- Rakes to clean up the discarded cups and trash

- Tables on which to set the cups

- Three to four pairs of surgical gloves per volunteer to aid in sanitary handling of the cups and water

- Special hoses with nozzles to control water flow to get the water from the source to the cans, if a municipal water source is being used. Consider using RV hoses, which are bacteria resistant and safer for drinking water, instead of potentially moldy garden hoses.

- Waxed—not plastic—8 oz. cups (Waxed cups are less slippery than plastic and do not splinter like plastic when stepped on.)

- A race communicator who can relay information back to the central command station when there is a medical emergency or other problem.

(***Note:*** If a sports drink that comes in powder or concentrate form will be provided, containers for mixing the drink at each aid station will also be needed.)

How Many Cups and How Much Water?

These two questions are the Holy Grail of the operation of aid stations and the most critical not to guess low (it is far better to store extra cups than to run out). Cooler weather events may be able to get by with *2-3 cups per participant per aid station*. This would mean a 500-runner 5K with start-finish water and one on-course aid station (3 stations total) would need between 3,000 cups (at 2 cups per runner) and 4,500 cups (at 3 cups per runner); a 2,000-runner 10K with start-finish water and two on-course aid stations (4 stations total) might plan on somewhere between 12,000 cups (at 2 cups per station) and 24,000 cups (at 3 cups per station). Hot-weather marathons and half marathons often use a figure of *8-10 cups per runner per aid station*. This means that a hot-weather marathon with start-finish water and 10 on-course aid stations (12 stations total) would need a range of 192,000 cups (at 8 cups per runner) to 240,000 cups (at 10 cups per runner)! *The bottom line is that you do not want to run out of cups (or water), so plan as if every race will experience hot, humid conditions.* All of these formulas will most likely result in leftover cups, but that is a far more palatable solution than running short.

To calculate the amount of water needed, simply multiply the number of cups needed by 6 ounces (.047 of a gallon), the amount of water placed into an 8-ounce cup. The resulting figures, which may bring images of the Hoover Dam to mind, should serve as testimony to the value of having standby water supply trucks on-site (if you are using bottled water) or to the value of an on-site water supply, so you are not faced with the task of transporting that quantity of water to the aid stations. Despite the logistical difficulty of providing sufficient cups and water, it is not a good idea to supply individual (8 or 16 oz) bottles of water to runners at the aid stations. In addition to the fact that this results in large amount of plastic to be cleaned up from the course and recycled, runners will often not drink an entire bottle of water and will discard it quickly, so there will be excessive waste.

Volunteers at Aid Stations

Volunteers with strong lungs are needed to work the aid stations, as they will have to make continuous verbal communications of information about the aid stations for up to several hours. Place the first volunteers about 25 yards in front of the aid station just to let the runners know that aid is coming up. Supply a few of these volunteers with bullhorns.

How the water and/or fluid replacement drinks are dispensed will depend on the number of volunteers there are compared with the number of participants in the race. If there are a large number of volunteers, some can be used to fill cups and put them on tables and others to hand cups to the runners as they go by. If there are fewer volunteers, they will probably have to fill the cups and put them along the edge of the table for the runners to take themselves, as they go by. It is preferable to have volunteers handing out the water, as that will prevent a runner from accidentally knocking over a table and taking out all the fluids on the table (as well as potentially injuring him/herself).

As the size of the race grows, it will reach a point where volunteers can no longer fill and replace the cups on the tables as fast as the runners can pick them up. At that point, cup separators will be needed in order to stack cups

on top of cups. Purchase water-resistant pieces of Styrofoam, foam-core (outdated sponsor signs or other foam-core signs may be perfect for this, since the printing on the signs will never be seen by the runners), heavy-duty cardboard, or pegboard sheets cut to the size of the water tables. Use these separators to make layers of water cups on the tables. This allows many more cups to be filled in advance. As one level of cups is used, simply remove the separator and start using the next layer down. Cups can be pre-filled to create several layers even before the first runners arrive.

Be sure to spread the aid station out so that lots of people are not crammed in one small area. Spreading things out will reduce the risk of someone tripping, as well as make it more likely that all runners who want aid will be able to get it. To hand out the cups, volunteers should stand in a stationary position with the arm holding the cup extended as the runners pass by. Instruct the volunteers to hold the cup gently, with just the thumb and pointer finger, instead of holding it with the entire hand. This type of grip allows a moving runner to easily grab onto the cup and take it from the volunteer's hand. It is preferable to use adult volunteers to hand out the cups, as a child might accidentally get bowled over by a runner trying to take a cup. If children are used to dispense water, at least wait until the elite and near-elite runners have gone by, as they are moving a lot faster than most of the pack. In addition, have both the adults and the kids rehearse in advance what will happen, so they can appreciate fully just how quickly it's going to happen.

If energy gels like Gu or gel alternatives will be handed out, make sure that these stations are separated from the fluid replacement stations, and remember that energy gels only need to be handed out for longer races (if at all) and in the later stages of these races. If energy gels or other similar products are distributed, keep in mind that the volunteers will have the additional

 GREEN TIP

Plan Aid Stations for Recycling and Composting

Design aid stations (as well as the start and finish areas) to incorporate recycling and/or composting into the plan, from both a space and equipment standpoint. In many municipalities, the typical aid station cup may be compostable. Check with local authorities to confirm their acceptability.

job of cleaning up the discarded packaging after the event. This can be an arduous task which may require hosing the discarded gel off the roadway.

Encourage aid station volunteers to be at their posts as much as 90 minutes or more in advance of the start for a large race, especially if they are working the first stop on the course where the runners are still tightly bunched. It takes a surprising amount of time to fill the cups and stack them on the tables.

Provide trash bins at the aid stations for the disposal of empty cups, but if (clean) trash cans are being used for dispensing the water into cups, make sure those cans are not mistaken for actual trash bins, or the drinking water will quickly become contaminated with used cups! Since most runners do not remain at the aid station while they drink, even if trash bins are provided, you will end up with a large number of discarded cups on the road, some of them quite a distance from the aid station. After all the runners have passed, it is important to clean up the cups and any other trash that was left behind. Cups can be easily collected with rakes and scooped into trash bags; energy gel packets are sticky and pose more of a problem for cleanup. For more information on post-race cleanup, see *Chapter 19—Post Race.*

Pre- and Post-Race Water

The pre- and post-race water operations are easier to operate than the on-course stops, simply because the clientele is not moving nearly as fast, if at all. There are nonetheless some special considerations for the management of these stations:

- *Location.* Make sure that the pre-race water tables are in a visible and accessible location in relation to where the runners will be lining up for the start. Consider large signs or banners to indicate where the water is located. Runners will get frustrated if the announcer dwells on the importance of drinking water before the race and they can't find it.

- *How the water is dispensed.* Pre- and post-race water are much more conducive to being

served in single-serving water bottles, since participants are not drinking it on the run. Using bottles provides excellent visibility for a potential bottled water sponsor. The downside of using bottled water is the cleanup of the bottles. If using bottled water, try to get water bottled in PET plastic containers. Recycle used bottles after the race.

- *Consider separating pre- and post-race water.* Examine how visible and accessible the water is for runners both *before* and *after* the race. Consider whether the staging area needs separate tables for pre-race and post-race water, even though both are in the same general area. Make sure the race announcer provides detailed information about where the water is located.

- *Format of tables.* Because these stations are not serving people on the run, look at a "hollow square" format for the staging area water. This format allows the water stop volunteers to set water out from the inside of the square and the runners to receive it along all four sides of the square.

Clocks and Split Times

While nearly every event, regardless of size, will have a clock at the finish line, runners also appreciate clocks along the course for noting their split times at mile marks. Even if back-of-the-pack runners wait six minutes before crossing the starting line, making the opening mile split a meaningless record of their pace for that mile, or if a wave start is used and the clocks show the accurate time for only participants in the first wave, digital clocks still remain a popular feature among runners.

Before race day, become very familiar with how to charge the digital clocks (most races charge them overnight the night before the race), what their battery life is, how to set and clear them very quickly, and how to start them when the gun goes off.

If clocks will be placed along the course, the

best way to start them simultaneously is to have a volunteer with a race radio or a cell phone at each clock. These volunteers are in direct communication with the timers (or other volunteers) at the start line as the race starts, so they can start their clocks at the same time. Alternatively, if the course is such that it is safe and feasible to drive the clocks to the mile markers *after* the race starts, all of the clocks can be placed in a van at the starting line and wired together. When the gun sounds, one button can be pressed to start all the clocks at once. As soon as the clocks are started, they can be driven out to the appropriate mile markers along the course. It will speed the mounting of the clocks if the tripods have been set out at each mile mark in advance.

Setting up and taking the clocks down is not hard; it only takes two or three minutes. As a result, depending on the course layout and length, you may be able to transport clocks from the early miles and set them up for use once again in the later miles. If this is planned, however, be sure that the van or truck will have time to transport the

clocks from one spot to another, even if there is some traffic.

Split Time Callers

Although the prevalence of Garmins and other GPS-based 'watches' now makes it very easy for runners to keep track of their own split times, some races that cannot afford clocks for each mile marker still choose to employ volunteers to call out split times at the mile marks. If you will use human time-callers, ideally try to assign split calling to people who have done it before. Don't give this job to a novice who might not understand how to do the job properly. Splits can be called every two seconds ("5:07…5:09…5:11," etc.)—so the split callers don't trip over their tongues—in a loud voice, with the minute called frequently, not just the seconds. Also, consider giving each split caller a bullhorn to help make the splits more audible.

If split timers are using their own watches to keep track of the time, it can't hurt to provide them each with a backup watch in case a battery dies or there is some other malfunction. Both watches should be started at the same time the race starts. Like the volunteers in charge of digital clocks described above, split timers should be in contact with the personnel at the start line via race radios or cell phones, so that they can hear the start of the event and start their watches simultaneously.

Lead Vehicles

If a race is very small and limited to secondary roads that remain open to traffic, it is possible that a race official may be able to lead the runners on a bicycle. As long as this official is very familiar with the course, there should be no problem. (Many low-key events may rely solely on arrows and

Phil Stewart

The lead vehicle caravan at the Boston Marathon. Frequently a race official will coordinate the movement of these vehicles with respect to each other to ensure the safety of the runners.

course marshals and not have a lead vehicle of any sort.)

However, as soon as there are road closures involved, it is nearly certain a police vehicle will be in front of the runners. The largest events will have a host of other vehicles, including press trucks, TV trucks, more police cars and motorcycles, sponsor vehicles, etc., creating a two- and four-wheeled armada at the front— and a need for a lead vehicle coordinator on the race committee, both to plan lead-vehicle movement in advance and to orchestrate it on race day.

It is a good idea to send a vehicle out to review the course between 15-30 minutes prior to the start, just to make sure the course is clear.

Coordinating with the Police

Since you are placing control of the event in the hands of a police officer who may have only received a copy of the course map just hours before the race, it is wise to take the opportunity to review the course with the officer in advance. Better yet, make a request to have someone on the race committee who knows the course well ride along with the lead officer. (Attitudes toward this type of request vary widely among police departments, but it doesn't hurt to ask.)

Keeping Everyone Else in Line

If the event will include a number of lead vehicles, designate one race official to be in charge. This official should maintain radio contact with *someone in each vehicle* and coordinate the movements of all of the vehicles. Be sure to work out the chain of command with the police in advance, so there will be no question as to who is in charge when a snap decision has to be made. Also, let the police know with whom they can communicate during the event.

The lead vehicle coordinator is responsible for

SIDEBAR

Lead Vehicle Management

Here is a checklist for lead-vehicle management for a larger race:

- Make sure the race is led by local drivers. Never use out-of-towners to lead a race.
- Never let TV stations or non-race personnel determine who rides in the lead vehicles or where the lead vehicles will go.
- Always use the smallest number of vehicles possible.
- Limit the amount of broadcast power used by the media, as some transmitting equipment can interfere with other essential race communications.
- Make every rider sign a waiver.
- Don't permit anyone to get on a lead vehicle without a reservation. Have a race official check in every rider.
- Don't use any banners on the course that could interfere with the lead vehicles.
- Use a second individual (possibly a police officer) on the media truck to keep unauthorized people off and to assist with communications.
- Drive the course before race day (in the media vehicle with the media vehicle driver) to check for tight turns and low-hanging branches.
- Have an advance vehicle drive over the course about 30 minutes before the start of the race, just to make sure the course is clear. (Officials on this vehicle can also remove unauthorized (non-sponsor) banners from the course.)
- Make sure drivers know in advance where vehicles exit the course. Have them accelerate out of sight of the lead runners before they exit, to avoid confusing the runners. Lead runners are notorious for following lead vehicles as they exit the course—even if they are only yards from a massive finish line structure.
- Have a protocol in place for passing and other maneuvers. Decide in advance if vehicles are supposed to pass on the left or right.

ensuring that all the lead vehicles negotiate the course without getting in the way of the runners. All vehicles should line up far enough ahead of the start line so that they don't have to jam on the accelerator to keep the runners from catching up to them (and thus possibly injuring someone in the process.) If possible, the vehicles should be lined up to the sides of the road at the start, just in case one of the vehicles fails to start. This will keep a disabled vehicle out of the way of the runners. Many courses have tight spots where the road narrows, and careful planning for these points is essential to avoid congestion and accidents. If the race has a wheelchair division that begins prior to the running event, a plan must be developed about how the vehicles are going to pass the wheelchair competitors.

Special Considerations for Media Vehicles

If an event is large enough to warrant one or more media trucks, be sure to arrange the convoy so that the media and photographers can get as clear a view of the runners as is (safely) possible. Prior to the race, describe to the media how close the media truck will get to the runners, and if there will be a TV truck between their vehicle and the lead runners. If so, consider arranging for the TV truck to drop in back of the media truck once or twice, to allow for closer viewing by the media and still photographers. (Some races place a still photographer on a motorcycle to ensure quality still photos showing the action.) Finally, be very clear about what point in the race the media vehicle needs to leave the leaders to get back to the finish line. Most races have media trucks accelerate to the finish with about a mile to go, to allow the media—especially photographers— time to get off the truck and get situated for the finish.

FayFoto/Boston

Photo and media trucks frequently feature a tiered platform to enhance visibility.

Other Considerations for Lead Vehicles

Be sure that all lead vehicles—especially the media vehicle, since it may have risers on it—can fit under any banners, low-lying tree branches, power lines, etc., on the course. With photographers and reporters looking backwards from the media vehicle, they are particularly oblivious to any approaching low-hanging branches, etc. and are at risk of serious injury. "Test drive" the media vehicle—with someone standing on the highest point—before race day, to identify any problem areas.

In addition, it is very important that a plan be made for the way vehicles will exit from the course. Each driver should know where he is to get off the course, where any people riding on the vehicle will get off, and where he is to park the vehicle so he won't be crowding the finish area when the winners arrive. Finally, make sure that the lead vehicles are well-serviced prior to race day (check the batteries) and that someone has an extra set of keys for each vehicle.

Sweep Vehicles

It is vital to have an official presence at the back end of the race as well—this can be a race committee member walking, a bicyclist, or a sweep vehicle. This sweep presence clearly defines where the race organizer's responsibility for the runners ends. Often, the sweep vehicle will pick up stragglers and give them a ride to the finish line. This function is very important in races that have time limits. In longer events, it may be necessary to have multiple sweep vehicles so when one is full of runners who are abandoning the race it can return to the finish line, while another vehicle continues to pick runners up. Some runners—especially in events with time limits—may resist boarding a sweep vehicle because they are determined to finish. Consider stocking the vehicle with food, water and first aid supplies, and staff it with sympathetic volunteers to make it a bit more tempting.

Discuss with law enforcement personnel how to handle any recalcitrant participants who simply will not leave the course. Race volunteers should never use force to remove a participant, for legal reasons. Frequently, police will use their squad car bullhorns to demand that

SIDEBAR

What Makes Lead Runners Go Off Course?

Few things are more embarrassing to a race director than having the leaders go off course, and few things will raise the wrath of frontrunners more quickly, especially if prize money is involved. (Plus, the media will make this the "story" of the race.) Although some race directors will include a course map with the registration form or on the website and state "It is the runner's responsibility to know the course," it is reasonable for runners to expect a well-marked course as one of the basics of the event. Following all the suggestions as outlined in this chapter is key, especially posting loud and assertive course marshals at key intersections and turns.

Some of the most frequent and high-visibility miscues have been in high-profile events with elite athletes. The difficulty arises because the lead pack has its attention transfixed on either the press truck or the lead police motorcycle for 98% of the race—the leaders are like greyhounds chasing the artificial rabbit at dog races—they will chase it wherever it goes. Suddenly, with the finish line in sight, the lead vehicle turns off on a side street to allow the leaders to cross the finish line unobstructed by the vehicle. As incredible as it seems to the spectators because the finish line is in plain sight, the lead runners follow the lead vehicle off the course and down the side street. Whether it is only a few strides or a city block, the leader has to regroup, turn around and return to the course and the complexion of the competition is forever changed.

The solutions to this problem include explaining to the elite athletes, in a pre-race technical meeting or at the starting line, exactly when the press truck or lead vehicle will exit the course, having the press truck leave the course at least half a mile before the finish line, and having extra course marshals at the precise vehicle exit point, who have been told in advance that the vehicles will be leaving at this point and who are prepared to redirect the runners if needed.

A second potential scenario for runners to go off course is if a lead runner—or group of runners—has opened up such a large lead on the pursuing pack that the pack no longer has the lead vehicles as a visual check. Ideally, it would be good to have a vehicle or a bicyclist drop back to provide reassurance to the followers. If this is beyond your capabilities, just reinforce to the course marshals the importance of their jobs in situations where the runners are greatly strung out.

individuals get off the streets and onto the sidewalks. Coming from police, these announcements will be more intimidating. Race directors should be firm about not recording times or places after a certain time, to remove the incentive for participants who refuse to clear the course.

The Finish

This section covers the activities, other than timing and scoring, that take place at the end of the race. (See *Chapter 17: Timing and Scoring* for a full discussion of timing and scoring.) Since many races use a common start and finish line area, many of the set-up issues were covered in the section in this chapter covering *"The Start."* Here are a few items that are unique to the finish line.

Finish Line Tapes

The peak moment for the race as an athletic event is when the winner breaks the tape. (The tape-breaking is done for both the male and female winners—and sometimes for the wheelchair champions as well.) One of the key finish line officials should take responsibility for making sure

the finish line tape is at the finish line. (The specifications for ordering a finish line tape are covered in *Chapter 11: Equipment, Supplies and Key Personnel.*)

Paradoxically, the holding of the finish line tape is a task frequently given to key sponsor representatives, who may never have attended a running event and have certainly never held a finish line tape before! Therefore, gather the key sponsor officials in the finish line area about 15 minutes before the winner arrives, and have someone on the race organization who is experienced in this task train them and remain close by throughout the time period when the tape is being used.

Plan to have the tape in place about five minutes before the first runner crosses, so photographers can frame their shots. The tape holders should be equidistant from the center of the finish line (consider placing a small mark on the pavement to indicate where each tape holder should stand). The tape should be held a little above hip level of the incoming runner. Most runners will raise their arms in a victory gesture when they break the tape, so their bodies will be stretched a bit. Given that the tape holders will not know the height of the winner, they will have to adjust the tape height as the winner is approaching it. Additionally, if the tape is being held for wheelchair winners, tape holders should receive special instructions so that the tape does not end up in the winner's face or tangled in the wheels of the chair. A two-part Velcro tape works best in these situations.

Make sure the tape is right-side up, with the logo side facing *away* from the runner's body. (Keep in mind that the finish shots will be taken from *behind* the finish line, so the logos should be facing the photographers.) If the tape consists of two parts held together in the center with Velcro, the officials must be told to hang on to the end of the tape and let the runner pull the Velcro

---

SIDEBAR

Prepare for Running Out of Items

It is a good plan to develop a strategy in advance should you run out of items distributed to runners after the race, such as medals and/or t-shirts. Have a system in place to quickly capture the bib numbers of all of the runners who do not get something that was promised to them. This can be as simple as alerting the volunteers and supplying them with clipboards, pens and paper to record the bib numbers of the runners who missed out. If the bib numbers have bar codes, you can use bar code scanners for this purpose. The complete information (including t-shirt sizes) for each runner can be obtained from the registration data. Volunteers should reassure the runners, who may be a bit cranky over not getting the item, that it will be sent out at no charge after the race (or whatever the policy might be).

free with the force of his/her body; if the tape is continuous, the officials should hold the tape gently and let the force of the finish gently draw it out of their hands.

It is wise to have a standby tape on hand in case the male winner decides to carry the tape off with him. This way, you will be set for the winning female. Last, if it is a close finish with multiple runners sprinting for the finish line, it may be best not to put the tape up at all and get the tape holders out of the way. Surprisingly, the finish line tape is not the legal finish line. (See *Chapter 14: Rules of Competition* about the relationship between the finish line and the finish tape.)

Post-Finish Line Processing

Once across the finish line, runners will enter a post-race processing area, with services provided in descending order of priority. If transponder timing is being used with disposable transponders,

runners will be free to move as quickly as possible through the processing area. Events employing reusable transponders will need to have volunteers to assist with the removal of the transponders. These races will require chairs for runners to sit on while removing the transponders, and collection buckets for the transponders. This system will slow down the movement of the finishers considerably, so if this is the timing method being used, make sure to have a large 'corral' area in which transponder removal will occur. (If conditions are hot, consider having some water for runners in distress before the transponder-removal area.) If pull-tag scoring is being used, the runners will enter the chutes where their tags are removed and placed on spindles by volunteers. (See *Chapter 17: Timing and Scoring* for details about pull-tag timing.) Medical services (covered in detail in *Chapter 8: Medical, Safety and Security*) should be located just past the

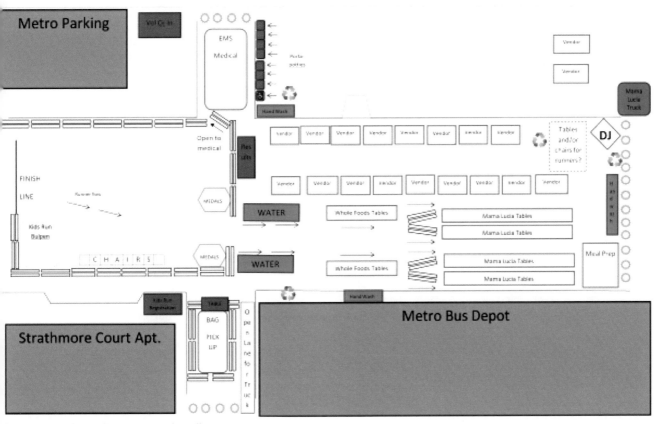

A post-race finish line processing diagram.

finish line, with vigilant medical personnel on hand to watch for runners in medical need.

Water and fluid-replacement drinks should be the next items for the runners to receive, followed by Mylar warming blankets, if they are being offered, food, and medals (if offered). For races with over 1,000 runners, and definitely for mega-races, it is best if the runners are cordoned off from the spectators with barricades throughout this post-finish processing. Place perky volunteers throughout the area to congratulate the runners. Give some of the volunteers bullhorns so they can let the runners know to keep moving through the post-race area and inform them about the activities that are coming up. Sprinkle medically-trained personnel throughout this area to keep an eye out

Phil Stewart

A medal rack can expedite the distribution of medals after runners cross the line.

for runners needing medical attention, as well. If finishers will be barricaded throughout this process, consider where they will be released into the general post-race staging area for family reunions, gear retrieval, and any post-race activities.

Medals

If the race is distributing medals to all finishers, have a system in place for this or it will significantly slow down the movement of runners through the post-finish area. Medals should be removed from their packaging and pre-strung in advance on some sort of rack system. It is a bad idea to keep the medals in a box or bin, because the ribbons will get tangled and it will be very difficult for the volunteers to distribute them. Have enough volunteers to hand out medals, so that the process is quick and efficient and the runners flow smoothly out of the finish area.

Post-Race Refreshments

Ideally, tents and tables for post-race refreshments should be located in the post-race staging area, some distance away from the finish line/immediate post-finish area. Runners often move quite slowly through the refreshment tent, so if the refreshments are too close to the finish line, you can very easily end up with a significant backup that could impact the remaining finishers as they cross the line.

How Much Post-Race Food?

Although less critical than running out of water or cups, running out of promised post-race food will light up social media with negative comments by those who miss out. Unless you advertise a big post-race party with lots of food, runners expect to receive 2-3 items post-race, such as a bagel, a banana or orange, and a granola bar. (Certainly food items should top the in-kind donation requests from sponsors. Most events with large post-race parties have supermarkets as sponsors.) If your volunteers encourage each runner to take one of each item, you should be safe if you order the same number of items as you have participants. (For more details on post-race refreshments, see *Chapter 11: Equipment, Supplies and Key Personnel*.)

Communications

● **Cell phones.** If the event is small and you plan to rely exclusively on cell phones for communications among key race personnel, make sure that all the key players have the cell phone numbers of everyone else. Prepare a master cell phone list and make sure that it is distributed to everyone on the network. Encourage the important players to pre-program some of the key numbers into their own cell phones. Some races—even those using radios—list the cell phone numbers on the back of laminated "All Areas" passes provided to key race staff. Remind people that text messaging is an option as well. In advance of the race, check to make sure there is good cell phone reception over the entire area of the course. Besides the possibility of coverage limitations, the biggest shortcoming of cell phones as a primary communication network is that they are generally limited to communication between only two people at a time. In addition, it is often very difficult to hear a cell phone ringing over the noise at the event site, and it's sometimes even difficult to feel them vibrate. Remind race personnel to check their phones often or to wear an earpiece, which has the additional advantage of freeing up the hands for other tasks.

The universality of cell phones also means that *any* person with a cell phone is a potential set of eyes out on the course. To tap into this network without overloading the communications network, publish a single cell phone number as the call-in number for any volunteer with a cell phone who sees an emergency on the course.

Police and EMS officials will have their own radio networks (with far broader coverage than just the race) that operate independently of the race's communications network. Therefore, be sure that someone on the race team is in a position to communicate with police and EMS quickly. This person may be designated as "Command Central" for the event. Tell all volunteers in advance that if someone calls "911" on the course in response to an emergency, to be sure to call the race director— or "Command Central"—to state that such a call has been initiated. The race director or "Command Central" will relay that information to the first responders and the event's medical team, and take action as needed.

● **Radios.** Once races grow past 500-1000 runners, the organizers should consider commercial-grade walkie-talkie radios. (See *Chapter 11: Equipment, Supplies and Key Personnel* for details on using this type of radio.) The biggest advantage of using a radio net is that multiple people can listen and/or provide input to address a problem.

The set-up of the radio network will depend largely on the size of the race. Have one main "operations channel," but be aware that once the communications network expands beyond 15-20 people, it will become cluttered, and more channels should be used for various sub-groups, with one communications coordinator who monitors all the channels and informs individuals of goings-on on the other networks as needed. Many races using radios also end up using cell phones for one-on-one conversations as a back-up. This can reduce the need for "off-line" conversations on different radio channels if the communication is just between two people.

It is most likely that the medical team will be the first group to have its own separate channel. This will allow communication between the medical team and race officials out on the course about any medical situation. By having a designated channel, this critical communication can take place without interference from conversations on the main channel and without wide broadcast of the nature of the medical matter.

A second separate channel might be set aside for any more-involved conversations that need to take place between a small group of race officials without the interference of the general race channel (or if the content of the conversation is such that it would be better not to have it heard by everyone on the net). In this case, one official on the main channel might say "Can we have all the officials who need to address 'Topic X' please turn to channel 3 to continue this conversation." This change will remove "Topic X" from being heard on the main network. The key is for the involved parties to remember to switch back to the main channel once the "private" conversation is concluded.

If the event has communications between the lead vehicle and the finish-line announcer, this is a good example of a two-way conversation that may be better handled by

cell phone between the spotters on the lead vehicle and the announcer's assistants. If it is handled on the radio net, be sure to put it on a separate channel, because the chatter can be fairly constant, potentially blocking out other important communications.

As a general rule, don't establish too many separate channels for communications. If this happens, people will inevitably forget what channel is for what (even if a list is supplied) or what channel they are on.

The key elements in making the communications system work are:

- Advance preparation
- Pre-race tests and simulations
- Volunteer education regarding how to use the radios
- A communications coordinator who monitors the radio net and suggests when people should move to separate channels. This person usually serves as the crossover link between the race and police/emergency personnel.

SIDEBAR

Emergency Grid Map of the Course

Imagine that an emergency announcement comes over the radio network announcing that a runner is down on the course. Would the volunteers know exactly how to describe where the runner is located to the medical team? Sure, some points on the course are easy—each mile, if mile markers are used—but how about points in between mile marks or off the course? Is an ambulance going to know exactly where "near the 4-mile mark" or the "infield adjacent to the finish line" is located? One solution to this problem is to create a grid map, which breaks the course down into smaller quadrants. The volunteer can relay the message "The runner is down in grid 6C and I need an ambulance." **See *Figure 8-1* in *Chapter 8: Medical, Safety and Security*** for an example of a Grid Map and a complete discussion of its use.

The Darman Group

A Speaker's Bureau

Representing:

- Race Announcers
- Pioneering Women Runners and Event Directors
- Olympians
- Motivational Speakers
- Sports Business Entrepreneurs

Looking for the perfect speaker for your next event, club meeting, banquet, or running clinic? Whether you want a speaker with inspiration, humor, advice, or a great race announcer, the Darman Group has the person for you!

Contact:

Jeff Darman
610.925.1976
jeff@darmangroup.com
www.darmangroup.com

ENGAGE YOUR ATHLETES AND FANS

MYLAPS EVENTMANAGER OFFERS EVENTS AND TIMERS WORLDWIDE THE MOST COMPLETE ENGAGEMENT PLATFORM IN THE INDUSTRY!

Registration

Timing

Eventapp

PhotoVideo

SocialShares

LiveTracking

EventResults

With modules like your own (branded) EventApp, LiveTracking, PhotoVideo, Social Shares and Event Results, combined with our worldwide timer network, MYLAPS offers a complete event solution.

LET'S ENGAGE YOUR FANS CONTACT US VIA MYLAPS.COM

MYLAPS EVENTMANAGER SUPPORTS YOU WITH

▶ Enhancing the event experience for participants

▶ Offering great exposure for your sponsors

▶ High quality modules, separately available, yet strong in combination

MYLAPS

EXPERIENCE **PROGRESS**

Phil Stewart

17 Timing and Scoring

THE BASICS

- Deciding to learn how to time an event and to invest in timing equipment more sophisticated than the most simple, small race system outlined in this chapter needs to be carefully evaluated. If you are involved with a single, modest sized event, it may make more sense to rent the equipment and hire the timing expertise needed from a local running club or event management company. If you are hoping to time and score multiple events, you might consider honing your timing skills and purchasing the equipment as outlined in this chapter.

  If you decide to engage a professional timing and scoring company, it can be a for-profit company specializing in timing/scoring running events or a local running club that contracts out services. Either of these groups can provide everything needed for finish line operations, plus they can work with volunteers, or provide their own, to make sure the finish line runs smoothly. The cost will vary depending on the level of service provided, but transponder-based timing and scoring should start between $2-$3 per registrant. (**Note:** If your race is very small, most timing companies will have a minimum fee they will charge regardless of the size of event. This applies to smaller races—generally less than 200 participants.) If other services are needed, such as equipment rental, registration services, or experienced personnel, etc., the cost will increase.

- For details about hiring a company, see **Hiring a Finish Line Company** later in this chapter.

- If the event is small (a few hundred participants at most) or confined primarily to a closed group, such as a PTA or church group, the pull-tag or index card systems may suffice. Otherwise expectations will be for a transponder-based system based on disposable transponders (often called a "chip") generally adhered to the back side of the runners' bibs (although a few systems still use reusable transponders that are returned after the race and often affixed to runners' shoes). Transponders are detected as runners cross mats laid down at the start and finish of the race or at strategic points out on the course. If you wish to time and score the event yourself or are looking to establish yourself as a timing and scoring business or as a race management expert for a running club, investigate purchasing the timing equipment and learning how to operate it. The cost of transponder-based timing systems has dropped significantly in recent years, with some systems available for purchase for $2000-$2500 for an entry level timing system and under $1.00 each for the transponders. Vendors will tout their "read" rates, which should be close to 98-99%. If the main use of the system will be for timing small events, you may want to consider getting re-useable chips. The upfront cost per chip is more ($1.50-$3.00), but it is a one-time fee and is significantly cheaper in the long run. Of course, whatever transponder system you choose, there will be a learning curve.

- An intermediate alternative might be to contact a local running club to fill in any gaps in expertise, equipment or personnel.

- USATF has a detailed publication that presents more technical detail about scoring than is possible here. See **Chapter 23: Resources** for information about this publication.

THE DETAILS

The anticipation of receiving their times and places from the event organizers is the reason most runners enter races—they want to know how fast they ran, how they did in comparison with their own performances at previous events of the same distance, and how they fared against other competitors—and they want to know quickly. In its most basic form, timing and scoring a race involves linking three pieces of data together—the runner's place, the runner's time, and the runner's identity—and then presenting this information. The purpose of this chapter is to outline the processes employed to accomplish this goal.

The advent of transponder-based (sometimes called "chip") timing systems in the mid-1990s, coupled with dropping price points, increased ease of use, and wider availability of these systems, has made this type of timing widely available to a large number of races. Today, some relatively small events (usually no larger than a few hundred participants) may still rely on the pull-tag system and even smaller events on the index card system for timing/scoring. An overview of all three systems is provided in this chapter, along with other considerations surrounding the timing and scoring of running events. Because transponder-based timing is the most widely used, it is covered first, followed by descriptions of the pull-tag and index card systems generally used for smaller events.

Three Methods of Collecting Data

Transponder-Based Timing

Transponder-based timing systems function through the use of RFID (radio frequency identification) technology. Without a doubt, transponder technology is the most dramatic development in timing since computers replaced 3" x 5" cards! There are a relatively small number of transponder system suppliers in the marketplace. Unfortunately, the transponders provided by each are unique to that company's system. This means that, if a transponder-timing system is purchased from a given company, the purchaser is limited to ordering and using that company's brand of transponders as well. (Some timing systems (very few) are "unlocked" and allow the use of any compatible chip on the market. Again, though, this is rare.)

Types of Transponders

- **Disposable transponders:** The disposable transponders that dominate the marketplace are made up of tiny transponders embedded on a strip that is generally adhered to the backside of a runner's bib number. The transponders are generally sold separately from the bibs, meaning that someone will have to individually adhere the strips to the backs of the bibs (a considerable task for large events). This task can be performed either by the race organizers/volunteers or the timing company, or, in some instances, the bib printers will provide this service, although they will need to know which type of transponder is being used and how the transponder is applied—some are vertical and some are

horizontal—and arrangements will need to be made for the transponders to be delivered directly to them. Some timing companies will actually create custom bibs for events, with the transponders already attached and ready to go.

- **Reusable transponders:** Reusable transponders come in a variety of different options, customized for different types of events (running, triathlon, cycling, skiing, etc.) Those used for most running events are either a quarter-sized piece of plastic (hence the name 'chip'), or an approximately 1" x 1" tag containing a transponder and an energizing coil. The transponders are tied into the runners' shoelaces, affixed to the shoes using a plastic tie, or worn on ankle straps. Each transponder is unique in that it contains a transponder code different from that of every other transponder. These reusable transponders are almost always *rented* by the race, so they must be collected at the end of the race.

Transponder System Hardware

The 'fixed' parts of a transponder scoring system consist of the following:

- **Antennae mats:** The antennae mats are set up at both the start and finish lines, and often at intermediate points on the course as well. Depending on the type of timing system used, these mats contain both transmitting and receiving signals, and as a runner properly wearing the transponder steps onto the mat, the receiving signal "reads" the unique code associated with each transponder. This code is then transmitted to the "readers," which are the hardware associated with the timing system (see below). Some of the newer timing systems replace or supplement the mats on the ground by mounting specialized antennae, either on the sides of the finish line or overhead. The use of these types of systems greatly depends on the event type.

- **Readers ("boxes"):** The readers are

connected by cables to the antennae mats and collect the transponder data from the mats.

- **A computer:** The data collected by the reader boxes is then transmitted to a computer, usually located in a separate tent, room, or van, for processing into results using scoring software.

How It Works

There are two main types of systems/chips used—Dual Frequency and UHF. Dual frequency systems typically have a transponder that is made unique by encoding within it a unique identifier code. Before the race, each runner's bib number is matched to a transponder number (and a corresponding code) in the scoring database. UHF systems most often have chips that match the bib number of the runner, which eliminates the need for a transponder ID/bib number reference. As runners cross the start mat, the antennae send out signals to transponders, creating a magnetic field that energizes the coil within the transponder and triggers the transponder. The transponder sends the signal with the unique ID/transponder number of that transponder to the receiving antennae in the mat. The data is transmitted from the mat to the reader that is then attached to the scoring computer and thus entered into the scoring system, indicating that the runner has started the race. The reader records a timestamp for that chip code that is used for calculating times. Upon crossing the finish line mat, the same thing occurs and this new information is then also entered into the system. The transponder numbers and times transmitted to the computer processing the results are then matched with the bib numbers. At that point, the scoring software calculates the elapsed time between the two reads, links it with the runner data, and the results are generated.

Gun Times and Net Times

One of the most revolutionary aspects of transponder-based timing was the introduction of "net times" and "gun times" to the lexicon of running terminology. Briefly, with a transponder

Side Antennae

Readers

Ground Mats
(contain antennae)

Phil Stewart

The key elements of a transponder scoring system are the mats, readers and transponders (on the bibs or attached to a shoe).

system, each runner's transponder is read at the moment he or she crosses the mat at the starting line. That read starts the clock running for that particular runner. The result is a unique or "net" time for each individual runner based entirely on when that runner's transponder crossed the start and the finish lines. Compare that with the traditional system under which *every* runner's time starts when the gun is fired—even the time for a runner who may have to wait ten minutes or more (if the field is very large) before crossing the starting line. These elapsed times, called "gun" or "start" times, may be equal to the net times in the cases of the few runners on the front row, but will be slower than the net times for the vast majority of the runners who started further back.

Net times were an instant hit with the vast majority of runners, because back-of-the-packers were no longer penalized for waiting to cross the starting line. However, rulemaking organizations such as USATF, for whom the order in which runners cross the finish line had always been sacrosanct in producing results, were flummoxed over how to handle situations in which a runner with a slower gun time placed in front of another runner with a faster net time. After grappling with this for a number of years as the acceptance of net times by the masses swept the country, USATF settled on a hybrid system that calls for the front runners to be timed by gun times while accepting net times for those further back in the pack. (For a complete discussion of USATF Rules regarding the use of gun times and net times see *Chapter 14: Rules of Competition.*) Also see **Sidebar— *A Closer Look at Gun and Net Times,* below**, for an example illustrating the difference between gun and net times.

Should a Transponder System Be Used?

For many race directors, the foremost question is one of cost, but directors should also be aware that transponder timing has a number of benefits that might make it worth the cost. These benefits include the ability to track runners at various points along the course if desired, a nearly real-time reading of the finishing times and places, announcers' mats for calling out names, and ease of detecting suspected cheaters. Plus, as cited earlier, runners' expectations have risen to the point where transponder timing is expected at nearly all but the smallest informal events. As a very general rule, estimates are that transponder timing will range somewhere between $2.00 to $3.00 per runner. Some points to consider:

- **Number of runners.** Races of a few hundred

SIDEBAR

A Closer Look at Gun and Net Times

Here is how the difference between gun and net times can be illustrated. Let's look at the impact of using net times on two masters (55-59 age group) competing for prize money in a championship half marathon with several thousand runners. Bob lines up on the front row with his toes just behind the starting line, and when the gun goes off Bob immediately starts running. Ed lines up aways behind the starting line (and behind Bob) and takes 60 seconds to cross the start line.

To the judges and observers at the finish line, Bob crosses the line 30 seconds ahead of Ed (1:12:44 to 1:13:14) and appears to have beaten Ed (based on *gun* time). However, if the race is being scored by *net* times, Ed is not penalized the 60 seconds he "lost" at the start, so his final *net* time becomes *1:12:14*, and he beats Bob by 30 seconds based on *net* time. Bob is furious and argues that he can't lose to a runner who crosses the finish line *after* him. Bob gets some relief from the USATF rules only if he sets an American age-group record. USATF allows net times to be considered for age-group records if the runner posting the record time is the first runner across the line in that age group! Otherwise, next time out, Bob will have to be sure to scout out his competition and line up nearby. In order to minimize the impact of the difference between gun and net times, race directors should consider setting aside a specific area or corral for their age-group competitors.

runners or fewer can be scored easily and effectively using one of the less expensive, more manual systems. Once past this size, transponder timing should be considered. Runners in larger races pretty much expect transponder timing these days.

- **Cost.** As mentioned, hiring someone to perform transponder timing may involve a considerable cost, so you will need to ensure that the race budget can accommodate it. If you decide to go this route, ascertain all the fees. Also, keep in mind that if reusable transponders are employed, the timing company may charge a fee for any unreturned transponders. Some timers charge for travel, as well. As more event-management companies enter the field, and as running clubs begin to acquire transponder-based systems, it should be easier to find a local provider of transponder-based timing and the associated cost should come down.

- **Compatibility with the scoring program.** Most transponder-timing companies work with the most popular running scoring software companies to ensure that their systems work with the scoring software. However, if custom software is used, problems may be encountered.

The following are the most significant advantages of transponder-based timing:

- **Simpler finish line management.** Transponder timing eliminates the need for finish line chutes —and potential backups— since the runners do not have to be kept in order once they cross the line. The finish line area clears more quickly.

[*Note:* If *reusable transponders* are employed, using them reduces the number of finish line personnel needed only slightly, as volunteers will be necessary to help runners remove the transponders and to collect them. Those jobs are definitely lower stress than working in the finish chutes. However, it can be hard to get the reusable transponders back. Event organizers are generally held responsible for any unreturned reusable transponders after the race. This fee varies, so be sure to check with the timing company. Most races warn runners of a pricey "lost transponder fee" in order to motivate them to return the transponders. Enforcement is difficult, however, so many races don't actually try to collect the fee. Non-return rates usually range from 0.5% to 1% of transponders issued.]

- **Cheating is made more difficult.** A transponder-based system makes tracking runners very easy. In an attempt to catch cheaters, some events will put mats down at various points along the course (in addition to the start and finish line mats). The transponders are read at these intermediate points. If a runner's transponder number is not recorded at the intermediate mats, a very strong case can be made that the runner did not complete the entire course. [This method is not foolproof, however, as an extremely small number of transponders can be misread or not read by the mats at all]. The intermediate splits produced by the transponders can also be checked to see if they make sense. If a runner finishes a 10K in 36:00 with transponder-documented splits of 27:00 for the first 5K and 9:00 for the second 5K (nearly 4:00 faster than the world record), there is reason to believe that the runner cut the second half of the course.

- **Accuracy and speed of results.** A transponder-based system produces more accurate results more quickly than can be achieved with the alternative methods of timing and scoring a race.

- **Professional image.** Simply put, transponder timing makes a race look more professional and thus generally more appealing to runners.

The following are the most significant challenges of transponder-based timing:

- **Transponders not read.** "Read rates" (meaning the percentage of transponders actually tracked at the start and finish mats) are in the 98-99.5% range for most of the major transponder companies. However, there will almost always be a 1% or less non-read rate, either due to faulty transponders or runners wearing heavy clothing over top of their bib numbers, blocking the transponders from being read. Un-read transponders may result in runners not showing up in the results or only showing up with a start time and no finish time, or vice versa. If the finisher whose transponder does not get read knows his finishing time, timers can generally reconstruct a finish time reasonably close to the time that was missed.

- **Extraneous transponder times:** The transponders will be read whenever they pass within a certain distance of the timing mats. This means if a runner crosses the finish line and goes back across the finish line to greet a friend, or if a finisher simply stands too close to the mat after finishing, the transponder will have an extra read related to the second trip across the mat. These extra reads will need to be identified and edited out of the results. For most timers, this is not a concern. Since the first occurrence of a chip read is used (except at the start where for the most part last read is used) any extra reads will just be junk and filtered out of scoring automatically. The event should consult the timing company if there is any question.

- **Determining when to consider gun times or net times as official.** USATF rules require gun times as the official times for the top finishers; back-of-the-pack runners demand net times as their official times, to compensate for the time lost waiting to start. At some point in the results process, timers will switch over from using gun times to net times as the official times. This can create anomalies in the results at the point where the switchover is taking place. See *Chapter 14: Rules of Competition* for details on USATF rules covering gun and net times.

- **Radio interference:** On extremely rare occasions, some sort of radio interference may cause problems with the transponder reads.

Should a Transponder System Be *Purchased*?

Initial purchasers of early transponder-based timing systems paid over $25,000 for the mats, hardware and software! After the initial investment, these purchasers had to rent the transponders each time they were used, at a cost of $1-$2 per transponder per event. This high cost meant that the investment only made sense for event management companies and running clubs scoring a lot of races. As more new transponder companies enter the marketplace, however, transponder systems are becoming much more affordable. With systems available for between $2000 and $2500, organizers of a *single event* may find systems within their budget range. The low-priced systems target the high school and college markets, but are just as applicable to single event organizers. Many events still elect to hire a seasoned transponder timing company or club.

Keep in mind that if your race organization decides to purchase a transponder-based timing system, you will need to ensure that individuals with the proper skills will be available to man this equipment. It takes some very technically-adept talent to make the transponder technology work at the race level. Significant time and training are needed to obtain solid expertise in the operation of the transponder timing system itself, as well as to integrate the system with the timing/scoring software that will be used. Most companies that sell transponder-based timing systems will include some level of training along with the purchase. Before purchase, inquire about both training and the availability of technical help, which operators may sometimes need immediately when they are on-site at an event. Another consideration must be the capability to store the mats and boxes, which are somewhat large and bulky.

The Pull-tag/Select Timing Method

Scoring runners using the pull tags from the bottom of runners' bibs was the timing and scoring system of choice before the advent of transponders in the 1990's. In its simplest form, just after runners cross the finish line, volunteers remove the perforated tag at the bottom of the bib and place it on a spindle in the order of finish. The tag contains the runner's identity, either in the form of a pre-printed label or a bar code. The timers at the finish line click a time for each runner on a printing timer. The times and the tags are later matched up, so that the identity from the pulled tag is linked with each time. Remember, pull tags only produce the equivalent of gun times. The system is reasonably straightforward as long as the event is small enough so at the peak density of finishers, runners can exit the chutes after their tags are removed faster than the finishing runners are entering the chutes. However, as races grow in size, the tag-removal process often cannot keep pace with the finisher rate, and back-ups can occur, sometimes causing the runners to stop before they even reach the finish line. To address this problem, in the mid 1980s, timers and scorers developed an elaborate *multiple-chute* system where deft volunteers open and close multiple chutes simultaneously to accommodate the peak finisher density. This is a carefully choreographed process. If an event is of sufficient size to need a multiple-chute system, it's better to opt for a transponder based system. If you are determined to use a multiple-chute system, it is strongly recommended that novices desiring to use this system obtain training from experienced groups.

A detailed description of pull-tag timing is provided below for novices contemplating a single-chute system. (A description of a multiple-chute system is provided as a sidebar.) Pull-tag timing is broken down into two components: capturing the runner's time and matching that time with the runner's place in the order of finish. Race scoring software has made it simple to put these two elements together once this data has been collected.

The runners' times are captured by a printer timer or printing machine (commonly known as a 'time machine'), which outputs (either to paper or directly to a computer) two pieces of information—place and time—repeated as many times as there are finishers. Basically, the operator just clicks a button each time a runner crosses the finish line, which triggers the machine to output the place/time info. Most modern time machines also have a keypad that allows for 'select timing,' meaning that the operator can enter in the bib numbers of as many of the finishing runners as possible, while also 'clicking' as they come across the line. This data serves as a useful backup for the collection of pull tags, described in the next paragraph (see details in **The Use of Select Timers and Select Times,** below).

Using this system, the runner information part of the timing equation is collected via the runner's bib number. At packet pick-up, each runner receives a unique bib that has been associated with that runner's personal information in the race database. Each bib number has a perforated, tear-off tag (pull tag) on the bottom. Prior to bib number pick-up, the scoring team generally places a label on the pull tag that contains the key identifying information for that runner—name, age, sex, and address (at least the city and state of residence). This pull-tag (with the label) is removed at the end of the finish chutes with the assistance of volunteers, and the tags are kept in the order that the runners finish. It is essential that the tags be kept in order to ensure the integrity of the results processes.

Most of these manual, pull-tag timing operations use the "stringer" method to collect the tags. Race workers wait at the end of a chute and as the runners finish, they either remove the perforated tags themselves or the race workers assist them. The race workers then slip the hole at the end of the tag over a "stringer," which can be a metal spindle (similar to a wire hanger twisted into a loop so the tags won't fall off) or a nylon cord stringer (a six-foot long length of nylon with a pointed metal tip at the front end and a metal loop at the other end).

With the ready availability of computer/tablet/smart phone-based scoring software, the database of runners, containing the registration information about each, can easily be paired with the information from the pull-tags and the time machine data. As the "stringer runners" bring completed strings of pull tags from the finish area, race workers in the results room either type in the bib numbers from the pull tags, or, in somewhat more sophisticated systems, scan barcodes from the pull tags. This results in a sequential listing of all runners who have finished, in the order that they finished—all that is needed is to link this order-of-finish with the times. Linking the two can be done by manually typing in the finish times in order, if a printing timer is used without a computer, or, as is much more common, the data can be easily uploaded from time machine into the scoring software and the order-of-finish can be linked with the times by the software.

For very small races with no access to computers, tablets or phones, a manual pull-tag system can be used, in which the scorers use a sheet of paper or a previously prepared "Manual Results Form" to record the basic information about the runner from the label on the pull tag or from the database, and then append that runner's finishing time. Simply put, the first finisher gets the first recorded time; the second finisher gets the second recorded time, etc. This process continues until all the runners have been given finishing times.

As a rule, each race that uses a pull-tag system for scoring should create and use a finish chute to keep the runners in the proper order as they cross the finish line. Station race personnel in the chute to help ensure that the correct order of finish is maintained. Chutes are created using stanchions, or metal/plastic poles mounted on a base (either cinder blocks with poles attached or heavy metal 18" square plates with 24" screw bolts screwed into the center of the squares and plastic or PVC poles inserted over the metal screws). Then a tape or rope is strung from beginning to end at the top of the stanchions or poles, starting at the finish line and extending back toward where the tag pullers are stationed. (**Note:** Unfortunately, the authors were unable to

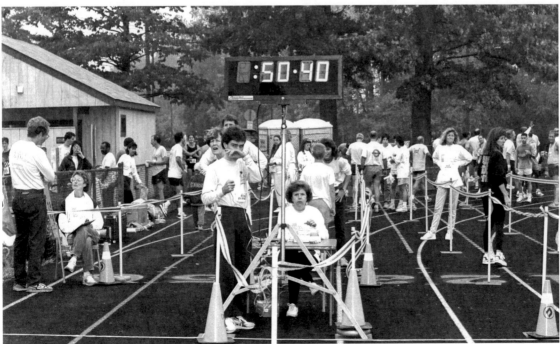

Bob Mallet

A chute system poised to process finishers.

SIDEBAR

The Challenges of a Multiple-Chute System

As a race grows in size, so does the need for additional chutes and more workers to ensure that runners in the chutes do not back up across the finish line. With multiple-chute systems, each chute requires its own herding and tag-puller teams. It is sometimes helpful to establish separate men's and women's chutes to reduce the volume of runners in a single chute and to allow independent scoring of the men's and women's races. In addition, in multiple-chute systems, consideration should be given to establishing a separate chute in the middle that serves as a zone to accommodate finish line workers.

Experienced finish line managers know how to determine the number of chutes needed for a particular event. Chutes will be "closed" as they fill and new ones opened simultaneously. The stringers from each chute are labeled sequentially, usually by use of a 3" x 5" card. These cards are prepared with these sequentially identifying numbers beforehand. For example, the stringer for the chute into which the winner of the race will be directed is labeled with a tag that says "number 1." The first tag on the stringer belongs to the winner and the tags from the runners who followed him are piled on top of his, until that chute closes because it has become full. The next stringer is labeled "number 2" and is used to collect tags from everyone who finished in the second chute. The process continues, with chutes opening and closing until the density of runners has decreased to the point where just one chute is needed.

The closing of chutes is usually done with *swing ropes*. A multiple-chute finish line system must be constructed to allow the swing ropes to completely close one chute while opening another one. Runners are directed by the forward-most people movers into the open chute, until the swing rope captain determines the potential for back-ups is imminent, and then the order is given to swing the rope so as to close that chute and open the other one. With this type of multiple-chute system, careful control of the sequential use of the chutes is vital. Thus, the numbering of the stringers is usually done by a race worker (chute plug) who runs ahead of the runners down a newly-opened chute and hands a numbered card to the tag pullers, who place it on the stringer. The chute plug then hurries back to the swing rope captain to repeat the process at the next chute opening.

As chutes open and close, race workers known as "runners" pick up full stringers, in order, and deliver them to where the results are being tabulated. In the results room (ideally away from the din of the race in a trailer or a building), the race scorer, either manually or with race-scoring software, performs the task of matching up the list of finishing times from the printer timer with the information from the pull tags that was previously entered in the database: runner name, age, sex and hometown.

Head spinning? Think transponders over a multiple-chute system.

locate an active manufacturer of the metal bases and bolts system, which means these would need to be custom made.)

It is better to err on the side of making chutes too long rather than too short. Chutes should be "tapered" from the front (nearest the finish line), narrowing toward the rear, as a measure to help control runner activity (switching places) within the chute.

The Use of Select Timers and Select Times

Unfortunately, nothing is perfect. Although

the manual scoring process described above is simple, errors can occur, and often do. While most errors are caused by runners not following procedures (running as bandits, changing places in the finish chutes, jumping out of the chute before their tags are pulled, or moving to another chute), timers can also hit the button on a timing machine erroneously and generate fictitious finish times in the system. To control and correct such errors, finish line managers often collect what are known as "select times." Select times are aptly named; they are times taken by a couple of independent individuals (different from the team being used for the pull-tag system) for *certain selected runners*. These select times represent the precise, actual finishing time for those selected participants. For very small events using only a basic printing timer for recording runners' times, the select timers can stand right at the finish line with a watch that was started with the race, and every five or ten seconds (depending on the density of the crowd) they can write down the bib number and actual finish time for a "selected" runner. It's usually not this manual, though. Most modern time machines have the capability to allow select timing with a little more ease. A spotter can call out the bib number of an approaching runner, and that number can be typed into the time machine; then, as that runner hits the finish line, the thumb button connected to the timing machine is pushed. This creates a specific finish time for a specific runner who has finished the race. Select times provide the results manager with accurate information he or she can use to adjust the results when finish times and runner identifications don't seem to match up.

The bib numbers of the select-timed runners are then compared to the bib numbers of the same runners obtained by the pull-tag system. If there are discrepancies (too many or too few pull tags as compared with the times produced by the printing timer or time machine), the times can be adjusted within the gap between the two select timed runners, since these times are "known" to be accurate.

As more runners finish the race, the practice is generally to print pages of results and to post them for the field to view. These results pages should be clearly marked as "Unofficial," pending the opportunity for race results workers to clean up the data by, for example, eliminating bandit information or discarding obvious extraneous clicks on the time machine. When all the anomalies have been resolved satisfactorily, the results can be declared official and final results can be posted on the event's website.

The Simplest Approach—Index Cards

Low-tech timing "systems" for very small or informal races rely entirely on the participants to make note of their times as they cross the finish line. Therefore, these events must have either an individual calling out times from a stopwatch, or have a digital clock mounted at the finish so the runners can see their own times—or both. The watches and/or the digital clock are the only equipment items needed.

Most events employing this method of timing use 3" x 5" index cards, numbered sequentially in advance, which are handed to runners as they cross the finish line. With this system, the runner completes the card with his name, age, and finish time, and either hands it to the scorer at the scoring table or pins it to a cork board, which is pre-numbered and contains enough space to pin the card next to the number indicating his finish place. Once all the runners have finished, the scorer collects the cards and generates the results.

This system is simple but effective, as long as the race isn't too large. The biggest shortcoming is the reliance on the runners to note their own finish times. Frequently, the runners fail to look at the finish line clock as they pass it. Only after they have passed the finish line do they remember to look back at the clock or at their watch, so the time they come up with is often a guess. This is not the sort of situation in which the director of a highly professional race would care to find him/herself, especially if there are prizes involved.

SIDEBAR

Hiring a Timing Company

As this chapter makes clear, timing and scoring a race, especially a large one, is a complex process for the uninitiated. If you are involved with a single event, it is probably worthwhile to hire an outsider to provide timing and scoring expertise and equipment. If you are considering hiring an event management company to operate the finish line and score the race, the questions to be asked include:

- *How long have they been in business?* The majority of race-timing companies that exist today are reputable firms that have kept up with technology, provide good service, and have maintained excellent relationships with their clients. But to be safe, ask a potential company about their past experience. You may want to check on insurance coverage as well.

- *Will they offer a written contract/proposal and references?* Most event management companies will provide a proposal that will include tasks to be performed, a timetable for those tasks, a fee schedule and, often, a list of the races with whom they have worked in the past. Contact those race directors! Always get references; you'll find that race directors are very honest and helpful when it comes to discussing their vendors.

- *Are they a full-service operation or do they specialize in finish line management specifically?* Changes in the industry over the years have meant that more companies have moved into offering other services, such as public relations, marketing, and sponsor sales. As long as you are handling those services successfully on your own, you're probably better off with a firm that specializes in finish line management and timing services only.

- *Do they contract out to other companies that provide specific services related to finish line management that they may not offer?* The use of sub-contractors may work just fine, or may cause unanticipated difficulties. Approach with caution any arrangement that leaves you without direct control over an element of your own race.

- *Who will supply the equipment that is needed?* What will the race organization have to rent or buy and what will be supplied by the timing company? This important consideration will have major impact on the race's "bottom line."

- *How many volunteers do they require the race organization to provide?* Does the timing company provide additional staff? How many? What specific skills will the company bring on race day and how many volunteers with what skills will be required from the race organization?

- *How are their fees determined?* Fees are generally calculated on a per-runner basis. However, there are often other costs that need to be agreed upon, such as accommodations/travel (and possibly per diem) if the company is not local and its staff needs to be housed on race weekend.

- *Create a spreadsheet.* As you contact companies to get information on services and pricing, create a spreadsheet so that you can compare the companies based on similar criteria. For a sample spreadsheet comparing timing companies, see *Table 17-A* on the next page.

Table 17-A

Sample Timing Company Comparison Spreadsheet

	COMPANY A	COMPANY B	COMPANY C
Contact	John Smith	Mary Jones	Dave Johnson
Email	john@abc.com	mary@def.com	dave@ghi.com
System used	Chronotrack	Ipico	MyLaps (B-Tag)
Scoring software	Customized	RunScore	RunSignUp
Text messaging	Not Offered	Yes	Not Offered
On Site Registration	Not Offered	Yes	Not Offered
Certificates	Not Offered	Yes	Not Offered
Online provider	Athletic Management, Inc.	SportsRegistration, Inc	Runners Registration, Inc.
Chip Price	$2.50	$2.45	$3.00
Chip Total @ 5,000	$12,500.00	$12,250.00	$15,000.00
Extra mats (3 sets)	$1,500.00	$1,800.00	$ 1,200.00
Other Finan. Considerations			
Travel	None Required	$1,000.00	$2,750.00
Hotel Rooms	None Required	$ 1,000.00	$ 1,500.00
Total	$14,000.00	$16,050.00	$20,450.00
Text messaging Addl Cost	(Not Offered)	$1,300.00	(Not Offered)
Other Races Worked:			
Race #1	JKL Half Marathon	MNO 10K	PQR 15K
Size	25,000	10,000	20,000
Race #2	STU 10K	VWX 5K	YZA Marathon
Size	33,300	30,000	16,000
Race #3	BCD 5K	EFG 10K	HIJ 10K
Size	48,000	15,000	20,000
Last Race Closest to Ours	KMO 15K on Jan 15	3 events on Mar 17	HLP 5K on Feb 15
First Race After Ours	TSR 10K on Jun 19	BBB Half Marathon on Jul 4	CCC 15K on Aug 15
Contractor Staff to be Onsite	7	5	7
Unused tags		Will be collected at the expo	
Notes	Offers rate reduction for multi-year contract	Offers printed out results as each runner crosses the line	Has a solid reputation

This index card approach can be made more sophisticated by coupling it with either a time machine, described above, or one of the race-timing apps available for smart phones or tablets (see **Mobile Apps for Race Timing** on the next page for more on this option). This will avoid the necessity for runners to note their own times. The time machine or app is started with the official start of the race and, at the finish, the elapsed time of every runner who crosses the finish line is recorded by simply clicking a button on the device. It isn't necessary for the person operating the timer to identify or recognize the runners. He or she is just recording places and times; identifying the runners is done separately. When the runners finish, they are given index cards as above, indicating their overall finish place. Runners provide their name and age to scorers on these cards, but do not have to worry about providing their time. Once all runners have finished, race scorers can then match up runner info from the cards with the times from the time machine or app based on finishing place.

Scoring Software

If you decide to score a race on your own, you will need to invest in specialized race scoring software. Software programs are available for both PCs and Apple computers. [**Note:** Be wary of well-intentioned technology buffs on the race committee or one of the race sponsors who may feel that designing scoring software from scratch is easy—there are plenty of peculiarities of running events that make this dicey.]

The scoring software is used for entering runner data on the front end (usually uploaded from the registration platform) and then using the race database thus created to score the event and produce results on the back end. Most of the scoring software companies will let you download a trial version of their scoring software so you can familiarize yourself with the look and feel of it. Here are some things to investigate:

On the "front end" or data entry side:

- Ease of creating custom data entry screens/fields; can screens be edited, new fields inserted (and is there a limit), and fields moved around once the data entry screen is set?
- Ease of uploading data from online registration, and of manual data entry, if this will be performed.
- Ease of searching for records already entered and making corrections.
- Can you "browse" the entire database or view only one record at a time?
- Can you assign bib numbers using the software, or must this be done by the timing company?
- Can the software be networked so data entry can take place from more than one computer at a time?
- Can the lists and reports needed for packet pick-up be easily generated?
- Can data be sorted on any field?

On the "back end" or scoring side:

- Can the software accommodate uploads from the timing system—either from a transponder-based system, a timing app, or a time machine?
- Can the software handle an array of special timing scenarios? These could include wave starts, special award categories (such as providing options for "double dipping"), age- and sex-grading based on established performance standards, team scoring with a range of specifications for open, masters, single-sex or mixed teams, etc., and multiple chutes (if using a multiple-chute pull-tag system). (See *Chapter 18: Awards, Awards Ceremonies, Entertainment and Results Posting* for an explanation of the array of possible award categories that can be offered.)
- Can results templates be easily created, in an appealing format?
- Can data be exported easily to Excel or other applications?

Mobile Apps for Race Timing

As mentioned above, another option for those who wish to manually time their own events without investing in expensive equipment is to use one of the mobile timing apps that are available for smart phones and tablets. These apps generally work like a time machine with scoring software included and thus are really only appropriate for smaller events, up to a few hundred participants. The registration database is uploaded to the mobile device in advance of the event. During the race, the operator simply 'clicks' a button when a runner crosses the finish and then selects or enters in the bib number, in order to link the runner info to the finish time. Results can then be posted to the internet (generally to the app's website) or downloaded. Although these apps are not free, they may provide a degree of professionalization to a small event at a much lower cost. As the technology advances, these apps are acquiring more and more advanced features that make them a practical and affordable option for many smaller events.

enable "editing" of results with any available data in order to determine a runner's time. With manual scoring systems, as previously noted, extraneous clicks of the timing buttons or the appearance of race "bandits" without numbers are problems that must also be resolved. Once the results are posted, participants will contact you regarding problems and raise questions about their finishing times as they appear in the unofficial version of the results.

Finalizing the Results

No matter how meticulous the scoring team is and what kind of scoring system is used (transponder-based or pull-tag systems with select times), the results will most likely require post-race editing, updating and correcting before being declared as official. These tasks can be facilitated by the scoring software. For example, despite the highly developed nature of transponder-timing systems, expect a 98-99.5% "read rate," which still means a few transponders will malfunction, resulting in missing times. (If transponder mats are located at the start and finish lines, there may be some misreads at the starting line mats that are correctly read at the finish line mats, or vice versa.) The bottom line is that the scoring software should

SIDEBAR

GPS/Course Measurement Discrepancies

Runners frequently tell race directors that there is a discrepancy between the distance their GPS says they ran and the advertised distance of the course. Often, these runners will argue that the course is 'wrong.' Tests performed by members of USATF's Road Running Technical Council have found that runners will generally get a reading indicating the course is 1% long. Understanding how GPS works will help the race director to clearly explain to concerned runners the two main factors that result in such discrepancies.

- GPS devices worn by runners have varying degrees of accuracy. These devices work by triangulation, meaning they need a clear view of at least three satellites at established intervals (1 second, 20 seconds, etc.) to get an accurate reading. Trees, buildings, and even the runner's body can interrupt the signal, making it less accurate at any time. Even when satellite contact is unobstructed, the best commercially available GPS units for running are only accurate to about 12 feet at any given time, and can sometimes be hundreds of feet off in accuracy.

- Certified courses are measured along the shortest possible route, a line that cuts all the tangents just one foot from the curb or road edge. Very few, if any, runners run the exact line that was measured, and since the measurement was taken of the *shortest* route, most runners will actually run longer than the measured distance. Weaving through other runners/not running in a straight line also increases the distance covered by the runner.

The USATF/RRTC position on GPS used by runners can be found at: http://www.usatf.org/Products-/-Services/Course-Certifications/USATF-Certified-Courses/Certify-Your-Course/Statement-on-GPS-Use-by-Runners.aspx

The posted results should be as complete and correct as possible, but set a deadline after which participants will not be allowed to request changes to the results. After a pre-determined period of time, possibly a day or two for a small race and perhaps three weeks to a month for very large races, post-race results should be declared final. Failure to set such a deadline could potentially have you making tweaks to the results years later! Make sure to inform all participants that there is a firm deadline for fixes, and what that deadline is.

After the results are official, you can pay any cash prize awards, distribute open and age-group prizes, and start planning for next year's race.

Presentation of the Results

The scoring software should allow preparation of a customized report that can be uploaded to the event website or formatted for a print publication, if necessary. Consider providing the results in three different ways—overall results in the order of finish, award winners, and searchable results, in which a runner can enter his/her name and pull up only his/her race time. If the event offers team competition or competition in other special divisions, include those results as well. Lastly, if the race has an app, make the results available there in addition to putting them on the race website.

- **Overall results:** This is the basic order-of-finish, including runner's name, sex, age, hometown and time. An additional option is to include place in age group and overall number of finishers in that age group. Most races provide separate listings for men and women. An alternative is to offer age-graded scoring. Age grading is a method of comparing times run by different ages over the same distance. It is discussed in more detail in *Chapter 12: Special Entrant Categories.*

- **Award winners:** A surprising number of events do not post a separate listing of the award winners on their websites. Without a list of award winners, viewers and the media are faced with the cumbersome task of extracting this information from the overall order-of-finish. Since the awards list needs to be generated for the awards ceremony, it should be easy to post the same information on the race website. If possible, include prize money won, if any.

- **Searchable results:** It is helpful to provide searchable results on the race website, in which a database containing the complete results can be queried by any field (last name, first name, city, state, age, etc.) contained in the database. Searchable results are offered by many online registration companies as an additional feature. Searchable results are more difficult to browse, so it is best to include them in addition to a complete listing in finishing order. An on-going searchable results database can be maintained, which allows runners to see their times for all the years they have run in the race.

Individual Results Notifications

Some races will send 'congratulations' emails or texts to each individual finisher, containing that individual's specific results, including info like overall placing, place in sex, place in division, etc. Some online registration services provide for this ability, as do some of the companies that provide virtual race bag services. This message also provides a final avenue for sponsor publicity, a final message from the race organizers, and maybe even a plug for the next year's event. Some timers can even include a link to a results correction form that will help aid in the "results inquiry" process.

BREAK THROUGH THE PACK.

What Motivates You?

Your passion for competition – and a chance to combine work with pleasure helping others achieve their dreams. You could say Race Directors help raise the self-esteem and self-confidence of tens of thousands of runners who accomplish their goals at the finish line. The responsibility of directing a race is enormous, with thousands depending on you. For you, there is no greater reward!

What Motivates a Runner?

For the novice it may be simply finishing their first race, or reaching a fitness goal. A runner's reward is crossing the finish line and the sense of accomplishment it brings. For the seasoned veteran it's improving their personal best, travelling to exciting destinations and the exhilaration of competition and cheering supporters.

Recognizing Achievement

Running a race is a substantial achievement, you deliver a well-planned race culminating at the finish line; race participants rightly deserve to experience the magnitude of their accomplishment. Your finisher medal has to measure up. Your duty is not only commemorating the event, but also exceeding the expectations of sponsors and finishers alike. A good finisher medal design will deliver both; but a great design leaves a lasting impression.

Ensure Repeat Performances

Creating a unique experience helps your event make a lasting impression, builds your race brand and secures the return of participants, sponsors, supporters and spectators. Making your event unique is entirely up to you, but when you consider the high-expectations of participants, why not turn to a proven producer of the top finisher medals in America?

The Results are Clear

Producing finisher medals that consistently exceed expectations is exactly what Maxwell Medals and Awards has been doing since 1978. Thousands of customers, both large and small, have chosen us as their awards vendor because of the outstanding value we provide.

The Maxwell Difference

Our personal approach to serving customers sets us apart from the competition because we are prepared to invest the necessary time to create the best medal for your event. We'll guide you through the entire medal design and ordering process. Simply share your medal design idea and we will transform it into a custom medal you will be proud to present and your participants will cherish.

To get started on your inspiring medal, contact us and experience the Maxwell Difference.

MAXWELL
MEDALS & AWARDS

1296 Business Park Dr.
Traverse City, MI 49686
Phone: 1-800-331-1383 Fax: 1-231-941-2102
Web Site: www.maxmedals.com

The Mallet Team

18 Awards, Awards Ceremonies, Entertainment and Results Posting

THE BASICS

- Hold the awards ceremony as soon as possible after the race is over. The later it is, the more likely it is that people will leave. Work with the race timers in advance to determine the most efficient way to obtain the results needed to conduct the ceremony. Keep the ceremony short, 30-45 minutes maximum. If you are giving out extensive age-group awards, move through them quickly or consider not announcing them on race day.

- Determine the awards structure in advance—decide how deep to go in each age group and whether double dipping will be allowed (see ***Double Dipping*** section below for description).

- Label the awards clearly and lay them out on a table well in advance of the start of the ceremony.

- Have at least two people working in tandem at the awards ceremony—one to announce the award winners and the other to hand out the award as the recipients come forward and to keep track of which awards have been picked up.

- Thank the sponsors at the awards ceremony. This will be the last chance to give the sponsors visibility at the event.

- Providing entertainment at an event can both keep the runners engaged during the event and help to keep them around longer after the event. "Entertainment" generally consists of some combination of food, drink, and live performers. (See ***Chapter 9: Insurance and Legal*** for a discussion of music licensing and serving alcohol, issues that must be addressed if the event has any type of music—live or recorded—or if alcohol is provided.)

- Post the results in a timely fashion. These days, runners at even relatively small races expect results to be posted as they become available at the race site (make sure to have a printer on site) and to appear on the race website no later than the evening after the race. If that isn't possible, post a notice on the website stating when results will be available. Expectations rise at larger races for results to be posted at race site kiosks or on mobile devices through a race app, or for each individual to receive his/her result by text message or email.

- Declare the results "unofficial" in order to allow time to review them. In most instances, the results will be correct for nearly all the runners, but there will likely be some adjustments made in the days (and weeks) after the race, most likely because of unread transponders or switched bibs.

- Pre-race, ask local businesses and sponsors to donate prizes that can be given away as random awards before and after the awards ceremony, to entice people to remain until the end. Inform race participants both pre- and post-race that this will happen. If a very large prize, such as a free trip, will be given away, announce it last and keep the crowd excited by making several announcements about the "big prize" yet to be awarded.

- Develop a plan for the post-race dissemination of results to local media and other outlets that might be interested. These outlets, and their contact information, should be determined in advance. Ask the outlets if they would like a short article about how the race unfolded, or if they would like any race photos.

THE DETAILS

For years, race awards ceremonies were designed to formally recognize the top performers at an event. However, today, for many events, the awards ceremony is only a part of the overall post-race entertainment program. More events emphasize post-race parties or concerts than advertise that awards will be given out on race day. Event directors should not lose sight of the fact that the award winners are only a fraction of the overall participants and they should look to balance the needs of the award winners with the needs of the masses, who may be more interested in the post-race music or other activities than in the age-group winners. Furthermore, advances in timing and results processing often allow for all runners, not just award winners, to be informed about their times and finish places before leaving the race site.

Awards

Who Will Get Awards?

The first decision that needs to be made regarding awards is who will receive them—will you give awards only to the top overall and age-group finishers, or will you provide participation awards to all finishers (medals are a perennial favorite). The awards structure should be part of the pre-race publicity for the event and should be included on the race website and in as many other forms of race communication as possible. Decide if the race budget will allow you to offer medals or another participation award. Awards such as basic medals and key chains average $2-6 each for as many runners as you have in the race (ornate or large customized medals can cost more). Individual awards can cost from $10 and up. If you give awards 3 deep to the overall winners and in 10-year male and female age groups from 14-and-under through 80+, you've quickly racked up over 60 individual awards and an awards budget in the $800-$1,000 range.

Runners participating in larger and more prestigious events (generally those with higher registration fees) will expect a deeper age-group awards structure and will also expect participation awards, especially in events of marathon or half-marathon distance, since these longer distances are considered a bigger achievement than a 5K. A small, local race should, at a minimum, try to budget for awards to the top 3 males and females and 3 deep in 10-year-age groups through 60-and-over. This totals 36 awards. Just keep in mind that, as participant numbers creep up, the

participants' expectations will grow as well. Once a race grows past 1,000-1,500 registrants, participants may expect awards to the top 10 overall and the top 3 to 5 finishers in 5-year age groups starting from 19-and-under through 70-and-over. Regardless of the awards structure you choose, the most important step is to be in close communication with the timing team regarding awards well in advance of the event. This will allow the timers to properly set up the scoring software in order to easily identify the appropriate award winners.

"Double Dipping"

"Double dipping" refers to a policy that allows a single runner to receive multiple awards. For example, in an event that allows double dipping, a 42-year-old male runner who places 8th overall in a race that gives awards to the top 10 overall *and* wins the 40-49 age-group division receives two awards—the 8th place overall *and* the first place 40-49 age-group award. A race that does *not* offer double dipping would give the same runner the 8th place overall award but would eliminate him from the age-group awards and elevate the second male 40-49 finisher to first place. Advocates of double dipping feel that if the runner is the 8th fastest in the race and the fastest in the 40-49 age group, he is entitled to both awards, because this reflects what actually happened in the race. Advocates of "no double dipping" like to spread the awards around to a larger number of individuals.

TIP

Special Award Categories

Some races offer special award divisions as a way to foster goodwill with municipal groups that help out, such as police and firefighters. Giving a trophy to the fastest state trooper, the fastest police officer and fastest firefighter from all of the jurisdictions that the event runs through may help to strengthen relationships with these groups and could be of great benefit in future years of the race, especially in the event of course changes or other tweaks requiring the involvement of municipal organizations.

Usually, the "open" award is considered a "higher" award category than an age-group award, so in a race without double dipping, age-group awards may be awarded to individuals who would *not* have received them in a race that allowed double dipping. There are strong opinions on both sides of the issue, and either format is considered acceptable, as long as the format is clearly spelled out in advance. Be sure to state on the race website, and anywhere else that race information is publicized, either "double dipping allowed" or "no double dipping."

Types of Awards

Runners have become more discriminating over the years, and when it comes to awards, they

Bix Seven Mile

The Bix 7 Mile, named after jazz trumpeter Bix Beiderbecke, gives trumpets to the winners.

expect more than the ubiquitous trophy topped with the figure of a runner. Most awards vendors today offer a broad array of wooden, lucite, stone, or metal awards that are more unique. Some race directors prefer custom awards that reflect something about the area or community where the race takes place. Local artists can be hired to create hand-crafted items, such as wood carvings or plaques, stained glass panels, blown glass pieces, pottery, clocks or paperweights, etc.—all for a cost. Be wary of choosing sized apparel items as awards, because award winners come in all shapes and sizes.

Gift cards/certificates are nearly always well-received, particularly at smaller races where most of the participants live in the area and can easily redeem them. Specialty running stores love the opportunity to further their relationship with local runners by providing gift cards or certificates for free shoes or apparel. (See **Chapter 12: Special Entrant Categories** for details about awarding prize money.)

Whatever you end up selecting, order the awards early. This is especially important if you are having the awards engraved or customized in some way; early delivery will give you enough time to have any errors or misspellings corrected. Allow longer lead times—up to six months—for hand-crafted awards. Most participant medals are produced in China, which adds weeks—if not months—to the delivery timetable.

It is helpful to select an awards vendor that is familiar with running events. There are a number of awards companies with experience dealing with running events that can be found online or by talking to other race directors.

Should an Awards Ceremony Be Held? If So, What Type?

The technological advances and the broadening participant base in the sport have combined to raise some basic questions about the relevance of traditional awards ceremonies. In small club races, a high percentage of non-award winners will probably know the award winners, which may induce them to stay for the ceremony to acknowledge their fellow runners and friends. In a race of 500 participants, it is possible that 2% of the finishers may be award winners. In a race of 5,000 that number drops to 0.2%. Announcing the top 10 overall and top 5 in a dozen male and female 5-year age groups will take close to an hour. Doing the age-group awards on-site also complicates matters if there is a problem that changes the age-group results after the person present at the ceremony has gone home with the award. Quite frankly, the majority of the participants would rather continue to enjoy the post-race party (if there is one) or mingle with their friends than take an hour to hear the names of top age-group finishers, many of whom won't even stay around to claim their awards. So, first decide if you even want to stage a formal, full-blown awards ceremony or possibly just include an abbreviated option.

If you wish to formally recognize each and every one of the award winners, the goals will be to keep the crowd around until the ceremony begins and to be very organized, so that the ceremony moves along as quickly as possible. A good post-race party (see section on *Entertainment*, below) will induce runners to stick around. One race holds its kids' races after the running of the main event and the awards ceremony. As a result, parents and their children often end up watching the awards ceremony while waiting for the kids' races to begin. Other races begin their ceremonies before the race is officially complete, while some of the stragglers are still coming in. During the ceremony itself, you may be able to hold the crowd if you have a talented announcer who keeps the excitement going. You

can also keep their attention by randomly giving away merchandise during the ceremony, interspersed with the distribution of awards. Even the most formal awards ceremony should last no longer than 30-45 minutes, with 20 to 30 minutes being a much more reasonable goal in terms of crowd retention.

There are a number of ways to abbreviate the awards ceremony. Clearly if prize money is offered or if there is a strong masters field, you will at least want to recognize those accomplishments, regardless of whether it adds time to the ceremony. Some races just call up the 'big prize' winners or the overall or open division finishers and mail out all the age-group awards later. Alternatively, some race directors choose to simply mention the names of age-group winners, without calling them up one at a time (or even just post a list of these winners), and direct them to a table where they can claim their awards. In short, it's important to strike a balance between recognizing the award winners and acknowledging that the rest of the participants may not have the time or desire to stick around for a long period of time after the event.

Regardless of the format that is chosen, the awards ceremony is generally the last public chance for event organizers to make a final impression on the participants. Therefore, it is important to ensure that the ceremony goes smoothly and efficiently, even though tired race officials may have little energy left. To optimize the chances of having the ceremony be fresh, timely, efficient, effective, and entertaining, designate a committee member whose sole responsibility is to handle the awards ceremony. The fatigued race director may plan, at most, a cameo appearance. This also frees up the race director to deal with any post-race issues.

Finally, remember that holding some type of awards ceremony is valuable, because it is usually the last opportunity for the media to interview and photograph the leading runners, as well as for the race organization to get stock photos. This ceremony is also the last race-day chance for sponsor recognition. Hang sponsor banners at the finish line/awards ceremony staging area where they will be easily visible, particularly to photographers. Many races have a backdrop banner with the race name and key sponsor logos and take photos of their award winners in front of this banner. Remember to recognize the sponsors at the start of the ceremony. Discuss sponsor recognition with the sponsors themselves, before race-day, as they may envision the ceremony as a good place for speeches by company officials. Although it is important to recognize sponsors, you want to prevent the ceremony from dragging; remember that *you* are the race director—maintain control. Sponsors seeking greater visibility at the awards ceremony might have a representative make a *brief* statement and then help greet the award winners.

Awards Ceremony Logistics

It is amazing how much can go wrong at an awards ceremony. A sound system that doesn't work, results that take so long to compile that only a few people are still present for the ceremony, and mix-ups over age-group winners are only a few of the many mini-disasters that can befall an awards ceremony. Below are a few tips to keep in mind when planning the awards ceremony that will help keep everything flowing smoothly:

- **Consider the size and layout of the facility.** If the awards ceremony is held inside, make sure that the space is large enough to accommodate the size crowd that is expected, but not so cavernous as to dwarf crowd participants and their families. You want it to look like there are lots of people at the ceremony, and it should be set up so there is some proximity between the audience and the presenters. For example, gyms often don't work well because the audience is too far from the action. If the ceremony will be held outside, make sure to have a contingency plan for bad weather.

- **Hold the ceremony close to the finish line.** Runners are less likely to go to the

ceremony if they have to walk a number of blocks to get there. Even if the time and location of the ceremony are included in pre-race information, a lot of runners may not bother to read the website or race instructions, so they may go home if the ceremony isn't within eyesight of the finish line.

- **Pre-test the sound system.** The best option is to test the sound system with a room full of people, as the acoustics are quite different than when the room is empty. If this is not possible, at least make sure the system works beforehand, and assign a volunteer the job of checking the sound level around the area during the ceremony and informing the sound team when adjustments are needed.

- **Arrange awards prior to the ceremony.** Arrange the awards in a way that permits orderly and quick distribution and is in sync with how they will be announced. Presenters shouldn't have to scramble to find the proper award.

- **Make the stage readily accessible.** Don't force runners who may be tired and stiff to clamber up onto platforms to receive awards—provide steps. Also, if there are wheelchair competitors, make sure to provide a ramp or other accommodation for them to reach the stage.

- **Take photos fast.** Awards ceremony photos are important: a local media outlet might want to publish them, the sponsors will probably want copies, and you will want to use them for PR purposes and on the race website. Don't let photo-taking slow down the ceremony though. Ideally, the winners' photos should be taken off-stage, against a backdrop of race and sponsor banners, as the awards emcee continues to hand out awards.

- **Keep track of the awards claimed.** Assign someone to keep track of who has picked up their award and who hasn't. This is especially important if merchandise or other non-customized awards are offered. The most efficient way to do this is to have an awards registrar stationed off the stage with a list of winners. Before each winner leaves the stage area, the volunteer checks off his or her name as having received the award. The list can be reconciled later with the leftover awards. This also serves as a double check to make sure no one has received the wrong award.

- **Be careful what you promise.** Don't make promises during the ceremony that you can't keep, such as telling runners in a particular age group to stay around because results will be available shortly, despite the fact that there's a problem and they may not, in fact, be available for hours. If you encounter scoring problems, let runners in the affected age group or groups know where they can go to get final results—for instance by checking the race website—and make sure that the awards

are mailed to the winners as soon as possible, once everything is sorted out. Runners are very understanding if they are given all the facts, but they don't like being told to wait around for something that isn't going to happen within a reasonable period of time.

- **Maintain contact with the scoring team.** Scoring teams generally closet themselves in a quiet room, tent, or trailer so they won't be disturbed as they work on the results. If all of the results are not available when the awards ceremony starts, have one of the race workers at the awards ceremony keep in radio or cell phone contact with a scorer to get reports on the scoring progress.

- **Make sure invited runners attend.** Whether you are paying prize and/or appearance money or expenses for elite runners to attend the event, it is reasonable to expect these invited runners to attend the awards ceremony, regardless of how well or poorly they ran. You and the elite runners should have an understanding in advance of what you expect of them, before you commit any money. Some runners feel that, if prize money is being offered, they are not being paid to do anything except run—and that means not attending the awards ceremony. If an invited runner runs poorly and fails to place in the top 10 or 25, you may allow him or her to skip the ceremony, but set the limits in advance on your terms.

Sample Format of an Awards Ceremony

Formal awards ceremonies will open with some brief thank yous and acknowledgements by the announcer, who will then move quickly into distributing the awards. Choose an experienced and skillful

---

SIDEBAR

Bands and Award Ceremony Logistics

Many races employ bands to keep the crowd entertained before and after the awards ceremony. In fact, for many races, the entire awards ceremony is merely a pause in the post-race concert, while others have gone one step further and replaced the awards ceremony altogether with music or other forms of post-race entertainment. See *Chapter 9: Insurance and Legal* for a discussion of music licensing issues that must be addressed if any type of music—live or recorded—will be played at the event.) Although a band can be a good way to keep the crowd engaged and to get them to stay for the awards ceremony, carefully consider the logistics of having the band and awards distribution on the same stage. Band equipment can leave little extra room for a podium or a place for the award winners to come up on the stage to receive their prizes. Even if there is room, they may be forced to step through a maze of wires and amplifiers. If you have a band, ideally you should have a riser or totally separate area for the awards ceremony, situated in front or to one side of the area where the band will play. A second option is to have the awards announcer on the stage but the awards themselves on tables in front of the stage. If neither option is feasible, at least have the band members move some of their equipment (quickly) to clear a passageway on the stage for the award winners.

announcer who is able to keep the crowd enthused and energized.

- **Opening comments:** If sponsors must speak or checks must be presented to charities, keep these activities brief.

- **Open awards:** The announcer will most often start with the open or overall awards for the women, followed by the men. In order to build interest, the award winners are announced in reverse order starting with the lowest place award winner and progressing to the race winner (if the awards go 10 deep in the open division, start with 10th place, then 9th place, etc.). This builds the suspense. Each award winner should have his or her place, name, hometown and time announced. If the event has prize money, the amount each runner earned should be announced as well.

- **Age-group awards:** The age-group winners can be announced either in ascending (1, 2, 3) or descending (3, 2, 1) order. The objective here is to move quickly.

- **Special awards (if any):** Following the age-group awards, announce special individual awards or team awards, if any.

- **Closing remarks:** At the conclusion of all the awards, make some brief closing remarks and announce the date of next year's race, if it has been set.

There are no hard-and-fast rules about the structure of awards ceremonies, so if you have reason to change this order for any reason, go ahead. Just remember to keep it as short as possible!

Challenges and Errors to the Distributed Awards

One of the perils of doing the awards ceremony right after the race is that a scoring error may be discovered (usually called to your attention by an aggrieved runner present at the ceremony) after all the awards have been given out. If someone challenges the awards while the ceremony is going on, try to have a race official

suggest gently to the individual that he or she wait until the ceremony is over and you have time to sort everything out. Once the ceremony is over, take the name and contact information of the individual, along with the nature of the challenge, and tell the person you will look into the matter with the timing team and respond in a day or two. Assure the individual that he or she will receive any award earned, but do not commit to anything until you have had time to review the facts. The noble thing to do is to ask all the affected parties to return their awards so they can be properly distributed. However, more than one director has taken the easy way out and simply ordered and given a duplicate award.

Dealing with Leftover Awards

Announce the policy for unclaimed awards on the race website and on any printed registration materials. Directors of smaller races generally do not make any attempt to get awards to runners who skip the awards ceremony, unless special arrangements have been made with the award recipient. Most directors of larger races, however, attempt to distribute the awards to their rightful recipients post-race. This is particularly true for events that do not give out age-group awards on race day, or those that simply allow runners to pick up the awards off stage on their own. Just be forewarned that shipping awards out (by mail or by UPS) is tedious and costly, and you can be certain that at least a few will be returned due to bad addresses, or may arrive damaged and require replacement.

If an event attracts foreign athletes, things can get even more complicated and expensive. A number of agents who represent foreign runners recommend sending the award to the agent, and giving him or her the responsibility of getting it to the athlete. *Age-group* awards for foreign athletes are probably not worth shipping abroad. While a 6th place overall finisher from Kenya might be interested in the overall award, he or she probably doesn't care (or know) about placing 2nd in the 30-34 age group.

Post-Race Entertainment

If the intention is to keep the runners on-site after they finish the race, some form of post-race entertainment is the most effective way to encourage them to stick around. For our purposes, 'entertainment' can include some combination of food, drink, and live (usually musical) performers. A race course that finishes in a nice, scenic or fun location where people like to hang out will be a strong inducement as well. Keep in mind that runners are generally more willing to stick around and socialize after an evening race, when they don't have somewhere else to rush off to immediately after they finish. Also, the question of whether or not to have a post-race party should

definitely take into account the time of year. People will not want to hang around after a run if the weather is too cold, unless there is a tent or other warm space. Likewise, if you plan post-race entertainment outside, make sure to have a contingency plan for bad weather.

"High Quality" Post-Race Food

While most races offer some sort of traditional post-race fare (bagels, bananas, oranges), more substantial or unique food, or a variety of different food options, will give an event something of a 'street fair' atmosphere, incentivizing runners to remain on-site to eat and socialize instead of just grabbing a bagel and heading for the car. Runners generally enjoy seasonally appropriate food—hot

Phil Stewart

The Boilermaker post-race party at a local brewery draws tens of thousands.

entrees/soup/chili in the winter or ice cream in the summer, for example. The options are limited only by your imagination and the event's budget.

Consider contracting with popular local restaurants, pizza/sandwich shops, etc. for these post-race food options. The cost of providing interesting food choices can add up quickly, so be sure to budget appropriately. Food vendors who are also sponsors of the event may be willing to provide some food as an in-kind donation, in return for the visibility they receive from the event—keep this in mind when you are initially procuring sponsorship. Supermarkets and grocery stores are extremely valuable sponsors if you are planning a post-race party. They can lean on their food and beverage vendors to come up with a variety of items.

Some food vendors will expect to provide the employees to serve the food, as opposed to just dropping off the food for the race volunteers to serve. Although this may constitute an additional expense, vendors that serve their own food most often come with their own permits, which not only may save the race the trouble of obtaining the appropriate permits but also eliminates the need for the volunteers to understand and comply with all the permitting minutia regarding safe handling of foods, particularly hot foods. The permitting process for serving food varies by jurisdiction, so make sure to research carefully the permitting requirements for the event well in advance. In summary, if food vendors are hired, determine whether they will serve the food themselves, whether they have their own permits, and whether they provide their own serving equipment/tents/ etc. (For more information, please see **Chapter 11: Equipment, Supplies and Key Personnel.**)

Beer/Wine

Many runners consider the enjoyment of a nice cold beer after a race to be one of the best forms of post-race "entertainment." Likewise, races (often through or around vineyards) that provide post-race wine are also growing in number and popularity. If the event's budget allows it, the provision of wine or beer at the post-race party can

Phil Stewart

Volunteers working feverishly to serve runners at the Quad City Times Bix Seven post-race party.

truly be a differentiator for an event. However serving alcoholic beverages is a serious undertaking with potentially negative consequences, and there are a number of very important points to consider before making the decision to serve alcohol at a race.

Many race directors shy away from serving alcohol primarily because of the potential liability involved, particularly regarding rowdy/dangerous behavior and/or participants (or volunteers) driving under the influence upon leaving the event. The most obvious way to prevent these problems (other than not serving alcohol) is to limit the number of drinks each person can obtain, through using drink tickets or marking the runners' bibs to indicate the number of drinks they have had. This also serves to restrict drink access only to event participants, but is by no means foolproof, as non-drinkers may transfer their drink tickets/bibs to drinking friends. Also be aware that, if volunteers will be used to monitor drink consumption, these volunteers may turn a blind eye to friends returning for more than their allotted number of drinks. It is also extremely important to make sure that only people of legal drinking age are able to get drinks, meaning that drink servers will either have to check IDs or that participants of legal drinking age need to be easily distinguishable from underage participants, using wrist bands or different colored bibs, for example. Again, these methods are far from foolproof.

Make sure to include appropriate language in the registration waiver to reflect that alcohol will be served, and to place the responsibility on the participant. An example of such language is "I understand that I am fully responsible for all of my own actions including the consumption of alcohol. I hereby expressly waive any and all liability that may arise related to my consumption of alcohol whether or not provided by the Event or any sponsor."

From a strictly logistical standpoint, if you wish to serve alcohol at a race, you will need to obtain both the proper permits from the local jurisdiction and appropriate insurance coverage.

Standard RRCA liability insurance *does cover* events that serve alcohol, *provided that the club/organization putting on the event is not "in the business of selling, serving, manufacturing, distributing, or distilling alcoholic beverages."* The inclusion of "serving" in this stipulation means that **races cannot use their volunteers to pour the drinks**. *Races should make sure that all of the servers are from the alcoholic beverage sponsor.* A less attractive option is to have beer served from a keg, with race volunteers handing out cups and monitoring the participants as they pour their own beer. The RRCA further states that, in order for liability coverage to be valid if alcohol is served at a race, there should be **no charge** for the drinks and the event registration should not make any reference to alcohol being included as part of the registration fee. If *outside* vendors *sell* alcohol at the event, incidents arising from the sale of alcohol are *not* covered by RRCA insurance and additional insurance will need to be obtained in these cases. Depending on the jurisdiction, events may be asked to secure a temporary liquor license, sometimes called an ABC license, even if they are not selling or serving the alcohol. If this is the case, the RRCA requires the event to secure a liquor liability endorsement, which as of this writing could range from $400-$700 or more. Clearly, you will want to determine if this is necessary long before deciding to provide alcohol at the event. Lastly, the RRCA states that if at any time the RRCA-insured event assumes responsibility for selling or serving the alcohol, or if the event is required to secure a temporary liquor license, that event must secure a liquor liability endorsement through the RRCA's insurer. (See **Chapter 9: Insurance and Legal** for further discussion of this topic..)

Concerts/Live Entertainment

The marriage of running and rock music propelled the Rock 'n' Roll series to national prominence in the first decade of the 21st century. The rapid growth of this series meant that music soon became an important staple for mid-sized and large events, not only for post-race entertainment but for on-course entertainment as well.

Recruiting and coordinating live entertainment can be a fairly significant job, even if that entertainment only constitutes a local band playing on the course or after the race. The race director should consider delegating this responsibility to a member of the race committee. The first step is to determine the type of entertainment to provide; and, just like with post-race food, this choice is only limited by the event's budget and the director's imagination. Consider choosing entertainment that reflects the unique personality of the local city/region. Local bands are always a favorite and may be fairly inexpensive (or even be willing to play just for the practice or exposure). Some races also employ 'cheerleaders' (often supplied by sponsors), drum lines, jugglers, stilt-walkers, local church choirs—the possibilities are boundless.

Performers can be found by word-of-mouth or booked through an agent.

In most municipalities, permits may be required for bands and other types of entertainment, unless these acts perform solely on private property (with the consent and written permission of the property owner, of course). As with all other types of permitting, make sure to fully understand all of the local ordinances and what is required, permit-wise, by the municipality. To avoid unpleasant surprises, particularly on race day, do this well in advance of contracting with any bands/performers.

Regardless of what type of entertainment is chosen, it is important that all performers be vetted carefully in advance for credibility. Listen to the music of a potential band to ensure that it is family friendly. If possible, check the reputations of the performers, particularly in regard to showing up (and showing up on time). Also, be aware that if any non-original music will be played at the event in any form (whether by a band, a DJ or the

Phil Stewart

Bands are usually a critical ingredient of post-race festivities. If the awards will be given out on the same stage, make sure you are able to move the band equipment aside quickly for the ceremony.

race organization through a sound system), a music license is required. (See **Chapter 9: Insurance and Legal** for more information on music licensing). In addition, if you charge a *separate fee* for a post-race concert (in addition to the race entry fee), an additional music license is required (two licenses—one for the event and one for the paid concert).

Create written contracts for the performers, in which as many details as possible are directly spelled out. Negotiate all fees in advance and clearly state the time they are to *arrive* as well as the times they are expected to start/stop playing. Work with the entertainers to determine whether they will bring their own equipment, *including generators and tents*, or whether they will expect certain items to be provided or delivered by the event. Encourage them to bring their own generators and other equipment; otherwise entertainment set-up can become a major pre-race distraction. If generators are needed, check with the municipal permitting authorities about any special requirements or restrictions. (Frequently, municipalities will require that generators have barricades surrounding them and have drip pans, so these must be arranged for each generator.) Determine where on-course performers can park and issue any necessary credentials. Determine whether you will allow bands the opportunity to sell their music at the event. If the band will be located along the course, establish clear rules regarding runner/band interaction (distribution of free merchandise, etc.), as you will want to keep the runners moving to avoid accidents. Based on local ordinances, make sure bands are aware of when they can start playing (for morning races) or when they have to stop playing (for evening races). List all of this information in the contract.

Establishing a solid relationship with the performers will help to ensure their willingness to return to the event in the future. Actions taken toward this end include promoting the performers on the event's website (even posting digital versions of their songs, if possible), allowing them the

opportunity to sell merchandise and meet their fans (perfect for an expo, if you have one), and engaging with them during the event's off-season by supporting them when they perform at local venues.

Posting Results

Advances in race scoring technology and use of the internet make results posting faster and more streamlined than ever before. This accelerated processing power has also increased runner expectations that the results will be available quickly. The use of transponder-based scoring systems means that race results can be posted on the race website and viewable via mobile devices practically in real time—meaning within moments of each runner crossing the finish mat. As in so many other areas, the runners' expectations about fast results rise with increasing race size.

One downside of this nearly instantaneous posting is that it does not allow time for checking the results for errors and subsequently making any corrections. Therefore, race directors should take every opportunity possible to warn runners that *the results are unofficial*. There is no question that accuracy has taken a back seat to speed in this super-charged fast-results era. Before any official results are released, the results should be reviewed very carefully to see if everything looks credible. This includes checking the times to see if they are realistic, making sure no women's names appear in the men's results (and vice versa), and checking for other possible anomalies, such as a 70-year-old man placing in the top 10.

"Real Time" Tracking and Results

A small but growing number of races at distances of 10K and longer are placing transponder timing mats at various checkpoints along the course, getting split time data as the runners cross the mats, and sending the data out by a text message (to individuals who have registered their cell phone numbers in advance) or some other method, while the race is still underway! This is a great way for spectators to be able to track a runner's progress. In addition, the text messages give the runner a record of his or her splits along the course. The intermediate splits can be particularly informative if the mats are placed at meaningful points along the course, such as the half-way point of any event, or the 10K point in a half marathon, etc. An alternative format is to post these split times to a website where they can be viewed by friends and families. This same technology can make the splits and final results available moments after the runners finish as well.

Posting Results in the Finish Line Area

Despite all of the technological advances in results processing, there is still some interest in having a printout of the results on site. If there is a printer at the race site, simply print out and post the results as they become available. Find a wall, the side of a truck, or a trailer in the awards area (or bring bulletin boards or "A-Frames," where you can post men on one side and women on the other side) and tape up the sheets that are printed out. This also serves as the "official posting" of the results for purposes of starting the protest period (*see Chapter 14: Rules of Competition for details about protests)*. This is still the most streamlined way for runners not only to see their own time but the times of those who finished around them. Indicate that they are "unofficial results." Runners will be checking them as they are posted, so you may be able to get a heads-up on any results issues, such as a problem with an award winner, while the scoring team is still present and working on the data. An increasing number of events set up results kiosks with a number of laptops or mobile devices, on which people can look up their times and places.

Posting Results on the Event Website

Even with the availability of nearly real-time results, it is still important to post the results on the race website as soon as possible, as was mentioned in *Chapter 6: Marketing and Promotions*. Runners will visit the site to see how they and their friends did. The ability to scroll through a long list of finishers may be easier on a website than on a mobile device. When runners visit the website to check their results, this is the perfect opportunity to get sponsor logos in front of the runners again, as well as to get them excited about next year's race. Today's runners expect to see the results on the website within a matter of hours after the end of the event. For more information about the various formats in which results should be posted, see *Chapter 17: Timing and Scoring*.

All-Time Searchable Results

As was mentioned in *Chapter 17: Timing and Scoring,* some races keep an on-going searchable database containing the results from every year the race has been held. This allows runners to see their times, or the times of any runner of interest, for every year they have participated in the event. In many instances, this feature can be developed by the online registration or scoring teams.

Results Booklets

The internet has dramatically decreased the number of events offering post-race results publications. However, some race directors and runners still like the idea of a results "booklet." This is a final way to say thank you and make the runners feel part of the event. Today, any results booklet is most likely to be in PDF format and either emailed as an attached file or posted on the website and included as a link in an email sent to participants and volunteers. Here are some things that can be included in the results booklet:

- **Results:** These should include an overall listing, as well as the award winners in the open and age-group divisions and team results (if any).
- **Photos:** Photos remind spectators, participants, and sponsors how much fun

everyone had and how successful the event was. Photos taken in front of sponsor logos also serve to put the sponsor's name in front of the participants once again. Including plenty of photos breaks up the monotony of pages and pages of results listings.

- **Race story:** Include details of how the men's and women's races unfolded, and stories of any other runners or happenings that make for interesting reading.

- **Race director's message:** This is a final opportunity for the race director to thank the runners, the sponsors, the volunteers and other key players.

- **Names of volunteers and organizing committee members:** This will make everyone feel like a part of the event.

- **Sponsor ads:** Include ads from the sponsors as a final avenue of exposure for them.

- **Race statistics.** Previous open and age-group winners, age-group records, number of registrants broken down by age and sex or state and country, and average age of race registrants makes for interesting reading.

A Final Note on Results Booklets: Set a goal to have the results booklet completed and posted/emailed within six weeks of race day. You'll find this to be a challenging standard, but if the results show up six months after the race, the final impression of the event will be the long time it took to produce the results booklet.

Dennis Steinauer

19 Post-Race

THE BASICS

Race-Site Teardown and Cleanup

- If at all possible, assign management of the dismantling of the race site (sometimes called "strike," a term borrowed from the theater) and cleanup to one of the committee members. Ideally, this person will have no duties other than cleanup, so he or she will be as fresh and enthusiastic as one can be about this task. You can certainly plan to help out, but knowing that someone else has the lead can be a big relief, since you may be exhausted or may be dealing with a post-race emergency of some sort!

- Likewise, have the volunteer coordinator assign cleanup duty to volunteers who are not assigned to do anything else. These people will be fresh and will likely do a better job than tired volunteers.

- Plan the dismantling and cleanup operation in advance and make sure to have all the necessary equipment such as trucks, handcarts, and supplies on hand, including plenty of trash bags, trash cans and rakes. Develop a timetable for dismantling so it will proceed in an orderly manner, minimizing the clogging of the site by contractors. Everyone will be in a hurry to remove whatever they brought. Some advance planning will help avoid chaos on the back end.

- Think about announcements that can be made to the runners after the race to get them to assist in the cleanup effort.
- Post-race cleanup is prime time to implement any recycling initiatives. Running events generate a considerable amount of trash, ranging from cups to clothes to banana peels. Develop a cleanup plan that incorporates environmental responsibility.

Off-Site Race Wrap-Up

- During the days immediately following the race, you will be dealing mostly with issues ranging from problems with the results, lost and found items, and participant critiques (positive and negative) about the event. If you ran out of any items promised to the runners, such as medals or t-shirts, figure out to whom you owe these items and how you are going to get them sent out, and then notify the runners when this will happen.
- Make sure all of the last minute pre-race instructions are removed from the website and anywhere else they might exist online, and replaced with the appropriate post-race announcements.

Follow Up

- Within a few weeks after the event, get the race committee together and go over all aspects of the event while they are still fresh in everyone's mind. If you wait six months to do this, the knowledge of what worked and what needs improvement will have faded away.
- Continue to make sure the event website is kept up-to-date. The following year's date should be posted prominently on the site. Be sure to remove items from the site that are no longer relevant after the race is over.
- Send out thank you's to sponsors, volunteers, municipal officials and anyone else who contributed to the success of the event.
- Have a party for yourself and key volunteers. Then take a break. You deserve it!

THE DETAILS

The moment the last finisher crosses the finish line, all of the anticipatory excitement and drama of the event dissipates faster than helium out of a punctured balloon—for both the participants and the organizers. With the adrenaline rush gone, everyone realizes just how tired he or she is. Unfortunately, the tasks that need to be done at this point are far more mundane, but no less important if you wish to produce a professionally executed event from start to finish. Be forewarned that it may take one to two months or more to wrap up a major event.

Site Teardown

Almost as soon as the final runner leaves the

race site, you will begin to tear down the site (the term "strike" is sometimes used to describe this activity). Similar to site set-up, you should develop a detailed timetable and plan. All of the vendors (porta-johns, tents, sound system, timing company, etc.), as well as the race's teardown volunteers will be in a big hurry after a long day. Additionally, if the event requires road closures, there may be a very tight timeframe for getting everything out of the way so that the roads can re-open. (Ideally, the entire teardown process takes place before the roads re-open, but you may not have that luxury.) This mass exit will need to be choreographed, so think in advance if there is any particular sequence the teardown needs to follow. For example, supplies have to be removed from tents before tents come down. Should the porta-johns be removed before the tents; should the sound equipment be taken down before the stage? Do the timing mats need to be removed right away in order for the roads to reopen quickly? How will water stop supplies and cones be retrieved from the course? All of these activities likely involve vehicles that will be competing for a limited amount of space on the roadway. The bottom line is that a site teardown plan is needed and someone must be responsible for enforcing that plan.

Site Cleanup

The post-event cleanup effort will help determine whether the event is welcome back to the same location the following year. If the event takes place in a neighborhood, don't leave

such a mess that the neighbors complain. If the event is on municipal property, the day-after-the-race "footprint" may determine whether or not a permit will be approved the following year. Many cities require that races pay a bond to cover cleanup and damage to the staging area (such as destruction to the grass due to trucks, etc.) Any costs incurred by the municipality after the race is over are usually liberally deducted from the bond.

If sufficient volunteers are available, try to assign fresh volunteers to cleanup duty. It is hard for volunteers to be motivated to do a good job of cleaning up if they have already been working for two or more hours. Instead, assign people whose only race-day job is cleanup (great for people who don't like to get out of bed early or for participants who may want to help out after they run the race). In addition, assign the role of coordinating the cleanup to a committee member who has not had any tasks prior to cleanup. Since you will have

Phil Stewart

Municipal authorities will be eager to reopen the streets as soon after your event as possible.

been working on little sleep for days, it will be a relief to know that cleanup is being handled by someone else. Just make sure to give the duty to someone you can trust to get the job done.

A little advance thinking can go a long way toward reducing the amount of post-race cleanup. Start by seeking cooperation from the runners in the pre-race instructions. At the race, have the announcer remind runners about cleanup, and then follow up by making sure to have plenty of trash cans placed throughout the staging area in strategic locations, such as near the post-race water and food tables. Use separate bins for recyclable items. Volunteers at water stops may be able to sweep up and bag used cups while the race is still underway, if rakes and trash cans/ bags are placed at the water stops.

Know how and when the trash will be collected. Plan to place all the trash together in a central location so it will be easy for the trash collectors to pick it up. If the event is being held on a windy day, make an extra effort to secure the trash bags so they will not blow away.

Discarded Clothing

If the event takes place in colder weather, many runners will overdress and simply discard garments once the race starts, or along the course. Consider placing receptacles for abandoned clothing in the vicinity of the starting line area and follow up with announcements for runners to use them. Some races ask runners to pass their discarded clothing gently over to the side of the road a few minutes before the race starts, where volunteers can collect it in an organized manner. If no instructions are provided, runners may simply hurl the clothing into the air during the euphoria of the start, making the items harder to collect (items ending up in low-hanging tree branches can be particularly nettlesome). Discarded clothing, if thrown onto the roadway, can also pose a tripping danger to the runners coming along behind. Tell the runners that if they will be discarding clothing items *during* the race, they should try to drop them off at an aid station instead of at any point along the roadway, so that race officials won't have to cover every inch of the course in order to clean up.

Work out an arrangement to donate the discarded items to a local homeless shelter, although the items may need to be screened to see which are suitable for donation and which are not. If the items will be donated, let the runners know that this will happen.

Food Donations

If usable food and bottled water or sports drinks are left over after the event, find out in advance if these items can be donated to a local food bank. (There are restrictions on what types of items most food banks can

Discarded clothing can be donated.

MarathonFoto

accept.) Also, arrangements will need to be made in advance to deliver the items. You may be able to earn some good will with the local police by letting them take any extra cases of bottled water or granola bars off your hands.

Post-race Communications

Even though you might want to crawl off into a hole and sleep once race day is over, you will not have this luxury for a while. Expect a deluge of emails, social media posts, and phone calls to start, possibly before you even get home or back to the office. People will be telling you what they liked and didn't like about the event, letting you know if their names don't appear in the results (or if their times are incorrect) or if they lost their keys. The list goes on.

Consider setting up an "out of office" email to let participants who contact you shortly after the event know that you will reply to their specific questions, but it may take a few days. Post something similar on the event's social media sites. At a minimum, make sure to update the final pre-race voice mail message and make posts on social media with something that indicates that

GREEN TIP

Recycling and Composting at Race Cleanup

In an effort to make events environmentally friendly, many race directors are trying to recycle more and more of the race supplies. Certainly, race cleanup offers opportunities to recycle paper products and plastic bottles and to compost any organic material such as food waste. If the event has a recycling program, make sure that the collection bins are clearly marked for trash, recycling and compost, and have signage indicating which items belong in which bin. Work closely with the waste removal company to identify recyclable and compostable materials and to ensure their diversion from the landfill. (See **Chapter 21: Before Next Year** for details about a Sustainability Plan.)

Bob Mallet

Post-race is the key time to implement your recycling initiatives.

the race is over! Although the initial round of communications may be intense, you will find that interest in the event wanes fairly quickly after a couple of weeks. This means that you should really hype things like purchasing race merchandise early on after the event, because sales will drop off rapidly as runners' attention transfers to their next race. Here are some suggestions about post-race communications. Organized race directors may prepare these responses in advance of race day, so that the communications simply need to be posted after the race.

- **Post-race email:** It's a good idea to send out a post-race email immediately after the event, thanking the participants and informing them of whom to contact with different types of issues, such as results corrections, general race feedback, lost and found, etc. Include a link to the race results and to the web store, if race merchandise is still being sold. If the event had a participant photographer, include information about viewing and purchasing photos. (The photography company will contact the participants separately, but it doesn't hurt to reinforce the availability of these photos in your own communication with participants.)

  If there was a shortage of t-shirts or medals on race day, expect a large volume of inquiries about those items. Take the offensive and address the plan for distribution of these premiums in the immediate post-race email as well.

- **General critique:** Encourage participants to send any feedback—positive or negative—about the race. Much of this will develop spontaneously on the event's social media sites such as Facebook and Twitter, as well as on external sites that encourage race reviews. Make sure these sites are being monitored closely after the event, so you will have an opportunity to provide "your side" of the story regarding any feedback. The post-race critiques will provide some information about what went well and what needs improvement in subsequent years. Consider

creating a post-race survey to collect participant feedback. Surveys can be set up online via a number of available platforms, and a link to the survey can be included in the post-race email. If you decide to use a survey, it's in your best interest to keep it short and simple ("yes and "no" or rating scales instead of "comments"), to encourage the greatest number of respondents. Offering some incentive to survey-takers will increase the number of respondents as well. Incentives can range from race swag, possibly given out at random to a predetermined number of respondents, to discounted registration for next year's event.

- **Results corrections:** Either the race organization (if the timing was done internally) or the hired timing company should have a standard, even automated, way to handle issues with race results. The most common method is an online "form" that runners can fill out with their name and bib number, type of problem ("not in results," "results are incorrect," or "runner data such as age and sex are incorrect," and "other.") Include a comments section, to allow for a more complicated written description of the problem. Everyone who submits a request for a correction should receive a response, even if it is that the results will not be changed (and why). If a timing company is used, communicate with the timers in advance to determine the method that will be employed to address these complaints. The most common issue they will face is that of transponders that were not read as the runners crossed the finish mat, resulting in missing times. Most seasoned timers can at least come up with a fairly accurate approximated finish time for these omitted participants by gathering information about runners who finished around them, or through the use of finish line photographs or streaming video of the finish. These same strategies should be used if you timed the race yourself.

  Due to issues like missing transponder

times, it is likely that corrections to the posted, unofficial race results will need to be made in the first few weeks after the event. Keep posting the most current set of results as they become available. Include an "as of" date, so viewers will know when the current updates were included. Indicate that the results are "unofficial" until you are ready to post an official set of final results. Some races wait as much as a month after the race to declare the results final, just to allow for any challenges to be heard and for the necessary changes to be made.

- **Keep the website and other social media current:** It is surprisingly common to visit an event's website a couple of months after the race and find that the site is frozen in time with most of the information (except for the posting of the results) exactly as it appeared before the race happened. Make a special effort to have the event's webmaster take down all of the information that is no longer relevant after the race. Post the following year's date in a prominent position, as well as anything that is firm about the following year's event, such as the official headquarters hotel, etc. Finally, have the webmaster check the site every few weeks, just to see if there are posted items with deadlines that may have expired or new information that is now ready to be posted. Don't let the website be stagnant. Any other forms of social media used by the event should also be updated to reflect that the race is over. Social media is an excellent way to stay in contact with many of the participants, so be sure to continue posting updates, photos, or other interesting information on a fairly regular basis throughout the year.

- **Photos and media releases:** Runners generally enjoy viewing photographs of the event once it is over. Consider establishing a photo gallery and include a link to this gallery on the event website. If you have the time (or a willing volunteer!) to do it, you can even ask participants to submit their own photos for posting in the gallery or on social media.

Publicize the photo gallery on social media. If any media releases were submitted after the race, consider posting these on the event website as well.

Thank You's

Be sure to send an appropriate "thank you" to all of the individuals, sponsors and organizations that contributed to the event. You may want to send all of the event sponsors a plaque or a framed race poster (if one was produced) or an item of race merchandise, along with the thank-you note. Some races have the awards vendor produce special thank-you plaques to send to key groups. Don't forget to make some gesture toward the municipal authorities and local police for the services they provided. For most of the contributors, a personal note from the event director goes a long way toward building long-term loyalty to the event. You might even want to get a card made with a photo from the race to use for these notes. Sponsors deserve a more detailed report showing the visibility that they received. (See *Chapter 6: Marketing and Promotions* for a discussion of a post-race sponsor report.)

The Wrap-Up Meeting

Try to schedule a final wrap-up meeting with the race committee within two to three weeks after the race. Give the committee some time to recover, but don't wait so long that things fade from memory. Suggest to the committee members that they check in with some of their running buddies to get feedback about the event. Some race directors ask for a written report from each committee member (be aware that it takes some persistence to get them to actually submit the report). When people initially sign on to serve in a key race-management role, consider telling them that a prerequisite of the job is agreeing to submit a post-race report shortly after the race. As an initial step, key race personnel could be asked to submit a short 5-10 bullet point report within 24 hours of the event, and then they could elaborate more over the following couple of weeks. This immediate feedback provides the race director with valuable information right away.

Make sure to have someone take detailed minutes at the wrap-up meeting. Each committee member should discuss things that worked well and things that did not, along with any suggestions for improvement for the following year. Keep the tone honest as far as where the race fell short, but not overly criticizing. Remain professional and polite regardless of how many things may have gone wrong. Once all the suggestions have been compiled, review them to determine which ones should be implemented in future years. Some suggestions may involve things that can be dealt with during the down-time before things really get under way for the next year's event.

Putting Things Away

If the event has storage space, it is a near certainty that most items will be brought from the race site and simply dumped on the floor of that space. Do not let more than a week or so pass before going to the storage space to begin the cleanup process. Everything related to water stops will need to be cleaned thoroughly (especially any containers that were used to mix sports drinks, or pitchers used to

pour them—some events simply discard the pitchers and replace them with new ones each year). Signs may need to be wiped clean and then laid out flat. Many items will simply need to be sorted, inventoried, and then put away neatly. Open every box and label what is in it. If there are leftover t-shirts, sort them into boxes by shirt size. (The shirts can be sold at a deep discount at next year's race.) Look for items that may have been damaged. It is better to find out that these items need to be replaced now rather than shortly before the next race. You will undoubtedly find a few items that don't belong to you. Try to return them, if it is feasible. Think about any items that can be thrown away or donated. Try to have at least one assistant to help out with the cleanup, and take that person to lunch afterwards!

Phil Stewart

Expect to take time in the weeks after the race to reorganize your storage shed.

CUCB

20 Special Types of Races and Participatory Events

THE BASICS

This chapter is designed to give an overview of a number of types of "specialized" running events and activities which, in addition to utilizing most of the race directing principles described in the previous chapters, have some unique characteristics and challenges. This is by no means intended to be a detailed description for each of these types of events. In most cases a reference for further details is provided at the end of each section.

Obstacle/Mud Runs and Uniquely Themed Events

- The popularity of obstacle/mud runs and other uniquely themed events took off around 2008, as runners and non-runners alike looked for new and different experiences. The rise of social media around the same time made these events exceptionally easy to promote.

- This genre of events can be divided into two branches—*mass participation experience events*, including color runs, glow runs, chocolate runs, etc., which are generally non-competitive, and *obstacle course runs (OCR)* or mud runs, which are more competitive and market themselves as "tough."

- With many of the mass participation experience events not timed, they may be easier to put on, depending on the technicalities of the unique experience provided. Any extra effort is often offset by the absence of timing/scoring, awards, etc. Depending on the experience provided, post-race cleanup may be more labor intensive (i.e. color runs).

- OCR and mud run-type events (sometimes called "MOB" events for "mud," "obstacles" and "beer") are complex to execute, starting with the creation of safe and creative obstacles or mud pits. Plans must be developed for the increased risk of injury due to the obstacles. Small-scale race directors or running clubs probably should shy away from directing these types of events, leaving them to professional series promoters well-versed in the complexities of staging them. These events are not covered under either the RRCA or USATF road race insurance plans. Insurance is available but is costly.

Trail Runs

- Trail runs run the gamut from trails in a city park to rocky trails over 12,000-foot mountain peaks. In more rural environments, race directors must exercise greater caution to ensure the safety of all of the participants.

- Although the courses for trail runs can be measured, they are not eligible for USATF certification due to the ambiguity of trails.

- Setting up services such as aid stations and medical support for trail runs in remote areas can be a challenge.

- The permitting process for trail runs can be far more complex than a standard road race. There are many Federal and State Agencies that may become involved in reviewing an application for a permit, depending on the location of the course.

Relay Races

- The guiding principle of organizing a relay is to make sure that everyone is in the right place at the right time. The organizers of most marathon relays provide extensive transportation systems to get out-going runners to the start of their relay legs and finishing runners back to the staging area. Staging a four-leg relay can be compared to putting on four road races in succession. Ultra-distance/overnight relay organizers rely on the participants to provide their own transportation.

- Both marathon and ultra-distance relays emphasize participation more than competition. There is little uniformity in either the number of legs in the relay or the length of the legs. Leg lengths are frequently determined largely by the location of suitable exchange zones. For this reason, most legs are odd distances, such as 4.3 or 6.7 miles in length.

- Transponder-based timing is a near necessity for accurate relay timing, with the mats being placed at the exchange points. Manual timing is labor-intensive and the splits from each leg have to be integrated into the final time. Most of the popular race scoring software packages have modules for team scoring.

- Novice race directors should perfect their race directing skills at a traditional road race before venturing into the relay business.

Kids' Runs

- The main goal of children's races should be to give children an introduction to running, with the emphasis on fun rather than on competition.

- A children's race should be a short distance—between 50 yards for toddlers and up to 1 mile for older children.

- The age range for children's races is usually 12 and under, although ages 5-8 seem to be the peak years for participation. Many events include "special needs" divisions for physically-challenged children who may need walkers, wheelchairs or adults alongside them in order to participate.

- Most directors of kids' runs find that things go more smoothly if all children are given the same prize for completing the event, regardless of their place. Kids love getting medals!

- Safety is paramount for children's races. Many children line up at the front and sprint as hard as they can when the "Go" signal is given, which can lead to children tripping and trampling on one another. To enhance safety at the start, use adult volunteers and have multiple heats. Parents will appreciate it if the race has a loop course where they can see their youngster for most, if not all, of the race.

- Once a child crosses the finish line, it is most important to make sure that he or she can be reunited with a family member. Use chutes and corrals to keep the kids in the finish area while their parents are looking for them, and make sure to have a Lost Child Tent where families can re-unite.

- Dealing with parents is one of the biggest challenges for the organizers of kids' runs. The younger the child, the more anxious the parent will be about whether their child is in trouble. Try to design the course and staging area so parents can see their child at all times. Generally, parents are allowed to run with the youngest participants, those ages 6 and under. Policies vary for children ages 7-12. If parents are allowed to participate, they are not required to pay the registration fee.

Cross Country Meets, Track Meets and Road Miles

- Cross country meets are typically run on golf courses or in open fields and generally range in distance from 3 to 7 miles. They are relatively easy to organize and manage compared with traditional road races. Cross country courses are not eligible for certification.

- Track meets are a good way to provide some variety to an organization's race schedule. Like cross country races, they are relatively easy to stage because they are contained on a track, and the logistics are much less demanding than those required for a typical road race.

- Road miles are popular add-ons to the menu of race distances.

Training Groups—In-person or Online

- Establishing a training group to prepare new runners and walkers for an event is a good way to build attendance at the event and can be a significant profit maker for the race or club. Runners are willing to pay for online training programs available through online coaching companies and are willing to pay significantly more for in-person coaching conducted by a running club, certified coach, or a local specialty running retailer.

- Finding the right person to motivate a training group is essential. The groups typically meet weekly and consist of a short talk on training, nutrition, injury prevention, etc., followed by a short group walk or run.

- Since most participants in training groups will be entry-level runners or walkers, make sure that both the training group and the event itself are slow-runner or walker friendly.

- The length of the training program should be determined by the distance of the event. Start a training group at least six weeks before the race for a shorter-distance event (5K, 8K, 10K), and ideally allow at least six months for a marathon training program.

- Training groups may help to foster goodwill within the municipality where the event is being held, which may facilitate the approval of permits and receipt of other city services.

THE DETAILS

As the number of both runners and standard road races has swelled over the last 25 years, the interest in doing "something different" has grown as well. Today, the running menu includes trail runs, relays, kids' runs, an entire new genre of often un-timed obstacle course runs, and variously themed events like mud runs, color runs, glow runs and more. [**Note:** We do not deal with triathlons in this book.] A number of types of special races are discussed separately below. We will focus on the organizational aspects that are different from those of a standard road race, so as not to repeat information from previous chapters.

Obstacle/Mud Runs and Uniquely Themed Events

The biggest difference between most of these types of unique events and traditional races is that these events tend to emphasize the experience of participating more than the competition. (There are some notable exceptions such as the Warrior Dash and Spartan Races obstacle series, which celebrate the machismo of the competitors.)

A large number of unique races cropped up nationally in the second decade of the 21st century, including The Color Run, Tough Mudder, Spartan Road Races, Hot Chocolate Runs and Warrior Dashes, just to name a few. Although some of these types of runs racked up some impressive registration numbers very quickly, a number of them just as quickly became overextended and eventually folded.

The focus on the experiential aspect over the competitive aspect means that many of the rigors of traditional road races, such as course certification and, in many cases, even timing and scoring, may not apply. Another big difference is that the traditional road course must be supplemented with whatever it is that makes the event unique—color spray stations, obstacles, glow sticks, mud pits, etc.

Impact on "Traditional" Race Audiences

As Obstacle Course Races (OCRs), mud runs and uniquely themed mass-participation running events began to proliferate, directors of traditional races wondered if the exploding numbers of participants in this new genre of races would affect participation in their events. Over time, two trends have emerged. First, the new genre of events largely appears to be drawing a different audience, one less focused on competition and more driven by a desire to do something new and exciting or challenging, and to share the experience with their friends, either in person, on social media or both. Participants in many of the uniquely themed mass-participation running events, such as color runs, tend to be younger than participants in traditional races, and predominantly female. The second observable trend seems to be that, after an initial period of dramatic expansion, the growth curve of these events appears to have slowed.

Social Media Savvy Needed

Organizers of OCRs and other uniquely themed events should be extremely fluent in all types of social media, including (at the time of this writing) Facebook, Twitter, Instagram, and Pinterest, because social media is the driving force behind the popularity of these events. Directors of these unique events should be ready to vigorously promote them using social media, far beyond simply replying to social media posts. It's a good idea to use committee members or race loyalists with the appropriate interest and experience to make sure the event has a very strong social media presence, beginning well in advance of the event and continuing even after race day.

MarathonFoto

Mud Runs require the construction of elaborate obstacles in addition to a mud pit.

Selecting a Venue

Some uniquely themed events, particularly those in the vein of color runs or glow stick runs, etc., may be able to use city streets, although the permitting authorities will need to be convinced that the course will be completely cleaned up afterwards, especially for runs that generate unusual or excessive trash or otherwise leave a mark on the local environment. If the municipalities say "no," attempt to arrange the course such that the unique aspects (think color points in a color run) that the municipalities object to are located on private property, such as in the parking lot of a private business (maybe even one that is a sponsor). Of course, you will need permission from the business owner, and the appropriate insurance, to do this. Nearly all OCRs and mud runs are held entirely on private property, in order to accommodate the construction or placement of the obstacles or mud pits.

Distances and Obstacles

With the emphasis primarily on the experience as opposed to the running, the distances of most uniquely themed, mass-participation running events are in the 5K to 8K range, although some may be a non-standard distance within this range. With a more casual audience, course certification, mile marks and even timing and scoring may not be necessary. Obstacle course runs tend to be longer, although most are less than a half marathon in distance. Organizers of some of the larger OCR event series have broadened their distance ranges from kids' OCRs, which are short, through ultra-marathon distance OCRs. The courses in the 10K to half-marathon range generally include 15-20 obstacles, which range from climbing walls, ladders, heavy items to be carried, ropes, mud pits and obstacles to be crawled under. Constructing obstacles and creating mud pits is beyond the scope of this book, but, needless to say, sturdy construction is critical for participant safety, which is a must. Construction of obstacles also adds a significant new line item to the event budget; by some estimates this can add a six-figure expense.

Colors

The colors used to coat color run competitors are primarily food coloring and corn starch. Count on using 1-2 pounds per participant. The concoctions can be made by hand or purchased from vendors on the internet in bulk or in pre-packaged bags convenient for throwing.

Races2Run

The after effects of a color run. The participants may clean up more easily than the streets.

Registration Fees

Registration fees for uniquely themed events may be 20-50% higher than fees for traditional events, despite the reduced requirements for some of the traditional aspects of race organization. Money saved on organizing expenses is plowed into the features that make the event unique, such as the cost of constructing the obstacles. The increased revenue may also be used to pay the higher insurance premiums (see below) and for elaborate post-race parties and entertainment.

Registration Limits

In the early days of this genre of uniquely themed mass-participation running events, social media promotion caused some events to go viral, and with no registration caps, the crowds overwhelmed both the organizers and the venues. Events planned for 10,000 participants attracted 25,000, causing significant shortages of runner amenities as well as big headaches for the law enforcement personnel trying to control traffic in and out of the venue. Subsequently, successful mass-participation events have set stricter registration limits, with some of the most popular events employing a lottery system.

In addition to the above concerns, the number of participants in OCR events must be controlled simply because of the limitations of the obstacles themselves. For either type of event, if the race is so oversubscribed that the organization breaks down, directors can be certain that the same social media response that spread the word about the event will quickly turn angry and ugly. Set realistic expectations about what size a specific venue can handle and stick to it.

Insurance

Uniquely themed mass-participation running events without obstacles are covered under RRCA and USATF insurance policies. Obstacle course runs are not covered by either the RRCA or USATF policies, so insurance will have to be purchased on the open market. Access to insurance is available through U.S. Obstacle Course Racing (www.usocr.com). Make sure it includes both participant and spectator liability. Expect the rates to be steep—as much as five to ten times the rates for running events. Some events simply tack an insurance fee onto the registration fee to help cover the additional cost. The range may be as high $15-$20 per participant for an event with difficult obstacles.

A Final Word

The creation and management of the obstacles in OCR events is significant and should make prospective organizers of this type of event think long and hard about staging one. Most of OCRs/mud runs are associated with a national series of some sort, with paid staff versed in the complexities of staging these events. On the other hand, adding a unique theme (color, glow sticks, etc.) to an event run on a traditional 5K course may be a nice addition to a running club's schedule of traditional events. Organizing a more traditional event with a unique theme woven in is far easier than staging an OCR/mud run and may serve as a gateway to bring new participants into the sport.

(Additional Resources: See *Chapter 23: Resources* for details about U.S. Obstacle Racing, which provides information for both obstacle race participants and event directors.)

Trail Runs

Here, we will focus primarily on shorter-distance trail events (shorter than marathon distance) held off-road, generally in an environment more rural than that of the traditional road race.

Limiting the Size of the Field

Most trail events can only handle a small fraction of the number of runners in a typical road race, due to the constraints of permits, course terrain, and logistics such as parking, aid station set up, and volunteer support. If the trail is less than 3' wide (single track), it will be difficult for the runners to run more than one abreast, and running abreast is actually discouraged because it can lead to erosion of the trail and damage to the natural environment adjacent to the trail. It is likely that permitting authorities will place a tight cap on participant numbers for most trail events, since these authorities are required to consider the environmental impact of staging an event on park or National Forest land. You will also want the runners to have a positive experience, and a conga-line of runners makes for a less-than-enjoyable outing. Think in terms of a maximum of hundreds of runners, rather than thousands.

Selecting a Course

As you plan a trail race, be aware that a challenging course will attract competitive runners and those comfortable with gnarly terrain, but may discourage some novice trail runners. By providing choices (for example, a tough 10K held in concert with a gentle 5K) the event will attract a wider range of participants. Of course, the distance

Phil Stewart

The finish of the Pikes Peak Ascent illustrates the challenges and thrills of trail running.

selected for the race may be pre-determined by the venue, as may be the number of runners the venue can accommodate. Be creative and consider offering double- and triple-loops to gain extra distance, or design a course with an out-and-back route if a loop isn't feasible, provided the trail is wide enough to accommodate runners going in both directions. Be sure the start area allows runners enough time to "thin out" before reaching single-track terrain. Once the course is set, take some runners out on the route to do a test run. Make adjustments if needed.

Parking for trail races can often be a significant issue. Scout out the location well in advance and determine whether ample parking exists near the start/finish line. Trailheads often have limited parking. If parking is limited, encourage carpooling or consider busing people to the start from a larger staging area. Be aware that busing will incur an additional expense and complicate the logistics. (*For details on busing runners, see* **Chapter 16: Race Logistics and Operations.**)

Obtaining Permits for Trail Runs

It is very likely that any race held on trails will require permits from either the U.S. Forest Service, a local parks department or other governmental agency, or permission from a private land owner. Permits often require a detailed safety and communications plan, a course map, a registration form, a preliminary race budget, and a

SIDEBAR

Who's Who Among Federal and State Agencies

Federal Agencies

- **National Park Service** (Department of the Interior, www.nps.gov): Probably the best known of the federal agencies, the National Park Service's jurisdiction ranges from the National Mall in Washington, DC to Yosemite National Park in California. NPS oversees 84 million acres of land. *Mission:* "...to promote and regulate the use of the...national parks...which purpose is to conserve the scenery and the natural and historic objects and the wildlife therein and to provide for the enjoyment of the same in such manner and by such means as will leave them unimpaired for the enjoyment of future generations."

- **U.S. Fish and Wildlife** (Department of the Interior, www.fws.gov): Holds jurisdiction over Chincoteague, Arctic National Wildlife Refuge and 500 wildlife refuges totaling 93 million acres. *Mission:* "To work with others to conserve, protect, and enhance fish, wildlife, plants and their habitats for the continuing benefit of the American people."

- **U.S. Forest Service** (Department of Agriculture, www.fs.fed.us): Determines multiple uses of forestland. Makes recommendations for "wilderness" or "non-wilderness" use of lands. Forest Service lands frequently surround National Park Service lands. Jurisdiction includes Finger Lakes, Kaibab, Lake Tahoe, Arapahoe-Roosevelt, etc. Oversees 191 million acres. *Mission:* "Caring for the land and serving people."

- **U.S. Bureau of Land Management** (Department of the Interior, www.blm.gov): Determines multiple uses of lands under its jurisdiction. Oversees 261 million acres, mostly in Western U.S., including Hells Canyon Wilderness and Santa Rosa (CA) Wilderness. *Mission:* "To sustain the health, diversity, and productivity of the public lands for the use and enjoyment of present and future generations."

State or Private Agencies

(collectively oversee 58 million acres)

- Fish and Game Agencies: Vary from state to state
- Others: State Parks, County Parks, City Parks, etc., vary from state to state

certificate of additional insured. (For a discussion about insurance certificates see **Chapter 9: Insurance and Legal.**) Some permitting agencies require that the event be put on by a 501(c)(3) nonprofit organization. If the event is staged by a for-profit entity, race plans may be curtailed before the permit process even begins. Be sure to secure insurance coverage and all necessary permits, including both public and private land permits and/or written authorization, well in advance of the event. The permit may require the posting of signs at trail heads and on the course, both prior to and during the event, as well as notifying (usually via letters) those residents living on or near land used or affected by the race. Close follow-up with all relevant agencies and individuals is imperative in order to ensure that all necessary requirements are fulfilled.

For trail runs, environmental impact trumps economic impact when it comes to issuing a permit. Here are some tips to ease you through the permitting process:

- **Determine who has jurisdiction over the area in which the event will run.** Much of the nation's forestland falls under a number of federal or state agencies, including (but not limited to) the National Park Service (U.S. Department of Interior), the U.S. Forest Service (U.S. Department of Agriculture), and the State Bureau of Land Management. Each group will have its own policies regarding use of forestland and will also have its own permitting process. Events that cross jurisdictional lines will need permits from all involved agencies.

- **Plan to apply for permits about a year in advance.** If the event requires an environmental impact study to be performed, this takes time (more on this below). Be prepared to convince the authorities that the club, group, or organization is experienced in putting on trail-running events, that the race will be sensitive to the environment (by using removable flagging instead of permanent flagging; trucking out the trash, etc.), and that the organization is committed to runner safety.

- **Locate the "mission statement" for the parkland.** This document may offer an initial clue about your chances of success. If the park's priority is something along the lines of "serving day-to-day visitors" you will be on stronger ground; if the mission is to "preserve the park land," you may have a tougher (but not impossible) sell; if it is to protect endangered species, consider alternative sites.

- **Find a runner or a running advocate in the parkland office.** Having such an individual on your side may greatly assist permitting efforts.

- **Try to schedule the event at an off-peak time or in an off-peak location.** Parks whose mission is to serve day-to-day visitors have the challenge of balancing the needs of event participants with the needs of hikers, campers, picnickers, and motorists who also want to use the park. Unfortunately, a running event during the peak fall foliage time goes right up against stiff competition from other park users. Since park officials tend to strive to please everyone, a few complaints from motorists or hikers about clogged roads can doom an event, even if the runners greatly outnumber the other park users. The bottom line is that an event will be evaluated to determine how much it will interfere with daily park use. Minimizing this interference will provide the greatest chance of success.

- **Strategies for more remote parkland.** Park areas primarily concerned with "preserving the park land" instead of "serving day-to-day visitors" are not necessarily completely off limits for trail races. However, the standard for approval may be more rigorous. Many parks of this type will want to study the impact the event will have on the plants and animals within the park. For example, permits may be denied during the spring nesting season but may be approved for other times of the year. Some parks require an "archeological" review for trail runs to determine the impact participants will have on the trail itself. Event directors may need to incur one-time charges for these types of studies, which can run between $500-1,000 for each study required. Some park areas may be pre-cleared for certain types of activities, which means studies are not necessary.

- **Determine and obtain necessary insurance coverage.** Start looking into insurance coverage early, as some agencies may not even consider a permit application unless it is accompanied with a certificate of liability insurance. The amount of liability insurance required is likely to be in the $1,000,000-3,000,000 range. Both the RRCA and USATF offer liability insurance programs that cover standard trail races. Frequently, federal and state organizations will want to be named as additional insured parties and will want certificates indicating this. This process takes time. Be a good risk manager, and consider such things as the amount of time it would take emergency transport to reach some of the remote parts of the course. Make sure the insurance policy covers these added risks—or obtain additional insurance riders if it does not.

- **Be pleasant, flexible, and willing to work with park officials.** The special needs of parklands may require modifications in the race plan for the staging area, the course, or the time of year. Park officials are not intrinsically anti-event, but they may have more needs to balance than do city officials. If you are inflexible or angry, this will likely only increase the resistance of park officials. Decisions of park officials can rarely be appealed, so attempting to go 'over the heads' of the individuals in the permit office is usually a poor strategy and will only serve to alienate permitting officials. Lastly, it can be helpful to your cause to include an option for making a donation to the park and/or one of its programs on the race registration form.

Course Measurement and Logistics

Although trail courses are not eligible for USATF certification due to the ambiguous nature of the terrain, the same methods outlined in *Chapter 4: The Course* can be used for measurement. Run or walk the course with an accurate GPS device to determine an approximate distance. Topographical maps are also beneficial in assessing the distance (as well as elevation changes), especially in more remote and hard-to-access areas. If part of the course is in a state or national park, trail distances may have already been measured and documented. Create a detailed course description and clear, accurate map for the chosen route. Use Trail Run Project, Strava, Garmin, or another .gpx mapping program for this purpose. Google Maps or Google Earth can be also be invaluable in preparing a course map.

A detailed course description and a map are a must, both on the event website and in any other informational materials about the event. Providing detailed course information will minimize calls or emails to the race director, especially given the fact that some runners will go out in advance of race day and run the course. Be specific about the terrain, elevation changes and potential hazards that may exist on the route. Indicate where the aid/support stations will be located and the amenities runners will find at each station. Also consider offering clothing suggestions for expected as well as unexpected weather conditions and temperatures, and advise runners about potential weather extremes. Provide course records and average times to indicate just how challenging the course is.

Marking the Course

To minimize the chances of runners going off course, consider some redundancy in the course markings, as well as "confidence" markings along the trail letting runners know they are going the right way, especially at trail junctions. Flour is often a preferred method of marking a course, since it dissolves after a few rainfalls. On the other hand, significant foot traffic (or rain) may remove a directional flour arrow before the last runner makes the requisite turn. It is therefore a good idea to supplement the flour with flagging, using some sort of removable flag (NEVER permanently mark either the ground or trees!). Place the flagging at eye level every 100 to 200 feet (remember that trail runners typically look down at the trail, not up in the trees), more frequently if junctions occur along the trail. Consider one of three options for flagging: the first involves tying colored trail-marking ribbon to tree branches; the second is to place small, brightly colored course-marking flags in the ground; and the third is a combination of the two. The chosen color should clearly stand out from the background and be visible to all competitors (including those who are color blind). In the registration information, make competitors aware of the type and color of flagging used and how often the markings will be found along the course. Whichever marking method is used, the entire course should be re-checked for consistent markings just prior to the start on race day.

Some race directors neglect to mark the course if it appears obvious that it is impossible to make a wrong turn. However, runners like to be reassured that they are on course, so this may mean that the course should be well marked regardless of its simplicity. Safety should always be the top priority. Provide additional markings for exposed tree roots, large rocks, or other natural, unmovable obstacles on the course, especially if they are easy to overlook but are in the runners' direct path.

Not a trace of the race should be left in the park after the event. This means that all flagging and course markings need to be removed following the event. This job should be performed by trusted volunteers, or possibly the race director, during a final course sweep after all runners have finished. Give course sweepers backpacks in which to place discarded flagging and any other trash they may find along the trail.

Course Logistics

Part of the safety plan for a trail race should

include placing aid stations along the course. Shorter-duration events (those lasting under 30 minutes) require few or no aid stations, but may require some support in terms of volunteers or medical assistance, depending on the terrain, the time of year, the weather conditions, and the potential for injuries. At minimum, water at the start/finish line and a first aid kit should be available. Longer events require more aid stations, but there is no general rule of thumb regarding exactly what the race should provide. Due to concerns about the environmental impact of trail events, many trail runs encourage participants to carry hydration packs/bottles, since many aid stations are going cup-less and only providing water for refilling water bottles.

Aid that is part of the finish line setup should include some type of fluid replacement, such as water or an electrolyte drink. Race timing should, of course, be located at the finish line and if computerized scoring is used, ensure that access to power is available, which may require a generator if utilities are not within reach of an extension cord. Power will not be a concern if only stopwatches or battery-charged digital clocks are used for timing.

Most events do not close their courses to other park users. It is a good idea to befriend any other groups of park users that you know will be in the park on race day, and perhaps ask them to volunteer or be supportive spectators. Further, if the group's members provide volunteer support, offering the group a donation or getting trail runners to volunteer for their events will build good will.

Compared with traditional road races, trail courses vary widely—some have very remote areas, for which recruiting volunteers or even paid support is difficult. Thoroughly consider the special challenges involved in a trail event long before race day and adjust both the logistics and volunteer needs accordingly.

Keeping Track of Runners

It is especially important to keep track of runners in trail races, to make sure that everyone who starts the race safely finishes. Require all registered runners to check in on race morning, even those who may have picked up their numbers the day before. If a runner drops out, he or she should report to the finish line or to a race official on the course so that all runners will be accounted for at the finish. This way, the volunteer sweeping the course won't have to search fruitlessly for a presumed-lost runner. Unfortunately, it is not uncommon for runners to check in at the start but never check back in at the finish line or elsewhere on course. In the pre-race announcements, be sure to explain the importance of doing so. If any runners are not accounted for at the end of the race, emergency officials should be contacted immediately and a large-scale search instituted. The remoteness of many trail runs make this imperative. Lost runner protocols should be developed with park police and emergency responders in advance of race day.

Additional Resources: For more details about organizing trail races, contact the American Trail Running Association (ATRA) at www.trailrunner.com. ATRA also provides a solid document outlining its "Event Standards Program," which provides fairly detailed instructions for new and experienced trail race directors at http://trailrunner.com/about-atra/events-standards-program/.

Relay Races

There has been dramatic growth over recent years in two types of relays—relays within existing marathons and long-distance relays, sometimes called "ultra-distance relays" or "overnight relays." Marathon relays are a good way to increase the number of runners at a marathon by providing an opportunity for people to participate while running a shorter distance as part of a relay team. Ultra-distance relays are generally point-to-point runs over long distances, such as the legendary Hood to Coast Relay, which extends 195 miles from Mt. Hood to the Oregon Coast, or the overnight American Odyssey Relay from Gettysburg to

Washington, D.C., or the Ragnar series held around the country. Although there are very serious participants in most every relay, relays generally fall more toward the "fun experience" side of the sport as opposed to the "competitive" side. One organizer referred to his overnight relay as "a 205-mile slumber party."

There are a number of other types of relay races that will not be discussed in much detail here, but the general details provided in this section will still apply. One example is the **Ekiden relay**. This is a variation of a marathon relay race imported from Japan. An Ekiden traditionally has two defined formats—a 5-person team format with legs (in this order) of 5K, 10K, 5K, 10K and 12.195K; or a 6-person format with legs of 5K, 5K, 10K, 5K, 10K, and 7.195K, although the number of legs, the distances of the legs and the total distance of the Ekiden can vary.

Marathon Relays

The Course

Nearly all marathon relays are run in conjunction with traditional marathons. The relay course is the same as the marathon course and the marathon and relay participants start together. Relay runner exchange points need not be at even mile marks—they can be set up in conjunction with marathon aid stations in order to double up on services.

Distinguishing Between Relay Runners and Marathoners

Relay runners should have bib numbers that are easily distinguishable from those of the marathon participants, so that the runners in each event will be able to tell each other apart. Some events make the relay bib numbers a composite of a team number plus a leg number such as "135-1," "135-2," "135-3," representing team 135's first-, second- and third-leg runners. Full marathoners are given sequential bib numbers as in standard races. Still, some marathoners can be a bit confused—and potentially thrown off pace—by the presence of marathon relay runners.

Team Numbers, Leg Lengths and Divisions

The length of each marathon relay leg is most frequently determined by the location of a suitable runner exchange zone, which can result in odd-distance legs lengths such as 4.3 or 6.7 miles. While the most frequent number of team members is 4, there are no fixed rules for the number of runners per team—this is up to the race director. With all the varying leg lengths and number of team members, marathon relay records are kept on an event-by-event basis, if at all.

In the drive to be all-encompassing, many events have a number of divisions for their marathon relays, including open men, open women, mixed teams, masters, grand masters, corporate teams, etc.

Registration Process

The key to the marathon relay registration process is to have all the team registrations come in together, rather than having the registrar figure out which people belong to which team. Most online registration platforms are equipped to handle team registrations. Online team relay registration generally requires that a team captain set up a team first (and pay the registration fee). If the team captain has the option to register the remaining team members, it is important that all team members still sign the required waivers somehow—either online or at packet pickup or on-site on race day. It's often easier to require all team members to register online individually after the team captain has set up the team. After they have registered as individuals, they can select their team from a drop-down list containing all of the teams that have already been set up. The details of how an existing team is selected during the registration process will vary according to the registration platform, but it is generally quite straightforward. If paper registration forms are still being used, require that all registrations for a team come in together with a single check for the entire team. In all team events, team member substitutions can be expected right up until race day, so make sure the race registrar understands the appropriate way to accomplish this using the chosen registration platform. In advance, review with the online provider the company's procedures for handling relay team registration.

Lastly, for safety reasons, keep track of who is running each leg of the relay. Capture this information from the team at some point before race day.

Transportation

Assuming that the marathon relay is not on a loop course with a common exchange point for every leg, you will be faced with the challenge of transporting outbound runners to the exchange points and bringing runners who have completed their legs back to the main staging area—all at different times. The easiest way to do this is to set up a continuous transportation loop between the start/finish area and the exchange points. Try to have enough buses so there is never more than a 20-minute gap between buses at any point in the circuit. If the course is point-to-point, this gets more complicated, because buses will need to make the circuit from both the start and finish areas. This is a good argument for having the start and finish lines close together if a marathon includes a relay component.

Timing and Exchange Points

As with any relay, timing each individual split is not an exact science. However, individual split times must be captured, because each individual relay team member will want his or her split time in addition to the final time for the entire team. If the event is using transponder-based timing, there will need to be transponder mats at every exchange point. With the mats in place, there are two options for scoring.

- **Single transponder used by the entire team:** For this method, there is *a single transponder* that may be attached to a bib, carried on a race belt or ankle/wrist strap, or laced into a shoe, and *is passed off from runner to runner at the end of each leg*. It is best to have the incoming runner cross the mat and then make the transponder exchange to the outgoing runner *after* crossing the mat. The incoming runner's finishing split becomes the starting split for the outgoing runner, although this will not take into account the time lost during the exchange. The advantage of this system is that the elapsed time on the single transponder is the total team time; the disadvantage is that the transponder needs to be physically passed from one runner to the next, like a baton in a track relay.

- **Separate transponders issued to each team member:** With this system, each runner on the team is registered as an individual and given a bib with a unique transponder. *Each runner's individual transponder is associated with his/her team.* The *incoming* runner's finishing transponder time is used as the *outgoing* runner's starting transponder time. The individual times are added up using the scoring software to obtain the team's total time. The advantage of this system is there are no hand-offs between runners; the disadvantage is the possibility of false transponder reads with more transponders around the mats at the exchange points.

- **Manual timing:** If manual timing is used at the exchange points, have a timer at each exchange who will take the split when the incoming runner crosses a line marking the start of the exchange zone. This split becomes the starting split of the outgoing runner as well. Most marathon relays do not use batons, but simply rely on a hand slap to mark the transition between the legs if there is no timing device to be exchanged. There are no rules governing the length of marathon relay exchange zones, as there are for track-and-field relays. Most events allow 30-50 yards after the transponder mat or split finish line to make the exchange.

Results

Although the marathon relay culture is somewhat laid back, you should still plan to make individual leg splits available in addition to the combined team time. Most timing/scoring software programs can handle this. If a relay option is planned as part of a marathon, be sure to talk to the race timers well in advance, as they will need to set up the scoring software properly to handle the inclusion of a relay into the event.

Ultra-Distance and Overnight Relays

Ultra-distance relays are truly the "Wild West" of the road racing world. Most long-distance relays cover a couple hundred miles, often on roads open to vehicular traffic. Most also require participants to provide their own transportation and their own aid. This creates a bit of a laissez-faire environment to these events, in stark contrast to the usually controlled environment of most road races.

The Course

The ultra-distance relay course is a key part of the event "experience," and these courses generally run across an entire state or between two well-known landmarks or along a particularly famous stretch of scenic trail or highway. Most distances average around 150 to 200 miles, although some are longer, and have leg lengths between 2.5 and 8 miles. The general assumption is that each runner will run 2-3 legs during the relay, so a 200-mile relay with 12 team members running 3 legs would work out to an average for each runner about 5.5 miles per leg; a 300-mile relay with a 12-person team works out to a little over 8 miles per leg. The size of the teams allowed and the number/lengths of the legs are entirely up to the race director.

Insurance and Permitting

The RRCA insurance policy *excludes* overnight relays unless they are held on closed, traffic-free courses, such as within parks. However, USATF does insure overnight relays. Insurance will need to be purchased on an event-by-event basis. Alternatively, insurance can be obtained from a private insurer, but this may prove more costly.

Do not assume that a relay does not require

permits just because no roadways will be shut down. Permits are always required if the course traverses federal land, such as national parks. The same almost always holds true for courses that include state parks. States and local municipalities all have differing permit requirements for overnight relays, so be sure to check on the requirements for every single jurisdiction that the course passes through. If the relay is point-to-point and extends for several hundred miles, the number of permits required can pile up.

Odyssey Relay

The exchange point in an overnight relay. The scenic courses can run a couple hundred miles. Participants run multiple legs on roadways that are not closed to traffic.

Registration Process

The registration process is similar to that of marathon relays or any other type of team event—a team captain creates a team and pays the fee, and then the other team members generally sign up, and sign waivers separately and then select the team they wish to join. The number of runners required to constitute a team is determined by the race director. Some long-distance relays have a 'standard' team size of 12-members, but also allow 'ultra' teams of 6 members (or even fewer) to compete. In a few instances, the team captains themselves can decide how many members will be on the team (up to a maximum number set by the race director).

Relay Logistics

If there is an upside to organizing an event as complicated as an ultra-distance relay, it is the fact that relay participants themselves shoulder many of the support functions normally provided by the race at traditional events. Ultra-distance relays would simply be cost- and labor-prohibitive if this were not the case. For example, the runners' vehicles are required to carry all of the water and other aid required by the team, saving the race organization this burden.

● **Runner safety:** The safety of relay participants should be the race director's primary concern. Anyone contemplating staging an ultra-distance relay needs to fully understand the intricacies involved in having runners spread out over miles of open roads, particularly at night. The course should be designed with runner safety in mind, and every mile of the course and every exchange point should be carefully studied for safety issues, specifically during the time of day when runners will be present. It is important to have clear, well-lit signage along the entire route, to make sure runners do not go off course and get lost, particularly at night. Do not assume that runners will rely on leg maps just because they are provided on the website or in runner instructions—signage is still crucial. Consider having volunteers, or better yet, local police or professional flaggers, at any and all intersections or areas that might prove even remotely dangerous—again, especially during the nighttime hours. Coordinate with local EMS in each town or jurisdiction that the course passes through so they will be on alert for any incidents during the relevant time frame.

- **Seeded start and time limits:** In order to reduce the amount of time the finish area has to remain open, and to thin out the flow of runners on the roadway (since the roads are not closed to vehicular traffic) during the relay, most ultra-distance relays reverse-seed their starts. This means that the slowest teams start first and the fastest teams last. In theory, this means that all the teams will finish within a narrower time frame. In keeping with the spirit of this type of relay, this also means that most of the teams are not competing head-to-head (except those who may have started at the same time).

Seeding relay teams is generally done by the honor system, with teams providing an approximate pace or finish time. Be aware that some teams may purposely provide a pace that is *slower* than they actually intend to run, just to get an earlier start time. This is a dangerous practice, as these teams will often arrive at the exchange points ahead of any volunteers or safety personnel. It's critical for relay directors to make participants aware that this 'sandbagging' is not allowed and will result in some sort of penalty for the entire team.

- **Exchange points:** An average 200-mile relay will have about 35 exchange points. Depending

on the course, many of these may be on private property, for which permission will clearly be required. Setting up such a large number of exchange points over such a great distance requires both tremendous organizational and relationship-building skills. Property owners need to be made aware that exchange points are busy places, with lots of foot and vehicular traffic, primarily consisting of larger vehicles, like vans. During the race, try to monitor each exchange area for any issues (excessive noise, trash, etc.) that may result in ill-will between the event and the property owner, limiting any situations that might damage the relationship or decrease the chances of being able to use that transition in future years.

- **How it works:** Most relays require that each team provide two support vehicles, one is called the "active" or "on" vehicle and the second is called the "stand-by" or "off" vehicle. The relay is usually divided into several primary exchange zones, with each primary exchange zone covering a number of legs/secondary exchange zones. The "active" vehicle makes the drop-offs and pick-ups at the secondary exchange zones until reaching a primary exchange zone. At this point, the "active" vehicle becomes the "stand-by" vehicle and can transport the runners who have finished to the next primary exchange zone. The "stand-by" vehicle, which is loaded with the participants for the next set of legs/secondary exchange points, becomes the "primary" vehicle. The two vehicles leapfrog each other to ensure that no one is spending an inordinate amount of time cooped up in a van.

- **Volunteers:** Most ultra-distance relays have a requirement that each team provides a specified number of volunteers to work the event, or they are assessed a 'volunteer fee' for each volunteer they do not supply. These fees are frequently donated to charity or may be used to hire necessary race-support personnel.

Most volunteers help at the transition points, directing traffic and keeping track of the teams that come through. The use of seeded start times has implications for volunteer management, because runners will be more spread out as they pass through the early transitions and become more concentrated as they approach the finish. Since volunteers should not be asked to work more than a few hours at a stretch, some transitions may require more than one shift of volunteers. Make sure that volunteer shifts overlap by at least 15 minutes, to account for late arrivals and adequate training/transition time. The increased density of runners passing through the later exchange points may necessitate a few more volunteers at these locations to keep things moving along smoothly.

- **Timing and scoring:** With such a large number of exchange points, most ultra-distance relays do not officially time each individual/each leg of the race, but instead focus on providing the overall time it takes for the team to complete the entire distance.

Additional Resources—The "Handbook"

If you are contemplating putting on an ultra-

distance relay, visit the website of an existing relay. Most established relays provide some sort of participant handbook, which has all the rules along with maps of each leg. Such a handbook will provide a far more detailed overview of the challenges involved in organizing this type of event. The team rules govern everything from substitutions, to policies about runners who drop out, to strict rules designed to minimize the relay's impact on the environment and neighborhoods. Breaking the rules can result in time penalties (30 or 60 minutes being added to a team's time) or disqualification. The handbook also includes a checklist of items that each support crew must have for its team members and details about running during nighttime and policies regarding extreme weather.

Kids' Runs

It is obvious to anyone who watches children at play that little ones love to run. Race directors and volunteers who tap into this energy by staging fun runs for children not only ensure a rewarding experience for themselves, but at the same time help to nurture future runners and encourage healthier lifestyles at a time when childhood obesity is at an all-time high.

A fun run for children should be just that—glorious fun. It should be non-competitive, in the sense that each child should be rewarded equally for completing the event, instead of emphasizing only the top finishers. Ideally, the age range for non-competitive kids' runs should be 12-and-under; children older than 12 are often already involved in competitive sports and probably have less interest in running purely for fun. The largest percentage of entrants will come from the younger age groups—interest in a kids' run is likely to peak by age eight. Some events have rolled back the oldest age group to ten-year-olds. See **Table 20-A** at left for typical age distributions at two kids' runs of different sizes.

Although kids' races should be pure fun for the children themselves, don't underestimate the

Table 20-A

Age Distributions at Kids' Runs

Age	Age 5-12 event with 300 participants		Age 0-12 event with 2,500 participants	
	%	Number	%	Number
1	n/a	n/a	5%	125
2	n/a	n/a	10%	250
3	n/a	n/a	10%	250
4	n/a	n/a	11%	275
5	21%	65	13%	325
6	20%	61	10%	250
7	13%	39	10%	250
8	16%	50	9%	225
9	11%	33	7%	175
10	7%	21	7%	175
11	7%	21	5%	125
12	6%	19	3%	75

amount of work, resources and manpower needed to manage a kids' event, even if it is an ancillary event at a larger adult race. Consider assigning a separate coordinator and, depending on the size of the kids' run, possibly an entirely separate committee, to focus on just this one area of the overall event.

Distances can be anything from 50 yards for toddlers (sometimes called a "diaper dash" or "diaper crawl") to one mile for older children. Most kids' runs offer several distances, and children can either be assigned a distance according to age, or the director can allow all kids to register for and run whichever distance they please.

Children's events can be stand-alone (i.e., held the day before a separate "adult" race, or at a time not linked in any way to the associated adult race, or simply not connected with any other event at all), or they may be closely tied in with an adult race, taking place just before, during, or just after the main race. The advantage of a stand-alone kids' run is that the focus is entirely on the children, and adult supervision is more readily available, since the adults are there solely for the sake of children and not to run their own race. The advantage of a kids' run that is part of an adult event is that the two events can share much of the same equipment, volunteers, and services, significantly decreasing the costs of putting on the kids' race. Many kids' runs allow parents to accompany their children during the run, without the parents having to register themselves. This is especially important for parents of children under the ages of 6 or 7 years old.

Table 20-B below shows the distances for a number of popular kids' runs and when the runs

Table 20-B

Kids' Runs at Several Events

Race name	When held	Distances
Army Ten Miler Kids Run Washington, DC	Day of 10M	5-7 years old: 100m
America's Kids Run Various military bases	Stand-alone *(not associated with any "adult" race)*	5-6 years old: 1/2 mile 7-8 years old: 1 mile 9-12 years old: 2 miles
Boilermaker Youth Run Utica, NY	Day before 15K	4-6 years old: 1/4 mile 7-8 years old: 1/2 mile 9-10 years old: 3/4 mile 11-12 years old: 1 mile
Cherry Blossom Kids' Run Washington, DC	Day before 10M	1/2 mile for all ages
Gasparilla Jr. Classic Tampa, FL	1 week before 15K	3-4 years old: 30 yards 5-6 years old: 1/8 mile 7-8 years old: 1/2 mile 9-10 years old: 1 mile
Quad City Times Bix 7M Davenport, IA	Day before 7M	1-and-under: 7-yard diaper dash 2-5 years old: 70-yard 6-7 years old: 1/2 mile 8-12 years old: .7 mile

were held in relationship to the "adult" event.

All aspects of a kids' run—refreshments, awards (medals are the favorite), music, warm-up exercises, and above all the design of the t-shirt—should be chosen to reflect the preferences of children. In particular, sponsors should be appropriate. If, for example, the major sponsor of a three-day running festival that includes a kids' run is a brewery, then it is wise to find a separate, more kid-friendly sponsor for the kids' run.

A kids' run tied into an adult race will generally have little difficulty attracting participants. Race directors of stand-alone kids' events can draw participants through local running clubs or YMCAs, or by working to establish training programs with local preschools or with PE teachers in the local elementary schools.

While some aspects of kids' runs make them easier to put on than adult runs (for example, the distances are short and there is no timing, multiple water stops are not necessary, no awards ceremony, etc.), some aspects of kids' runs present different challenges, which will be addressed below.

Special Considerations

Registration

- **Registration fees and t-shirts:** The registration fees for most kids' runs are low, especially relative to the escalating registration fees seen over recent years for adult races. There are still a few kids' runs that are free! The registration fee usually includes a youth-size t-shirt (youth sizes are generally Youth S (6-8), Youth M (10-12) and Youth L (14-16). Youth L shirts may not be vastly different in size from Adult XS or S shirts).

- **The registration process:** A critical factor in the registration process—whether it is done online or by paper registration forms—is to capture information about both the child and the parent, guardian or responsible adult *who will accompany the child on race day*. It is important to make sure this information does not get mixed up, so it is clear who is the child and who is the responsible adult. Ask for details about any special medical conditions, allergies, or other special needs of the child.

Maria Prince

The challenge at a Kids Run is to encourage the kids to avoid over-exuberance at the start.

See *Chapter 9: Insurance and Legal* for a sample kids' run waiver. If an online registration provider is being used, set up the form to allow one adult to register multiple children.

Linking Kids and Adults

The highest priority for a kids' run is a foolproof and efficient way to reunite kids with their parents at all times. It is critical that information about the child and the responsible adult be printed on a label located on the child's bib. Some races go a step further and give the adults a wristband with the same information printed on it. Volunteers will only release children to the adults with the matching information.

Other Logistical and Safety Concerns

- **Course:** Keeping children safe should be the primary concern. The course can be on a track, a closed road, a bike path, or around a field, but it is recommended that the course be a loop or an out-and-back so that parents can see both the start and finish of the event and can easily link up with their children at the finish. Some children may not be able to read signs and may be unfamiliar with the purpose of cones and directional arrows, so there should be plenty of course marshals along the route, each one within sight of another. An additional safety item, and a favorite with children, is to have a "rabbit," frequently in costume, on a bicycle, leading the way and making sure the public clears the course.

- **Water and porta-johns:** Most kids events mimic the amenities provided at adult runs if for no other reason than to provide "teachable moments" to kids about running events. It is useful to have pre- and post-race water, even if not much will be consumed. Of course porta-johns need to be ordered, and it may be good to have more handicapped units to allow parents to assist children, if necessary. Certainly the 1 to 100 ratio is more than adequate.

- **Announcer:** Using an announcer who is experienced in announcing Kids' Runs is important. The announcer needs to be calm but upbeat and able to clearly explain how the event will function and the event's timetable. If the event will feature multiple heats within each age group, the announcer should explain this structure to the adults.

- **Start:** In their eagerness, children often trip over one another at the start. To minimize this, plan multiple small heats by age (usually between 30-50 kids is ideal, although some events have larger heats). Some events line the kids up in multiple lines behind the starting line, with 10' or so of space between each line to allow a little more space at the start. Put adult volunteers in the first few rows to keep children amused and calm, and to signal the start of the run in a low-key way. Watch out for parents who stay on the course until the very last minute, taking photos or videos—they may also pose a safety risk to running children.

- **Parents running with their children:** Most Kids' Runs will allow parents to run along with their children in the younger age categories (6 and under). Some parents will insist on running with their children. Whatever policy you adopt, make it abundantly clear in all advance publicity, and then be flexible. Many events include a "special needs" heat for children of all ages with physical disabilities; other events make provisions to have special needs children participate with their age group. Parents usually run with their special needs children.

- **Finish and post-race reunions:** In a large kids' event with many finishers, getting the children and parents reunited can be a challenge. Even though there are no timing concerns, chutes and barricades are an ideal way to help not only with the efficient distribution of the medals or ribbons, but also to slow the kids down and prevent them from dispersing into the crowd too soon. A secure corral entirely enclosed by barricades (see an example in **Figure 20-1** below) beyond the chutes allows parents to catch sight of their children and await them at the various exits. In addition, a reunion location for children and their families should be well-located and publicized.

- **Medical:** Bruised/scraped knees and elbows resulting from falls are usually the major medical problem seen at kids' runs, so be sure that the medical team has plenty of Band-Aids and ice. Asthma attacks may also occur. And, depending on the time of year, bee stings and concomitant allergic reactions may happen—so make sure the medical team is well-prepared to treat potential anaphylactic reactions as well.

- **Post-race food and water:** If food is served, be sure to indicate if it contains nuts for the protection of children who are allergic.

- **Lost-child policy:** Think through and publicize widely—both in the pre-race instructions and through the race-day announcements—how lost children will be reunited with their parents. It is best to have a clearly marked, centrally located "Lost Child" area, well staffed with volunteers who can soothe crying children and panicked parents. A direct channel of communication between the lost child area and the race announcer is critical, so that the announcer can announce lost children on a timely basis, repeat the announcements as needed, and stop making them once the reunions are made. Also, prior to the event, have a discussion with local law enforcement personnel regarding how children who are not reunited with their parents will be handled. Some police departments have very rigid lost-child protocols that require lost children to remain in police custody until the parents are located.

Communication

Don't assume that all the parents of the children entered in the event are runners themselves or are even

Figure 20-1

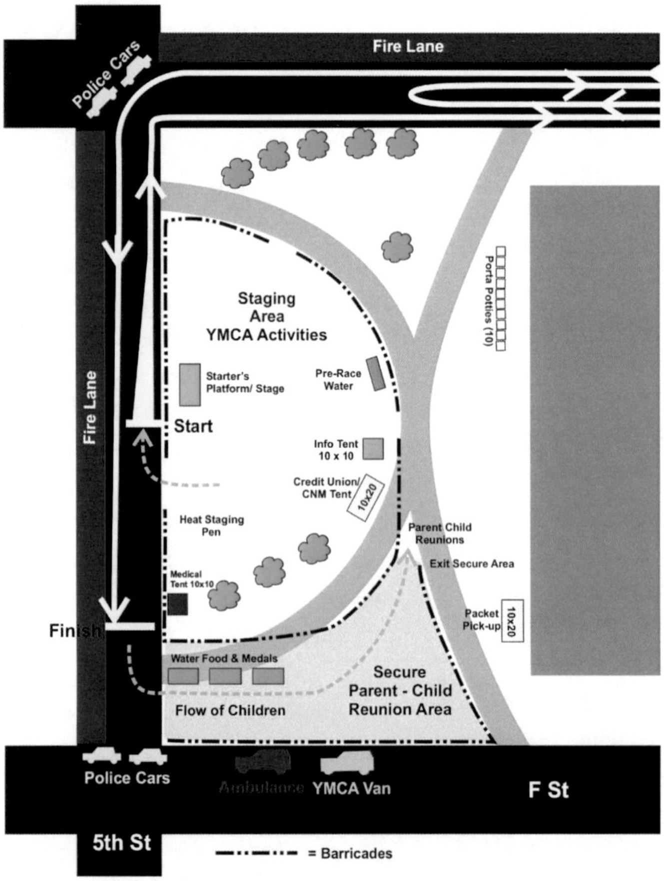

Reuniting parents and kids after a Kids' Run is imperative. Using a secure corral entirely enclosed by barricades can facilitate reunions in a safe area.

familiar with race procedures and running jargon. It is important to have as much information as possible, using very basic terminology, on the event website and registration form. No matter how clear the instructions, be prepared for a large number of questions about seemingly basic matters, such as whether the bib goes on the child's front or back, what the child should eat before the event, what the child should wear, whether the event will be held if it rains, etc.! Large, clear signs are important at the race site, but a good sound system and a knowledgeable announcer are even more critical.

Additional Resources

Details about kids' running programs are available on the RRCA website at http://www.rrca.org/our-programs-services/programs/kids-run-the-nation/resources/youth-running-events

Cross Country Meets

Many long-time runners got their start running cross country in high school or college and have fond memories of the team camaraderie that the sport engenders. Staging a cross country race will enable these runners to reconnect with their memories. Incorporating a cross country meet into a running club's schedule also provides a nice alternative to a steady diet of road races. Cross country races in the U.S. traditionally take place during the fall, although they can be scheduled at any time of year. Internationally, cross country events may take place during the winter months leading up to the IAAF World Cross Country Championships, which is held in odd numbered years in late March, or the Pan Am Cup, held in even-numbered years in late February or early March. USATF conducts its club cross country championship in late November or early December and its individual cross country championships (used to select the U.S. team to compete in the IAAF event) in early February.

Here are some points to consider in the staging of a cross country race.

- **Distances:** Most cross country events range in distance from three to seven miles. Cross country courses cannot be certified, and it is more acceptable than in standard road races to have "odd" distances, such as 5.2 miles, etc. This gives the organizers greater flexibility in setting up courses. For the record, the IAAF and USATF standard distances are 10K for men and 8K for women; the NCAA Championships are 10K for men and 6K for women. Masters men's and women's events range from 6K (masters women of all ages) to 10K (masters men under 60) to 8K (masters men 60 and over). The bottom line is any distance within these ranges is acceptable.

- **Types of courses:** Many cross country events are held on golf courses or other wide-open parks. When designing a course, make sure it does not narrow too quickly right after the start; you want to allow runners to thin out before reaching any narrow sections. Some courses do incorporate portions on trails. In general, however, cross country courses are different—more wide open—than trail running courses. For example, the NCAA mandates a minimum width for championship courses of five meters. Cross country courses are often designed to have multiple loops, so that coaches and spectators can see how the race is unfolding without having to walk long distances. At the international level, a standard world course is a 2K loop.

- **Marking the course:** Most cross country courses are marked with a combination of flags and powdered arrows (lime, flour or temporary spray paint). Be cognizant that if there are multiple heats or multiple loops, powdered arrows will degrade as more and more runners pass over them. The flags should be in pairs so the runners will be expected to "split" the flags, meaning run between them like a slalom course in skiing.

Chris Lotsbom

Cross country races generally take place in the fall on golf courses or other open off-road venues.

Each set of flags should be easily visible from the preceding set. If possible, incorporate a final straightway to the finish line, so runners can see the finish and plan their finishing kicks.

- **On-course amenities:** Because of the shorter distances of cross country courses, aid stations are generally not set up on the courses. Obviously, both pre- and post-race fluids should be available. There should also be medical aid on site, as with any road race. The medical team may see more sprains, cuts and abrasions from falls than in a traditional road race, especially if the course has narrow, twisting sections on trails. A common feature of cross country meets is a golf cart or gator with a medical person trailing the last runner.

- **Timing and scoring:** Cross country is historically a team sport, so you may want to consider keeping with this tradition and

incorporate teams. However, more informal meets may not have a team element. Many events use transponder-based timing, although smaller meets may just hand out index cards at the finish. Participants will appreciate mile marks and split times on the course, even if the overall distance is an odd distance. If a team competition is included, USATF rules call for the *results to be calculated based on place*, by adding up the finish places of the scoring runners. The low score wins. Cross country teams generally consist of seven runners, with the top five being included in the scoring. The non-scoring runners, called "pushers," serve to push back the places of members of other teams. For example, if seven runners from Team A come in the first seven places and the top five score, Team A totals 15 points (1+2+3+4+5) from its scoring runners and its non-scoring "pushers" occupy 6th and 7th place. This means that the first

Team B runner, finishing 8th, will score 8 points instead of the 6 points that person would score if the places of the pushers were not included in the team scoring. Some events that choose not to use USATF rules may score the teams by combined time (adding the times of the scoring runners, with the lowest combined time winning). (For a complete discussion of Team Scoring, see *Chapter 14: Rules of Competition.*)

Additional Resources

Detailed rules about the conduct of cross country meets are contained in the USATF Rule Book available on the USATF website at www.usatf.org. Many of these rules may be more technical than required for informal meets, but they provide an overall framework for conducting a cross country event.

Track Meets

Long-time runners who didn't start out by running cross country may have had their first running experiences on a track and field team. According to the National Federation of State High School Associations, track and field is the top participatory sport for girls and second highest for boys. As with a holding a cross country meet, including a track meet in a running club's schedule

can help runners return to their racing roots and provide additional variety in the type of races available.

Outdoor track and field in the U.S. is primarily a spring sport, with high school and college seasons typically starting in March and early April and culminating in State and National Championships in May and June. Early and mid-season meets are usually an assortment of dual meets and Invitationals. The USATF Outdoor Championship meet is held annually in late June (the Olympic Trials are held at this meet every four years) and the IAAF World Championships are held every other August in the odd numbered years. Low-key running club track meets are frequently held on summer evenings when the temperature is warm and there is light later into the evening.

While the NCAA Championships have 21 track and field events for both men and women (and high schools a slightly lesser number), a track meet for a *distance-oriented running club* will likely include only a handful of these events and none of the field events. For a variety of reasons—including marginal interest, lack of equipment and liability concerns—the only races a road race director of a stand-alone track meet is likely to want to hold are some mix of the 800 meter, the 1500m/1600m/1-mile, and the 3000m/3200m/2-mile, 5,000m and 10,000m. If you want to be more adventuresome, some relays can be

Hayward Field in Eugene, OR is the most celebrated track in the U.S. *Chris Lotsbom*

added, such as the 4x400m, 4x800m and distance medley (legs of 1200, 400, 800 and 1600m, in that order) relays. A small number of clubs still hold one-hour track runs that are scored by the amount of distance participants can cover in exactly 60 minutes, and 24-hour track relays, which are team relay events consisting of one-mile legs with generally ten people on a team. These relays are scored by the amount of distance teams cover in 24 hours. These events require extensive documentation, either by volunteers or transponder mats, of the laps or miles covered by each participant.

Logistics

Track meets are relatively easy to organize and manage, and the logistics are much less demanding than those required for a typical road race. The first priority is to locate an available track. Check with local high schools and colleges to determine the procedure and cost for renting the track. If the event will be held in the evening, ask whether there is an additional charge to use the track lighting—in many cases there is. Also check to see if you can arrange to open the building that provides access to the bathrooms. Both USATF and RRCA insurance policies cover track meets, although the school may request to be listed as an additional insured party on the policy.

In staging a track meet, there is no need to be concerned with road crossings, course marshals at intersections, police support, course layout or remote aid stations. Also, the course map is extremely easy to draw! In addition to the registration, refreshment and timing crews that are used at traditional road races, you'll also need a starter, an announcer and two or three volunteers to help the runners keep track of the number of laps they have completed and to direct finishers into the chute.

Depending on the total number of runners expected at the meet, you'll likely want to hold heats. These can be done either by age groups or finishing time; you'll likely find that finishing times make more sense, as you'll be better able to control the time schedule of the meet and the heats will be more competitive. Rough guidelines for the number of runners in each heat are 15 for the 800m, 25-30 for the mile, 35-40 for the 2 mile and 8-10 teams for the relays. The announcer will need to be diligent about announcing the upcoming events and keeping everyone informed about the time table—especially if you begin to fall behind the published schedule. The announcer might say something like "lining up on the track now is the first heat of the men's 1-mile run; this will be followed by the first heat of the women's mile, which should start in about 15 minutes..." With so many individual events, it is important for everyone to know the schedule. Two sample track meet schedules are provided in **Table 20-C** at left.

Due to lapping and the need to provide each runner with a clear path to the finish line, you'll

Table 20-C

Sample Track Meet Schedules

Going Green Track Meet:

6:45 PM	Young Runs of 1/4 and 1/2 miles
7:00	Two Mile—First Heat 12:00 minutes and faster
7:15	Two Mile—Second Heat 12:00-14:00
7:35	Two Mile—Third Heat 14:00-17:00
7:55	Two Mile—Fourth Heat 17:00 and slower
8:20	One Mile—First Heat 6:00 and faster
8:30	One Mile—Second Heat 6:00 and slower
8:45	4×400m Relay 5:00 and slower
8:55	4×400m Relay 5:00 and faster

Midsummer Night's Mile:

Heat 1 - Runners with expected times greater than 8:45.
Heat 2 - Runners with expected times greater than 7:50 up to 8:45.
Heat 3 - Runners with expected times greater than 7:00 up to 7:50.
Heat 4 - Runners with expected times greater than 6:15 up to 7:00.
Heat 5 - Runners with expected times greater than 5:45 up to 6:15.
Heat 6 - Runners with expected times greater than 5:20 up to 5:45.
Heat 7 - Runners with expected times greater than 4:50 up to 5:20.
Heat 8 - Runners with expected times of 4:50 or less.

likely want to set up the finish chute and timing equipment in the outer lanes. If transponder timing is used, this could require as many as 3 lanes (or perhaps just 2 lanes for a manual scoring system) for the timing mats and chutes, so an 8-lane track (or some space outside the outer lane) is preferable. However, a 6-lane track will also suffice, although you might want to reduce the heat sizes by several runners to reduce overcrowding in the first lap or two.

Additional Resources

Detailed rules about the conduct of track meets are contained in the USATF Rule Book, available on the USATF website at www.usatf.org. Many of these rules may be more technical than required for informal meets, but they provide an overall framework for conducting a track meet.

Road Miles

In 1981, just five years after launching the five-borough New York City Marathon, New York Road Runners President Fred Lebow started the Fifth Avenue Mile—a point-to-point race down one of the world's most famous avenues—as a second venture to bring high profile running events to the streets of major cities around the world. The road miles were designed primarily as spectator events, with fields generally limited to world class milers. The New York City model was quickly emulated in major cities around the world, including Paris, Rome, Copenhagen and Toronto. Although the Fifth Avenue Mile continued, interest in road miles faded until the 2010s when an organization called Bring Back the Mile rekindled interest. Today the organization coordinates a mainly U.S.-based circuit of road miles for all ages. Road miles are generally run on point-to-point courses down city streets, although a few—such

as the BAA Mile—feature criterium-style courses to enhance spectator interest. The logistical advantages of a road mile over a longer race are fewer and shorter time limits for street closures. Elite heats should be kept small—20-30 individuals maximum—and should be scored on gun times. Less competitive heats may have several hundred and may be created based on sex and age-group (frequently middle school, high-school, college, open and masters) or by anticipated finishing time. These heats may be scored on net times. Depending on the number of entrants and the number of different categories, a road mile event may have 10-12 separate heats.

Road miles, such as the BAA Mile shown here, have gained popularity in recent years.

For details about the Bring Back the Mile circuit, visit www.bringbackthemile.com

Training Groups and Programs

Many races, running clubs and specialty running retailers have had success offering multi-week training workshops to help people prepare for a specific event. Although running seems like a pretty straight-forward sport, it is intimidating to many—especially the total non-athlete, those who have become unfit in recent years, or otherwise active people who are new to running. Even casual joggers often think that entering a race is only for "real" runners. A gradual, progressive, structured, training program in a group setting, or through daily emails with short "how-to" talks, can educate, motivate and nurture these potential participants into becoming new registrants, as well as your most appreciative fans!

These programs, which can be in-person, online, or a combination of both, can benefit everyone—the training group participant, the event, the sponsors, the club and the community—in many ways. Training programs also increase the base of runners participating in the sport of running, which is good for the future health of both participants and the sport itself. In most cases, when races offer a pre-race training program, participants pay an additional fee for the program. Thus, conducting a training group can be a revenue producer for an event or club. Fees for programs vary depending on what is offered and whether the program is online-only or involves in-person training. Participants can enroll in the training program when they register for the race. If the race has an apparel or shoe company sponsor, consider outfitting the training program participants in the sponsor's brand.

In-Person Training Programs

In-person training programs are a great way to build both enthusiasm and event loyalty. However, in-person programs require participants to travel to a specific location (or rotating locations) to participate. Training programs add to the workload of what may be an already stretched race committee. If an event has an appropriate sponsor or a specialty running retailer involved with it, individuals from these companies may be willing to conduct the program from their location. Here are some of the logistics involved with in-person training programs and some guidance on conducting them successfully.

- **Who will lead the program?** This certainly is the first and most important challenge. It's critical to find a running enthusiast with good organizational and leadership skills. Consider whether you, or anyone on the race team, knows someone with the requisite skill set. Here are some possibilities:

  - **A certified coach:** Both the RRCA and USATF have coaching certification programs. The RRCA program focuses solely on coaches of distance running events, while USATF's program includes certification for various track and field events. Details appear in the "Additional Resources" section below.

  - **Teacher:** A physical education teacher or most any teacher who loves the sport of running will probably have the necessary skills to communicate, motivate and educate the trainees.

  - **Good runner:** Sometimes this is a benefit. But be sure the runner can empathize with complete beginners. Sometimes a top local standout can appear too talented and intimidating to newbies. The person chosen to lead the training has to want to spread the gospel of fitness. Many times, an average runner can be more motivating than a star. ("If she could do this when she's got a job, two kids and was 20 pounds heavier, then I can, too!")

  - **Healthcare sponsor:** Sometimes a local hospital or healthcare provider may be willing to take on the responsibility of a training program as part of its sponsorship and community outreach. The hospital or healthcare provider may provide the staff to give the talks and monitor participants' progress.

- ◆ **Specialty Running Retailer:** A local specialty running retailer may take on this job—after all, brand new runners need everything (shoes, clothes, watches, etc.)!
- ◆ **A vociferous enthusiast:** A general race/ running enthusiast (or two or three) could fit the bill, as long as the individuals are knowledgeable about safe training, willing to ask for help from experts when needed, and enjoy helping people improve. Training is a very rewarding job! Willing individuals

may find that sharing the responsibility for the training program with another friend or two makes the task less daunting. Ask the race committee for recommendations and invite those people to consider it—they're often flattered to be asked. Frequently, these enthusiasts will enroll in one of the certified coaching programs outlined above.

- ● **Where should the training be held?** Some obvious places in the local community may come to mind. A park with pedestrian trails is ideal, if it's conveniently located for the target audience. Sometimes a healthcare sponsor or fitness facility has safe paths or a good running route on or around their property.

Phil Stewart

The Students Run LA training group gathers for their graduation race at the LA Marathon.

Local tracks and school parking lots are other options. Even quiet residential streets offer opportunities. When selecting a location for the training program, keep the following in mind:

- **Safety:** The training course should be safe from vehicles, safe from any criminal element, easy to follow so that people don't get lost, etc. Also, trails or roads should have even surfaces or any existing hazards should be well marked.
- **Convenience:** Try to make the meeting location convenient to participants' workplaces or homes.
- **Parking:** The meeting location should have adequate, convenient (and ideally, free) parking.
- **Toilets:** Facilities should be clean, functioning and open at the time the training will be held. If there aren't any bathroom facilities available, consider renting a porta-john for the duration of the program (and locking it between sessions). Porta-john rental can be fairly affordable, so check with local vendors. If there are not going to be any toilets or porta-johns available at the training location, be sure to let the participants know.
- **Congregating place and/or speaker system:** Most of the time, participants can sit on the ground or stand while listening to a speaker or while the day's workout is being explained, but amphitheaters, pavilions, or inside rooms are nice, especially if someone will be talking to the group for more than a few minutes. A speaker system may not be necessary, depending on the group size, but a portable microphone might be a worthwhile investment if the attendance is large.
- **How long should the training last and when should it be held?** The timing of the training program depends on:
  - **The target audience:** If you want to develop brand new walkers and runners out of couch

potatoes, you'll need to offer a longer program. If you want to take an existing casual runner and get him or her ready for the race, program duration may be shorter.
  - **Length of program and event distance:** Marathon training programs should last 3-6 months; 5K training programs 6-12 weeks. Middle distance (10 miles, half marathons, etc.) may fall in the middle.
  - **Time of the year and other considerations:** Selection of a meeting time will be dictated in part by things like darkness and heat. After-work programs allow for the largest audience, since stay-at-home parents or students can make this time, as well as those who work nine-to-five. For those reasons, a 6:00 PM workshop works well. If it's dark at 5:00 PM during the span of the program, however, an after-work meeting time probably won't work unless the location is well lit. If darkness is an issue, try for a weekend morning program, but bear in mind that this can conflict with other family obligations. Mid-day programs will definitely limit the audience. After-school times are good for teachers.
- **How should the program be marketed?** Make the training program part of the race promotion, assuming you have the lead time to do so. Put program information on the race website and advertise using social media. Also consider sending a blast email with program details to the target audience, and even to past participants. Paper flyers can also be posted at workplaces, fitness centers, specialty retailers, and grocery stores. Don't be afraid to market the program to existing runners—they are the enthusiasts and influencers and will recruit others.
- **Waivers:** When people sign up for the training program, they should sign a waiver specific to the program and separate from the waiver that they sign when they register for the race. Be sure to indemnify all parties involved in providing the training.

Other Considerations

- **Topic suggestions:** The talks at the beginning of each training session might cover training principles, nutrition, shoe and sports bra selection, injury prevention, safety, stretching, motivation, etc. Keep the talks short and very basic (15 minutes maximum).

- **Liability insurance.** This is absolutely essential for any training program. Get it through a local running club, the race itself, the host sponsor or store, etc. RRCA and USATF insurance policies both cover training programs.

- **Reward attendance.** Make participants earn their graduation shirts—don't give them out until after the program is over, and consider requiring them to attend a certain number of classes. Although the "graduation" race may miss out on some early exposure, participants will be more motivated to complete the program.

- **Get help.** Invite friends to help mentor the participants so that more individualized attention can be offered. Get experts in to speak on topics in which the program leaders aren't fluent.

- **Base the training on time, not miles.** A mile may be too far for many beginners. Base the program on the *amount of time* participants have run. A reasonable beginner's goal might be to walk or run for stretches of five minutes, not to run or walk a whole mile.

- **Invite walkers.** Walkers also enjoy the camaraderie of training in a group setting. Some walkers may even eventually become runners if the program is gradual enough and they are motivated by those around them. However, walking in itself is good exercise and a worthwhile achievement—welcome walkers into the training program and into the event, if possible.

- **Gender-specific.** All-women's workshops can draw a large attendance, especially for beginners. Co-ed classes sometimes limit the number of women because they are self-conscious and worry whether they can keep up.

- **Make it fun!** People tend to enjoy those things that they can do successfully, so make the progression very gradual, and be sure to make it fun! Praise and motivate the runners as much as possible.

- **Publicity.** Offering a 6-12 week training program leading up to the event can bring additional exposure 4-5 months prior to race day.

  - ◆ Spread the word about the training program widely on social media. Encourage interested individuals to share the information with their friends.

  - ◆ Search out and pitch the human interest stories among the training group participants. Or invite a media or political celebrity to participate in the program. If a local celebrity is involved, this can provide the program some nice publicity—you could 'follow' the celebrity trainee from class day #1 to graduation and on to the race, posting details of his/her progress on social media. Some traditional media outlets may also publicize the training schedule in a public service column, or give it air time, increasing the reach of the program.

  - ◆ Certain sponsors (healthcare facilities, doctors, specialty retailers, etc.) can offer speakers on certain topics and thus be incorporated into the educational aspect of the program and, in doing so, gain exposure.

  - ◆ If participants enjoy the program, they often become the event's biggest promoters. They will want to share their newfound enthusiasm with others.

- **Community service.** Programs promoting healthy lifestyles for locals are a great way to give back to the community that is hosting the event. This sort of community service may even help you negotiate with the city or county and possibly lower some costs for use of their facilities and personnel.

Online Training Programs

The number of online training programs has expanded greatly in recent years. These programs use email, social media, Smartphone apps, and devices like FitBits and Garmins to help runners train remotely, on their own. When runners register and pay the fee for these programs, they usually supply details about their current training routine, including weekly mileage, etc. This enables the online vendor to create a program targeted to the individual. Participant fees can very widely depending on the level of individual service and length of the program, ranging from free to several hundred dollars a year. Runners can easily collect data about their daily runs, their vital signs, etc., which can either be studied by a remote coach or entered into some sort of automated training software. The number of companies providing these programs and services continues to grow. An event director can choose one of these programs and tie it in to his/her event. Generally, if you decide to use an online program, you will essentially be licensing the online company to offer coaching in return for a percentage of the income earned by the company.

The biggest advantage of online training programs is their convenience. Program participants can train from their homes or workplaces according to their own schedules—they do not have to block out specific times each week for meeting up with the group, or worry about traveling to the location of the trainings. However, participants in online programs miss out on the both the fun and camaraderie of training with others and the specific, real-time coaching feedback that is only really available in an in-person training environment.

Additional Resources

- For details about RRCA certified coaches visit: http://www.rrca.org/our-programs-services/programs/coaching-program

- For details about USATF certified coaches visit: http://www.usatf.org/Resources-for---/Coaches/Coaching-Education.aspx

Dennis Steinauer

 # Before Next Year

"The first year we did it, it was a complete disaster. I didn't know what the [heck] I was doing. It was a real embarrassment to me. That's why I did it the second year."

> — Ed Froehlich, Director, Quad-City Times Bix 7 Mile, on his first year as race director. The race now attracts over 19,000 entrants and pays out over $50,000 in prize money.

"The speed with which you improve your event is exceeded only by the velocity of the runners' demands."

> — Tim McLoone, Former Director, New Jersey Waterfront Marathon

THE BASICS

- There are a number of activities to consider in the months after the previous event is concluded and before the following year's event planning gets under way in earnest. These include:

- **Conducting a participant survey** to obtain feedback about the runners' experiences at the event.

- **Assessing the event's sustainability efforts** by collecting stakeholder feedback. Sustainability questions can be incorporated into a participant survey, but sponsors, vendors, volunteers and municipal officials should also be polled.

- **Undertaking an economic impact study (**for large events of several thousand or more runners) to provide demographic data for prospective sponsors and spending data for city officials to use as justification for closing the roads and providing city services.

- **Documenting event organization and procedures** in the form of an "Operations Manual."

- **Formulating a contingency or disaster plan** to determine responses to a variety of emergency situations.

- **Hosting a committee retreat** where a long-range plan can be developed in a relaxed environment well-removed from the pressures of the event.

- **Taking care of yourself** a bit after the stresses and rigors of staging the race, rejuvenate yourself and avoid race director (or committee member) burnout during the "off-season."

THE DETAILS

After the race is over, the results are finalized, the unclaimed awards shipped out, and the thank-you letters sent, a race director might feel a strong temptation to go into hibernation for six months. There are a number of activities, however, that can be extremely beneficial to the event and are better done during the "slow" or "off" season. This chapter outlines a number of longer-term activities that might be considered, along with a section dealing with race director burnout (which also is best addressed during this time).

Participant Surveys

Event Feedback Surveys

Surveys are a great way to find out how the participants felt about various aspects of the race. Armed with the survey results, you can determine what was done well and which areas need improvement. If you plan to do a survey, aim to send it out within a few days (or at least no more than a week) after the race in order to maximize the response rate.

There are a number of online survey platforms that are easy and inexpensive to use, with SurveyMonkey (www.surveymonkey.com) being the most popular tool as of this writing. Facebook also offers opportunities to create surveys to be posted on Facebook pages. While some online survey platforms are free to use, most charge a small monthly fee for access to all of the features of the platform or for sending out multiple surveys within a given timeframe. Survey platforms generally help with everything, including designing the survey, emailing/distributing the survey, maintaining contact lists (including an option for people to opt out of future surveys), and tabulating the results. Some online registration companies provide survey services as well. It may take a few hours to learn how to create and send electronic surveys, but the time will be well spent. Once the survey is created, take the survey yourself or test it out on a few friends to see if it is intuitive. Make changes as needed. Analyze the data submitted by the survey testers to see if the survey questions actually provide the data you are looking for. Be patient before hitting the "send" button to release the survey to the public.

Kinds of Questions to Ask on Surveys

When creating your survey, break out the various facets of the event and ask participants to use a scale to rate how the event performed or rated in each area. Some areas might include: pre-registration procedures, packet pick-up, registration fee, awards categories, t-shirts/premiums, prizes/awards, availability of porta-johns, the course, starting procedures, crowd control, mile markers, aid stations, finish line, parking, race start time, pre-race events, post-race events, and sustainability initiatives/efforts. This is only a sampling of the areas runners can be questioned about—tailor the survey to the particular event. Include an opportunity for participants to add comments to supplement their answers. Although "comments" can't be tabulated, they provide extremely valuable feedback without the rigidity of ratings or simple "yes" or "no" responses.

In addition to requesting information about each area of the race, participants might be asked to rate the *importance* of each function. This helps with better allocation of resources, allowing more time and energy to be channeled into improving those functions that matter most to the runners. For example, if low scores are received about shower and changing facilities, but the runners indicate that this is a function they really don't care about, then improvements are probably not needed. Better to use those resources improving the starting procedure, if runners indicate that this is very important to them and they feel it wasn't handled as well as it could have been. Conversely, there may be some highly rated functions that the runners don't care about much. For example, if high ratings are received for the fact that a large number of team award categories are included, but runners rate this as very low on the importance scale, then some of the categories can potentially be eliminated—saving money on awards without negatively affecting runners' perceptions of the event. It is important to keep some perspective— no event can be everything to every runner— choices have to be made, and the survey can help make these decisions.

Don't make the survey too long; most runners will want to be able to complete it in less than five minutes. It is probably best to send out the survey within a few days to no more than a week after the race. Although runners are usually pretty responsive to requests for feedback (response rates may run as high as 30-40%), it sometimes helps to offer a premium, such as a free registration for next year's race, to a couple of people randomly selected from those who complete the survey. [**Note:** go to www.random.org for a handy, free program that will select random numbers within a given range of numbers.]

Social Media Feedback

If the event was small, or if a survey just seems like an overly formal method of collecting feedback, paying close attention to social media is another great way to obtain relevant information about how the event was received by the participants. In the hours and days after the event, closely monitor the postings on the event's social media sites/pages and keep notes of consistent themes or any improvements suggested. Consider asking simple, direct questions such as "what could we do better next year?" or "what did you like best about the event?" Again, keep track of the responses, especially opinions expressed by multiple people. Using social media for this purpose is a great way to establish a personal rapport with race participants. Try to respond to *all* comments, even if it's with a simple "thank you for your input" or "let's take this conversation offline."

Be aware that social media is a double-edged sword. While it can be a great way to engage with participants and obtain feedback, it can also serve as a very public way for participants to rant about the race if they are unhappy. Be prepared for some vocal, negative comments. Address them calmly and tactfully, taking the discussion offline, if necessary. Some event directors actively monitor social media and remove negative posts that are 'out of line.' Use this power sparingly, however—many participants consider it a kind of censorship. Determine in advance what types of posts to disallow—for example, those containing profanity or language that is personally attacking can be considered fair game for removal, while general complaints, even if perceived as 'unfair,' should probably stay. No matter how negative the comments get, remember that your response defines you (and the event!) Stay professional and don't take anything personally.

If you receive negative comments on social media, you may want to delay responding for a brief time to see if the negative comments get reinforced, either with "likes" or comments. It is possible that a negative comment from a disgruntled individual may simply fade away, meaning nearly no one else felt the same way. However, if a comment "goes viral," be prepared to post the event's explanation quickly.

Economic Impact Surveys

As mentioned in **Chapter 13: Municipal Relations,** economic impact statistics for larger events can be extremely useful to show local municipalities exactly how the road race benefits the community. An economic impact study analyzes the amount of money that participants, their family members and friends spend in the community while in town for the event, on such items as hotels, restaurants, shopping, and entertainment. These studies also capture direct spending done by the race organizers in conjunction with the race. From these figures, additional statistics can be derived, like additional tax revenue and even employment opportunities the event generates for the local area.

A positive economic impact within the community can help cities and towns justify closing city streets and providing municipal support for the event. While there are standard survey assumptions and methodologies—the most basic of which is to define "out-of-town visitor" as anyone who travels more than 50 miles to the event—there is still wide variation from survey to survey. Both the organization undertaking the survey and the municipality using the survey like to be able to tout impressive figures to justify support of the event, which means that there is a tendency to create reports that produce astronomical figures for the economic impact.

Economic impact studies consistently show that marathons have a greater impact than shorter distance races, since marathoners tend to stay in the area for longer periods of time, bring more family and friends to spectate, and do more celebrating in the form of dining out or even shopping afterwards. Economic impact studies

from major marathons like Boston and New York show impacts of over $100 million dollars as of this writing (see **Table 21-A**).

Many event directors will turn to a local college or university and approach a marketing or business professor, asking him/her to perform such a survey as a class project. Alternatively, there are companies who will conduct these surveys on a contract basis. As a last resort, information can be gathered by the event director, using one of the electronic survey companies mentioned above. One downside of doing the survey internally is that it lacks the imprimatur of an organization or business experienced in conducting these surveys, which may cast doubt on the methodology with the municipalities reviewing the results. Although the survey can be conducted electronically, many survey groups rely on interviews taken over the course of race weekend, generally at the race expo. The interviewers (this is where working with a class of students really pays off) ask attendees if they traveled more than 50 miles to get to the event. If the answer is no, the interviewer thanks them and moves on. If the individual answers "yes," the interviewer proceeds to a list of additional questions, which might include:

- How many nights are you staying in town?

- Are you staying in a hotel or with a friend or family member?

- How many people came with you on your trip?

- How many meals will you eat in restaurants during your stay?

- What other entertainment will you attend while in town (movies, professional sports games, theater performances, etc.)?

- How much do you anticipate spending on the following during your stay:
  - Hotel
  - Food
  - Shopping
  - Entertainment
  - Transportation

CHAPTER 21 - Before Next Year

* Sight-seeing
* Race Expo

The same set of questions can be asked of both spectators and expo vendors.

In order for the results to have validity, the survey should be administered to between 5 and 10% of the race participants. The results from this sample can then be extrapolated to cover all of the runners in the event.

In addition to participant, vendor, and spectator expenditures, include the expenditures incurred by the race organization in staging the event. The event's financial statements and tax records should provide a clear picture of how much money the event organization is bringing to the city and state.

Once the dollar amounts contributed by the event have been established, the amount of additional sales tax revenue provided to the city by the event can be calculated by using the local tax rates in the area.

A Word About Multipliers

All of the spending discussed above is what is known as "direct spending," which refers to expenditures made as a direct result of the race itself. Some organizations will include "multipliers," which take into account that the money spent by race organizers and by runners results in further money being spent in the city as a result of the initial outlay of cash. For example, if a runner comes to town for a race and buys a meal in a restaurant and tips the waiter, the waiter now has more money to spend. If he spends that money in the city, the expenditure is considered an economic impact of the event based on multipliers.

TABLE 21-A

Economic Impact of Various Events

Listed below are economic impact figures released by a number of large marathon and non-marathon events in recent years. Differences in methodology make a direct comparison of these figures challenging.

Event	Year	Participants	Claimed impact
Austin Marathon	2016	3,169 marathoners; 8,108 marathoners, 790 5K	$25.3 million
Boston Marathon	2015	30,000	$181.9 million
Chicago Marathon	2013	30,000	$253 million
Cowtown Marathon	2016	28,000 in multiple events	$10.1 million
500 Festival Half Marathon	2013	30,000	$19.7 million
Fredericksburg Historic Half Marathon	2013	7,806 finishers in half marathon, 10K, 5K combined	$21 million
Honolulu Marathon	2012	31,000 entrants	$130 million
Marine Corps Marathon	2013	30,000 entrants	$88 million
Miami Marathon	2013	11,656 in marathon, half marathon	$15.8 million
New York City Marathon	2014	50,000 finishers	$415 million
Rock 'n' Roll Las Vegas Marathon	2015	46,000 entrants	$226 million

Page 445

Multipliers can boost the direct spending from two to five times. However, the use of multipliers is controversial within the survey industry and many firms have abandoned using them.

Once economic impact data has been collected and if the figures are impressive (as they usually are), don't keep it a secret! Plan to let the media know about those numbers—either at a race press conference or via a press release or on the event website. Be sure to trumpet the data before tight-fisted municipal government personnel as well.

Demographic Surveys

Demographic surveys are designed to gather demographic data about event participants for use in approaching sponsors. (Frequently, a demographic survey will be coupled with an economic impact survey, although demographic surveys should be drawn from *all runners* in the event, not just those from out-of-town.) Considerably less complicated than an economic impact study, the basic questions in a demographic survey include such things as sex, age, household income, and education level. Additional questions can be tailored toward specific sponsor categories such as "Do you plan to purchase any of the following in the next two years: a car, a new home, a boat, a Smartphone, a large screen TV, etc.," or "Are you the person in your family who makes decisions about health care or about investments?" Demographic surveys can be performed using the electronic survey tools outlined above in *Event Feedback Surveys.*

If it is the first year of the event, or if a survey isn't feasible, some general demographics of runners can be found on the websites of the industry trade association Running USA (www.runningusa.org), the Road Runners' Club of America (www.rrca.org) or from advertising "kits" provided by running publications. Some online registration companies may also provide demographic data aggregated from the runners who use their services.

Operations Manual

As an event grows in size and complexity, it is a good idea to prepare an "Operations Manual" of some sort. This document is key for anyone stepping in to take over the event in an emergency or simply as an outline to cover a planned transition, or even just to keep track of how things are done from year to year. The procedures for most races likely reside only in the minds of the race director and the committee members or team captains charged with various pieces of the overall race management. The challenge—and it is not a small one—is to get the key information out of the minds of these individuals and into one document, and then to keep it reasonably up to date. It may be useful to distribute this document to all of the team captains to broaden the number of people who have an overview of the entire operation. And after you create an Operations Manual, be sure that it doesn't just sit in a drawer or file cabinet somewhere. Keep updating it each year!

A good place to start when you want to create an Operations Manual is to have the race director and all of the team captains write up their own job descriptions in detail, including a timetable for undertaking these activities. In addition to the write up, they should include the contact information for any vendors, as well as any other important documents, maps or forms. If you are dealing with an all-volunteer race committee, it will probably be difficult to get this documentation—for some reason it simply never rises to the top of their "to do" list. A volunteer may put in many hours at the aid stations, but be unable to find 2-3 additional hours to prepare a report on this job. The individual in charge of collecting this information will need to be persistent.

The Operations Manual consists of the compilation (and editing) of these individual documents, plus any other event documents, into an overall plan for the event. Plan to update this manual at least every two to three years.

Below is an outline for an Operations Manual. Although the items to be included will vary from event to event, the categories in this outline provide a useful starting point:

- Organizing committee contacts

- Race contacts (vendors, etc.)

- Timeline for race week

- Equipment and supplies: items, quantities, and vendors

- Food and refreshments: items, quantities, and vendors

- Signage, including text of signs; notation of in stock, missing, to be ordered; sizes

- Volunteers: number needed, number signed up, arrival and departure times; location of assignment, additional notes.

- Buses: quantity, report-to location, timetable of service, contact

- Porta-johns: quantity, location (very detailed, with maps), contact

- Vehicles: vehicle type, location, time to be at location

- Credentials: printed samples of each type of credential; quantities of each to print

- Officials: judges, jury of appeals, official timers, outline of protest procedures

- Communications: cell phone numbers of key personnel, radio list

- Transponder timing instructions

- Aid stations: locations; items to be delivered; supply list by station, set-up of each station, time schedule

- Awards: outline of speakers, outline of awards to be given out, equipment needed

- Race announcements: starting line announcements, finish line announcements

- Staff lodging: rooming list at race hotel with check-in and check-out dates

- Merchandising: items offered and cost

- Key printed items: course map including certification papers, start and finish line staging area maps, official vehicle passes, participant certificates, etc.

Once the initial Operations Manual has been prepared, the biggest challenge will be to keep it current from year to year.

Contingency Plan

A contingency plan addresses how the race organization would respond to a variety of emergency situations. The theory is that it is better to anticipate worst-case scenarios in advance than to have to think on your feet once they arise. Be aware that, in a post-September 11th, post-Boston Marathon bombing world, race directors may have less control over the fate of their events than they did previously. As plans are developed to deal with threats like a bomb or explosive device on the course, etc., it is best to obtain input from law enforcement officials and to determine at what point these officials would need to take over. Plans to deal with an injury or death should be coordinated with local EMS providers. The contingency plan should include all of the necessary emergency contacts both inside and outside the race organization, and a clear outline of who will serve as the official race spokesperson and handle media requests for information. Sample statements should be drafted to deal with each type of incident. In addition, it may be useful to provide team captains with an "Incident Report Form," to help them record details of the incident while it is still fresh in their minds.

Some scenarios you might wish to address in a contingency plan include:

- Race cancellation due to terrorism or other municipal emergency. There may be separate procedures for cancellation the week before, the day before, and on race day. The plan should include race suspension and course evacuation protocols.

- Race cancellation or delay due to inclement weather

- Serious injury or death

- Assault

- Fire on or near race course
- Gas leak on or near race course
- Power outage
- Protest march on or near course
- Theft
- Traffic accident
- Vandalism
- Lost persons

Directors of large events with extensive municipal involvement may be able to set up a "tabletop exercise" with law enforcement personnel and emergency responders. (The municipality may charge a fee for the exercise.) With all of the key personnel and decision makers in one room, the convener outlines various emergencies and the group collectively addresses how their agency or organization would respond. This meeting also provides an excellent opportunity for all of the players involved in developing the emergency response to meet one another. Ideally, the tabletop exercise should be held well in advance of race day, in order to allow time for implementing the protocols that are developed. The protocols should become part of your Contingency Plan as well.

Sustainability and Social Responsibility Plan

To create a sustainability and social responsibility plan, make a commitment to yourself and the race team to take the time needed to thoroughly address the task at hand. Ultimately, you'll want to come up with a set of realistic goals and measurable objectives for reducing the event's environmental footprint and enhancing its social impact. You'll also want to develop a working list of tactics to undertake. The goal may be simply to add one new initiative to the "menu" each year. As you sit down to develop a sustainability plan, here's a list of general questions that might prove helpful:

- Specifically, what are the goals and objectives in regard to producing a more sustainable event?

- What level of support and enthusiasm does the event's leadership team bring to the table?
- How will you publicize the intentions and plans to maximize awareness among stakeholders of what you are trying accomplish?
- Who among the event's sponsors, vendors and civic partners will support these efforts?
- Who will actually manage this aspect of the event on a day-to-day basis? (In an ideal world, at least one committee member should be dedicated to leading the sustainability efforts, and sustainability should be their only area of responsibility.)
- How will initiatives that cost money be funded?
- How will success be measured?
- With whom and how will accomplishments and lessons learned be shared?

Here are some broad areas to look at for sustainable and social responsibility initiatives:

Procurement Policy

Having a clearly defined set of criteria for procuring the vast array of goods and services required to put on a responsibly produced event will go a long way toward achieving the goals and objectives outlined in the sustainability plan; development of plans and policies go hand-in-hand. A comprehensive procurement policy can be a powerful tool for preventing unnecessary costs and waste, while providing positive pressure on suppliers to offer a more responsible range of products.

As an example, consider reducing packaging. Some race organizers have asked t-shirt vendors not to package shirts in individual plastic bags. Eliminating individual bags reduces expenses for the sponsor/vendor and also prevents a huge headache for race organizers. Similar requests for reduced packaging are also being made of awards manufacturers, especially those who produce medals.

There are some ways to reduce costs as well as decrease the environmental footprint of the event. A number of races have begun to ask their participants to opt-in to receive a t-shirt or medal— an a la carte type choice—reducing both the expense of purchasing more t-shirts and medals than are actually needed and the need to dispose of large quantities of unwanted and unclaimed race premiums. Events can also save a great deal of money and eliminate unnecessary printing and paper use by producing a PDF results book and eliminating a printed registration form. Reusing event signage, eliminating single-serve plastic water bottles, and distributing virtual goody bags are other examples of procurement decisions that eliminate a lot of waste and, in most cases, reduce expenses.

Of course, there are some procurement decisions that may lead to additional expense. If the decision is made to provide a more responsibly produced t-shirt, for example, you'll pay a premium for t-shirts made from organic cotton or recycled PET plastic. Race participants may be willing to pay extra for such a t-shirt, or the race budget may be able to absorb the additional cost. One thing is certain: providing a more responsibly produced t-shirt is a great way to make a very visible statement about the event's commitment to sustainability.

Resource Management

Tracking waste diverted from the landfill through recycling and composting efforts, measuring the amount of traditional and/or renewable energy used, calculating the carbon footprint of event operations, and avoiding wasteful use of water are all key components of a robust resource management plan. The Council for Responsible Sport *(see **Sidebar** on next page)* awards a range of credits

in its certification scheme for achieving certain waste diversion benchmarks: one credit for 60% diversion, a second credit for 75% diversion, and a third credit for 90% diversion of waste from the landfill. Depending upon the location of the race, however, it may be that even 60% diversion is initially unattainable. That's why a good long-term waste diversion goal focuses on a 10% reduction per year, which can be achieved by making conscious procurement choices as well as improvements in on-site sorting of waste and local infrastructure capabilities.

Calculating carbon footprints and measuring energy use are certainly not as straightforward as tracking waste diversion, but they are equally important to race organizers who truly want to produce a more sustainable event. After all, you can't manage what you don't measure. If the race team lacks expertise in these areas, reach out to a local college or university for help.

Access and Equity

Running events may be inaccessible to individuals based on social, economic, cultural, or

Bob Mallet

During the "off season" is a good time to evaluate and update your greening initiatives.

physical barriers that could be addressed and/or prevented by event organizers. Think about ways to reach out to underrepresented groups in the community, and develop ways to reduce any barriers to their participation.

Community Legacy

An economic impact survey (see above) is one very good way to measure an event's community legacy. Other positive community impacts worth accounting for include promoting local nonprofits and/or actively fundraising for them, as well as directly contributing to the development of community infrastructure (for example, clearing or enhancing a trail used by local runners and walkers).

Most running events do a better job in the area of social responsibility (access/equity and community legacy) than they do on the environmental front. Community outreach, charity fundraising and supporting local businesses are key components of most races. Nevertheless, access/equity and community legacy are areas that deserve their own focus, as a comprehensive plan is developed for enhancing the social impact of the event as well as reducing the event's environmental footprint.

Stakeholder Sustainability Feedback

Regardless of your interest in pursuing certification from the Council for Responsible Sport (*see **Sidebar** below*), in preparation for any long-range planning retreat, it's a good idea to ask the stakeholders what they think of the various sustainability initiatives undertaken by the event, however modest or ambitious they may be. In addition to your own evaluation of efforts to reduce the event's environmental footprint and enhance its social impacts, ask the event's stakeholders what worked well and what could be improved. Stakeholders are people actively involved in the event (participants, spectators, volunteers, vendors, sponsors, municipal officials, etc.), and their feedback can be tremendously helpful in measuring success against certain objectives, particularly those that require active participation, like improving waste diversion, maximizing use of public transportation, or meeting the accessibility needs of special populations.

Some ways to get feedback that can be used to gauge stakeholder perceptions and observations of sustainability initiatives include face-to-face interviews, online surveys, group meetings or focus groups, and suggestion boxes at the event.

SIDEBAR

Council for Responsible Sport

The Council for Responsible Sport is an Oregon-based nonprofit organization that certifies events, based on their performance, against the Council's certification standards. Founded in 2007, the Council has certified scores of running events around the world—from grassroots fun runs to big-city marathons. At the time of publication of this edition of *Organizing Running Events*, v4.2 of the Council's certification standards was in effect. With 61 credits available, events that achieve 45% of those credits earn basic certification, while silver, gold and evergreen levels of certification are granted to events that earn 60, 75 and 95% of the Council's certification standards, respectively. For more information about the Council and the services it offers, please visit www.CouncilForResponsibleSport.org

Long-Range Planning Retreat

At least every few years during the "off season," it may be a good idea to consider some type of retreat or planning session for the entire race committee, or for at least the highest level players/executive board. This retreat may be built around some type of social function such as a picnic. The objective of the retreat is to do some long-range planning—where would the team like to see this event in 3, 5, or 10 years—in a more relaxed, expansive

SIDEBAR

Sample Sustainability Plan

There is no perfect plan, but here's an example of a plan for producing a more responsible running event:

Goals and Guidelines:

- Reduce the environmental footprint by taking a year-by-year approach to adopting increasingly aggressive green standards

- Continually strive to expand climate-friendly and environmentally responsible initiatives for all race-related activities

- Maximize participation of underrepresented community groups

- Measure impacts in quantifiable terms and communicate successes and shortcomings in a timely and transparent manner

Long-term objectives:

- Achieve certification by the Council for Responsible Sport (see *Sidebar on previous page*), then strive for higher levels of Council Certification

- Minimize carbon footprint through rigorous conservation and mitigation efforts

- Reduce overall waste by 10% each year, based upon baseline figures for recycling, composting and materials sent to the landfill

- Involve community groups that serve underrepresented populations to identify and remove barriers to participation for their constituents

- Involve sponsors, vendors and contractors in sustainability efforts

First-year objectives:

- Make going green a goal of every race committee member

- Maximize use of public transportation; involve 50% of public transportation users in bike ridership and/or carbon offset purchases

- Develop a comprehensive solid waste management plan for both pre-race and race-day opportunities and challenges

- Establish a "scholarship" fund to underwrite registration fees for disadvantaged youth

- Build awareness of social/environmental responsibility among participants, sponsors, vendors and contractors

First-year tactics—focus on transportation impacts and solid waste management:

- Maximize use of mass transportation to expo and race

- Offer bike valet parking at expo and on race day

- Sell carbon offsets via race registration and at expo

- Offset the carbon impact of elite athlete travel

- Explore alternative fuel and renewable energy options for race-day vehicles and start/finish area power needs

- Eliminate printed registration forms and results book (pdf version of results book will be available)

- Provide recyclable goody bags made with recycled material

- Recycle plastic water bottles and all other recyclable materials

- Compost aid station cups and post-race food waste

- Establish baseline metrics upon which to measure future solid waste management efforts

- Grow participation in wheelchair competitions

atmosphere, at a time when the key players are not so intensively focused on executing the current year's event.

This retreat may be the opportunity to examine the mission of the event as well as other related questions: Does the event exist primarily to provide a top-notch experience for runners, or is it to raise funds for charity? Should the event offer masters prize money? Should the event allow double dipping for awards? Should the event add a pasta dinner or a road mile the night before the race? Does anyone have any ideas to boost attendance, to keep the race fresh? The list could go on, but the key idea is to have these discussions in a relaxed, informal atmosphere.

Race Director Burnout

After many months of hard work and building tension, you—and the key players on the organizing committee—may experience some kind of a letdown when the event is over, either immediately or several weeks or months later. Perhaps it is because you are no longer the center of attention (while this may be a burden in the lead-up to the event, it is exhilarating as well), or because something did not go as well as planned. You may question how you were ever able to get up enough energy to put on the event in the first place and feel a knot in the pit of your stomach when you think of doing it again.

The aftermath is a time to keep things in perspective—remember that people are more likely to complain about than to praise an event. (It's astonishing that a runner who feels wronged by a mixed-up age-group award seems to equate the experience with the eruption of Mt. Vesuvius.) When you hear criticism, remember those runners who did *not* criticize (while learning from the criticism if it has validity). Unless the event was a disaster, those who are happy far outnumber the critics. Remember that in the scheme of life, *this is only a road race*, one of thousands that take place year-round. If there were imperfections, they can be fixed or addressed the following year.

Here are some suggestions for dealing with burnout:

- *Realize that, no matter what you do and how many compliments you receive, you are going to have to suffer through complaints.* Being overly sensitive to the negative won't help your already over-taxed psyche. If you're particularly sensitive to negative comments after the race, have someone screen email and social media for a few weeks, putting aside the negative comments until you are mentally ready for what may not even be constructive criticism. Why let some obnoxious runner upset you because he didn't like the t-shirt?

- *Delegate the post-race responsibilities as much as you can.* One race director has described it like this: It's like the morning after a good party. You go downstairs, and all the cups are all over, and someone put a cigarette butt out in your best rug. Most of the post-race activities—scoring, getting the race results out, arranging transportation back for the athletes, paying leftover bills—hold little glamour. So what can you do? Make sure that those sorts of cleanup jobs are in the hands of good (and fresh) committee members. Give those jobs to people who haven't already done a lot on the race, as they will be more likely to tackle the tasks with eagerness.

- *Know your personal limits.* It can be flattering if you are contacted by a local reporter or another race director anxious for advice, but the higher your profile, the more calls and emails you are going to get. If you find you are spending too much time on the phone or answering emails, or being asked to speak at too many functions, know when to say "no."

- *Find a balance between the race and other commitments.* The totally involved race director has little time left for himself, his family and friends, or for leisure and vacation. Make sure that you aren't sacrificing too much of your personal life for the race. Be especially careful of this in the weeks after the race. If it's your full-time job, go home at 5 PM. If it's an after-hours avocation, only give it two hours instead of five hours each night. If things can wait, let them. If you can, plan a vacation about a month or so after the race. By that time all the little post-race details will be mostly taken care of, and you can relax guilt-free.

- **Plan well, both for you and the race workers.** If you put on a number of races a year, make sure to schedule breaks throughout the year.

- **Reward yourself and the key people in the organization.** Offer yourself and the key race personnel gift certificates, running shoes or apparel (especially if you have a shoe or running apparel company as a sponsor), or a trip to another race or a race directors' meeting. This is a good way to get everyone fired-up for next year. Also, give your workers as much public attention as you can. Some people work just for the satisfaction of doing a job well, but they will always appreciate it when their efforts are recognized and applauded.

- **Remember that you're supposed to love what you are doing.** "If this weren't a labor of love, I don't think I could do it," says one major race director. "The fact is, I really found something in life I love doing." Another commented that his job is to provide thousands of people the stage to live out their athletic fantasies. It doesn't get much better than that.

Final Words

While most race directors derive a great deal of satisfaction from doing a good job, race directing can be a challenging, difficult, and at times seemingly thankless task. When race directing is done well, it looks easy, like anyone could do it. Most race participants have no idea what lies "under the hood" of a well-organized event. Although the event planning industry—of which

race directing is a subset—has grown in recent years, many race directors have had little formal training; most were runners who eventually volunteered to help at a race, then found themselves drafted into the role of director. The best race directors continue to learn on the job, always seeking new ways to enhance their events. Below, we describe some of the areas where race directors might find they can continue to improve their performance, thereby bettering their event.

- **Pay attention to the details.** To really put on a successful event, you have to pay attention to the commonplace tasks that are a part of every road race. Neither participants nor sponsors are going to come back if things don't go smoothly because race directors didn't think things through. Obviously you can't do everything yourself and must delegate authority, but it is critical to make sure that everything is planned for and that everyone is following the proper course of action. You can't make proper decisions if you aren't well-informed. If you are not a detail-oriented person, make sure that someone in the race organization is. The legendary Fred Lebow, who brought the New York City Marathon from the obscurity of a multi-lap event in Central Park to prominence, was a true visionary, but he was ably assisted during the race's growth by the detail-oriented Allan Steinfeld, who was there to take care of all of the more mundane tasks.

- **Be a promoter.** No race is going to last long without the support of sponsors, so always keep the goals of the sponsors in mind. Be sure to talk with the sponsors at length about what their goals are and how you can help them achieve those aims. The more you can creatively help the sponsor reach the public, the more the sponsor will think their investment in the race is worth the expense.

- **Don't procrastinate.** Problems are not going away if you try to ignore them; odds are they will only get worse. Face problems head on as they arise rather than hoping they will fade away. In addition, try to imagine potential problems and how to solve them *before* they arise. The more procedures are created for addressing every eventuality, the more likely problems will be minimized.

- *Don't try to be everything to everyone.* Remember that you are a human being with strengths and weaknesses. Assess your personality and try to evaluate your weaknesses objectively. Then assign more qualified people to work in those areas that you feel are not your strengths.

- *Break the event down.* If you start to think about all the things you have to do as race director, it can be overwhelming. Break the event down into doable tasks and assign someone on the race committee to be in charge of each task.

- *Make sure the event is safe and enjoyable for the runners.* Obviously, the number one priority should be the safety of all involved with the event. Beyond that, do all you can to make the runners feel special and to ensure that they have an enjoyable experience. Make sure that the volunteers understand these goals as well and do what they can to promote them.

- *Be innovative.* There are thousands of events out there; to make a race stand out, you must think creatively. Of course you never want to sacrifice safety or sound organization in order to have an innovative event, but there are many things you can do that won't compromise those goals.

- *Plan ahead.* Dave McGillivray, Director of the Boston Marathon and a number of other major races, says that he pretends that every event he does is two weeks earlier than its actual date. That way, he always has a cushion in case something unexpected arises. While this approach might not work for everyone, it does serve to show how important pre-race planning is, even to experienced race directors. If you leave a lot of tasks until the last minute, you might not have time to get to them all, especially if something unforeseen comes up.

- **Stay on top of technological advances in the sport:** The development of new technologies and consolidation of existing technologies continues to take place at a breathtaking pace. Resist the temptation to succumb to what may appear to be a technological assault on our craft. Embrace and take the time to learn about new technologies and decide if they are right for your event.

- *Learn from others.* Other race directors are an excellent source of ideas, tips, and advice. Look at what other races of similar size and with similar demographics are doing to attract runners and promote their sponsors' interests.

- **Become an RRCA Certified Race Director:** If you have read this manual, you are well on your way. Consult http://www.rrca.org/our-programs-services/programs/race-director-certification for details.

Phil Stewart

22 Organizing and Managing a Running Club

*The material in this chapter is adapted and condensed from the Road Runners Club of America's instructions about "***How to Start a Running Club***." The complete version of this material is available at http://www.rrca.org/resources/club-directors.*

THE BASICS

- **Know when to start a club.** Many running clubs begin as a group of friends or co-workers who decide to get together for occasional group runs or to travel to races. When the group is small and informal, the need for official structure might be minimal. However, these groups can grow quickly. As the group grows, it's important to consider forming a club to protect group members from liability exposure.

- **Hold an initial meeting to determine an organizational structure and staffing**. Elect a board of directors. Determine the mission of the organization and discuss the legal responsibilities of the board. Decide how often the board will meet, as well as the kinds of organized activities the club will undertake. Determine whether designated committees will be needed to head those activities. Join the Road Runners Club of America (RRCA).

- **Adopt governing policies.** A number of written policies are important for managing a running club. Some policies are required for nonprofit status and others are simply good practice.

- **Establish a method for membership management.** How will the club keep track of and communicate with members? How long will a membership term last? Who will do this work?

- **Give plenty of consideration to financial matters.** Even if a club starts as a small and informal group, sound financial procedures are key to the health and growth of the organization. Create a club budget and determine how the accounting will be performed. Define the role of the treasurer and of a possible finance committee.

- **Plan for transitions.** Every organization with an elected board of directors will experience turnover on a regular basis. Undertake the necessary procedures to make these transitions smooth and to prevent loss of institutional knowledge.

THE DETAILS

Getting Started

Many running clubs start out as a group of friends or co-workers who decide to get together for periodic group runs or to travel together to races. When the group is small and informal (10 people or fewer), the need for official structure might be minimal. However, small informal groups can grow quickly, as new friends are invited to join and they subsequently invite *their* friends to join in group runs. All of a sudden, the group of five running buddies has morphed into 25 people showing up to run on a Saturday. When participation in a group run reaches 10 or more, this is the point at which formation of a more formalized running club should be considered, in order to protect each other from potential liability exposure.

To establish a club, reach out to key individuals in the community who are interested in promoting local running, such as local high school cross country coaches, employees of local running stores, and the city recreation department. Recruit these individuals and organizations to promote the new club. Various low-cost ways to advertise include sending emails to friends, posting information on social networking websites, and posting on the bulletin boards of gyms, running/fitness stores, and recreation centers. If starting from scratch, solicit preliminary feedback from people about what they are looking for in a running club. Use this knowledge to set up an exploratory meeting to discuss the mission and formation of the club.

The Planning Meeting

A good way to entice people to come to an initial planning meeting is to schedule it with a coinciding social activity or run. Remember that the meeting should be at a convenient place and time. A practical place might be an office conference room, a local high school, a recreation center, someone's house.

Here are some important points for the initial meeting:

- *Have a clear agenda for the meeting and a meeting leader.* Assign someone who is not the meeting leader to take notes documenting the meeting.

- *Collect names and contact information for all attendees.* Start a contact list. These people will probably take on leadership positions with the new club.

- *Discuss the purpose of the club and the general types of activities and/or events in which the club will engage.* These activities might include group runs, training programs, races and social gatherings. Clubs may be established primarily to put on races or fun runs to benefit either the club itself or other organizations in the community. Clubs may also be organized to support youth running programs, cross country clubs, or to serve any number of additional functions, with the goal of promoting running as a healthy lifestyle choice and an enjoyable sport. Draft a mission statement that clearly captures the intended purpose of the club. The mission statement document will help to keep the club 'on track' as it grows and diversifies.

- *Decide on a club name.* Determine some branding strategies for the club, such as a logo, a slogan, or any other important branding needed to identify and promote the club.

- *Form a board of directors.* Elect officers who are willing to dedicate time and hard work to develop the club. The minimum possible number of elected officers is usually three, but this requirement varies by state. More information about the board of directors can be found later in this chapter.

- *Approve a set of bylaws.* Come to the meeting prepared with a draft set of bylaws for the club. New clubs are encouraged to use the RRCA's sample running club bylaws (available at http://www.rrca.org/resources/club-directors/start-a-club) as a template for creating their own bylaws. The bylaws should include voting requirements for club decisions, including elections. Revise the bylaws as needed, based on feedback at the meeting, and approve them or table

SIDEBAR

Sample Mission Statements

Mission Statement for the 60,000-Member New York Road Runners:

Over the past 59 years, we have grown from a local running club to a global champion of the running movement. We are the world's premier community running organization, and our efforts and events serve all runners and active individuals, from beginners to professional athletes: the young, the elderly, and the underserved of all abilities.

We impact the lives of over 430,000 people annually, from New Yorkers throughout the five boroughs to runners around the world, through a wide variety of events and programs for people of all ages and abilities.

It is our unique nonprofit model, which teams contributions from corporate, foundation, and individual donors with earned income from our best-in-class events, that makes all our efforts possible.

Together with the help of all of NYRR's members, supporters, participants, and partners, we're working hard to fulfill our mission of giving all people everywhere a reason to run. Today, tomorrow, and for life.

Mission Statement of the 300-Member Hunter's Creek Running Club, Orlando, FL

Hunter's Creek Running Club strives to share our love of competitive and cooperative running by bringing people together from all walks of life, to move in the same positive direction. We work to provide a family oriented, happy, healthy, enthusiastic atmosphere to run and socialize while supporting our community and charitable organizations. We hope to use our passion for running to build friendships, provide encouragement, and improve ourselves with no regard to age, cultural differences, gender, pace or experience. Our goal is to learn and grow through our shared experience, and to leave no runner behind.

- *Establish corporate status.* Determine if the club will be a nonprofit organization and whether it will get its nonprofit designation from the IRS or through the RRCA's group exemption with the IRS. New clubs are highly encouraged to join the RRCA and use the group exemption benefit of RRCA membership. More information about the RRCA can be found below. Some clubs elect to organize as an LLC and are not eligible for nonprofit status. These clubs are considered for-profit entities.

- *Consider incorporating the club in the state in which it will operate.* Incorporation is optional and requirements vary by state. The RRCA highly recommends that clubs be incorporated in order to protect the board of directors from liability. Incorporated organizations must adopt formal governing procedures including by-laws, hold regular meetings, maintain minutes, and keep the state informed of changes in board officers. The incorporation process registers and protects the organization's legal name. In most circumstances, regular members, board members, and employees cannot be held personally liable for a corporation's debts and activities. The corporation itself is liable while members' personal funds and assets are protected. However, members can be held liable for intentional negligence and misappropriated funds. Foundations, government agencies, and banks are often more willing to do business with incorporated nonprofits than unincorporated organizations. They recognize nonprofit corporations as legally responsible and more likely to meet their obligations.

- *Establish a budget.* Outline the club's expected expenses along with the likely sources of revenue. More details on club revenue and expenses can be found later in this chapter.

- *Discuss how insurance will be obtained.* Insurance coverage is absolutely critical. The RRCA offers its member clubs affordable general liability insurance, which covers all club activities including group runs, races, social events, meetings, etc. Clubs can also choose to obtain insurance through an independent provider if they are not members of the RRCA.

- *Determine membership dues.* Membership dues are often the primary revenue stream for a new running club. Membership dues vary by club, based on location, type of membership, events/programs included and the budget of the club. Most clubs set their annual dues between $20-$35 for individual memberships and may offer a family membership for a higher fee.

- *Establish a board meeting schedule.* Also, establish schedules for group runs and social gatherings, as well as dates for any races or events that will be held in the upcoming year.

Join the Road Runners Club of America

It may already be obvious from some of the information provided above that all new running clubs are highly encouraged to join the Road Runners Club of America (RRCA). The RRCA is the oldest and largest national association of running organizations. Their mission is to champion the development of community-based running clubs and events that serve runners of all ages and abilities in pursuit of health and competition. RRCA membership provides important benefits to member clubs, including nonprofit exemption status, comprehensive and affordable insurance for club events and activities, and a plethora of other advantages. Clubs can also join USATF through their local USATF associations.

After the running club is established, it must

be continuously cared for in order to stay in good standing, from both an IRS standpoint and from a civic standpoint. The minutes taken at club meetings are the permanent record of the proceedings and should be clear, accurate, brief and objective. Minutes should be shared with club members.

Club Staffing

Board of Directors

Most running clubs are nonprofit entities run by a board of directors. The board of directors should include a chair/president, vice president, treasurer, secretary, and an agreed-upon number of at-large members. Often, boards contain an odd number of members to help avoid repeated ties when voting. The RRCA requires at least three board members and recommends up to nine. A majority of those members cannot be related parties.

Board meetings should take place at regularly scheduled intervals. Board members and committee members should attend these meetings, and club members in good standing should be invited to attend as well.

Legal Responsibilities of the Board of Directors

As a collective body, the Board's role is to ensure that the organization functions within a framework that supports its mission. The primary responsibilities of the board are encapsulated by three duties: duty of care, duty of loyalty, and duty of obedience. Duty of care means each board member ensures that he/she is reasonably informed and actively participating. Duty of loyalty means that each board member serves in the best interest of the organization. Duty of obedience means each board member complies with applicable laws, adheres to the bylaws, and is a guardian of the mission

The board of directors of any nonprofit has

several important legal responsibilities, as outlined below. (Adapted from *Ten Basic Responsibilities of Nonprofit Boards* by Richard T. Ingram, Ph.D., and *Legal Responsibilities of Nonprofit Boards*, by Bruce R. Hopkins, JD.)

- Adhere to local, state and federal laws pertaining to nonprofit organizations
- File accurate reports required by local, state and federal governments in a timely fashion
- Keep records of lobbying activities and expenditures
- Protect the organization's staff from harm and ensure compliance with OSHA standards
- Maintain personnel policies that include a grievance policy
- Register with the appropriate state agencies before launching fundraising campaigns
- Adhere to the organization's bylaws and articles of incorporation and amend them as necessary
- Provide for an independent annual audit of the organization's financial statements and activities
- Publish an annual report to provide to members and includes financial statements

Other legal responsibilities running club boards should undertake:

- Adopt recommended policies to protect the integrity of the club
- Ensure well-written contracts with independent contractors that outline clear deliverables, clear payment terms, and clear ownership of works-for-hire by the club
- Ensure appropriate trademarks are filed and maintained to protect the brand and identity of the club
- Respond immediately to complaints filed by members and/or take legal threats seriously by reviewing them with the RRCA, if the club is a member of this organization. If a lawsuit is filed, the insurance company will appoint counsel for the club and manage the lawsuit.

Elected officers, along with volunteer-run committees or appointed program directors, should be responsible for carrying out the work of a volunteer-run club. Larger clubs with the financial capability may hire paid staff to manage club activities, under the direction of the board of directors. Keep in mind that not everyone involved in the management of club activities has to be a board member.

Committees are a great way to divide the workload and engage club members. The board can choose to set up various committees to tackle specific projects. Committees can be made up of board members, general club members, or some combination thereof.

Governing Policies

One important job of the board of directors is to draft, adopt and implement the policies that will guide the effective functioning of the organization as it grows and changes. Some of the policies that should be considered by the board of any running club are listed below.

- **Conflict of Interest Policy:** The officers, directors, and employees of a running club owe a duty of loyalty to the organization they serve, which requires that they act not in their personal interests or in the interests of others, but solely in the interests of the organization. Officers, directors, and employees must have undivided allegiance to the organization's mission and may not use their positions, information they have about the organization, or property of the organization in a manner that allows them to secure financial benefit for themselves or their relatives.

- **Ethics Policy or Code of Conduct:** Adopting a Member Code of Conduct policy is a good opportunity to outline the type of atmosphere the club is trying to create, especially as club membership increases. A Code of Conduct establishes a baseline expectation of behavior for all members, and it should also outline what members should do if they feel that

another member is violating the club's Code of Conduct policy. The Code of Conduct policy should be included on membership forms, ideally under the waiver of liability.

A Code of Conduct policy does not need to be complex. Here are the basic points to include in such a policy:

- Show respect to fellow club members at all times
- Always show respect and appreciation for the volunteers who give their time to help the club and/or the club's event(s)
- Never yell, taunt, or threaten physical violence upon another member of the club, a volunteer or an event spectator
- Never use abusive or vulgar language, or make racial, ethnic or gender-related slurs or derogatory comments at club events
- Never make unwanted sexual or physical contact with other members
- Always report violations of the Code of Conduct policy to the board of directors in writing

- **Protection for Whistleblowers:** In 2002, the Sarbanes-Oxley Act was passed. The Sarbanes-Oxley Act makes it a federal crime for any organization—nonprofit and for-profit alike—to retaliate against a "whistleblower" who reports illegal activity. A board-approved whistleblower policy is required for nonprofits under Sarbanes-Oxley. The Sarbanes-Oxley Act also forbids the purging of documents when any organization—nonprofit or for-profit— is under federal investigation.

- **Criminal Background Check for the Treasurer and/or Staff Responsible for Money:** As a guideline, the RRCA recommends having a volunteer treasurer undergo a criminal background check to ensure there is no history of theft or financial fraud. The results of criminal background checks should be kept strictly confidential, and only authorized individuals should have access to the reports. If a background check discloses a criminal conviction for a theft-related or fraudulent crime within a 15-year period, this person should be disqualified from a position involving the handling of funds.

- **Criminal Background Check for Anyone Working with Youth:** Coaches, assistant coaches, volunteers, or employees engaged in working with legal minors on behalf of a club or event must submit to a criminal background check. Criminal background checks should be performed on an ongoing basis throughout the year. The President of the running club or event, or a duly authorized official, should manage any criminal background check procedure on behalf of the youth event or youth running program. The results of the criminal background checks should be kept strictly confidential, and only authorized individuals should have access to the reports.

If a background check discloses a criminal conviction for a violent crime against a person—including a sex offense—within a 20-year period, this person should be disqualified from working with youth.

- **Privacy Policy & Legal Notice:** A Privacy Policy outlines for club members how the club will use their personal information. RRCA member clubs are encouraged to use the RRCA privacy policy as a template. A Legal Notice outlines ownership rights for the content found on a club's website or other information owned by a club, such as contact lists, event registration lists, etc. Clubs are encouraged to use the RRCA legal notice as a template.

Membership Management

Most clubs start small with a group of friends, but if the running community is active, the club can grow quickly. A running club should designate someone as the membership coordinator, if that position is not included as part of the board of directors. The job of the membership coordinator is to maintain a listing of the members, collect annual membership dues, and report dues revenue to the Board. The membership coordinator may also assist with communication efforts to the membership by working with the newsletter editor, the webmaster, or the social media coordinator for the organization. One important job of the membership coordinator is to ensure that all club members sign an annual waiver of liability for all activities they participate in related to the club. All clubs that are part of the RRCA are required to obtain waivers from their members as part of the RRCA insurance program. (See *Chapter 9: Insurance and Legal* for a sample club participant waiver.)

In this day and age, most running clubs use an online system for membership management. An online system can assist with collecting and archiving waivers, gathering emergency contact and important medical information from members, auto-renewal, and much more.

Financial Management

Even if a running club is very small, sound financial practices are crucial to keep the club afloat. The larger a club gets, the more complicated its finances will become. No matter the size of the club, however, it is important to open a bank account in the name of the club, using the club's Federal Employer Identification Number (EIN). Clubs and events should maintain a checking account or bank account in a board-approved financial institution. Incorporating the club may be required to open a bank account. Members of the board or individual members of a club should **never** be allowed to comingle the club's finances with their personal checking accounts.

Budget and Accounting

Come up with the probable categories of revenue and expenses and project dollar amounts for each of these categories. For a list of common categories of revenue and expenses, *see Sidebar on next page*. Set a budget period/fiscal year.

When drafting the budget, be realistic about the revenue the organization can generate. Inflating the revenue budget simply to exceed the budgeted expenses can lead to an actual deficit at the end of the year. Be sure to have a contingency plan if revenue falls short of expectations, to minimize the likelihood of a deficit at year's end.

SIDEBAR

Common Running Club Revenue and Expenses Categories

Revenue

- Membership dues (individual and family)
- Club sponsorship
- Program fees (create a subcategory for each program)
- Contributions
- Race registration fee revenue (create a subcategory for each race)
- Race sponsorship
- Donations collected
- Sales of club clothing/merchandise
- Misc. revenue

Expenses

- Program expenses (create a subcategory for each program)
- Race expenses (create a category for each race)
  - Permit fees
  - Contractors
  - Finisher items
  - Prize money
- Contributions or grants given
- Equipment
- Office supplies
- RRCA membership—dues & insurance
- Board meeting expenses
- Club clothing
- Membership recruitment & retention
- Staff (as needed)
- Depreciation of assets (timing systems, clocks, etc.)
- Misc. expenses

The Role of the Treasurer

The treasurer of an organization is typically an elected or appointed member of the board. In a volunteer-run organization, the treasurer is responsible for keeping full and accurate accounts of all revenue (receipts) and expenses (disbursements or checks).

Here is a sample job description for a board treasurer:

- Oversee the budget planning process
- Ensure adequate revenue is available to achieve the budgeted expenses
- Safeguard the organization's assets
- Draft financial policies for board approval
- Anticipate and report financial problems
- Ensure the board receives regular and accurate financial statements and that the board members understand the information presented
- Ensure federal, state, and local reporting takes place

Internal Controls

The board should ensure that there are policies in place to protect the organization from fraud or theft. These policies are often referred to as internal controls. An important aspect of internal controls is segregation of duties. In a volunteer-run organization, oftentimes full financial management is delegated to the treasurer. However, this is not the best practice to ensure against theft or fraud.

The financial management process in a running club involves at least five steps:

- Receive revenue (dues, sponsorship, donations, etc.)
- Deposit revenue items into a board-approved bank account
- Write checks drawn from the board-approved bank account
- Reconcile the statements from the board-approved bank account
- Report the financial status of the organization to the board

The treasurer should not be expected to handle every aspect of the financial management process. Instead, the treasurer, in agreement with the president or chair of a board, may appoint one or more individuals to assist with the process. The finance committee may also serve in this capacity if there is no staff support. By engaging more than one individual in the process, important divisions of duties are created.

To assist with segregation of duties in the absence of paid staff, clubs and events should consider the following:

- Require all checks to be co-signed.
- Have an individual other than the treasurer receive a copy of the bank statement, ideally the president or board chairperson. The statements should include images of the cancelled checks. This individual should be free to question any check drawn from the club/event checking account or question any deposit made into the account.
- Ensure documentation of revenue received—photocopy or scan checks.
- Ensure documentation of expenses paid—

SIDEBAR

Important Financial Questions the Board Should Be Able to Answer

- Is the club showing a profit or loss this month/quarter?
- Is there a projected profit or loss for the end of the year?
- What needs to be done to address a loss?
- Are the revenue sources (dues, race registration, sponsorship) increasing or decreasing?
- Does the club have a diverse source of revenue or is it dependent on a single source?
- Are key expenses under control?
- Does the club have sufficient reserves?
- Is the cash flow projection adequate?
- Are revenue and expenses on track with the budget?
- Is the budget consistent with the club's mission, strategic plan, and vision statement?

---

maintain copies of invoices and note the check number and date paid on the invoice.

- Ensure bank statements are reconciled. If the treasurer reconciles the bank statements, have another individual review the reconciliation report. Failure to reconcile bank accounts in a timely manner can mask serious cash flow problems.

Taxes

There are several types of filings that even small, nonprofit running clubs are required to provide. Consult with a local tax professional or accountant to make sure all necessary taxes are filed appropriately. (See **Chapter 2: Getting Ready—Incorporation, Taxes, Budgets and Finances** for details about tax filing.)

RunBlogRun™

\+

the shoe addicts

\+

RUNNING NETWORK LLC

Represented By

FORTIUS
MEDIA GROUP, LLC

P.O. Box 6450, San Jose, CA 95150, U.S.A. • Global mobile: +1608.239.3785
Global fax: 302.792.7484, Attention: Larry Eder
email: fortiusmedia@gmail.com • blog: runblogrun.com

 # Resources

For further exploration, a list of publications, organizations, electronic press release aggregators, and websites that are referenced in this book is included below. In addition, a list of running event suppliers—who have generously supported the publication of this manual—is included as well.

Publications (print and online)

Course Measurement and Certification Procedures

http://www.usatf.org/events/courses/certification/manual/

This publication, compiled by some of the most experienced course certifiers in the U.S., is available for free from the website listed above. The course certification process is explained in great detail. Published by USATF's Road Running Technical Council.

Contact: USATF, Road Running Technical Council, 130 East Washington Street, Suite 800, Indianapolis, IN 46204.

Phone: 317-261-0500

How to Conduct a Wheelchair Race: Guidelines for the Administration of a Wheelchair Road Race Division, by Brad Hedrick, Martin I. Morse, and Ann C. Walters.

Available: Free under "Resources" at www.rrm.com

Currently out of print but downloadable for free from the Road Race Management website, this 28-page book published in October 1994 succinctly covers nearly every facet of wheelchair race management. A supplement provides guidance on key wheelchair rules.

Contact: The University of Illinois, Division of Rehabilitation Education Services, Recreation and Athletics—Road Race Book, 1207 South Oak, Champaign, IL 61820.

Phone: 217-333-4606

International Association of Athletics Federations (IAAF) Road Running Manual

http://iaaf-ebooks.s3.amazonaws.com/IAAF-Road-Running-Manual/sources/index.htm

The world governing body for track and field, race walking and road running publishes a race director's manual available at the link above. It reads a little like something produced by the United Nations, but contains some useful information, especially for anyone considering a championship level event.

Contact: IAAF, 6-8, Quai Antoine 1er, BP 359, MC 98007 Monaco Cedex.

Phone: +377 93-10-88-88

International Association of Athletics Federations (IAAF) Rules

https://www.iaaf.org/about-iaaf/documents/rules-regulations#rules

IAAF Rules of Competition available for download as a .pdf document

Contact: IAAF, 6-8, Quai Antoine 1er, BP 359, MC 98007 Monaco Cedex.

Phone: +377 93-10-88-88

Road Race and Finish Line Management Manual

http://www.rrtc.net/finishline/contents.html

This publication, compiled by some of the most experienced finish line experts in the U.S., is available for free from the website listed above. It contains a very detailed description of finish line management, complete with density graphs and more. Published by USATF's Road Running Technical Council, it is a bit dated (last updated in 2001), but contains excellent information.

Contact: USATF, Road Running Technical Council, 130 East Washington Street, Suite 800, Indianapolis, IN 46204.

Phone: 317-261-0500

Road Race Management Newsletter

http://www.rrm.com

Available to members of Road Race Management, *RRM Newsletter* covers news and organizational facets of race directing.

Contact: Phil Stewart, Road Race Management, 4963 Elm St., Suite 106, Bethesda, MD 20814.

Phone: 301-320-6865

Road Runners Club of America Handbook

www.rrca.org

Handbook published by RRCA, covering race and club organization from the largest U.S. grassroots running organization. Currently in digital format only.

Contact: RRCA, 1501 Lee Hwy., Suite 140, Arlington, VA 22209.

Phone: 703-525-3890

Road Runners Club of America Kids Run the Nation Program Guide

www.rrca.org

Guide for teachers, coaches, or program leaders interested in implementing a youth running program or club. Companion publication for kids: **Kids Run the Nation**.

Contact: RRCA, 1501 Lee Hwy., Suite 140, Arlington, VA 22209.

Phone: 703-525-3890

USATF Competition Rules

http://www.usatf.org/About/Competition-Rules.aspx

Rulebook contains all the rules for track and field and road running from USATF, the national governing body. New rules and amendments to existing rules are added every two years. Available for free by download.

Contact: USATF, 130 East Washington Street, Suite 800, Indianapolis, IN 46204.

Phone: 317-261-0500

Organizations

Abbott World Marathon Majors

www.worldmarathonmajors.com

Umbrella organization of six Abbott World Marathon Majors events. Advocates efforts to advance the sport, raise awareness of its elite athletes, and increase the level of interest in elite racing among running enthusiasts.

Adaptive Sports USA

www.adaptivesportsusa.org

Advocacy organization that engages, evolves and empowers individuals with disabilities to be involved in adaptive sport through education, coaching and advocacy.

American College of Sports Medicine (ACSM)

www.acsm.org

Sports medicine and exercise science organization dedicated to advancing and integrating scientific research to provide educational and practical applications of exercise science and sports medicine. Promotes "flag system" to indicate heat risk at running events.

American Trail Running Association (ATRA)

http://trailrunner.com/about-atra/events-standards-program/

Organization promoting trail running for participants and organizers. ATRA has also produced a solid document for trail running event standards that provides a fairly detailed account for trail run directors.

Association of Road Racing Statisticians (ARRS)

www.arrs.net

Statistical clearing house for road running events. Tracks world and national records based on its criteria; provides prize money statistics, race histories and competitive levels for selected events; publishes athlete rankings, lifetime prize money earned, and copious other elite athlete and race statistics.

Bring Back the Mile (BBTM)

www.http://bringbackthemile.com/

An advocacy organization to promote and celebrate the classic one-mile distance. Provides a steady stream of mile-focused media releases and stories. Conducts a national circuit of road miles in the U.S. and promotes road miles outside the circuit. A good resource for groups considering staging a road mile event.

Collegiate Running Association (CRA)

https://www.collegiaterunning.org/

An association dedicated to providing and supporting opportunities for NCAA-eligible college athletes to earn prize money at road races.

Council for Responsible Sport (CRS)

www.CouncilForResponsibleSport.com

A nonprofit organization that certifies events based on their performance against the Council's sustainability and social responsibility certification standards. Provides support and advice for event directors and volunteers who aspire to incorporate sustainability practices into their events.

International Association of Athletics Federations (IAAF)

http://www.iaaf.org

World governing body for "Athletics," which includes track and field, race walking and road running. Sets rules for international competition, enforces drug testing bans, and oversees activities of athletics National Governing Bodies worldwide. Offers road race labeling program for events meeting criteria.

International Institute for Race Medicine (IIRM)
www.racemedicine.org
International collective of medical professionals that seeks to further research and education and promote best medical practices in marathons and other endurance road races around the world.

National Center for Spectator Sports Safety and Security (NCS4)
www.ncs4
Research center devoted to the study and practice of spectator sports safety and security. Provides security resources and training for event directors.

PRRO Circuit
www.prro.org
Organization committed to promoting "Clean Sport" running events. Conducts an annual circuit of prize money events, with a rotating Circuit Championship, which self-fund drug testing.

Road Race Management (RRM)
www.rrm.com
Membership organization for event personnel, running clubs, and running industry businesses. Members receive *Road Race Management Newsletter,* published 11-times yearly, containing articles, news, and commentary about the organizational side of long-distance running. Organizes annual event directors meeting and trade exhibit.

Road Runners Club of America (RRCA)
www.rrca.org
Largest membership organization for running clubs, running events and running event management companies. Extensive resources and programs for event directors. Provides liability and other insurance policies for events.

Running USA
www.runningusa.org
Membership-based trade association for the running industry. Provides extensive statistical reports on industry trends, race sizes, demographics, etc. Organizes annual industry meeting.

USA Track & Field (USATF)
www.usatf.org
National governing body for track and field, race walking and road running. Sanctions events and certifies courses. Sets rules of competition for sanctioned events. Selects U.S. international teams and conducts U.S. Olympic Track & Field and marathon trials. Provides resources for event directors and sells liability and other types of insurance.

U.S. Anti-Doping Agency (USADA)
www.usada.org
National anti-doping agency for Olympic sports including road running. Manages anti-doping program, results management processes, drug reference resources, and all athlete education for all United States Olympic Committee-recognized sport national governing bodies.

U.S. Obstacle Course Racing (USOCR)

www.usocr.com

A national association dedicated to the sport of obstacle course racing. Provides support for both obstacle course professional and casual participants, event directors of OCR events, sponsors and vendors. Provides support for current and potential event directors.

Electronic Media Release Aggregators

These media outlets aggregate media releases from running events and either post them on their websites or send out emails with links to the releases on a daily or weekly basis. Most national and regional running publications offer these same services.

Endurance Sports Business News (OSE Productions)

www.oseproductions.com/newsletter.html

Free aggregator of endurance industry press releases distributed by email.

Endurance Sports Wire

www.endurancesportswire.com/

Charges a fee to include releases for individual events and organizations to a large number of industry, event and media outlets. The public can sign up to receive daily or weekly aggregated releases for free.

Road Race Management

www.rrm.com

Posts running industry releases for free in the "News" section of its website and considers releases for inclusion in periodic "Enews" emails distributed to members.

RRCA

www.rrca.org

National grassroots running association posts running news for free.

Running USA

www.runningusa.org

Running industry trade association posts running event and business news on website and includes in emails.

Websites

Below is a list of websites sorted by the chapter in which the website first appears. Some may appear in multiple chapters. Note that these websites were valid as of the date of publication.

Forward

www.rrca.org
www.rrm.com

Chapter 1: Taking the Plunge
www.rrca.org/about/governance/
www.usatf.org

Chapter 2: Incorporation, Taxes, Budgets and Finances
www.eftps.gov
www.irs.gov

Chapter 4: The Course
www.gmap-pedometer.com
www.google.com/earth/
www.jonescounter.com
www.mapmyrun.com
www.mapquest.com
maps.google.com/maps
www.microsoft.com/streets/
nationalmap.gov/
www.topozone.com/
www.topomaps.usgs.gov
www.usatf.org/events/courses/measurers
www.usatf.org/Products-/-Services/Course-Certifications/USATF-Certified-Courses/Certify-Your-Course.aspx
http://www.usatf.org/routes/map/

Chapter 5: Sponsorship
www.active.com
www.athlinks.com
www.cvent.com
www.databarevents.com
www.racedirectorresource.com
www.raceresultsweekly.com
www.roadracemanagement.com
www.runnerspace.com
www.runsignup.com
www.sponsorship.com
www.sportfilm.com
www.surveymonkey.com

Chapter 6: Marketing and Promotions
calendar.runningnetwork.com/
www.cherryblossom.org
www.coolrunning.com
www.CouncilForResponsibleSport.org
www.facebook.com
www.flotrack.org
www.instagram.com
www.LetsRun.com

www.linkedin.com

www.marathonguide.com

www.pinterest.com

www.plus.google.com

www.runnersworld.com/race-finder

www.snapchat.com

static.googleusercontent.com/media/www.google.com/en//webmasters/docs/search-engine-
optimization-starter-guide.pdf

www.twitter.com

www.youtube.com

Chapter 8: Medical, Safety and Security

www.zunis.org

Chapter 9: Insurance and Legal

- *ASCAP General FAQ:* www.ascap.com/licensing/licensingfaq.aspx#general

- *ASCAP Guide to Using Copyrighted Music:*
  www.ascap.com/~/media/655449c494b748ba89edc4864655e1b6.pdf

- *Better Business Bureau Guide to Music Licensing:* www.bbb.org/council/for-businesses/toolkits/
  bbb-brochure-music-in-themarket-place/

- *BMI Website:* www.bmi.com/news/entry/

- *SESAC FAQ:* www.sesac.com/Licensing/FAQsGeneral.aspx

- *U.S. Copyright Law:* www.copyright.gov/title17/

Repertory Searches

Use the links below to find out which artists are represented by each agency—but be aware that co-licensing is common!

- **ASCAP**—www.ascap.com/Home/ace-title-search/index.aspx
- **BMI**—repertoire.bmi.com/StartPage.aspx
- **SESAC**—www.sesac.com/repertory/terms.aspx

Chapter 12: Special Entrant Categories

www.achillesinternational.org/

www.adaptivesportsusa.org

www.bringbackthemile.com

www.bringbackthemile.com/tour

www.collegiaterunning.org

www.dopingsanctions.com

www.paralympic.org

www.prro.org

www.rrmonlineguide.com

www.rrca.org/our-programs-services/programs/rrca-championship-series/hosting-an-rrca-
championship-event

www.runnersworld.com/tools/age-grade-calculator

www.usantidoping.org

www.usatf.org/groups/EventDirectors/bids/process.asp

www.worldmarathonmajors.com

Chapter 14: Rules of Competition

www.arrs.net

www.iaaf.org

www.iaaf.org/competitions/iaaf-label-road-races

www.rrtc.net

www.usatf.org/About/Competition-Rules.aspx

www.usatf.org/about/directory/info.asp?parent=Administrative+Division&group=Officials+Committee

Chapter 17: Timing and Scoring

http://www.usatf.org/Products-/-Services/Course-Certifications/USATF-Certified-Courses/Certify-Your-Course/Statement-on-GPS-Use-by-Runners.aspx

Chapter 20: Special Types of Races and Participatory Events

www.blm.gov

www.fs.fed.us

www.fws.gov

www.nps.gov

www.rrca.org/our-programs-services/programs/kids-run-the-nation/resources/youth-running-events

www.trailrunner.com

trailrunner.com/about-atra/events-standards-program/

www.usocr.com

Chapter 21: Before Next Year

www.random.org

www.runningusa.org

Chapter 22: Organizing and Managing a Running Club

www.rrca.org/resources/club-directors

Chapter 23: Resources

www.acsm.org

www.activeendurance.com

www.ashworthawards.com

www.champ-sys.com

www.darmangroup.com

www.databarevents.com

www.ecprint.com

www.electronumerics.com

endurancesportsmedia.com/

www.endurancesportswire.com/

www.hastyawards.com

www.iaaf.org/about-iaaf/documents/rules-regulations#rules
iaaf-ebooks.s3.amazonaws.com/IAAF-Road-Running-Manual/sources/index.htm
www.lesliejordan.com
www.marathononline.com
www.maxmedals.com
www.orbiter.com
www.oseproductions.com
www.racemedicine.org
www.registrationsaver.com
runningnetwork.com
www.strideawards.com
www.symbolarts.com
www.usada.org
www.usatf.org/usatf/files/62/626ff37e-feed-4ec3-8c40-758ddda9af8a.pdf

Industry Suppliers

The following companies have generously supported the publication of the Second Edition of ***Organizing Running Events: The Complete Guide to Staging a Successful Road Race***. They represent many of the leading suppliers to the running industry. Companies are organized by category.

Apparel

Champion System
www.champ-sys.com
Champion System provides the finest quality custom technical apparel for a wide range of sports and activities which can be customized with virtually any design. Sublimation printing.
Contact: Champion System, 218 Richardson Street, Brooklyn, NY 11222.
Phone: 718-383-8855

Leslie Jordan, Inc.
www.lesliejordan.com
Custom printed performance apparel, wicking tech T's - Wholesale prices.
Contact: Leslie Jordan, Inc., 1930 NW 24th Ave. Portland, Oregon 97210.
Phone: 800-935-3343
Email: ljsales@lesliejordan.com

Awards

Ashworth Awards
www.ashworthawards.com
Unique custom awards including medallions, awards, lanyards, plaques, pins, coins, belt buckles, bottle openers and more.
Contact: Ashworth Awards, 41 Richards Ave., North Attleboro, MA 02760.
Phone: 800-325-1917

Hasty Awards

www.hastyawards.com

Custom awards including medals, lucite awards, plaques and more designed by professional artists from your ideas and artwork.

Contact: Hasty Awards, 1015 Enterprise St, Ottawa, KS 66067.

Phone: 800-448-7714

Maxwell Medals & Awards

www.maxmedals.com

Providers of high quality finisher medals and other die cast products, acrylic and glass awards, lapel pins, t-shirts and more.

Contact: Maxwell Medals & Awards, 1296 Business Park Dr., Traverse City, MI 49686.

Phone: 1-800-331-1383

Stride Awards

www.strideawards.com

Custom race medals and finisher medals for runners. Styles include 3D molded, acrylic, cutouts, full color, multi-piece, sliders, stand metal and wood styling.

Contact: Stride Awards, 83 Vermont Ave., Unit 3, Warwick, RI 02888.

Phone: 401-431-5959

Symbol Arts

www.symbolarts.com

One stop shopping for all your event needs including medals, awards, key chains, pins, coins, apparel, patches and more.

Contact: Symbol Arts, 6083 South 1550 East, Ogden, UT 84405.

Phone: 801-475-6000

Bibs (Numbers)

Electric City Printing

www.ecprint.com

Event solutions including custom tyvec bibs, wrist bands, transponder application, event accessories, event brochures, onsite bib printing.

Contact: Electric City Printing, 730 Hampton Rd., Williamston, SC 29697.

Phone: 800-277-1920

Marathon Printing, Inc.

www.marathononline.com

Custom designed bibs, stock bibs and race accessories for any kind of event all over the globe.

Contact: Marathon Printing, 390 NE 9th St., Gresham, OR 97030.

Phone: 503-255-4122

Clocks

Electro-Numerics

www.electronumerics.com

Manufacturer and distributor of digital clocks and printing timers for events.

Contact: Electro-Numerics, Inc., 42213 Sarah Way, Temecula, CA 92590.

Phone: 800-854-8530/951-699-2437

Consultants

Tatreau Consulting

tatreau@comcast.net

Event design and event management consulting.

Contact: Chris Tatreau, Tatreau Consulting, 98 Plymouth Rd., PO Box 139, Gwynedd Valley, PA 19437.

Phone: 215-628-1981

Equipment Rental

Tatreau Consulting

tatreau@comcast.net

Event design and management consulting. Rental of extensive inventory of event equipment including barricades, start-finish structures, signage and more.

Contact: Chris Tatreau, Tatreau Consulting, 98 Plymouth Rd., PO Box 139, Gwynedd Valley, PA 19437.

Phone: 215-628-1981

Insurance

RegistrationSaver

www.registrationsaver.com

Event cancellation insurance available for purchase by race participants. Provides coverage in case policy holders cannot participate due to a covered peril or if the event is cancelled.

Contact: Milena Glusac, Marketing Manager, Registration Saver Program, Next Wave Insurance Services, 100 West A St., Suite 675, San Diego, CA 92101.

Phone: 619-708-2510

RRCA

www.rrca.org

Nation's largest organization of running clubs and event members. Provides support for running clubs and event members. Sells liability and other types of insurance.

Contact: RRCA, 1501 Lee Hwy., Suite 140, Arlington, VA 22209.

Phone: 703-525-3890

USATF
www.usatf.org
National Governing Body for track and field, road running and race walking. Provides support services for race directors. Sells liability and other types of insurance for events.
Contact: USATF, 130 East Washington Street, Suite 800, Indianapolis, IN 46204.
Phone: 317-261-0500

Media

Fortius Media Group
www.runningnetwork.com
Represents 25 Running Network Publications. Editor of *Run Blog Run* blog. International content provider.
Contact: Larry Eder, Fortius Media Group, P.O. Box 6450, San Jose, CA 95150.
Phone: 608-239-3785

MarathonGuide.com
www.marathonguide.com
Online registration services for events. Website devoted to marathons including schedules, editorial contact, statistics, reviews and more.
Contact: John Elliott, MarathonGuide.com, 750 Spruce St., Boulder, CO 80302.
Phone: 917-627-3434

Road Race Management
www.rrm.com
Membership organization for event personnel, running clubs, and running industry businesses. Members receive *Road Race Management Newsletter,* published 11-times yearly, containing articles, news, and commentary about the organizational side of long-distance running. Organizes annual event directors meeting and trade exhibit.
Contact: Phil Stewart, Road Race Management, 4963 Elm St., Suite 106, Bethesda, MD 20814.
Phone: 301-320-6865

Meetings

Road Race Management Race Directors' Meeting and Trade Exhibit
www.rrm.com
Oldest annual race directors' meeting and trade exhibit. Seminars, social events and trade exhibit of running industry suppliers.
Contact: Jeff Darman, Road Race Management Race Directors' Meeting, 110 East State St., Suite 15, Kennett Square, PA 19348.
Phone: 610-925-1976

Online Services

Active.com

www.active.com

On-line registration, race management software. race apps. Technology to drive new participants to events and to collect data insights. Properties include IPICO Timing and Virtual Event Bags.

Contact: Active Network, 717 North Harwood Street, Suite 2500, Dallas, TX 75201

Phone: 888-906-7622

Databar Events

www.databarevents.com

One-stop services for event directors including online registration, event marketing and promotion, awards, apparel, equipment rental, event management, race timing and more.

Contact: Databar Events, 2908 Meridian East, Edgewood, WA 98371.

Phone: 253-770-7338 ext 260

MarathonGuide.com

www.marathonguide.com

Online registration services for events. Website devoted to marathons including schedules, editorial contact, statistics, reviews and more.

Contact: John Elliott, MarathonGuide.com, 750 Spruce St., Boulder, CO 80302.

Phone: 917-627-3434

MyLaps

www.mylaps.com

Timing systems and services to suit the needs of professional timers, event organizers, track and club owners and federations, as well as individual racers and athletes.

Contact: MyLaps North America, 2030 Powers Ferry Road (South East), Suite 110, Atlanta, GA 30339.

Phone: 678-816-4000

Organizations

Road Race Management

www.rrm.com

Membership organization for event personnel, running clubs, and running industry businesses. Members receive *Road Race Management Newsletter,* published 11-times yearly, containing articles, news, and commentary about the organizational side of long-distance running. Organizes annual event directors meeting and trade exhibit.

Contact: Phil Stewart, Road Race Management, 4963 Elm St., Suite 106, Bethesda, MD 20814.

Phone: 301-320-6865

RRCA

www.rrca.org

Nation's largest organization of running clubs and event members. Provides support for running clubs and event members. Sells liability and other types of insurance.

Contact: RRCA, 1501 Lee Hwy., Suite 140, Arlington, VA 22209.
Phone: 703-525-3890

USATF

www.usatf.org

National Governing Body for track and field, road running and race walking. Provides support services for race directors. Sells liability and other types of insurance for events.
Contact: USATF, 130 East Washington Street, Suite 800, Indianapolis, IN 46204.
Phone: 317-261-0500

Speakers

Darman Group

www.darmangroup.com

Speakers bureau featuring running luminaries past and present.
Contact: Jeff Darman, Darman Group, 110 East State St., Suite 15, Kennett Square, PA 19348.
Phone: 610-925-1976

Suppliers

Heatsheets

www.heatsheets.com

Heatsheets blankets, plain or custom imprinted, serve as all-weather, reflective insulation solutions for heat, wind, cold and rain. Ponchos and capes also available.
Contact: Stephanie Deigan, 2 N. LaSalle St., Suite 1200, Chicago, IL 60602.
Phone: 773-337-3887

Transponder Timing

MyLaps

www.mylaps.com

Timing systems and services to suit the needs of professional timers, event organizers, track and club owners and federations, as well as individual racers and athletes.
Contact: MyLaps North America, 2030 Powers Ferry Road (South East), Suite 110, Atlanta, GA 30339.
Phone: 678-816-4000

Orbiter

www.orbiter.com

Transponder timing systems for rent or purchase for use by.professionals and novices at events and schools and for fitness testing.
Contact: Orbiter, 13500 Pacific Ave S. Tacoma WA, 98444
Phone: 253-627-5588

Index